CACHE LEVEL 3 EXTENDED DIPLOMA

cache
nurturing achievement

Children and Young People's Workforce

EARLY LEARNING AND CHILD CARE

Maureen Smith, Teena Kamen,
Jo Irvine, Mary Armitage,
Corinne Barker

Orders: please contact Bookpoint Ltd, 130 Milton Park, Abingdon, Oxon OX14 4SB. Telephone: (44) 01235 827720. Fax: (44) 01235 400454. Lines are open from 9.00 - 5.00, Monday to Saturday, with a 24 hour message answering service. You can also order through our website www.hoddereducation.co.uk

If you have any comments to make about this, or any of our other titles, please send them to educationenquiries@hodder.co.uk

British Library Cataloguing in Publication Data
A catalogue record for this title is available from the British Library

ISBN: 978 1 4441 5606 5

This Edition Published 2012
Impression number 10 9 8 7 6 5 4 3 2 1
Year 2015, 2014, 2013, 2012

Cover photo © Amelia Fox – Fotolia
Typeset by Datapage (India) Pvt. Ltd.
Printed in Italy for Hodder Education, An Hachette UK Company, 338 Euston Road, London NW1 3BH.

Contents

Additional free material on the web at www.hoddereducation.co.uk/cache covering unit CP 18: Supporting science and technology development in children and/or young people

Acknowledgements

I would like to thank my colleagues at Wakefield College for their support and encouragement. Thanks also to the early years students who continue to inspire me. Special thanks to my dear friend Sue Smith who has helped to keep me organised over the years.

Corinne Barker

Photo credits:

All photos © Andrew Callaghan, except:

Figures: 1.17 © Zakharov Evgeniy – Fotolia; 1.18a–h © Photographs by John Oates, from http://www.open.edu/openlearn/body-mind/childhood-youth/early-years/attachment-parents © The Open University 2012; 3.2 © Carolyn A Mckeone/Science Photo Library; 3.4 © Jaren Wicklund – Fotolia; 3.5 © Dr. P. Marazzi/Science Photo Library; 3.6 © Dr. P. Marazzi/Science Photo Library; 3.7 © CDC/Science Photo Library; 5.4 © ruzaimy – Fotolia; 5.13 © auremar – Fotolia; 6.1 © Monkey Business – Fotolia; 6.8 © Warrick Page/Getty Images for UNICEF; 10.3 © Georgios Kollidas – Fotolia; 10.4 © The Granger Collection, NYC/TopFoto; 11.2 © Monkey Business – Fotolia; 11.4 © Roger Bamber/Alamy; 11.6 © MBI/Alamy; 11.9 © Julie Voigt/ArtForSmallHands.com; 11.10 © bobo/Alamy; 11.12 © Visions of America, LLC/Alamy; 11.15 © Heini Kettunen/Alamy; 12.9 © Jeff Gilbert/Alamy; 12.10 © Frank Baron/The Guardian; 12.11 © Monkey Business – Fotolia; 13.5 © Photofusion Picture Library/Alamy; 13.9 © Losevsky Pavel/Alamy; 13.12 © Sally and Richard Greenhill/Alamy.

Figures 8.7, 11.13, 12.15, 13.6, 13.7 © Justin O'Hanlon.

Illustrations by Barking Dog Art (Figures 2.1, 3.3, 5.1, 5.2, 8.1, 8.2).

SECTION 1

Mandatory units

1 Extending understanding of theories of children and/or young person's care or development (CP 1)

2 Understand the role of policies in children and/or young people's settings (CP 2)

3 Maintaining the health of children and/or young people (CP 3)

4 An introduction to leadership and management (CP 4)

5 Supporting the development of study skills (CP 5)

6 Working with families of children and/or young people (CP 6)

7 Working as part of more than one team (CP 7)

8 Supportive approaches to behaviour management (CP 8)

9 Formal recording for use within the work environment (CP 9)

10 Research to support practice when working with children and/or young people (CP 10)

Chapter 1 Extending understanding of theories of children and/or young person's care or development (Unit CP 1)

The aim of this chapter is to increase awareness of theories and their benefit to children and young people's care or development.

Learning outcomes

1. Know the role of theories in informing practice when working with children and/or young people.
2. Be able to apply theories to workplace practice.
3. Understand the relevance of identified theories in relation to own workplace practice and personal development.

Section 1: The role of theories in informing practice when working with children and/or young people

This chapter looks at the use of theory to inform practice when working with children and/or young people. There are many theories of development – in this chapter, we look at the theories that are most relevant to the study of children's and young people's care, development and learning: behaviourist theories, psychoanalytic theories, humanistic theories, social constructivist theories, attachment theory and experiential learning style theory. In many cases, these theories offer competing views on childhood development and this presents one of the challenges in putting these theories into practice.

Behaviourist theories

Behaviourist theories (or behaviourism) are based on the assumption that learning occurs through interactions with the environment and that all behaviours are acquired through a person's interaction with their environment. Behaviourists believe that internal thoughts and motivations cannot be used to explain behaviour. Instead, they suggest that we should look only at the external, observable causes of human behaviour, rather than thoughts and feelings, which cannot be observed.

Behaviourists are concerned with how external forces can be used to control behaviour. For example, B.F. Skinner (see pages 3–5) considered that all thinking and learning are based on responses to rewards and punishments received within our environment.

Ivan Petrovich Pavlov (1849–1936)

Pavlov was a Russian biologist who studied animal behaviour. His experiments involved teaching dogs to salivate in response to the sound of a bell. Before giving the dogs their food, Pavlov rang a bell. Eventually, the dogs began to salivate when the bell rang, even when there was no food. The dogs had learned to respond to the bell sound with their salivating reflex. This type of learned response or behaviour is called a conditioned reflex. Pavlov extended his ideas concerning conditioning to human psychology. He believed that human behaviour consists of many conditioned reflexes that are triggered by external influences.

Principle	Description	Example
The unconditioned stimulus	The unconditioned stimulus is one that unconditionally, naturally and automatically triggers a response.	When you smell one of your favourite foods, you may immediately feel very hungry. So in this example, the smell of the food is the unconditioned stimulus.
The unconditioned response	The unconditioned response is the unlearned response that occurs naturally in response to the unconditioned stimulus.	In this example, the feeling of hunger in response to the smell of food is the unconditioned response.
The conditioned stimulus	The conditioned stimulus is a previously neutral stimulus that, after becoming associated with the unconditioned stimulus, eventually comes to trigger a conditioned response.	In the earlier example, suppose that when you smelled your favourite food, you also heard the sound of a whistle. While the whistle is unrelated to the smell of the food, if the sound of the whistle was paired multiple times with the smell, the sound would eventually trigger the conditioned response. In this case, the sound of the whistle is the conditioned stimulus.
The conditioned response	The conditioned response is the learned response to the previously neutral stimulus.	In this example, the conditioned response would be feeling hungry when you heard the sound of the whistle.

Table 1.1 The basic principles of classical conditioning

Key term

Behaviour – a person's actions and reactions, and their treatment of others.

Classical conditioning – the learning process that occurs through associations between an environmental stimulus and a naturally occurring stimulus. For example, Pavlov's dogs learnt to associate an environmental stimulus (a bell) with a naturally occurring stimulus (the smell of food).

Conditioned reflex – a learned response or behaviour.

Activity

A fun experiment in classical conditioning is available to do at: www.simplypsychology.org/classical%20conditioning.swf.

Summarise your findings about classical conditioning and share them with the group.

John B. Watson (1878–1958)

According to Watson, psychology should be the science of observable behaviour. In his most famous and controversial experiment, known as the 'Little Albert' experiment, Watson (and a graduate assistant named Rosalie Rayner) conditioned a small child to fear a white rat. They accomplished this by repeatedly pairing the white rat with a loud, frightening, clanging noise. They were also able to demonstrate that this fear could be generalised to other white, furry objects. The ethics of this experiment are often criticised today, especially because the child's fear was never deconditioned.

Research Activity

1. Find out more about the 'Little Albert' experiment. For example, take a look at: http://psychology.about.com/od/classicpsychologystudies/a/little-albert-experiment.htm.
2. Share your findings with a group of students or colleagues.

B.F. Skinner (1904–1990)

Skinner was an American psychologist who discovered that the behaviour of rats could be

Figure 1.1 The 'Little Albert' experiment (Watson, from Swenson, 1980)

controlled by food rewards. One of Skinner's best-known inventions is the 'operant conditioning chamber' (the Skinner box). Skinner showed how positive reinforcement worked by placing a hungry rat in the box, which contained a lever in the side As the rat moved about the box, it would accidentally knock the lever; as soon as it did so, a food pellet would drop into a container next to the lever. The rat quickly learned to go straight to the lever after being put in the box a few times – the consequence of receiving food if it pressed the lever ensured that the rat would repeat the action again and again (McLeod 2007a)

This experiment demonstrates Skinner's idea of operant conditioning. Unlike Pavlov's classical conditioning, where an existing behaviour (salivating for food) is shaped by associating it with a new stimulus (ringing of a bell or a metronome), operant conditioning is the rewarding of an act that approaches a new desired behaviour.

This idea of operant conditioning can be applied to any situation where the required behaviour is reinforced with a reward. Skinner believed that positive reinforcement (rewards) and negative reinforcement (sanctions) both contribute towards an individual's motivation for learning and behaviour. Skinner applied his findings about animals to human behaviour and developed teaching machines that enabled students to learn step by step, revealing answers for immediate feedback (reward).

Activity

In your own words, explain the difference between classical conditioning and operant conditioning.

Some of the key concepts in operant conditioning involve the use of reinforcement and punishment. Reinforcement is used to *increase* appropriate or desired behaviour. Reinforcement takes place when something the child likes (such as a smiley face or sticker) is offered to them to increase the frequency of the desired behaviour (e.g. sitting still during assembly or story time). When the desired behaviour is demonstrated by

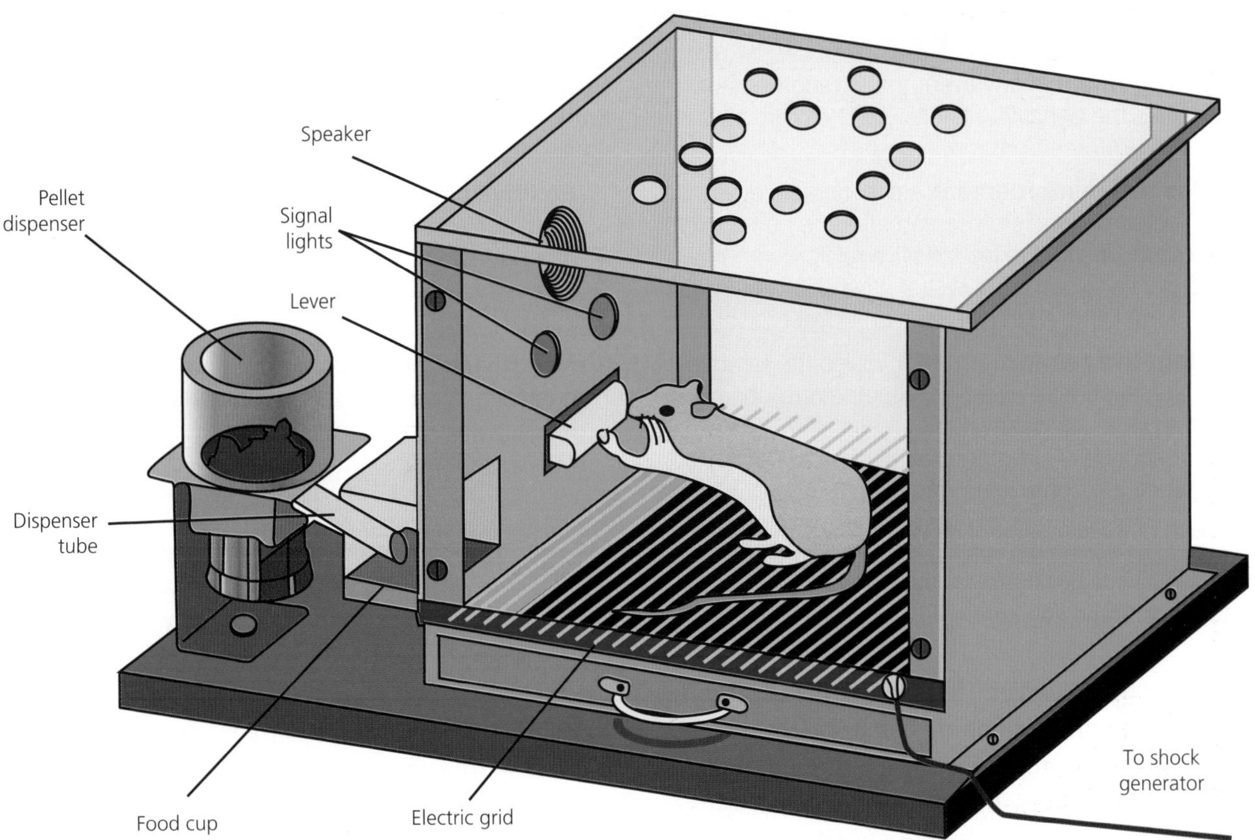

Figure 1.2 The operant conditioning chamber (the Skinner box, http://www.simplypsychology.org/operant-conditioning.html)

the child, then the reinforcer or reward (e.g. the smiley face or sticker) must be given. Examples of reinforcers (rewards) may include: child's choice of favourite activity; smiley faces, stars or stamps; stickers or badges; merit points and certificates; mention in praise assemblies or a special book.

Punishment is used to *decrease* inappropriate or undesirable behaviour. When a child is making noises during assembly or story time, the adult may reprimand the child in order to stop or decrease the behaviour. If the child stops making noises after the reprimand, the reprimand is an effective punishment. Examples of punishments or sanctions include: time outs; verbal reprimands; suspension of privileges; temporary removal of favourite object or activity.

Within the reinforcement and punishment model (see Table 1.2), there are two aspects:

1 **Positive** – which means you are giving something in response to the behaviour.
2 **Negative** – which means you are taking something away in response to the behaviour.

Key term

Operant conditioning – behaviour dependent upon what happens *after* the response to a stimulus.

Punishment – the presentation of an adverse event or outcome that causes a decrease in the behaviour it follows

Reinforcement – any event that strengthens or increases the behaviour it follows.

Activity

List examples of reinforcement and punishment from your own (or your children's) experiences as a pupil or student.

Social learning theory and the work of A. Bandura (1961, 1965 and 1973)

Albert Bandura is a key researcher linked with social learning theory. Bandura built on the work of

Reinforcement	Punishment
Reinforcement is any event that strengthens or increases the behaviour it follows. There are two kinds of reinforcement.	**Punishment** is the presentation of an adverse event or outcome that causes a decrease in the behaviour it follows. There are two kinds of punishment.
1. **Positive reinforcement** is a favourable event or outcome that is presented after the behaviour. In situations that reflect positive reinforcement, a response or behaviour is strengthened by the addition of something, such as praise or a direct reward.	1. **Positive punishment** (sometimes referred to as punishment by application) involves the presentation of an unfavourable event or outcome in order to weaken the response it follows.
2. **Negative reinforcement** involves the removal of an unfavourable event or outcome after the display of a particular behaviour. In these situations, a response is strengthened by the removal of something considered unpleasant.	2. **Negative punishment** (also known as punishment by removal) occurs when a favourable event or outcome is removed after a particular behaviour occurs.
In both of these cases of reinforcement, the behaviour **increases**.	In both of these cases of punishment, the behaviour **decreases**.

Table 1.2 Some key concepts in operant conditioning

Skinner outlined earlier. He thought that children learned through conditioning and reinforcement but also by observing and imitating. Bandura thought that children acquired many skills and behaviours simply by watching and listening to others around them. However, children mainly copy (model) the behaviours and skills of those who are important to them – that is, people who:

- they like and respect
- have high status
- are similar to them (e.g. same sex, around same age)
- have desirable possessions or characteristics.

For many children, the practitioners who work with them fall into some of these categories so they will model your behaviour.

Bandura also looked at how children learn aggressive behaviour. In 1973, he conducted the Bobo doll study. Three groups of nursery school children watch a short film with different endings. Each child sees an adult punching a plastic doll. In one film, the children see the adult rewarded, in the second the adult is punished and in the third there is no reward or punishment. After the film, the children are given an opportunity to play with the doll. The children who had seen the adult rewarded and the children who had not seen any consequences were equally aggressive to the doll. The group who had seen the adult punished were less likely to be aggressive. Bandura concluded that all the children had learnt the aggressive behaviour but that what they went on to do was influenced by what happened to the adult.

There are many criticisms of this type of artificial experiment and it is difficult to be certain how far Bandura's findings would be true in a more natural situation. However, there are possible implications for how we work with children from the Bobo doll study. We know children will imitate aggressive behaviour so we want to minimise the amount of aggression they are exposed to. Dealing with aggressive behaviour firmly and consistently so that children see there are negative outcomes may lead to reduced imitation of the behaviour. Sometimes, if the situation is not dangerous, ignoring aggressive behaviour and withholding attention are sufficient to discourage copying.

How behaviourist theories support meeting the needs of children

Behaviourist theories can be useful in meeting some aspects of children's needs, especially helping children to demonstrate appropriate behaviour – for example, using positive/negative reinforcement and positive/negative punishment.

Positive reinforcement occurs when a reward is given after the child demonstrates appropriate behaviour, which then increases the frequency

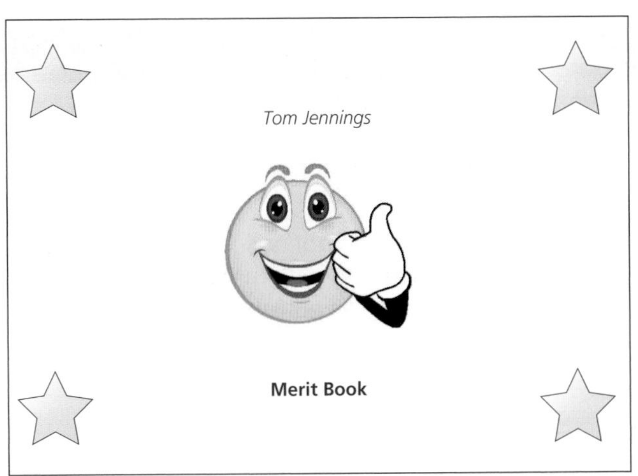

Example cover

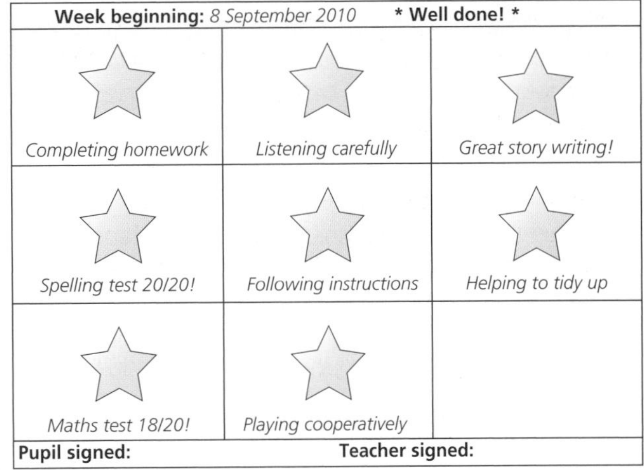

Example page

Figure 1.3 Positive reinforcement occurs when a reward is given after the child demonstrates appropriate behaviour, which then increases the frequency of that behaviour

of that behaviour. For example, Tom is finding it difficult to finish his homework. As Tom is interested in video games, his mother makes an agreement with him that he can earn stars for every homework task he completes on time; she will then exchange the stars for cash so that Tom can purchase video games or accessories. Tom now regularly completes his homework on time; positive reinforcement has occurred because the frequency of the appropriate behaviour increased due to the reward (reinforcer).

Negative reinforcement occurs when something the child dislikes is removed after the child demonstrates the appropriate behaviour. For example, Sarah rarely completes her class work, even though she is capable of doing the work. The teacher stands near Sarah and keeps verbally prompting her to get on with her work. However, Sarah does not like the teacher's frequent prompts and so she gets on with her work. The teacher walks away and leaves Sarah to get on with her work. Sarah continues to finish her work to avoid further prompts from the teacher; negative reinforcement has occurred because the frequency of the appropriate behaviour increased due to the removal of the unwanted prompts.

Positive punishment occurs when something undesirable is introduced to the child to reduce the occurrence of an inappropriate behaviour. For example, Denzel is playing about and not listening to the instructor during sports practice. The instructor tells Denzel to take a 'time out' on the bench; positive punishment has occurred because the instructor is trying to decrease the frequency of the undesired behaviour through the presence of the punishment.

Negative punishment occurs when something desirable is removed after the occurrence of inappropriate behaviour. The most common form of negative punishment is the removal of privileges and can be effective in reducing unwanted behaviour in the short term. For example, Tamika constantly chats to her friends during class, despite frequent reminders by the teacher to stop. The teacher does not allow Tamika to go out to play with her friends at break time; negative punishment has occurred because the teacher is trying to decrease the undesirable behaviour by removing a desired event.

The impact of the behaviourist theories on practice

Of course, in reality, people do not respond exactly like Pavlov's dogs. However, there are many ways in which classical conditioning can be applied to work with children and young people. For example, classical conditioning techniques are useful in the treatment of phobias or anxiety problems as practitioners are able to apply classical conditioning in the setting by creating a positive environment to help children overcome anxiety or fear. Pairing an anxiety-provoking situation, such as performing in front of a group, with pleasant surroundings helps the child learn new positive associations. Instead

Strengths of behaviourist theories	Weaknesses of behaviourist theories
Behaviourist theories are based upon observable behaviours, so it is easier to quantify and collect data and information when conducting research.	Behaviourist theories are based on a one-dimensional approach to behaviour and do not account for free will and internal influences, such as moods, thoughts and feelings.
Effective therapeutic techniques such as intensive behavioural intervention and behaviour analysis are all rooted in behaviourist theory. These approaches are often very useful in changing destructive or harmful behaviours in children, young people and adults.	Behaviourist theories do not account for other types of learning, especially learning that occurs without the use of reinforcement and punishment.
While behaviourist theories are not as dominant today as they were during the middle of the 20th century, they still remain an influential force in psychology. Outside psychology, animal trainers, parents, teachers and many others make use of basic behavioural principles to help teach new behaviours and discourage unwanted behaviours.	People (and animals) are able to adapt their behaviour when new information is introduced, even if a previous behaviour pattern has been established through reinforcement.

Table 1.3 Some strengths and weaknesses of behaviourist theories

of feeling anxious and tense in these situations, the child will learn to stay relaxed and calm.

The work of Watson and others set the stage for behaviourist theories, which soon rose to dominate the field of psychology. While behaviourist theories became less popular after 1950, many of the concepts and principles are still widely used today. Conditioning and behaviour modification are still widely used in therapy and behavioural training to help children change problematic behaviours and develop new skills.

Operant conditioning, Skinner's most widely acclaimed work, is based on a system of both positive and negative reinforcement. Children, parents and practitioners all benefit when positive reinforcement techniques are used to guide children's behaviours, making for a more pleasant and respectfully run setting. Even babies and very young children respond well to a system where rewards exist, repeating behaviours when they bring big smiles and hugs from a caring adult. Using positive reinforcement to encourage appropriate behaviour can help practitioners to encourage children's continued cooperation. Computer-based self-instruction programmes use many of the principles of Skinner's techniques. Effective teaching requires learners to respond to new information and receive feedback on their performance *before* advancing to the next step; in addition, the sequencing of the steps is critical. More recently, research into Skinner's work in this area has led to breakthroughs in teaching children to communicate more effectively, especially those with autistic spectrum disorders.

Research Activity

1. Select an article about behavioural theory – for example, an article from a psychology/childcare magazine, journal or website. (See 'Useful resources' at the end of this chapter.)
2. Explore the relationship between this article and a recent news story relating to children's behaviour and learning.
3. Evaluate the connection to your own life, personal interests and your practice when working with children/young people.

Psychoanalytic theories

Psychoanalytic theories originated with the work of Sigmund Freud. Through his clinical work with patients suffering from mental illness, Freud believed that very early childhood experiences and unconscious desires influenced behaviour. Based on his observations, he developed a theory that described development in terms of a series of psychosexual

Dear:..
You have used your:

Listening Skills......................
Speaking Skills......................
Thinking Skills......................
Looking Skills......................
Concentrating Skills..............

And we are really happy that you are trying so hard.

Positive Press © developed by Jenny Mosley

Figure 1.4 Effective teaching requires learners to respond to new information and receive feedback on their performance before advancing to the next step (image based on the 5 Skills Notelet Pads from the Five Skills Series – Jenny Mosley Consultancies www.circle-time.co.uk. Call 01225 719204 for a free catalogue)

stages (see Table 1.4). According to Freud, conflicts that occur during each of these stages can have a lifelong influence on personality and behaviour.

Sigmund Freud (1856–1939)

The Austrian physician Sigmund Freud believed that very early childhood experiences are responsible for how people think and feel in later life. Depending on these experiences, people are either well or poorly adjusted to their everyday lives. Freud considered that most of our thinking is done on a *subconscious* level and is therefore beyond our control.

Freud's theory of psychosexual development is one of the best known, but also one of the most controversial. Freud believed that personality develops through a series of childhood stages during which the desire for sexual pleasure would focus in turn on different areas of the body.

This psychosexual energy was described as the driving force behind behaviour. If these psychosexual stages are completed successfully, the result is a healthy personality. If certain issues are not resolved at the appropriate stage, fixation can occur. Until this conflict is resolved, the individual will remain 'stuck' in this stage.

Key term

Fixation – a persistent focus on an earlier psychosexual stage.

Criticism of Freud's theory of psychosexual development

Freud's psychosexual stage theory is controversial as it is based mostly on male psychosexual development and has very little about female psychosexual development. Freud's theory is based on the recollections of his adult patients, rather than the actual observation and study of children over a period of time. In addition, basing current adult behaviour on a specific childhood experience

Psychosexual stage and age range	Area of the body
The oral stage **Birth to 1 year**	**Mouth** If fixation occurs at this stage, the individual would have issues with dependency or aggression. Oral fixation can result in problems with drinking, eating, smoking or nail biting.
The anal stage **1 to 3 years**	**Bowel and bladder control** If parents take an approach that is too lenient, an anal-expulsive personality could develop in which the individual has a messy, wasteful or destructive personality. If parents are too strict or begin toilet training too early, an anal-retentive personality develops in which the individual is stringent, orderly, rigid and obsessive.
The phallic stage **3 to 6 years**	**Genitals** Freud believed that boys begin to view their father as a rival for the mother's affections. However, the boy also fears that he will be punished by the father for these feelings, a fear Freud termed castration anxiety. Freud believed that girls instead experience penis envy, which was never fully resolved, and that all women remain somewhat fixated on this stage.
The latent stage **6 years to puberty**	**Sexual feelings are inactive** The latent period is a time of exploration in which the sexual energy is still present, but it is directed into other areas, such as intellectual pursuits and social interactions. This stage is important in the development of social and communication skills and self-confidence.
The genital stage **Puberty to death**	**Maturing sexual interests** During the final stage of psychosexual development, the individual develops a strong sexual interest in the opposite sex. This stage begins during puberty but lasts throughout the rest of a person's life. Where in earlier stages the focus was solely on individual needs, interest in the welfare of others grows during this stage. If the other stages have been completed successfully, the individual should now be well-balanced, warm and caring.

Table 1.4 Psychosexual stages

is very vague as the length of time between cause and effect is too long – other factors may have contributed to the adult behaviour.

Activity

Find out more about Freud's theories. A great starting point is www.all-about-psychology.com/sigmund-freud.html, which includes an interesting video about Freud.

Melanie Klein (1982–1960)

Klein met Sigmund Freud at the 1918 International Psycho-Analytic Congress in Budapest, which inspired her to write *The Development of a Child*. Through Klein's work, the technique known as play therapy emerged and is still used extensively today in psychotherapy. With Klein's technique, instead of lying on a couch and free associating, the child had a simple playroom with a collection of their own small toys, as well as play materials like paper, crayons, strings, a ball, cups and a sink with taps, which provided maximum opportunities for the child's own imagination to be expressed. The adult also used simple and age-appropriate language when interacting with the child, including using role play where the child acts as a strict teacher and the adult is the naughty child (Anderson 2008).

Key term

Free associating – the technique of exploring the unconscious mind by encouraging a person to articulate words and thoughts that are associated with key words provided by a psychoanalyst.

Activity

Find out more about Melanie Klein's views on psychology – for example, her ideas about play therapy. You could start by looking at: http://psychology.about.com/od/profilesofmajorthinkers/p/klein_bio.htm.

Anna Freud (1895–1982)

The youngest of Sigmund Freud's six children, Anna was extraordinarily close to her father. The majority of her education was from the teachings of her father's friends and associates. While she was heavily influenced by her father's work, she was far from living in his shadow. In the 1930s, Anna helped to run a nursery school for poor children in Vienna where the children were allowed to choose their own food and had the freedom to organise their own play. Her work here enabled Anna to observe infant behaviour and experiment with feeding patterns. After the outbreak of the Second World War, Anna set up the Hampstead War Nurseries, which provided foster care for over 80 children of single-parent families and where she helped children to form attachments by providing continuity of relationships with the nursery staff and by encouraging mothers to visit as often as possible.

Her own work expanded upon her father's ideas, but also created the field of child psychoanalysis. Anna Freud had a profound influence on Erik Erikson, who later went on to expand the field of psychoanalysis and ego psychology.

Activity

Find out more about Anna Freud's views on psychology – for example, her ideas about child psychoanalysis. You could start by looking at: http://psychology.about.com/od/profilesofmajorthinkers/p/bio_annafreud.htm.

Erik Erikson (1902–1994)

Much like Sigmund Freud, Erikson believed that personality develops in a series of stages. Erikson also believed that a sense of competence motivates a person's behaviours and actions. Erikson's psychosocial stage theory is concerned with becoming competent in an area of life. If the stage is handled well, the person will feel a sense of mastery; if the stage is managed poorly, the person will emerge with a sense of inadequacy. According to Erikson, in each stage a person will experience a basic conflict that acts as a catalyst for development.

Activity

Test your knowledge of Erik Erikson's theory of psychosocial development in this quiz: http://psychology.about.com/library/quiz/bl_eriksonquiz.htm.

How psychoanalytic theory supports meeting the needs of children

The pioneering work of people such as Anna Freud is important to our understanding of both recognising and meeting the individual needs of young children. For example, Anna's work at the Hampstead Clinic in London supported the idea of using a key person to help young children form attachments, as well as involving parents in the care of their children. Anna's concept of tracking children along a developmental timeline also supports meeting children's needs. For example, a child keeping pace with most of his or her peers in terms of eating behaviours, personal hygiene, play styles, relationships with other children and so on could be considered healthy; when one aspect or more of a child's development seriously lags behind the rest, the clinician could assume that there is a problem and could communicate the problem by describing the particular lag. Psychoanalytic theories show that supporting children's needs (especially in early childhood) is essential to children's overall development. This includes meeting children's

Psychosocial stage	Basic conflict	Important events	Developmental outcomes
Stage 1: Infancy (birth to 18 months)	Trust vs. mistrust	Feeding	Children develop a sense of trust when caregivers provide reliability, care and affection. A lack of this will lead to mistrust.
Stage 2: Early childhood (2 to 3 years)	Autonomy vs. shame and doubt	Toilet training	Children need to develop a sense of personal control over physical skills and a sense of independence. Success leads to feelings of autonomy; failure results in feelings of shame and doubt.
Stage 3: Preschool (3 to 5 years)	Initiative vs. guilt	Exploration	Children need to begin asserting control and power over the environment. Success in this stage leads to a sense of purpose. Children who try to exert too much power experience disapproval, resulting in a sense of guilt.
Stage 4: School age (6 to 11 years)	Industry vs. inferiority	School	Children need to cope with new social and academic demands. Success leads to a sense of competence, while failure results in feelings of inferiority.
Stage 5: Adolescence (12 to 18 years)	Identity vs. role confusion	Social relationships	Teens need to develop a sense of self and personal identity. Success leads to an ability to stay true to yourself, while failure leads to role confusion and a weak sense of self.
Stage 6: Young adulthood (19 to 40 years)	Intimacy vs. isolation	Relationships	Young adults need to form intimate, loving relationships with other people. Success leads to strong relationships, while failure results in loneliness and isolation.
Stage 7: Middle adulthood (40 to 65 years)	Generativity vs. stagnation	Work and parenthood	Adults need to create or nurture things that will outlast them, often by having children or creating a positive change that benefits other people. Success leads to feelings of usefulness and accomplishment, while failure results in shallow involvement in the world.
Stage 8: Maturity (65 to death)	Ego integrity vs. despair	Reflection on life	Older adults need to look back on life and feel a sense of fulfilment. Success at this stage leads to feelings of wisdom, while failure results in regret, bitterness and despair.

Table 1.5 Summary of Erikson's stages of psychosocial development

psychological needs, not just their physical needs, by providing a caring, nurturing and appropriately challenging environment.

As a practitioner, you should encourage children's self-reliance, self-esteem and resilience by:

- engaging with and providing focused attention to individual children
- treating children with respect and consideration as individual people in their own right
- demonstrating understanding of their feelings and points of view

Figure 1.5 Providing a caring, nurturing and challenging environment

- encouraging children to take decisions and make choices
- communicating with children openly and honestly in ways that are not judgemental
- helping children to choose realistic goals that are challenging but achievable
- praising specific behaviour that you wish to encourage, as well as directing any comments, whether positive or negative, towards the demonstrated behaviour not the child.

You should work with colleagues and other professionals, as required, to encourage children's self-esteem and resilience – for example, providing opportunities to encourage children's self-reliance, positive self-esteem and self-image (see page 12). You may need to work with other professionals (e.g. counsellors, psychologists or social workers) to promote the well-being and resilience of children with special needs.

Research Activity

1. Select an article about psychoanalytic theory – for example, an article from a psychology/childcare magazine, journal or website. (See 'Useful resources' at the end of this chapter.)
2. Explain the link between the article you selected and an aspect of psychoanalytic theory (e.g. psychosexual stages or psychosocial development).
3. Summarise and analyse the article – for example, identify the strengths and weaknesses of the relevant psychoanalytic theory.

The impact of psychoanalytic theory on practice

Psychoanalytic theory had great influence during the first half of the 20th century. Psychologists inspired by Freud expanded on his ideas and developed theories of their own. For example,

Figure 1.6 Play therapy

Erikson's psychosocial stage theory describes growth and change throughout the lifespan, focusing on social interaction and conflicts that arise during different stages of development.

Melanie Klein had a significant impact on developmental psychology and her play therapy technique is still widely used today. She also emphasised the role of the mother–child and interpersonal relationships on development.

Anna Freud created the field of child psychoanalysis and her work contributed greatly to our understanding of child psychology. Anna introduced the concept of 'developmental lines', which emphasises the nature of child development as a continuous and cumulative process, which includes the assessment of a child's total personality rather than isolated parts.

Research Activity

1. Explore the relationship between the article you selected for the previous research activity (on page 14) and a recent news story relating to children's psychological development.
2. Evaluate the connection to your own life, personal interests and your practice when working with children/young people.

Humanistic theories

During the 1950s, humanistic theories of psychology began as a reaction against behaviourist and psychoanalytic theories, which dominated psychology at the time. Behaviourist theories study the conditioning processes that produce a person's behaviour, while psychoanalytic theories concentrate on understanding the unconscious motivations that drive a person's behaviour. Humanistic thinkers view these theories as failing to take account of personal choice. Humanistic theories focus on each individual's potential and stress the importance of growth and self-actualisation.

Abraham Maslow (1908–1970)

Abraham Maslow developed a hierarchy of needs that has influenced a number of different fields, including education. According to Maslow's hierarchy, there are five levels of needs:

- **Physiological needs**: these are biological needs, consisting of the need for oxygen, food, water and a relatively constant body temperature. They are the strongest needs because, if a person is deprived of all needs, the physiological ones come first in the person's search for satisfaction.
- **Safety needs**: when all physiological needs are satisfied and are no longer controlling thoughts and behaviours, the need for security becomes active. Adults have little awareness of their security needs, except in times of emergency. Children often display signs of insecurity and the need to be safe.
- **Belonging needs**: when physiological and safety needs are satisfied, the need for love, affection and belongingness can emerge. Maslow states that people seek to overcome feelings of loneliness and alienation. This involves both giving and receiving love, affection and the sense of belonging.
- **Esteem needs**: when the first three needs are satisfied, the need for esteem can become dominant. These involve needs for both self-esteem and the esteem a person gets from others. Humans have a need for a stable, firmly based, high level of self-respect and respect from others.
- **Self-actualisation needs**: when all of the above needs are satisfied, then the need for self-actualisation is activated. Maslow describes self-actualisation as a person's need to be and do that which the person was 'born to do'. 'A musician must make music, an artist must paint, and a poet must write' (Simons *et al.* 1987).

Children's needs

Every child has these basic needs (**PRICELESS**):

- **P**hysical care: regular, nutritious meals; warmth; rest and sleep.
- **R**outines: a regular pattern to the day; clear explanations for any changes.
- **I**ndependence: encouragement to do things for themselves and make choices.

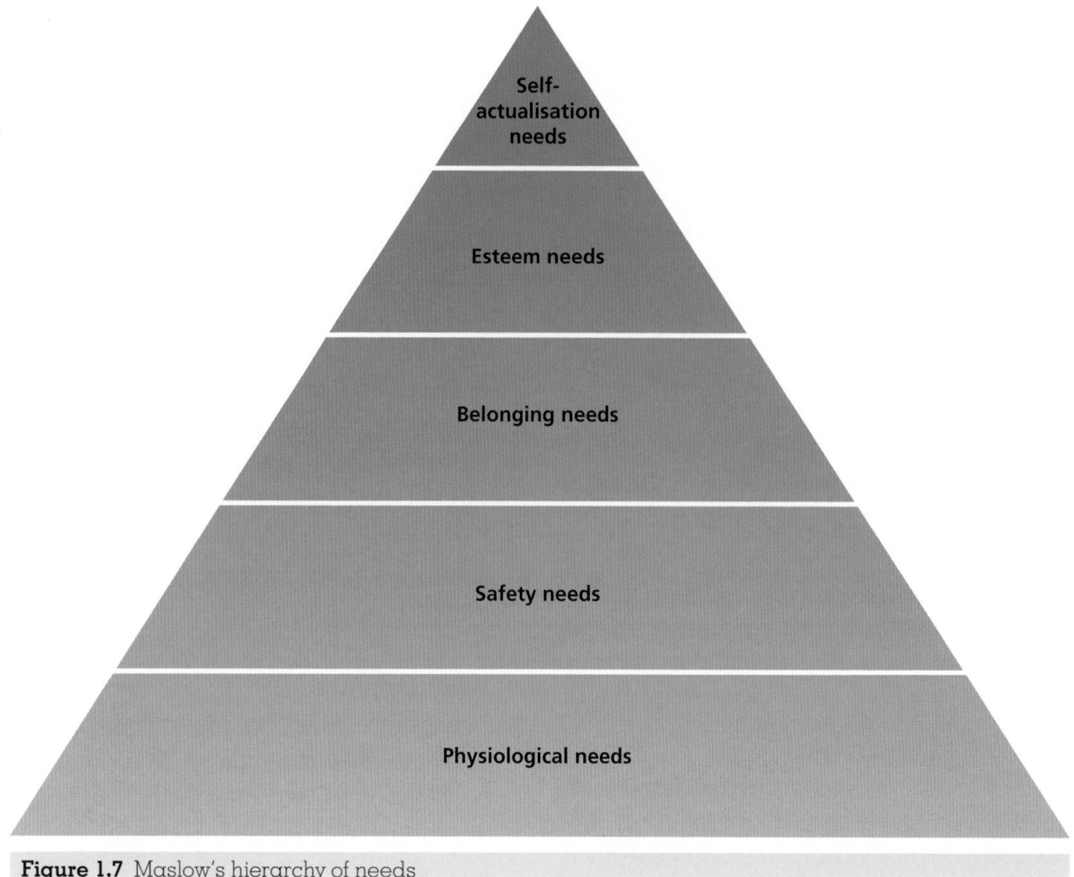

Figure 1.7 Maslow's hierarchy of needs

- **C**ommunication: opportunities for talk and interaction with others.
- **E**ncouragement and praise: for attempts as well as achievements.
- **L**ove: from parents or carers that is unconditional.
- **E**ducation: appropriate to age and level of development.
- **S**incerity and respect: including honest and courteous treatment.
- **S**timulation: opportunities to explore the environment and tackle new challenges.

Activity

Using the 'PRICELESS' list above, place children's needs in what you think is the correct section in Figure 1.7.

Carl Rogers (1902–1987)

Carl Rogers believed that every person has the potential to achieve their goals, wishes and desires in life. When, or rather if, they do so, self-actualisation takes place. He believed that humans have one basic motive – to fulfil their potential and achieve the highest level of being human (i.e. achieve self-actualisation). Like a flower that will grow to its full potential if the conditions are right, so a person will flourish and reach their potential if their environment is good enough. Unlike a flower, the potential of the individual person is unique and we are thought to develop in different ways according to our personality. (McLeod 2007b)

The self is composed of concepts unique to each person. The self-concept includes three components:

1 **Self-worth** (or self-esteem) – what we think about ourselves. Rogers believed feelings of self-worth

developed in early childhood and were formed from the interaction of the child with the mother and father.

2 **Self-image** – how we see ourselves, which is important to good psychological health. Self-image includes the influence of our body image on inner personality. At a simple level, we might perceive ourselves as a good or bad person, beautiful or ugly. Self-image has an effect on how a person thinks, feels and behaves in the world.

3 **Ideal self** – this is the person who we would like to be. It consists of our goals and ambitions in life and is dynamic (i.e. forever changing). The ideal self in childhood is not the ideal self in our teens or late twenties, etc.

(McLeod 2007b)

Rogers believed that people are inherently good and creative. They become destructive only when a poor self-concept or external constraints override the valuing process. Rogers believed that for a person to achieve self-actualisation they must be in a state of congruence. This means that self-actualisation occurs when a person's *ideal self* (who they would like to be) is consistent with their actual behaviour (self-image). Rogers describes an individual who is actualising as a fully functioning person. The main determinant of whether we will become self-actualised is childhood experience. A person's ideal self may not be consistent with what actually happens in the life and experiences of the person. Hence, a difference may exist between a person's ideal self and actual experience. This is called incongruence (McLeod 2007b)

Key term

Congruence – where a person's ideal self and actual experience are consistent or very similar.

Incongruence – the difference between a person's ideal self and actual experience.

Self-actualisation – when we feel, experience and behave in ways which are consistent with our self-image and which reflect what we would like to be like, our ideal self.

Activity

Find out more about Carl Roger's views on psychology – for example, his ideas about self-actualisation. You could start by looking at: http://www.nrogers.com/carlrogersbio.html.

Incongruent

Self-image

Ideal self

The self-image is different from the ideal self.

There is only a little overlap.

Here self-actualisation will be difficult.

Congruent

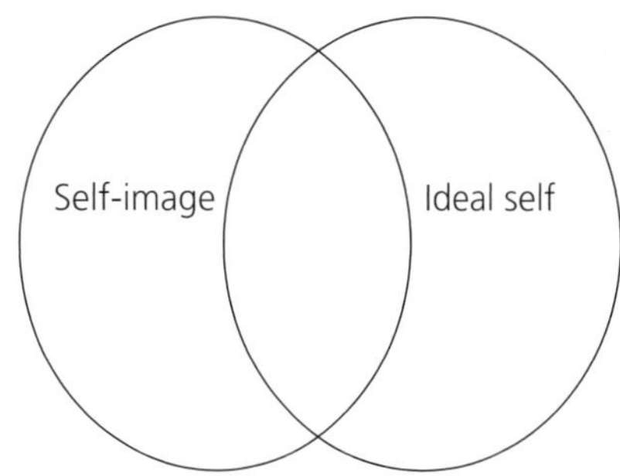

The self-image is similar to the ideal self.

There is more overlap.

This person can self-actualise.

Figure 1.8 Incongruent and congruent (Source: Saul Mcleod, website: http://www.simplypsychology.org)

Mia Kellmer Pringle (1921–1983)

Mia Kellmer Pringle (founder and first director of the National Children's Bureau) laid the foundations for the current focus on prevention and early intervention and on the importance of the first five years of life and the role of parents. Mia always saw children 'in the round'. Mia's personal childhood experience and her training and work as a psychologist led to her definitive book *The Needs of Children*, first published in 1975. Her book draws on the work of John Bowlby and Donald Winnicott, as well as her own clinical practice. Mia's themes in this book are the importance of: the early years of life to later development; the environment in which children grow; and children's social and emotional needs, as well as their physical needs. Failure to meet these needs has long-term consequences. Parents have a key role in meeting their children's needs, and parenting should be better supported and taken more seriously. (Pugh 2006)

Activity

Find out more about Mia Kellmer Pringle's views on psychology – for example, her ideas about children's needs. You could start by looking at: www.nurseryworld.co.uk/news/716362/Putting-children-first/?DCMP=ILC-SEARCH.

How humanistic theories support meeting the needs of children

In the past decade, there has been a major shift in attitudes towards children's rights. In the past, children's rights were mainly concerned with children's basic welfare needs. Now, as well as their basic rights to life, health and education, children are viewed as having a much wider range of rights, including the right to engage in play activities, to express their views and to participate in making decisions that affect them directly. Children's rights, as stated in the UN Convention on the Rights of the Child, are clear and universal: they apply to all children. Also, while children's individual needs may differ, they all have the same rights. Children's rights are based on their needs, but emphasising rights rather than needs demonstrates a commitment to viewing and respecting children as valued citizens (The Children's Rights Alliance for England: www.crae.org.uk).

Every child has individual needs as a special and unique individual. Each child perceives the world differently and interacts with other people in different ways. Each child views the world in an individual way due to different life experiences. Every child experiences different social and environmental factors, which, together with genetic differences, help to create a unique combination of personality, knowledge and skills.

As an individual, each child belongs to various social groups – that is, their family, local community, school and wider society. When working with children, you must appreciate the uniqueness of every child, while ensuring that the needs of both the individual and the group are met (Brennan 1987). How each child reacts to the learning environment depends on individual needs and life experiences. Some children see the learning environment as an exciting challenge and are well motivated to learn. Some children find the learning environment extremely daunting and may experience learning difficulties. Some children see the learning environment as boring or uninviting and may demonstrate signs of difficult behaviour.

Every child has social and emotional needs that should be met by the setting through:

- assistance in adjusting to new learning environments
- help in relating comfortably with other children and adults
- opportunities to interact and play with other children
- opportunities to find out about people and the world they live in.

Every child also has individual educational needs, requiring:

- opportunities to explore the environment
- adult assistance to aid knowledge and understanding
- activities that are appropriate to individual abilities and development.

Some children may have special or additional needs, requiring:

- special equipment or resources
- modified surroundings, e.g. wheelchair access, ramps
- extra learning support to access the national curriculum
- a special or modified curriculum.

About one in five children have special educational needs and the majority of these children are educated in mainstream settings. Children with special educational needs have additional needs arising from a physical disability, a learning difficulty or an emotional or behavioural problem. Children with special educational needs may require learning support to enable them to access the curriculum. One of the responsibilities of the practitioner may be to provide intensive learning support for an individual or small group of children with special educational needs to ensure that the needs of all children can be met in an inclusive way. You may work as part of the special educational needs team and your role may involve supporting children identified as having special educational needs, including those with individual education plans (IEPs) and/or statements of special educational needs.

Carl Rogers viewed children as having two basic needs: positive regard from other people and self-worth. Rogers believed that people need to be regarded positively by others – we all need to feel valued, respected, treated with affection and loved. Positive regard is to do with how other people evaluate and judge us in social interaction. Rogers believed feelings of self-worth developed in early childhood and were formed from the interaction of the child with the mother and father. As a child grows older, interactions with significant others will affect feelings of self-worth. (McLeod 2007b)

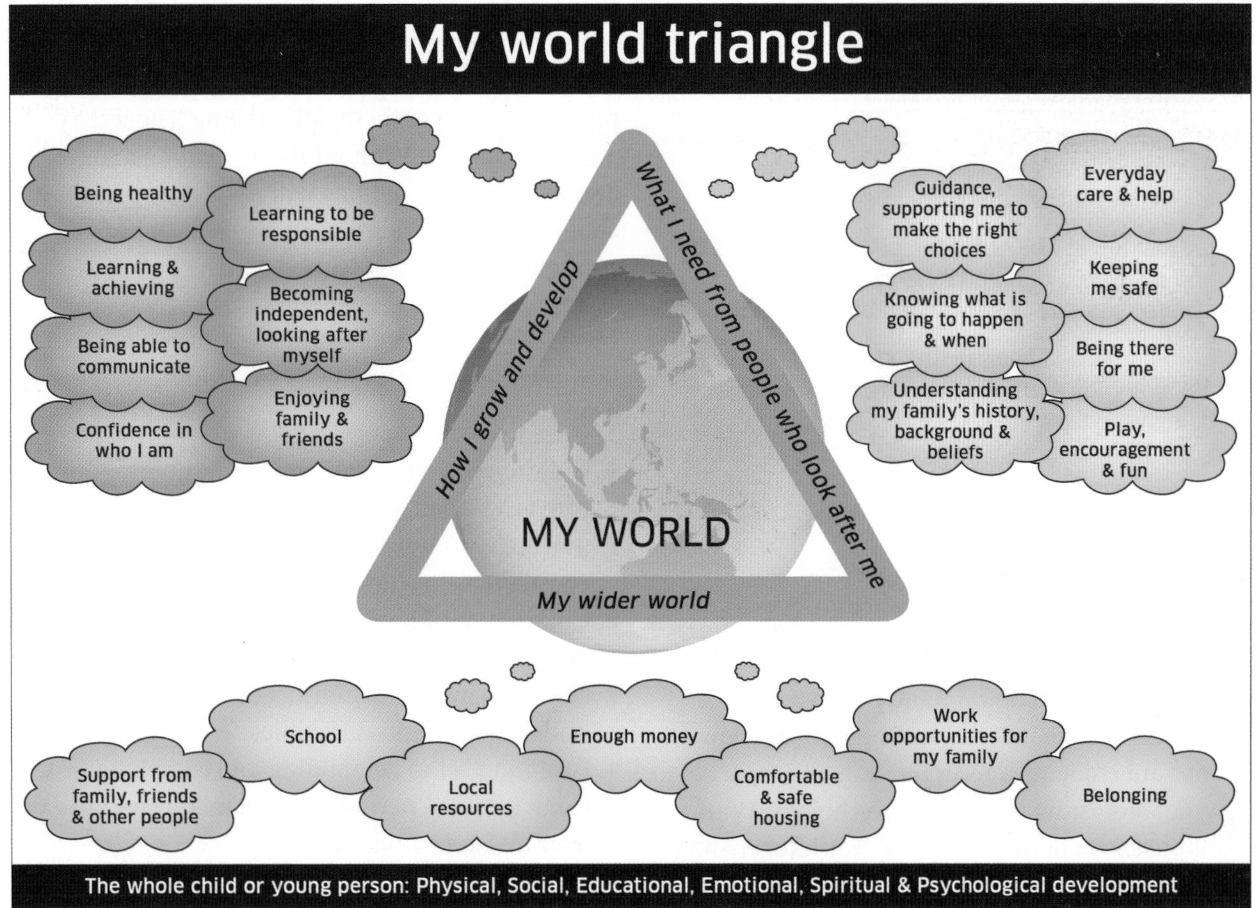

Figure 1.9 Meeting children's needs: My World Triangle (source: Scottish Government, www.scotland.gov.uk)

Strengths of humanistic theories	Weaknesses of humanistic theories
A major strength of humanistic theories is that they emphasise the role of the individual. They give more credit to the individual in controlling and determining their state of mental health.	Humanistic theories can be too subjective. The importance of individual experience makes it difficult to study and measure humanistic phenomena objectively. For example, we cannot objectively tell if someone is self-actualised. We can only rely on the individual's own assessment of their experiences.
Humanistic theories also take environmental influences into account. Rather than focusing solely on a person's internal thoughts and desires, humanistic theories also credit the environment's influence on the individual's experiences.	Another major criticism is that observations are unverifiable – there is no accurate way to measure or quantify these qualities.
Humanistic theories continue to influence therapy, education, healthcare and other areas.	While some research has showed support for Maslow's theories, most research has not been able to substantiate the idea of a needs hierarchy.
Humanistic theories helped remove some of the stigma attached to therapy and made it more acceptable for normal, healthy individuals to explore their abilities and potential through therapy.	Other criticisms of Maslow's theory note that his definition of self-actualisation is difficult to test scientifically. His research on self-actualisation was also based on a very limited sample of individuals.

Table 1.6 Some strengths and weaknesses of humanistic theories

Research Activity

1. Select an article about humanistic theory – for example, an article from a psychology/childcare magazine, journal or website. (See 'Useful resources' at the end of this chapter.)
2. Explain the link between the article you selected and an aspect of humanistic theory (e.g. children's needs or self-actualisation).
3. Summarise and analyse the article (e.g. identify the strengths and weaknesses of the relevant humanistic theory).

The impact of humanistic theories on practice

Many psychological theories focus on what is considered to be abnormal behaviour, but humanistic theories take a more positive and holistic view of the individual. Abraham Maslow's theories are enjoying a resurgence due to the growing interesting in positive psychology. With his emphasis on human potential, Carl Rogers had an enormous influence on both psychology and education. Rogers agreed with most of what Maslow believed, but added that for a person to 'grow', they need an environment that provides them with genuineness (openness and self-disclosure), acceptance (being seen with unconditional positive regard) and empathy (being listened to and understood). Without these, relationships and healthy personalities will not develop as they should, much like a tree will not grow without sunlight and water. (McLeod 2007b)

Most of Mia Kellmer Pringle's key messages are now integral to current policy developments. For example:

- Children are our future, and their upbringing and care is a skilled, responsible and demanding job in which the community as a whole should invest considerable resources.
- Children need love and security, new experiences, praise and recognition, and responsibility.
- Failure to meet children's needs in the early years leads to long-term difficulties.
- Parenting is too demanding and complex a task to think it can be performed well merely because we have all been children.
- The school curriculum should include human psychology, child development and preparation for parenthood.

Figure 1.10 Children are our future, and their upbringing and care is a skilled, responsible and demanding job

- Pre-school education should be expanded, and care and education should be integrated.
- 'If even half of what we know were accepted with feeling and applied with understanding by all who have the care of children, then the revolution brought about in children's physical health in the past 40 years might well be matched by a similar change in their psychological well-being' (Pugh 2006).

Research Activity

1. Explore the relationship between the article you selected for the previous research activity (on page 20) and a recent news story relating to children's emotional and social needs.
2. Evaluate the connection to your own life, personal interests and your practice when working with children/young people.

Social constructivist theories

Social constructivist psychologists believe that human behaviour can be understood by studying how people think and learn. This includes the work of Piaget, Vygotsky and Bruner. The social constructivist view of intellectual development takes into account more recent research concerning how children think and learn within the context of home, school and the wider environment. Social constructivism integrates children's intellectual and social development within a useful framework. It moves away from the idea that the development of children's intellectual abilities occurs in stages at particular ages and that adults simply provide the means for this natural process. Instead adults assist children's intellectual development as part of the social process of childhood. Age is not the critical factor in intellectual development; assisted learning can and does occur at any age. The key factor is the learner's existing knowledge and/or experience in connection with the current problem or learning situation.

Jean Piaget (1896–1980)

A Swiss biologist, Jean Piaget used observations of his own children, plus a wider sample of children, to develop his theories of cognitive development. Piaget's theories of cognitive development have had a major influence on early education for more than 40 years. Piaget believed that children went through different stages of cognitive development based on fixed ages. Within these stages, the children's patterns of learning, or schemas as he called them, were very different from adult ways of problem-solving. He also believed in the importance of young children learning through action and exploration of their environment using their sensory motor skills. According to Piaget, children are *actively* involved in structuring their own cognitive development through exploration of their environment. Children need real objects and 'concrete experiences' to discover things for themselves. The adult's role is to provide children with appropriate experiences in a suitable environment to facilitate the children's instinctive ability to think and learn. Cognitive development occurs in four set stages, which are universal – they apply to all forms of learning and across all cultures (see Table 1.7).

Piaget viewed children as thinking and learning in a different way from adults. Not only do children have less experience of the world, but their understanding of it is shaped by this entirely different way of looking at their environment. Children will only learn when they are 'ready' for different experiences as determined by their current stage of cognitive development.

Piaget did not see language and communication as central to children's cognitive development because this development begins at birth, before children can comprehend or use words. Young children's use of language demonstrates their cognitive achievements, but does not control them. He does see the importance of language at later stages. Young children are egocentric. They are unable to see or understand another person's viewpoint. This also means they are unable to convey information accurately or effectively to others.

Piaget believed that children interact with their environment to actively construct their knowledge and understanding of the world. They do this by relating new information to existing information.

Stage	Cognitive development
Stage 1: Sensori-motor – 0 to 2 years	• Babies and very young children learn through their senses, physical activity and interaction with their immediate environment. • Babies and very young children understand their world in terms of actions.
Stage 2: Pre-operations – 2 to 7 years	• Young children learn through their experiences with real objects in their immediate environment. • Young children use symbols (e.g. words and images) to make sense of their world.
Stage 3: Concrete operations – 7 to 11 years	• Children continue to learn through their experiences with real objects. • Children access information (using language) to make sense of their environment.
Stage 4: Formal operations – 11 years to adult	• Older children, young people and adults learn to make use of abstract thinking (e.g. algebra, physics).

Table 1.7 Piaget's four stages of cognitive development

Piaget called this interaction: assimilation (the need for further information); accommodation (the need for organised information); and adaptation (the need for revised/updated information). All new information has to be built on existing information; there needs to be some connection between them. Similar information can be stored as it relates to existing information. Discrepant information cannot be stored because it is not related to existing information. Piaget described internal mental processes as schemas and the ways in which they are used when thinking as operations. Mental processes or schemas do not remain static; they continually develop as we acquire new information and extend our understanding of the world.

Research by people such as Margaret Donaldson suggests Piaget underestimated young children's cognitive abilities – the use of appropriate language within a meaningful context enables three- and four-year-olds to use logical thinking and to understand concepts such as the conservation of number, volume and weight. For example, the number conservation task, which involves two identical rows of objects where young children agree that there are the same number in each row until the adult moves the objects in one of the rows so that it is longer than the other row – although the number of objects remains the same, young children will say the longer row has more objects (see Figure 1.12). However, when this task is done using a 'naughty' teddy bear to upset the arrangement of the objects, then young children can state that the number of objects remains the same. The task has to *make sense* to the young child and the adult needs to use language that the child can understand.

Donaldson also challenged Piaget's claim that children under seven years old are highly egocentric – that is, they cannot see things from another person's point of view. Piaget's evidence for this claim included the 'mountains' task, in which young

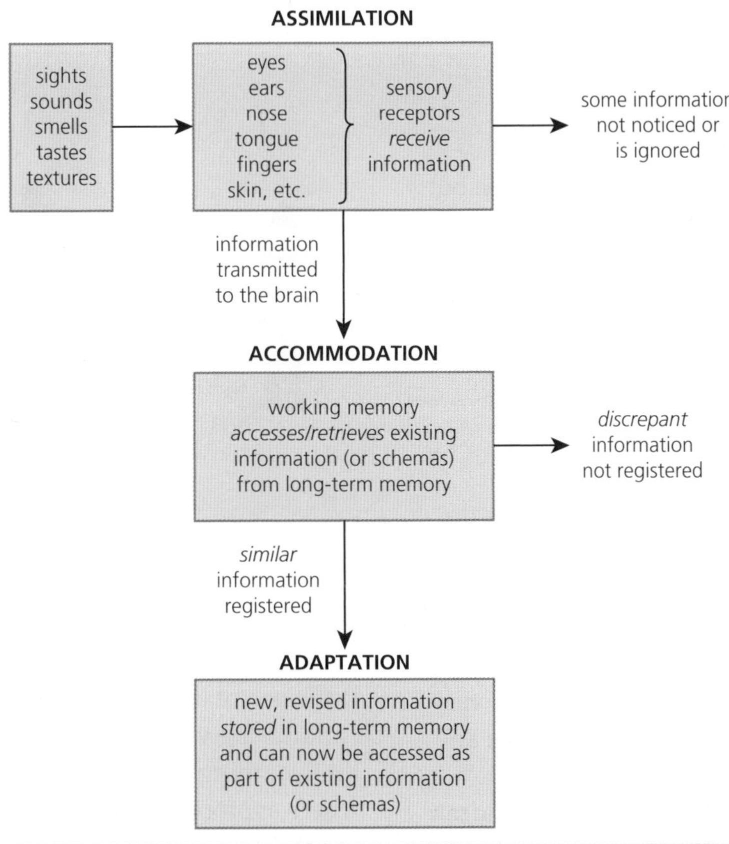

Figure 1.11 Understanding assimilation, accommodation and adaptation

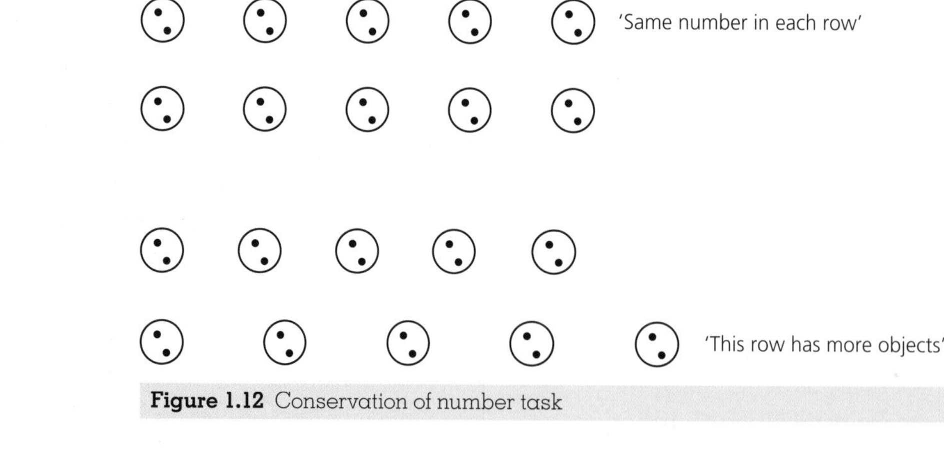

Figure 1.12 Conservation of number task

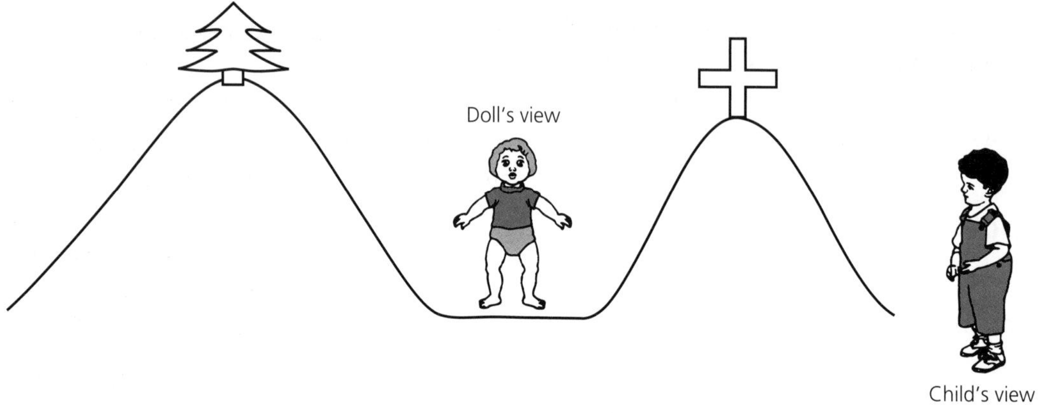

Figure 1.13 Piaget's 'mountains' task

children had to indicate what a doll would see but instead would state their *own* view of the situation (see Figure 1.13). Piaget described this as *egocentric illusion*.

Donaldson states that there is evidence which strongly suggests that Piaget's claim was incorrect. For example, 'the policeman and little boy' task devised by Martin Hughes showed that even three- and four-year-olds could assess the policeman's viewpoint and hide the little boy where the policeman would not be able to see him (see Figure 1.14). This is because the task makes sense to young children – they can understand what they are supposed to do because even very young children can understand the motives and intentions of the policeman and the boy. The 'mountains' task is too abstract and the children do not understand what they are supposed to do. (Donaldson 1978)

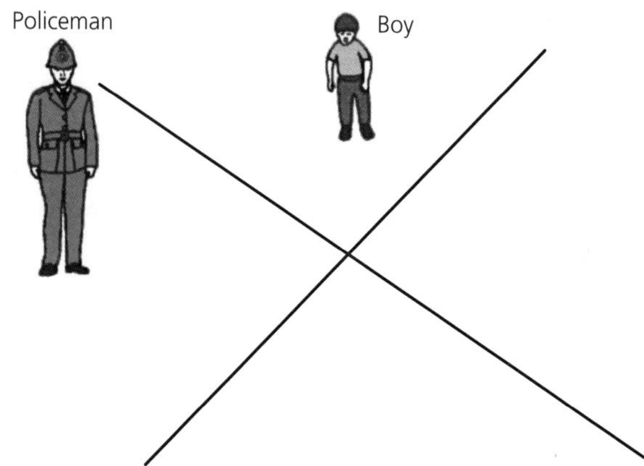

Figure 1.14 The 'policeman and little boy' task (Hughes)

Revisions of Piaget's work demonstrate that young children are very capable thinkers as long as their learning takes place in meaningful contexts where appropriate language is used to facilitate the children's understanding. Language is seen as having a key role in children's development

– children use language to develop their understanding of the world around them. In later life, Piaget recognised the importance of social development in connection with the development of cognitive skills. Social interaction helps stimulate and formulate intelligence. Prior to this, Piaget had concluded that cognitive development progressed parallel to social development but was not influenced by it. In his earlier work, Piaget did recognise the role of peers in children's cognitive development – a child on their own might be unable to solve a problem but working with other children could reach a solution. One of the most valuable contributions Piaget makes to our understanding of children's cognitive development is that children's thinking and learning are an active process rather than one of passive absorption.

Key term

Cognitive – intellectual abilities involving processing information received through the senses.

Schemas – term used mainly by Piaget and Froebel to describe internal thought processes.

Activity

- Make a list of the main points of Piaget's theories of cognitive development.
- Which points do you think accurately describe children's thinking and learning? Give examples from your own experiences of working with children.

L.S. Vygotsky (1896–1934)

The Russian psychologist Lev Semonovich Vygotsky argued that the social interaction between children and other people enables children to develop the intellectual skills necessary for thinking and logical reasoning. Language is the key to this social interaction. Through language and communication, children learn to think about their world and modify their actions accordingly. Like Piaget, Vygotsky was concerned with the active process of cognitive development, but there were also many differences between their viewpoints (see Table 1.8).

Vygotsky considered adults as having an active role in fostering children's cognitive development. So while children are active in constructing their own intellectual processes, they are not lone explorers; children need and receive knowledge through interaction with other children and adults. Vygotsky (and later Bruner) viewed the adult as supporting children's cognitive development within an appropriate framework (see 'scaffolding' on pages 26–9).

Adults support children's learning by assisting the children's own efforts and thus enabling children to acquire the necessary skills, knowledge and understanding. As children develop competent skills through this assisted learning, the adults gradually decrease their support until the children are able to work independently. With appropriate adult assistance, young children are able to complete tasks and to solve problems which they would not be able to do on their own. It is important that adults recognise when to provide support towards each child's next step of development and when this support is no

Piaget's viewpoint	Vygotsky's viewpoint
Egocentric young child separate from others for a long period of development (0–7 years) but gradually becomes socialised.	Young child is a social organism who develops awareness of self through interactions with others.
Peer interaction can be helpful. Adults provide rich and stimulating environment but too much adult interference can be harmful. Teaching by adults inhibits young children's 'natural' development.	Social interaction with children and adults is crucial. The adult's role in teaching new skills is very important – for example, providing assisted learning situations within each child's zone of proximal development (see Figure 1.15).
Thought develops independently of language.	Language is a tool for thought.

Table 1.8 Differences between Piaget and Vygotsky's viewpoints

longer required. Vygotsky used the idea of the zone of proximal development, or area of next development, to describe this framework of support for learning (Tharp and Gallimore 1991). Children can be in different zones for different skills or tasks. Each activity has its own zone of proximal development (see Figure 1.15).

The zone of proximal development can be represented in four stages. For example, children learning to read may progress in this way:

- **Stage 1**: learning phonics, decoding and comprehension skills with assistance of childcarers, parents, teachers, teaching assistants (assistance from others).
- **Stage 2**: sounding out difficult/unfamiliar words, reading aloud to self, lips moving during silent reading, etc. (self-help).
- **Stage 3**: reading competently using internal prompts (auto-pilot).
- **Stage 4**: new words, complicated texts, learning to read in a different language, etc. require further assistance (relapses to previous steps).

Activity

Draw your own diagram showing how the zone of proximal development could apply to:

- your own learning (e.g. learning to cook or learning to drive)
- a child's learning (e.g. learning to write or learning a new mathematical skill).

Jerome S. Bruner (1915–)

The American psychologist Jerome S. Bruner emphasises the importance of the adult in supporting children's thinking and learning. Bruner uses the term scaffolding to describe this adult support. Picture a builder using scaffolding to support a house while it is being built. Without the scaffold, the house could not be built, but once the house is finished, the scaffolding can be removed. The adult supports the child's learning until they are ready to stand alone. Bruner also emphasises the adult's skills of recognising where and when this support is needed and when it should be removed. The structuring of children's learning should be flexible; the adult support or scaffold should not be rigid; it needs to change as the needs of the child change – that is, as the child gains knowledge and understanding and/or acquires new skills.

The adult supports children's learning and development by:

- providing learning experiences within a meaningful context
- adapting tasks and learning experiences
- selecting appropriate materials for each child's needs and abilities
- encouraging children to make choices about what they want to do and when.

Bruner believed that any subject can be taught to any child at any age as long as it is presented in an

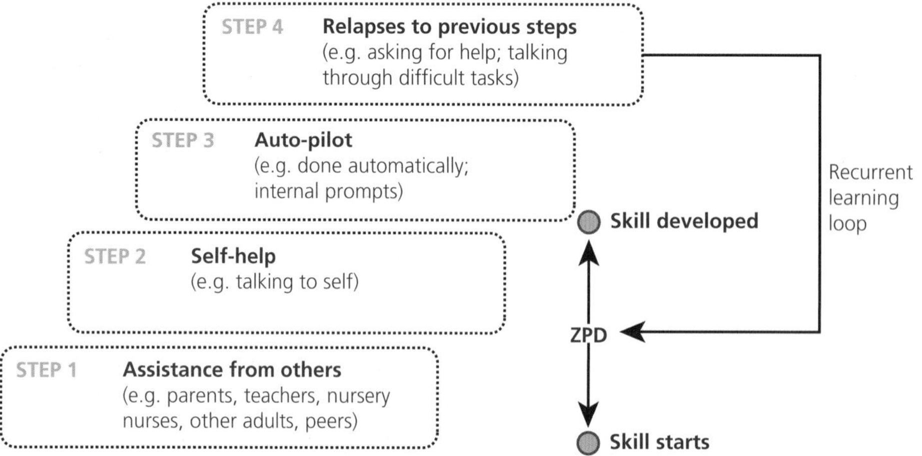

Figure 1.15 The zone of proximal development Source: adapted from Tharp and Gallimore (1991, p. 50)

appropriate way. Learning does not occur in pre-determined stages, but is dependent on linking knowledge to children's existing knowledge in a holistic way.

Bruner's sequence of cognitive development is divided into three areas:

1 **Enactive**: understanding the world through action (relates to Piaget's sensori-motor stage).
2 **Iconic**: manipulation of images or 'icons' in child's thinking about the world (corresponds to Piaget's pre-operational stage).
3 **Symbolic**: use of language and symbols to make sense of the world (similar to Piaget's operational stage).

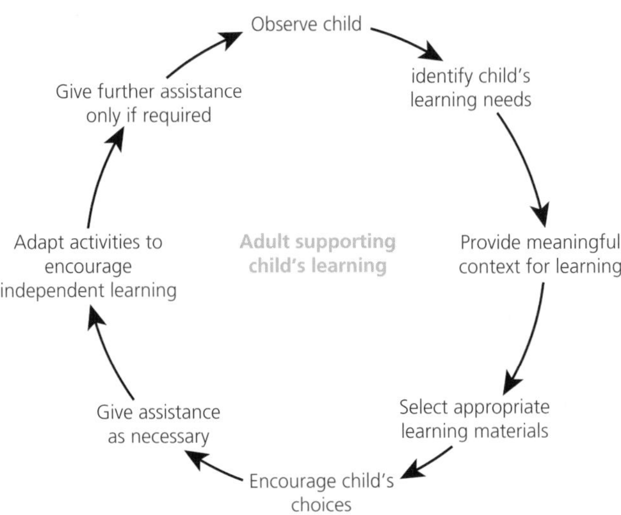

Figure 1.16 Scaffolding: supporting a child's thinking and learning

Bruner views language as central to children's thinking and learning and stresses how language is used to represent experiences and how past experience or knowledge is organised through language in ways which make information more accessible. Language connects a person's understanding of one situation to another. The adult has a particular role in establishing effective communication to encourage and extend children's thinking and learning. Adults use language to: capture children's interest and direct their attention; develop children's problem-solving abilities; assist children's understanding of concepts; encourage and extend children's own ideas; and negotiate choices with children.

Key term

Scaffolding – Bruner's term for adult assistance given to support child's thinking and learning. As child develops competence, the adult decreases support until child works independently.

Zone of proximal development – Vygotsky's description for a child's next area of development where adult assistance is only required until the child has developed the skill and can do it independently.

Activity

- Summarise the main points of Vygotsky's and Bruner's theories concerning children's thinking and learning.
- Think about how these ideas relate to your experiences of working with children.

How social constructivist theories support meeting the needs of children

As appropriate to your particular role, you will need to plan, implement and evaluate curriculum plans according to the requirements of your setting. When planning, implementing and evaluating curriculum plans, your overall aims should be to: support *all* the children you work with; ensure each child has full access to the relevant curriculum; encourage participation by all children; meet children's individual learning and development needs; build on children's existing knowledge and skills; and help all children achieve their full potential.

It is vital that *all* children have access to a stimulating environment which enables learning to take place in exciting and challenging ways. To develop into healthy, considerate and intelligent adults, all children require intellectual stimulation as well as physical care and emotional security. Intellectual stimulation through play and other learning opportunities allows children to develop their cognitive abilities and fulfil their potential as individuals.

The children you work with will be constantly thinking and learning – for example, gathering new information and formulating new ideas about themselves, other people and the world around them. Social constructivist theories support meeting children's needs by stressing the importance of providing children with opportunities to:

- explore their environment and/or investigate new information/ideas
- discover things for themselves through a wide variety of experiences
- feel free to make mistakes in a safe and secure environment using 'trial and error'
- develop autonomy through increased responsibility and working independently
- encourage and extend their knowledge and skills with appropriate support from adults (and other children)
- learn to make sense of new information within an appropriate curriculum framework.

Research Activity

1. Select an article about constructivist theory – for example, an article from a psychology/childcare magazine, journal or website. (See 'Useful resources' at the end of this chapter.)
2. Explain the link between the article you selected and an aspect of constructivist theory (e.g. schemas, scaffolding or zone of proximal development).
3. Summarise and analyse the article (e.g. identify the strengths and weaknesses of the relevant constructivist theory).

The impact of social constructivist theories on practice

Piaget's ideas have had enormous influence on developmental psychology. He changed how people viewed the child's world and their methods of studying children. His ideas have been of practical use in understanding and communicating with children, particularly in the field of education – for example, active learning (see pages 46–8).

Figure 1.17 Adult supporting children engaged in a writing activity

The theories of Vygotsky and Bruner are relevant to teaching and learning – for example, 'scaffolding', in which an adult or more advanced peer helps to structure or arrange a task so that a new learner can work on it successfully.

Research Activity

1. Explore the relationship between the article you selected for the previous research activity (on page 28) and a recent news story relating to children's intellectual development and learning.
2. Evaluate the connection to your own life, personal interests and your practice when working with children/young people.

Attachment theories

Babies develop a strong attachment to the people they see most often and who satisfy their needs. One attachment is usually stronger than the others and this is usually to the baby's mother, but the attachment can be to another family member or anyone outside the immediate family who spends a significant amount of time with the young child, such as a grandparent or nanny. The security of these early attachments is essential to babies and young children because they provide a firm foundation for promoting emotional well-being, positive relationships with other people and confidence in exploring the environment. These early attachments enable children to feel secure about their relationships and to develop trust in others. Security and trust are important elements in young children's ability to separate from their parents and carers in order to develop their own independence and ideas.

John Bowlby (1907–1990)

John Bowlby's theory was that, to ensure a child's mental health, the child required a continuous relationship with *one* mother or mother substitute. If not, the child would be psychologically damaged by the deprivation experienced. Bowlby believed there was a parallel between the animal instinct for *imprinting* and the human need for *attachment* between mother and child. This belief was a firm foundation of Bowlby's theory of maternal deprivation. An important concept in Bowlby's

1. A child has an innate (i.e. inborn) need to attach to one main attachment figure (i.e. monotropy).	Although Bowlby did not rule out the possibility of other attachment figures for a child, he did believe that there should be a primary bond which was much more important than any other (usually the mother).
2. A child should receive the continuous care of this single most important attachment figure for approximately the first two years of life.	If the attachment figure is broken or disrupted during the critical two-year period, the child will suffer irreversible long-term consequences of this maternal deprivation. This risk continues until the age of five.
3. The long-term consequences of maternal deprivation might include the following: delinquency; reduced intelligence; increased aggression; depression; affectionless psychopathy.	Affectionless psychopathy is an inability to show affection or concern for others. Such individuals act on impulse with little regard for the consequences of their actions. For example, showing no guilt for anti-social behaviour.
4. The child's attachment relationship with their primary caregiver leads to the development of an internal working model.	This internal working model is a cognitive framework comprising mental representations for understanding the world, self and others. There are three main features of the internal working model: (1) a model of others as being trustworthy, (2) a model of the self as valuable, and (3) a model of the self as effective when interacting with others.

Table 1.9 Main points of Bowlby's attachment theory (McLeod 2007c)

theory of maternal deprivation is attachment theory, which suggests that the mother–baby attachment is unique and unlike any other relationship the child may have with another person. This instinctive attachment which a child has to one mother figure is described as monotropy.

Key term

Attachment – the strong bond between baby and parent (usually the mother) or to another family member or anyone outside the immediate family who spends a significant amount of time with the very young child, such as a grandparent or nanny.

Maternal deprivation – the psychological damage experienced by a child due to the lack of a continuous relationship with *one* mother or mother substitute.

Monotropy – instinctive attachment and unique relationship between a baby and one mother figure.

Activity

Find out more about John Bowlby's views on attachment – for example, his ideas about monotropy. You could start by looking at: www.simplypsychology.org/bowlby.html.

Michael Rutter (1934–)

Bowlby's theories have been strongly criticised as children are able to form many attachments and distinct relationships with other family members and day care staff. The term 'maternal deprivation' has been described as unsatisfactory. Michael Rutter disagrees with the term maternal deprivation as stated by Bowlby because children can experience deprivation in other ways, not just through separation from their mothers. Children can also experience maternal deprivation within the family setting, even if the mother is actually present (Rutter 1991).

Instead, Rutter prefers the following definitions of deprivation:

- **Privation**: the child has no opportunity to form secure attachments/relationships.
- **Disruption**: the child experiences broken attachments/relationships due to death or other separation.
- **Distortion**: the child experiences distorted family relationships due to marital discord, inconsistent treatment or any form of abuse.

Bowlby's theory suggests that any family, no matter how 'bad', provides children with the care they need so that they do not experience maternal deprivation; children in 'good' residential care do less well than children in 'bad' homes. Rutter suggests that children in 'bad' families are suffering distortion; the children are still experiencing deprivation even though they remain in the family setting. Children can experience violence, cruelty or neglect at the hands of their mothers (and fathers); many children can and do receive better care away from their biological parents in foster homes, small residential homes or with adoptive parents.

Activity

Find out more about Michael Rutter's views on attachment – for example, his ideas about maternal deprivation. You could start by looking at: http://as-psychology.pbworks.com/w/page/9174253/DeprivationPrivation.

Mary Ainsworth (1913–1999)

Most attachment research is carried out using babies and young children, so psychologists have to devise subtle ways of researching attachment, usually involving the observational method. The psychologist Mary Ainsworth provided research offering explanations of individual differences in attachment. She devised an assessment technique called the 'strange situation' in order to investigate how attachments might vary between children. Her experiment was set up in a small room with one-way glass so the behaviour of the infant could be observed. Infants were aged between 12 and 18 months. The sample comprised about 100 middle-class American families.

The experiment was conducted by observing the behaviour of the infant in a series of eight three-minute episodes, as follows:

1 Stranger joins parent and infant.
2 Stranger talks to parent then plays with infant.

1. *Stranger joins parent and infant.*

2. *Stranger talks to parent then plays with infant.*

3. *Parent leaves infant and stranger alone.*

4. *The stranger stays and plays with infant.*

5. *The parent returns and stranger leaves.*

6. *Parent leaves; infant left completely alone.*

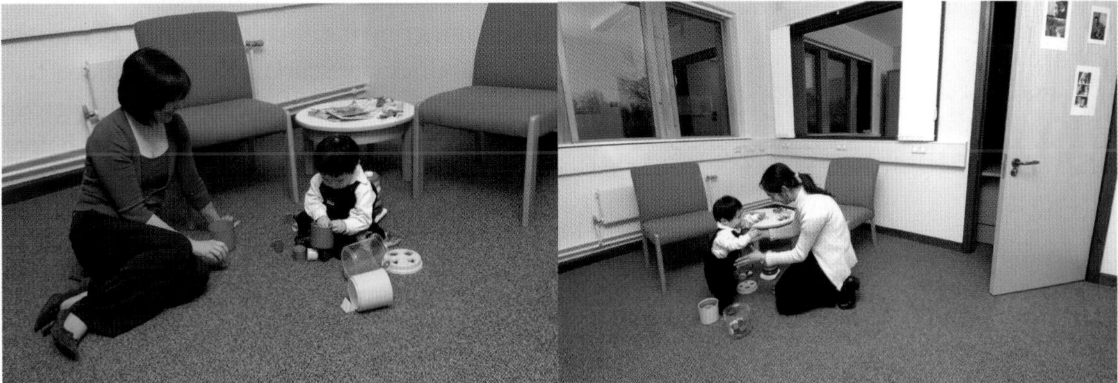

7. *Stranger returns.*

8. *Parent returns and stranger leaves.*

Figure 1.18 The 'strange situation' (**Source:** The Open University)

	Secure attachment	Resistant attachment	Avoidant attachment
Separation anxiety	Distressed when mother leaves.	Infant shows signs of intense distress when mother leaves.	Infant shows no sign of distress when mother leaves.
Stranger anxiety	Avoidant of stranger when alone but friendly when mother present.	Infant avoids the stranger – shows fear of stranger.	Infant is okay with the stranger and plays normally when stranger is present.
Reunion behaviour	Positive and happy when mother returns.	Child approaches mother but resists contact, may even push her away.	Infant shows little interest when mother returns.
Other	Will use the mother as a safe base to explore their environment.	Infant cries more and explores less than the other two types.	Mother and stranger are able to comfort infant equally well.
Percentage of infants	70	15	15

Table 1.10 Mary Ainsworth's strange situation – three attachment styles (McLeod 2008)

3 Parent leaves infant and stranger alone.
4 Stranger stays and plays with infant
5 Parent returns and stranger leaves.
6 Parent leaves; infant left completely alone.
7 Stranger returns.
8 Parent returns and stranger leaves.

Ainsworth's set of observational studies using the 'strange situation' revealed three distinct forms of attachment ('attachment styles' – see Table 1.10).

Activity

Find out more about Mary Ainsworth's views on attachment – for example, her ideas about the 'strange situation'. You could start by looking at: www.simplypsychology.org/mary-ainsworth.html.

How attachment theories support meeting the needs of children

According to Bowlby, separation from their mothers causes intense distress in very young children, particularly in the critical period between the ages of seven months and three years. Following reunion with their mothers, detachment may still continue, leading to contradictory feelings towards their mothers, alternating between being clingy and being hostile. Bowlby believed that continued and persistent periods of this sort of separation caused permanent psychological damage. Although young children do experience distress when first separating from their mother when starting nursery or school, it is short-lived and has no lasting effects on children's psychological development. Long-term effects *have* been found in children in residential care; teachers' reports indicate behavioural problems in such children with effects including extreme need for adult attention and difficulties in making friendships with peers (Tizard 1991).

These effects can also be apparent in young children who have been mothered at home, where they are used to one-to-one with their mother and so sometimes find it difficult to be part of a group (e.g. in nursery or school). Research shows that children who have attended nursery/playgroup or been cared for by a relative/childminder before they start school are often more independent, better able to interact with their peers, more willing to share and cooperate with other children, more sociable towards unfamiliar people and less timid or shy. However, there was no difference in the percentage of behavioural difficulties between children cared for by their mothers and children who have attended day care prior to nursery or school (Tizard 1991).

Research Activity

1. Select an article about attachment theory – for example, an article from a psychology/childcare magazine, journal or website. (See 'Useful resources' at the end of this chapter.)
2. Explain the link between the article you selected and an aspect of attachment theory (e.g. attachment styles or maternal deprivation).
3. Summarise and analyse the article (e.g. identify the strengths and weaknesses of the relevant attachment theory).

The impact of attachment theories on practice

The theory of maternal deprivation is related to social, cultural and even political ideas. For example, Bowlby's theory of maternal deprivation was established in the 1950s following post-Second World War anxieties concerning the care of children in residential nurseries. His theory may also have been politically motivated by the fact that when men returned from the war they wanted the jobs back that had been done by women during the war. Many women had enjoyed being part of the workforce and were reluctant to give up their freedom and status. Women were made to feel guilty about going out to work; the theory of maternal deprivation effectively blackmailed women into staying at home for the sake of their children's psychological well-being.

In the UK today, women are still viewed as children's primary caregivers. Mothers who work are seen by some as not being maternal, especially if their children are under five years old (Stoppard 1990). Some people still feel that mothers should stay at home and not go out to work. Children do not have to be cared for solely by their mothers; there is strong cross-cultural evidence that a child can make strong and secure attachments with five or more 'caretakers' (Woodhead 1991).

Bowlby himself recognised that the *amount* of time children spend with their mothers is not the crucial factor; it is the *quality* of the time spent together, not the *quantity*. *Quality* is also the key factor in children's other attachments. There is no evidence that quality day care has a detrimental effect on young children and it is unlikely that young children will suffer psychological damage because their mothers work (Tizard 1991).

Recent research suggests that mothers should stay at home or only work part-time until their children are 18 months old as employment started after a child is 18 months or part-time work at any time has no negative effects. Also, young children have better cognitive outcomes when cared for by paid, qualified childcarers rather than by unpaid carers (such as a friend, relative or neighbour), especially if their mothers work full-time (Gregg *et al.* 2005).

Research Activity

1. Explore the relationship between the article you selected for the previous research activity (on page 33) and a recent news story relating to children's attachments and settling into new situations.
2. Evaluate the connection to your own life, personal interests and your practice when working with children/young people.

The nature versus nurture debate in children's development

The debate over the contributions of nature (inheritance) and nurture (the environment) to child development is one of the oldest issues in psychology. All the theories covered in this chapter have influenced the debate to some degree. Today, most psychologists believe that it is an interaction between these two forces that causes development. Some aspects of development are distinctly biological, such as puberty, but the onset of puberty can be affected by environmental factors, such as diet and nutrition.

Nature versus nurture in language development

The nature theory, put forward mainly by the linguist Noam Chomsky, states that babies are *born* with some knowledge of language. He argues that language systems are too complex to be acquired solely from being copied from and/or taught by adults. Language is innate and all humans have a genetic predisposition towards using language.

Chomsky concludes that humans have a 'language acquisition device' (LAD), which allows them to process and to use language. To reinforce this argument, Chomsky points out how all children appear to learn language in the same way and that the early stages of language are the same for all children. For example, all children (whatever their community language) first learn to speak using *holophrases* (one-word utterances to convey whole sentences), followed by *telegraphic speech* (sentences of two or three words to convey meaning).

The nurture theory originates from the work of the philosopher John Locke and was developed by behaviourists such as Pavlov. This theory suggests that a baby is born with a mind like a *tabula rasa* (a clean slate). This means that babies have to learn *everything*, including language, from scratch. Language has to be learned in the same way as any other skill. Children's parents and other carers shape the way in which children learn language by encouraging the required sounds (and then words), while ignoring others. Children learn language by copying sounds, words and phrases around them and through the positive reinforcement of their attempts to communicate.

Social constructivists (like Bruner and Vygotsky) believe that a mixture of both nature *and* nurture is essential for language development. Although Bruner agrees with Chomsky that there is a language acquisition device (LAD), he does not think this is enough. He argues that there also needs to be a 'language acquisition support system' (LASS). By this, he means that the child's family and the whole context in which the child learns language are important. Social constructivist theory suggests that young children acquire language as a means

Figure 1.19 Language arises from the need to understand the environment and from social interactions with others

to communicate more effectively than can be done through non-verbal communication alone. This theory is similar to the behaviourist tradition in that children *learn* language through their interactions with others. However, social constructivist theory differs in that even very young children are seen as active participants in their own language development. For example, research has shown that babies can initiate and control pre-verbal 'conversations' with their parents, rather than the other way round; babies make adults pay attention to them through body language, crying and babbling and they end 'conversations' with adults by breaking off eye contact or simply falling asleep! The role of the adult in children's language development is to provide the social context in which meaningful communication can take place. This theory also stresses the strong link between language acquisition and children's cognitive or intellectual development.

Nature versus nurture in cognitve development

Is children's cognitive development derived from their genetic inheritance (nature) or the result of their upbringing and experiences (nurture)? This is one of the questions concerning children's cognitive (or intellectual) development. If a person's cognitive skills are dependent on heredity (nature), then it is possible to believe that people are born with a predetermined level of intelligence that remains the same all their lives – they can only be as intelligent as those intellectual abilities permit. However, if a person's cognitive skills arise as the result of their environment (nurture), then it is possible to believe that people are as intelligent as their learning experiences allow.

Research indicates that the development of children's cognitive abilities depends on *both* nature and nurture – babies and young children have a *predisposition* towards learning, which is activated by *environmental triggers* such as social interaction, language and learning opportunities. For example, research with twins (separated and raised in different environments) shows that genetics is a key factor because the twins had similar IQ scores despite their different life experiences. While research on children from ethnic minority groups has shown that environment is also important because where there was racial discrimination the children did less well educationally, but when their families moved to areas where there was little or no discrimination, these children's IQ scores were the same as non-minority children. Intelligence is not determined by just one factor, similar to the way children's language and communication skills are affected by other factors (see above).

Nature versus nurture in emotional and social development

Research indicates that, in the same way as babies inherit their physical characteristics (e.g. hair and eye colour), they also inherit genetic information which contributes towards their personality development. Children inherit their particular temperaments, which are then influenced by the environment they are raised in. Researchers agree that personality is derived from a combination of inheritance (nature) and environment (nurture).

Studies of young babies show they already have distinct temperaments or personality types. For example, one study found that 40 per cent were 'easy-going', 10 per cent were 'difficult', 15 per cent were 'slow to warm up' and 35 per cent did not fit any category (Fontana 1994)! Remember that labelling personalities is not really a good idea as every child is a unique individual.

Environmental factors also affect children's emotional development. Consistent and loving care from a parent/carer who is sensitive to the child's particular needs enables the child to feel secure and to develop self-worth. Physical care is not enough – every child needs love and attention from their parent and/or carer. Having at least one secure and personal relationship with a parent/carer enables a child to form other relationships (see the section on attachments from page 29).

Different cultures within society may have different cultural expectations relating to behaviour and emotional responses, including the expected roles for men and women. For example, parents do treat boys and girls differently (often subconsciously), such as giving girls more cuddles or expecting boys to be tougher. Family size may also affect children's personality. For example, children in large families may find it more difficult to get their parents' attention and this may affect their emotional (and social) adjustment in group settings, but may have positive benefits, such as increased independence and ability to take turns. Some research studies indicate that the position of children in the family may also affect their personality. For example, first-born or only children are more likely to be conscientious, cooperative, sensitive and academically ambitious; second-born or middle children are more likely to be outgoing, aggressive and competitive; the youngest child in the family tends to be the most sociable, spontaneous, passive and lacking in maturity. However, these differences in personality are probably due to the way in which adults treat the children rather than birth order. For example, first time parents are more likely to be anxious and overprotective of their first-born or only child; parents may be more relaxed with the second-born or middle child, who in turn may feel they are in the older child's 'shadow'; the youngest child may be 'babied' by the rest of the family.

Children's emotional (and social) development may also be affected by other factors, such as:

- special needs and/or difficulties at birth (e.g. premature baby, forceps or caesarean delivery), which are often stated as being the cause for a baby being 'difficult', but this is more likely to be the result of the adult's treatment of the child, which then affects the child's behaviour (e.g. over-anxiety due to low birth weight of a premature baby or concerns over a child's special needs)
- family circumstances, such as parental separation/divorce, single-parent families, step-families
- death, abandonment or other permanent separation from parent
- adoption, foster care or other temporary/permanent residential care.

These factors do not necessarily have negative effects on children's emotional development; there are usually additional factors (such as financial hardship or inadequate substitute care) which can lead to poor social adjustment and/or emotional difficulties.

Key term

Nature – genetic inheritance or biological factors; the characteristics a person is born with.

Nurture – environmental/social factors which influence a person's characteristics/skills (e.g. early childhood relationships and experiences).

Social context – *any* situation or environment where social interaction occurs (e.g. home, early years setting, local community).

Activity

What is your own opinion regarding children's development and the nature versus nurture debate? Give a detailed account, using examples from your own experiences of working with children.

Neuroscience and brain development

Neuroscience is the study of the brain and nervous system. It is an area of study that has developed a wide range of theoretical approaches to many areas of children's growth and development. The use of imaging techniques of the brain, in part, has made this possible.

In recent years, investigation into babies' developing brains has provided insights relevant to the work of early years practitioners. Shore (1997) provides an overview of some of the research and states that, throughout the entire process of development, beginning before birth, the environment plays a key role in brain development and the 'wiring' that takes place in babies' brains. A warm and loving environment that meets individual children's needs is important in supporting positive brain development. There is more information about the effects of stress on a baby's developing brain in Chapter 6.

The importance of physical activity for young children's learning has been supported by brain-based investigation. Early years practitioners have known for decades that sitting young children down to learn in a formal way is not the most effective form of supporting learning. Healy (2004) translates some of the key findings into practical ways of supporting learning and development.

A number of companies have attempted to use the research into brain-based approaches to learning to support their products and services. Some have developed materials that claim that specific activities for children can exert effects on different parts of the brain. Lindon (2012) states that 'research reviews (Howard Jones undated, about 2008; Blakemore and Frith 2000) raise some serious questions over claims from some of the commercial brain-based learning programmes.'

Neuroscience has already made an important contribution to the understanding of children's learning and development. It is clear, however, that there is much more research needed to understand how the brain works and how learning can best be supported.

The work of early educators

As well as basing early years provision on key theories of how children learn, current early years practice has also grown out of the theories developed by early educators.

Friedrich Froebel (1782–1852)

Froebel emphasised the importance of physical activity and exploration involving real experiences. He greatly valued play, especially creative play, finger plays, songs and rhymes, and emphasised the importance of symbolism, making one thing stand for another. He stated how symbolic behaviour is best developed through play, especially imaginative and pretend play, and developed play activities and materials to promote symbolic play. Froebel also felt that children could be helped to think by being introduced to opposites (e.g. hard and soft) and this was a theme followed through in the play materials he used.

Froebel emphasised that everything in the world was linked together and that children perceived the world best through integrated activities. He stressed the importance of encouraging art, literature, natural sciences, mathematical understanding and the appreciation of beauty.

Froebel was concerned with the 'whole child' – for example, he believed children should wear comfortable clothes that allowed them to move about freely and that they should have a simple but healthy diet. Froebel recognised that parents are the child's first educator and stated that teachers should be like 'mothers' to young children. He welcomed parents into schools and into the 'communities' where the children were cared for.

The influence of Froebel on current practice

Most mainstream early years provision in the UK is based on Froebelian principles and, although most of his ideas are now taken for granted, in his lifetime they were groundbreaking.

Current mainstream settings encourage learning through first-hand experiences, and play remains central to provision for children's learning, including language development through rhymes and finger plays. Most early years settings encourage imagination to flow freely in play, and symbolic play is acknowledged as being very important for children's development.

Children's development is now encouraged through the provision of a wide range of materials and activities tailored to the needs of the individual child. Current best practice still emphasises creativity, science and the humanities, and learning opportunities are integrated across curriculum areas. Current mainstream early years setting also place a strong emphasis on positive relationships, social development and value partnerships between the parent/carer and the educator.

Key term

Symbolism – making one object stand for another.

Susan Isaacs (1885–1948)

Susan Isaacs worked in the Froebelian tradition but was also influenced by Melanie Klein. Isaacs believed that play gave children the opportunity to think, learn and express feelings.

Isaacs saw parents as the main educators of young children and felt that nurseries should be an extension of the home. She felt that children should remain in nursery until the age of seven before starting school and that careful records should be kept of each child at the nursery. Through these records, she demonstrated that children actually regressed after starting formal school.

Margaret McMillan (1860–1931)

Margaret McMillan was also unfluenced by Froebel. She believed in learning through first-hand experiences and emphasised feelings and relationships, as well as the physical aspects of movement and learning. McMillan believed that play helped a child to become a 'whole person'.

McMillan believed in the introduction of nursery schools as an extension of not just the home but communities themselves. She emphasised the value of the open air and introduced gardens for families to play and explore. She believed in partnership with parents, who developed with their children in the nursery environment.

Margaret McMillan first introduced school meals and medical services and stressed the importance of having trained adults to work with children.

The influence of McMillan and Isaacs on current practice

Margaret McMillan has had a powerful influence on the provision of nursery education in the UK and many of her principles are widespread today.

Early years settings give opportunities for physical, social, imaginative and creative play and encourage the expression of feelings. Active learning is encouraged through the provision of a wide range of materials and equipment, together with a skilled and qualified workforce.

Isaacs and McMillan's views on the nursery school as a community and extension of the home are followed through today as parents are invited into schools and seen as partners in the care and education of their children. As well as being a community in itself, early years settings extend provision into the community and become part of the wider community as well.

Other important influences on current practice include the following:

- Children are given access wherever possible to outdoor areas and are encouraged to use make gardens and use natural materials.
- Health, nutrition and medical services are part of childcare provision.
- Observation of children and accurate record keeping is emphasised in early years settings.

Maria Montessori (1870–1952)

Maria Montessori was a doctor who practised in a poor part of Italy and who spent a good deal of time observing children, especially those with special needs. Montessori believed that children go through periods in their development when they are more open to learning particular skills and concepts.

Unlike McMillan and Isaacs, Maria Montessori did not emphasise play or the free flow of ideas. Children were encouraged to work through the graded learning activities before undertaking creative activities. The emphasis was on a carefully prepared environment where the child would be able to solve problems independently, building self-confidence, analytical thinking and the satisfaction that comes from accomplishment.

The Montessori method involves a series of graded activities through which every child progresses, working through specially designed Montessori materials – for example, solid geometric forms, knobbed puzzle maps, coloured beads and various specialized rods and blocks. Each material isolates one quality for the child to discover – for example, size, colour or shape. The materials are self-correcting so, for example, when a piece does not fit or is left over, the child can easily see what went wrong.

Maria Montessori did not think there was a need for adult 'correction'. She believed the role of the adult was limited to facilitating the child's own activity and the teacher was known as the 'directress'. Allowing the child to become independent was emphasised. Montessori thought children should work in a quiet and peaceful environment of total concentration.

The influence of Montessori on current practice

There are many Montessori schools in the UK within the private sector and some Montessori classes and schools in mainstream education. In early years provision today, Montessori ideas and materials are sometimes used, such as graded sizes of particular shapes, such as small, medium and large blocks.

Current mainstream practice is more likely to intervene and support the child to work through activities and to encourage group work.

Rudolf Steiner (1861–1925)

Steiner was a strict vegetarian, as well as a believer in reincarnation. Steiner believed in childhood as a special phase of life and that the young child needs a protected environment in which all-round development can take place. He believed that a child's temperament was important to overall development and learning. As well as intellectual progress, Steiner emphasised spiritual, moral, social, artistic, creative and altruistic (caring for each other) development. He did not emphasise what is taught but how and when it is taught.

Steiner believed that young children need to be protected from formal learning and to learn through imaginative and creative play using simple tasks and activities with natural materials. In Steiner schools, the learning opportunities are often repeated as many times as necessary so that all children, including those with special needs, feel confident.

Steiner stressed the importance of community and relationships with other people and, in Steiner schools, the same teacher stays with the child for several years. Steiner placed emphasis on correct food and a balance of rest and activity.

The influence of Steiner on current practice

Schools that follow Rudolf Steiner's principles are called Steiner-Waldorf schools in the private sector in the UK.

Mainstream settings believe in early childhood as a unique phase of life that is more than just preparation for adulthood and that the individual child's needs and personality are important. As in Steiner-Waldorf schools, establishing relationships is valued and reaching out and serving the community is considered part of the nursery's role.

However, mainstream settings consider the content that is being taught as well as the process of learning. Also mainstream settings do not emphasise spirituality as much as Steiner.

Section 2: Applying theories to workplace practice

Understanding theoretical approaches to how children learn and develop may influence practice by improving:

- the quality of early education provision
- the structure of the learning environment
- the provision of materials and equipment
- the communication between adults and children during learning experiences
- the adult expectations of children's development.

Theoretical approaches to how children learn and develop increase adults' awareness and understanding of the importance of:

- observing and assessing children's development very carefully
- listening to children and the way they express ideas

- taking account of children's interests and experiences when planning learning opportunities.

Planning and organising environments for children

It is important to plan and organise an environment for children and families that is welcoming and user-friendly. This involves planning and providing an enabling physical environment for children, including adapting the environment to meet children's needs (according to their ages, abilities and any special needs) and ensuring that any barriers to participation are addressed. It also involves organising space and resources to meet children's needs within an accessible, comfortable and stimulating environment. You should provide a caring, nurturing and responsive environment where children and their families feel valued and respected. You should also facilitate children's personal care by encouraging children to care for themselves as appropriate to their ages, needs and abilities.

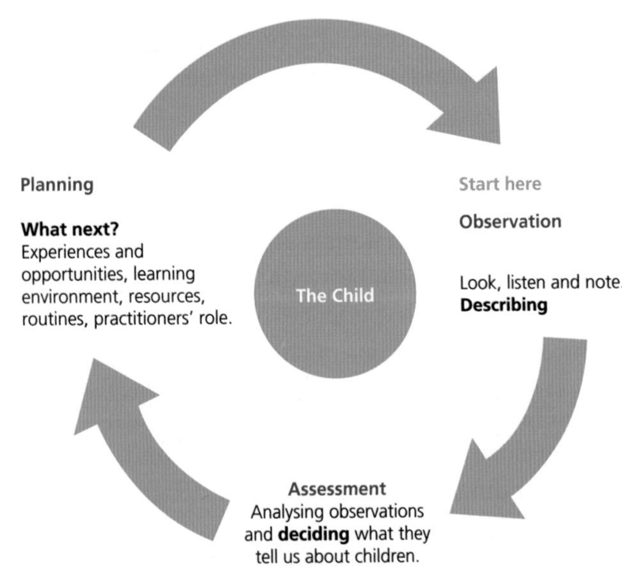

Figure 1.20 Planning to support each child's learning and development (**Source:** 'Development Matters in the Early Years Foundation Stage', 2012)

Planning for children and/or young people's care and development

You will need to plan provision for the children you work with based on your assessment of their developmental progress. You should recognise that children's developmental progress depends on each child's level of maturation and their prior experiences. You should take these into account and have realistic expectations when planning activities and routines to promote children's development. This includes regularly reviewing and updating plans for individual children and ensuring that plans balance the needs of individual children and the group as appropriate to your setting. You should know and understand that children develop at widely different rates but in broadly the same sequence.

When planning provision to support children's and/or young people's development, it is essential to always look at the 'whole' child or young person. This means looking at *all* areas of their development (e.g. **S**ocial, **P**hysical, **I**ntellectual, **C**ommunication and language, **E**motional) in relation to the particular aspect of development or learning you are focusing on. We therefore refer to children's and young people's development as holistic, with each area being interconnected. For example, when observing a pupil's writing skills, as well as looking at their intellectual development, you will need to consider the pupil's:

- physical development (fine motor skills when using a pencil or pen)
- language development and communication skills (vocabulary and structure of language used during their writing)
- social and emotional development (interaction with others and behaviour during the writing activity).

Key term

Holistic – looking at the 'whole' child or young person (e.g. *all* aspects of the child or young person's development).

More detailed information about children's holistic development can be found in *CACHE Level 3 Diploma: Children and Young People's Workforce – Early Learning and Child Care* (Meggitt *et al.* 2011, Chapter 5, pp. 49–66).

Following your observation and assessment of a child's development, learning and/or behaviour, your recommendations can provide the basis for planning appropriate routines and/or activities to encourage and extend the child's skills in specific areas. Effective planning is based on children's individual needs, abilities and interests, hence the importance of accurate and reliable child observations and assessments. Depending on the type of setting, you may also need to plan provision based on the requirements for the relevant curriculum framework – for example, the 2012 Early Years Foundation Stage.

Activity

Describe how *you* plan provision to promote children's development in your setting. Include examples of any planning sheets you use.

Implementing a plan for care or development of children and/or young people

Good preparation and organisation are essential when implementing plans to promote children's development, including:

- having any instructions and/or questions for the child or group of children ready (e.g. prompt cards, worksheet, work card or written on the board)

8.00 8.30 10.00 11.30 12.30 2.30 5.30 6.00

DAY	BREAKFAST	HELP CHILD DRESS	MORNING ACTIVITIES	SNACK	MORNING ACTIVITIES	NAP TIME	LUNCH	AFTERNOON ACTIVITIES	SNACK	AFTERNOON ACTIVITIES	TEA	BABY-SITTING
MONDAY			Ice breakers e.g. name games Mystery bag Construction toys		Play in garden Story Rhymes/ songs	Child's washing Prepare lunch		Playgroup (meeting with parent, exchange vital info).		Playgroup Children's TV Prepare tea		
TUESDAY			Library (with parent)		Play in garden Story Rhymes/ songs	Child's ironing Prepare lunch		Painting Small-scale toys		Jigsaws Simple games Children's TV Prepare tea		
WEDNESDAY			Visit the park (with parent)		Construction toys Story Rhymes/ songs	Tidy child's bedroom Prepare lunch		Playgroup (local shopping with parent)		Playgroup Children's TV Prepare tea		
THURSDAY			Swimming (with parent)		Jigsaws Simple games Story Rhymes/ Songs	Wash swimming costumes etc. Prepare lunch		Play in garden Small-scale toys		Drawing/ colouring Make playdough Children's TV Prepare tea		Quiet games Bath time Bedtime Story
FRIDAY			Junk modelling Playdough		Play in garden Story Rhymes/ songs	Clean child's bedroom Prepare lunch		Playgroup (stay as adult helper)		Playgroup Children's TV Prepare tea		

Figure 1.21 Example of a weekly routine

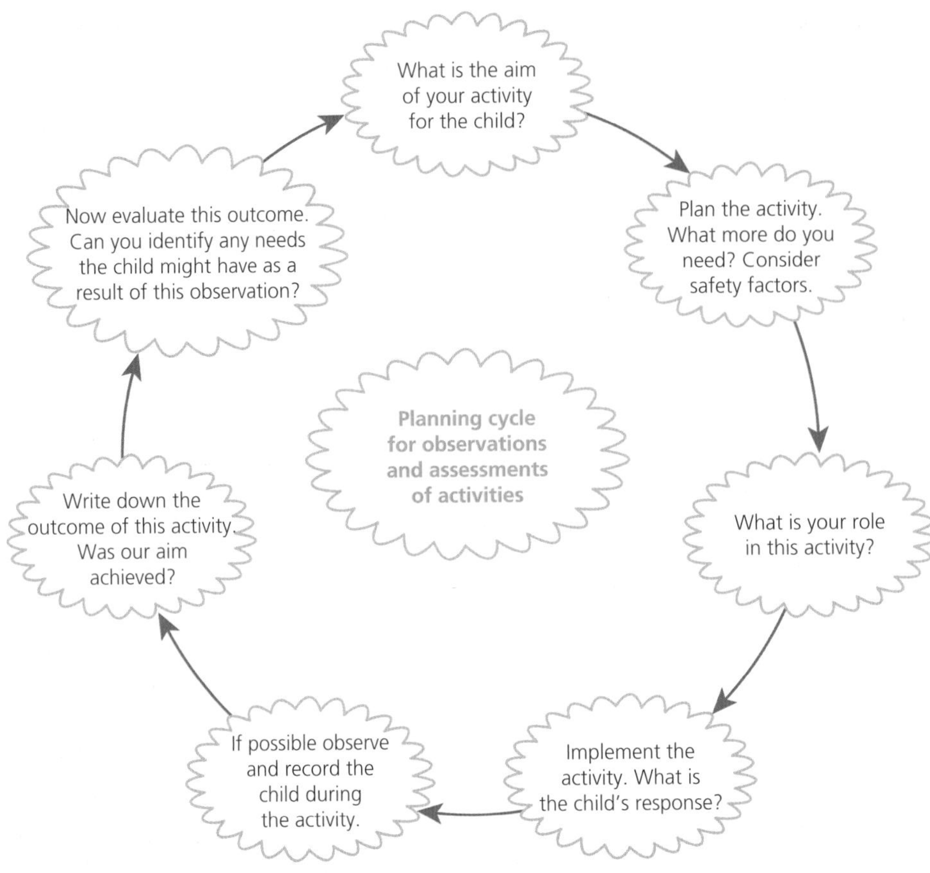

Figure 1.22 Planning children's activities (**Source:** Jackie Harding and Liz Meldon-Smith, 2001)

- ensuring sufficient materials and equipment, including any specialist equipment
- setting out the materials and equipment on the table ready or letting the children get the resources out for themselves, depending on their ages and abilities.

Implementing a plan for care or development of children and/or young people may involve the following:

1. Giving out any instructions to the children.
2. Showing children what to do – for example, demonstrate a new skill or technique.
3. Keeping an individual child and/or group on task.
4. Clarifying meaning and/or ideas.
5. Explaining any difficult words to the children.
6. Assisting children with any special equipment – for example, hearing aid or a dictaphone.
7. Providing any other appropriate assistance.
8. Encouraging the children to tidy up afterwards as appropriate to their ages and abilities.
9. Remembering to maintain the children's safety at all times.

Evaluating the implemented plan in relation to identified theories and workplace practice

After you have planned and implemented a care routine, play opportunity or learning activity, you will need to evaluate it. Some evaluation also occurs during the routine or activity, providing continuous assessment of a child's performance.

It is important to evaluate the routine or activity so that you can:

- assess whether the routine or activity has been successful (e.g. the aims and objectives or outcomes have been met)

- identify possible ways in which the routine or activity might be modified/adapted to meet the individual needs of the child or children
- provide accurate information for the senior practitioner, setting manager or other professionals about the successfulness of a particular routine or activity.

The senior practitioner, setting manager or your college tutor/assessor should give you guidelines on how to present your routine and activity plans. If not, you might find the suggested format in Table 1.11 useful.

Title: *brief description of the activity*
Date and time: *the date and time of the activity*
Plan duration: *how long will the activity last?*
Aim and rationale: *the main purpose of the activity, including how it will encourage development, learning and/or behaviour. The rationale should outline why this particular activity has been selected (e.g. identified particular pupil's need through observation; links to topics/themes within the group, class or setting). How does the activity link with any curriculum requirements?*
Staff and setting: *the roles and number of staff involved in the activity, plus the type of setting and the age range of the setting.*
Details of the pupils(s): *activity plans involving an individual pupil or small group of pupils should specify first name, age in years and months, plus any relevant special needs; activity plans involving larger groups should specify the age range and ability levels.*
Learning objectives for the pupil(s): *indicate what the child or children could gain from participating in the activity in each developmental area:* ***SPICE*** *(Social, Physical, Intellectual, Communication and language, Emotional).*
Preparation: *what do you need to prepare in advance (e.g. selecting or making appropriate materials; checking availability of equipment)? Think about the instructions and/or questions for the pupil(s); will these be spoken and/or written down (e.g. on a worksheet/card or on the board)? Do you need prompt cards for instructions or questions?*
Resources: *what materials and equipment will you need? Where will you get them from? Are there any special requirements? Remember equal opportunities, including special needs. How will you set out the necessary resources (e.g. setting out on the table ready or the pupils getting materials and equipment out for themselves)?*
Organisation: *where will you implement the activity? How will you organise the activity? How will you give out any instructions the pupils need? Will you work with pupils one at a time or as a group? Are there any particular safety requirements? How will you organise any tidying up after the activity? Will the pupils be encouraged to help tidy up?*
Implementation: *describe what happened when you implemented the activity with the pupil(s). Include any alterations to the original plan (e.g. changes in timing or resources).*
Equal opportunities: *indicate any multicultural aspects to the activity and any additional considerations for pupils with special needs.*
Review and evaluation: *review and evaluate the following:* • *the aims and learning outcomes/objectives* • *the effectiveness of your preparation, organisation and implementation* • *what you learned about development and learning in relation to the identified theories* • *what you learned about planning activities in the context of workplace practice* • *possible modifications for future similar activities.*
References and/or bibliography: *the review and evaluation may include references appropriate to development, learning and behaviour, including relevant theories. Remember to include a bibliography of any books used as references or for ideas when planning the activity.*

Table 1.11 Suggested format for planning activities

Planning for children and/or young people's care and development based on identified theories

Planning based on behaviourist theories

Skinner believed that positive reinforcement (rewards) and negative reinforcement (sanctions) both contribute towards an individual's motivation for learning and behaviour. His theory forms the basis for behaviour modification, which involves using positive reinforcement to encourage acceptable behaviour and ignoring all but harmful unwanted behaviour. For example, working on one aspect of behaviour at a time and rewarding the child for any progress, no matter how small. See Figure 1.23.

The basic principles of behaviour modification are as follows:

- **P**raise and reward acceptable behaviour
- **R**educe the opportunities for unwanted behaviour
- **A**void confrontations
- **I**gnore minor unwanted behaviour
- **S**tructure appropriate sanctions
- **E**stablish clear rules, boundaries and routines.

Key term

Behaviour modification – changing behaviour using techniques such as positive reinforcement (rewards) and/or negative reinforcement (sanctions).

In Practice

Think about the basic principles of behaviour modification.

1. Observe a child who regularly demonstrates challenging or unwanted behaviour during group activities. In your assessment, include information on:
   - ❑ the child's behaviour during the activity
   - ❑ the child's communication skills
   - ❑ how the adult responds
   - ❑ how the other children respond to the child's behaviour
   - ❑ how to monitor the child's future behaviour

   how to encourage the child to behave more appropriately.
2. From the information in your observation, plan and implement a step-by-step approach (e.g. behaviour modification) to encourage the child to behave in more acceptable ways. Remember to include appropriate rewards (and sanctions).
3. Analyse the outcome of the implemented plan in relation to this behaviour theory and your workplace practice.
4. Evaluate the benefit of using behaviour theories to underpin the planning for children and/or young people's care or development.

Planning based on psychoanalytic theories

Children need the freedom to develop their independence in ways that are appropriate to their overall development. Some children may need more encouragement than others to become increasingly independent and less reliant on other people. Children gain independence by developing self-help skills, making choices and decisions, and taking responsibility for their own actions. Most children start wanting to do things for themselves from about 18 months to two years. While young children want to do things for themselves (e.g. getting dressed, making things), they may become frustrated if they are not successful in doing those things. Many conflicts arise between young children and other people as children increase their independence and expand the boundaries of their world.

Adults caring for children should avoid *inhibiting* the child's need for independence as

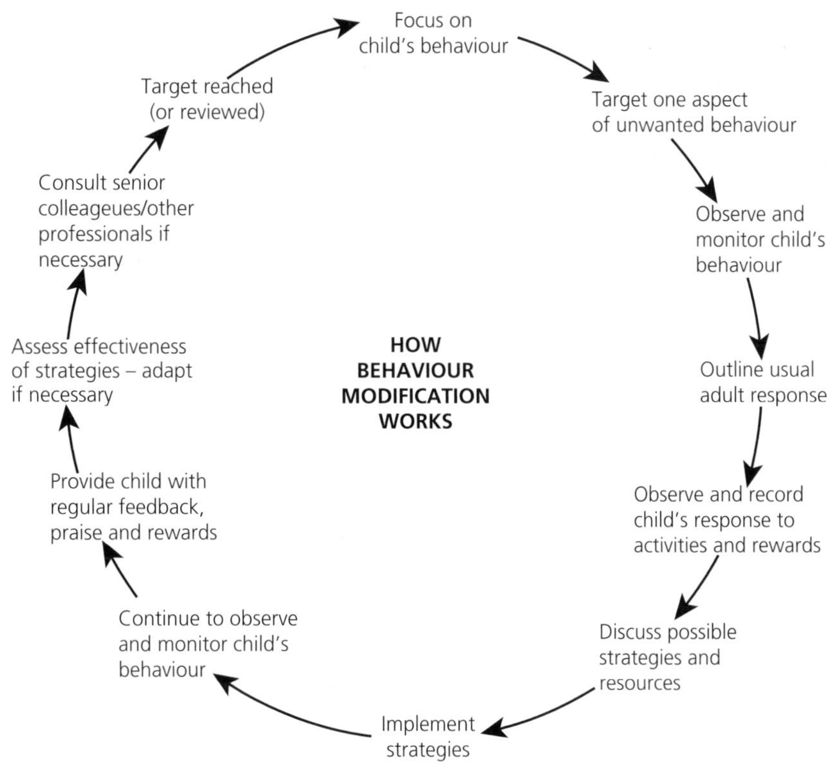

Figure 1.23 Using behaviour modification techniques

this can lead to either emotional dependence, excessive shyness and an overcautious nature *or* emotional detachment, anti-social behaviour and a rebellious nature. Adults should also avoid *unrestricted* independence as the child may be exposed to danger and physical harm (e.g. from fire, boiling water, traffic) and/or the child may become selfish and unable to recognise the needs and rights of others. Adults should strike a balance between these two extremes. You should provide a balance between allowing for the *individual* child's need for independence and providing supervision with appropriate guidelines for socially acceptable behaviour, which takes into account the needs of *everyone* in the setting.

Encouraging children's self-reliance is an important part of helping them to develop their independence and resilience, which will enable children to face life's demands and challenges in preparation for their adult lives. Encouraging self-reliance involves helping children to develop:

- independence (or autonomy) – for example, the ability to think and act for themselves
- dependence on their own capabilities and personal resources
- competence in looking after themselves
- trust in their own judgement and actions
- confidence in their own abilities and actions.

In Practice

Think about encouraging children's self-reliance.

1. Observe a child demonstrating self-help skills, such as feeding themselves, washing hands, getting dressed/undressed (e.g. for PE) or tidying up. Assess the child's ability to perform the skill independently. Outline the adult's role in developing the child's self-reliance in this area.
2. From the information in your observation, plan and implement a routine which will encourage the child's self-help skills.
3. Analyse the outcome of the implemented plan in relation to psychoanalytic theory and your workplace practice.
4. Evaluate the benefit of using psychoanalytic theories to underpin the planning for children and/or young people's care or development.

Planning based on humanistic theories

As a practitioner you should be sensitive to children's needs. There are universal needs that are necessary to all children; these needs are physical or biological needs, such as food, drink and shelter, that are essential to survival. Then there are psychological needs, such as love, affection, secure and stable relationships, friendships, intellectual stimulation, independence; these needs are essential to maintaining the individual's quality of life.

Remember that children's *individual* needs vary. Meeting the needs of children in childcare settings, especially where children are grouped according to age, can be difficult. Some children will have developmental needs which are in line with the expected norm for their chronological age, while others will have needs which are characteristic of much younger or older children. In recognising and attempting to meet children's needs, you should consider each child's age, physical maturity, intellectual abilities, emotional development, social skills, past experiences and relationships.

The development of self-image is strongly linked to self-esteem. Self-image can be defined as the individual's view of their own personality and abilities, including the individual's perception of how other people view them and their abilities. This involves recognising ourselves as separate and unique individuals with characteristics which make us different from others. Respecting children and helping them to develop a positive self-image and identity goes a long way towards providing a caring, nurturing and responsive childcare environment. Consistent, loving care from a parent/carer who is sensitive to the child's particular needs enables children to feel secure and to develop self-worth.

Five ways to promote children's emotional well-being and resilience

You can help children to develop emotional well-being and resilience by:

1. **Developing their self-awareness**, including helping children to establish a positive self-image and to recognise their own feelings.
2. **Helping them to handle and express feelings** in appropriate ways (e.g. through creative, imaginative and physical play).
3. **Encouraging their self-motivation** by helping children to establish personal goals (e.g. developing self-control and self-reliance).
4. **Developing their empathy for other people** by encouraging children to recognise the feelings, needs and rights of others.
5. **Encouraging positive social interaction** by helping children to develop effective interpersonal skills through play and other cooperative group activities in the play setting and in the local community.

Key terms

Norm – the usual pattern or expected level of development/behaviour.

Self-image – the individual's view of their own personality and abilities, including the individual's *perception* of how other people view them and their abilities.

Planning based on social constructivist theories

An essential part of all learning experiences is active learning – not just for children but for adults as well. For example, at college you may find that learning situations take the form of workshops, group activities and discussions, rather than formal lectures. Children (and adults) learn by *doing*.

In Practice

Think about supporting children's emotional needs.

1. Observe a child during imaginative play or creative activity. Focus on the child's emotional development. In your assessment, comment on:
   - ❑ the child's imaginative and creative skills
   - ❑ the child's ability to make choices or decisions
   - ❑ the child's use of language to express needs and/or feelings
   - ❑ the role of the adult in promoting the child's emotional development
   - ❑ suggestions for further activities to encourage or extend the child's emotional development, including appropriate resources.
2. From the information in your observation, plan and implement an activity which will support the child's emotional needs.
3. Analyse the outcome of the implemented plan in relation to humanistic theory and your workplace practice.
4. Evaluate the benefit of using humanistic theories to underpin the planning for children and/or young people's care or development.

Lectures would be a waste of time for children. Indeed, traditional lectures *are* a waste of time even for adults! This is because the average attention span of an adult is 20 minutes. (This is probably why commercials are shown about every 15 to 20 minutes on television.) The average attention span of a child is considerably less, more like five to ten minutes, or even as little as two to three minutes, especially for very young children and some children with cognitive difficulties or behavioural difficulties.

In all learning situations, it is important to provide information in small portions with plenty of discussion and activity breaks to maintain interest and concentration. It is essential that children become *actively* involved in the learning process. Learning needs to be practical, not theoretical. Children need *concrete* learning experiences (e.g. using real objects in a meaningful context). This is why providing appropriate play opportunities is so crucial to all children's learning and development.

Active learning encourages children to be:

- **C**urious
- **H**andy at problem-solving
- **I**maginative
- **C**reative.

Through active learning, children use play opportunities to encourage and extend the problem-solving abilities that are essential to developing intellectual processes. Play activities provide informal opportunities for children to develop ideas and to understand concepts through active learning and communication. Language is a key component in children's thinking and learning. Play is an invaluable way to provide opportunities for language and to make learning more meaningful, especially for younger children. Play enables children to learn about concepts in a safe and non-threatening environment.

Children need a combination of real and imaginary experiences to encourage learning. This is why play is an important aspect of young children's thinking and learning. Play opportunities are particularly useful for encouraging children to develop mathematical and scientific skills. Younger children need to handle real objects and materials to understand basic concepts – for example, in mathematics, using objects for counting and addition, such as buttons, cones or interlocking cubes. Once children have plenty of practical mathematical experiences, they can cope more easily with abstract concepts, such as mental calculations and algebra.

Play activities are effective in developing children's thinking and learning by providing opportunities for:

- well-motivated learning
- challenging and interesting learning experiences
- taking responsibility for their own learning and gaining independence
- cooperative work between children
- developing problem-solving skills and improving concentration
- encouraging imagination and creativity.

Figure 1.24 Play is an essential part of the active learning process

In Practice

Think about the active learning process.

1. Observe a child involved in a play activity. In your assessment, include information on:
   - ❑ the learning objectives for the activity
   - ❑ the intellectual skills demonstrated by the child during the activity (e.g. concentration, memory skills, imagination and creativity, mathematical or scientific skills, language and communication skills)
   - ❑ the level of adult support provided during the activity
   - ❑ suggestions to encourage and extend the child's development and learning.
2. From the information in your observation, plan and implement a play activity for the child which involves the active learning process. Include information on:
   - ❑ the intended learning objectives for the play activity
   - ❑ the organisation, resources and staff required
   - ❑ any special requirements (e.g. specialist equipment)
   - ❑ the support to be provided by adults.
3. Analyse the outcome of the implemented plan in relation to theories relating to active learning and your workplace practice.
4. Evaluate the benefit of using these theories to underpin the planning for children and/or young people's care or development.

Planning based on attachment theories

A meaningful relationship with a key person enables very young children to form a secure attachment to the adult. A very young child's relationship and attachment to a key person provides an excellent context in which the child can feel safe to express and make sense of their emotions (Gillespie Edwards 2002).

The key features of an effective key person system

- The same practitioner is responsible for the physical needs of a very small number of individual babies and toddlers as very young children need to be able to recognise the face of the person who changes them, feeds them or wakes them from a nap.
- The key person responds sensitively to individual babies and toddlers, knows their preferences and develops personal rituals of songs, smiles and enjoyable 'jokes'.
- The key person develops a friendly relationship with the child's parent(s), sharing ideas about the very young child and communicating important information about the day or the child's state of health.
- The key person observes, assesses and records the learning and development of their key children.

Lindon (2002)

The revised Early Years Foundation Stage (effective from September 2012) also emphasises the importance of a key person. Each child must be assigned a key person. Providers must inform parents and/or carers of the name of the key person, and explain their role, when a child starts attending a setting. The key person must help ensure that every child's learning and care is tailored to meet their individual needs. The key person must seek to engage and support parents and/or carers in guiding their child's development at home. They should also help families engage with more specialist support if appropriate (Department for Education 2012).

To cope with, prepare for and accept transition and transfer, children need:

- reassurance from adults to maintain their feelings of stability, security and trust
- adult assistance to adjust to different social rules and social expectations
- help in adapting to different group situations.

Factors that may affect children's transfers and transitions include:

- the child's age and level of maturity
- previous experiences in other settings, which may have been positive or negative
- special needs (e.g. physical disability, sensory impairment, communication difficulties, behavioural and/or emotional difficulties)
- moving to a new area, county or even country
- special family circumstances (e.g. parental separation or divorce, bereavement, serious illness, etc.)
- returning to the childcare setting after a prolonged illness or accident.

Key term

Key person – the member of staff with whom a child has more contact than other adults within the setting; this adult demonstrates a special interest in the child (and their family) through close daily interaction.

Transition – the process of adjusting to a new situation. A transition may involve the **transfer** from one setting to another or changes within the same setting. For example, home to childminder's home, nursery, playgroup or school; one year group or Key Stage to another; primary school to secondary school; secondary school to college or work. A transition may also involve other significant transfers or changes in the child's life, such as: death or serious illness of a family member or close friend; parental separation or divorce; moving house; going into hospital; arrival of a new baby.

Figure 1.25 The key person can help the young child to deal with separation anxiety when making the transition to the setting

In Practice

Think about the role of the key person.

1. Identify the factors that may affect new children starting at your setting. For example:
   - ❑ each child's age and level of maturity
   - ❑ any previous experiences in other settings
   - ❑ any special needs (e.g. physical disability, sensory impairment, communication difficulties, behavioural and/or emotional difficulties)
   - ❑ the family circumstances of each child
   - ❑ the changes in expectations and activities required of the children.
2. Devise a plan to help new children to settle into your setting – for example, developing an effective induction programme for children that helps them to understand the new expectations and activities within the setting. Include information on:
   - ❑ working with parents to ensure a full understanding of the transition process
   - ❑ encouraging parents to share information that may affect their children's emotional security
   - ❑ identifying the support the children will need to make a successful transition, including any special requirements
   - ❑ the role of the key person (e.g. recognising and responding promptly to signs of emotional distress; using different techniques to calm, reassure and distract individual babies and children who are distressed; acknowledging and communicating respect for the very young children's feelings; reassuring parents during the transition process).
3. Analyse the intended plan in relation to theories relating to attachment and your workplace practice.
4. Evaluate the benefit of using these theories to underpin the planning for children and/or young people's care or development.

Section 3: The relevance of identified theories in relation to own workplace practice and personal development

To be an effective practitioner requires a sound theoretical base. For example, a practitioner working with a distressed child who is struggling to settle into a new setting may find a useful link between theory and practice in Bowlby's theory of attachment, particularly his concept of separation response (protest, despair and detachment), as this may help to illuminate the practitioner's understanding of this child and, in turn, help the parent(s) to understand and to tolerate certain behaviours. Using theory to guide practice should not involve becoming lost in concepts that are difficult to understand or locked in professional jargon that sets practitioners apart, but it should result in acquiring a greater understanding about what constitutes effective practice (Trevithick 2000).

Drawing conclusions regarding the relevance of identified theories

As a practitioner, you need to know and understand the techniques of reflective analysis: questioning what, why and how; seeking alternatives; keeping an open mind; viewing from different perspectives; thinking about consequences; testing ideas through comparing and contrasting; asking 'what if?'; synthesising ideas; and seeking, identifying and resolving problems (NDNA 2004).

Self-evaluation is needed to improve your own professional practice and to develop your ability to reflect upon routines/activities and modify plans to meet the individual needs of the children you work with. You should also be able to draw conclusions regarding the relevance of identified theories to your own work role.

In Practice

Look back at the activities you planned and implemented in the previous section. For each activity, evaluate your own practice by considering the following:

- ❑ How relevant were the identified theories to your own work role?
- ❑ Was your own particular contribution appropriate?
- ❑ Did you choose the right time, place and resources?
- ❑ Did you intervene enough or too much?
- ❑ Did you achieve your intended goals (for example, objectives/outcomes for the child or children and yourself)? If not, why not? Were the goals too ambitious or unrealistic?
- ❑ What other strategies/methods could have been used? Suggest possible modifications.
- ❑ Where could you get further information or advice about linking theory and practice (for example, from senior practitioners, other professionals, the internet, libraries, journals)?

Reflecting on own practice in relation to the use of theories

Effective practice requires committed, enthusiastic and reflective practitioners with a breadth and depth of knowledge, skills and understanding. To be an effective, reflective practitioner, you should use your own learning to improve your work with children and their families in ways which are sensitive, positive and non-judgemental. You can reflect on your own professional practice by making comparisons with relevant theories and appropriate models of good practice (e.g. the work of more experienced practitioners within the setting).

Through initial and ongoing training and development, you can develop, demonstrate and continuously improve your:

- relationships with both children and adults
- understanding of the individual and diverse ways that children develop and learn

- knowledge and understanding in order to actively support and extend children's learning in and across all areas and aspects of learning
- practice in meeting all children's needs, learning styles and interests
- work with parents, carers, the wider community and other professionals (Department for Education and Skills 2005).

In Practice

1. How do you monitor the processes, practices and outcomes from your work?
2. Give examples of how you evaluate your own childcare practice, including:
   - ❑ self-evaluation
   - ❑ reflections on your interactions with others
   - ❑ sharing your reflections with others
   - ❑ using feedback from others to improve your own evaluation.
3. Describe how you have used theories to solve problems and improve practice.

Developing a personal development plan

You can take part in continuing professional development by identifying areas in your knowledge, understanding and skills where you could develop further. You should develop and negotiate a plan to develop your knowledge, skills and understanding. You should seek out and access opportunities for continuing professional development as part of this plan. You should use opportunities for continuing professional development to improve your professional practice (NDNA 2004).

To develop your effectiveness as a professional childcare practitioner, you should be able to identify your own **SMART** personal development objectives:

- **S**pecific: identify exactly what you want to develop, such as the particular skills you need to update or new skills you need to acquire (e.g. first aid or ICT skills).
- **M**easurable: define criteria that can be used to measure whether or not your objectives have been achieved (e.g. best practice benchmarks, course certificate of attendance or qualification).
- **A**chievable: avoid being too ambitious; set objectives which you know are attainable.
- **R**ealistic: be realistic about what you want to develop.
- **T**ime-bound: plan a realistic time frame within which to achieve your objectives.

You should discuss and agree these objectives with those responsible for supporting your professional development. This includes developing and negotiating a plan to develop your knowledge, skills and understanding further (e.g. a personal development plan). For example, you may consider that some of your work tasks require modification or improvement and discuss possible changes with your line manager. Or you may feel that you lack sufficient knowledge and skills to implement particular activities and need to discuss opportunities for you to undertake the relevant training. To achieve your personal development objectives, you should make effective use of the people, resources (e.g. the internet, libraries, journals) and other professional development or training opportunities available to you.

When assessing your personal development and training needs, you need to consider:

- your existing experience and skills
- the needs of the children you work with
- any problems with how you currently work
- any new or changing expectations for your role
- information and/or learning needed to meet best practice, quality schemes or regulatory requirements.

In Practice

1. Identify your own **SMART** personal development objectives.
2. Develop a personal development plan. Include information on:
   - ❑ your existing strengths and skills
   - ❑ opportunities for improving your work using knowledge gained from this unit
   - ❑ the skills and knowledge you still need to improve
   - ❑ examples of opportunities for continuing your professional development.

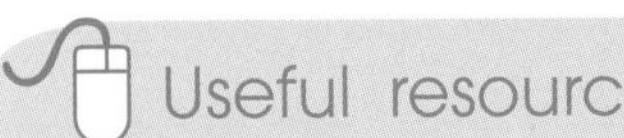

Useful resources

Organisations and websites

Anna Freud Centre

The centre was established in 1947 by Anna Freud to support the emotional well-being of children through direct work with children and their families, research and the development of practice and training mental health practitioners. www.annafreud.org

Foundation Years

Developed by 4Children, this is the 'one stop shop' for resources, information and the latest news on the foundation years. The website provides advice and guidance for practitioners on working effectively with parents as partners in their children's learning.
www.foundationyears.org.uk

Siren Films

Siren Films produces high-quality DVDs covering a wide range of topics, such as the first year of life, two-year-olds, play, attachment and key person, three- and four-year-olds, early literacy and schemas in toddlers.
www.sirenfilms.co.uk

Books

Anderson, R. (2008) *Melanie Klein and child analysis*, The Melanie Klein Trust, www.melanie-klein-trust.org.uk/ra2009.htm (accessed April 2012).
Bandura, A. (1965) 'Influence of models' reinforcement contingencies on the acquisition of imitative responses', *Journal of Personality and Social Psychology*, 1: 589–595.
Bandura, A. (1973) *Aggression: a social learning analysis*, Englewood Cliffs, NJ: Prentice Hall.
Bandura, A., Ross, D. and Ross, S.A. (1961) 'Transmission of aggression through imitation of aggressive models', *Journal of Abnormal and Social Psychology*, 63: 575–582.
Blakemore, S. and Frith, U. (2000) *The implications of recent developments in neuroscience for research on teaching and learning*, a consultation paper commissioned by the Teaching and Learning Research Programme, ESRC, www.tlrp.org/pub/acadpub/Blakemore2000.pdf.
Boeree, C.G. (1998) *Personality theories: Anna Freud 1895–1982*, http://webspace.ship.edu/cgboer/annafreud.html (accessed March 2012).
Brennan, W.K. (1987) *Changing special education now*, Milton Keynes: Open University Press.
Bruce, T. (2011) *Learning through play: for babies, toddlers and young children*, London: Hodder Education.
Bruce, T. (ed.) (2009) *Early childhood: a guide for education students*, 2nd edition, London: Sage Publications.
Chasnoff, I.J. (2011) 'Catch 'em being good! The only form of discipline that works is positive reinforcement', *Aristotle's Child*, 27 May, *Psychology Today* website: www.psychologytoday.com/blog/aristotles-child/201105/catch-em-being-good-0 (accessed March 2012).
Cole, J., Clark, S., Hirschheimer, S., Martyn, T. and Morrall, J. (2001) *Helping young children learn through activities in the early years*, London: Hodder & Stoughton.
Department for Education (2012) *The Early Years Foundation Stage: setting the standards for learning, development and care for children from birth to five*, London: DfE.
Department for Education and Skills (2005) *Primary national strategy: KEEP – Key Elements of Effective Practice*, London: DfES.
Donaldson, M. (1978) *Children's minds*, London: Fontana.
Fontana, D. (1994) 'Personality and personal development', in D. Fontana (ed.) *The education of the young child*, Oxford: Blackwell.
Gillespie Edwards, A. (2002) *Relationships and learning: caring for children from birth to three*, London: National Children's Bureau.
Glenn, A., Cousins, J. and Helps, A. (2003) *Behaviour in the early years*, London: David Fulton Publishers.

Useful resources (cont.)

Gopnik, A., Meltzoff, A.N. and Kuhl, P.K. (1999) *The scientist in the crib: minds, brains, and how children learn*, New York: William Morrow & Co. Inc.

Gregg, P., Washbrook, E., Propper, C. and Burgess, S.M. (2005) 'The effects of a mother's return to work decision on child development in the UK', *Economic Journal*, 115(501): F48–F80.

Harding, J. and Meldon-Smith, L. (2000) *Helping young children to develop*, London: Hodder & Stoughton.

Harding, J. and Meldon-Smith, L. (2001) *How to make observations and assessments*, 2nd edition, London: Hodder & Stoughton.

Healy, J. (2004) *Your child's growing mind: brain development and learning from birth to adolescence*, 3rd edition, New York: Three Rivers Press.

Hobart, C. and Frankel, J. (2005) *A practical guide to activities for young children*, 3rd edition, Cheltenham: Nelson Thornes.

Howard-Jones, P. (undated, circa 2008) *Neuroscience and education: issues and opportunities*, London: Teaching and Learning Research Programme, www.tlrp.org/pub/documents/Neuroscience%20Commentary%20FINAL.pdf.

Lindon, L. (2002) *Good practice in working with babies, toddlers and very young children*, London: Sure Start.

Lindon, J. (2007) *Understanding children and young people: development from 5–18 years*, London: Hodder Arnold.

Lindon, J. (2012) *Understanding child development 0–8 years*, 3rd edition, London: Hodder Education.

McLeod, S.A. (2007a) *Skinner – operant conditioning*, Simply Psychology website: www.simplypsychology.org/operant-conditioning.html (accessed March 2012).

McLeod, S.A. (2007b) *Carl Rogers*, Simply Psychology website: www.simplypsychology.org/carl-rogers.html (accessed April 2012).

McLeod, S.A. (2007c) *Bowlby attachment theory*, Simply Psychology website: www.simplypsychology.org/bowlby.html (accessed May 2012).

McLeod, S.A. (2008) *Mary Ainsworth – strange situation*, Simply Psychology website: www.simplypsychology.org/mary-ainsworth.html (accessed April 2012).

Meggitt, C., Kamen, T., Bruce, T. and Grenier, J. (2011) *CACHE Level 3 Diploma: Children and Young People's Workforce – Early Learning and Child Care*, London: Hodder Education.

NDNA (2004) *National occupational standards in children's care, learning and development*, Brighouse: NDNA.

Pound, L. (2005) *How children learn: from Montessori to Vygotsky – educational theories and approaches made easy*, Salisbury: Step Forward Publishing Ltd.

Pugh, G. (2006) *Putting children first*, Nursery World website: www.nurseryworld.co.uk/news/716362/Putting-children-first/?DCMP=ILC-SEARCH (accessed March 2012).

Rutter, M. (1991) *Maternal deprivation reassessed*, London: Penguin.

Shore, R. (1997) 'What have we learned?', in R. Shore *'Rethinking the brain'*, New York: Families and Work Institute.

Simons, J.A., Irwin, D.B. and Drinnien, B.A. (1987) *Psychology – the search for understanding*, St Paul: West Publishing Company.

Stoppard, M. (1990) *The new baby care book*, London: Dorling Kindersley.

Tharp, R. and Gallimore, R. (1991) 'A theory of teaching as assisted performance', in P. Light, S. Sheldon and M. Woodhead (eds), *Learning to think*, London: Routledge.

Tizard, B. (1991) 'Working mothers and the care of young children', in M. Woodhead, P. Light and R. Carr (eds), *Growing up in a changing society*, London: Routledge.

Trevithick, P. (2000) *Social work skills: a practice handbook*, Buckingham: Open University Press.

Vargas, J.S. (2005) *A brief biography of B.F. Skinner*, The B.F. Skinner Foundation website: www.bfskinner.org/BFSkinner/AboutSkinner.html (accessed March 2012).

Woodhead, M. (1991) 'Psychology and the cultural construction of children's needs', in M. Woodhead, P. Light and R. Carr (eds), *Growing up in a changing society*, London: Routledge.

Chapter 2 Understand the role of policies in children and/or young people's settings (Unit CP 2)

In 2005, when launching a new guide to developing policies for early years settings, Steve Alexander, who was then Chief Executive of the Pre-School Learning Alliance, said, 'All settings have a responsibility to provide high-quality services for parents and families. Clear policies help to ensure that parents are aware of how settings are run, how their children will be cared for and their own responsibilities when using the service.' This statement highlights the importance of policies for services and settings for children and young people.

Policies and procedures are vitally important in almost all work settings as they provide the framework in which people work. In children and young people's settings, they are particularly helpful as they will set the standard for high-quality working practice. Policies and procedures define the ethos and values of the setting and clearly outline the expectations for practitioners, other professional groups and service users – that is, children, young people and their families. Although we explore in this chapter how policies and procedures are seperate and different, most of the chapter looks at these as one – that is, where the learning outcomes relate to policies, this will normally assume an associated procedure.

Settings and services will approach policies and procedures in different ways and with different emphases. For example, although important in all settings, a local authority social services department may emphasise safeguarding, whereas in a school setting there may be more emphasis on learning. In social services, there will be great detail in both policies and procedures and a wide range of circumstances to which the policy applies will be outlined.

Policies and procedures are only effective if they are followed. If they gather dust on a top shelf and are not living documents, they will not be effective in meeting legal requirements and improving practice.

Learning outcomes

1. Understand the role of policies within a children and/or young people's setting.
2. Understand the requirements which underpin a policy.
3. Understand how to develop a policy for a real work environment caring for children and/or young people.
4. Understand how to implement a policy in a real work environment caring for children and/or young people.

Section 1: The role of policies within a children and/or young people's setting

The difference between the role of policies and the role of procedures in the workplace

Policies

Policies are principles, rules and guidelines to help an organisation to reach its medium and long-term goals and are used to help people make decisions. They often indicate the strategy the setting or service will use to attain its aims and are based on what can realistically be delivered. Policies must be legal (i.e. not break the law) and will also explain the ethos of the setting or service. Policies are designed to be read by people external to the organisation as well as those within as they indicate what the organisation believes and takes seriously – that is, the core principles and values of the setting and the quality standard to be met. One purpose of a policy is to communicate to employees the goals of the organisation. Policies are usually not too detailed and state its aims – what has to be achieved and why. They include how the setting or service operates and help employees understand their roles and responsibilities. Policies are normally written down and may be a legal requirement in some settings. They are often published in an easily understood booklet or other format that is widely accessible.

Policies are not the same as contracts, which are formal agreements between service providers and service users. These contractual agreements are normally in place before the child or young person starts in a setting. A contract will vary between settings, but is likely to include:

- business arrangements and fees
- method of payment
- hours.

The contract may specifically state that the service users will accept the policies and procedures of the setting or service. Some settings include the policies and procedures as part of the contract; others may present these as separate documents.

Policies should flow out of the aims of the setting or service and reflect its values and ethos. The same key themes should be seen to a greater or lesser extent in all policies and procedures. For example, equality, participation, empowerment and partnership are key values which all settings and services should embed in their policies and procedures.

Procedures

Procedures provide the 'doing' element of the policy. They define in more detail the processes, activities, actions or ways of acting that must be followed to accomplish tasks or solve problems. Procedures are very useful to people within settings – for example, they may be fixed steps to be followed correctly and in order. Procedures can form the basis of standard routines, such as waste disposal. In other cases, it can be more difficult to define these when they attempt to cover values, attitudes and individual behaviours. For example, a policy may say that practitioners will treat children or young people with respect and value their opinion, or it may include statements such as 'respond sensitively to children and young people'. A procedure that reflects these policy aims is very important but more difficult to define and measure.

In most settings or services, there are written procedures for almost every area of work as they clarify what needs to be done and how it is to be done. Sometimes procedures are passed on verbally and through established work practices.

Sometimes a policy is combined with a procedure and, for other situations, they are separate. For example, a safety policy may be combined with a procedure in one statement; it will state that the policy aim is to keep children safe and avoid accidents but it will also provide a clear procedure to follow when accidents occur.

A shortened example of the difference between policy and procedure is shown in the following box.

Difference between policy and procedure

Policy

Our policy is to work in partnership with parents and to encourage their participation in every aspect of nursery life.

Procedure

1. Every new parent is given copies of the partnership policy and procedure.
2. Parents are shown round the setting and familiarised with participation opportunities.

3. Parents are actively encouraged to attend meetings by addressing possible barriers to their attendance.
4. Parents who wish to do so are actively encouraged to participate in daily activities in the setting:
   - helping in the session
   - helping with outings
   - preparing materials
   - supporting cooking and other activities
   - hearing readers in schools
   - utilising specialist skills, such as music.
5. Parents who wish to do so are encouraged to participate in management and governance of the setting in areas such as planning, fundraising, community activities and family learning projects.

Activity

Develop a policy for children's safety when outside in the sun. Using the policy, develop procedures to support the policy.

The purpose for the use of policies when working with children and/or young people

As stated in the introduction to the chapter, policies are vitally important in almost all work settings as they provide the framework in which people work. Clear policies and procedures that are understood and followed by staff are essential and may be a requirement of registration.

There are different areas covered by policies in services for children and young people. For example:

- human resources, staffing and employment
- health and safety
- safeguarding and protection
- equalities
- play and learning
- disability and special educational needs.

Within each of these categories, there is a range of different policies with associated procedures. For example, health and safety may include:

- fire safety
- emergencies
- safety checking
- dealing with a critical incident
- equipment and resources
- no smoking
- waste management
- manual handling
- supervision
- safety off site
- sun safety
- administering medicines
- behaviour management.

As well as these, there are likely to be numerous other policies – for example, animal welfare and safety – depending on the type of setting.

Figure 2.1 Policies and procedures

Examples of policies and procedures

Taken from 'Your Essential Guide to Policies and Procedures' (2011) by National Day Nurseries Association (NDNA). Web sample of policies, 1 March 2012.

Medication

When dealing with medication of any kind in the nursery, strict guidelines will be followed.

Prescription medication

- Prescription medicine will only be given to the person named on the bottle for the dosage stated.
- Medicines must be in their original containers.
- Those with parental responsibility of any child requiring prescription medication should allow a senior member of staff to have sight of the bottle. The staff member should note the details of the administration on the appropriate form and another member of staff should check these details.
- Those with parental responsibility must give prior written permission for the administration of each and every medication. However, we will except written permission once for a whole course of medication or for the on-going use of a particular medication under the following circumstances:
    1. The written permission is only acceptable for that brand name of medication and cannot be used for similar types of medication, e.g. if the course of antibiotics changes, a new form will need to be completed.
    2. The dosage on the written permission is the only dosage that will be administered. We will not give a different dose unless a new form is completed.
    3. Parents should notify us IMMEDIATELY if the child's circumstances change, e.g. a dose has been given at home, or a change in strength/dose needs to be given.
- The nursery will not administer a dosage that exceeds the recommended dose on the instructions unless accompanied by a doctor's letter.
- The parent must be asked when the child had last been given the medication before coming to nursery; this information will be recorded on the medication form. Similarly when the child is picked up, the parent or guardian must be given precise details of the times and dosage given throughout the day. The parent's signature must be obtained at both times.
- At the time of administering the medicine, a senior member of staff will ask the child to take the medicine, or offer it in a manner acceptable to the child at the prescribed time and in the prescribed form. (It is important to note that staff working with children are not legally obliged to administer medication.)
- If the child refuses to take the appropriate medication then a note will be made on the form.
- Where medication is 'essential' or may have side effects, discussion with the parent will take place to establish the appropriate response.
- Wherever possible, ask parents to request that GPs prescribe the least number of doses per day, i.e. three times daily, rather than four times daily.

Non-prescription medication

- The nursery will administer non-prescription medication for a period of three days, dependent on the medication or the condition of the child. After this time medical attention should be sought.
- If the nursery feels the child would benefit from medical attention rather than non-prescription medication, we reserve the right to refuse nursery care until the child is seen by a medical practitioner.
- If a child needs liquid paracetamol or similar medication during their time at nursery, such medication will be treated as prescription medication with the *onus being on the parent to provide the medicine/*nursery

providing one specific type of medication should parents wish to use this.

- On registration, parents will be asked if they would like to fill out a medication form for a specific type of liquid paracetamol, which can be given in the case of an increase in the child's temperature. This form will state the dose to be given, the circumstances in which this can be given, e.g. the temperature increase of their child, the specific brand name or type of liquid paracetamol and a signed statement to say that this may be administered in an emergency if they CANNOT contact the parent.
- If a child does require liquid paracetamol during the day and the parents cannot be contacted then the nursery manager will take the decision as to whether the child is safe to have this medication based on the time the child has been in the nursery, the circumstances surrounding the need for this medication and the medical history of the child on their registration form.
- For any non-prescription cream for skin conditions, e.g. Sudocrem, prior written permission must be obtained from the parent and the onus is on the parent to provide the cream, which should be clearly labelled with the child's name.
- If any child is brought to the nursery in a condition in which he/she may require medication sometime during the day, the manager will decide if the child is fit to be left at the nursery. If the child is staying, the parent must be asked if any kind of medication has already been given, at what time and in what dosage, and this must be stated on the medication form.
- As with any kind of medication, staff will ensure that the parent is informed of any non-prescription medicines given to the child whilst at the nursery, together with the times and dosage given.
- The nursery DOES NOT administer any medication unless prior written consent is given for each and every medicine.
- In the case of medication that may need to be given to a child due to them becoming ill during the day, e.g. liquid paracetamol for temperature reduction, parents will be contacted as soon as possible to ensure all details are correct and that they agree with the dosage being given.

Injections, pessaries, suppositories

As the administration of injections, pessaries and suppositories represents intrusive nursing, they should not be administered by any member of staff unless appropriate medical training is given to each member of staff caring for this child. If this causes a problem in providing appropriate care of a child, please consult *Ofsted/*Social Care & Social Work Improvement Scotland (SCSWIS)/*Care and Social Services Inspectorate Wales (CSSIW).

Staff medication

The first aid box for staff should be kept in a readily accessible position, but out of reach of the children.

First aid boxes should only contain items permitted by the Health and Safety (First Aid) Regulations Act 1981, such as sterile dressing, bandages and eye pads. No other medical items, such as paracetamol, should be kept in the first aid box.

Storage

All medication for children must have the child's name clearly written on the original container and kept in a closed box, which is out of reach of all children and under supervision at all times. If this box is left unguarded at any time throughout the day, we have a procedure in place to ensure the safety of any child or adult in the nursery, including visitors, parents and siblings able to access the area.

Emergency medication, such as inhalers and epipens, will be within easy reach of staff in case of an immediate need, but will remain out of children's reach and under supervision at all times.

Any antibiotics requiring refrigeration must be kept in an area inaccessible to children.

All medications must be in their original containers or they will not be given. All prescription medications should have the pharmacist's details and notes attached to show the dosage needed and the date the prescription was issued. This will all be checked, along with expiry dates, before staff agree to administer medication.

Internal use only	Insert date
This policy was adopted on	
Signed on behalf of the nursery	
Date disseminated to staff	
Date for review	

Activity

Find out which policies and procedures are used in your setting. Give examples of separate policies and procedures and where policies and procedures are written in one document.

You will note that this medication policy is comprehensive and detailed as it covers an important area of the nurseries' work for which clear and mandatory guidance is required.

An example of a separate policy and a procedure is shown in the box below. The procedure is not complete and is not presented as a model of good practice but to clarify the differences between policy and procedure.

Example of a hand-washing policy

Policy

Practitioners and others in the setting will minimise the spread and risks of infectious diseases between children, carers, other staff and visitors by conforming to recommended hand-washing guidelines and standards. Effective hand-washing significantly reduces the risk of cross-infection for both serious and minor diseases.

Procedure

To effectively use hand-washing to prevent the spread of infectious disease, practitioners should:

- ensure that facilities for washing hands using soap and running water are available in the immediate vicinity of areas where children and adults:
  - use toilets or change nappies
  - deal with food
  - handle animals
  - use outdoor areas.
- ensure effective drying of hands with individual towels, disposable paper towels or automatic hand-dryers
- ensure that liquid soap or individual soaps are used, rather than hand gels or shared soap bars
- ensure that children and young people are aware of the need to use liquid soap and running water and to rub their hands vigorously whilst counting to ten or singing a short song.

And so forth...

In Practice

Identify a situation when a policy or procedure is followed in your setting. Observe how the policy is implemented and consider how your own practice could be improved in the policy area.

Supporting change

Although this chapter talks about change being a key outcome in relation to the implementation of policy, in many circumstances the best way of presenting this is in terms of policy evolving, rather than an imposed change. This is because deeply embedded change takes a long time and cannot easily be achieved by a directive from management.

Policies have the potential to change practice and this makes them a key tool to support change. The impetus for change may come from managers and/or other stakeholders, such as people from the private, voluntary or public sector. Local or central government may enforce change through changing laws and regulations. In the private sector, change may be required by owners or shareholders. Change can be at different levels. It can be superficial, when the change is barely noticeable. This can be because there is reluctance to change at all levels of the organisation. Staff may pay lip service to a new policy or procedure and not embed it deeply into their practice or believe in it. Real change that is embedded deeply within the culture and practice of the setting requires ongoing effort and commitment at all levels of the setting or service.

An example from recent years is the move from child protection to safeguarding. This is not just a change of terminology but reflects a fundamental change in attitude and philosophy. Safeguarding is a wider and more active concept than protection and includes not just protecting children, young people and vulnerable adults but actively promoting their welfare. It was embodying this through laws and regulations from government that enabled changes in practice. Almost all settings in England will now have a safeguarding policy, which includes a child protection policy. The new EYFS statutory framework (2012) has made further changes but still emphasises the importance of policies and procedures. DFE (2012) states:

> 'Providers must take all necessary steps to keep children safe and well. The requirements in this section explain what early years providers must do to: safeguard children; ensure the suitability of adults who have contact with children; promote good health; manage behaviour; and maintain records, policies and procedures.'

It is important for managers responsible for introducing new policies and procedures to ensure that people are well prepared for change and that, where possible, change is not rushed or imposed without a full exploration of why it is needed. Chapter 4 looks at the process of managing change.

Meeting legal and regulatory requirements

There are legal requirements for policies and procedures to be in place, particularly when settings are regulated. Regulated settings are those subject to laws and regulations and almost all settings for children and young people fall into this category. Many settings, such as early years day care, have to be registered and then regularly inspected to make sure they meet the legal and regulatory requirements. In England, these are the requirements set out in the Early Years Foundation Stage (EYFS). Wales and Northern Ireland have equivalent regulations that must be met.

Policies are important in all areas of work but especially in circumstances involving health and safety or safeguarding. For example, clear procedures when providing intimate care will mean that practitioners are protected against allegations of improper conduct. The welfare and safety of the child or young person always come first and the practitioner has a duty of care towards them. Policies and procedures for health and safety of food are vital – for example, where a child has a severe food allergy. Children have died in day care settings where practitioners have not followed procedures and checked individual children's records for allergies.

The EYFS requires early years settings to maintain the records, policies and procedures that are required for the safe and efficient management of the settings and to meet the needs of the children.

Ofsted guidance (2010) 'Using the early years evaluation schedule' states that:

> 'The EYFS Inspectors should take into account:
> - the maintenance of records and implementation of policies and procedures required for the safe and efficient management of the Early Years Foundation Stage and for ensuring that children are safeguarded and their needs are met.'

Guidance to inspectors emphasises the importance of policies and procedures, which must be effectively and consistently implemented. Without these, settings are unlikely to achieve an 'outstanding' or 'good' grading in their Ofsted report or may face heavier sanctions.

Standardisation and consistency of approach

A real benefit of policies and procedures is that they help standardisation within the service, with each practitioner working in similar and predictable ways to achieve the goals of the setting or service. In early years settings, parents/carers will be reassured to know that all practitioners deal in similar ways with the wide variety of circumstances that may occur in day-to-day work with their children. How issues are dealt with should not depend, for example, on how practitioners are feeling that day or whether the child is thought to be 'difficult', but should be based on the policies and procedures in the setting. This is not to be confused with issues about meeting an individual child or young person's needs. Policies and procedures are normally written to enable individual needs to be met.

Avoid misunderstandings

Clear, well thought-out policies and procedures can help a setting or service avoid misunderstandings and reduce ambiguity. When all concerned are clear about policy and procedure, this helps to avoid embarrassment and misunderstanding. For example, it is not always possible to keep a person's confidence, especially, for example, when concerns about a child or young person's welfare are expressed. Practitioners can use the policy as a basis for stating that they have no choice but to escalate the information (e.g. speak to a supervisor or report safeguarding concerns). Other issues, such as racist comments or poor behaviour, may also be covered by policies and procedures to which practitioners can refer.

Where good-quality policies and procedures are developed and implemented effectively, this enables a setting or service to work professionally and consistently. Where policies are applied consistently and fairly, they can clarify difficult situations and reduce frustration, enabling a better working environment.

Improve health, safety and welfare

All settings working with children and young people should establish and maintain a safe and enriching environment. They all also need to be clear about how to respond if concerns about children and young people's health, safety and welfare are raised. Policies and procedures establish a clear framework for safe and effective practice. They are particularly important when dealing with issues and activities that are critical to health and safety, safeguarding and where legal liabilities and regulatory requirements are involved.

Provide standards for high-quality working practice

In children and young people's settings, policies and procedures will help to set a benchmark/standard for high-quality working practice. Policies and procedures should clearly outline the expectations for practitioners, other professional groups and service users – that is, children, young people and their families.

Improve efficiency

Policies and procedures improve efficiency and save practitioners time. Practitioners know what to do and have the confidence to proceed knowing they are following agreed policies and procedures.

Demonstrate values

Policies and procedures also demonstrate the principles and values of the setting. Although sometimes required for regulatory purposes, the effective use of high-quality policies and procedures, such as anti-discrimination and equality, can be a demonstration of the values held by the setting.

Protection

Where policies and procedures are followed, the practitioner will be meeting legal and organisational requirements and ensuring that the child or young person gets the most appropriate support. For example, a bullying policy will lead to a child or young person being given relevant support.

Policies and procedures protect both the child or young person and the practitioner from inappropriate responses or behaviour. In recent child sexual abuse cases, practitioners were taking inappropriate photographs of young children on their mobile phones. As a result, many settings operate a ban on mobile phones in the workplace. This ban would be backed up by a policy which practitioners sign up to before starting work.

Case Study

A previously active and lively young person has become sullen and withdrawn. The support worker asks her what is wrong. The young person says she is receiving texts that are upsetting her and she does not know what to do. The support worker is not sure what to do either so tells her to ignore the texts and stop worrying. The young person mentions this to another support worker, who tells her to contact the police as this is unacceptable. Eventually it turned out that neither support worker recognised this as serious cyber-bullying and did not know that policies and procedures existed to deal with this situation.

What are the potential problems associated with this setting? How could things be improved?

Section 2: The requirements which underpin a policy

The relevance of legislation to policy development

Legislation and regulations have already been mentioned as certain policies and procedures are required to be in place by law. Policies and procedures will be written specifically to meet legislation and regulatory requirements, but in many cases will add value by enhancing and developing the minimum requirements. Where settings take time to develop their own policies, this means they will be relevant and meaningful for their own setting or service. They will also be developed in such a way as to be practical for the setting. It is no use having a beautifully written policy with sound aims and objectives that it is impossible to implement.

A good policy will cover minimum requirements but go further by specifying in more detail what is required and the quality expected in the provision. For example, minimum requirement for a policy may state:

> 'Outdoor play areas will have approved floor surfaces to ensure child safety.'

Enhanced requirements may include detailed information such as:

> 'The playground surface should be free of standing water and debris that could cause someone to trip and fall, e.g. rocks, tree stumps, and tree roots.'

Research Activity

Select a policy and/or procedure in your setting (e.g. health and safety). Investigate why the policy is required and the laws or regulations that underpin it.

The relevance of policies in assisting service users and staff

Policies and procedures assist service users and staff by providing clear direction about what to do in specific circumstances. Service users will be able to understand their rights and what they can expect as these will be outlined in the policy. For example, an admission policy may include details of the catchment area of a setting and will also include details of an appeals procedure if the child is refused a place.

For practitioners, a policy and procedure should leave them in no doubt about the correct actions to take in certain circumstances. For example, all settings will have a safeguarding policy and a procedure for reporting concerns. Most settings have a whistleblowing policy, where practitioners may report concerns about colleagues or others in the setting. When followed, these policies and procedures act as a safety net for staff. In difficult and sensitive situations, a clearly written set of actions to take is reassuring and protects staff from unfair blame.

Some policies and procedures, such as safeguarding or food safety, are critical for the welfare of children and young people. Other policies may contain statements of good practice and these may make a huge difference in the quality of the experience for children and young people. For example, there may be a policy for animal health and safety. This policy will focus on the welfare of the animals in the setting but can also include material on how the child or young person is protected whilst actively involved in animal care. Practitioners understanding this policy will know that children and young people are expected to be involved in care of animals in the setting.

The relevance of policies and procedures in informing practice

Developing policies and procedures that meet high-quality standards and reflect evidence-based practice is a key element in driving up standards and developing practice. For example, many residential childcare settings have policies and procedures covering:

- immunisation and screening
- behaviour management
- nutrition and diet
- exercise and rest
- personal hygiene
- sexual health
- the effects of alcohol, smoking and other substances
- HIV and AIDS and other blood borne diseases.

Each of these areas provide the opportunity for practitioners to develop practice. In some cases, this forces the pace of change. Changes to policies may mean more training opportunities are required to introduce new forms of practice. This can provide a basis for change even where practitioners may be reluctant. One of the first things the setting may consider is a training needs analysis, which identifies needs associated with specific policies. This can be undertaken, for example, using a formal survey, or as part of an appraisal system. The idea being that individual as well as group training needs are clearly identified.

The introduction of the EYFS provided a framework for most early years providers to follow. This included the development of policies and procedures that may not have been required before. Childminders have also been included in this change of practice, even though the requirements for written policies may be less stringent.

Activity

Choose an area of work requiring a policy and develop your own version of the policy. Develop a set of clear procedures to implement the policy. Test out whether a small sample of people understand what you mean in the policy you have developed. Take their views into account and make changes to your policy. Does it still meet your original requirements?

The relevance of costs to policy development

Policies and procedures do come with associated costs. For example, there may be costs associated with:

- developing new or enhancing existing policies
- employing someone to develop the policies
- printing and distributing
- training and supporting practitioners
- change management.

Costs will be a factor in setting fees for parents/carers or in the extent of local authority provision. Central government has sometimes in the past funded or part funded major changes, such as the introduction to new curricula, but this is likely to be more difficult in the future. In times of austerity, when money for new development is tight, it may be that the effect of this is to prevent or minimise the development of new policy. Sometimes new policy is forced through, but the reality could be that other areas of provision may become weaker.

Case Study

A voluntary sector service supporting disabled children and young people had planned to introduce new ways of working. In particular, they had planned to introduce a new behaviour management policy designed to minimise the number of aggressive outbursts in their settings and to create a calmer, more supportive environment. They costed this new approach and developed a number of policies, procedures and protocols designed to support its introduction. A key element was staff training and holding a number of events designed to help parents and carers understand and support the approach by, for example, continuing the behaviour management methodology at home. Before they could start this major change, they learned that their grant was being cut and the money to do this in the ways planned would not be available.

This service did proceed with the change but on a reduced scale, reducing the impact and the speed and effectiveness of the proposed change.

The relevance of a requirement for new resources for policy development

The previous section on costs applies equally to this section. Policy development may or may not require new resources, depending on its nature and scope. Resources may include almost anything required to develop or implement policy. For example:

- human resources
- physical resources, such as buildings or equipment
- consumables.

If the policy development is minor – for example, enhancing a small part of an existing policy – it may be that there is little extra resource required in developing policy and in its subsequent implementation. If policy development covers a new area of work or requires new staffing resource, the impact on costs and resources will be significant. Outdoor facilities may require development in some circumstances or access facilities, such as provision for wheelchairs. Access facilities for disabled people are now required by law (under the Equality Act 2010, building on the Disability Discrimination Act 1995). Settings may have to close down if they do not comply with new laws. Sometimes funding is available to support change, but this is increasingly rare, and often changes have to be funded in other ways, such as raising fees to parents or freezing pay.

Monitoring implementation of policy

New policies can only be effectively monitored if policy aims are clear to practitioners, service users and others involved. Effective monitoring can let the setting or service know if:

- policies and procedures have been implemented (or ignored)
- procedures have worked well
- there are any unintended consequences
- adaptations to policies and procedures are required
- greater flexibility is needed.

In some cases, measuring the effectiveness of a policy is more difficult, especially if it relates to behaviour change or even changes to attitudes. Practitioners may resent new policy and, although they give lip service to it, nothing much changes on the ground. A good example of this is changes to behaviour policies. Practitioners need to be involved in the development of this type of policy and engaged right from the start. How they deal with children or young people's behaviour should be based on this policy, but much depends on the preparation and training given to practitioners who may have a strong culture of dealing with behaviour in a different way. Monitoring a policy can be challenging to some practitioners, so it has to be done with fairness and sensitivity. Sometimes it involves asking for feedback from service users, including children. Confidentiality may not be easily maintained and children, young people, families and carers should be encouraged to make open and honest evaluations.

Whatever aspect of the setting or service is affected by policy change and development, monitoring and measuring impact are essential to make sure changes are effective in meeting policy aims. When new policies or changes to existing policies are introduced, it is good practice to set up a system of evaluation to see if the changes are effective or need adaptation. For example, if a new policy regarding reaching families who have traditionally been hard to engage with is launched, some way of measuring its effectiveness is required. It is no longer enough simply to gather anecdotal information in which practitioners or managers might comment informally: 'We seem to have more families from a particular estate.' Now more than ever, settings need concrete evidence. In this case, the policies and procedures may define what constitutes a 'hard-to-engage' family. It may be a family from an estate or other types of family, such as those where English is an additional language.

Both monitoring the processes involved in the new policy and procedure and the outcomes should be included. The outcomes may be easier to determine as this involves counting how many more are coming to the setting. However, simply measuring outcomes is not enough. In the above policy, a 10 per cent increase in hard-to-engage families using the setting could be seen as success. However, the process of engaging with families may be so flawed that the 10 per cent could have been 25 per cent with better ways of working.

Case Study

In order to monitor a policy change, it is also important to define what success looks like. A setting has found that its outdoor play policy has been challenged as it restricts access to particular times and weather. The new policy makes outdoor areas accessible at all times, regardless of weather, unless there are exceptional circumstances. The setting has decided that success for this policy will take the form of:

- 80 per cent or more of individual children using and enjoying the outdoor area over a week
- children engaging in sustained periods of outdoor play and learning
- children moving independently from indoor to outdoors
- outdoor curriculum/learning goals being met
- the whole outdoor area being utilised appropriately by children
- supervision being appropriate and adequate.

These indicators of the success of the policy are measurable and staff are involved in observations, assessments and reflections.

Case Study (cont.)

The measure of success is able to be based on hard numerical and observational evidence, as well as considering 'soft' issues, such as whether having easy and open access to outdoors is fun and enjoyed by children.

Monitoring of the new policy initially focused on issues such as:

- identifying how children use the outdoor space
- identifying how many children use the space and for how long
- monitoring how curriculum resources are used
- identifying whether there is easy access to boots and warm clothing when required
- identifying whether children are linking outdoor and indoor learning experiences
- removing barriers when they are identified and monitoring outcomes.

New policies can only be effectively monitored if policy aims are clear to practitioners, service users and others involved. Monitoring will have a cost implication, but this might be far less than if the changes had not been made.

The impact of policies on service users

The potential impact of policies on service users is significant. Policies make clear what can be expected in the setting. Policies provide a clear framework for the operation of the setting, from an admissions policy through to a policy supporting transitions as the child or young person moves on.

Policies and procedures help service users and practitioners:

- to have thorough and comprehensive discussions with new service users
- demonstrate to service users that this is a formally constituted business
- prevent any misunderstandings
- set the boundaries and expectations
- together with a contract, provide a basis for any required legal action
- provide clarity about what is acceptable in the setting
- provide clarity about the consequences of infringement of the contract or where policies and procedures are ignored.

When parents/carers enrol their child or young person, it is important to provide them with written copies of relevant documents and to go through them verbally to make sure their importance is understood. Service providers and users sign and keep a copy of the agreements. Service providers have to deal with this in a professional way but also show understanding to parents/carers' concerns. Written policies do help to clarify expectations for both sides. If service providers or users want to change elements of the contract or do not accept policies and procedures at a later date, the signed agreements give a good basis for discussion.

The impact of policies on staff

All the above discussion on the impact of policies on service users is relevant to this section. In addition, polices provide additional security for staff to help them to respond in predictable and consistent ways to everyday and unusual activity. For example, staff will apply a behaviour policy frequently in everyday work but are unlikely to have to utilise an emergency policy and procedure for lost children very often, if ever.

Changes to policies and procedures affect staff both personally and professionally. The change they are implementing or supporting may be outside their area of competence. They may feel threatened and anxious and not able to work effectively. Leaders and managers need to be able to support staff effectively and not rush the pace of change.

Policies and procedures will assist practitioners when dealing with potentially difficult issues, such as equalities. Sometimes parents/carers do not understand the basis of the setting's policies regarding equalities and may see them as irrelevant

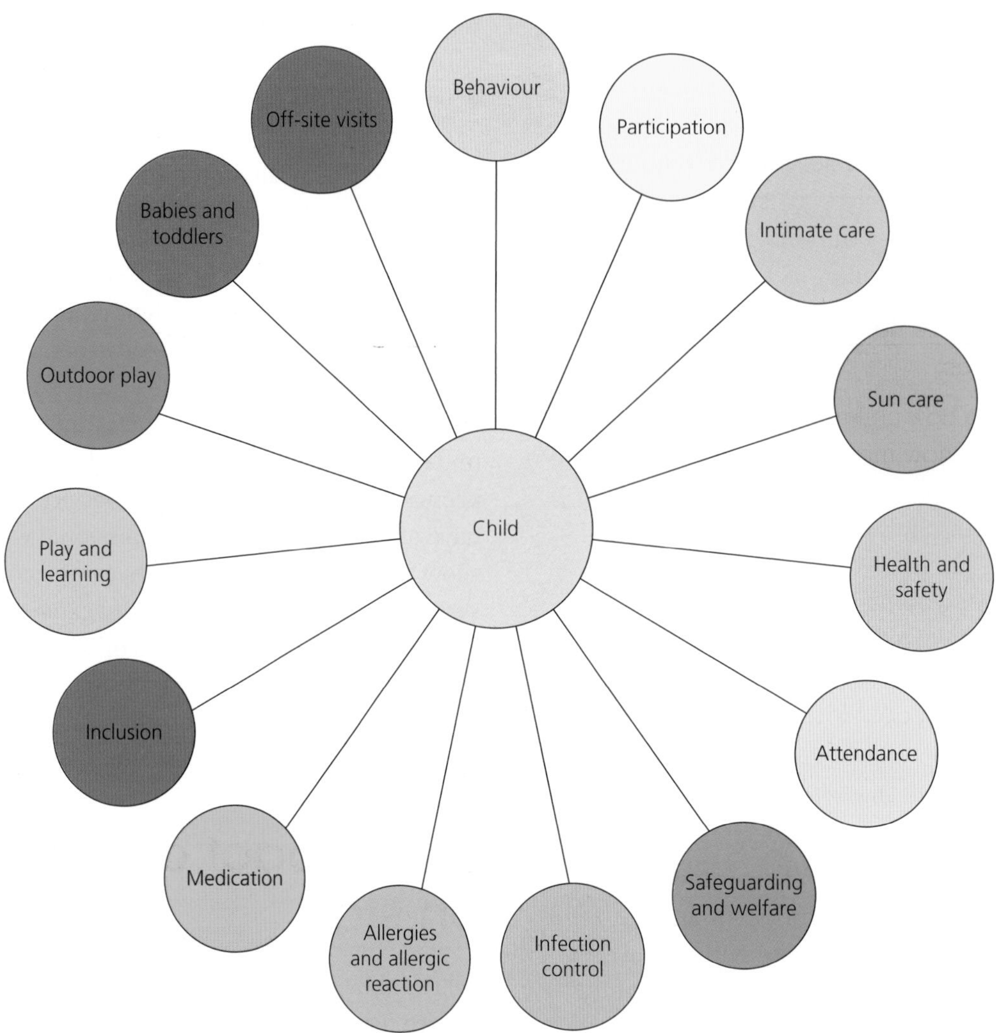

Figure 2.2 This chart does not include all the policies and procedures that are developed to support children and families. From your experience in your setting/s, list any gap areas.

or wrong. Policies will have been explained at enrolment and practitioners can remind parents/carers and other stakeholders that these are the baseline for good practice. Issues of behaviour can also be challenging and the same arguments apply.

Policies also support staff with their employment rights and responsibilities – for example, pay, conditions of service and confidentiality.

The impact of policies on communities

Policies and procedures within settings and services for children and young people may have an impact on the community. For example:

- Cost policies may encourage or discourage parents/carers to use services; greater use may lead to higher levels of parental employment.
- Effective inclusion policies may mean greater take-up from hard-to-reach groups in communities.
- Greater inclusion of hard-to-reach families may lead to better outcomes for children and young people.
- Policies emphasising participation of fathers can support development in areas where gender stereotypes are strong and can lead to a greater involvement of fathers in their child's life.
- Involvement of parents/carers can lead to community development projects.
- Involvement of parents/carers in the work of the setting can lead to an increase in confidence,

empowerment of parents and a greater sense of ownership of the setting and service.

- Where settings have a policy of including parents in their child's learning, this can lead to involvement of the whole family in family learning projects, such as adult literacy and numeracy.

Research commissioned by the Pre-School Learning Alliance (2004) found that pre-schools play a wide-ranging, active role in supporting communities, delivering a 'range of tangible benefits for children, parents and wider communities'. The researchers revisited a number of pre-schools in areas of social and economic disadvantage to assess their contribution to the overall strengthening of communities. It concluded that:

- as well as providing high-quality services for children, the pre-schools continue to have a strong emphasis on involving parents in the day-to-day running of the settings and supporting parents in their own learning and development
- the pre-schools are supporting the expansion of the early years workforce, with a striking number of people moving from parent to volunteer and from volunteer to permanent member of staff
- the pre-schools are continuing to help support social inclusion, by helping often very isolated parents to build their own social networks within the community.

The PLA website (www.pre-school.org.uk/media/press-releases/134/pre-schools-play-in-invaluable-community-role-says-study) states the following:

> 'The research shows that pre-schools have gone from strength to strength and are still performing an invaluable community role. The follow-up study demonstrates that as well as the many benefits these pre-schools provide for children, they continue to provide a wide range of personal, social and economic benefits for parents.'

Pre-school settings were found to provide a great deal more to parents and families than high-quality childcare alone:

> 'The role they play in engaging parents in their child's and their own learning, in supporting routes to qualifications and in combating social exclusion is seen as crucial to sustaining healthy communities.'

The impact of policies on other stakeholders

Key term

Stakeholder – a person, group or organization that has direct or indirect stake in an organisation because it can affect or be affected by the organisation's actions, objectives and policies (source: www.BusinessDictionary.com). A key stakeholder refers to people, groups or organisations that have a significant stake and are most affected.

Policies impact on other stakeholders according to circumstances. Examples of other stakeholders are:

- health professionals
- police and law enforcement
- multidisciplinary teams
- local or central government
- funders
- social services
- voluntary organisations
- support services for families, children or young people (e.g. autism teams)
- language support services
- inspectors and regulators.

Other professional groups will generally support the policies and procedures within a setting but need to be clear what these are. Inspectors and regulators clearly have an interest in the setting's policies and procedures, as they will form part of what is inspected.

Sometimes there is conflict between the policy of a setting and other stakeholders – for example, when confidential information is requested. Generally, unless there are legal or safeguarding issues, a setting's confidentiality policy must be respected. Strong policies and procedures give a clear message to other stakeholders, and this clarity assists and supports partnership working.

Progress check

Develop a leaflet explaining to new staff why policies and procedures are needed and the benefits they bring to settings.

Reflective practice

Reflect on the way you implement a procedure. How do you know that your implementation of the procedure is accurate and effective? How can you improve your practice?

Section 3: Developing a policy for a real work environment caring for children and/or young people

Developing or updating a policy for a real work environment has some challenges. Policies must be workable and their impact measurable.

Many settings adopt a whole-systems approach, which looks at how all the policies work together within the setting or service. Settings will look at:

- their current practices
- their structures
- their working environment and culture
- potential unforeseen consequences.

Some settings view this like a jigsaw puzzle. They consider whether a new or amended policy will prevent the pieces fitting together well. If not, they need to think about how this new policy or existing policies in other areas might need to be amended. There is useful information relating to this approach in the SCIE Participation Practice Guide 06.

Considerations when developing a policy

The importance of language level when developing a policy

Policies and procedures are only effective if they are followed and clearly understood. Therefore, they must be understood by everyone who needs to use them. In early years settings in England, Ofsted inspectors will consider the extent to which policies and procedures are available to, and understood by, parents and others (Ofsted 2009). Language level is important when considering the format and presentation of policies and procedures.

The language used in policies must be clear and accessible to parents/carers, children, young people and practitioners. Generally, policies should be written in plain language and be brief, clear and to the point. During the development of policies and procedures, the materials need to be tested with a sample of parents and others to make sure they are clearly understood. The 'Plain English Campaign' has some useful information about the Crystal Mark (www.plainenglish.co.uk), which is their seal of approval for the clarity of a document. However, there are costs associated with getting this approval, which may be out of reach for many small-scale settings for children and young people.

Where people cannot speak or read English or have other issues, such as sensory impairments or learning difficulties, other ways of ensuring they understand policies and procedures must be developed. Sometimes interpreters are used or materials translated into other languages. All these have cost implications. Sometimes settings can get assistance from local communities or local authorities with these tasks. However, communicating effectively with parents/carers, children and young people and other stakeholders in this process is important and is not an optional extra.

Case Study

The kind of language that appears in policies can sometimes be gobbledygook! A rare example:

> 'We are a setting that values strategic high-level input from professionals representing the full breadth of thinking and enterprise of our industry. This input is utilised in the most cost-effective way to bring about a paradigm shift in our strategic and operational thinking.'

Find examples of how language used in policies and procedures can be hard to understand. Rewrite them in plain language.

The importance of an aim and rationale when developing a policy

When developing a policy, the aims and rationale should be clearly defined; they are closely linked. The rationale, or reason, for a policy often comes first. Why is the policy being developed, for what purpose? Having decided why a policy is required, the specific policy aims are then worked out. Very often aims and rationale are directed by law or in regulations, but these have to be translated into accessible language that enables change to be achieved.

Policy aims and rationale are frequently associated with change – change in the ways of working or in procedures to be followed. If the aims and rationale are not clear:

- there will be difficulties in measuring whether it has been successful
- people will not really understand what they have to do.

What can and cannot be done when developing a policy

When developing a policy, it is important to involve all stakeholders – that is, parents/carers, other professionals, children and young people. Even where children and young people may not be able to verbally express their views, ways need to be found to overcome this as their input is often the most important. Generally, age or developmental level will determine how this is done.

It is best if policy development and changes are not forced on people. It is important to make sure everyone affected understands why change is needed and, where possible, they are respectfully persuaded through logical argument and further training. For example, if new research or changes to legislation are driving change, making sure everyone understands the implications is necessary to avoid resentment.

Policies and procedures will clearly identify what can or cannot be done in terms of the area they cover, but in themselves they cannot change individual attitudes or prejudices. What they can do is to state clearly how practitioners and others must behave in the setting or service and their individual responsibility for issues, such as confidentiality outside the work setting. For example, where a parent/carer is openly racist and the child repeats racist abuse, there should be clear procedures to follow. This means the parent must not allow their personal prejudices to come into the setting or their child may be excluded. The seriousness of this should be made clear as the parent/carer will have 'signed up' to the policy on admission.

Practitioners also must not behave in ways which are prejudiced or discriminatory. Sometimes this is difficult to define. For example, a practitioner may really care for a particular child with special educational needs, but an overwhelming desire to protect the child may mean that there are low expectations of achievement. In turn, this is working against a policy which states that learning and achieving are central and every child will be encouraged to reach their potential.

Time constraints when developing a policy

There are likely to be time constraints when developing a policy. Developing policy is time consuming as it will require staff and service users' time to develop an effective and useful policy. However, there may be pressure from regulators such as Ofsted to make sure that effective policies are in place. In some cases, regulators such as Ofsted will withdraw registration if effective policies are not in place within a set period. This may mean practitioners need to be trained and service users involved and informed, and a period of trialling may also be required. This takes time and costs money but may be critical to the success of the policy.

Market forces also may put pressure on providers to develop and advertise clear policies to reassure and encourage parents/carers, children and young people.

Exemptions to the policy

At the time of development of a policy, any exemptions to the policy should be made clear, but in a setting or service these are normally rare. Exemptions at national level can sometimes be more easily identified – for example, foreigners are exempt from the 'one child' policy in China. In England, there is guidance for exemptions from parts of the EYFS statutory framework. Such exemptions will be reflected in the setting's policies and procedures, and service users will be made aware of these.

In schools, sometimes children or young people can be exempted from religious assemblies and RE lessons. Schools policies and procedures will make this parental right clear.

Research Activity

Look into the policies and procedures in your setting and in local services to consider the range of circumstances where children, young people or families may be exempt from particular policies. Select examples of particular exemptions and develop a list of points in favour of or against the exemptions.

Person responsible for implementation

People responsible for implementation of policies will either be named personally or more often reference may be made to their role (e.g. the manager or qualified first-aiders). In some cases, their responsibility will also be to make sure that others in the setting understand the policy and procedure and to monitor their effectiveness. They may also be required to check that the policy and procedure are being implemented correctly.

Many policies and procedures form the basis of work with children and young people. Often all practitioners and other professionals/colleagues will be bound by the policies (e.g. safeguarding, health and safety, behaviour, confidentiality). Within these policies, certain people may have particular responsibilities – for example, the health and safety policy affects everyone but there are named first-aiders within the policy with specific responsibilities. Equally, within safeguarding, there is a general policy for all, but some people will have specific responsibilities, often a manager or senior professional, to take forward a set of actions.

Activity

Examine health and safety (or other) policies in your setting – there may be several covering one topic. Identify the actions that are general for everyone and those that are specific to a named person.

Case Study

In recent years, there have been a number of high-profile cases of inappropriate photos being taken of young children in nurseries, which have been circulated across the internet. This is the sexual abuse of vulnerable young children. In many settings, mobile phones are now banned. Settings have clear policies and procedures covering this.

Check out what actions the policies and procedures require you to take in your setting if you see someone using a mobile phone in a banned area, no matter how innocent the call.

 Progress check

Develop a short briefing paper for other learners on the key points to take into account when developing a policy for a real work environment. Working in a group, use the headings given in this section to develop a policy and present it to a larger group.

A system for monitoring, evaluating and reviewing a policy

Key term

Monitoring – monitoring is about collecting data/information to help determine whether objectives have been met. Monitoring will need specific indicators on which to measure progress. Data is best collected systematically – that is, in a planned, organised and routine way. Data is best collected at set times – for example, weekly or monthly but may be more frequent depending on circumstances.

Evaluation – evaluation is the systematic and objective assessment of any activity including projects or policy implementation. This helps lessons to be learned and changes to be made.

Review – very similar to an evaluation, a review is a critique or revision and includes looking back at something – that is, a critical re-assessment or reconsideration.

Monitoring, evaluation and review are required:

- because, if results are not measured, it is impossible to tell success from failure
- because, if success cannot be seen, it cannot be recognised, rewarded and built on
- because, if success is not identified, failure will not be identified and cannot be put right
- to determine if it is possible to save resources and improve value for money
- to improve accountability
- to provide a better service for children, young people and families
- to keep ahead of national policy changes
- to incorporate best practice from research.

Monitoring, evaluation and review are linked activities that complement each other. Monitoring often describes the processes involved in policy implementation at any given time measured against policy aims. Evaluation gives evidence about why policy aims are or are not being achieved and why this might be the case. When monitoring finds that things are going off track, evaluation can clarify this and suggest a change of approach. Review feeds into both activities and looks back at how things were and are now changing – that is, what works and what does not work.

Policies and procedures should be transparent and accessible by all who use the setting or service. They should be reviewed regularly in consultation with staff and any other stakeholders. Real collaboration is important for the effective implementation of policies and procedures; in this way, all stakeholders involved can reach agreement and ownership and a commitment to carry out the actions needed to make the policy work. Policies should be dynamic and flexible, not set in stone. This will ensure they meet the needs of the environment in which the setting or service operates. Regular monitoring, evaluation and review are needed to keep up-to-date with the changing world, new research or legal requirements. In a customer-focused environment, the needs of the customer are also important.

Policy monitoring, evaluation and review help settings to sharpen up their accountability and business outcomes, but primarily should focus on the outcomes for children and young people.

Monitoring, evaluation and review help with the detailed work involved in:

- formulating outcomes and goals
- developing outcome indicators
- gathering baseline information on the current condition
- setting specific targets and dates for reaching them
- regularly collecting data to assess whether the targets are being met
- analysing and reporting results
- learning from the experiences

- accounting for resources
- using information gained to make changes to policy, procedures and practice.

There are several ways in which settings review the effectiveness of changes to or the introduction of new policies and procedures. Review is always needed to make sure the aims of the policy are being met. It involves a systematic collection of information about the processes and outcomes of changes that have taken place in a setting or service as a result of new policies. Monitoring policy implementation is covered earlier in this chapter.

In order to monitor, evaluate and review the impact of policies, the policy aims should have been determined at the outset. The achievement of policy aims can be measured through setting a series of smaller targets if this is required.

Monitoring, and evaluation and review are closely linked, as Table 2.1 below suggests.

Monitoring	Evaluation and review
Clarifies objectives of policy change	Analyse why expected changes were or were not achieved
Checks how activities in the setting link to the policy objectives	Assess whether specific activities have contributed to success or otherwise
Can link performance assessment and appraisals to policy objectives through setting targets for individuals and teams	Assess whether performance targets have been achieved and why
Collects ongoing data and measures actual changes as a result of policy	Evaluate unintended consequences and suggest changes to policy or implementation
Reports progress and gives early warning of problems	Analyse achievement and suggest potential improvement

Table 2.1 Monitoring, and evaluation and review

Case Study: An example of monitoring the process of implementing a new policy

In an out-of-school setting, a new bullying policy is introduced. Most young people are closely involved and fully participate in its planning and implementation. Practitioners have planned to monitor the implementation of the new policy:

- informally through everyday work
- through structured observations
- through interviews with individual young people
- through small groups.

The above was supported by a series of structured questions and also took into account informal feedback. For example, young people were asked if practitioners intervened too quickly or too often. Did the intervention by practitioners support young people being bullied or did it make things worse? Did the bullying worsen off site? Did it draw embarrassing attention to individual young people?

Example of a monitoring, evaluation and review system for a new policy

A nursery has a behaviour policy that has been identified as weak, with practitioners dealing with children's negative behaviour inconsistently and with different degrees of success. The nursery has undertaken a review of the policy and found it lacked detail and was not clear to practitioners, who had little training in managing behaviour. It did not involve parents in supporting behavioural goals.

The nursery has been observing children and areas within the nursery to gain information about the flashpoints and has some hard evidence about how many outbursts of difficult or challenging behaviour have been experienced in particular rooms, with particular children and in circumstances such as walking in corridors or in the outdoor play area. This has provided them with a baseline with which to measure improvement. They have planned to evaluate the policy after two months and then again every three months until it is well established.

The new policy seeks to strengthen and make consistent the approach to negative behaviour. The new policy spells out the aims. For example:

- to ensure a safe and secure emotional and physical environment for children
- to work in partnership with parents/carers in supporting children's development and behaviour
- to encourage children to respect themselves and others and to take responsibility for their actions
- to promote kindness, understanding and compassion
- to encourage understanding of fairness and inclusion
- to reduce episodes of difficult behaviour by introducing a programme that rewards positive behaviour
- to introduce 'circle time' to discuss feelings and what is negative/positive behaviour.

The policy also outlines procedures to follow in circumstances when behaviour is difficult. For example:

- recognise and respond appropriately to minor behaviour difficulties, such as being clear when behaviour is not acceptable, using positive statements, labelling the behaviour not the child, etc.
- use direct but non-confrontational language
- use an individual education plan to identify behavioural targets
- be aware that children may demonstrate negative behaviour when hungry, tired or bored and deal with those circumstances in a consistent way.

Specific aims have been identified as, for example:

- fewer aggressive outbursts in particular areas
- noting and meeting individual needs for quiet periods, a snack or more stimulation
- effective reflective practice recording of antecedents to work out why the behaviour changed and became negative, and the role of the practitioner if relevant.

Actions to enable effective monitoring

- Staff have all been trained in the agreed system to manage behaviour.
- Clear, transparent and consistent guidelines have been introduced and shared with parents, whose comments have been incorporated.
- Practitioners have been encouraged to reflect on their practice in this area and reflective practice recording documents have been provided.
- Simple monitoring forms have been introduced to encourage observation and assessment of children's behaviour at key points in the day/week.
- Monitoring forms are also being used in key places in the nursery to see if the area itself needs to be redesigned – for example, a long, empty corridor encourages running, and children pushing at a narrow point.

- Practitioners are encouraged to prioritise completion of forms fully and accurately.
- Practitioners are given feedback on the results of their monitoring and how it is being used to make the policy more effective.
- Regular feedback is obtained, both formally and informally, from service users and other stakeholders through questionnaires, meetings or individual conversations.
- Staff meetings and training days include a session or item on the new policy implementation.
- Practitioners and service users are made aware of data protection in terms of the monitoring.

Actions to enable evaluation

- After two months, initial monitoring data is collated and measured against the baseline to check for improvements or other changes.
- Nursery undertakes self-evaluation.
- Self-evaluation is checked with stakeholders for accuracy.
- All feedback is checked against aims of policies.
- A brief report of findings is prepared and shared.
- A simple graph of hard data is developed to demonstrate findings.

Additional actions for next round of monitoring and evaluation

- Changes are made to the layout of the nursery where problem areas have been identified.
- Individual practitioners are encouraged to continue to participate and incorporate their observations into everyday work.
- Individual performance targets are set for practitioners in terms of monitoring children's behaviour and using the new behaviour management system.
- Further training sessions are planned.
- Parent groups are encouraged to attend meetings to discuss policy evaluation.

Section 4: Understand how to implement a policy in a real work environment caring for children and/or young people

The necessity of communicating the use of new/revised policies within the real work environment

New or revised policies will impact on all stakeholders in different ways. Managers and those responsible for new policy development need to take into account the impact on different groups of people and be sensitive to their needs. It takes time to adjust to change and, wherever possible, new policies should not be rushed in. To get the best out of policy change, it is important to take people with you, and allow them to see why change is needed and the potential benefits to them as individuals and to the organisation. For example, cost-cutting will not be welcomed, but if this is undertaken to ensure the survival of the service or setting, people are more likely to see the necessity and work with it.

Communication of any change needs to be effective and multidimensional. It can involve:

- speaking
- listening
- reading
- writing
- encouraging
- understanding
- consulting
- debating

- translating
- interpreting
- reflecting
- various media.

The capability of the leader/manager in communicating the changes in policy and the vision of the setting is centrally important. As has been said throughout the chapter, any changes need to be transparent and based on dialogue with all stakeholders.

Communicating the use of new/revised policies to staff

Staff need to understand and be aware of policies and procedures in order to implement them effectively. This can be done through:

- a positive and thorough induction into employment in the setting
- ongoing training
- easily understood and accessible printed or electronic information
- personal and professional development
- staff meetings
- appraisals and performance management
- 'champions' of the new policies.

All of these methods give the opportunity for managers and others to communicate information about new and revised policies. It is also important to communicate new approaches or procedures through example and modelling good practice. Managers and senior staff should be clear about what is required and enthusiastic about the proposed changes. Sometimes settings have a 'champion', who supports the changes being introduced and is a point of contact for staff with queries or concerns.

Reflective practice

Reflect on the way you were introduced or inducted into the policies and procedures of your setting. Did you have enough information to implement these? What questions could you have asked that might have helped your understanding?

Communicating the use of new/revised policies to stakeholders

Communicating new policies is vitally important but how this is done will depend on the stakeholders concerned. Most stakeholders will have been involved in some way in developing new policy and procedures. Occasionally, change can lead to conflict but this needs to be worked out in a professional way and agreement sought. All professionals working with the setting need to be clear about new policy in order to make sure their approach is supportive and consistent. If there is conflict between professionals, this could lead to problems for service users.

Where other professionals work within the setting, it may be valuable to invite them to shared training and/or allow time for the impact of new policies to be discussed, individually or across agencies. Printed or electronic versions of the policies and procedures should be available.

If stakeholders are parents/carers, time will be needed to consult with them on the initial proposals as there may be opposition to the plans. For example, parents may object to changes to a catchment area or to other aspects of admissions policy. As key stakeholders, their input is important and policies should be adapted to meet their requirements if this is possible. Once the policy is ready for implementation, time should be given to explain what might happen. Parents/carers should expect to be asked for feedback and to share any problems promptly. Information can be passed on and discussed, for example:

- in parent meetings and interviews
- using leaflets or electronic media
- using texts or internet to relay feedback
- on noticeboards and in letters home
- using interpreters or translation services
- using appropriate aids to communication.

In many settings, the full participation of children and young people in decisions affecting their lives is central, and changes to policies and procedures should be explained carefully. Ideally, children and young people will have been part of the initial consultations and will be involved in drawing up the policy, according to their age and abilities. Feedback from children and young people often focuses on how much they value being listened to.

Communicating the use of new/revised policies to service users

As we have commented above, service users are normally included in the development and implementation of new policies. However, some service users may have missed out on the consultation procedure and settings will have to work with this group to make sure they are fully informed as to the implications of the policy. Written information should always be available on noticeboards or in leaflet form. Letters to parents/carers are sometimes used. In addition, this information should be freely available on websites or in news sent by text to parents. It is important to recognise the specific communication needs of stakeholders – for example, the need for translation or interpretation, or the use of assistive technology.

Different approaches to promoting the use of policies within the work role

Promoting the use of policies in the work role is the responsibility of all practitioners, as most policies will have direct relevance to their work. Some practitioners will have particular responsibility as their work role may cover specialism in that area of work. For example, everyone is involved in implementing care and education for disabled children, but a special educational needs coordinator will have specific responsibilities. One of their responsibilities may be to work with other practitioners to help them to follow the special educational needs policies and support children appropriately. However, the main responsibility for new policy development and implementation will lie with leaders and managers of the setting or service.

Leadership and management

Leaders and managers need to understand how change works and the processes involved. They need to be aware that change is challenging for practitioners and service users. Some will find it difficult and need a good deal of support to manage change. Key areas that managers and leaders need to take into account when promoting the use of policies are shown in Table 2.2.

Chapter 4 talks about different styles of leadership and management and there is more information there that can be applied to policy change. Management and leadership styles will influence how new policies are promoted in the setting. The two opposite extremes are the autocratic, on the one hand, and the democratic (participative), on the other. In practice, the style will vary according to the personality of the leader and to the culture of the organisation but also to the specific situation.

Autocratic approach to promoting the use of policies

Autocratic leadership provides clear expectations of the policy change, including what, where, when and how to do it. It is sometimes called a 'top down' or 'command and control' style. This style of leadership and management can be over-controlling and dictatorial and does not listen to people. The changes may be introduced in a way that does not allow time for people to understand, support and become engaged with the issues. Many settings find that autocratic leadership and management does not work, and there is high staff dissatisfaction and a high turnover. This is bad for children and for the business in private settings. Attempting to change policy and practice in this way is unlikely to work well.

In emergency situations when a change is urgent, perhaps after mistakes have been made in a setting, a more autocratic approach may be needed.

Areas to take into account	Comment
Celebrate achievements	Give appropriate reward and recognition for what is good and has worked well.
Fairness, openness and transparency	These should be at the heart of policy change and development. The need for transparency and openness to take people on the journey towards a shared vision.
Reasons for change should be very clear	Why change is required and the outcomes expected should be discussed with all stakeholders.
Change and maintenance of policies and procedures needs leadership and direction	Change will not 'just happen'. It needs clear and consistent leadership.
Change takes time	Change happens all the time but deep change takes time to embed.
Change is costly	Change is costly in energy, time and resources.
A team culture and identity	A collective, shared vision is important for policy development.
Being inclusive is important	Involve parents/carers, children and young people and a wide range of stakeholders wherever possible.
Effective collaboration, positive relationships and effective communication is at the heart of policy change and development	Listen, be flexible and adaptable and be seen to avoid change for change's sake. Use effective multidimensional ways of communicating the reason for and potential benefits of change. Work together to develop specific plans for achieving policy aims.
Reflective practice is good practice	Encourage all practitioners to be reflective in all areas of practice but, to embed change, encourage reflection in the area of policy development. There is a need to allow change to emerge from reflective practice and existing systems of evaluation.
Professional development	Encourage lifelong learning and building a learning community (see Chapter 4).

Table 2.2 Promoting policies in a real work environment

Democratic approach to promoting the use of policies

A democratic approach is thought to work better and to engage people. Effective democratic leaders and managers offer guidance, encouragement and direction. Stakeholders are listened to and given the opportunity to influence the policy. This approach is respectful to stakeholders and will help them to understand the reasons for change and allay anxieties. The ELEYS Study (2006) found that effective leaders in early years settings were able to identify and articulate an ambitious collective vision and to ensure consistency among staff. This required a shared understanding of setting practices and processes and the use of reflective practice. In particular, planned and managed change is crucial – that is, a change such as a new policy is often inevitable, but how the process is managed is the greatest influence on its success.

Policy champions

These are people identified as having special responsibility for supporting change. Sometimes champions are selected to represent particular groups, but where policy is changing in a setting it is sometimes useful to use the 'champion' systems. Champions may or may not be experts in the policy area but they should be trained in the area and in the changes being implemented. They are key people to whom others can go for information about the changes and who act as a point of contact with management, where necessary, to report on implementation. For example, when it was recognised that children and young people needed a greater voice in decisions affecting their lives, participation policies were introduced in many settings. Participation champions were one way of helping settings to change their practice.

Case Study

A setting wishes to introduce an effective policy for participation. They know that children and young people have the right to participate fully in decisions and services affecting their lives and should be given effective support and choices. They are aware that the culture and practices in the setting currently do not support effective participation, although practitioners are supportive.

The setting was keen to involve practitioners, children and young people, and parents/carers in developing the policy. The setting looked at its current practices and developed a strategy to encourage participation and to work with parents/carers and other professionals. They developed a 'participation champion' role and looked at how the new policy affected key areas of work, including other policies, practices and procedures. In discussions with staff and in training sessions, the area of listening to children and young people was identified as weak due to structural reasons – for example, not enough time at key points in the day, weak implementation of key person role early in the morning and in the evenings. Several changes were made to rotas and to the daily routines to support participation.

Describe how changes to existing policies or the introduction of a new policy for participation (or another area) might affect your setting.

How to evaluate the implementation of policies within the real work environment

The evaluation of the implementation of policies is covered earlier in this chapter, with an emphasis on new policies. In a real work environment, the implementation of policy is an ongoing activity for both new and existing policies, but there are constraints on what can be done, such as:

- finding time to evaluate and reflect in a busy work environment
- the costs associated with evaluation and reflection
- the commitment of staff to evaluation
- the commitment of other stakeholders
- the difficulty in making changes and adaptations as a result of the evaluation.

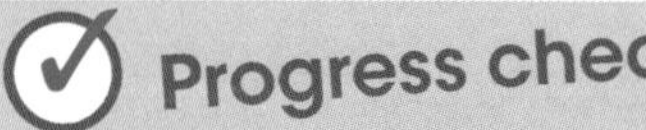

Identify the key stages in evaluating a policy. For each stage, develop a short paragraph of guidance, including suggestions of how to overcome difficulties. Write a short account of the benefits to a setting of regularly monitoring, reviewing and evaluating their policies.

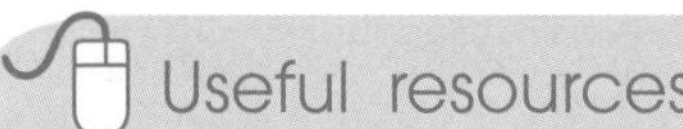

Useful resources

Organisations and websites

Pre-school Learning Alliance
www.pre-school.org.uk

National Day Nurseries Association
www.ndna.org.uk

National Childminding Association
www.ncma.org.uk

Social Care Institute for Excellence
www.scie.org.uk

The Fostering Network
www.fostering.net

Books

Department for Education (2012) *Statutory framework for the Early Years Foundation Stage*, London: Department for Education.

McGivney, V. (NIACE) (2004) *The impact of pre-schools in the community: a follow-up study*, Leicester: Pre-school Learning Alliance.

Ofsted (2009) *Early years self-evaluation form guidance: guidance to support using the self-evaluation form to evaluate the quality of registered early years provision and to ensure continuous improvement*, Manchester: Ofsted.

Ofsted (2010) *Using the early years evaluation schedule: Guidance for inspectors of registered early years settings required to deliver the Early Years Foundation Stage*, Manchester: Ofsted.

Pre-school Learning Alliance (2008) *Policies and procedures for the Early Years Foundation Stage* (electronic access only), **https://shop.pre-school.org.uk/A080E**.

Siraj-Blatchford, I. and Manni, L. (2006) *Effective leadership in the early years sector: the ELEYS study*, London: Institute of Education, University of London.

Siraj-Blatchford, I., Sylva, K., Muttock, S., Gilden, R. and Bell, D. (2002) *Researching effective pedagogy in the early years (REPEY)*, Institute of Education, University of London and Department of Educational Studies, University of Oxford.

Wright, P., Turner, C., Clay, D. and Mills, H. (2006) *The participation of children and young people in developing social care. Participation Practice Guide 06*, London: Social Care Institute for Excellence.

Chapter 3 Maintaining the health of children and/or young people (Unit CP 3)

It is important for children and young people to be in good health so that they can engage completely with the world around them and therefore have the best opportunity to reach their full potential. As a childcare worker, you have an important role to play in helping to ensure the children and young people you look after are healthy.

As part of your ongoing practice, you are responsible for promoting children and young people's health with children themselves, their families and carers. You have a key role in maintaining the health of those children or young people in your care and identifying and supporting children or young people who may become unwell, or who have ongoing health problems while you are caring for them. Dealing with children's health means that you will be cooperating closely with the families and carers of the children or young people you work with.

The aim of this chapter is to provide practitioners with an understanding of the factors that affect the health and well-being of children and young people, so that they are able to act as role models, providing care that promotes children's health and supports children and young people, their parents and carers to maintain good health.

You need to be aware of how public health services promote child health and the role of the health services generally in maintaining children's health and preventing poor health outcomes. It is important to consider ways in which you and your setting can support child health programmes and services. For further information on the government's Healthy Child Programme, see www.dh.gov.uk/prod_consum_dh/groups/dh_digitalassets/@dh/@en/@ps/documents/digitalasset/dh_118525.pdf.

Learning outcomes

1. Understand the importance of workplace policies and procedures when dealing with ill health in children and/or young people.
2. Understand the role of the practitioner in supporting an unwell child and/or young person.
3. Understand possible factors affecting health in children and/or young people and how to promote health.
4. Be able to support children and/or young people to improve their health.
5. Understand how to respond to illness in children and /or young people.
6. Understand how immunisation aims to prevent harmful diseases in children and young people.

Section 1: The importance of workplace policies and procedures when dealing with ill health in children and/or young people

Policies are important documents that state the principles of the organisation, set out in written form, and that guide management decisions about how the workplace operates. Policies are the rules that provide the justification for your practice and ensure the organisation acts in accordance with the law.

All organisations must have policies to ensure they do not break the law – for example, in relation to health and safety at work or employment law. Childcare settings need to be registered in order to operate, so are legally obliged to meet certain requirements, which include staff ratios and qualifications. For example, recruitment policy in a day nursery would need to ensure that all staff have been checked by the Criminal Records Bureau (CRB) as required by law and as part of safeguarding children and young people. More detailed information on policies and procedures can be found in Chapter 2.

It is crucially important that you follow government recommendations and guidelines when developing your policies for maintaining children and young people's health and well-being and for dealing with ill health in the setting because this is based on research that identifies what is effective.

Putting in place evidence-based practice for maintaining children's health ensures that you will be implementing best practice in your setting. By embedding this in organisational policies and procedures, you are not only protecting children and young people's health and well-being; you are also safeguarding your organisation and yourself from any risks and challenges to your practice.

Policies need to be monitored to make sure everyone follows them and to see how well they are working. It is usually the manager's responsibility to decide if any changes are needed by regularly reviewing all the policies to make certain they are up to date with current and emerging practice or, for example, to meet a change in the law.

Key term

Policies – these are written statements about how you will operate in a specific area of practice.

Procedures or routine methods are established that detail how work activities should be carried out in order to comply with a particular policy; they are the actions needed to implement a particular policy. In short, policies say what you should do and procedures state how you should do it.

If you are an independent practitioner, working mostly alone with children and/or young people, you must comply with the legal requirements of your role and should still follow government recommendations and guidelines about promoting health and well-being in the same way as other childcare settings. You will find it both helpful and good practice to write down the key principles underpinning your practice in the form of policies so that you can share these with parents and carers as and when required. It will also provide evidence for inspections.

It is important to recognise the difference between organisational policy and the contract you might have with parents/carers to look after their children or young people. Both group settings and childminders need to have a contract with parents/carers, which sets out the care arrangements and clarifies the roles and responsibilities of both parents/carers and the setting. The contract should state what the organisation's policies are and parents/carers should understand that, by signing the contract, they agree to abide by the policies. This is especially important in the case of accidents and emergencies or the child becoming unwell.

It is important to understand that most legislation (Acts of Parliament) will have associated regulations, which state how the law is intended to be applied in practice.

The role of workplace policies and procedures when caring for an unwell child and/or young person

Workplace policies are intended to protect children and young people's health, safety and well-being so that the risk of children being unwell or coming to harm in the childcare setting is minimised.

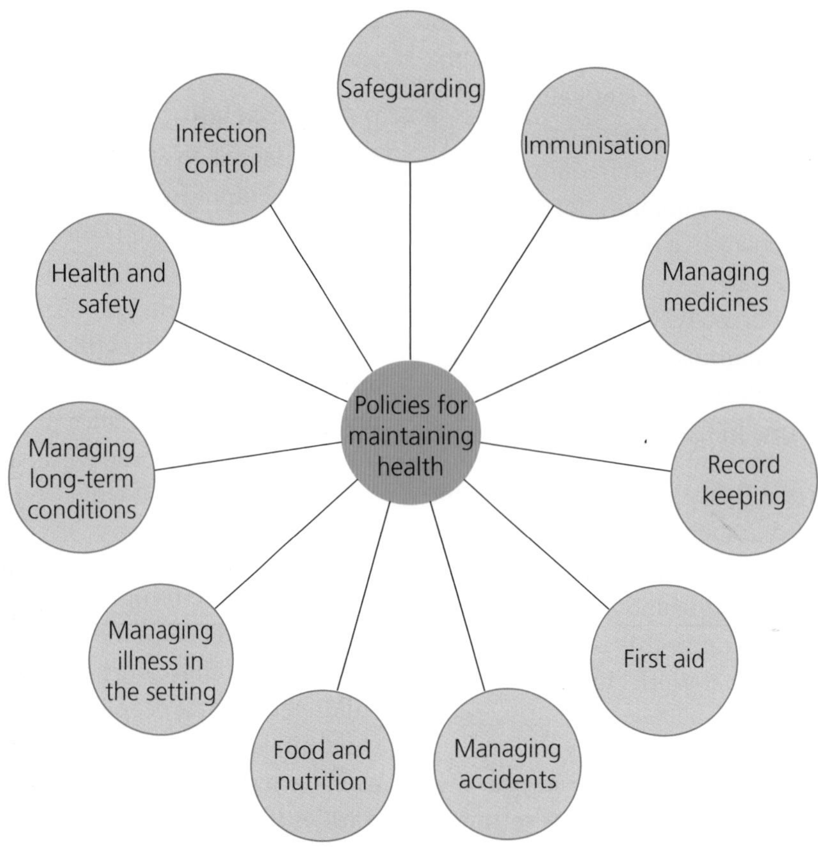

Figure 3.1 Policies for maintaining health

If you work in a group setting, you are likely to be operating as part of a team of people with different skills and levels of responsibility. Therefore, it is important to have policies and procedures in place so that everyone is clear about their individual accountability for the health and well-being of the children and young people in their care and that practitioners understand what to do if a child or young person becomes unwell.

If you work alone, you still need information about the health of the children you care for and have procedures in place to deal with a sick child, so that the other children in your care are protected at the same time. You will probably want to develop a 'Managing illness/sick child' policy.

There are a number of different policies that have a role in protecting and maintaining the health of children and young people, and there can be sometimes be overlap between them. Policies should also consider the health of staff and colleagues, since, for example, some childhood illnesses can have serious consequences for adults who are exposed to them, especially when pregnant. These principles also apply if you work alone, say, as a childminder, because many childhood illnesses are highly contagious and can quickly spread within and outside your setting.

It is good practice for policies to state their aims or rationale, as it clarifies the purpose, which helps when developing a policy and the associated procedures. The following are examples of policies concerned with the health and well-being of children and young people.

Health and safety policy

A health and safety policy should be proactive in preventing accidents. Larger organisations may have a designated Health and Safety Officer, who will be responsible for ensuring that the underlying procedures are in place to implement the policy. In smaller settings, it is likely that the manager will take on this role; independent practitioners, such as childminders, will need to ensure that they have emergency procedures in place and that parents/carers are made aware of these.

The aims of an organisational health and safety policy might state, for example:

> *'The purpose of Happy Days' health and safety policy is to ensure that the health and well-being of the staff and children are protected while on the premises, and that any risks to health or safety are identified and minimised in accordance with the Health and Safety at Work Act 1974 and associated regulations.'*

While all staff should ensure health and safety is of paramount importance, a health and safety policy will identify specific roles and responsibilities of individual staff, and is likely to include procedures for the following:

- **Accident prevention** – daily risk assessment of the indoor and outdoor environments, including reporting risks, defective equipment, obstructions, spillages, near misses, etc. The policy will include reporting procedures for defective equipment.
- **Risk assessment** of the capabilities of the children and young people when engaging in learning activities and when planning outings and visits.
- **Fire safety**, including arrangements for testing equipment, evacuation procedures and emergency measures. A member of staff may be designated as the Fire Safety Officer, who is responsible for regularly testing the fire alarm and practising the fire safety drill with the children or young people.
- **Reporting and recording procedures for accidents and illness**, including the documentation – for example, forms, accident book and RIDDOR (Reporting of Injuries, Diseases and Dangerous Occurrences Regulations 1995; see www.hse.gov.uk/riddor).
- **Hazardous substances** – the policy will cover procedures for assessing risk from harmful substances in the setting, such as cleaning products (e.g. bleach) and other potentially toxic substances and the arrangements for storing, handling and using them safely in accordance with the Control of Substances Hazardous to Health Regulations 2002 (see www.hse.gov.uk/coshh/index.htm).

Record keeping policy

The aims of this policy are to ensure that the setting has important information about children's health. The policy will include the legal requirements of record keeping, such as confidentiality, together with arrangements for sharing important information with other professionals and the circumstances in which this is permissible under the requirements of the Data Protection Act 1998. The policy should also have procedures in place for making sure all staff are aware of any health issues the children or young people may have. This is particularly important when children have allergies (e.g. a nut allergy) since a severe allergic reaction can result in death.

There should therefore be procedures in place for recording the following:

- **Health information** about the children or young people being cared for, including any previous or ongoing health conditions, allergies, medications and immunisation status.
- **Special requirements** – making staff aware of any special requirements an individual child needs, such as special diet.
- **Specific assistance** – making staff aware of what specific assistance a child or young person with additional needs might require so that they can fully join in with activities, outings, etc.
- **Contact details** for parents/carers and the child or young person's GP, including who to contact first in case of an emergency or if the child is ill and, because many people work and may be temporarily unavailable, who else may be contacted.
- **Personal information** – keeping records containing personal information confidential in accordance with the UK Data Protection Act 1998.
- **Arrangements for sharing information** – the Data Protection Act states when and in what circumstances information can be shared; for example, in situations where the child's life or safety may be at risk. It is good practice to regularly share information with health professionals to help the early identification of vulnerable children and support the Common Assessment Framework (Draft NICE Guidelines: Social and Emotional Well-being – Early Years).

The procedures should state who is responsible for collecting the information, how other members of staff should be informed (e.g. through regular staff meetings or daily briefings) and who is responsible for making sure everyone is aware of their responsibilities for confidentiality, including the boundaries of confidentiality (e.g. the manager or deputy manager, or an allocated person to whom this responsibility has been delegated).

Infection control policy

The purpose of an infection control policy is to prevent cross-contamination and the spread of infections and disease. Germs rapidly multiply and infections are easily spread when people are in close contact with each other, especially coughs and colds, which are passed on through the droplet route (e.g. sneezing). Children are very susceptible to infections, especially in the early years, because their immune systems are still immature. When developing a policy for infection control, you will need to understand how infections and diseases arise so that you can consider, in the first instance, all the methods by which infection can be spread within the setting – for example, through sharing toys, through close contact between children and adults within and outside the setting and through personal hygiene practices.

Key term

Pathogen – something (an organism) that causes disease in humans, such as a virus or bacteria.

It is also important that you are aware of the role of universal or standard precautions for infection control, that these form an integral part of your policy and that you can apply them through your written procedures for the regular cleaning and management of the areas which are most likely to harbour infection, such as toilet areas and bathrooms. The key principle behind universal precautions is that all body fluids are treated *as if they are infected*, primarily because, without a blood sample, it is impossible to identify individuals who are infected from those who are not. Clearly,

Precaution	Description
Routine hand-washing	Involves following proper procedures and using effective techniques, e.g. using liquid soap, covering all surfaces of hands and fingers and rubbing all for at least 30 seconds, rinsing under running water and drying thoroughly with disposable towels. Hand-washing is the most effective method of preventing infection.
Personal protective clothing	Use disposable gloves and plastic, waterproof aprons whenever you are likely to come into contact with body fluids. Personal protective clothing is worn according to the level of risk identified, hence additional protection such as face masks, goggles and special footwear are not usually necessary in childcare settings.
Disposing of waste safely	Use separate bags according to your local authority regulations (found on the local website or on www.directgov.co.uk). For example, yellow for potentially infected material.
Dealing with soiled clothing	Place in a plastic bag to take home; use a professional laundry service or wash using industrial washing and drying machines. Soiled laundry should be laundered separately using a pre-wash cycle and washed on a hot wash according to instructions.
Dealing with spillages	Soak up with paper and dispose into infected waste bag. For blood and other body fluids, soak affected area with a solution of bleach (one part bleach to ten parts water) before cleaning with disinfectant and allowing to dry thoroughly.

Table 3.1 Universal precautions

adopting universal precautions will protect everyone in the setting from most pathogens and reduce the risk of cross-contamination and infection.

Sources of infection

Infections and diseases are caused by micro-organisms (microbes or germs). These are present everywhere, although not all micro-organisms cause infection. Microbes that can cause infection are known as pathogens. The human body has a variety of defences available, so conditions have to be right for pathogens to thrive, breed and become sufficiently numerous to overcome the body's defences.

Pathogens are spread by any of the following means:

- **Direct contact** – in which microbes are spread through body fluids, such as saliva (through kissing), blood, urine, faeces, nasal discharge or other infected body fluids (e.g. the pus from boils, abscesses, etc.).
- **Indirect contact** – in which pathogens are spread through touching hands or objects, such as toys, bedding, toothbrushes, water, food, animals and animal faeces.
- **Airborne** – in which pathogens are spread through the air, carried on airborne particles such as dust or in respiratory droplets (e.g. sneezing or coughing).
- **Water** – some pathogens breed in water, such as legionella pneumophila, which causes Legionnaires' disease.
- **Arthropods** – these are insects or bugs such as mosquitoes, lice, ticks and fleas that can carry infection, which is transmitted to humans through biting, sucking or burrowing under the skin. Sometimes their droppings are also sources of infection.

The principles of infection control are intended to prevent the spread of disease and infection by any of these routes.

Procedures to control infection in the setting include:

- **Routine and regular cleaning** of the setting, including floors, toys, equipment and hard surfaces. Also routine cleaning of food preparation and storage areas.
- **Cleaning products and methods**, including different cloths/mops for floors and surfaces, methods of cleaning, suitable cleaning agents and safe storage of these (see COSHH regulations).
- **Dealing with accidental spillages**, especially those which may be contaminated (see Table 3.1).
- **Hand-washing** procedures for staff and children/young people (see Table 3.1). For example, when and how often hands should be washed and personal hygiene (e.g. uniforms, practical clothing, dealing with personal hygiene issues in children or staff).
- **Nappy changing procedure**, including disposal of soiled nappies.
- **Personal protective clothing** – for example, gloves, aprons or similar to cover personal clothing and when to use them (see Table 3.1).
- **Food handling and storage** procedure – for example, stock rotation, proper storage of raw and cooked food.
- **Infectious illnesses and diseases** notification and exclusion procedure (see 'Sick child policy' on page 90).

Food and nutrition policy

Food and nutrition are of crucial importance to the health of growing children and young people and poor diet in the early years of life can have long-term health consequences (see Section 3). It is important to recognise that children, especially young children, have significantly different nutritional requirements to adults (see Table 3.2, Section 3), so it is crucial that you follow government guidelines and recommendations for feeding babies, children and young people.

Food and nutrition requirements are set out in the Early Years Foundation Stage (EYFS) Framework and the food standards for school lunches, which can be found in 'Guidance for food and drink provision in early years settings (March 2010)' issued by the School Food Trust (see www.schoolfoodtrust.org.uk).

Additional information can be found on the following sites:

- The Department of Health's document Birth to Five: www.dh.gov.uk/en/Publicationsandstatistics/Publications/PublicationsPolicyAndGuidance/DH_107303

- NHS Choices: http://www.eatwell.gov.uk/agesandstages/children/yrtoddler/
- The Department of Health's Start4Life campaign: www.nhs.uk/start4life.

The aims of the guidelines and hence your food and nutrition policy are to ensure that children and young people receive a balanced diet that meets their nutritional needs and helps to develop good eating habits for the future. A suggested policy statement to demonstrate this might be along the lines of:

> *'Happy Days nursery is committed to providing a nutritious and well-balanced diet for all the children we care for, in line with government recommendations. We provide food and snacks that evidence shows to be the most suitable for the age and needs of your child and we will be pleased to discuss any special dietary requirements your child may have, including during weaning. We provide dedicated facilities to support mothers who choose to breastfeed so please let us know how we can help.'*

Procedures to implement your policy are likely to include:

- **Breastfeeding** – arrangements for supporting breastfeeding mothers (e.g. a quiet room and comfortable chairs, provision of drinks, etc.). This is also likely to include arrangements for expressing and storing breast milk.
- **Weaning** – best practice and government recommendations should be built into weaning plans for individual infants and included in the procedures followed by staff.
- **Sterilisation** of feeding equipment and feed preparation procedure.
- **Healthy snacks** – what snacks will be provided and how they contribute to the overall energy and nutritional requirements of children and young people.
- **Special diets** – how the setting is able to accommodate special diets (e.g. for diabetic children) and what contribution, if any, parents/carers need to make (e.g. providing gluten or wheat-free products for children with coeliac disease or wheat allergies).
- **Drinks** – having drinking water freely available, for example, and details of what drinks will be offered in the setting.

First aid policy

Individuals caring for children must be registered with Ofsted (Office for Standards in Education, Children's Services and Skills), the government regulatory body responsible for inspecting the suitability of care offered to children and young people. It is a requirement of registration that childminders have a current, appropriate first aid certificate. Similarly, group childcare providers must make sure that at least one person caring for children at any given time has an appropriate first aid qualification (i.e. a paediatric qualification if caring for children up to puberty). You can find information on the criteria such a course should cover at www.ofsted.gov.uk/resources/guide-registration-childcare-register.

It is important that any paediatric first aid certificate includes specific training in paediatric resuscitation because there is a significant difference between adults and children who require resuscitation, both in the reasons for cardiac arrest (when the heart stops beating) and in the treatment. In adults, the heart usually stops first and they stop breathing as a result. In children, up to puberty and early adulthood, they stop breathing (respiratory arrest), which then causes the heart to stop. Resuscitation is a combination of rescue breaths and chest compressions; you can find more information from the Resuscitation Council (UK) at www.resus.org.uk.

Some causes of respiratory arrest in children include:

- choking
- severe asthmatic attack
- severe allergic reaction (anaphylactic shock)
- electric shock
- severe burns
- severe epileptic fit
- head injury
- poisoning
- drowning.

The aims of a first aid policy are to ensure that, when accidents occur or in emergency situations, immediate care is provided to the child or young person until medical assistance is available. The key purposes of first aid are:

- to **prevent** further injury
- to **preserve** life
- to **promote** recovery.

The following procedures should be included in a first aid policy:

- **Accident and emergency procedures** – the response of the first person on the scene and procedure for summoning medical assistance (999).
- **Designated first aider**/first aid coordinator responsibilities.
- **Emergency contact** procedure, including information and contact numbers.
- **First aid box** – procedure for checking and replenishing contents, including responsibility for this.
- **Anaphylaxis** procedure, including emergency interventions (e.g. EpiPen administration). For more information on anaphylaxis, see www.anaphylaxis.org.uk, www.allergyuk.org/severe-allergy-and-anaphylaxis/anaphylaxis or www.resus.org.uk/pages/reaction.pdf, as well as NICE guidelines (www.nice.org.uk/Search.do?x=25&y=12&searchText=+anaphylaxis&newsearch=true#/search/?reload).

In addition to a first aid qualification, staff looking after allergic children should seek medical training on how to manage severe allergic reactions. This may be available from their local health authority. They should also work closely with the parents of any allergic child.

General information can be obtained from The British Allergy Foundation, Deepdene House, 30 Bellgrove Road, Welling, Kent DA16 3PY (0208 303 8525 or their helpline, 0208 303 8583) or from their website (www.allergyuk.org).

Medicine policy

It is important to have a policy in place for managing medicines that children and young people may need to take. This is particularly relevant if you look after children who have long-term conditions or who may be unable to manage their medication without help. You may be required to supervise the child or young person to administer his or her own medication. It is important that you do not administer any medication to a child or young person unless you are authorised to do so by a parent or medical practitioner and your organisation's policy permits this.

Your policy should cover the safe storage of medicines and be clear about restrictions on who is able to administer medicines, the range of medications that can be given and under what circumstances. These may be either regular medicines because of an ongoing health condition (e.g. inhalers, insulin) or occasional medicines, such as antibiotics. In addition, a medicine policy should cover the emergency administration of medicines – for example, EpiPen for allergic reactions or analgesics such as paracetamol or ibuprofen to reduce pain and fever.

Procedures in place to implement the medicine policy are likely to include the following:

- **Arrangements for storing medication** – for example, labelling. Some medicines need storing in the fridge.
- **Consent** form/authorisation from parents/carers.
- **Administration** of medicines – for example, who is authorised to give medicines in the setting or supervise children/young people self-medicating.
- **Recording** of medicines given, including time and by whom.
- Procedure for **administering analgesics** (links with sick child policy; see below).

It is good practice to ensure that staff are trained in the administration and storage of common medicines before being allocated responsibility, to make sure they have the knowledge and skills to administer medicines safely. See Chapter 2 for more details of the National Day Nurseries' (NDNA) sample policy on medication (pages 58–60). Also see the Department of Health's guidance on managing medicines in schools: www.education.gov.uk/schools/pupilsupport/pastoralcare/b0013771/managing-medicines-in-schools.

Activity

1 Draw up the procedure for the administration of medicines in your setting.

2 Develop forms for:

a) parental consent

b) recording medication.

Managing illness in the setting (sick child) policy

Children can become unwell quite quickly and without much warning. Because young children cannot always explain how they feel in ways that adults can understand, childcare workers need to be aware of the signs that a child or young person is unwell (see Section 2). It is also important to note that some diseases are notifiable by law (see below).

The aim of a sick child policy could be stated as, for example:

> *'Happy Days nursery is committed to promoting the health and well-being of all the children attending the setting; this is crucially important so that children can learn and fulfil their potential. In order to help us keep our children healthy and protect both children and staff, we ask for your cooperation by not bringing your child to nursery if s/he is sick, unwell or showing signs of being unwell. If your child becomes ill while at nursery, we will make sure they are cared for appropriately and inform you as soon as possible.'*

Procedures might include:

- **Exclusion** procedures – these are important to prevent the spread of infection.
- **Managing the sick child** procedure – comforting the child, taking appropriate action, including seeking medical advice if necessary and immediately if the child is in danger.
- **Informing parents** procedure – this might be the responsibility of the key worker or nursery manager/childminder, using the emergency contact numbers.
- **Reporting** – procedure for reporting any signs of illness in the child to the parents/carers.

Some diseases are so serious that they must be reported (notified) by the GP to the authorities (currently the Health Protection Agency) so that any outbreak can be monitored and dealt with as a public health issue.

The following diseases are notifiable:

- diphtheria
- hepatitis A, B and C
- HIV/Aids
- measles
- meningitis
- mumps
- pertussis (whooping cough)
- rubella
- scarlet fever
- typhoid and para-typhoid
- tuberculosis.

As you can see, the list includes many infections that commonly affect children, including all illnesses that are currently preventable by immunisation. For guidance on exclusion, see: www.hpa.org.uk/Topics/InfectiousDiseases/InfectionsAZ/SchoolsGuidanceOnInfectionControl.

Safeguarding policy

Keeping children safe is a crucial aspect of maintaining health and well-being; a child who is being neglected, maltreated or abused is vulnerable to both physical and mental ill health. It is a requirement of all settings that a policy for safeguarding children is in place so that all childcare workers know what action to take if they suspect a child is being ill-treated, including the correct processes for referral and reporting. If you are not sure whether a child or young person is being maltreated, it is better to take action than not.

It is good practice to publish statements of the key aims of your setting's policies and safeguarding is no exception. Such a statement might be set out as follows:

> *'At Happy Days nursery, we take our duty of care to keep the children we look after safe from harm*

very seriously. We believe the welfare of the child is paramount, as stated in the Children Act 1989. Our staff are carefully recruited and vetted and undertake regular accredited training and development in Child Protection. We work in an open and transparent way with both parents and children to ensure their safety.'

The procedures underpinning a safeguarding policy should cover the following areas:

- **Child protection**, including the designated person for child protection, for example, liaising with other agencies, using the Common Assessment Framework.
- **Safe working practices** – for example, personal care procedures and the guidelines regarding visibility; respecting personal boundaries with young people; age-appropriate contact with children and young people who are distressed and in need of comfort and reassurance; the importance of challenging and recording when such guidelines are broken.
- **Training and development** – for example, the arrangements for regular staff training and what this should cover; when to suspect child maltreatment; recognising signs of abuse; awareness of risk factors (child, family, community); dealing with disclosure; what action to take – reporting and recording; dealing with parents/carers.
- **Reporting procedures** – for example, who to report to and in what format, including reporting the behaviour of other staff that might cause concern; how to contribute to multi-agency processes for dealing with child protection; record keeping and confidentiality.

For further information and guidance on good practice, see: http://publications.nice.org.uk/when-to-suspect-child-maltreatment-cg89/guidance.

Immunisation policy

Why have an immunisation policy? Immunisation is the most effective method of preventing a range of serious illnesses, many of which caused death or disability in the past. One consequence of routine vaccination is that we have lost our fear of diseases such as polio and measles because we are not aware of the devastating consequences that were all too frequent before immunisation. In recent years, there has been some controversy about the safety of immunisation, especially in relation to a suspected link with autism. However, the research upon which these fears were based has now been thoroughly discredited.

It is not currently compulsory to have children immunised in the UK. However, childcare settings have a responsibility and a duty of care towards all the children they look after, as well as the staff. The prevention of disease requires a given number of people to be immune to the disease and vaccination is the best way to ensure this (see 'Key term: herd immunity' in Section 6, page 114).

Because of this, the immunisation of children wishing to attend the setting cannot be a matter for individual parents to choose. While it is acceptable for adults to take risks with their own health, by failing to immunise their children, they risk serious harm to other children and adults, and leave their own children exposed to the risk of serious disease, which may have long-term consequences. This can be argued to be contrary to their own child's best interests and poses unacceptable risk – because it is preventable – to others. Childcare settings have a clear role to play in supporting this important aspect of public health.

> **'The Healthy Child team, led by a health visitor working with other practitioners, should check the immunisation record (including the personal child health record) of each child aged up to 5 years. They should carry out this check when the child joins a day nursery, nursery school, playgroup, Sure Start children's centre or when they start primary school. The check should be carried out in conjunction with childcare or education staff and the parents.'**

Source: NICE (http://publications.nice.org.uk/reducing-differences-in-the-uptake-of-immunisations-ph21/recommendations#recommendation-1-immunisation-programmes)

A policy statement about immunisation could we worded as follows:

> *'Happy Days nursery is committed to promoting and supporting the health of all the children attending the nursery. We therefore expect parents to have their children immunised in line with the UK immunisation schedule, in order to protect all the children from preventable diseases. We work closely with the health services and will be happy to discuss your child's immunisation requirements with you.'*

Procedures underpinning the setting's immunisation policy could include the following:

- **Recording and updating** the child's immunisation status in the setting's child health records.
- **Liaising with health professionals** – for example, the Healthy Child team to facilitate the uptake of immunisations.
- **Identifying vulnerable children** who may not have been immunised or who have an incomplete record and helping parents arrange for them to be immunised.
- **Ensuring staff are fully immunised**, encouraging and facilitating this where necessary.

Some settings may be able to allow immunisation to take place on the premises and this could also be built into the policy.

Managing long-term conditions policy

Some children attending the setting may have specific health needs or possibly suffer from a long-term condition. In most cases, the parents and the individual child will be able to manage their own condition. However, staff need to know what to look for if the condition should deteriorate while the child is in the setting and what actions must and must not be taken. Details should be documented in the child's records.

Common long-term conditions include allergies, diabetes, asthma and eczema. However, you may also be caring for children who have treatable conditions such as heart defects and are awaiting surgery, or those who have disabilities. From time to time, some conditions can become worse – for example, due to changes in temperature or weather conditions, or if the child contracts a cold. In some children, eczema can be worse in hot weather and asthma can sometimes be affected by exercise or by very cold weather conditions.

A suggested policy statement might be:

> *'Happy Days nursery offers an inclusive and holistic learning environment for all children, including those with special requirements. Our trained staff are able to support children with a range of needs, including those with long-term health conditions. It is our policy to discuss your child's particular needs and agree an individual learning and support plan with you.'*

Procedures may overlap with other policy areas – for example, recording children's allergies and communicating these to the other staff or following infection control procedures when dealing with eczema. It is good practice to develop an individual care plan for children with long-term conditions in partnership with the parents.

Guidance on eczema and asthma can be found on the following websites:

- Atopic eczema in children: http://publications.nice.org.uk/atopic-eczema-in-children-cg57
- Guidance on the use of inhaler systems: http://publications.nice.org.uk/guidance-on-the-use-of-inhaler-systems-devices-in-children-under-the-age-of-5-years-with-chronic-ta10.

Activity

Develop a policy for managing allergies in the setting, including first aid and emergency procedures for managing anaphylaxis. Include the following areas:

- common allergies (food and non-food)
- procedure for communicating allergic information within the setting
- identifying children who are at risk of anaphylaxis
- recognising signs of anaphylaxis
- emergency treatment of anaphylaxis in the setting
- recording and reporting procedures
- a plan for monitoring and reviewing the policy.

The importance of implementing the workplace policies and procedures in relation to ill health

Policies can be described as 'living documents' because, although a policy may be written down, until it is implemented, it remains an intention. In other words, it states an aim or purpose, which has to be followed up by action.

This is why policies are always underpinned by procedures, which describe the actions that need to be taken for the policy to be implemented. To assess the effectiveness of a policy, it has to be monitored. This means that someone – usually the setting manager – has to be responsible for regularly checking that members of staff are following the procedures and routinely evaluating the policy to make sure it is up to date, reflecting current effective practice.

Policies are important to ensure the setting, and the people working in the setting, follow the law. In relation to children's health, managers need to make sure that childcare workers have been properly trained to carry out health-related activities in the setting, including dealing with accidents, allergies and caring for children who become unwell. They also have a wider role in promoting health and supporting healthy lifestyles. In situations where children have come to harm in a childcare setting, investigations usually reveal a failure to follow proper policies and procedures, often accompanied by a failure of communication. This clearly affects the reputation of the setting and can lead to prosecution in extreme cases.

Useful websites for keeping up to date include:

- National Institute for Health and Clinical Excellence: www.nice.org.uk
- Department of Health: www.dh.gov.uk
- Ofsted: www.ofsted.gov.uk
- Health and Safety Executive: www.hse.gov.uk
- Health Protection Agency: www.hpa.org.uk
- Department for Education: www.education.gov.uk
- National Childminding Association: www.ncma.org.uk.

It is particularly important to implement policies and correct procedures when dealing with ill health in children and young people because, unless you are clear about your roles and responsibilities, including the boundaries of your role and the limits of your competence, you could either intervene in situations where professional medical care is essential or fail to intervene when a child or young person is at serious risk. For example, although it is rare, it is not unknown for children to have died in nursery settings as a result of allergic reactions – only eight children have died over the last ten years out of a population of approximately 13 million under-16s in the UK.

In life-threatening situations, it is better to act than not. The Resuscitation Council points out that children have failed to receive resuscitation when they desperately needed it because the adults present had not been specifically trained in paediatric resuscitation, did not feel confident in attempting resuscitation on children and were afraid of being penalised if their efforts failed. If you have been trained in resuscitation techniques, it is better to attempt resuscitation than fail to save a life.

Activity

Draw up and carry out an induction programme for a new member of staff, explaining the importance of policies and procedures to:

- the child or young person
- the family/parents/carers
- the staff.

Demonstrate how you implement the policies and procedures in your setting.

Summary

Workplace policies are essential to ensure the health and safety of children and staff in the setting. They reassure parents that their children are being cared for professionally and that they are at least as safe as they would be if cared for at home – if not more so as the majority of accidents for children under five years old take place at home. In addition, parents can be confident that, if their child becomes unwell in the setting, all the staff will know what to do and appropriate action will be taken to manage their illness until the parent or medical help is able to take over.

We have identified that policies are only worthwhile if they are properly implemented, monitored and reviewed regularly to make sure they keep up with best practice and meet legal requirements. This ensures that the staff in the setting are not inadvertently breaking the law. Policies are implemented through everyone following set procedures, so that everyone is clear about their roles and responsibilities, thus minimising any likelihood of poor practice.

Activity

1. Review your setting's sick child policy, including the reasons for the policy and arrangements for monitoring.
2. Carry out research to identify best practice in managing children who become ill in the setting.
3. Write a report comparing and contrasting your setting's policy with best practice, making recommendations for any changes that could be made and the rationale for your recommendations.

Section 2: The role of the practitioner in supporting an unwell child and/or young person

If a child becomes unwell in the setting, it will be important to know whether they have any underlying health issues that may have either contributed to them becoming unwell or which might be responsible for their illness; this information should be clearly documented in the child's records. For example, children who are diabetic may have episodes of hypoglycemia (low blood sugar) because their diabetes is not well controlled. Similarly, if a child with diabetes contracts an infection, it is likely to destabilise their diabetes, making it more difficult to control.

It is important for childcare workers to be able to recognise signs and symptoms of illness in the children or young people they care for in order to act responsibly and in the child's best interests. Practical action may be needed; however, for the most part, children who are ill in the setting need reassurance, comfort and monitoring.

For general information on managing long-term conditions, see www.education.gov.uk/schools/pupilsupport/pastoralcare/b0013771/managing-medicines-in-schools.

Common signs that a child or young person may be unwell

The signs that a child or young person is feeling unwell often vary according to the particular illness and the age of the child or young person. Whereas older children are able to articulate or explain how they are feeling – for example, 'I feel hot', 'My head hurts', 'I feel sick' – babies and young children lack the vocabulary. Because of this, it is important to know the difference between signs of illness and symptoms of illness. Young children often complain of 'tummy ache' when they feel unwell, whatever the cause of their illness. This is generally believed to be due to enlargement of the lymph nodes (or glands), part of the immune system, which fights infection; some of these are located in the abdomen. Because children's immune systems and immunity are still developing, and they frequently come into contact with pathogens they have not encountered previously, their lymph nodes are often slightly enlarged.

Key terms

Signs of illness – these are physical and can be observed (e.g. a raised temperature).

Symptoms of illness – these are what the person experiences (e.g. feeling feverish, chilly and shivering).

Common signs and symptoms of illness include the following:

- **Raised temperature** (above 37 degrees Celsius or 99 degrees Fahrenheit) – the child looks flushed and feels hot, and they will usually be quiet and more subdued than usual, listless or sleepy. It is important to note that young children do not perspire because their temperature regulation mechanisms are underdeveloped; similarly they can quickly become feverish. If the temperature is very high, febrile convulsions can occur so it is important to make sure the temperature is as controlled as possible.
- **Vomiting** – when a child is unwell, the body's energy reserves are directed at fighting infection so other body functions, including digestion, slow down and the tendency is for the stomach to then empty itself. Any infection can cause vomiting; it does not always indicate gastroenteritis (inflammation of the stomach).
- **Diarrhoea** – this may or may not be a sign that the child is unwell. Many toddlers suffer from loose stools that are related to diet as new foods are being introduced and tolerance to these depends on the type of food and the maturity of the digestive system. If the diarrhoea is accompanied by either raised temperature or vomiting, it is usually a sign of illness.
- **Pulling on an ear** – this can indicate earache, especially if the temperature is raised.
- **Loss of appetite** – this accompanies most illness in children and young people.
- **Incessant crying** and a need for comfort in babies and young children, including tearfulness, being 'clingy' and not wanting to be alone.
- **Drowsiness**, lethargy and listlessness.
- **Abdominal pain** – this is difficult to check without examination. Asking the child to point to where it hurts is not always helpful, so it is best to note that the child has complained of tummy ache and report it along with other signs and symptoms.

Signs of serious illness that need immediate medical attention include the following:

- **Rapid breathing** or difficulty breathing (e.g. when the movement of the ribs is obvious), especially if lips and fingernails are blueish as well.
- **Excessive drowsiness** – for example, if the child is slow to respond or difficult to rouse.
- **Cold or discoloured hands and feet** with a warm body. However, this should only be regarded as a serious symptom in older children or if there are other signs of illness because young babies often have cold hands and feet.
- **Abnormal colour** – too pale, very flushed or blueish.
- **Pains** other than stomach ache (e.g. in the arms or legs).
- **Signs of meningitis** (see Section 5, page 108).
- **Accidents** – especially if the child has lost consciousness at all or a fracture is suspected.

Many of the signs and symptoms will be present together and it is important to record them all to provide parents/carers or medical practitioners with a complete picture so that effective decisions and appropriate action can be taken.

Long-term conditions

If a child or young person has a long-term or pre-existing condition, you will need to be aware of what to look out for in case the condition becomes acute – for example, an asthma attack, diabetic episode or epileptic fit.

It is good practice to have agreed the action to be taken in such situations with parents/carers and the child or young person themselves. Such agreements can form the basis of a care plan and protocols for staff to follow in case of emergencies.

For information on epilepsy, see www.epilepsy.org.uk/professionals/education.

For information on asthma, see www.asthma.org.uk/about-asthma/what-to-do-in-an-asthma-attack.

For more information on managing children with diabetes in schools and childcare settings, see www.childrenwithdiabetes.com/uk and the report of the UK Children With Diabetes Advocacy Group.

The roles and responsibilities of the practitioner if a child and/or young person is unwell

In most group settings, one childcare professional will be in charge of a small group of children; the number of children in a particular group will depend on the age and capabilities of the children and will comply with registration ratios. This person will be the key worker for the children in the group. It is the responsibility of the child or young person's key worker to observe the children or young people they work with as part of their duty to assess the learning and development of the child or young person. As such, they will be expected to notice any signs that the child is becoming unwell or is actively ill.

The key worker will be expected to follow the setting's policy and procedures for dealing with illness, which should include reporting their concerns to the nursery manager or senior worker in the first instance. Decisions should be taken jointly regarding the appropriate course of action (e.g. checking for symptoms or administering medication).

In the case of children with long-term conditions who become unwell at nursery, it is good practice to have an individual care plan drawn up with the parents for managing the particular condition and this should include any action that should be taken if the situation is urgent.

It is important to contact the parents or carers to make arrangements for the child to be collected and looked after at home as soon as possible – this is best for the child who is unwell and the other children in the setting.

Until the child is collected, the manager should make arrangements for a member of staff to remain with the child who is unwell or to check their condition regularly if they are fit to be left (e.g. if they fall asleep). It is important that the child is assessed regularly – every ten minutes or so – to make sure their condition has not deteriorated.

If the situation becomes urgent and the child's condition worsens (e.g. febrile convulsions, unconsciousness or severe asthmatic attack), then medical assistance should be summoned immediately and the parents informed. The child will need to be accompanied on any hospital visit by a member of staff until the parents arrive.

The nursery manager will need to ensure that there are sufficient members of staff to cover such emergencies, perhaps by having staff on standby, for example. The manager will also need to ensure that staff have the appropriate training to deal with emergencies for those children with long-term conditions, such as diabetes, allergies or epilepsy, in which medication may need to be administered as a first response.

Actions to be taken by the practitioner

The actions required by the practitioner will, of course, depend on the situation and the child or young person in question. The appropriate response is likely to be quite different if, for example the child has an accident, from the response if the child has a long-term condition that has deteriorated or if the child or young person becomes unexpectedly ill in the setting.

The child and/or young person

As a childcare practitioner working with small groups, you will get to know the children in your care quite well, so you are in a good position to pick up on signs that they may not be well – for example, changes in usual behaviour. If you suspect a child is becoming unwell, you should take the following actions.

- Observation and assessment: you need to observe the child and note any differences from normal, including behaviour, appetite, complaints and anything unusual.
- Monitoring: you need to monitor the child throughout the session and take note of any improvement or deterioration in the child's condition.
- Recording: it is advisable to record your observations in the child's records, making sure you stick to what you observed or what the child said, rather than speculating on what might be the matter.

You need to be clear about lines of accountability and who is responsible for making decisions in relation to the child's well-being. Any action or intervention, such as giving medication, needs to be carefully documented, following the setting's procedures and providing the parents/carers have given written permission. Other actions are likely to include removing the child to a safe, quiet space if they are too poorly to participate in activities. They may need distraction if distressed or in pain and all will need comfort and reassurance from familiar childcare workers/their key worker.

If the situation is urgent – for example, if there has been an accident – it is important to remain calm and not panic. The designated first aider should deal with the injured child, following procedures, and other staff should focus on the remaining children, who may be frightened and concerned for their friend. If you are a sole practitioner, you need to implement first aid and call medical assistance (999) if necessary and the parents/carers at the first opportunity.

Other children and/or young people

Other children in the setting may be aware when a child is unwell and are likely to be curious, especially if the sick child is removed from the main area to a quiet space or designated medical room. It is best to explain, using simple language, that 'Bobby is feeling poorly and has gone to be quiet while he waits for his mummy or daddy to come and take him home', keep calm, reassure the children and distract them – perhaps with a group activity. If the child has vomited or had a fit, or any other significant physical reaction, this must also be explained simply at the time, not just ignored. Witnessing other children being ill can frighten some children.

In accident situations, you may need to gently question the other children to confirm what actually happened, especially if you did not see the moment of the accident yourself. Write down what the children actually say, in their own words. This is necessary for medical staff and so that parents have a clear understanding that accidents can happen despite rigorous risk assessment, as you cannot plan for all eventualities.

Reporting procedures

It is crucial to report any accidents or illness to your line manager or responsible person (e.g. first aid officer); failure to do so can leave individual practitioners or the organisation at risk of legal action in some circumstances. Filling out correct forms and completing daily records is an important aspect of this. Forms could include accident/incident forms (RIDDOR), medicine forms, health records, etc. There should be protocols in place for when to call emergency services (999) or to phone the NHS helpline. It is also helpful to liaise with local health services and, although it is the parent/carer's responsibility to report the child's health issue to the GP, it would be helpful to ensure this happens.

Parent(s)/carer(s)

Whenever a child is unwell in the setting, a decision has to be taken regarding whether it is possible for them to remain until they are collected at the usual time or whether to contact parents immediately. The point at which parents are informed of the child's condition will be the decision of the manager. However, in emergency situations or with serious incidents, the parents should be contacted at once. Similarly, if a child has vomited and is clearly unwell, parents should be contacted and asked to collect the child in line with managing illness in the setting (sick child) procedures. It is important, when speaking to parents, to reassure them that appropriate action has been taken and their child is safe. You should clearly state the condition of the child and what action has been taken, and arrange for the child to be collected either from the setting or from the medical treatment centre, confirming the time they are likely to arrive. Bear in mind, it may take parents/carers some time to make arrangements to leave work and make their way to the setting.

Completing workplace records

When completing workplace records, the importance of accuracy cannot be overstated. Such records can provide evidence that the setting acted properly and in good faith, with the safety and well-being of the child paramount. As such, it is very important that you only document what you observed yourself, not what other people saw. You can include the information and opinions of other staff, providing you make clear that is what it is.

Section 3: Possible factors affecting health in children and/or young people and how to promote health

While there are many factors affecting the health of children and young people, socio-economic factors, including overall income levels, have been consistently demonstrated to underlie many of the issues. Income levels can affect people's choices and access to a healthy lifestyle, which in turn affects children's health.

Children and young people need educating on how to live healthy lifestyles and good role models from the people around them, including childcare workers.

Possible factors which influence health in children and young people

Food and nutrition are important because they not only impact on growth and development in the early years but can impact on achievement as well as set up eating habits for a lifetime.

Food, diet and nutritional factors affecting health

The guidance on infant feeding is clear, evidence based and available to the public. The government appoints the Scientific Advisory Committee on Nutrition to carry out research and examine the evidence before advising on infant feeding practices. This forms the basis of health and nutritional advice to parents given by health professionals and made available to parents (e.g. Birth to Five and the Healthy Child programme).

However, decisions about feeding and diet are very personal and parents may choose not to follow such advice. Children's health over their lifetime is affected by the food choices that are made for them and that they, in turn, make for themselves. As a childcare professional, you should be aware of what current guidelines are and the evidence on which it is based. You have a responsibility to follow government guidelines for the children in your care and help parents to make informed choices about their children's diet, starting from the very early days. You should also be aware of the likely consequences for the child's health if parents choose not to follow such advice and suggest they discuss any issues with a health professional. You should be clear that it is the policy in your setting to follow government recommendations on food, diet and nutrition (see www.schoolfoodtrust.org.uk/download/documents/pdf/early_years_food_and_nutrition_guidance.pdf).

Young children's nutritional needs are quite different from adults. Because of their small size and hence small stomachs, they need what are known as 'energy dense' foods. These are foods with a lot of calories in small portions. However, it is important that these foods provide proper nutrition, not just a lot of calories. For example, you could say that chocolate is an energy-dense food because it contains a lot of fat and sugar. However, it does not contain much nutrition, such as vitamins or minerals. It is better to offer starchy foods, such as peanut butter sandwiches or cheese, and things like dried fruit instead of chocolate.

Common factors affecting babies' and young children's diets are as follows:

- **Overfeeding** due to anxiety – for example, feeding the baby first when it is crying instead of working out if the baby is crying for some other reason. If the baby's natural mechanism for regulating appetite is regularly overruled, it stops being effective, predisposing the child to obesity.
- **Weaning too early** – before six months of age. This tends to happen more frequently if the baby has been overfed.
- **Unsuitable foods** introduced too early – for example, tea, chocolate, biscuits, breakfast cereal, cow's milk.
- **Too much milk** due to a delay in weaning off breast or bottle. With breastfeeding, the milk gradually reduces as solid food is introduced and the infant only takes what it needs. If bottle-fed, this is controlled by the parent and sometimes the balance is wrong. If the child is refusing solids, parents tend to overcompensate by giving milk.
- **Poor family diet**, including an over-reliance on pre-prepared or microwavable meals.
- **Instant baby foods** – while these are convenient and can be used as part of an infant feeding regime, they are high in water content, bland and low in nutrition. Babies fed exclusively on these often have difficulty adjusting to a normal diet and can turn into 'fussy eaters'.
- **Maternal anxiety** – mothers are afraid to let a young child go without food and, if solids are refused, give milk to make sure they are fed (see above). It helps to introduce a cup and water to drink and wean off the bottle or breast, except for the bedtime feed, once solid food is an established part of the diet.

Older children and young people's eating habits will be determined by the type of foods they have been exposed to and their own food preferences, in turn influenced by household eating habits and advertising.

Case Study — Infant feeding

Sue McGregor is the single, teenage parent of Nathan, who you have agreed to look after as a registered childminder specialising in supporting young mothers. Nathan is almost six months old and Sue has started to work part-time for three days per week. Nathan has started weaning and has two meals per day. There is a family history of eczema and asthma.

Sue has brought Nathan's food for the day, which is:

- a jar of egg custard and rice
- a baby yogurt
- a chocolate flake.

1. Identify the advantages and disadvantages of this diet for Nathan.
2. Describe how you might support Sue in feeding Nathan according to government guidelines.
3. What are the risks to Nathan's health of this diet?
4. Identify three reasons why Sue might be offering such a diet to Nathan?

Girls			Daily energy	Boys		
Age (years)	Weight (kg)	Height (m)	needs (kcal)	Age (years)	Weight (kg)	Height (m)
1–1½	10.80	0.80	1050–1200	1–1½	11.06	0.80
2	13.50	0.90	1250–1400	2	13.97	0.91
3	15.50	0.97	1450–1550	3	15.47	1.00
4	17.29	1.04	1555–1650	4	17.74	1.06
5	19.41	1.11	1700–1850	5	20.32	1.11

Table 3.2 Average height and weight of ethnic Caucasian (white) children

Information on infant feeding can be found at:

- Department of Health: www.dh.gov.uk
- The Scientific Advisory Committee on Nutrition: www.sacn.gov.uk
- Food Standards Agency: www.food.gov.uk.

The influence of exercise or recreation and leisure on health

Babies and young children are very active as a rule and it is important that they have plenty of opportunities to play both indoors and outdoors.

Exercise helps to strengthen bones and muscles and helps to prevent obesity. This is important because the number of children who are either obese or in danger of becoming obese is increasing rapidly. Obese children are more likely to develop health conditions such as diabetes, and extra weight also puts a strain on joints and the heart.

All children need opportunities for exploring the outdoor environment to increase their confidence. It is important to have a balanced approach so that calculated risks can be taken which enable the child to feel a sense of achievement and heightened self-esteem, while minimising obvious dangers. It has been suggested that children of parents who are risk-averse lack confidence and are less able to manage risk, leaving them in more danger.

The influence of rest, sleep and/or lifestyle on health

Sleep is crucial for babies, children and young people. During sleep, the brain replenishes the chemicals that influence the functioning of the central nervous system – the neuro-transmitters such as dopamine and noradrenaline. These particularly affect coordination, mood and behaviour. It is therefore no surprise that sleep difficulties, including insufficient sleep, are associated with behavioural problems in children, including hyperactivity and difficulty concentrating.

Children need more sleep than adults because they are growing physically, but also because their brain is developing. During sleep, the day's events get processed and this often forms the basis of dreams. It is also thought that sleep is necessary for the development of memory and it is also important for achievement.

A toddler needs between ten and twelve hours of sleep per day, although this does not all have to be at night. Most young children benefit from a nap during the day. However, even if they do not sleep, it is important to have a rest period during the day.

Adolescents also experience a growth spurt, including in brain development. It has been suggested that, in adolescence, a person's 'body clock' alters, changing their sleep patterns and making it more difficult for them to get up in the morning. Adolescents need as much sleep as young children because of this growth spurt so it is most unfair to label them as 'lazy' when they are undergoing a biological process.

As a result of changing lifestyles, children and young people of all ages have more access to technology than previously. Research has indicated that using technology such as mobile phones, television, computer games and ipods can stimulate the brain and make it more difficult for children and young people to "switch off", particularly as playing games and social networking are extremely popular communal activities shared with friends. Many of these devices are small, portable and can be used anywhere – including in bed, so it is more difficult for parents to prevent over-use.

Poor sleep habits impair performance and this can have a profound effect on the ability to achieve potential and on mental health in the long term. It is important, therefore, to help parents and children establish good sleeping patterns – for example, by insisting on switching computers off, having a wind-down period, and leaving mobile phones downstairs.

The influence of preventing infection on health

Children can easily catch infections, particularly in a group setting as infections are quickly passed from one person to another. This is why it is important for the setting to have an infection control policy and pay attention to hygiene. Many children suffer from frequent upper respiratory infections, especially if they are regularly exposed to cigarette smoke. This can have a lasting effect, causing such problems as, for example, glue ear or chronic chest infection. Glue ear is particularly problematic as it impairs hearing and can therefore affect speech. Children who cannot hear well may be thought to be naughty or not paying attention. It can also affect their confidence and ability to form relationships with peers.

Some children also suffer from repeated diarrhoea – so-called toddler diarrhoea. If it is accompanied by vomiting, it is usually due to infection and the child should be excluded. Some children, however, suffer from diarrhoea for no apparent reason. They are usually of normal weight and healthy with a good appetite. It has been suggested that it is caused by food intolerance or following an infection. However, its cause is unknown, although it has been associated with excessive drinking. Stools typically contain undigested food and are frequent and watery.

Children who have chronic infections usually miss a lot of schooling in the early days, which impacts on overall school achievement unless they are actively helped to make up for lost time.

Emotional and social influences on health

Children need supportive relationships with adults who care for them in order to provide a secure basis from which to explore the world. This includes developing friendships and becoming part of a group. Clearly, any issue that impacts on a parent's ability to care for a child, such as parental physical or mental ill-health, or substance abuse, will have a corresponding affect on the child or young person's mental health and wellbeing: the child/young person can feel powerless and overwhelmed in the face of such problems. Similarly, bullying can make a child or young person feel excluded from friendship groups, and recent studies show that even very young children can suffer from clinical depression, with some victims of bullying, including cyber-bullying (using technology and social networking), taking their own lives.

One of the most significant influences on children's social and emotional health is child maltreatment, which means physical, emotional, intellectual or sexual abuse, neglect, bullying or harassment. Evidence shows that children who have been maltreated are much more likely to suffer from depression as children and go on to develop mental health problems as adults.

Emerging research on brain development suggests that the constant fear experienced by children who are abused can affect the way the brain develops, with lifelong consequences. For very young children, neglect can affect their ability to form strong attachments (see Chapter 6 page 197 onwards), and in severe cases, such neurological changes can result in Reactive Attachment Disorder (see: www.psychnet-uk.com for more information).

Brain scans have demonstrated the difference in children's brain development and particularly in the amygdala – the structure that is involved in processing many of our emotions, such as fear, anger and pleasure, and motivations, particularly those that are related to survival. The amygdala is also responsible for determining what memories are stored and where the memories are stored in the brain. It is thought that this difference between those who have suffered abuse, including neglect, and others who have not is based on how huge an emotional response an event invokes, how often it is repeated and how long it continues.

Academics have concluded that what matters for every child are:

- secure attachments to carers
- good-quality childcare provided by people who are interested in the child
- interest and love from parents and carers.

If these are not available within the family, action has to be taken to ensure that they are provided elsewhere. Just as food is necessary to nourish growth, security, positive regard and loving kindness are necessary to nourish brain development (see http://publications.nice.org.uk/social-and-emotional-wellbeing-in-primary-education-ph12).

The role of advertising in relation to possible health factors in children and/or young people

Advertising is a powerful marketing tool used to influence what people buy. Things that are promoted through advertising are generally aspirational and the lifestyle they portray is not easily available to ordinary people with average incomes. Advertising has been blamed for many things, including encouraging people to get into debt, which has a detrimental effect on family life.

The influence of advertising on food, diet and nutrition

Adverts are thought to affect what children know and understand about food and it is believed to influence their food choices and, by default, what parents buy, which is the point of advertising. The effect is separate from other factors such as parental eating habits, and the foods that are promoted through advertising tend to be less healthy than evidence-based recommendations for healthy eating (research commissioned by the Food Standards Agency, 2003). In other European countries, such as Sweden, manufacturers are not allowed to target advertising at children (e.g. during children's programmes). In the UK, there have gradually been more restrictions on what can be advertised during peak viewing hours for children, including food.

Infant formula and 'follow on' milks are aggressively marketed during times when it is expected that women will be watching TV and it is rare to see a breastfeeding mother on the television. This reinforces the idea that artificial (bottle) feeding is normal and, as all the research demonstrates that breast milk is the ideal food for infants, it is counter-productive, going against the government's own guidance.

How advertising can affect exercise or recreation and leisure

It has been argued that there are gender differences in advertising material that tend to reinforce traditional gender roles, although this is less marked than it used to be.

In terms of exercise, recreation and leisure, there are many products that are advertised by footballers and sportsmen, for example, and many adverts showing men being active (e.g. swimming, playing sport). For women, the emphasis tends to be on looks and appearance, and food treats such as chocolate or sweet things. There are far fewer adverts that show women playing sport or being active, except when carrying out housework.

The effect of this on children and young people is likely to be a reinforcing of traditional stereotypical gender roles and a lack of encouragement for girls to get involved in physical activities such as sport.

The influence of advertising on rest, sleep and/or lifestyle

Children can be highly influenced by what is shown on television, which is why adverts are regulated to ensure children are not exposed to adult or unsuitable material. However, many children watch a lot of TV and sometimes this is unsupervised. Unsuitable material can leave children feeling vulnerable or frightened, which may lead to nightmares. TV can interfere with the development of good sleeping habits and it is recommended that children have an hour of 'wind down' or quiet time before bed as part of developing a sleep routine.

Television adverts are carefully chosen to complement the programmes they are shown with and this includes lifestyle. For example, during a James Bond film, there may be adverts for high-performance cars. Adverts are aimed at selling and they showcase the 'ideal lifestyle', which is often unattainable. This can lead to feelings of discontent and disenchantment.

The influence of advertising on prevention of infection

The role of advertising in preventing infection is to promote products that kill germs. They include household products that suggest anti-bacterial wipes are all that is needed to keep homes clean and germ-free. Many of the personal hygiene products are untested and some have been considered to be unsafe (e.g. vaginal deodorants for women). Many of the chemicals in adult personal hygiene products have not been tested and some are known carcinogens in other species.

Products for children are more tightly regulated, especially since children are smaller and thus more at risk from toxic chemicals. However, an anti-bacterial chemical used in many products has been linked to an increase in allergies. Similarly, arachis oil, derived from peanuts and found in some creams, has been linked to peanut allergy in children.

In terms of babies and children, many products are advertised that are unnecessary and may even contribute to poorer health outcomes. For example, dermatologists have tried to discourage the use of baby wipes, as they seem to be associated with eczema, due to the different chemicals the wipes are impregnated with.

The most effective method of preventing infection is to ensure personal hygiene, particularly frequent hand-washing.

The influence of advertising on emotional and social health

Advertising can affect emotional and social health in a negative way because it aims to make people dissatisfied so they will want to purchase goods and services. In other words, it is intended to stimulate consumption. The branding is powerful; nevertheless many of the products advertised are beyond reach for a majority of people. This has led to children and young people being bullied as some brands, especially expensive designer brands, are seen as high status and hence confer status on the wearer.

Children and young people can be made to feel very vulnerable, particularly during adolescence, when the desire to fit in with peers is part of forming a separate identity from parents. This can lead to low self-esteem and, in extreme cases, self-harm. Other young people might turn to crime in an attempt to secure money or goods to boost their status.

While younger children do not feel the same pressure of brands, it is still the case that there will be certain toys or games that are seen as the best and children will strive to have them. Manufacturers compete to be the toy that is the 'must have' every Christmas and advertising contributes enormously to this.

As long as brands, goods and products are intimately bound up with status, wealth and self-esteem, advertising will continue to contribute indirectly to poorer mental health.

Activity

Describe the role of the Advertising Standards Agency in the regulation of adverts.

Possible ways of promoting health

Health promotion is only effective if it is able to get a clear message across to the target audience in a meaningful way. It is therefore important that, when promoting health among children and young people, age, gender and a range of factors are considered when designing a campaign. It is helpful to have a focus group made up of a representative sample of your target audience.

Health promotion in itself does not change behaviour; however, it can stimulate discussion and make people think. Some people may change behaviour as a result and if sufficient people are motivated to change – the 'critical mass' – then the new behaviour becomes more socially acceptable than the previous behaviour. An example of this is smoking among young people, which is considered socially unacceptable in some groups and an unappealing habit to have on a date!

It is important to use things that are of interest to children and young people to act as a vehicle for promoting health messages. If there is a particular area in which a message is needed, you need to stimulate the interest first before you can deliver the message.

Food, diet and nutrition

There has recently been a great deal of work done in relation to healthy school meals and raising awareness of healthy eating among children. A number of strategies were used to get children interested in food and ready to try new foods, since children and adults sometimes tend to stick to the things they know and like. If the diet is poor and children are only exposed to a limited range of foods, it becomes more difficult to eat healthily.

Suggested ways of engaging children's interest in food include the following:

- Ask children to bring in an item of food that they are unfamiliar with and get small groups of children to find out about their novelty food. These foods could then be tasted by each child in the group and compared. Another strategy would be to incorporate the foods into a meal or dish that the children help to cook.
- Put together a cookbook with recipes from around the world – this works well in multicultural settings. Alternatively, hold an open day for parents and ask everyone to bring a national or regional dish and be prepared to swap recipes.
- For older children, find out about 'celebrity diets' and examine them for their nutritional content – this activity could raise awareness of the problems of dieting.

Exercise or recreation and leisure

Health promotion activities in this area could include the following:

- Dancing competitions or children inventing their own dance routine. This could be linked to recommendations for exercise and learning how exercise is necessary for your body throughout life.
- Games and sport – for example, examining athletes and their lifestyle, including diet and nutrition, rest and sleep, training routines and compare to children's own lifestyles, getting the children to suggest what changes they could make and how they think they would benefit. Progress charts and prizes for most improved over a month could be provided as an incentive.
- Making music could be used as a health promotion activity in several ways. For example, the dangers of music that is too loud and how it damages hearing, with children making suggestions on how to avoid this, perhaps inventing some ear protectors.

Rest, sleep and/or lifestyle

Health promotion activities could cover issues such as the following:

- Computer games – do children think they are influenced by computer games? Is this positively or negatively? Is there a difference for boys and girls? What actions can children take to enhance the positive and minimise the negative?
- Alcohol and drugs could be the focus of health promotion activities for young people – for example, designing their own programme and carrying it out with peers.
- Importance of sleep – for younger children, look at sleep in pets and animals (e.g. hibernation) to raise awareness of its importance. They could then develop an individual 'sleep plan' and try it for two weeks before evaluating it (e.g. has it made a difference to how they feel?).

All of these activities could be included in a lifestyle quiz or questionnaire to carry out as a competition.

Prevention of infection

Health promotion topics that are helpful in this area include personal hygiene. For example:

- The importance of hand-washing and how to do it. Activities could include when to wash, why to wash and how to wash hands. Posters, demonstrations, competitions, using different soaps/cleansers, making a video, using the laboratory to check bacteria on hands before and after washing for older children, etc. would all help to get the message across.

- For older teens, a health promotion activity about sexually transmitted infections could be integrated into PHSE lessons. As there is a lot of material available on this subject, an activity to compare and contrast approaches and evaluate their likely impact on young people could be helpful.

Emotional and social aspects

Health promotion activities in relation to social and emotional health must be very sensitively handled as it may touch on personal issues that the child or young person is not ready to deal with. However, the following topics can be helpful for children and young people to consider:

- Bullying: what it is and how children and young people can deal with it. It is likely that the setting has an anti-bullying policy and it might be useful to review it as part of a health promotion activity to see how it could be improved so that children and young people are empowered and their resilience and self-esteem improved.
- Gangs – good or bad? An activity to examine different friendship groups, why they are important, etc. This activity could include how people behave in groups, how individual young people can choose positive friendship networks rather than negative ones and what makes a good friend.

Section 4: Support children and/or young people to improve their health

The aim of health promotion is to encourage people to exert control over their own health. In relation to children and young people, this means helping them to be as independent as possible so that they can manage health-related issues that are within their control – for example, personal hygiene or road safety. For improving other aspects of healthy lifestyles, children and young people are dependent on their parents. Therefore, you need to design a health promotion activity with the children or young people you care for that will have an impact on parents and that children can help to encourage at home.

Plan and implement an activity to promote the health of children and/or young people

You can use the suggestions in Section 3 to develop a health promotion activity or devise you own. The key criteria to consider are as follows:

- Who is the promotion activity for?
- What message are you trying to convey?
- Myth busting – what does your target audience know already?
- How is the activity going to empower your target audience?
- How will you measure success (evaluation)?

Once you have answered all these questions, you will need to devise an action plan. This should clearly show the roles and responsibilities of all those involved (e.g. devising questionnaires). You will need to put timescales on your action plan and include a review of the plan.

Evaluate the outcome of the health promotion activity

You will need to develop some evaluation criteria for your activity – what measures will you use to tell whether your activity has been successful and has achieved your overall aim? You may need to include short-term evaluation criteria and longer-term criteria because it is not always easy to see what impact health promotion has on longer-term behaviour change. Your evaluation criteria, however, should cover the outcome of the promotional activity:

- For the learning of the child/young person, questions might include the extent to which the child or young person understands the health message behind the promotional activity and whether they will have more control over their own health as a result of the activity (empowerment). It is difficult to measure this objectively, but you can ask the child or young person themselves via interview or questionnaire, which you can tape or video (as long as you have parental permission).
- For the potential influence on the family, you might need to interview parents. Your evaluation should allow for parents wanting more information about the health message. For example, if they ask you to refer them for help to stop smoking following a promotional activity in this area, this would indicate some success. The health of the child will be improved as a result.
- The involvement of the team within the work environment is about how you work as a member of a team and how the roles were allocated and carried out according to your action plan for implementing the activity. You will need some criteria against which to measure performance and this could be built into your plan at the beginning.

Reflect on own role within the health promotion activity which supported children and/or young people to improve their health

Reflective practice is important for childcare workers. Once you have completed your evaluation, you can examine your findings and reflect on how you could improve it or what you might have done differently. It is important to say how you think any changes would have improved the outcome of the promotional activity – that is, the extent to which your health message was received and acted upon and the extent to which it empowered the child or young person to improve their own health.

Section 5: How to respond to illness in children and/or young people

It is relatively rare for children or young people to be in the setting while suffering from serious infectious diseases, especially if there is an immunisation policy and an exclusion procedure in place, as part of a managing illness policy (see Section 1). Most children and young people who are poorly with highly infectious diseases should be cared for at home and, unless you are working with looked-after children, or are the sole carer in a home setting, you are unlikely to be required to care for children in the acute stages of their illness.

Nevertheless, there are some children who have not been vaccinated and pose a risk to themselves and others. It is therefore useful if you become familiar with the signs and symptoms of some of the infectious diseases.

Symptoms of common infectious illnesses

A rise in confirmed measles cases in England and Wales in 2011 was reported by the Health Protection Agency, with 496 cases being reported from January to May 2011, compared with just 374 cases for the whole of 2010. There was also a significant outbreak of measles on Merseyside in 2012; the majority of cases were among children under five, babies and toddlers, and young adults who were not vaccinated as children.

Measles

Measles is a highly contagious viral infection spread by droplets. It is a notifiable disease so must be reported by the GP in order for action to be taken to prevent an outbreak. Signs and symptoms include:

- raised temperature – sometimes as high as 40C
- symptoms of a common cold – runny nose, cough, sore throat, etc.

- diarrhoea
- grey or white patches on throat and enlarged lymph glands in the neck
- rash beginning on head and neck (usually behind the ears) and spreading to the legs, then the rest of the body – reddish-brown in colour; once the rash appears, the temperature will start to return to normal
- eyes which have a pink colour to the whites (conjunctivitis) and are sensitive to light.

The incubation period for measles (time between coming into contact with the virus and developing symptoms) is 7–14 days and people are infectious from four days before the rash appears until five days afterwards. During the few days before the spots erupt, red patches known as Koplik's spots appear on the inside of the mouth, confirming measles, especially with other symptoms.

Complications, although rare, can include:

- febrile (fever-related) convulsions (fits)
- pneumonia due to secondary (usually bacterial) infection
- infection of the middle ear (otitis media), which in extreme cases can lead to deafness
- inflammation of the brain (encephalitis) and its coverings, called meninges (meningitis), which can lead to developmental delay.

For more information and to see what a measles rash looks like, see the video on www.nhs.uk/conditions/measles/Pages/Introduction.aspx.

Chicken pox

Chicken pox is another highly infectious illness caused by a virus (varicella zoster) spread by droplet infection. Chicken pox is more common in children but the virus can also cause shingles in adults who have had chicken pox. Adults with shingles can cause chicken pox in others who have not been exposed to it. Symptoms of chicken pox include:

- raised temperature – sometimes as high as 40C
- symptoms of a common cold – runny nose, cough, sore throat, etc.
- a highly itchy rash, which starts off looking like tiny, fluid-filled blisters (vesicles), appearing in clusters mostly on the trunk, but can appear on the limbs and face.

The incubation period for chicken pox is 10–21 days, with the most infectious period being a day or two before the rash appears to about five days after, or when all of the vesicles have dried up and formed crusts.

Complications from chicken pox are fairly rare but the spots can leave scars if they are scratched, especially if they become infected. However, certain groups (e.g. pregnant women, very young babies, people on chemotherapy or steroids and anyone who has a weakened immune system) may experience more serious complications, including:

- congenital varicella syndrome in the unborn babies of pregnant women, leading to shortened limbs, cataracts and growth retardation
- premature birth or neonatal (newborn) chicken pox
- secondary bacterial infections, particularly chest and skin infections
- encephalitis (inflammation of the brain), which can have serious long-term consequences (e.g. developmental delay)
- viral pneumonia.

If expectant mothers come into contact with chicken pox, they can be offered a specially prepared vaccine called immunoglobulin, which contains antibodies to help fight the infection. People with weakened immune systems (immunocompromised) can be given anti-viral drugs as well as immunoglobulin if necessary.

Because chicken pox is so dangerous to pregnant women and their unborn babies, it is crucial that children with suspected chicken pox are kept away from pregnant mothers and the signs and symptoms are recognised before the spots appear.

Meningitis

The term meningitis means inflammation of the protective coverings of the brain – the three meninges. It is a general term covering several different types of meningitis, caused by either certain bacteria or a virus, and it is a notifiable disease. Many people – about 10 per cent of the population – carry meningococcal bacteria in their throats without ill effect and it is rare that they overcome the body's defences to cause meningitis. There are different groups of meningococci, the two main ones being Type B and Type C, which used to cause 35–40 per cent of meningitis cases. Since vaccines were introduced for Type C in 1999/2000, there has been a significant reduction, with only two deaths under 20 years of age in the last five years, compared to 78 in the year prior to vaccination. Meningitis is not highly contagious.

- Bacterial meningitis – the most serious type caused by one of several bacteria: meningococcal, pneumococcal, streptococcal, Hib (haemophilus influenzae type B), TB and E-coli. This is a life-threatening disease – one in ten people die – and there are serious long-term health consequences if survived.
- Viral meningitis – often caused by an enterovirus (one which lives in the intestines), it is usually much milder and, although it can make people feel very unwell, there is less likelihood of serious complications and lasting damage than with bacterial meningitis. Recovery, however, is usually slow.

The signs and symptoms of meningitis are similar, irrespective of the causal agent (pathogen). They include:

- high temperature/fever with cold hands and feet – all age groups
- pale, blotchy skin, spots or rash – all age groups
- food refusal or loss of appetite
- vomiting – all age groups
- drowsiness and floppiness (babies and young children); unresponsiveness and difficulty to rouse (older children and teens)
- rapid breathing, often accompanied by grunting (babies and young children)
- high-pitched or unusual cry (babies and young children); confusion and irritability (older children and teens)
- tense, bulging fontanelle (soft spot in babies); headache (older children and teens)
- stiff neck and dislike of bright lights – all age groups
- muscle pain, often severe (older children and teens)
- convulsions – all age groups.

Not all of these signs and symptoms need to be present at the same time but if meningitis is suspected, medical help must be sought. If the condition of a child or young person suddenly deteriorates (e.g. convulsions begin), medical assistance is urgently required.

The most serious symptom is the rash that does not fade under pressure because this is a sign of meningococcal septicaemia (blood poisoning), which is a medical emergency. The rash can be checked using the glass test – if a glass is pressed against the rash and the rash does not fade, it is septicaemia. It is important not to wait until there is a rash. **If any combination of the above symptoms is present, you should suspect meningitis and seek immediate help**. You can get further information, including a video of the 'glass test', at www.meningitis-trust.org/meningitis-info.

The consequences of meningitis are serious because it can lead to brain damage and developmental delay. Complications include the following:

- **Physical difficulties**, especially following meningococcal septicaemia, because the toxins produced damage blood vessels and blood-flow to all major organs, skin and muscles. This may cause muscle weakness, scarring and in extreme cases there may be loss of limbs. Acute headaches are not unusual and there may be clumsiness due to impaired spatial awareness, hearing loss (very common) and/or sight loss. There is often tiredness and fatigue, which can last for many months.
- **Learning difficulties**, including reduced attention and concentration, short-term memory loss, difficulty in number and word recognition. Speech and communication difficulties are not unusual. A significant number will have a reduced IQ.

- **Emotional and behavioural difficulties**, including depression, personality changes, loss of confidence, mood swings and anxiety.

It is estimated that 15 per cent of meningitis survivors experience significant long-term health problems. It is therefore crucial that, if you have a child or young person in your care who has survived meningitis, you are aware of any consequences for their health and development. They may need additional observation and assessment, together with extra help to reach their potential.

Mumps

Mumps is an infection of the parotid (salivary) gland, usually transmitted through saliva, either by direct contact (e.g. kissing) or by droplets from an infected person. It is a viral illness and a notifiable disease, as are all illnesses that can be prevented by immunisation.

The signs and symptoms of mumps include:

- raised temperature
- headache
- swelling of the parotid gland under the angle of the jaw on one or both sides.

The swelling in mumps is characteristic. However, the incubation period is long, at 14–21 days, and it can be transmitted (passed to others) for several days before the swelling becomes apparent until several days afterwards. It is not as infectious as chicken pox or measles but can have complications if other glands are involved, especially the ovaries and testes.

Complications from mumps can include swelling of the ovaries or testes. There is no strong evidence to support the common belief that orchitis – swelling of the testes due to mumps – causes sterility in men.

Less frequent but more serious complications include aseptic (not caused by a pathogen) meningitis due to inflammation of the meninges, pancreatitis (inflammation of the pancreas), neuritis (inflammation of nerves), arthritis (inflammation of joints), mastitis (inflammation of breast tissue), nephritis (inflammation of the kidneys), thyroiditis (inflammation of the thyroid gland) and pericarditis (inflammation of the membrane covering the heart). As you can probably see, words ending in '-itis' mean 'inflammation'.

Responding to possible signs and symptoms of these common infectious illnesses

Your response to children suffering from suspected infectious illnesses should follow the general principles for unwell children described in Section 2.

With the exception of meningitis, the response to possible signs and symptoms of measles, chicken pox and mumps is to give priority to reducing the fever (high temperature) and keeping the child or young person as comfortable as possible. It is helpful to have a quiet corner with a folding chair-bed or large bean-bag for the child to lie down on – children who are unwell may be very sleepy. Staff should be able to monitor the child easily, so having them alone in a separate room is inadvisable unless there is someone available to stay with the child. Babies should be placed in a cot or pram.

Reducing fever

Babies and young children have poorly developed temperature control mechanisms and can quickly become feverish when suffering from infection. If left unchecked, this can sometimes result in fits – febrile convulsions – which resemble epileptic fits and are both frightening and distressing, although harmless in the long term. Convulsions usually occur when the temperature reaches above 38C, or 100.4F.

It is important to take the child's temperature and monitor it regularly to see if it is getting worse. You can take a child's temperature using a fever strip, placed on the forehead, which will give you an approximate reading. More accurate readings are obtained by using a regular digital thermometer in the mouth, armpit or ear. It is important to take the temperature from the same site each time and accurately record it so that you can tell the parents or medical staff.

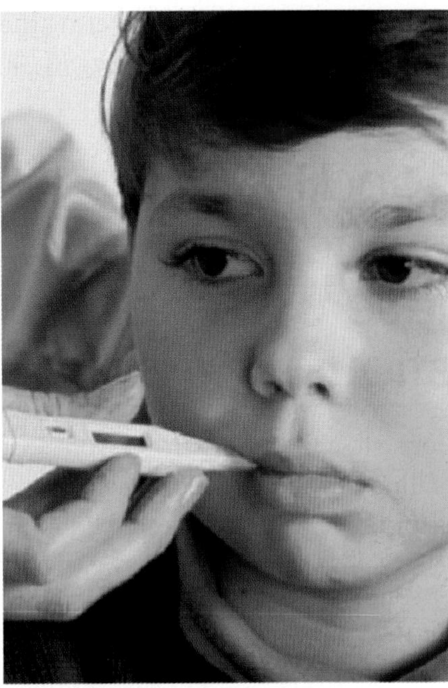

Figure 3.2 A digital thermometer

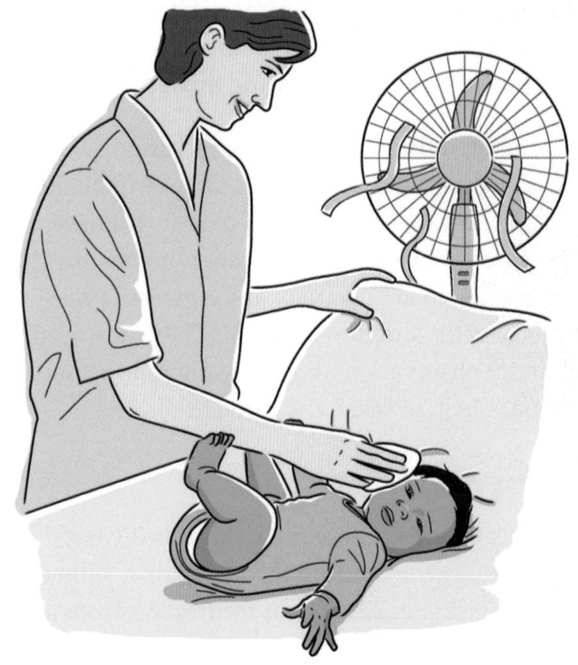

Figure 3.3 Tepid sponging

To reduce the temperature of children who become unwell in the setting, it is advisable to give paracetamol or ibuprofen syrup specially formulated for children, provided you have parental consent.

You can remove some of the child's outer clothing and place a fan nearby to blow cool air across the child. You must make sure you monitor this as temperature can reduce as quickly as it increases. It is best to have an oscillating fan so that the air is not blowing constantly on the child in the same place (e.g. the face).

If the child's temperature remains elevated, you can sponge the face and limbs with lukewarm water and allow it to evaporate – this is called **tepid sponging** and mimics the body's natural mechanism when we perspire and it evaporates, cooling us down.

It is also important to make sure the child continues to drink to avoid becoming dehydrated. Sips of cool water are best, given frequently. Make a note of how much has been taken. If the child will not drink, they may take sugar-free ice lollies or suck on an ice cube if they are old enough. This is particularly helpful if the child has chicken pox in the mouth or is suffering from mumps.

If the child has chicken pox, it is important to try and reduce the itching and prevent scratching. Applying calamine lotion is a tried and tested method, although it can be messy; cooling gels are an alternative. Nails should be kept short and clean to prevent infection and cotton mittens or gloves (or old socks!) can be worn at night to help prevent scratching during sleep. It is best **not** to tepid sponge a child with chicken pox. Children with chicken pox may be given paracetamol or ibuprofen, but they must never be given aspirin as this can cause Reye's syndrome, a dangerous condition causing liver and brain damage.

If a child has mumps, treatment is about reducing fever, giving fluids and general care. A warm facecloth held against the swelling can help with any pain.

If you are asked to care for a child with measles, it is best to place them in a dimly lit place to help with the photophobia (dislike of bright light). Give plenty of fluids as above – warm lemon and honey can be soothing if the child is old enough to take it. Children with measles often have a cough, and a bowl of water by the radiator or a humidifier to moisten the air will help. There is no point giving cough medicine, although paracetamol or ibuprofen will reduce fever.

Figure 3.4 Chicken pox

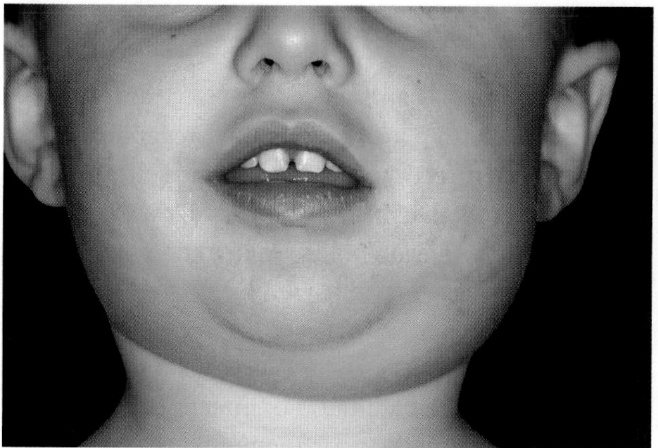

Figure 3.5 Mumps

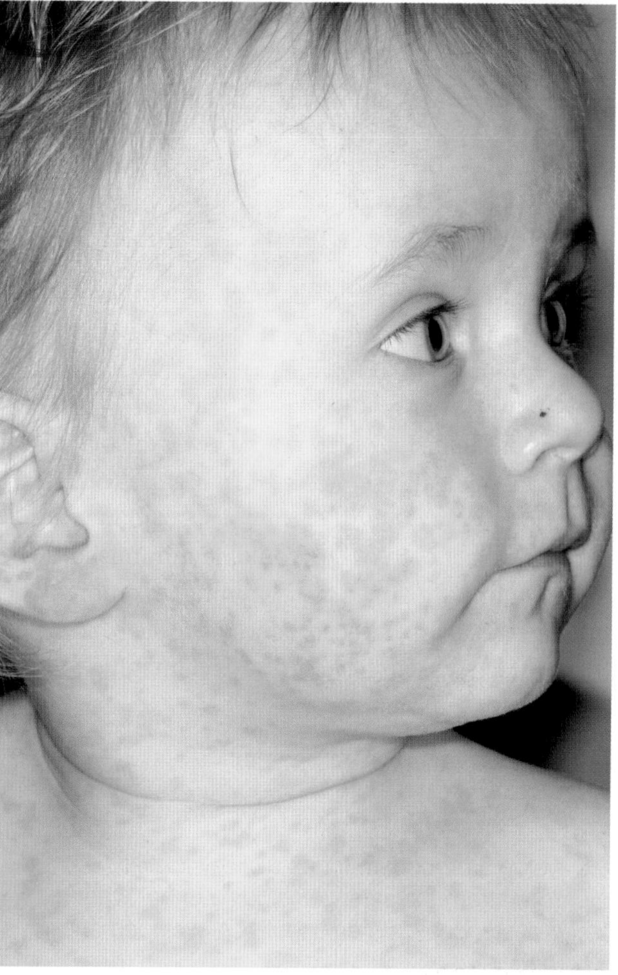

Figure 3.6 Measles

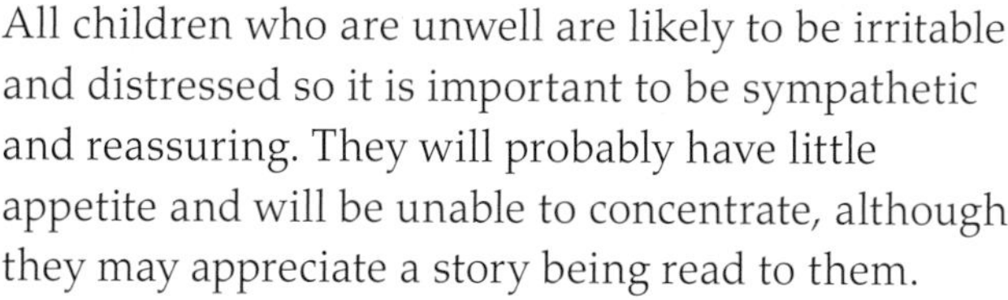

All children who are unwell are likely to be irritable and distressed so it is important to be sympathetic and reassuring. They will probably have little appetite and will be unable to concentrate, although they may appreciate a story being read to them.

The importance of recognising and responding to common infectious illnesses in children and/or young people

It is important to be able to recognise common infectious diseases so that other children and staff can be protected as far as possible and so that the individual child or young person can receive appropriate treatment.

It is also crucial that you know which infections are notifiable (these are the diseases that are preventable by immunisation) so that the appropriate authorities can be informed and action can be taken to prevent an outbreak.

For example, in the measles outbreak in 2012 in Merseyside, staff from the Health Protection Agency (HPA) worked with the local health services to identify and follow up all the people who had been in contact with the 441 suspected cases of measles. They discovered that the majority of cases were in children under five who had not been vaccinated at 13 months, as advised in the immunisation schedule. The majority of the others were teenagers and young adults who had not been vaccinated as children. This is an example of how herd immunity (see 'Key term' on page 114) can break down when insufficient people have been immunised to offer protection to the population as a whole (see Section 6).

The advice from the HPA to people suffering from measles was to avoid contact with others, especially pregnant women and babies too young to be immunised. They were told to stay away from schools, nurseries and workplaces until at least four days after the rash appeared. They were also advised to telephone health services – GP surgeries, A&E departments – for advice if they suspected measles, so that contact with others could be minimised. All these actions are aimed at containing an outbreak of infectious disease because, as we have seen, some of these infections can have seriously damaging long-term health implications.

Activity

Develop a procedure for excluding sick children from the setting, including under what circumstances children should be excluded and for how long.

1. State the arrangements for informing parents of the exclusion policy and procedures.
2. Identify which notifiable infections are covered by immunisation.
3. Explain who is responsible for notifying and the action they should take.

Summarise workplace procedures when dealing with a child and/or young person who has a possible common infectious illness

Workplace policies and procedures have an important role to play in helping to prevent the likelihood of infectious diseases in the setting through a proactive immunisation policy, together with a comprehensive policy on dealing with sick children through temporary exclusion and other measures. Coupled with a robust infection control policy, these policies protect everyone in the setting and minimise the likelihood of infectious diseases breaking out, while supporting public health initiatives to prevent outbreaks of infectious disease in the community, thus minimising the long-term health consequences of infectious diseases. The NICE website has guidelines on infectious and notifiable illnesses/diseases. See: www.nice.org.uk.

Activity

Indicate whether you think the statements given in the table below are true (T) or false (F). If you are unsure, put don't know (DK).

Question	T, F, DK
If a child's temperature is above 37.5C/99F, the child is unwell and should see a doctor.	
A child's body temperature normally varies according to the time of day.	
If the temperature is taken by mouth, the reading may be above normal because the child has just had something hot to eat or drink.	

Question	T, F, DK
When a child has a fever, it is important that they drink plenty of fluids.	
Children with fevers often do not eat for several days. This does not matter as they will make up for it when they are better.	
When a child is ill and has a fever, it is a good idea to give paracetamol or ibuprofen.	
When a child is ill and has a fever, it is a good idea to keep them warm and well wrapped up.	
When a child is ill and has a fever, it is a good idea to sponge them with tepid water.	
When a child is ill and has a fever, it is a good idea to fan them with cool air.	
Infections with rashes are usually more serious than infections without.	
Rashes due to infections get better if antiseptic cream is rubbed on the rash.	
A child who is unwell and develops a rash that looks like tiny bruises needs to see a doctor straight away.	
Rashes in children with infections can sometimes be caused by the antibiotic medicine they are given and not the infection at all.	
A child with meningitis may not seem very ill but just be a bit irritable, clingy and off their food.	
There is still a risk of meningitis in children who have been given the meningitis C vaccine.	
Children with meningitis may complain of headaches and dislike bright lights.	
Nearly all children who contract meningitis either die or suffer brain damage, despite modern drugs.	
If a child has meningitis at nursery or school, it is **very likely** that other members of the group will get it too.	
It is important that a child with diarrhoea and vomiting should drink plenty of fluids.	
For a child with diarrhoea and vomiting, it is more important that the child continues to eat rather than drink.	
A child who is vomiting needs large drinks of water; sips are no good.	
You can tell how ill a vomiting baby is by checking how often the nappy is wet.	
Medicine to stop diarrhoea, such as that used on holiday, is useful for treating children with diarrhoea.	
Most children with diarrhoea need to see a doctor for antibiotics to cure them.	
Diarrhoea in young children is always infectious.	
Antibiotics are useful to cure sore throats in children.	
Antibiotics are useful to cure runny noses and bad colds in children.	
Antibiotics are useful to cure chesty coughs.	
Antibiotics are useful to cure bad attacks of wheezing due to asthma in children.	
Antibiotics are useful to cure earache in children.	
Antibiotics are useful to cure chicken pox.	

Section 6: Understand how immunisation aims to prevent harmful diseases in children and young people

Children and young people are more susceptible to common illnesses and diseases because their immune systems are undeveloped. One of the key ways in which children and young people's health is protected is through immunisation. When babies are born, their organs and bodily systems are immature, which makes them vulnerable. Because the immune system is underdeveloped at birth and continues to mature throughout the early years, infants are especially susceptible to infection so it is crucial to start vaccination as early as possible for maximum protection.

For example, unimmunised children who contract a preventable disease such as measles may infect a baby who is too young to be immunised or who has not yet completed the full schedule. Children who develop rubella may come into contact with a member of staff or another parent who is pregnant, exposing their unborn baby to the risk of serious abnormalities if they themselves have not been immunised or their immunity is weak.

What is immunity?

Immunity is the body's ability to protect itself by resisting and fighting infection; it includes physical barriers to infection such as the skin, as well as special cells – lymphocytes – and antibodies, which are substances produced by the body to fight infection. Lymphocytes create antibodies to attack bacteria and other infectious micro-organisms. Antibodies are produced to fight specific infections.

Passive immunity

Some protection is transferred to the infant from the mother in the form of antibodies, which pass through the placenta and into the baby's blood before the baby is born, and through breast milk after birth, providing the baby is breastfed. These antibodies have been produced by the mother to fight infections that she herself has encountered; however, this protection, known as passive immunity because it is passed on through the mother rather than being created by the baby, only lasts from a few weeks to a few months, depending on the duration of exclusive breastfeeding and the strength of the mother's immunity.

Active immunity

Active immunity is provided by the individual's own immune system; it can be produced when an individual contracts an infection or disease, or the body can be stimulated to produce antibodies through vaccination (immunisation). Vaccines are developed using the organism that causes disease, but which is either no longer alive (known as inactivated) or which has been treated so that it is harmless (known as attenuated). The body responds to the organism as if it were alive by producing antibodies so that, if they subsequently come into contact with the disease, they will be protected against it.

The immunisation schedule in England and Wales starts at eight weeks after birth, when passive immunity will be waning. Vaccination is carried out to stimulate the infant's immune system to respond and develop its own active immunity. Even if the infant is being exclusively breastfed, there is no way of assessing the extent of any passive immunity from the mother so it is safer to immunise than not.

Childcare workers should understand the concept of **'herd immunity'** (community immunity). The principle behind herd immunity is that the more people who have immunity to a particular disease, the less opportunity it has to spread. This means that even people who have no immunity are better protected because there is much less likelihood of an outbreak.

Key terms

Herd immunity – the percentage of a group who need to be immune to a disease to contain it within the group and prevent it causing an outbreak.

The percentage of people who need to have immunity in order for the whole population to be protected depends on the specific disease; however, it ranges between 70 and 95 per cent. This means, for example, that 85 per cent of the population will need to be vaccinated against diphtheria in order to prevent transmission so that everyone is protected. The idea of herd immunity underpins the programme of universal immunisation.

Activity

Develop an immunisation policy for your setting.

The National Immunisation Schedule for children and young people from birth to 18 years

Children in the UK are routinely immunised against diphtheria, tetanus, pertussis (whooping cough), polio, a specific type of influenza virus (Hib), a specific type of pneumonia (pneumococcal virus or PCV), a specific type of meningitis (meningitis C), measles, mumps and rubella (German measles), starting at eight weeks and at intervals until the child is three years and four months. When children reach adolescence, they need a booster injection of some of the early vaccines to establish lifelong immunity. Different vaccines are given at different times and in different combinations to ensure maximum protection and minimum complications. Girls are also offered vaccination against the human papilloma virus (HPV), which is associated with cervical cancer.

Key terms

Vaccination – the process of introducing a harmless pathogen (see 'Key term' on page 86) into the body to stimulate the production of antibodies so that the individual becomes immune to that disease.

Immunisation – the body's response to vaccination by creating immunity. Sometimes the terms are used interchangeably.

The immunisation schedule is developed from research-based evidence of the behaviour and transmission (epidemiology) of communicable diseases. It is the role of the Joint Committee of Vaccination and Immunisation (JCVI), an independent expert advisory body, to review all the available evidence and make recommendations to the Department of Health, who then decide on the UK vaccination policy. UK vaccine policy is published in the 'Green Book', which is available on the Department of Health website for doctors and public health professionals to refer to.

The JCVI also advises the Secretary of State for Health in Scotland, Wales and Northern Ireland on the diseases that are preventable or potentially preventable through immunisation. This means that, because the immunisation schedule is based on evidence, in practice the immunisation schedule is the same in all the countries of the UK. The schedule is regularly reviewed and updated in the light of new knowledge and evidence.

The diseases currently within the scope of the UK immunisation schedule are serious diseases that can be fatal and often cause significant, permanent damage for children who survive.

BCG (Bacillus Calmette-Guerin) protects against tuberculosis and was routinely given to young people in secondary school. However, it is now offered as a targeted programme for babies, children and young adults considered to be at higher risk of TB. These are:

- children born or who live or have lived in areas where there is a high rate of TB
- children whose parent or grandparent was born in a country where there is a high rate of TB.

For children at risk, it is recommended that those babies less than 12 months old have the BCG and that older children are tested and vaccinated if needed.

Disease	Threshold (percentage needed to ensure herd immunity)	Transmission route and incubation period	Symptoms, causes, effects and complications
Diphtheria – caused by bacteria *corynebacterium diphtheria*	85%	Saliva. Two to five days. Infective period: up to four weeks.	• Affects respiratory tract, forming a grey membrane that can obstruct breathing • Produces a dangerous toxin (poisonous substance) that attacks the heart and central nervous system. Complications – paralysis and damage to the heart muscle, proving fatal in 10 per cent of cases.
HIB – caused by bacteria *haemophilus influenzae*	Not known because the bacteria causes a number of different diseases	Airborne and droplet. Carried in nasal passages.	• Meningitis (inflammation of the brain coverings) • Septicaemia (blood poisoning) • Epiglottitis (swelling and obstruction of the throat) • Septic arthritis (joint infection) • Osteomyelitis (infection of the bone). All of these effects can be fatal or cause long-term damage or disability.
Measles – viral infection caused by a *paramyxovirus*	83–95%	Airborne. Ten days. Infective period: days 10–18. Rash appears about day four.	• Rash • Fever • Cough, runny nose, sneezing • Conjunctivitis. The complications of measles are life-threatening and include: • severe conjunctivitis • inflammation of the small intestines • pneumonia • encephalitis (inflammation of the brain), causing brain damage in 40 per cent of sufferers • death from encephalitis.
Mumps – viral infection caused by a *paramyxovirus*	75–86%	Airborne and droplet. 14–21 days. Infectious for several days before swelling appears.	• Characteristic swelling under the ear caused by inflammation of the salivary gland on one or both sides • Can affect other glands, including pancreas, testes and ovaries. Complications can include: • deafness due to inflammation of the ear • viral meningitis • encephalitis • infertility.

Disease	Threshold (percentage needed to ensure herd immunity)	Transmission route and incubation period	Symptoms, causes, effects and complications
Pertussis (whooping cough) – bacterial infection caused by bacterium *bordetella pertussis*	92–94%	Airborne and droplet. 7–10 days. Infectious period: days 7–21 after infection.	• High temperature • Loss of appetite and feeling unwell • Runny nose, cough, sneezing • Coughing spasms with characteristic 'whoop' on breathing in. Complications are more common in children under six years and include: • pneumonia • vomiting • convulsions • brain damage • death.
Poliomyelitis (polio) – viral infection by one of three types of *poliovirus*	80–86%	Faecal-oral. 3–21 days. May be infectious for six weeks.	• Sore throat • Loss of appetite • Nausea and vomiting • Diarrhoea. Causing: • meningitis • paralysis • death due to paralysis of the respiratory muscles or brain stem damage.
Rubella (German measles) – viral infection caused by a *togavirus*	80–85%	Airborne and droplet. 14–21 days. Infectious from seven days before the rash to five days after it has gone.	Rash on face spreading to body and limbs. Complications are rare but include: • encephalitis • thrombocytopenia (affects clotting ability of blood) • joint pain (adults) • polyneuritis (Guillain-Barre syndrome), causing muscle weakness and sometimes paralysis. Rubella in the first ten weeks of pregnancy causes foetal damage in 90 per cent of cases, including: • deafness • learning difficulties • cataracts • heart defects • growth retardation.

Disease	Threshold (percentage needed to ensure herd immunity)	Transmission route and incubation period	Symptoms, causes, effects and complications
TB (tuberculosis) – caused by *mycobacterium* NB – vaccination is targeted, not universal	Heaf test given to check reaction to TB protein prior to vaccination, which is only given to those with no response	Airborne and droplet.	• Cough, sometimes blood-stained • Fever • Loss of appetite • Failure to thrive. Causing: • broncho-pneumonia • fluid around the lungs • collapsed lungs • TB spread throughout the body. Lungs are most commonly affected but TB can also affect kidneys, bladder, bones and ovaries/testes.
Tetanus	N/A	Via skin (e.g. open wound)	Bacterial infection. Tetanus is not contagious so herd immunity offers no protection. Everyone needs to be immunised individually.

Table 3.3 Diseases covered in the UK immunisation schedule

The role of immunisation in the health of children and young people

Children are routinely immunised in the UK against a range of different diseases, which are now relatively rare. For example, before the polio vaccine was introduced in 1955, there were 6,000 cases per year, mostly affecting children and young adults. Polio is a viral infection affecting the central nervous system; it attacks the spinal cord causing paralysis of the muscles by damaging the nerve supply. It commonly affects the limbs and the inter-costal muscles (between the ribs), which are necessary for breathing. There were widespread outbreaks of the disease in the UK, prior to the introduction of vaccines, and sufferers whose breathing was affected were placed into a machine called an 'iron lung', which used compression and decompression to artificially inflate the chest wall.

There is no cure for polio, which is specific to humans and frequently results in death or, for those who are lucky enough to survive, permanent paralysis with muscle wasting. For example, Ian Dury, the famous rock musician, was a polio survivor. He maintained that he caught the disease aged seven from a swimming pool and it permanently affected his left arm and right leg with partial paralysis, hence his famous stick and limp.

The success of routine immunisation is demonstrated by the fact that, in 1948, there were 241 deaths from polio in England and Wales; today there are none and there have been no new cases reported since 1998. This is not the case across the rest of the world, however, and polio still leads to paralysis for thousands of children.

Similarly, smallpox, caused by a viral infection and responsible for thousands of deaths and permanent damage, has now been eradicated entirely worldwide so vaccination is no longer required.

Figure 3.7 An iron lung

Summary of published information about the improvement to children and/or young people's health in relation to immunisations

While immunisation against some diseases has been extremely successful, others, particularly those regarded as childhood illnesses, such as mumps and measles, have had a more erratic take-up in the UK and still affect unvaccinated children, sometimes with devastating consequences, including lifelong disability and, in the worst cases, death.

The measles vaccine was introduced in 1968 and the measles, mumps and rubella (MMR) vaccine in 1998. Since that point, the incidence of these diseases steadily declined until recently, when the uptake of the MMR vaccine in the UK began to fall and herd immunity was compromised.

This was mainly due to a loss of confidence in the vaccine by parents, influenced by a highly publicised medical paper suggesting a link between the MMR vaccine and autism/bowel disease. This paper was theoretical and based on a very small sample of children. The data behind the theory has since been rigorously tested and over 200 further experiments have been unable to replicate the original findings. The theory has therefore been discredited; there is no evidence to indicate any link between MMR and autism and the safety of the vaccine is confirmed.

Measles has been eliminated in Finland; before 1975, there were 15,000 cases a year but there have been no cases since 1996 due to high vaccination rates. Meanwhile, measles causes 500,000 deaths per year in Africa and 800,000 a year worldwide. For more information on vaccinations, see www.nhs.uk/Planners/vaccinations/Pages/miracles.aspx.

Activity

1. Find out how the incidence of measles has changed in the UK between 2000 and 2012.
2. Identify any differences between the four countries of the UK.

Useful resources

Organisations and websites

Allergy UK
www.allergyuk.org

Anaphylaxis Campaign
www.anaphylaxis.org.uk

Asthma UK: what to do in an asthma attack
www.asthma.org.uk/about-asthma/what-to-do-in-an-asthma-attack

Children with Diabetes
www.childrenwithdiabetes.com/uk

Department of Health's Birth to Five
www.dh.gov.uk/en/Publicationsandstatistics/Publications/PublicationsPolicyAndGuidance/DH_107303

Department of Health's Healthy Child Programme
www.dh.gov.uk/prod_consum_dh/groups/dh_digitalassets/@dh/@en/@ps/documents/digitalasset/dh_118525.pdf

Department of Health's Managing Medicines in Schools
www.education.gov.uk/schools/pupilsupport/pastoralcare/b0013771/managing-medicines-in-schools

Department of Health's Start4Life campaign
www.nhs.uk/start4life

Epilepsy Action: guidance for education professionals
www.epilepsy.org.uk/professionals/education

The Food Standards Agency
www.food.gov.uk

Health Protection Agency: guidance on infection control in schools and other childcare settings
www.hpa.org.uk/Topics/InfectiousDiseases/InfectionsAZ/SchoolsGuidanceOnInfectionControl

HSE: Reporting of Injuries, Diseases and Dangerous Occurrences Regulations 1995
www.hse.gov.uk/riddor

HSE: Control of Substances Hazardous to Health Regulations 2002
www.hse.gov.uk/coshh/index.htm

Meningitis Trust: meningitis information
www.meningitis-trust.org/meningitis-info

National Childminding Association
www.ncma.org.uk

Useful resources (cont.)

NHS: measles
www.nhs.uk/conditions/measles/Pages/Introduction.aspx

NHS: vaccinations save lives
www.nhs.uk/Planners/vaccinations/Pages/miracles.aspx

NICE: atopic eczema in children
http://publications.nice.org.uk/atopic-eczema-in-children-cg57

NICE: guidance on the use of inhaler systems
http://publications.nice.org.uk/guidance-on-the-use-of-inhaler-systems-devices-in-children-under-the-age-of-5-years-with-chronic-ta10

NICE: guidelines on anaphylaxis
www.nice.org.uk/Search.do?x=25&y=12&searchText=+anaphylaxis&newsearch=true#/search/?reload

NICE: reducing differences in the uptake of immunisations
http://publications.nice.org.uk/reducing-differences-in-the-uptake-of-immunisations-ph21/recommendations#recommendation-1-immunisation-programmes

NICE: social and emotional well-being in primary education
http://publications.nice.org.uk/social-and-emotional-wellbeing-in-primary-education-ph12

NICE: when to suspect child maltreatment
http://publications.nice.org.uk/when-to-suspect-child-maltreatment-cg89/guidance

Ofsted: guide to registration on the Childcare Register
www.ofsted.gov.uk/resources/guide-registration-childcare-register

Resuscitation Council (UK)
www.resus.org.uk

School Food Trust: guidance for food and drink provision in early years settings
www.schoolfoodtrust.org.uk/download/documents/pdf/early_years_food_and_nutrition_guidance.pdf

Chapter 4 An introduction to leadership and management (Unit CP 4)

Effective leadership and management are crucial to the success of all settings and services for children, young people and their families. This includes social care settings, children's centres, nurseries, schools and other services for children and young people. Leadership and management are often defined as processes that influence others to work towards the aims and purposes of the setting or service – that is, influencing other people's thinking and behaviour. Sometimes they are thought of as functions, duties and responsibilities. The advantage of seeing leadership and management as processes is that there is more flexibility and the processes of leading and managing can change and adapt to circumstances – that is, they can be active processes, rather than static functions or roles.

Leaders and managers occupy key roles in a setting or service. The leader and the manager set the ethos and standards and therefore directly influence outcomes for children.

Learning outcomes

1. Understand leadership and management theories, styles and models.
2. Understand the skill sets required to be an effective leader and/or manager.
3. Understand how to create a sense of common purpose for team working.

Section 1: Leadership and management theories, styles and models

The differences between leadership and management

Leadership and management are separate processes that are closely linked and affect each other. Leadership tends to be about 'what' the purpose, focus and direction of the setting or service should be and about influencing others to support this. Management tends to be about 'how' to achieve the desired outcomes for the setting or service. A leader can be a manager, but a manager is not necessarily a leader. However, if a manager is able to influence people to achieve the goals of the service or setting, without using formal authority to do so, then the manager is demonstrating leadership.

There is potential confusion between the terms leader and manager. Over the years, they have often been seen as one process or as being overlapping processes. In some countries, 'educational administration' is an umbrella term to describe both. In recent years in the UK, there has been an increasing emphasis on the role and function of the leader, which is felt to be more strategic in terms of outcomes for children and young people.

Although leading and managing are different roles, in some settings they may be fulfilled by the same person – that is, a leader-manager – whereas in other settings they will be covered by different people. Either way, the functions of leadership and management are different, although they may overlap. These differences are explored below.

Leadership

Leadership is about setting the way forward – the direction of travel. It also includes monitoring progress towards achieving the setting and service goals and overall effectiveness. Leadership is about change and development. It does not take place in a vacuum but within a context and environment, in a given place and at a specific time. Leadership is affected by research and by international, national, regional and local policies and direction. It is about influencing, and the process of inspiring, motivating and engaging others to achieve the objectives of the setting or service. Human needs for value and respect are important; effective leaders recognise this and strive to create an environment that supports the energy and talent of their people.

Research Activity

In recent years, a new role has appeared that is designed to lead practice in early years settings. This is a key strategic role and is called the 'early years professional status' (EYP). It has been introduced because research such as EPPE (2004, 2007), as well as international research, has shown that more highly qualified staff in early years settings leads to better outcomes for children. It is an example of how research and government policy has directly affected leadership in early years settings for the benefit of children.

Research the role of the early years professional and answer the following questions:

- Why was the EYP status introduced?
- How do people become EYPs?
- What does this tell you about the importance of leadership?

Key term

Vision – how things will look in the future.

Mission statement – a statement that encapsulates the vision.

Strategic planning – planning to align the human, physical and financial resources to achieve the objectives of the setting or service.

Examples of leadership functions are as follows:

- providing a clear vision and mission statement
- defining tasks and objectives
- innovating
- setting the focus, purpose and direction
- establishing a positive culture
- motivating
- establishing attitudes, values and behaviours that support the vision and culture
- setting the desired outcomes, goals, targets and performance indicators
- aligning human and financial resources
- strategic planning (together with managers)
- evaluating
- modelling positive leadership attributes
- being an agent for change
- handling crises and uncertainty.

Examples of leadership qualities are as follows:

- being approachable
- being organised
- communicating effectively
- being knowledgeable and sharing knowledge
- having empathy
- being technically competent
- not being arrogant or bossy
- having enthusiasm
- having integrity
- being tough but fair
- having high but realistic expectations
- being tactful and respectful of people
- being innovative and creative
- being solution focused
- being a problem solver
- being able to make decisions.

The effective leader will motivate and encourage other people, equip them to do their job and empower them to give their best. Effective leaders will inspire people to participate fully to achieve the aims and objectives of the setting or service.

Leaders are required not only to set the focus, purpose and direction but also make sure there is an appropriately skilled workforce in place. The workforce will need to be organised in order to be effective and able to do the right things, in the right way, at the right time and in the right place. As well as this, financial planning may be part of their remit and the effective leader will make sure the financial resources are there.

Finally, leadership involves monitoring progress, reporting on outcomes and being accountable to others for the work of the setting or service. This accountability may be wide-ranging – for example, in the private sector, it may be to shareholders or customers; in the public sector, this can include central and local government and ultimately users, such as children and families.

Key term

Strategic leadership/management – this is about the ongoing management of strategy for a setting or service, which involves evaluating and controlling its activity. It is a high-level activity and can cover the development of a mission or vision for the setting or service and what has to be done to fulfil that mission. It takes into account changing circumstances, new technology, new competitors and new economic, social or political environments. This can include developing objectives, marketing, tactics, policies and procedures, assessing risk and setting the framework for meeting regulatory requirements. In a children's service context, the strategic management may be part of the local authority, together with the setting or service head. In the private sector, this will be managed partly by management committees or by owners and will be influenced by shareholders.

Operational management – people who monitor and manage the day-to-day operations of the setting or service.

Team – a team is any group of people organised to work together interdependently and cooperatively to meet the needs of their setting or service by accomplishing its purpose and goals (source: adapted from 'What is a team?': http://humanresources.about.com/od/teambuilding/f/teams_def.htm).

Management

In some settings and services, managers operate at a strategic level. In others, managers have an operational and, in some cases, an administrative function. Management involves working with others in daily systems and processes to ensure high-quality services. Management is often broken down into smaller subtypes of management, such as project management or change management, and these processes can be undertaken by managers with a wider remit. Sometimes individual managers are skilled project managers and this may take up all their time.

General management functions include:

- recruiting and training the workforce
- inducting new staff
- coordinating the workforce
- dealing with discipline and accountability
- handling grievances
- deploying human and financial resources to specific roles and tasks
- forming effective teams
- ensuring everyone does their job to a high standard
- planning to achieve the objectives of the setting or service
- reviewing and adapting policies and practices
- reporting on progress towards objectives
- being accountable to the leader for progress
- managing time effectively for self and others
- using IT and equipment effectively
- setting up, monitoring and updating planning and reporting systems
- setting up, monitoring and ensuring probity of financial systems (e.g. budgets, profit and loss, cash flow)
- giving presentations
- planning and running meetings
- communicating effectively for business purposes (e.g. letters, reports project plans)
- caring for customers
- managing the requirement for a duty of care
- meeting regulatory requirements.

Managers are often thought of as supporting the way things are and not as agents of change. Leader-managers have to cope with both supporting change and maintaining the systems and processes to ensure effective running of the service or setting. This can bring about tensions between the roles and the aims and processes involved.

Case Study Pre-school playgroup

A small rural playgroup has 24 children and six employed practitioners working different shifts. It relies heavily on parents/carers to help meet registration requirements. The person in charge of the pre-school is accountable to a management committee made up of parents and local organisations. The management committee together with the person leading the group, and with input from practitioners and parents, set the vision and mission for the playgroup. The person in charge deals with the curriculum and resources of the setting, the finance and staffing issues and is involved with hands-on work with children on a regular basis.

How helpful are the concepts of leadership and management in this setting? Analyse who is responsible for which aspect of the leadership and management processes.

Leaders and managers

Both leaders and managers will bring their own experiences and knowledge to the situations in which they find themselves. How they lead or manage will depend on circumstances such as:

- their personal values (e.g. how do they feel about their role, about delegating responsibility or about empowering others?)
- their ability to cope with uncertainty
- their confidence in the people they are leading or managing
- their background and training
- their personal 'comfort zone'
- the characteristics of the people being led or managed (e.g. are they new, do they like clear directions or do they prefer to make some decisions for themselves?).

Different theories, models and styles of leadership

There has been much written and researched about leadership, but most agree that, over the last 60 years, there has been a move from a command-and-control type of leadership towards a more flexible way of leading. Leaders operate at different levels. For example, some will lead a small team, whereas others will operate at the strategic level for an organisation, or even a whole country. In terms of services and settings for children and young people, effective leadership is highly valued as it improves outcomes and provides a more stable and consistent basis for services.

Key term

Theories – ideas or propositions, commonly regarded as correct, that can be used as explanations and predictions – for example, Einstein's theory of relativity (based on the definition on Dictionary.com).

Model – a systematic description of a system or process.

Leaders and followers

To be a leader, you are required to have followers, but this does not happen automatically. The best leaders will draw from all of the items in the following list:

- their position in the setting or service
- their personal authority or charisma
- their knowledge.

Followers may not recognise the authority of a leader simply by their position in the organisation. Leaders in settings or services may have formal authority but others may have informal authority or influence. A leader in a setting or service may not have a formal position but may emerge informally as the choice of the group. Leaders may need to have specific knowledge or charisma to ensure they have followers.

Leadership theories and models

It is important to be aware that there are many ideas about leadership and a good deal of research, much of which is overlapping or uses different terms to mean the same or similar things.

It is useful to think of leadership theories as based on either (i) the idea of leaders being task focused, or (ii) the idea of leaders being people/relationship focused. A leader who is task focused, as the term suggests, is focused on the task itself and getting the results required. A leader who is relationship focused is more interested in the people and their welfare, as well as getting the best out of them. Most leaders are somewhere in between. The theories and models below may have a focus on task or person, but each leader will interpret this in the light of their own situation.

As you read about leadership, you will find that the terms 'leadership theory' and 'leadership model' are often used interchangeably. Leadership styles are also confused with theories and models of leadership.

Models are generally based on theories, but it is sometimes difficult to see a clear link, and theories are presented as models, and vice versa. Models will normally derive from one or more theoretical approaches. For example, Adair's (1997) 'action centred' leadership model is a widely used and respected model that draws on different theories – for example, Maslow's hierarchy of needs, motivation theory and personality theory.

The following are examples of different types of leadership theories and models, and are presented as separate items. In practice, settings and services may utilise a combination of approaches based on what is best for them. The aims and values of organisations are also important – for example, a sales organisation might use a transactional theory with tight controls for performance. In children's services, theories and models that emphasise and value people are more likely to be useful.

Naturalistic theories

1 **The great man theory**. This is based on the idea that leaders are born, not made. The theory holds the view that political leaders such as Winston Churchill and military leaders such as Nelson are born with the necessary qualities. Although the great man theory has its roots many centuries ago, when leadership was thought of as a male quality, it still persists today.
2 **Trait theories**. These theories follow on from the 'great man' approach. The theory takes the view that there are certain inborn traits that make people better leaders. It does not explain why some people who also have these traits may not be leaders.

Behavioural theories

Behavioural theories are based on the idea that people can learn to become leaders but are not born that way. They learn through observing other leaders and by being taught leadership skills.

Transactional theory takes the view that leadership is based on a system of rewards and punishments and a clear chain of command. Leaders are in charge and instructions are to be followed, and it is on this basis that employees gain rewards. Here, the rules are more important than the people.

Context or situational theories

These theories are based on the view that the context or situation determines how the leader operates.

Contingency theory is a further development of situational theory. This theory argues that no one leadership theory or style is appropriate for all situations and that leaders have to be versatile and switch their style according to circumstances. This approach is focused on finding the best solution for the circumstances. 'Systems' approaches (see Model 4 below) are often included in this theory.

Transformational leadership theory

This is a theory based on the relationships formed between leaders and followers. Transformational leaders motivate and inspire others to achieve the goals of the setting or service. The focus is on supporting people to have a sense of purpose beyond narrow self-interest. These leaders want each follower to achieve their potential and they focus on supporting the effective performance of individuals.

Models

1 **Participative/democratic leadership models**. These are based on changing the balance of power between leader and follower so they become more equal. Participative models view the input of others to leadership as important. Leaders encourage participation and contributions from group members into decision-making. In this way, there is more 'buy in' at all levels of the service or setting. There is less competition between people and more collaboration when everyone has a chance to input into decisions.
2 **Distributed leadership model**. This is a type of participative/democratic leadership model. Distributed leadership describes when leadership responsibilities are shared across a setting or service. This is often in the form of leadership teams who, although they have different levels of decision-making responsibility according to individual circumstances, are able to influence the overall decisions that are made. For example, head teachers in schools may have overall authority but individual teams can strongly influence decisions and policies for the school. Belbin (2004) and other researchers describe this type of leadership model in detail.
3 **Facilitative leadership model**. This model is linked to transformational leadership. It is designed to facilitate leadership rather than impose decision-making. Facilitative leaders have a genuine interest in the individual and what they have to contribute. They are interested in team members' values and attitudes. Facilitative leaders often coach their team members and demonstrate how to reflect on practice. Such leaders are able to help individuals to see alternative points of view and will encourage debate.
4 **System models**. This type of model is said to operate effectively where there are significant challenges and uncertainties. It shows how a leader's thinking and actions are linked to the larger systemic structures within an organisation. It is an attempt to avoid fragmenting the work of the setting or service. A systems approach would encourage leaders of a team to make sure the team goals and activities fitted in with the whole service. This can be very complex and, if there is lack of trust and poor understanding of the whole service, this can act as a barrier, with individuals feeling undervalued.

Case Study

A successful team working to support children and young people with additional needs has a goal to gain additional funding from a local charitable trust. Gaining this funding could mean other parts of the service that are less successful may lose out. A systems approach to leadership might mean that this goal is not pursued in the light of the needs of the whole service. There is a tension here between an individual team's goals and that of the whole setting or service. This means that setting goals for teams must be carefully thought out to avoid causing conflict and demoralising people.

Adair's action-centred leadership model (1997)

This is an example of a leadership model that is simple to understand yet widely used and helpful for leaders building teams. Adair describes the core roles of leadership as three equal, overlapping and interdependent circles or spheres. The circles represent:

- achieving the task
- building and maintaining the team
- developing the individual.

Adair suggests that, when something significant happens in one of the three circles, it will have consequences in the other two.

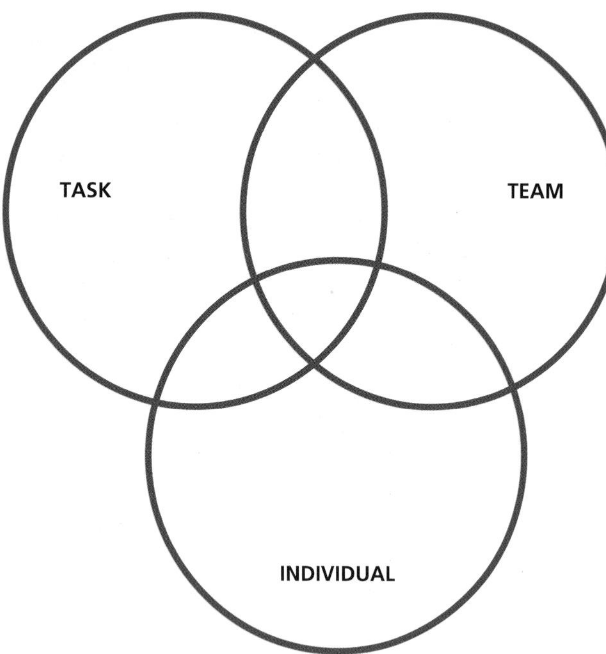

Figure 4.1 Action-centred leadership model

Adair's model suggests that:

- the task needs a team, as one person working alone is not sufficient
- if the team needs are not met, the task will suffer and individual members of the team will not be satisfied
- if individual needs are not met, the team's performance will suffer and achieving the task will be more difficult.

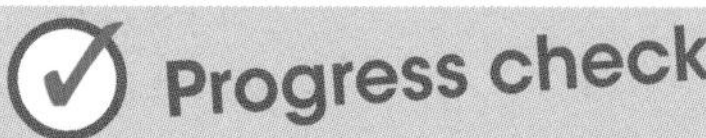

Look at the theories and models of leadership described above. Drawing on your own experience and reading, explain which types of leadership you have seen in action. Explain how your knowledge of theories and models has helped you to make sense of your experience.

Different styles of leadership

For many years, leadership styles have been divided into three main areas, based on the work of Lewin (1939). These are outlined in Table 4.1.

Most leadership styles that are used today fall somewhere into these categories but may combine different styles according to circumstances. In particular, democratic/participative styles are valued as they are seen to be more effective in care and education settings.

Hersey and Blanchard's leadership styles

Hersey and Blanchard (1977) identified four different leadership styles for contrasting situations.

1. **Telling** (high task/low relationship behaviour). This style closely defines goals and focuses on directing workers. It was found to be used particularly with new staff or where work was low-level, time-constrained or repetitive. A danger is that workers are viewed as being unable or unwilling to do a good job.
2. **Selling** (high task/high relationship behaviour). This is sometimes known as the coaching style, where leaders focus on training, counselling and staff development. Most of the direction is given by the leader but there is encouragement for people to 'buy into' the task. This style is more effective when workers are willing to work but lack the required skills or maturity.
3. **Participating** (high relationship/low task behaviour). In this style, decision-making is shared between leaders and workers and the role of the leader is to facilitate. The style involves high support and low direction and is used when workers are skilled and able but have other issues (e.g. they may lack confidence or be inexperienced).
4. **Delegating** (low relationship/low task behaviour). Here the leader identifies the task but the responsibility for carrying it out is given to workers. This style is most effective when the workers are competent, motivated and experienced.

Other leadership styles

Paternalistic style

This is where leaders make decisions in the best interests of their workers usually after consultation. It is more motivating than the autocratic style as it usually involves some two-way communication and

Leadership style	Key features	Comment
Autocratic	Provides clear expectations of the task, including what, where, when and how to do it. Decisions are made by the leader. Sometimes called a 'top down' or 'command and control' style.	Can be over controlling and dictatorial, not listening to workers. More difficult to move from this style to a democratic style. This style is less creative than others and is often used when leader has greater knowledge or time is short. It can be demotivating. Transactional leaders often fall into this category.
Democratic or participative	Thought of as the most effective style. Leaders offer guidance and encouragement. They participate in work with the group. Group members are given the opportunity to input into leadership but final decision usually rests with leader. The style is facilitative and encourages others to take decisions.	Respectful approach. Group may be less productive but input is usually of higher quality. Group members are usually more engaged, motivated and creative. Style is motivating but mistakes can be made if workers are not experienced or knowledgeable to take decisions. Group decision-making does not always work well.
Laissez-faire or delegated	This style is the least effective. Leaders offer little guidance and leave decision-making to group members.	Style can be useful where there is a high level of expertise in the group but can lead to poor motivation and lack of clarity about roles. This style leads to less cooperation and independent working. Leaders may not know what is going on in their area of responsibility. If they are completely indifferent, this may indicate they do not really care about the organisation.

Table 4.1 Leadership styles

workers feel their needs are being met. This style does slow down decision-making, though, and is still rather autocratic.

Pace-setting style

This is a leadership style where managers lead by example and are role models for their workers. Managers set high standards of personal performance that they then expect workers to copy. It is possible for workers to feel overwhelmed by this style as they may feel they will never achieve the standards.

Toxic leadership styles

Sometimes leaders who may be abusive or leave a service or setting in a worse state than when they arrived are called 'toxic leaders' (Whicker 1996). There are many styles of leadership that could come into this category, such as 'narcissistic', which tends to describe leaders who are egotistic, vain or conceited. Damage can also be done by leaders who are insecure or overambitious or have poor social and interpersonal skills.

Moral leadership styles

Leaders may be driven by a strong moral code, such as caring for the environment or religious beliefs. Moral leaders emphasise the importance of values in leadership and the ethical justification for actions taken. Some leaders lead by allowing their actions to speak louder than their words (i.e. lead from behind, not in front). This type of leader may give credit to other people rather than taking it themselves but will take the blame if things go wrong. They are focused on seeing the organisation succeed.

Case Study

The children and young people in an out-of-school club are encouraged to share and cooperate in an atmosphere of mutual respect and trust. The leader/manager of the group has recently left and has been replaced. The new manager is instituting a range of formal measures to increase the scope of the setting and to make it self-financing. She has called a meeting and informed the staff of the changes that are to be made. It includes rotas, deployment and a review of policies and procedures, which she is getting external help to do.

What pressures might the new leader/manager be experiencing? How might the staff be feeling? What style of leadership is being imposed? Discuss how the leader/manager might change her style to be more open?

Reflective practice

Describe one or more occasions when you have been involved in leadership or have undertaken a leadership initiative. Reflect on:

- what you did
- how you did it
- how successful it was
- what you learned from it.

Different theories, models and styles of management

Theories, models and styles of management are often confused and there are many of them. This section covers just a selection of approaches as management studies is a huge and growing area of work. It is important to remember from earlier in the chapter that, although managers may also have a leadership role, management as a set of processes is distinct. Management skills will vary according to the level in a service or setting. For example, a room supervisor in a nursery will need technical skills, such as caring for and educating babies and young children, and 'people' skills for managing a small team. The owner of a nursery chain may need strategic management skills and commercial and financial skills, as well as people skills. They may not need technical skills in caring for children. There are different levels of management depending on the size of the service or setting and how it is organised. Some organisations are 'flat', with very few layers of management between the senior manager/s and the rest of the workforce. Others are more hierarchical, with several layers of management that tend to form a pyramid structure. This is where senior management is at the top of the pyramid, followed by layers underneath, each having progressively less power and authority.

For example:

Supervisor – this is usually the lowest level or most junior management position. The authority of a supervisor will depend on the setting or service. A supervisor is usually responsible for the day-to-day performance of a small group or team. They are usually experienced in the work being undertaken but may not have any special skills. Supervisors will guide and support people to achieve the goals of the setting or service and recommend changes to more senior staff.

Middle manager – middle managers are normally responsible for seeing that senior management decisions are implemented. They may be project managers for specific projects and can often have the power to hire or fire people. Often it is this layer of management that is the first to go if a company is downsizing.

Senior manager – this level of manager can be at the top of a setting or service, or there may be additional levels above. They have major responsibilities for the success of the service or setting. Some settings or services have several senior managers reporting to a chief executive officer (CEO). Senior managers normally have middle managers or supervisors reporting to them. Senior managers are responsible for planning, directing, monitoring and controlling people and their work.

Management theories

Scientific management theory

This theory was first introduced by Taylor (1911). It argued for a move away from personal and individual management styles to a more 'scientific' approach. He felt this would be fairer to workers who had suffered under the industrial revolution and would lead to better relations between workers and managers. The scientific approach involved breaking down tasks into small subtasks and making sure the subtask was undertaken in the 'one best way' set by the management. This approach led to more efficiency in industry. Whilst breaking down tasks was useful, it also led to a more negative 'stop watch' approach, which 'dehumanised' the workforce. This approach still operates today, especially in industry.

Command and control (Fayol 1916)

This is the classical school of management, which emphasises command and control. Fayol suggested that the functions of management are fivefold – planning, organising, commanding, coordinating and controlling. His theory is further detailed in his 14 principles of management. His writing was not translated into English until 1949.

Human relations theory (Mayo 1933)

This theory disproved scientific management theory and took the view that taking into account human needs was important. It was based on the 'Hawthorne work experiments', which found that the social dynamics of the work team was more important for productivity than the 'one best way'. Human relations theory supported the value of teamwork and allowed workers to make changes to the way they did things to avoid boredom. This approach is still used today in areas such as 'quality circles', team-building activities and participatory management.

Bureaucracy (Weber)

Max Weber emphasised the idea of an ideal bureaucracy that would work towards its goals in the most efficient manner. A bureaucracy is based on a pyramid structure – that is, a hierarchical chain of command with layers of management. This is the basis of many big organisations, such as parts of the civil service and in some settings and services for children and young people. Weber felt that, in an ideal bureaucracy, decisions are made based on rules, regulations and relations.

Weber warned that bureaucracies would depersonalise people and, in doing so, get rid of human feelings and emotions. He felt that each human being would feel like a cog in a wheel, only interested in becoming a bigger cog. This is something bureaucracies have to try to avoid.

Maslow's theory (1943)

Maslow's hierarchy of needs is well known. It is often presented as a diagram but is listed in the text below. The first level of need must be met before people can progress to the next level, and so forth. In terms of management, it is not until the first four levels of need are met that creativity and potential are really released.

1. Physiological – such as hunger, thirst, shelter and sleep.
2. Safety – security, stability and freedom from attack.
3. Love and belonging – friends, family, partners, identification.
4. Esteem – success, self-respect, mastery, achievement.
5. Self-actualisation – self-fulfilment, realisation of potential, creativity.

Drucker (1954)

Drucker thought of management as more than an activity undertaken by a class of people. He thought of it as a discipline that could be taught and studied. He introduced many new concepts into management theory. His work is still influential today and forms the basis of commonly found approaches to management (e.g. management by setting objectives). His theory emphasised five key management concepts:

1. Setting objectives
2. Organising
3. Motivating and communicating
4. Establishing measurements of performance
5. Developing people.

Senge (1990)

Senge's theory introduced the idea of the 'learning organisation', which is popular in modern management, although difficult to achieve in a world of 'quick fixes'. This theory emphasises the need for modern organisations to be flexible and able to adapt and survive. Organisations need to have the commitment of all their employees in order to perform well and to continue to be creative. Senge identified five basic disciplines that must be incorporated into management in order for the organisation to succeed:

1 Systems thinking: the ability to see the whole, rather than focusing on the individual parts.
2 Personal mastery: the ability to be in 'a continual learning mode'. Here individuals are not afraid to admit they do not know something but are willing to continually learn.
3 Mental models: understanding that individuals have assumptions that influence how they understand the world and how they take action.
4 Building shared vision: a real vision that encourages people to excel and learn because they want to.
5 Team learning: because people need to be able to act together and learn from each other in order to achieve maximum creativity and innovation.

Key term

Emotional intelligence (EI) – emotional intelligence describes an ability to understand and recognise your own and others' feelings and be able to manage feelings appropriately. Emotionally intelligent people respond appropriately to other people's emotions and can use their feelings to motivate, plan and achieve.

Soft skills

Although not strictly a model of management, knowing about 'soft' and 'hard' skills helps to see why management is changing. Soft skills in management are increasingly recognised as important in helping the setting or service to achieve its goals. Soft skills are linked to 'emotional intelligence' and interpersonal skills, but where this is an area of difficulty for managers, appropriate training and practice can develop effective soft skills. The difficulties of doing this should not be underestimated, as behaviour patterns are hard to change. Managers who have to change their style may find they revert to their old ways if there is not appropriate support. Systems such as 360-degree feedback are sometimes helpful. This involves providing managers with feedback from all involved in their work, including the people they manage and others, such as parents and children and young people.

Soft skills include:

- communicating (face to face, electronic, written, telephone)
- listening
- building relationships
- networking
- teamwork
- negotiating
- team building
- flexibility
- coping well with stress and pressure
- time management
- having a positive work ethic
- motivating
- delegating
- influencing
- presenting
- facilitating
- mentoring and coaching
- empathy
- assertiveness
- conflict management
- creative thinking
- managing difference and diversity
- problem solving
- being solution focused.

Other skills, sometimes known as 'hard skills', relate to the technical aspects of the job and include:

- technical skills, such as the use of software
- understanding company procedures
- handling finance
- administration

- decision-making
- managing information
- business skills.

Managers today need to have both hard and soft skills.

Progress check

Write a person specification for a manager of a childcare service – that is, a list of everything you would need to see in a future manager, such as their qualifications and personal attributes. Check whether you have included both soft and hard skills.

Team management

When discussing leadership earlier in the chapter, we considered the idea of leading teams. This section builds on that earlier material but focuses more on team management. The two sections do, however, overlap and should be considered together. Teams are very important in settings and services that work with children, young people and families. A team is a group of people coming together to collaborate in order to reach a shared goal or task, for which they are accountable to one another as well as to others. Teams can be two or more people – for example, in a children's centre with responsibility for an age range (e.g. a baby room). They can also be management teams, placement teams, outreach teams, multidisciplinary or inter-agency teams, special needs teams, integrated teams, and so forth. Teams make best use of human resources as ideally each member is committed to the other members.

Tuckman (1965)

Tuckman explained how groups come together for a particular purpose and move through stages of development to achieve their purpose. It is a well-known model and widely used by for people responsible for building teams.

The five stages are:

- forming
- storming
- norming
- performing
- adjourning.

Stage	What happens
Forming	People come together for the first time and the group is formal. The interaction is between the leader and the group members.
Storming	Individuals assess what is in it for them. Reactions to other group members are being formed and decisions about whose ideas will dominate. The group argues in order to establish position.
Norming	Teams begin to have a clear purpose and members begin to see what is in it for them. Agreement is reached about the team purpose and who does what and how.
Performing	Members now put the team ahead of themselves to make sure they perform well and deliver what is required. Members listen to and assist each other.
Adjourning	This is the stage of winding up the team and starting afresh. It is based on the recognition that teams have a 'life' beyond which they may become complacent. Teams may need support as they experience a sense of loss and face up to change.

Table 4.2 Tuckman's five stages of team development

This model has become a blueprint for how teams develop and helps managers understand how to lead the team at particular stages of development.

Belbin (1981, new edition 1996)

Belbin set out to establish how to make a good team and identified roles which contribute to teams becoming effective and doing what is required of them. He identified eight team roles, set out in Table 4.3. Belbin found that all the roles need to be present to make an effective team and are as important as technical skills or previous experience. Sometimes team members undertake more than

Role	Description	Potential difficulty
Plant	Innovator, ideas person, creative, unorthodox, knowledgeable and imaginative	Can be individualistic, disregarding protocol and rules
Resource investigator	Extrovert, enthusiast, communicator with contacts outside team, likes new ideas and responds well to challenge, energetic	Can be lazy unless under pressure, quickly loses interest
Chairman	Calm, self-confident, decisive, social leader of team, guides and keeps people involved	Not likely to be creative or have great intellect
Shaper	Energetic, highly strung, concerned to get things done, challenges and opposes inertia and complacency in team	Can be abrasive, impatient and short-tempered
Monitor evaluator	Unemotional, hard-headed, careful/prudent, usually very able thinker, takes time but is good at assessing and monitoring progress, rarely wrong	Can be cold and distant, unlikely to motivate others
Team worker	Sensitive to others, good at networking and setting up support outside team activities	Concern for team and team spirit may lead to job not being completed
Company worker	Organiser who turns the plans into tasks, conservative, hard-working with common sense, methodical	May lack flexibility and be resistant to change
Completer finisher	Ensures team delivers, orderly and careful, good at follow-up and meeting deadlines, ensures team maintains a sense of urgency	Anxious perfectionist who worries about team and delivery

Table 4.3 Belbin's team roles

one role, so the model can work even in a small team. The model works best when used openly in a setting or service and where workers in specific roles are recognised. In practice, managers need to apply the model flexibly as roles may overlap and there may be situations where workers only lean towards some roles (i.e. they are not fixed in concrete).

Learning styles

The concept of learning styles is popular today and there are a variety of models used. There is more about learning styles as applied to children and young people in Chapter 8. Understanding learning styles is not limited to knowing how people learn but is applied in slightly different ways in management. The work of Kolb (1984) on experiential learning and Honey and Mumford (1986, 2000) led to questionnaires, manuals and systems being developed to help ascertain a person's learning style.

There are four commonly recognised learning styles in management:

- **Activists**: those who like to immerse themselves fully in new experiences and who act first and consider consequences later.
- **Reflectors**: those who like to stand back and observe and who tend to be cautious until they have all the facts.
- **Theorists**: those who like to think through problems in a logical manner and are keen on basic assumptions, principles, theories, models and systems thinking.
- **Pragmatists**: those who like to put theories into practice and who are impatient with long-winded discussion.

Managers who understand their own learning style and that of their team are more able to meet the needs of the team. They will ensure the team's strengths are utilised and avoid placing people in the jobs they find less rewarding or more difficult to achieve.

If you want to find out more about learning styles, there is a mass of information on the internet. For example, see www.open2.net/survey/learningstyles.

Team building

There are many examples of theories and approaches to team building that you can investigate further. For example:

- **Myers–Briggs type indicator**. This looks at key features of individuals, such as extroversion/introversion, thinkers/feelers, and so forth. It is designed to help people understand themselves and others within their team.
- **Social identity theory**. This looks at how individuals define themselves in terms of their group identity.

Change management

There are several models of change management because, in today's world, constant change is part of a manager's territory. Recognising that change is stressful and potentially damaging to a service or setting is important. It is not enough to impose change from above as this can lead to low morale and conflict. Managers need to make sure that the workforce is fully involved and understands the reasons for change and the possible impact this will have on them. This all takes time and managers have to build in sufficient time during the planning stage. If workers need new skills, the manager will need to give training choices and opportunities.

Lewin's change management model (1958) still applies today and provides the basis for more up-to-date variations. It recognises that change is difficult but that acceptance takes place in stages. His three-stage model uses the analogy of a block of ice and is known as 'unfreeze–change (move)–refreeze'. Unfreezing is the most stressful – the process of melting the ice, which means preparing the setting or service for change. This means explaining to the workforce why things have to change and tackling entrenched ideas and ways of working. It is useful to have arguments that support the need for change, such as the declining use of the service or setting, which is threatening its survival, or increased demands being met by competitors. The second stage is the actual period of change. It is the stage when the workforce begins to accept the change and sees benefits for themselves. Managers will need to recognise that this takes time and build in time for doubts and concerns to be discussed.

Refreezing is the third stage, where the changes become an established part of the setting or service and stability returns. Training may be needed at this stage, or earlier, and feedback systems should be put into place.

Case Study

In a day nursery, the manager comes in one day and calls a staff meeting after the children have left. At the meeting, the staff are told they will be extending the hours of the nursery to provide a wider range of services across an extended age range. This will enlarge the nursery by one-third and is to happen in two months' time. Staff are told that the rotas have been worked out to make sure everyone is treated fairly.

Comment on the way this big change has been introduced. How do you feel the staff might be feeling? Develop a plan covering the steps that should be taken by managers wishing to introduce this change.

Project management

Project management usually refers to managing a temporary or short-term activity with a defined beginning and end. There are usually specific outcomes that are required – for example, a project to consult young people on the use of playing fields, or projects to consider the impact of lower funding for children's centres. There is a mass of software available for project planning and management (e.g. PRINCE2, Microsoft Project or MacProject). Project management demands some of the same skills as more general management but additional skills are sometimes required, such as the ability to use software effectively or to apply for funding for specific projects. Negotiation skills are important for all managers but project managers whose project may seem to others in a service to be insignificant sometimes have to work hard and exercise leadership to persuade, inspire and involve others.

Performance management

Performance management systems are widely used in settings and services today. Systems can cover both individuals and team performance, for all levels of staff, from the lowest to the highest. Performance management is conducted in different ways in different organisations and is part of the overall way an organisation aims to achieve its goals. Properly implemented, it can be used as a tool to support people and enhance their contribution. Managers and supervisors undertaking performance appraisals need to be well trained and understand the goals of the organisation. Performance management normally follows a cycle similar to that shown in Figure 4.2.

For individual team members, performance management can take the form of an annual or more frequent appraisal interview where their performance is discussed and individual goals are agreed and included in a set of performance goals/targets. These should be kept as simple as possible. It is useful to use a standard pro forma to formally record the agreements. Verbal feedback and agreements should not be used. New staff may require frequent performance interviews. Targets should be agreed between the manager and individual team members and, where necessary, negotiated with the help of others. The annual interview should be backed up by regular support meetings and informal feedback so that it does not contain any surprises.

To work effectively, individuals must:

- have agreed job descriptions
- agree and set objectives that enable them to clearly understand the outcomes and goals they need to meet and the timescales for meeting them
- agree the tools, resources, training needs and other support they can expect in order for them to do the job

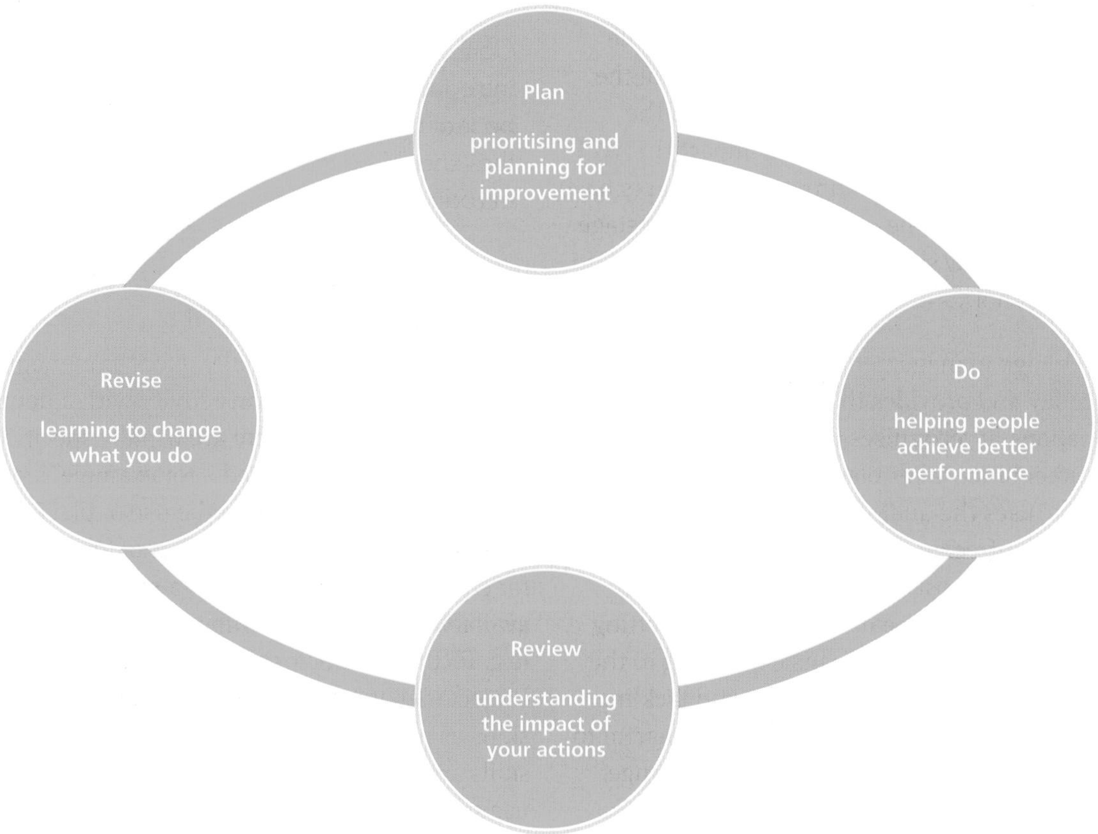

Figure 4.2 Planning and performance cycle

- understand how their performance will be measured and when appraisals will take place
- understand what is in it for them – for example, promotion, recognition, better pay.

There are difficulties in linking good performance solely to pay and conditions as these rewards may not be possible. Many people gain enormous satisfaction from their own personal achievement and this should be encouraged. Other forms of rewards may be helpful, such as training and development, away days, health club membership and time out.

By carrying out realistic and sensitive appraisals of performance and by setting SMART objectives (see Chapter 5), managers can help individuals to focus on what can be achieved, as well as provide a fair measure of progress. Equally, managers can demotivate by conducting hostile, unfair and damaging performance appraisals.

Management styles

The information on leadership styles is applicable to this section on management styles, so please see the earlier information on pages 128–9. Although the management styles described below can apply to leaders, they may be more relevant to managers. Remember, most managers will use more than one style of management.

Affiliative leadership and management style

This relates closely to the democratic leadership style and is intended to create positive feelings of harmony in the setting or service. It depends on creating an emotional bond between managers and workers and between workers. This can be successful but there are concerns that too much familiarity can cause lack of respect and possible conflict.

Bureaucratic style

This is a style used by managers who like rules and work to them. These managers will expect everything to be done according to the rules, policies and procedures. This management style can stifle creativity and become harsh and unfeeling. Managers who use this style may lack confidence and derive their authority from the rules, not by relying on or using their own skills and attributes.

Defensive management style

This is a negative management style that is the hallmark of a blame culture. Managers using this style are often harsh and blame others for the failure of their management. This style demotivates and leads to lack of trust.

Progress check

Taking into account all the leadership and management styles you have covered, which do you feel is the most desirable/undesirable? Give reasons for your answers.

Activity

In any area of your life, think about the managers you have encountered. What management styles have you seen in operation? What has been the impact of the different management styles you have experienced?

How different theories, models and styles of leadership and management can be applied to different situations

Leaders and managers often have to vary their management style according to the situation they encounter. If they are not able to do this, they will find it more difficult to achieve the aims of the setting or service. Earlier in the chapter, we looked at context or situational theories of leadership, which are about finding the best solution for the situation. It is from this theoretical perspective that this section is written.

Examples of common situations that require different responses from managers and leaders are outlined in Table 4.4.

Situation	Leadership and management implications
Experienced and confident workers	Where workers are knowledgeable and experienced, value their independence, are committed to the goals of the organisation and enjoy taking responsibility, managers may use a fully participative style. If the conditions are less favourable, leaders/managers may use a more autocratic style.
New workers	More 'telling' is involved (i.e. direct management). High-quality induction is important, as is closer monitoring and feedback. There is often a less participative management style until the manager knows the new worker and a level of mutual trust is established.
Not achieving goals	Leader and manager may have to explore different approaches based on the underlying reasons. They first need to discuss sensitively why the team or individual is not achieving. If there are genuine difficulties that can be sorted out, adequate support or training may be sufficient. If worker/s are not supporting their team and the goals of the setting or service, this may require a more autocratic style of leadership.
Changes to the setting or service	Change management is an area in its own right. Change should not be imposed without adequate time, explanation and support. Managers need to recognise that the workforce will be going through the stages of change and be aware of their needs.
Conflict	This depends on the degree of conflict and who is involved. Where managers are in conflict situations with workers, this may need external help and support. Managers should not just close down and become autocratic or opt out from their responsibilities. Neither approach will work. If workers are in conflict, managers will need to draw on their 'soft skills' (i.e. negotiation, persuasion, communication), as well as their 'hard skills'. Hard skills may involve applying human resources' policies and procedures rigorously.
New team	Leaders/managers will need to recognise the stages of team formation and development (Tuckman, Belbin) and make sure this is supported and fair.

Table 4.4 Common situations and leadership/management responses

Case Study

A leader/manager of a day care centre has expanded its services to include outreach work and has recruited six new workers to add to its existing 12. At the same time, one of the key middle managers has gone on maternity leave and another has resigned. One of these posts has been replaced temporarily from the pool of new workers and another has been advertised internally. There is a good deal of tension and uncertainty in the work team and the normal participative, democratic management style is not working. Sickness rates have risen and workers are openly expressing their lack of confidence in the future.

How is the existing team likely to be feeling and what are their support needs? How should change be managed in this situation? How might leaders and managers need to adjust their normal style to cope with the current situation?

Section 2: The skill sets required to be an effective leader and/or manager

Already in this chapter, we have looked at the features that provide an indication of effective leadership and management. This section considers these in more detail. What is clear is that, to be effective, leaders and managers must be flexible and able to assess situations and apply a range of models and styles to meet a range of needs. Needs can be focused on themselves (i.e. their needs as leaders/managers), the needs of the workforce or the needs of the situation in the setting or service.

Attributes that contribute to success as a leader or manager

Being able to inspire and motivate others

This has already been discussed earlier but enthusiasm, knowledge and technical competence help leaders to lead and managers to manage effectively. Individual leaders' and managers' styles will vary, but to inspire confidence in other people and to encourage them to share the aims and goals of the setting or service are critical. Effective leaders are often described as tough but fair and able to be decisive and take action. Personal integrity is also important as people need to be able to trust leaders and to model their behaviour and attitudes. Effective leaders and managers in children's services need to work within an ethical framework and issues such as social responsibility, sustainability and values will form part of their role.

Activity

Think of leaders you have worked with at different times. What sort of leadership styles have you observed? What attributes have you seen in leaders you admire? Do you have experience of leaders whose style was not helpful? Describe this experience while maintaining confidentiality.

Being a good communicator

Communication includes, speaking, listening, reading and writing. They are all important but often in a busy environment it is listening that suffers. Practise active listening, which focuses on the other person without distraction, including, for example, maintaining eye contact and not glancing at your watch. Using active listening enables you to:

- hear what is being communicated
- check understanding through questioning and clarification
- pick up on key ideas
- recognise non-verbal communication
- provide feedback
- provide a response
- focus on content, not how the message is delivered (e.g. repetition).

Remember, if you are only partly listening, you will not hear what is really being communicated. The other person will cut short their attempts to give you a full picture. Pretending to listen is not helpful as this may lead the other person to believe you are agreeing to something when all you are doing is nodding or making encouraging noises, but not really hearing. If you are aware that you are not an effective listener, do something about it – for example, role play, discussion exercises.

Activity

Are you a good communicator, especially a good listener? Check your communication skills. Find out if people can understand you clearly by getting them to feed back. Apply this to written, telephone, electronic or spoken communication.

Test out your listening skills – get feedback from others by asking them the questions below. Speak to people close to you who you can trust. If you do not want to be challenged and possibly offended, answer the following questions yourself, honestly.

Do I talk more than listen?

Do I interrupt too much?

Am I often distracted?

Do I try to solve your problems?

Do I finish your sentences?

Do I jump to conclusions too quickly?

Do you often sense I am not listening?

Do I try to do other things at the same time as trying to listen?

Being able to build trust

Building trust is a key area of leadership and management. This involves taking time to get to know people, respecting them and treating them as though they are trustworthy. A setting or service that is secretive and hides information from some and not others discourages trust. Building trust means treating people with respect and valuing them. Valuing equality and diversity also builds trust as people feel they are important and their differences are a positive asset not a barrier. It is important for leaders and managers to be approachable and to be empathetic with the people they lead. Leaders and managers need to be seen to treat people fairly and equally, being responsive to their individual needs, strengths and weaknesses. Arrogance and bossiness will not get the best out of people.

Being able to encourage, manage and support change

Change is a key feature of modern society. Settings and services that cannot change, adapt and update will not succeed. Leaders and managers need to understand the change management process and plan for it when introducing change. Change may not be for commercial reasons but, for example, to take on board new evidence of good practice, changes in government policy or changes in ownership.

Measuring what matters

This is a phrase often heard in management. Services and settings need to measure what is important, not concentrate on things that are easy to measure. Everyone in the setting or service needs to know what constitutes success – in children and young people's services, what matters is outcomes for children and families, and everything else flows from that. For example, staff retention rates can easily be measured and, although important to the individual concerned, the main issue for the service is how this will directly affect children's experience – that is, too much change upsetting their attachment to key people. It may also indicate wider problems within the setting or service, which may have a knock-on effect on outcomes for children. For example, if people feel undervalued, they will seek to move elsewhere.

Managers and leaders should expect to have their performance managed in a similar way to the people they manage. It is normal today to have performance indicators and targets. This is covered in more detail later.

Other issues that need careful measurement will include financial probity where public or private money is concerned. Meeting regulatory requirements is also a key focus for managers, but this should never be an end in itself. Regulatory requirements are normally based on minimum standards and provide a baseline on which to build a high-quality setting or service.

Being able to motivate others

This is an important attribute for leaders and managers and is covered in Section 2.3 (see pages 126–7).

Being able to train and develop others

An important role for leaders and managers is to train and develop others. Instead of feeling threatened by other people's success, effective leaders will always seek to improve the skill base of their workforce and help them to do their jobs well. Understanding training needs in relation to the needs of the setting or service and to meet the aspirations of the workforce is an important attribute. Leaders and managers who coach their workforce use a leadership style that empowers people to reach their potential. Coaching is a term that is changing but usually involves confidential one-to-one conversations with individuals about their goals or aspects of the work that they wish to develop. It may include looking at how they impact on other people, respond to situations, take personal responsibility and learn from their experience. Coaching can improve performance and enhance job satisfaction.

In some circumstances, mentoring is another feature of effective leaders and managers. Mentors are professional colleagues with experience who can help you assess your training and professional development needs. However, not all leaders and managers can be mentors and not all mentors are leaders and managers. Mentoring is most effective with participative, democratic leaders and managers who take on the role of 'a wise and trusted professional friend'. Mentoring from a senior colleague can really help people to make good decisions about professional development.

Being able to assure quality

Quality assurance is designed to make sure settings and services are doing the right things in the right way, whereas quality control is designed to check whether the results of actions taken are producing the expected results. These functions and processes are both formal and informal. There are formally recognised quality assurance schemes, as well as informal quality processes. Before leaders and managers can implement quality procedures, they need to be clear about what constitutes high quality in the setting or service and aspire to it.

Reflective practice

List your activities for a day when you are in the work setting. Identify the attributes or skills you used. Did any of these involve leadership or management? Did any involve influencing other people's behaviour or attitudes?

The importance of encouraging others to take the lead and the ways that this can be achieved

Already in this chapter, we have looked at types of leadership and management that will support democratic decision-making. This is said to be important as shared decision-making leads to greater commitment to the goals of the setting or service and greater job satisfaction and empowers people to move forward. Command and control models of management are no longer seen as producing the best outcomes.

Ways of encouraging others to take the lead can include:

- staff meetings and shared decisions
- building self-worth and confidence
- specifically delegating leadership and management activity and decisions
- additional training opportunities
- coaching and mentoring systems
- effective performance management systems
- reward systems, such as promotion and/or improved pay and conditions
- providing choices
- support in managing and assessing risk
- giving dedicated time to individuals to encourage and support
- following up and providing feedback.

In order to take the lead, most people need to feel confident in their abilities and to feel that management are behind them and will support them. Additional training needs must also be recognised. People may need a good deal of 'hand holding' to start with, but success builds on success. In many cases, managers or leaders can specifically delegate responsibilities to people in their team. This is often more effective in increasing engagement as it demonstrates to the person and to others that the individual is valued and trusted.

People who feel powerless and have low self-esteem are less likely to want to lead, so leaders and managers should work on raising self-esteem through positive reinforcement – that is, praise and rewards based on realistic appraisals. Increasing responsibility in a carefully managed way is also effective as it allows people to test their abilities and to achieve beyond their expectations.

Case Study

Miranda is a nursery assistant who has recently achieved a Level 3 qualification. She has several years' experience and has been asked to take responsibility for four-year-olds in the nursery and to improve the liaison with local schools in preparation for the children to move on. Miranda is overwhelmed by the new responsibilities outlined to her and asks her manager for help and advice. Her manager suggests that the new responsibilities are phased in so she has three months to familiarise herself with the work with four-year-olds and can make some visits to local schools with another member of staff. Miranda is also offered some

Case Study (cont.)

training for working with children who are moving towards the end of the EYFS.

Outline the ways in which the manager is supporting Miranda and suggest additional support that may help her to take on the new role.

How to encourage, motivate and support individuals to achieve

The information in earlier sections and above also relates to this section. Encouraging, motivating and supporting people to achieve is an important part of a leader's or manager's role. Effective leaders and managers know that employment in children's and young people's services is normally undertaken by people who have a 'heart' for the work and want to make a difference to the lives of children, young people and families. Leaders and managers should have high but realistic expectations of people who work for them. Low expectations can become a 'self-fulfilling prophecy' for the workforce. This can be on an individual or a team level. If not much is expected, the message is that the people involved cannot be trusted, cannot succeed or cannot achieve at a higher level than their current position. It is demotivating and depressing and will directly impact on outcomes for children and young people as they will encounter people who have no real enthusiasm for their work. Taking a 'one size fits all' approach to encouraging, supporting and motivating is also unlikely to work as individual needs must be met and personal contributions valued.

Motivating people is at the heart of effective leadership and management. People need recognition and to be valued and many organisations provide the opposite. Managers who try to control people can produce a dependent culture and high levels of passivity. This stifles creativity, new ideas and energy, which can benefit the setting or service. This can lead to:

- higher levels of absence
- high staff turnover
- passivity and indifference, which can spill over into relationships with other colleagues or with children and families
- gossip and moaning.

Understanding human motivation is a science in itself. People have different motives and their motives change over time. Motivation can be internal to them, which means that a person gets satisfaction from the task itself (i.e. seeing a job well done for the satisfaction that brings, and not for an external reward). People who are motivated in this way gain a sense of personal pleasure in achievement, especially of appropriately challenging tasks. This motivation will not last if the tasks are clearly impossible or beyond their expertise, or if they become bored or are put under excessive pressure.

External motivation is where people need an external reward to keep them going. A person who is extrinsically motivated may or may not like what they are doing but will continue for the reward. For children and young people, this reward may be a good grade in a subject they do not like or a reward sticker for a child who sits still. For adults, the rewards can be money, status or other things.

Adair (1987) introduced the idea of the 50:50 rule, in which he suggests that half a person's motivation is from within and half is from the external environment. He suggests that an important factor influencing external motivation is the quality of the leadership they encounter.

Adair suggests that there are eight rules for motivating people:

- be motivated yourself
- select motivated people
- treat each person as an individual
- set realistic but challenging targets
- understand that progress itself motivates
- create a motivating environment
- provide relevant rewards
- recognise success.

One of the most motivating factors for people is to work for someone who is themselves enthusiastic and knowledgeable about their work, someone who can inspire and encourage success in meeting the aims and goals of the setting or service. This has been discussed throughout the chapter and the qualities in a leader or manager have been explored.

People are motivated by different things. For example, some are motivated by money, whereas others may need constant challenge or warm, approving relationships. Managers and leaders need to find out what motivates their staff and build on this as meeting people's needs is as important as meeting setting or service needs. This is difficult for some people to recognise but the ultimate goal of better outcomes for children may depend, at least in part, on meeting the needs of the workforce.

Performance management can be an effective way of motivating and building up people to take on more responsibility and, therefore, increase their sense of achievement.

Case Study

A children's centre leadership and management team has decided to look at its own performance. They have drawn up a list of important areas to consider. These include ensuring that:

- the focus, goals and objectives of the centre are clear
- the culture of the centre is positive and constructive
- staff morale is high (e.g. there is a low staff turnover)
- practitioners are active and engaged
- outcomes for children are being met
- children, parents and carers are involved and participate
- policies and procedures are adhered to and effective
- practitioners are appropriately skilled and experienced
- there is a learning and reflective culture.

Develop brief notes on each of the above, saying why these are important features.

Progress check

What opportunities do you have in your life to exercise leadership? What skills and behaviours do you need to develop to develop leadership potential?

Section 3: How to create a sense of common purpose for team working

A group of people is not necessarily a team. Being a team requires more than simply working together or alongside each other. A team is a group of people working interdependently towards a common purpose. In an effective team, members have a commitment to each other and their work together is greater than the sum of its parts. Team members should have a chance to contribute, coach and mentor, learn from and work with other members. Teams work best when they have a shared sense of ownership of the task and a clear sense of purpose.

How to communicate a common goal within the work environment

Working together towards a common goal can be a powerful way of building teams and developing commitment to the aims of the setting or service. Team cohesion and having shared, common goals is closely linked to how well the team performs. It can make the difference between being a real team or simply a group of people working on the same project or in the same department. There is more about the theory behind effective teamwork earlier in the chapter (Tuckman, Belbin). Teams are all different and are composed of human beings with different needs and behaviours. As teams get to know one another, they may move from a fairly superficial way of working together to something deeper, based on shared experience and understanding. It is the deeper differences that may take a while to become exposed but dealing with them leads to greater commitment and shared goals. The manager's role in communicating a team vision or common goals will vary according to the circumstances and individuals, but it is in part to inform and facilitate a positive working environment, to set clear expectations and responsibilities and to let the team do their job.

Communicating common goals also means communicating the values of the setting, such as being inclusive and encouraging participation. To communicate this effectively, leaders and managers must be clear about the goals themselves before working with others. If they are not clear, this can sow seeds of confusion and doubt in people working for them. In many cases, the goals themselves may have been agreed in the work environment through a process of consultation, listening and sharing between colleagues and managers and with the participation of children, young people and families. Common goals may also involve people from outside the setting or service who have responsibility for outcomes for children, young people and families. There are many ways of communicating a common goal and some are outlined below.

Ethos of the setting or service

The general ethos of the setting or service can communicate its values and goals to both staff members/colleagues and service users, such as children, young people, carers and families. For example, a friendly and helpful welcome when people come into the setting or when they phone can communicate the goals of the setting, which may include providing support to families or reaching out into the community. The ethos of the setting should normally be inclusive and not create barriers to participation. Information should be easily available in a form that everyone can access. Sometimes this means providing forms and leaflets in different languages or using visual information, such as pictures and diagrams. The ethos of the setting or service can also indicate the standard or quality of service expected.

Effective teams

Teams that work well together have:

- a common understanding of what needs to be done next, by whom and by when in order to achieve team goals
- clear leadership
- shared priorities and clarity about constraints
- opportunities to deal with misunderstandings and conflict in open and transparent ways
- an understanding of when goals have been achieved.

Staff/team meetings can assist members to understand the goals of the team. This can be done overtly through discussion or activities. Staff/team meetings that are collaborative and allow people to speak in a 'safe' and 'no blame' environment are powerful ways of supporting work towards a common goal. When people find staff/team meetings well run and productive and look forward to this time together, this cements the understanding of common goals and does not feel like a waste of time.

Teams often have ground rules that they have agreed. Ground rules often include:

- open and honest discussion
- no interruptions during meetings
- confidentiality
- everyone pulling their weight and fulfilling their obligations
- confrontation and disagreement being kept constructive
- a focus on solutions, not finger pointing
- a need to spend time together
- development of trust.

There is a tension when teams are expected to meet goals but individuals in the team either cannot or will not work towards these at an appropriate quality level. Managers need to be aware of people in the team who, for whatever reason, are not meeting their responsibilities or are not being heard, and deal with these situations. If they are not dealt with effectively, these situations can deflect a whole team from achieving its goals.

Participation

Allowing participation in setting goals is very motivating and makes it much clearer to people what they are being asked to do and why. Staff should know their particular role in getting tasks done and when to allow a more senior person to do a certain task. Leaders and managers must not assume everyone understands the goals or values of the setting or service. Sometimes staff are kept in the dark because people do not share their knowledge, either because they are insecure and want to create an illusion of power or because they are too busy or genuinely unaware that people are misunderstanding. Staff should know what achieving goals looks like and be able to rejoice in their team's success.

Role models

The leader or manager must be a positive role model to other colleagues. Treating others with respect leads colleagues working in a setting or service to treat their work and people they meet with respect. In services and settings for children, young people and families, how we treat people forms an important part of our goal.

Training and development

Opportunities for feedback and updating skills should be provided on a personal basis and taken advantage of by team members. Training and development needs are usually discussed in performance appraisals or supervision times. On other occasions, people will identify needs outside formal arrangements and request specific training to help them to do their job. Leaders and managers need to make sure their team members are up to date and that training opportunities are widely publicised and fairly allocated. A key way in which training and new knowledge can be disseminated is through a cascade approach, in which people share their learning. Shared training experiences across different levels of the setting or service also support work towards common goals. This is particularly the case if leaders and managers share in some of the training and it is not then seen as 'them' and 'us'. In some circumstances, parents/carers can also benefit from sharing in the training.

Performance management

This aspect of management has been covered earlier in the chapter (see pages 136–7). It is a powerful way of ensuring that the team works to common goals as individuals and teams normally have performance targets and shared goals to reach.

Encouraging creativity in the team

Creativity is a valuable asset in any team and does not mean divergence from common goals. Teams who are properly managed and allowed to be creative and come up with their own group and individual solutions will work together and support each other. Managers need to be aware that individuals may become submerged in a team and their voices and ideas can be lost – there should always be space for individual ideas. Teams need to be vigilant so that they do not become too inward-looking or shout down anyone who might disagree with the way things are done. Teams should be safe places for people to explore new ideas, without feeling threatened for upsetting the applecart.

How to identify individual needs and motivate others towards common goals according to their needs

Section 3.1 covers much of this assessment criterion, and identification of individual needs has been covered already in the section on performance management (see pages 136–7). In addition, feedback from colleagues, as well as children, families and carers, may sometimes indicate a training need. This has to be sensitively handled and the team member should be offered appropriate training in a supportive way. Sometimes people have worked well for many years in a setting and understand the job role well. If they are required to undertake new training, this can cause resentment, so managers often have a whole-team approach to updating staff, rather than singling out individuals.

In addition to training needs, people may have personal needs that are hampering their ability to do the job well. These needs may be outside the workplace or may relate to situations in the workplace, such as harassment or hostility. Either way, they may affect how people work. Formal or informal meetings between managers and staff should help to discover where there are problems and the types of support that may be available. Sometimes people do need to have 'time out', work fewer hours, work more hours, take sick leave or have a change of environment. There is a limit to how much settings can do, but every effort should be made to support people in times of difficulty. Confidentially is important and systems are normally in place for 'whistleblowing' when there are serious issues. If there are issues between managers and staff, this can be difficult to deal with, but attempts should be made with a third party present – this is normally covered in the setting's policies and procedures. There are legal requirements in cases of workplace difficulties and there will be systems in place to deal with grievances. If this is taking place, for example, in a small-scale work setting, it makes the issue challenging and difficult.

How to encourage and support others to make the best use of their ability to achieve common goals

This assessment criterion has underpinned much of the material in Section 3 and in other parts of the chapter. It is important to encourage and support people to make the best of their ability and achieve common goals, both for the sake of the service or setting and for the individual themselves. Making the best of their abilities means people must be aware of the scope of their individual potential, and this can be difficult. Many people have a sense of failure through difficult personal experiences and through educational failure. Although it may not be possible to overcome this completely, a good workplace experience can help by:

- not setting people up to fail by giving them goals that they cannot achieve for whatever reason
- providing good support through training and development
- individual managers and supervisors providing sensitive, high-quality, individual feedback and recognition
- providing opportunities for progression and promotion, sometimes through changing job roles internally or by encouraging them to move on.

Although it may seem wrong to support a valued colleague to move on to another job, this is sometimes the best thing to do. People will value the organisation that supports them in this way. Another way of looking at it is that people who are not supported to move on when they are ready can sometimes become frustrated, bored and unhelpful to the team.

How to encourage reflection on achievement of common goals

Encouraging common goals by team reflection

Reflection is well-established good practice in services and settings for children, young people and their families. Reflecting is defined in different ways but essentially means thinking seriously or contemplating upon something. When we refer to reflective practitioners, we usually mean the processes involved in looking at professional effectiveness – that is, strengths and weaknesses and determining areas for further development. It is closely linked to being able to think critically about our own practice and that of others. Work by Kolb (1984) and Schön (1983), amongst others, sets out the theoretical basis for reflection. Schön speaks of reflective practitioners who are not just skilful or competent, but 'thoughtful, wise and contemplative'.

Schön describes 'reflection in action', which is the kind of reflection that occurs as events take place. It is contrasted with 'reflection on action', which takes place after the events.

Some types of teams, such as family therapy teams, are used to 'reflection in action' as they reflect together as a team with their clients. In most cases, team reflection is 'reflection on practice', taking place after events. Teams can reflect on their performance in different ways, such as:

- in staff meetings
- on staff development days
- during performance appraisals
- in informal meetings.

During formal or informal meetings, leaders and managers may decide to undertake some activities to highlight team effectiveness. These can include basic activities, such as team building, learning how teams can cooperate, contribute and communicate better, and identifying team roles and who undertakes them. Many settings will encourage activities such as:

- games
- team energisers
- quizzes
- puzzles
- workshops
- problem-solving activities
- obstacle courses
- teamwork strategies
- treasure hunts.

These activities are all designed to help the team work together more effectively and reflect on their team performance. They should be carefully managed as they have the potential to be destructive, as well as being useful.

Activity

Develop a checklist to see if a team is working together. Consider the following questions:

- Did the team members have conflicts and power struggles?
- Did everyone participate or did some remain outside the action?
- Did some people do all the work?

If you decide to measure a team activity using the above list, do not use it as a reason to criticise others – instead, be positive and constructive.

Progress check

Cookie making

Work with others to bake and sell cookies, or something similar, to fellow learners for a good cause, such as 'Children in Need'. Reflect on each stage of the activity and suggest how the team could work better in the future. Find out if team roles emerged. Relate this to Tuckman's and Belbin's theories (see pages 228–30 and 134).

Reflective practice

Undertake a team activity with other learners where common goals for the activity were agreed in advance. Analyse your own contribution to the team activity. Reflect on how you contributed and collaborated. How did your team members react to you and to each other? How could you improve your teamwork? Explain how the activity supported achieving common goals?

Encouraging common goals by individual reflection

Individuals should all reflect on their own practice and make this part of their working norm. When people reflect on what is important to them in a work situation, they will often need to check with managers and supervisors that they are on the right lines and working in an acceptable way. They may also request further training. This can be a chance for managers to support them to work towards common goals. Use of reflective accounts or diaries as a basis for supervision or appraisal meetings can also be useful in highlighting development needs and reviewing job roles.

Case Study

Phil has worked in a day care setting for some years. He is now working as a member of an outreach team, concentrating on work with parents and carers, especially fathers. The outreach team has been set targets to involve more fathers in their children's learning, especially those who have been identified as disengaged. Phil feels he is sufficiently trained to do his work well but feedback from other people suggests he should have further training in areas directly related to his job role. Phil has been asked to keep a reflective diary of his day-to-day work with fathers and to meet with the manager after a month to discuss any specific training needs.

Identify the issues that exist in this case study. How will keeping a reflective diary encourage Phil to work towards common goals?

Useful resources

Organisations and websites

National College for School Leadership
www.nationalcollege.org.uk

The Teaching Agency
www.tda.gov.uk

New Leaders in Early Years
www.newleaders.org.uk

Early Years Handbook
www.teachingexpertise.com/publications/early-years-handbook-2316

Championing Children Resource Book
www.education.gov.uk/publications/standard/publicationDetail/Page1/CWDC%200001

Elton Mayo's Hawthorne Experiments
www.accel-team.com/motivation/hawthorne_03.html

Books

Adair, J. (1987) *Effective motivation*, Guildford: Talbot Adair Press.

Adair, J. (1997) *Leadership skills*, London: Chartered Institute of Personnel Development.

Belbin, R.M. (1996) *Management teams: why they succeed or fail*, new ed., Oxford: Butterworth-Heinemann.

Belbin, R.M. (2004) *Management teams*, 2nd edition. Oxford: Elsevier, Butterworth-Heinemann.

Department for Education and Skills (2005) *Championing children*, London: DFE.

Drucker, P.F. (1954) *The practice of management*, New York: Harper and Brothers.

Fayol, H. (1949) *General and industrial management*, London: Pitman and Sons.

Hersey, P. and Blanchard, K.H. (1977) *Management of organizational behavior: utilizing human resources*, 3rd edition, New Jersey: Prentice Hall.

Honey, P. and Mumford, A. (1986) *Using your learning styles*, Maidenhead: Peter Honey Publications.

Honey, P. and Mumford, A. (2000) *The learning styles questionnaire*, Maidenhead: Peter Honey Publications.

Kolb, D.A. (1984) *Experiential learning: experience as the source of learning and development*, Upper Saddle River, NJ: Prentice Hall.

Lewin, K. (1958) 'Group decision and social change', in E.E. Maccoby, T.M. Newcomb and E.L. Hartley (eds), *Readings in social psychology*, New York: Holt, Rinehart and Winston, pp. 197–211.

Lewin, K., Lippit, R. and White, R.K. (1939) 'Patterns of aggressive behavior in experimentally created social climates', *Journal of Social Psychology*, 10, 271–301.

Maslow, A.H. (1943) 'A theory of human motivation', *Psychological Review*, 50, 370–396.

Mayo, E. (1933) *The human problems of an industrial civilisation*, New York: MacMillan.

Schön, D (1983) *The reflective practitioner*, New York: Basic Books.

Senge, P. (1990) *The fifth discipline*, New York: Doubleday.

Useful resources (cont.)

Sylva, K., Melhuish, E., Sammons, P., Siraj-Blatchford, I. and Taggart, B. (2004) *The effective provision of pre-school education (EPPE) project: final report*, London: DfES and Institute of Education, University of London.
Taylor, F.W. (1911) *The principles of scientific management*, New York: Harper and Brothers.
Tuckman, B. (1965) 'Developmental sequence in small groups', *Psychological Bulletin*, 63: 384–399.
Whicker, M.L. (1996) *Toxic leaders: when organizations go bad*, Westport, CT: Quorum Books.

Chapter 5 Supporting the development of study skills (Unit CP 5)

When you start to study a new subject, it can be very challenging, especially if you have found study difficult in the past or you have not studied for a long time. It is worth remembering that most people are concerned at the start of a course of study and you will not be alone. However, studying a vocational diploma such as you have chosen will be rewarding as well as challenging. You will have the opportunity to work with children or young people alongside your study, so you can put theory into practice. This really helps your understanding of the subjects covered. People are always surprised at how much there is to learn about for work with children or young people. This is because the work is complex and demanding, as well as inspiring and fun. To prepare yourself effectively for your course of study, check out the study skills you will find helpful and put them into practice. Doing this will really help you to cope with the demands of the course.

There are different approaches to study skills and there is a good deal of material on the internet. However, use these with caution as some will be helpful and others will confuse. Many of the approaches are linked to specific views of learning, especially adult learning – for example, learning styles and mind-mapping. Some of these are touched on in this chapter. This chapter covers areas involving research and practice. The policies and procedures of the setting for confidentiality and permissions should always be followed – for example, parents' and child's permission to study development or to take and use photographs.

Finally, when preparing for a course of study, remember to look after yourself – have enough sleep, eat healthily and do not get too stressed!

Learning outcomes

1. Understand the role of study skills.
2. Understand how to source information when planning a project or piece of writing.
3. Understand how to present information.
4. Be able to present information that is fit for purpose and relevant to target audience.
5. Understand the need to evaluate the process involved in gathering and presenting information.

Section 1: The role of study skills

What are study skills?

Study skills are techniques and skills that increase a person's ability to study, effectively – that is, to research, prepare and pass assignments and tests/exams. Study skills are useful to help you get the most out of your reading and research. They can help you produce better work and save time.

Study skills can be learned and applied to all or most fields of study. Some people differentiate study skills from study strategies but there are many similarities. Study strategies may refer to individual learning styles or may be related to the subject being studied, such as technology, music or art. An example of a study skill is effective note-taking, but an example of a strategy could be practising reading music or playing an instrument for three hours per day. As part of your course you are required to undertake different types of assessment including extended assessments. You will need to carefully read the guidance provided for you and take time to understand what is required. For the extended assessments, you will need to understand how to research and present material, and how to extract data and summarise key themes. This can be challenging, and you will find that this chapter will help you to undertake these assessments and to demonstrate your knowledge, understanding and skills.

Methods of flexible reading

When you start a piece of reading, you need to determine what the purpose is. Do you want to find out details? Do you want a general impression? To be an effective reader, you will need to vary your style of reading according to its purpose. Reading for the purpose of studying is different from reading, for example:

- books for pleasure
- poetry
- an instruction manual
- a sacred text (which may be studied but for different reasons)
- a newspaper.

Books and poetry can be read quickly, often with enjoyment and emotional satisfaction and with no need to remember the content. With an instruction manual or sacred text such as the Bible, you may have to read some of it in great detail. Reading for study purposes is different as you need to understand it and remember the key concepts and general content. There are a number of reading styles that can be used when studying. These are explained later in the chapter.

Study reading (academic reading)

How you read particular material will depend on why and for what purpose. For example, if you want to get a flavour of something in social studies, you might 'scan read' many sources of information and opinion. If you want information and research on nutrition, you may need to 'focus read' relevant material in great detail. Different study purposes might include:

- browsing/skimming to get a general impression
- getting background for the bigger picture
- fact finding
- focusing on detailed information and argument.

When you start a course, you will have to cope with a significant amount of reading, whether in books, journals or online. You are not expected to read everything line by line as you may have done in the past but you need to learn to read efficiently. An initial *scan* of material can lead to *skim* reading, which can then lead to *detailed, focused* reading within the same chapter or passage. A key aspect of study reading is 'active reading'.

Active reading

Active reading is reading in order to understand. Active readers are involved with their reading; they will question, predict, compare, draw conclusions and evaluate as they read. You will learn much more from active reading than passive reading. In terms of study, passive reading is often wasted time as your mind is not actively engaged with the content.

Active reading uses several techniques, such as:

- knowing what you are looking for – starting off by listing questions for which you want answers and checking if you have found out what you want to know
- making notes
- discussing your reading with other people
- choosing easier material first and working up to the more difficult material
- taking regular breaks, about every 20 minutes
- reading aloud to help understanding
- noting headings or key words on a card or in a notepad
- highlighting or underlining important sections of text or where more research is needed
- putting key areas of learning into your own words
- looking away from time to time and asking yourself questions about the material you are reading.

Critical reading

As well as being an active reader, you need to be a critical reader. Being critical of what you read is very important. You may not be an expert in the subject but you should not simply accept what authors say. Almost all authors/researchers come from a particular perspective. They may have a point to make and leave out the other side of the argument. It is good practice not simply to see *what* is said but *how* it is said. Recognising the author's purpose is important. Does the author seek to persuade you to a particular view? Is the writing biased in any direction? It is not always easy to see this but it can sometimes be very obvious – for example, when reading newspapers or advertisements. Some newspapers will provide arguments and statistics to support current government policy, while others will argue to prove the opposite. Advertisers clearly want to influence people to use particular products and will provide selective, biased and one-sided information to give the message – for example, 'these nappies are the best and everything else is inferior'. You will be able to see through much of this and you should apply the same critical approach to academic reading.

When you read material ask the following questions:

- What is the topic being covered?
- Is it based on reliable evidence or is it someone's opinion?
- Does it come from a particular point of view/ perspective?
- What conclusions does the author reach?
- Does it make sense in the wider context of what you know?
- What has been left out?
- Does the author use reasoned argument or emotional hype?
- What do reviews of the material have to say?

Formats for reading

Many people now use electronic books and read from the internet but some people prefer reading from paper. This may be a book or printout from the computer. Be aware that reading for long periods from a computer screen can be harmful.

Targets for reading

Reading study materials, whether in books or online, is likely to be more difficult than reading other types of materials. You need to understand and remember what you are reading. You are also likely to read more slowly and have to read material more than once. Many people find that they need to set targets – that is, what and how much they will read and what they need to find out. Do this before you start to avoid losing focus, getting tired or bogged down in detail. Prepare a list of questions before you start and keep updating as you are reading.

Practical issues

Try not to read when you are very tired, although this may be difficult. Make sure you are not straining your eyes. If you need glasses, make sure to wear them. Check that you are using a font size that is comfortable for you to read and that the lighting meets your needs (not too dim or too bright). Use natural light where possible. Check if reading coloured print or black print on a coloured background is difficult for you and avoid this if possible. If you keep having problems seeing and reading properly, go to your GP or local optician for an eye test.

Making a start

You may well be given little choice about the basic text books you read as these will have been developed for your course, but for other material you need to be sure not to waste your time and energy. Before starting to read a particular text or article check:

- the contents page
- the index
- the publisher's comments
- the chapter headings and sub-headings
- the chapter summaries.

Make a decision about whether the material is useful at that point. Select useful sections to focus on, rather than starting at the beginning, and make notes. When you make notes from your reading, remember to:

- summarise key points
- paraphrase into your own words
- synthesise what you read (integrate different strands into a whole)
- evaluate and comment on your reading
- compare what you have read where this is appropriate
- clarify the sources of your reading in case you come back to it later or want to quote some of the material in your own work.

When you start to study a new area, you will find all sorts of new vocabulary and acronyms that you will have to learn. Get familiar with the meanings by reading as many times as you need to so it is clear. Focus on key points, not the surrounding detail, as you can go back to that later.

Key term

Acronym – an acronym is a word formed from the initial letters or numbers of a name, such as DFE for Department for Education or C4EO for the Centre for Excellence and Outcomes in Children and Young People's Services. Sometimes an acronym combines initial letters or parts of a series of words, such as AWOL for absent without leave or CACHE for the Council for Awards in Care, Health and Education. Sometimes acronyms only capitalize the first letter, so, for example, UNICEF becomes Unicef. It is not always clear which version to use so keep the full set of capitals if unsure.

Speed reading

Speed reading is a skill that you can learn but it may mean breaking old habits. It is not simply about reading faster but more efficiently. There are many people selling speed-reading techniques, as you will find on the internet. Buzan (2003) is a well-known writer in this area and his work also includes mind maps, which are useful when note-taking and developing ideas. How fast you read depends on how you were taught to read, how you read now and how much you have been a reader throughout your life. It also depends on your concentration span and how interested you are in the material. How well the material is written is also a factor as some authors are easier to read than others.

It is important when learning to speed read that you:

- start and practise on something simple that you have already read
- use a large font in the first instance
- only speed read where this is helpful (e.g. not poetry, legal documents or a friend's letter or email)
- do not read when you are tired or are finding concentration difficult
- try not to read when you are really pressed for time.

There are different techniques involved in speed reading but most will include the following:

- Read blocks of words and understanding their meaning – slowly increasing the number of words in a block that you can read means you will read faster.
- Hold the material (books or printouts) further away from your eyes than normal. This may help you to read blocks of text rather than individual words.
- Read from the middle to get an overall impression.
- Look for bold headings or paragraph divides to help you structure your reading.
- Avoid 'sub vocalising' – that is, hearing the words you read in your head. Check if you do this by reading a passage from this book. Many of us read in this way and limit the speed of reading to how long it takes us to speak (i.e. approximately 240–300 words per minute).
- Avoid rereading – that is, going back time and again to reread words and sentences to see if you understood them correctly. If you do this, it is possible to lose the flow of what you are reading.
- Run a pencil or card along the line you are reading to stop you going back.
- When you are reading, do not tense your eye and facial muscles to focus. Allow your eyes to move gently across the page and quickly down to the next line.

- Take frequent breaks to prevent getting tired or straining your eyes.
- Do not try to read when the TV is on or where there is a lot of background noise. Distractions must be kept to a minimum.
- It is important not to work your way through line by line. Look up and down at the page layout and only read what is critical for your understanding.
- Practise for at least ten minutes daily.

In Practice

Check how fast you read a set amount of material and note the result. After a period of trying out speed-reading techniques, test yourself with the same material. Keep practising till you see a real improvement.

Scan reading

We have already referred to this study skill a number of times, which highlights its importance. Scanning is similar to when you are looking for a name in a phone book. You are not reading every detail but running your eyes across the page, looking for some key details. You might need to scan read when you are looking for a specific piece of information. You need to be able to move your eyes quickly over paragraphs, lists, diagrams and other material until you find what you want to know. Practice by looking up an address in the telephone directory and being aware of how you do this. Some people read every name and address but this is very slow and inefficient. You need to learn to scan effectively. If you find you do read everything, you will need to practise scanning on a daily basis.

Skim reading

Skimming is reading to get at the gist of the material – that is, getting the general meaning without concentrating on the individual words. You might skim through a newspaper or magazine article to get at the key messages but not the detail. You might start with the contents page or headings of an article or book and skim read the rest.

Many people skim read as a preview to a more thorough read. If you are in a library or online, you might skim read material to see if it is likely to be useful for your study.

Research Activity

Some people use the SQ3R technique for study reading. SQ3R stands for Survey, Question, Read, Recall and Review. Research where this technique started and how it has been developed over the years. Write a paragraph for each heading, explaining the meaning. Test out the technique yourself or with other people and report if it is effective.

Activity

There is a famous Woody Allen saying, 'I took a speed-reading course and read *War and Peace* in 20 minutes – it's about Russia.' Get hold of a textbook chapter, a magazine or internet article about any subject and skim read it for ten minutes. What have you found out?

Ways of using reference sources

In preparation for an assignment or an exam, there will be a need for you to refer to different sources of information. Different sources of information and academic referencing are covered in more detail later in the chapter.

Reference sources are used to:

- broaden your knowledge and understanding
- help you to understand the research or evidence base for current knowledge of the topic
- help you to come to conclusions about your topic
- convince your assessor or marker that you have a wide understanding of the topic.

Different ways of using reference sources can be summarised as:

- reading and researching around the subject to get a breadth of information
- looking in more detail at specific aspects

- finding out different points of view
- using your reference source to demonstrate your understanding – for example, if you agree or disagree with other people's points of view, you can use references to argue your point
- highlighting important points by quoting the work of others
- emphasising your own conclusions in the light of research.

Reference sources can be used as direct quotes within your writing or used to inform your work without directly quoting. Using references and a bibliography validates your work (i.e. gives it legitimacy) as it shows you have looked at others' work and research and thought through your own viewpoint. Always make sure you give credit for other people's work, either as a direct reference or in a bibliography. See pages 179–182 for more information.

You should use more than one reference source – do not base your work on just one book or article. Look for different sources and quote them in your work. Make sure they are reliable sources. If they are printed, it is easy to check the author and publisher but if you come across material that seems simply to provide opinions (e.g. blogs on the internet that are simply someone's opinion), do not use this. Make sure your information sources are not too narrow as it is better to look at the subject as a whole to begin with, before looking at specific details. For example, look at material on overall development, then social and emotional development, before focusing narrowly on attachment theory.

Taking notes

You will need to take notes as you read material or listen to lectures. Making notes helps you to remember what you have read or heard. Most of us are unable to remember in any detail unless we do this. If you take notes in lectures, review them within 24 hours or you will have forgotten their meaning and relevance. There are many different ways to take notes. Some people can take neat, orderly notes that are easy to read and understand, whereas others might write untidy lists or single words that cannot be understood by anyone except the writer. You may write on already printed material to enhance its content but many people use separate notebooks. Always write the date on your notes and your sources. For example, if you are in a local library or listening to a visiting lecturer, make a note of the subject, name of lecturer, date and venue to remind yourself. Be as neat as you can as this will help you to remember what you meant. In the end, it does not really matter how you take notes so long as the notes do their job and are meaningful for you.

Some useful note-taking methods are as follows:

- Read through the material first, then reread and make notes as this will help with recall.
- Make a list of headings for information that is essential.
- Use different coloured paper or folders to separate types of information.
- Do not rewrite what is in the text you are reading unless it is a heading.

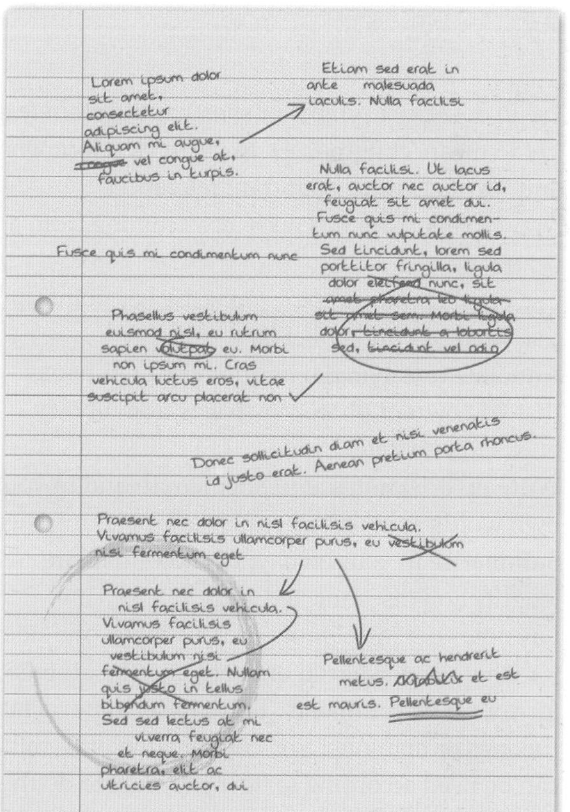

Figure 5.1 Notes can be tidy or untidy but must work for you

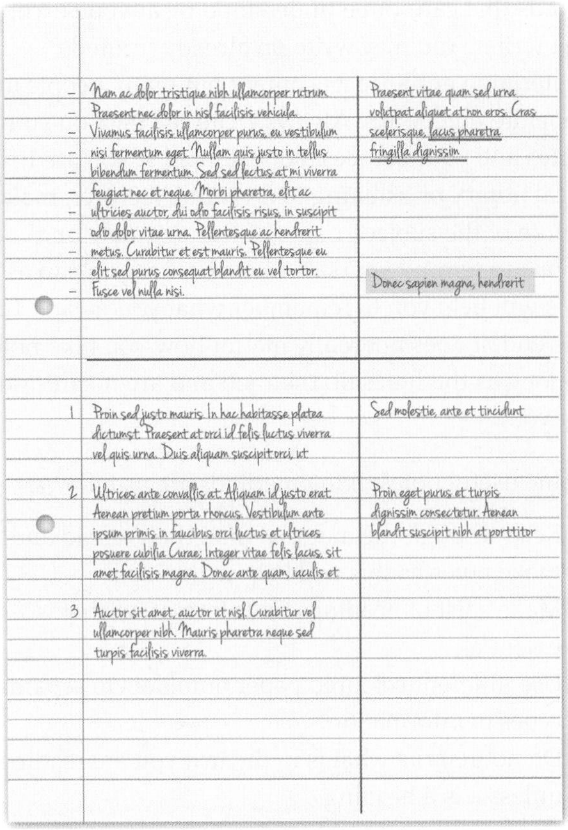

Figure 5.2 Tidy notes come easily to some people

- Try to develop a symbol or shorthand system (e.g. 'ch' to mean 'children', 'D' to mean 'development' and * to signify an important reference).
- Draw spider diagrams with ideas coming from a central point.
- Use highlighting pens to emphasise key points only.
- Use headings and bullet lists.
- Annotate text material in printouts or in books that you own or photocopy pages from library books to annotate.
- Write up brief notes at greater length and in your own words as soon as possible after making them.
- Summarise in your own words notes that are lengthy and disconnected.
- Lay notes out in columns – for example, one side for what you have read or heard and the other side for your own comments. This can separate facts, theories or opinions. Any combination of layouts can be used according to how you wish to do this.
- Make numbered lists, tables or diagrams.
- Note paragraph and page numbers that are especially relevant.
- Keep detailed records of where the information has come from (this is very important) – for example, author's name, full title, date and place of publication, website address.
- When you intend to use direct quotes, make sure your notes have enough information for you to reference these appropriately.

Mind maps

Key term

Mind map – a mind map is a diagram used to represent words, ideas, tasks or other items linked to and arranged around a central key word or idea. Mind maps are used to generate, visualise, structure and classify ideas, and as an aid to studying and organising information, solving problems, making decisions and writing (source: Wikipedia). The concept was developed further by Tony Buzan (2000).

Mind maps are ways of taking notes using diagrams. They are more compact than traditional notes and are normally restricted to one side of A4 paper. You can add to the mind map by incorporating new information. There are many software packages, such as 'Mindmaker', to help you develop mind maps, some of which are free for students. You can also create mind maps by drawing freehand and these are straightforward to do (see Figure 5.3). If you want to know more about mind maps, check out *The Mind Map Book* by Tony Buzan. It seems a complex concept but it is worth seeing if it works for you.

Using abbreviations

Key term

Abbreviation – Dictionary.com defines an abbreviation as a shortened or contracted form of a word or phrase, used to represent the whole, such as Dr for Doctor, US for United States and lb for pound.

We can all think of abbreviations that are commonly used in our sector, such as QCF (Qualifications and Credit Framework) or ml (millilitre). We need to be careful when using abbreviations as they can confuse people outside the area of work and can be misunderstood,

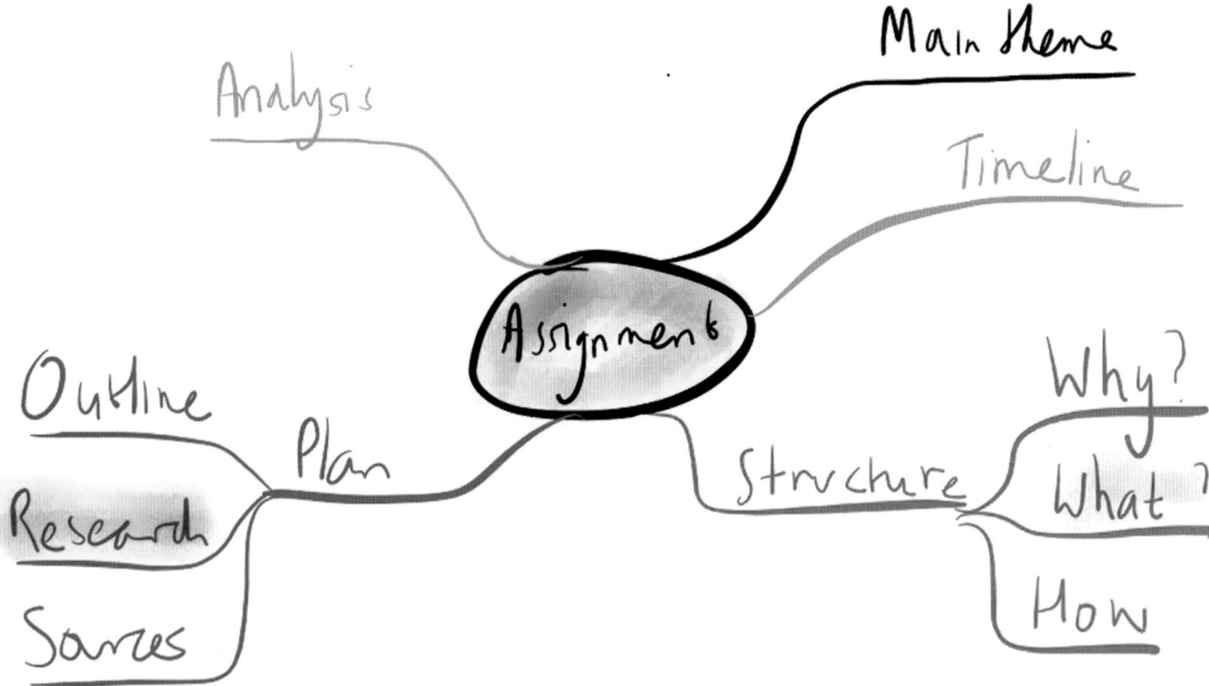

Figure 5.3 Example of a mind map drawn by a student

sometimes with serious consequences. An acronym is a type of abbreviation.

When presenting your academic work, you should be careful not to use too many abbreviations or acronyms. Assessors or markers sometimes see this as a form of 'alphabet soup' as it makes the writing less easy to understand. If you have to use many acronyms/abbreviations, develop a glossary and attach this to your work.

When using acronyms in academic writing, you must always write the words in full the first time you use them and the abbreviation or acronym in brackets afterwards. From then on, you can use the abbreviation. For example, 'The nursery has three qualified Early Years Professionals (EYPs) who work across the various rooms. The EYPs are able to support families with children under five years who have special educational needs.' Abbreviations are not used in certain places in documents, such as the title page, and current practice is not to use a full stop after an abbreviation.

1. Using numbers when writing should be consistent and most people write as follows:
   - 1–10 are normally written as full words (e.g. seven, one).
   - 11 onwards are written as numbers (e.g. 21, 1,019).
2. Roman numerals are sometimes used to number a list (i.e. i, ii, iii, iv…).
3. Other common abbreviations used in academic writing are:
   - *et al.* – and others
   - NB – note well (use when important information is being presented)
   - ibid. – when referencing, this means the source is the same as the one already cited
   - e.g. – for example
   - i.e. – that is.

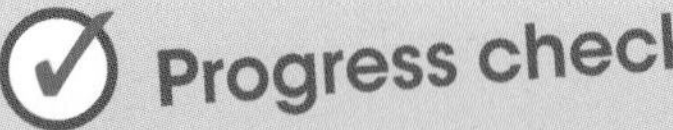

Progress check

Develop a piece of academic writing and use the above abbreviations accurately and appropriately. Demonstrate the accurate use of abbreviations, acronyms and numbers.

Managing time

Time management is one of the best ways to ensure you succeed on your course. Most of us find it difficult to fit everything in our lives but with some simple changes we could find we manage our time more effectively, rather than let it run away with us. The best way of managing your time will be individual to you. For example, some people may have caring responsibilities and others may have part-time jobs. Also some people are better studying in the morning, whereas others are better later in the day. Based on your individual lifestyle, you should plan carefully how you will approach your study – for example, for short-term planning, use tools such as 'to do' lists and daily/weekly plans and for long-term planning use monthly or termly plans. Make sure you are realistic and do not get overtired.

Key term

SMART – the acronym SMART is used widely in goal setting. It has variations in what the letters mean (see brackets). When setting goals, people should check that they are Specific, Measurable, Attainable, Realistic and Timely.

Progress check

Test your own goals to see if they are:

Specific – is the goal clear and specific?

Measurable – ask questions starting 'how much' or 'how many' to help you find out whether the goal is measurable. Can you tell if and when it will be achieved? You need to know what success or failure in achieving your goal will look like.

Attainable – is the goal achievable? Is it too challenging or not challenging enough? Check your commitment by asking if you are willing to work towards this goal.

Realistic – do you have enough time, knowledge and/or resources to meet the goal?

Timely – do you have clear timelines for achieving your goals? Remember, allowing too much time can also affect your performance.

Action planning

Action planning for your study is very important and includes a number of different practical steps. Remember, this is not action planning for your life but how to get the best out of your course and achieve the best results you can.

Practical steps in your action plan are covered in summary below. These include:

- setting goals
- prioritising
- making 'to do' lists
- planning your study environment
- starting the task
- keeping to task
- medium and long-term planning.

Setting goals

Setting goals is designed to help you succeed. Set a clear target for your study period (e.g. researching a topic, writing an assessment). Set personal SMART goals, checking they are not unrealistic but at the same time are sufficiently challenging. If you set goals that are too easy, you will be less motivated to achieve them. Challenging goals are more motivating as you feel a strong sense of satisfaction when you achieve them. However, it is important to break the tasks down because, if they are too complex and demanding, you may be overwhelmed. This is especially true if you under a tight deadline.

Goals also need to be clear and unambiguous, otherwise you will never be clear when you achieve or do not achieve them. For example, 'I will read and make notes on Chapters 5–7 of the set textbook' is more motivating than 'I will read parts of the set textbook.'

Prioritising

You prioritise to make sure that you concentrate and focus on the most important issues you have to deal with in terms of your study. Think very hard about deadlines and what has to be done to achieve these. Prioritise your study, preparation and assessment time. Some people give items priority numbers – for example, Priority 1 needs to be done first and preferably today. If you are working on your computer, do not start the day answering emails and then keep looking at emails or any new shopping opportunities that float across the screen. In terms of email, file messages or action immediately, otherwise you will spend a lot of time reading and rereading the same items.

Making 'to do' lists based on your study priorities

Do not try to do too much work from your list. Your priority 'to do' list should not contain more than 4–6 items. They should not include items such as 'walk dog', though you can include a 'take a break' reminder. Make sure you are keeping a careful eye on the volume of work you are setting yourself. Focus on one task at a time and do not try to multi-task when you are studying. 'To do' lists must be specific, as in the examples in Table 5.1.

Planning your study environment

Set aside somewhere you can study and let people around you know what is happening. If you have a choice, do not choose somewhere where you will experience constant interruptions. Minimise distractions from whatever source (e.g. turn the phone onto silent, make sure you have everything you need at the start of the study period). If you are used to music in the background, choose tunes without vocals or complicated rhythms that will distract you. Work out the needs of the task and whether you will have to go elsewhere for information (e.g. college library, local service providers). Plan blocks of time for study – around 45–50 minutes is a good time to allow before taking a break. Make sure you take regular breaks! It is better to take a break when you are at an interesting part of your study so you do not dread going back. Try to do the most complex work when at your most alert and study in daylight hours as this is more efficient. Do not study after a big meal and be surprised that you are struggling!

Starting the task

Do not put off what you are going to do. Make a start and get over the hurdle of picking up your pen or computer and put something down on paper. Suddenly the weight of the task is eased a little. Postpone other unnecessary activity until later. Your electronic media should not dictate your timetable!

Keeping to task

Review your progress regularly, at least once a week, and identify resources to help on an ongoing basis. Save time ultimately by reviewing notes and ideas before lectures. After lectures, review lecture notes

Vague and unhelpful	Specific and helpful
Look at child development book.	Read Chapter X, pages 200–235, of Master's book on child development. Reread Chapter Z conclusions.
Go to shops.	Buy red binder and coloured pens for placement from Smith's.
Write up notes from last lectures.	Check last two sets of notes from child health lectures and follow up references on computer.
Find out about next placements.	Make an appointment with tutor to discuss next placement to include discussion on: Dates Times Place Contact phone number Supervisor name and details Specific goals of placement.

Table 5.1 Examples of helpful and unhelpful entries in a 'to do' list

Figure 5.4 Try to study when you are alert

and materials within 24 hours of the lecture as you will remember much more if you do this. Make sure you allow correct amount of time for tasks – for example, most people need to allow two hours' private study for every hour of lecture time. Start well before deadlines and allow sufficient time.

Short-term planning

This is most useful on a week-by-week basis. Look at your course timetable and work out what you need to do over the next 1–4 weeks. There are many planning formats you can use. Figure 5.5 shows an example of a short-term plan, but you should use a format that works for you. You will need to make sure you enter all your deadlines and commitments into this plan. Then use the spaces to allocate your study times.

Long-term planning

Any plan needs to work for you. Include all personal and college commitments and deadlines. The plan can cover the whole term or half a term and could look like the example shown in Figure 5.6.

Motivation to study

It is important that you remain motivated to do your best in your course. Sleepwalking your way through is not helpful and will lead to lost motivation. Early on in your course, you will have discovered if the subject and potential employment is right for you. If you feel this is for you, stick with it for the ultimate satisfaction of achieving a positive goal. Work out for yourself what motivates you or what acts as a negative motivator.

Motivation can be divided into extrinsic and intrinsic. Extrinsic motivation is often associated with external rewards, such as getting a good grade, getting more money or getting a better job. Intrinsic motivation is more to do with personal satisfaction, the pride in achieving a goal. Both types of motivation are important.

Before you start to study, try to get into the right frame of mind. Do not bang the chair and slam the keyboard. Turn off music or the TV and try to clear your mind. Take a few minutes to breathe deeply. Some people use visualisation to see themselves studying and achieving. There are other techniques, such as saying encouraging words out loud or having a cup of coffee in a certain chair next to your desk. Having a ritual helps some people to get into the mood for study.

Time	Mon	Tues	Wed	Thurs	Fri	Sat	Sun
7am					Prepare outline for assignment		
8am	Placement	Work out queries for tutorial		Placement	Read through notes from last social studies lecture		
9am		Visit library to check subject database			Social studies		
10am		Tutorial					
11am		Ensure assignment is given in for 2pm deadline			Write up notes from social studies		
12pm		Check placement notes			Lunch break		
1pm		Lunch break			Outline planning for assignment		
2pm		Study period. Assignment for Unit 4			Continuing planning		

Figure 5.5 Example of a short-term study plan

Week	Mon.	Tues	Wed	Thurs	Fri	Sat	Sun
1		Term begins		Placement induction			
2	Placement starts			Placement. Assessor initial visit		Visit family	

Figure 5.6 Example of a longer-term plan

Activity

Make a list of things that have motivated you in the past. For example, pleasing others, pleasing yourself, financial motivators, treats, tutor support, family support. Make another list of things that have demotivated you. For example, task too hard or too easy, lack of support, too tired, having to use maths or computers. Ask why you are motivated or demotivated and think how you could change or improve your attitude. Finally identify likely sources of support.

Bearing in mind we are all different, some practical strategies to keep motivation going include:

- tackling the most difficult aspect first and then moving to easier or more interesting topics later
- dividing harder areas into chunks of learning
- taking regular breaks
- building in treats for small and larger successes (e.g. going for a swim, having a chocolate bar, buying a longed-for item of clothing, taking a holiday)
- planning well and planning for success
- using positive language and not dwelling on the negative
- using photos and positive messages around the house to remind you of your goal
- socialising with people who share your goals or who understand and support you
- understanding that everyone fails sometimes and we can learn from failures.

Activity

Select an assessment that you will be required to undertake as part of your study. Based on the previous section of text, develop a detailed plan that includes all the steps you need to take to complete the assessment.

The importance of developing study skills in relation to personal achievement

Study skills can enable you to achieve and reach your personal goals. They can help you succeed in the course you are doing by enabling you to read, understand and process information more efficiently and speedily. In this way, you can:

- set goals
- succeed in your course objectives
- achieve at higher levels than you have in the past
- become an independent learner
- be more confident in your abilities
- train yourself to read efficiently and with understanding
- develop organisational skills
- develop planning and time management skills
- work with less stress
- encourage those around you
- develop your thinking skills
- improve your memory.

There are many advantages to improving your study skills and the time is worth investing. You will save time in the end and you will be more likely to achieve your full potential. For example, it is not worth being held back by long-standing reading habits that are inefficient and frustrating. When you become frustrated in your learning, it is easy to opt out and ultimately miss out on a rewarding career.

Study skills are important in terms of efficiency when studying but also they are helpful life skills. Organisational skills and improved confidence are very important for every aspect of life. For example, when entering work you will need organisational skills in every aspect of work, from getting up in the morning and then throughout the day.

An appropriate level of confidence and positive self-esteem is helpful for getting and keeping employment.

Critical reading skills are linked to critical thinking. Being able to read and think in this way is helpful in life as it will enable you to analyse information, and question and judge the value and accuracy of what you are experiencing. These skills enable you to assess risk more effectively and weigh up advantages and disadvantages.

Developing your writing skills is also important. Being able to write briefly and effectively is a valuable skill in employment and throughout life.

Reflective practice

Reflect on the way you have read this section of the chapter or another textbook. Have you learned anything about the way you read? Have you been able to read more quickly and apply the appropriate reading techniques? How has that made you feel as a learner? Reflect on what training and/or practice you need to improve.

Case Study

Ana is a capable and knowledgeable early years practitioner with a Level 2 NVQ in Children's Care, Learning and Development (CCLD). She has decided to move forward with her study and hopes one day to get a degree. In the meantime, she is studying for a Level 3 qualification, which Ana hopes will enable her to move on in her studies.

What are the aspects of work at Level 3 that might be the most challenging for Ana? How can developing better study skills help her to achieve a good outcome in her assignments and tests?

Assess your own areas of weakness when studying. For example, is it reading too slowly, weak understanding, getting bogged down in detail, not being able to express yourself well, spelling, or something else. Plan how you will use study skills to help your weaker areas.

Section 2: Sourcing information when planning a project or piece of writing

You will need to be able to source information to help you when you are undertaking projects, essays or other written work. Although you will have ideas of your own, you will still need to find further information. It is important to provide an evidence base for your ideas as you cannot make statements (assertions) without being able to back these up with research. This is always a challenging activity but it is key to developing high-quality work. Also, you need to reference any material you use to avoid plagiarism. Plagiarism is covered on page 180.

The different stages involved in planning a piece of writing or project

There are different ways of planning a piece of writing or a project or assignment and all require time, effort and thought. Planning covers what you want to write and how you want the final product to look. If you do not plan well, you may find you read far too much non-relevant material, collect too much information, which becomes confusing, and are late with your work. You might find it helpful to think about what a good piece of writing or a project should look like. The following are points to think about:

- It is interesting.
- It answers the question.
- It shows my hard work and understanding of the subject.
- It gives evidence that I have read about the topic.
- It reads well and is well structured.
- It includes references.
- Spelling and grammar are to a good standard.
- Where appropriate, it draws on my practical experience.

A piece of writing may include an essay, a report, a case study or child observations. The purpose of each activity is different and you will find that you need slightly different skills.

Essay

Dictionary.com defines an essay as 'a short literary composition on a particular theme or subject, usually in prose and generally analytic, speculative, or interpretative'. Some essays have to be tightly structured and do not really give much room for creativity. Other essays are more free-flowing – for example, an essay title such as 'My dream holiday', as opposed to 'The role of bath houses in Roman Britain'.

As part of your course you are likely to have to undertake an extended essay. You will be required to plan the structure of the essay and to organise your information logically. Although essays will vary according to an individual's approach and the topics covered, they often follow a similar format.

Possible essay format:

1 An introduction that sets out the aims of the piece of the essay in relation to the title. This is normally quite short and will cover briefly the main areas you intend to include and why. The introduction should enable the reader to know what the essay is going to be about and possibly your reference sources. Do not go into any detail. In some cases, you will need to define briefly any difficult concepts or words so the reader knows where you are coming from.
2 The body of the essay develops the theme. It will include a series of paragraphs for each main theme. For example, you may need to have paragraphs explaining or comparing theories you are covering, or the values and principles that are relevant to the assessment theme. You should include a key sentence at the beginning of each paragraph that sets out the main points you are going to make and that links back to the title of the essay. For example, an essay that is entitled 'The importance of play for children's development' might have a paragraph on physical play. You could introduce that paragraph by saying: 'Physical play underpins many areas of development. It supports both fine and gross motor skills, but also the skills of locomotion, balance, strength and agility'. This statement shows you are intending to cover these areas in the paragraph. Use each paragraph to demonstrate your knowledge and understanding, and give examples to make your points clear. You should also link your work to underpinning theories or research where this is relevant. In many cases, including both positive and negative aspects shows the depth or your understanding.
   Try to link the paragraphs to remind the reader what you have covered and where you are going next.
3 Finish with a conclusion that summarises the main points and any conclusions you reach. Sometimes it is useful to consider briefly the implications of your findings. For example, if the essay was about raising the age of starting school to six years, how would this affect families? Remember that a conclusion does not normally introduce new information.

Check whether your essay is well structured by trying to write the content in one sentence. If you have difficulty, this might mean you need to divide the paragraph or omit some content.

Report

There are many different types of reports, each with their own formats and conventions – for example, medical reports, business reports, management reports and feasibility studies. Dictionary.com defines a report as 'an account or statement describing in detail an event, situation, or the like, usually as the result of observation, inquiry, etc.: *a report on the peace conference; a medical report on the patient.*' An academic report has some similarities but also some differences to this definition. An academic report will put forward ideas as arguments, backed up with evidence and in a logical sequence. A report is expressed in objective, unemotional language, which may include some scope for creativity, but this is limited.

Reports require clear, concise presentation of material and include text and diagrammatic formats. A report will be presented in sections with headings. For example:

- Introduction
- Background information
- Methodology
- Purpose and scope of report
- Conclusions.

Describe	Write or speak about the topic or activity, giving detailed information
Explain	Make clear, detailed information giving reasons, and showing how or why.
Outline	Identify or briefly describe the main points.
Compare	Examine the subjects in detail, looking at similarities and differences.
Evaluate	Review evidence from different perspectives and come to a valid conclusion or reasoned judgement.
Discuss	Give a detailed account, including a range of views or opinions.
Analyse	Break the topic down into separate parts and examine each part. Show how the main ideas are related and why they are important.
Justify	Give a satisfactory explanation for actions or decisions.
Illustrate	Give clear information or description with examples (e.g.: spoken, written, pictures, diagrams).
Summarise	Give the main ideas or facts in a concise way.
Apply	Explain how existing knowledge can be linked to new or different situations, or in practice.

Table 5.2 Some examples of key task words in titles of essays, projects or assignments (adapted from CACHE 'How to...' A Guide to Assessing CACHE QCF Qualifications, Version 1.2, 2010)

Case study

Wikipedia defines a case study as 'an intensive analysis of an individual unit (e.g. a person, group or event) stressing developmental factors in relation to context'. Case studies are designed to provide a thorough analysis of a situation or process. It will have many similarities with a report structure but will 'drill down' to a greater depth. The conclusion of a case study should suggest solutions to any problems that the 'case' has identified, either prior to or during the study. An example of a case study could be to investigate the reasons why a setting is not achieving its growth targets or why a setting is successful in reaching families.

Stages in planning are different according to individual circumstances but most include the following.

Deciding on the requirements of the assessment task

1 Analysing what is required and being clear about the task.
2 Checking out task words that state what you are being asked to do (see Table 5.2). For example, are you being asked to 'critically evaluate', which would be an in-depth piece of work, or 'describe', which may be broader but in less depth.
3 Checking what the 'content' words really mean. For example, is information about child development required across all age ranges or just one? Does 'play' include outdoor and indoor and does it refer to adult or child-led play, or both?
4 Narrowing content requirements down even further using techniques such as headings, mind maps or brainstorming.
5 Checking out how many different issues you have to consider.
6 Deciding if a structure is implied in the title, such as using set research, and presenting diagrams and graphics.
7 Taking into account technical requirements and guidelines from college – for example, word limit and reading lists.

Deciding how to go about the assessment task

1 Planning early (i.e. before you start writing).
2 Planning your time to give the opportunity to complete the task through stages, such as first draft, revising, editing, proofreading and final draft.

3 Pausing and thinking as you plan.
4 Jotting down early thoughts in a notebook.
5 Deciding what you already know and what you might need to investigate.
6 Planning what will go into the introduction, the body of work and the conclusions.
7 Researching and analysing information sources.
8 Initial reading round the topic but remaining focused.
9 Noting any initial ideas and organising into logical sequences.
10 Noting sub-groups of ideas that could form paragraphs.

Planning your structure

- Work out how you can introduce the topic and set the scene.
- Develop the main headings for the writing or topic, usually about three or four.
- Check the task words in the title of the work and make sure your structure reflects these (e.g. 'evaluate' might require greater emphasis on argument and conclusions).
- Under each heading, list the points you wish to make.
- Estimate how many paragraphs you will need for each point.
- Estimate word numbers for each point in context of overall word count.
- Start to think about how you will present your findings/conclusions.

The difference between primary and secondary data

Primary data

Primary data is original, first-hand material that is collected by the person undertaking the research. It is often seen as the best type of data as it has not yet been interpreted. However, this is not always the case as it depends on the circumstances of the data collection. In your work on the course, you may undertake some limited primary data collection, such as interviewing other learners.

Key term

Quantitative and qualitative data – quantitative data usually refers to numerical data (i.e. data that can be measured and counted). This data often appears as a graph or table. Qualitative data deals more with descriptions and things that can be observed but not easily measured.

For example, if you have a group of children, your quantitative data will refer to:

- how many children
- how many girls/boys
- how many three-year-olds
- how many children with special educational needs.

Your qualitative data might cover very different issues, such as:

- children's attitudes to learning
- parents' values in relation to education
- facial expressions
- emotional states
- attitudes to disability.

It is possible to express qualitative data in numerical form – for example, how many parents support the school – but this is a crude form of analysing something that is quite subtle and with many potential variations and underlying attitudes.

Secondary data

Secondary data is that which is collected by someone other than the user – for example, material from textbooks, surveys, records and data collected through research. Secondary data is used because it saves time and is cost effective. In many cases, quantitative data such as family or child health statistics is very expensive and time consuming to collect and would not be feasible for most researchers. In longitudinal studies, it is the only way to use historical findings – for example, from a long-term study such as EPPE (2004). Qualitative data such as that obtained through interviews, focus groups and observations is easier to obtain but cannot capture historical data. Most secondary data has already been through a process of interpretation and analysis and this is often useful when you are writing an assignment or project.

Examples of relevant secondary data are:

- Child Poverty surveys: www.cpag.org.uk/povertyfacts.
- The Effective Provision of Pre-School Education (EPPE) Project: the first major study in the United Kingdom to focus specifically on the effectiveness of early years education. The EPPE project is a large-scale, longitudinal study of the progress and development of 3,000 children in various types of pre-school education (http://eppe.ioe.ac.uk/). It is now taking the cohort through to later schooling through the Effective Pre-School, Primary and Secondary Education (EPPSE) projects.

Research Activity

Sources of secondary data vary. They may use qualitative or quantitative data and they will be of variable quality and validity. Find examples of secondary research in an area of your choice. Prepare a report outlining the research and the reasons why you think it would be useful for your coursework.

Key term

Valid – validity refers to data being fit for purpose and relevant. It must be possible for the results to be checked to ensure they are accurate and not just a result of random chance.

Reliable – this means that the data is free from error and provides repeatable and consistent results.

Sources of information

There are many sources of information that you may draw on when studying and preparing assessed work. These include:

- lecture and course notes
- library books/chapters
- e-books
- government reports
- the internet
- professional journals
- dictionaries
- thesauruses.

Please note that social media – for example, Facebook or Twitter – are rarely suitable sources for academic writing.

Accessing lecture and course notes is normally straightforward as you will be given these in class and will take your own notes. College libraries will be able to provide textbooks, including e-books, journals and relevant reports.

Libraries

Libraries now have a range of information sources under one roof. There is usually a reference section where you can find newspapers, maps, atlases, encyclopaedias, dictionaries, local information and much more. The book section in a local library will normally be divided into fiction and non-fiction, which will be in separate areas of the library. This will be different in a college or school library as these may not stock fiction but instead focus on textbooks, subject-based e-books, online and paper journals, databases and so forth. Books may be available in large type for those with poor eyesight as well as 'talking books' (on cassette) for blind and partially sighted readers.

Always attend any college induction for using library facilities as this will help you to get the best out of these resources. Every library will be laid out in a different way and getting familiar with your library is important. When you find the section of the library that stocks relevant books, make a note of where this is.

Catalogues

Most libraries now have an electronic catalogue, although some still have paper card indexes. If you are searching a computerised catalogue by title, do not search using the 'a' or 'the' at the start of the title. If you are searching by author of the book, these are usually listed by their last names. In a paper card catalogue, you will search alphabetically.

If you know what you want to read but do not know the title of a specific book, try a subject search. Be specific. If your subject is very broad, you may find that too many results come up. For example, if you want a book on child development and type in 'development', you will get hundreds of different results (e.g. land development, animal development, product development). If you are too narrow, this may also be a problem. If you want to know about two-year-old children's motor skills, you may not get this in the catalogue but it may be covered in searches such as 'child development' or 'under 5s child development'. Keep trying by searching using different words until you get what you want. In some cases, there will be a subject database and this will make the search easier.

The use of key terms is important as these are what you will enter in the database. If you, for example, are researching 'the effects of stress on a child's developing brain', the key terms to enter in the database might be 'child', 'brain' and 'stress'. You will need to use joining words such as 'and', so you should enter key phrases like 'stress and child's brain'. Practice makes perfect so try this out a number of times, changing the key words if necessary.

For specialist magazines, articles or journals, the same search principles will apply.

Classification systems

Most academic libraries will sort books into subject areas and then by author, title and date, according to its chosen classification system. Libraries use classification systems to arrange books and other library materials on the shelves so they can be easily retrieved. They allow items about the same subject to be shelved together.

Examples are of classification systems are:

- Dewey Decimal Classification System (DDC)
- Bliss Classification System (BC).

Dewey Decimal Classification System

DDC is a hierarchical number system that organises all human knowledge into ten main categories. Each of these categories is divided and subdivided according to the subject:

- 000 Generalities (includes computing)
- 100 Philosophy
- 200 Religion
- 300 Social sciences
- 400 Languages
- 500 Natural sciences and mathematics
- 600 Technology (applied science)
- 700 The arts
- 800 Literature
- 900 Geography and history.

The Dewey system is very widely used but can be confusing. For example, 'child rearing and home care of persons' is 649, whereas child psychology is 155.4 and child development can appear under 305.231, 612.65 or 155.4.

Bliss Classification System

Bliss is a classification system that provides distinct rules and its aim is to be more adaptable for libraries. It is designed to allow for subjects to be put in different locations following its own rules that must be consistent. Bliss uses the letters of the alphabet to classify information. More letters are added as the subject becomes more specific. Most subjects are three or four letters long. Examples are:

- ILK – Developmental psychology by age
- IM – Children, child development
- IMM – The family, family relations.

Rather than knowing the technicalities of classification systems, it is important for you to know enough to be able to use them effectively. The library staff are normally the best people to help you.

Accessing information from the internet

You will need to be careful when accessing information from the internet. In particular, you need to ensure that you are using a reliable and ethical source. There is a vast amount of easily accessible information on the internet from many countries and in many languages.

Typing key words into a search engine can bring up far too much irrelevant information so be as specific as possible. Use sites from well-known and preferably UK-based organisations, such as the NSPCC or National Children's Bureau.

Compare different methods of analysing information or data

Your analysis will depend on the type of research or assessed work you are doing. In terms of any kind of research, a good analysis begins with clear questions, a representative sample of people or situations and careful interpretation of the data. This is necessary if your results are to be useful. If you are undertaking a survey using a quantitative method, you will find it useful to use a computer program to help you analyse the data. You can also draw up a table and enter data by hand. You may use percentages or whole numbers, depending on what is most helpful.

If you are analysing information from a literature review or using course notes and information from an essay, you will be undertaking a similar process to that described earlier in the chapter.

Computer data analysis

Data and information analysis is a process that has several steps within it. Analysis of information or data covers numerical and other types of data/information as varied as hair colour, addresses and names, or detailed information from neuroscience or astrophysics. The processes are usually similar and include the following:

1. Data cleaning is where initial data or information is inspected for errors, such as missing entries. At this stage, all the original data should be kept.
2. Transforming data is when initial findings are manipulated, if this is required, to make sense of the information or to check if it is significantly different from other studies.
3. Modelling data is used to highlight, organise and structure useful information to get data ready for input into a database. Unstructured data or information can be found in word-processed documents or emails and this is unusable in a database.

Using computer software is common to help with data analysis and there is a range of programs that can be useful – for example, SPSS or Excel. Once the data or information is in a usable format, the main analysis can take place. There are many different types of analysis, some of which are highly specialised and complex.

Spreadsheets

Spreadsheets such as those created using Excel or paper-based equivalents are useful tools to look at data and make sense of it. You can look at trends and may find some unexpected results.

Examples are given below of some of the common types of analysis. These types of analysis present data in an easily understood format from which you can draw conclusions and make recommendations.

Graphs

Graphs display data in visual formats that make it easy to understand – for example, bar charts, pie charts and line charts.

Simple tables

These tables show the possible responses, the total number of respondents for each part and the percentage of respondents who selected each answer. Table 5.3 shows a simple example.

Red	8 children	40%
Blue	4 children	20%
Yellow	4 children	20%
Pink	2 children	10 %
Green	2 children	10%
Purple	0 children	0%

Table 5.3 Favourite colour

More complex tables

More complex tables are most often used to compare subgroups of information (e.g. demographic groups). Table 5.4 shows an example.

Colour	Number of children	Percentage of children	Girls	Boys
Red	8 children	40%	3	5
Blue	4 children	20%	1	3
Yellow	4 children	20%	2	2
Pink	2 children	10 %	2	0
Green	2 children	10%	0	2
Purple	0 children	0%	0	0

Table 5.4 Favourite colour by gender

Filtering

This technique allows you to select particular subsets and look at these in more detail. Researchers can often find patterns or trends by filtering data. For example, if you were looking at data on children's colour choices, you could do this over several weeks just concentrating on girls.

Regression analysis

Regression analysis considers what factors have led to a specific outcome – you work backwards to see why people answered in the way they did. In the case of the children's colour choice favourites, you might ask what factors made the sample of boys prefer red and blue to all other colours.

Qualitative and quantitative data

The methods used to analyse information will also depend on whether the data is qualitative or quantitative.

Qualitative data

For qualitative data, the researcher may analyse as the research progresses and keep refining in response to emerging themes. For example, a researcher may prepare a detailed interview schedule for work with parents and find (a) it does not get the information that is required and (b) it raises other issues. The interview detail is changed as a result.

Quantitative data

Large-scale surveys such as questionnaires will normally have been tested/piloted in advance to check that they work well and get the information that is needed. Statistical techniques are important in quantitative data analysis and can be difficult

Methods of analysing qualitative data	Description
Thematic analysis	Data is analysed by theme. For example, parents are asked what they think about pre-school provision in the area. It soon becomes clear that most parents' responses include comments about public transport. This is then included as a specific theme and parents with cars are compared with those without.
Comparative analysis	This is very similar to thematic analysis. Data from different people/sources is compared and proceeds until the researcher feels all the key areas are covered. The public transport example above includes both thematic and comparative analysis.
Discourse analysis	This method looks at people's speech and how they talk about subjects. Researchers might look at the type of vocabulary and language used and the way people converse. For example, do they listen and take turns or disregard these conventions? Researchers will look, for example, for insights into how people talk to each other and what factors, such as age or income, affect this.
Computer software can help with the analysis of qualitative data, especially content data. However, it cannot interpret sensitively or capture the nuances or contradictions of some research findings.	

Table 5.5 Examples of methods used for qualitative data

for some people. Most will now use computer software for the analysis. The techniques may include averages, frequency counts, scales and other means.

Reporting

After collecting and analysing all the data, the next stage is to report your findings. The research chapter (Chapter 10) has details of this final stage, which is not required for this unit.

Explain how to select relevant information or data for inclusion in a piece of writing or project

When you receive information about a required piece of writing or a project, it will normally be as part of or at the end of a period of study for a unit of your qualification. You will therefore have information from your tutor, such as unit reading lists or course notes. This can be your starting point. Reading through course notes will help you to gain an outline of what you need to do and what you need to know. However, researching relevant information is not straightforward. You will need to keep re-visiting ideas, and adding and exploring new ones.

Planning your project or piece of writing is covered earlier in the chapter and this will include:

- analysing what is required and being clear about the task
- deciding what you already know and what you might need to investigate
- researching and analysing information sources.

Deciding relevant information sources may be constrained by what is available but many learners need some guidance. You will normally find that a number of seemingly relevant articles will come up as a result of an internet or another type of search. Carefully select materials for use in your work only if they are:

- relevant – do they relate well to the task?
- current – are they up to date?
- valid – see 'Key term' on page 167
- reliable – see 'Key term' on page 167.

It is not always easy to know whether material you find meets the criteria above and it may be necessary for you to discuss with people who can help you. In most cases, you can apply the criteria yourself. It is worth looking at the following websites and publications, but there are many more:

- Government (Department for Education, Department of Health)
- Universities, such as University of London, Institute of Education
- sector organisations – for example, Pre-school Learning Alliance, National Childminding Association, Barnardo's, NSPCC, British Association of Adoption and Fostering, National Children's Bureau
- Nursery World, Children Today, Times Educational Supplement.

If you have to undertake a project or piece of writing about a subject of your choice, it can sometimes be difficult to select what you wish to research. Remember to follow your interests as this will keep you motivated. It may be worth your while to consider available resources before making a final choice of topic. If you select a narrow topic that has not been researched by others, you will find it difficult to make progress.

Using statistics

Using statistical data is not as difficult as it sounds. If you are researching a topic – for example, smoking in pregnancy – there is a good deal of detailed statistical information available. You need to use this sparingly but you might want to include a chart showing, for example, how many pregnant mothers smoke or how many give up in pregnancy, and so forth. Figure 5.7 shows at a glance some useful information about smoking in pregnancy across the UK.

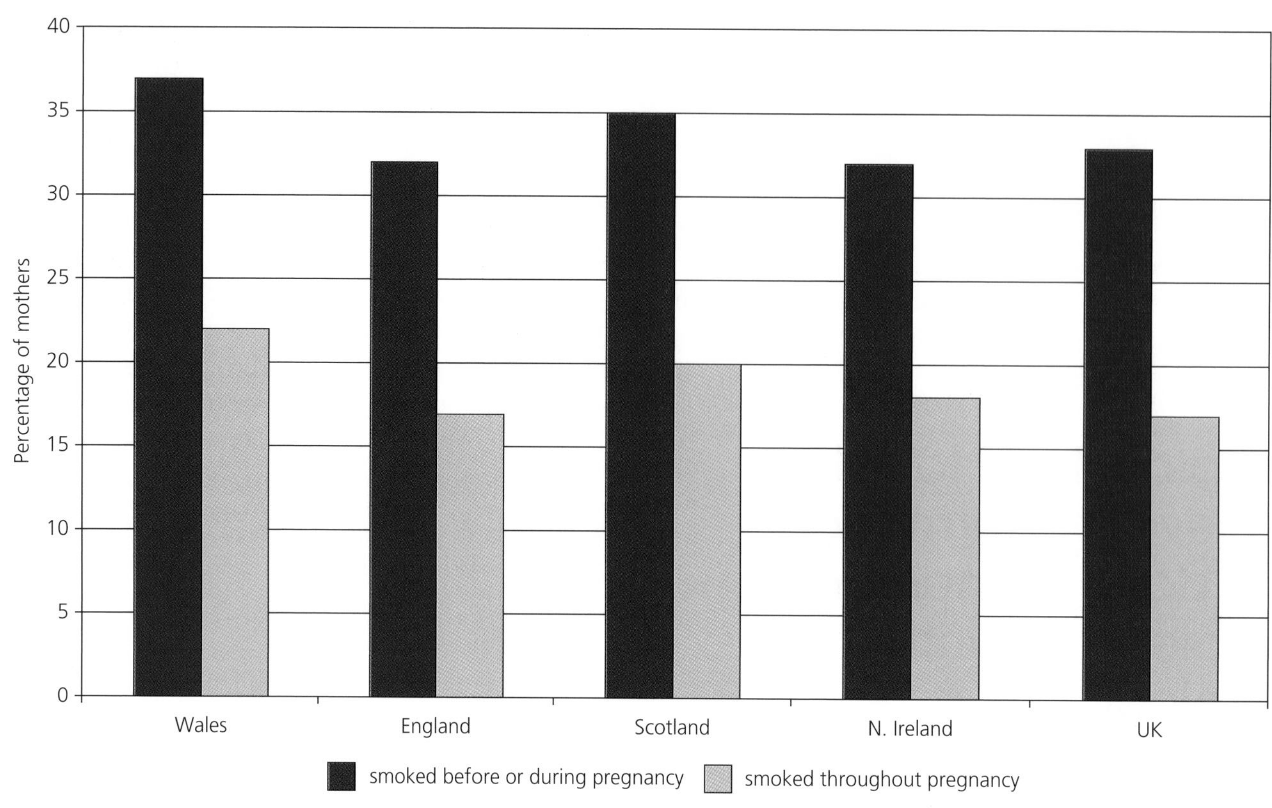

Figure 5.7 Mothers smoking during pregnancy, by country (2005)
Source: Smoking in Wales: Current Facts (2007), Wales Centre for Health

Case Study

Based on the information provided in Figure 5.7, a local newspaper in Wales contains the following headline: 'Wales is the worst country for smoking in pregnancy: babies in Wales are being born to mothers who smoke, even though they know it harms their babies.' The article goes on to blame health professionals and others for this situation. Even though the headlines do represent the statistical facts, a lot is left out, such as the age of mothers, how many cigarettes they smoked, the types of jobs they do, levels of education and so forth. Clearly the writer is taking a particular angle to shock people and to make a point by blaming health professionals.

Do you think the article is a fair representation of the situation?

Critical thinking

Being critical of what you read is very important. You may not be an expert in the subject but you should not simply accept what authors say. Almost all authors/researchers come from a particular perspective. They may have a point to make and may leave out the other side of the argument.

When you read material, ask the following questions:

- What is the topic being covered?
- Is it based on reliable evidence or opinion?
- Does it come from a particular point of view/ perspective?
- What conclusions does the author reach?
- Do they make sense in the wider context of what you know?
- What has been left out?
- Does the author use reasoned argument or emotional hype?
- What do reviews of the material have to say?

Section 3: How to present information

Presentation is key to a positive outcome for your work. Tutors, assessors and markers are human beings and, if your work is difficult to read and the information is hard to sort out, you may be marked down. This applies even when you have included some good-quality content. In business, work or study contexts, being able to present formal information effectively and clearly is important for the success of whatever you are undertaking.

Compare and contrast different formats for formal presentation of information or data

The formats for formal presentation of data will vary widely according to the circumstances and purposes of the data. However, they all require information to be presented in a well-structured, consistent way. Before preparing information or data:

- set your objectives
- assess who will read the information or data
- decide on the information you will need
- prepare a format and framework
- test and redevelop the format and framework as you go.

Formal presentations can take the form of:

- academic writing, such as projects, assignments, verbal presentations or essays
- formal letters – letters written for formal purposes (e.g. from banks, solicitors, hospitals or schools), which normally contain important personal or business information
- structured reports (e.g. for research, marketing or business activities, or formal reports, such as those needed in safeguarding cases)
- verbal presentations to individuals or groups
- case studies.

The next section covers some of these formats to enable you to compare the key features in an academic context.

Academic writing

An academic project/report is an assessment device to enable you to demonstrate your knowledge and understanding of a subject area or to present research you may have undertaken. Your style of writing is important. You should not write as you speak but instead use complete paragraphs and sentences. You should not use shortened or abbreviated words such as 'don't' or 'isn't', or words such as 'OK'.

Example of formal language

Incorrect:

I think that the parents of kids in this nursery all need to be told the rules.

Correct:

It is important that the rules are clearly displayed and available for parents.

Activity

Think of some key messages your setting may wish to give to people outside the environment who are new to using the service. Write out the key messages 'correctly' and 'incorrectly' for use in formal communications.

You will need to introduce new concepts or terminology gradually and explain each of these as you go along. You will need to pitch the writing at the correct level and structure it to meet the requirements of the task. For example, are you being asked to "describe', 'evaluate' or 'compare'. The material should be presented in a logical sequence, with paragraphs following on from each other and appropriately linked. For example:

Children's development is very individual but usually follows the same pattern. The pattern of development is explored in the next paragraph.

Title page	Unit number and title of work. Course title. College name. Your name. Date.
Contents	List of contents and page number of where the content can be found. You can also include an 'abstract', which is a brief summary of the report.
Introduction	Introduce the writing or project and state briefly your understanding of it and what you are setting out to do.
Methodology	A paragraph stating how you went about the work. For example, literature review, survey, internet research. Include everything you have used and referred to.
Results	Present the results using a mixture of lists, graphs, writing and pictures, as is relevant to your work. Do not use 'over the top language'. Keep your comments brief and factual and state your findings. Develop your argument and present your case.
Conclusions	This is where you pull together the key points of your findings. There should not be anything new in this section.
References	List of references you have used.
Appendices if used	If you have undertaken a survey or there is additional information that does not sit in the body of the report, attach it here. Make sure you have made reference to the Appendix in the report to justify it being there.

Table 5.6 Example of a report format for academic writing

The pattern of development refers to the sequence of development, which is the order in which development usually occurs, and the rate of development, which is the expected timeframe in which development occurs…

It is important not to make statements that you cannot back up with evidence, such as 'all children who drink orange juice have bad teeth'. Use your work to provide evidence of your reading, research and developing knowledge.

Table 5.6 includes components that you might use in an academic report. You may include more or less than those included here, according to your individual work.

Diagrammatic formats

Key term

Diagram – a sketch, outline, drawing or plan that demonstrates relationships between things or the parts or workings of something. For example, a diagram of a school classroom or a car engine.

It is said that a picture is worth a thousand words and this is also true of diagrams. They can be used to present complex information in a way that is simple to understand and to interpret. Here are some examples of different diagrams.

Figure 5.8 Example of a line graph: percentage of children living in poverty in recent years, before housing costs or after housing costs
Graph by Child Poverty Action Group, www.cpag.org.uk (Actual child poverty rates are from the DWP's Households Below Average Income 2009/10; projected child poverty rates are from the Institute for Fiscal Studies)

Line graphs

From the line graph in Figure 5.8, you can see at a glance that the percentage of children living in poverty when housing costs are taken into consideration has risen and slightly fallen over a number of years. The graph also indicates how this might develop in the future. This information is much more difficult to explain in words.

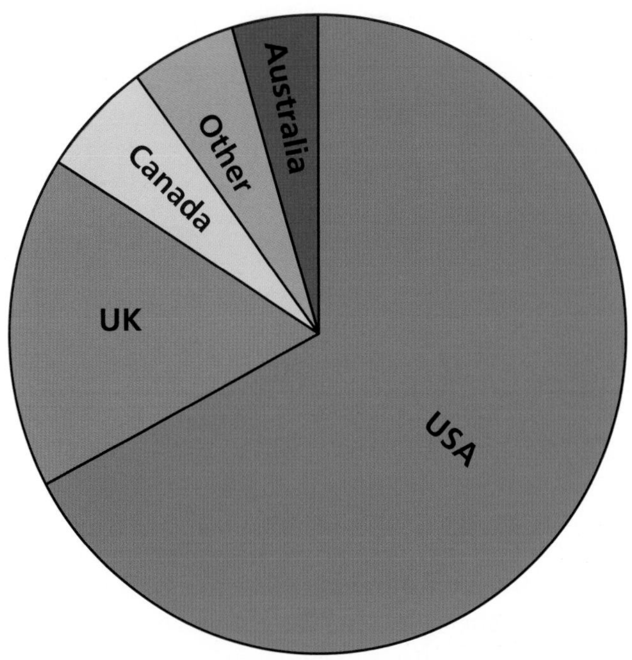

Figure 5.9 Example of a pie chart: relative numbers of native English speakers in the major English-speaking countries of the world (**Source:** Wikipedia)

Charts (such as pie charts and bar charts)

Pie charts are normally circles that are divided up according to percentage information (dividing up a pie). Again, information is easy to see at a glance.

Venn diagrams

Venn diagrams are a visual way of presenting sets of information and may consist of two or more circles or sets, which demonstrate similarities and differences.

In the imaginary example in Figure 5.10, we have three sets of individuals: the first group (A) own cars, the second are those who own a flat-screen television (B) and the third (C) own their own home. Where the three sets overlap, these fortunate individuals own all three and, where only two overlap, only two out of the three items are owned.

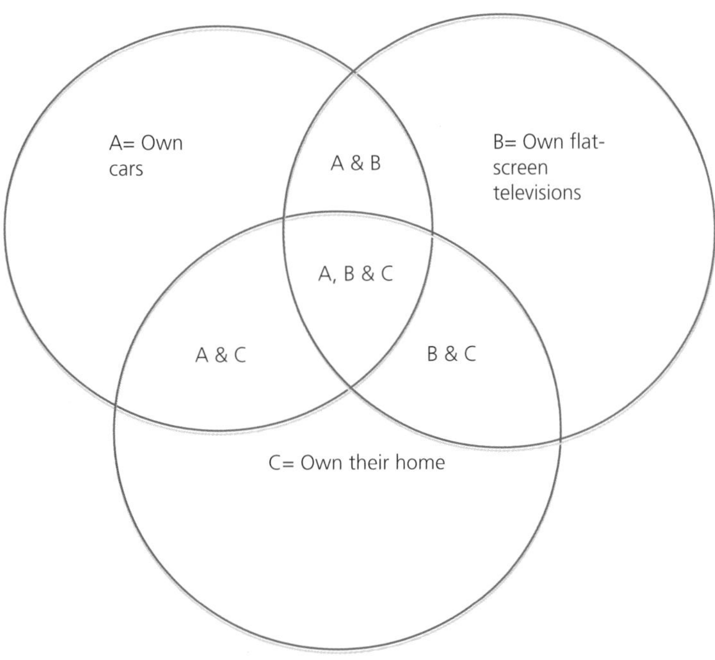

Figure 5.10 Venn diagrams and how they are used

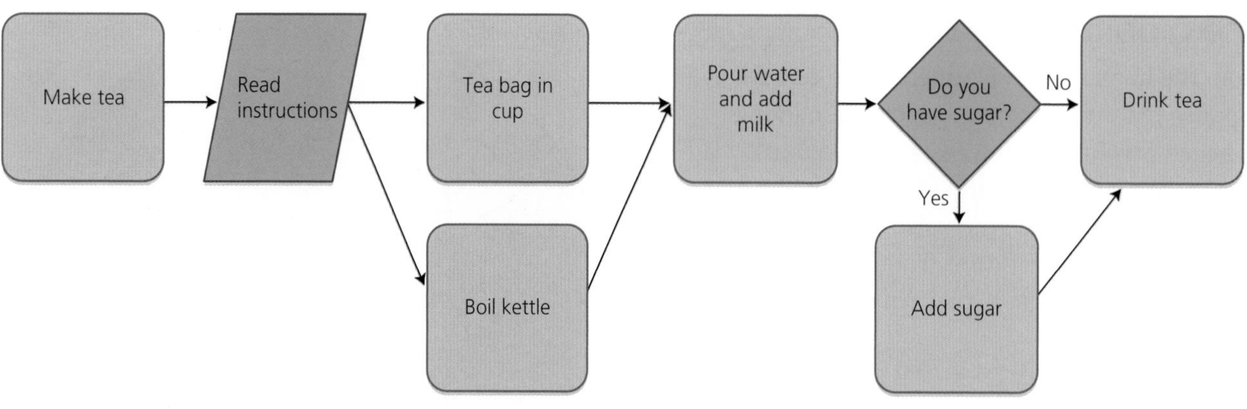

Figure 5.11 Example of a flow chart

Flow charts

Flow charts normally represent a process. They can be simple or complex, and use symbols or words. Flow charts can picture a straightforward process or something through which there are different routes. In Figure 5.11, a flow chart has been developed about a simple, everyday activity.

> **Activity**
>
> Develop a simple flow chart about another everyday activity.

Personal or company details
Name
Address

Recipient's details
Name
Title
Company
Address

Date of letter

Your reference: XYZ

Dear Sir or Madam,

Undelivered Goods

I am writing to let you know that I have not received the goods I ordered and paid for three months ago. I have not received any reason for the delay and require the goods urgently.

I would request that you look into this matter immediately and either despatch the goods or refund the money.

Yours faithfully,

Signature

Name
Enclosure
Cc: Name to receive copy

Figure 5.12 Example of a formal letter

Formal letters

Formal letters normally follow a set format with some individual variations. Figure 5.12 shows an example of a formal letter.

People tend to read business letters quickly to find out the main points. Make your key points early in the letter, if possible in the first sentence or two. Letters should be single spaced and many people use a typeface and font size that is set by their organisation. For personal letters, some people prefer to use a 'serif' font, in which small lines are added – for example, Times New Roman. These additional lines are used to link words together better, thus making it easier to read. They are also seen by some as classical or conservative, whereas fonts without serif (sans serif) are more modern. It is a matter of individual taste.

Leave a line between paragraphs and use short, succinct sentences that leave no doubt as to your meaning. Keep your paragraphs as short as possible.

Space your letter so it looks good on the page and keep it as central as possible (do not have the letter crowded into the first third of the page). Try and keep the space above and below the text roughly equal. It is best to keep the letter to one page as people tend not to read beyond the first page.

In the first paragraph, tell the recipient the nature of the issue. In the final paragraph, make sure you tell the recipient what you want them to do or what you can do for them.

When you sign the letter, use your name with your title in brackets (e.g. Jenny Fisher (Mrs)).

Figure 5.12 shows an example of a personal formal letter, which the author wrote recently. It is an example and not intended to be a model for people to follow.

Additional points

- Recipient details always go on the left-hand side of the page.
- Your address goes on the right but many business letters do not include a name here.
- The purpose of the letter has been included in bold before the first sentence. This is optional but widely used today.
- If you know the name of the person, then use this. Otherwise, use 'Sir or Madam'.
- The date can go either side of the page underneath address details – always include a date. In some countries, dates are presented differently from the UK. Here, it is normal to place the date before the month (e.g. 3 June 2011, 3/6/11, 03/06/2011 or any other combination).
- Include any reference number, NHS number or other relevant details.
- End the letter with 'Yours sincerely' if you have written to a named person and 'Yours faithfully' if you have written to 'Sir or 'Madam'.
- Avoid everyday or slang language.
- Avoid vague terms, such as 'nice'.
- Do not use words like 'you're' – use 'you are'.
- Try not to use emotional language, such as 'you give a rubbish service'.
- There are arguments about whether to use full punctuation but some recipients, such as future employers, may prefer this.

Verbal presentations

These are a useful way of presenting information. They can be used alongside a written report as a way of presenting key findings or features. A verbal presentation can be made without supporting materials but this is uncommon and less likely to provide an opportunity for you to demonstrate your understanding. Sometimes all that is required to support a verbal presentation is a brief outline or 'abstract' of your work, but your tutor will guide you about the course requirements. It is very important to be clear about what you want to say before you start, otherwise it is easy to become nervous and to lose the plot completely! It is useful to practise the whole presentation beforehand. This helps you to find out how long it takes and where the areas of weakness might be.

Many verbal presentations use computer programs such as 'PowerPoint' to illustrate key points. Preparing PowerPoint slides is fairly straightforward and you can use pictures, photographs and colour to enhance your presentation. Key points to bear in mind in any verbal presentation are as follows:

- Keep it as simple as possible.
- Use bullets and short phrases.
- Try not to put too much information on each slide – for example, three or four points max.
- It should be possible to scan read everything on a slide in less than 15 seconds.
- Do not use too many slides.
- Keep the font size as large as possible without going too close to the edge of slide (check if you can see clearly from the back of the room).
- Spell-check your slides and get someone else to read them through to check for clarity and to spot errors.
- Pictures and graphs are valuable to reduce the number of words on the slides.
- Choose your background carefully and do not use complex or fussy patterns.
- Use colour, artwork and pictures sparingly but for maximum effect.
- Use the first couple of slides to introduce yourself and the work.
- Follow through logically from introduction, to findings to conclusions.

It is very important that you speak about each point you list on the slide and understand what you want to say. Be prepared to answer questions that people may ask. If you do not know the answer, do not be frightened to say so.

Professional reports and proformas

Although as a student you are unlikely to have to prepare a real professional report for assessment purposes, it is useful to be aware of how these might be structured. Also there may be occasions when you are required to contribute to these in your work placement. Professional reports are made for many reasons – for example, reports on a child or young person's learning and developmental progress, reports for courts in safeguarding cases, reports on a child or young person's health and so forth. Each local area will use slightly different report structures with set headings (i.e. a proforma). For example, in the case of concerns for a child or young person's safety, the proforma may include as a minimum:

- family background and profile
- family environment
- timing and description of significant events
- individual child/young person profile
- sibling profiles if relevant
- child or young person's development
- parenting capacity
- child or young person's wishes and feelings
- implications for child or young person's future safety, health and development
- future plan of intervention
- recommendations.

The Common Assessment Framework uses a set of proformas that can be found on the Department for Education website at: www.education.gov.uk/childrenandyoungpeople/strategy/integratedworking/caf/a0068970/the-pre-caf-and-full-caf-forms.

Case studies

Case studies are undertaken for many reasons. For example, in children and young people's services or in academic work, it is common to undertake a formal case study of a family. The structure of this will vary widely but will very much follow a report format. However, there will be in-depth material about the child and family. Information will be subject to the policies and procedures of the setting with regard to confidentiality and gaining permission from the family and child or young person. If you undertake a case study, you may wish to use headings such as:

1. Reasons for the study – have you got a hypothesis about this family, such as poor housing causing the children to be ill?
2. Background information
3. Methodology – how you are undertaking the study
4. Evidence/research – what evidence base/research you will draw on in the study
5. Family and environment – such as community support, housing, employment status, income and family history
6. Child development needs – this may be supported by observations, professional reports and assessments

7 Parenting capacity – as a learner, it is unlikely that you will be making judgements about parenting capacity but you need to be aware that this is an important area in safeguarding cases and for other types of assessment
8 Conclusions and recommendations – for example, for future monitoring
9 Bibliography.

Not all these headings will be required and others may be more relevant according to the situation.

Explain what is meant by particular terms when presenting information or data

Formatting

This refers to the form, layout or arrangement of information or data. When people talk about 'formatting' a document on computer, they usually mean presentation formats such as:

- font type (e.g. Arial, Times New Roman, Copperplate)
- font size
- UPPER or lower case
- normal, **bold** or *italic*
- margins (the size of the white space around a document)
- line spacing (the size of the space between lines)
- line and page breaks
- page layout (landscape or portrait)
- headers and footers.

Activity

Develop a document on your computer using Word or a similar program. Use as many formatting features as possible. Highlight and explain how these improve the appearance of the document.

Fit for purpose

Something that is fit for purpose is good enough to do the job it was designed to do. The term came from industry and quality management where processes and outputs are measured against quality standards or customer requirements. In terms of presentation of writing or projects, everything contained in these should meet the stated requirements of the assessment.

The material in the writing or projects must:

- be relevant
- be presented on time
- be written at an appropriate level
- give appropriate detail
- be correctly structured
- meet the required standards.

Relevant for the audience

Written work and project work must be relevant for the audience or intended recipient. For example, if you are asked to develop a leaflet for parents or a story for five-year-olds, you will need to tailor the material to the age, abilities and needs of the audience. You will also need to take into account the purpose of the writing or project. For example, you may include graphs and diagrams for an assessment for your tutor but you are not likely to use these in materials to be used with young children.

Spell-checking

This refers to the checking of spelling, whether by hand as you read through or write a document or by using a spell-check program on a computer. Spell-checks on computers may give you options that you may have to further check using a dictionary. Some spell-checkers also include a grammar check and these can be useful. Always spell-check before you present your material as bad spelling and poor grammar will detract from your finished work.

Proofreading

This means to read and reread a document to find errors and mark corrections in spelling, punctuation and grammar. Proofreading is not the same as editing, although there are some similarities. Generally when you proofread you are not making changes or adaptations to content. In practice, when preparing your work for assessment, proofreading will also include checking for sense, layout and readability. A good proofread will check the different layout elements, such as headings, paragraphs, illustrations, colours, fonts and so forth. Carefully proofreading your writing or project before presenting for assessment will ensure your work is the best you can make it.

Academic referencing

Academic referencing within your own writing

Academic referencing is very important to ensure that you do not take the credit for other people's work. When you use other people's work, research or writing and do not reference it correctly, this is called plagiarism (see below). Throughout your study, you will build on the ideas of others as you develop your own understanding, and this is part of learning. Where you use these ideas in your work, you should normally acknowledge the source of the information. It is easy to omit this step unknowingly or through carelessness but it is important to guard against it.

Quotations can be:

- paraphrases – sections reworded in your own language to clarify
- summaries – concise versions covering key points
- direct quotes – taken directly, word for word, from the author's work.

Plagiarism

A tutor or assessor reading through plagiarised work can usually tell if there are issues of concern. Sometimes learners link together sentences from different sources and it is obvious that they have not written it themselves as the style is different and the content does not make sense. At other times learners take large chunks of information from the internet or from another person's work and this is usually obvious as well. Your own thoughts and ideas are very important and, while you can draw from others' ideas, you must interpret them and make sense of them yourself. It has to be your own work and must demonstrate your understanding of the subject and how you have thought about the topics covered. Your views are important and, although they may not be the same as the authors' views, they are valid so long as you give a reasoned argument and can back them up.

Developing and being confident in your own writing style will help you to do this and practice makes perfect. If English is an additional language for you, it is still important for you to write in your own words, even though this may contain grammatical errors. Your tutor and assessor will explain where you can get help to improve your English.

Referencing systems

There are different recognised academic referencing systems, which are formalised ways of referencing, as follows:

- Harvard, also known as the author–date system
- MLA (Modern Language Association of America)
- APA (American Psychological Association)
- MHRA (Modern Humanities Research Association)
- Chicago and CBE.

The Harvard system is considered here in more detail.

This section has drawn ideas from the 'Bournemouth University Guide to Citation in the Harvard Style', September 2010: www.bournemouth.ac.uk/library/citing_references/docs/Citing_Refs.pdf (accessed September 2011). You can refer to this document for a full explanation of the Harvard system.

Harvard is a popular system. Here the sources of the information are contained in brackets in the text. Footnotes and endnotes are not used. The name of the author, date of the publication and relevant page numbers are included. For example:

'M. Smith (2010) discussed the subject of bedtimes with parents.'

or

'Jones states that all children should be in bed by 9pm (Jones 2010, p. 34).'

If there are two authors, both names should be quoted but, for more than two, the reference should only include the first author's name with the addition of *'et al.'* – for example, Jones *et al.* (2010). If the author's name is not given but only the organisation, you should quote this in full – for example, 'Department for Education', rather than 'DFE'.

The rest of the information is contained in a list of references at the end of the piece of work and includes the title and publication details. References should be given in alphabetical order using the (first) author's name. Publication details should include the publisher's name and the place of publication. The following is an example of a section of references according to the Harvard system. You might find this at the end of a piece of work.

1. Bruner, J. (1990) *Acts of Meaning*, Cambridge, MA: Harvard University Press.
2. Piaget, J. (1962) *Play, Dreams and Imitation in Childhood*, London: Routledge and Kegan Paul.
3. Vygotsky, L. (1978) *Mind in Society*, Cambridge, MA: Harvard University Press.

Diagrams, graphs and figures

If you use diagrams, graphs or figures from other sources, you should always reference them in the same way as text.

Internet references

Although there is no set way to cite internet references, you will need to indicate the source of your information. This will include:

- the name of the author
- the title of the page as given in the taskbar at the top of your browser
- the title of the site as given on the homepage
- the date the page was last updated
- the date you accessed the page
- the full internet address (URL) of the page.

If essential information is not available, a note should be made of this (e.g. publication date not known). If there other information is available, such as a copyright date or ISBN, include this.

Figure 5.13 Studying is hard work

Example of an internet reference

Title: Centile Charts and Assessing Growth, Patient.co.uk

Author: Dr H.W.

Last updated: 29 September 2009

Date accessed: 12 September 2011

URL: www.patient.co.uk/doctor/Centile-Charts-and-Assessing-Growth.htm

Using academic referencing for information sources

Key term

Bibliography – a bibliography is a list of the sources you used to get information for your writing or project. It is included at the end of your work, usually on the last page.

Academic referencing of information sources is normally presented in the form of a bibliography or list of books and other materials you have read and which have influenced how you developed your writing or project. If you have paraphrased, summarised or directly quoted from books or other materials, you will use the Harvard referencing system outlined above in your own work or another recognised system. If you have simply read through other useful and informative material, which has helped you to think through issues, you can list these at the end of your work without always referencing in the text. Information is given below of how you should list various information sources in your bibliography. You could group the sources into type, such as those below (e.g. Books, DVDs), and then list the sources alphabetically within each type.

Magazines or journals

Author's surname, initials (year of publication) 'Title of article', *Name of magazine/journal*, volume number: page numbers.

For example, McLoyd, V.C. (1998) 'Socioeconomic disadvantage and child development', *American Psychologist*, 53: 185–204.

Books

Author's surname, initials (year of publication) *Title of book*, Place of publication (e.g. London): Publisher.

For example, Lindon, J. (2012) *Understanding child development 0–8 years*, 3rd edition, London: Hodder Education.

Newspapers

Author's surname, initials (date and edition if available) 'Title of article', *Name of newspaper*, section (e.g. leader column, supplement), page number/web address.

For example, Marmot, M., Sir (15 February 2012) 'Children denied opportunity to live up to their potential', *The Telegraph*, Health, available at: www.telegraph.co.uk/health/healthnews/9083313/Children-denied-opportunity-to-live-up-to-their-potential.html.

People interviewed

Surname, initials (date of interview) Occupation. Position or job title.

CD-ROMs

Title of disk (date created) Any other information, such as author or version.

Section 4: Presenting information that is fit for purpose and relevant to target audience

Convey information for an agreed audience

In order to fulfil the requirements of this learning outcome, you will need to use the information in Section 3 to help you prepare information. You are required to demonstrate how you convey information to an agreed audience in the formats already discussed. These are:

- report formats
- diagrammatic formats
- letter formats.

You may be able to draw on other assessments for other units to develop this information and your tutor will provide the relevant guidance. It is likely that your assessment will expect you to use experience from your workplace or placement. The following list provides examples of work you could develop and present to meet the assessment criteria. For a report on aspects of work with children or young people, in consultation with your tutor, you could include:

- a survey on advertisements relating to health, presenting findings using diagrams, graphs or tables
- an analysis of attitudes to aspects of healthy living, presented in a table or pie/bar chart
- a letter to parents
- minutes of meetings
- an event sample of behaviour issues, presented in diagrammatic format
- child observations
- assessments of learning and development
- learning materials for children that include use of ICT.

4.2. Demonstrate referencing, proofreading and spell-checking

You are required to demonstrate how to:

- reference sources of information
- proofread
- spell-check.

Use what you have learned in Learning Outcome 3 to reference correctly avoiding plagiarism, and proofread accurately, including reading for sense. Spell-check your work before submitting for assessment, but do not rely solely on a computer spell-check programme. Read through and check spellings that you are unsure about. If you have specific problems with writing and spelling, make sure you use any available sources of help and support.

Section 5: Evaluating the process involved in gathering and presenting information

This learning outcome requires you to reflect on the importance of:

- identifying sources of information
- gathering information
- planning
- presenting information
- analysing information.

In everything you do as a practitioner working with children and young people or managing services, you will need to be able to critically evaluate the effectiveness of what you are doing. You do this to make sure you offer the best possible service and continually update and improve your own practice.

Being reflective in gathering and presenting information is a powerful way of making sure that you are able to achieve the best you can. There are a number of models you can use to assist reflection, some of which are outlined below.

Kolb (1984)

This is a theory that considers learning through experience. Kolb developed an experiential learning cycle. It consists of four different stages of learning through experience. You can enter the cycle at any point so long as you complete each stage in the correct sequence. Kolb's work suggests it is not enough just to have an experience but you need to reflect on it in order to learn. To be able to develop new concepts, you also need to plan and test out this new learning.

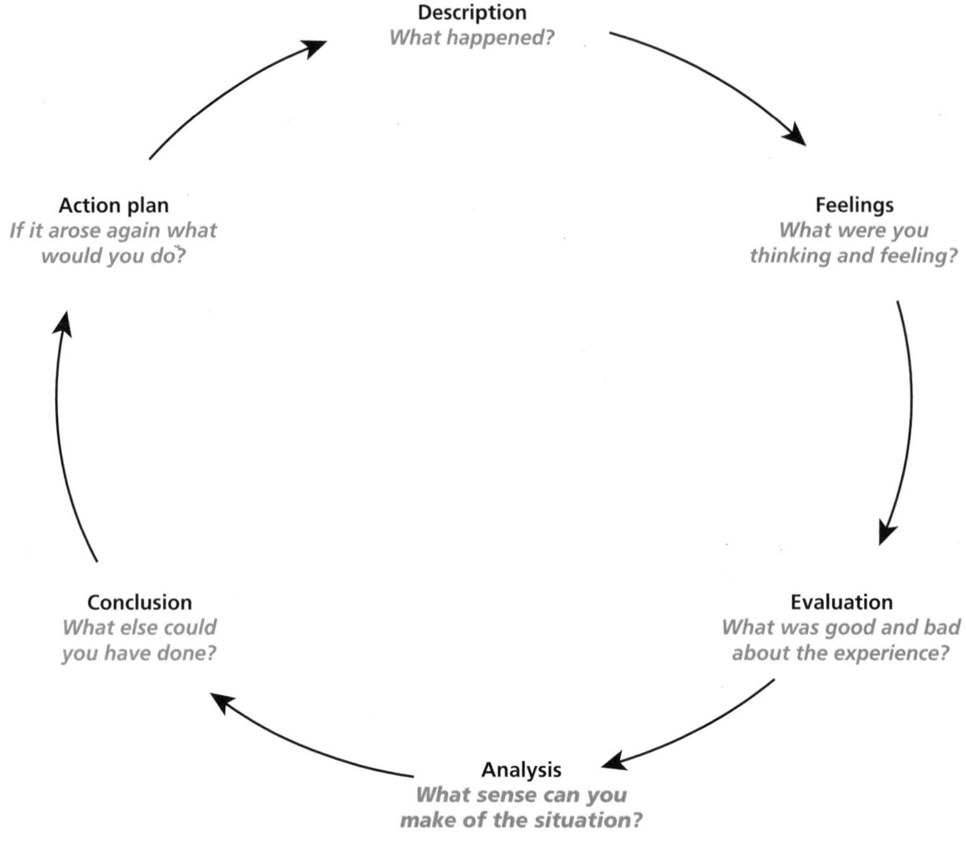

Figure 5.14 Gibbs reflective cycle (**Source:** www.brookes.ac.uk)

Gibbs (1988)

The Gibbs reflective cycle is named after Professor Graham Gibbs from the University of Oxford. It is often used within the health professions and is useful for developing your practice.

The Gibbs reflective cycle is very helpful when you need to think about an experience with a child or family.

Learning styles

Knowing your own learning style and building on your strengths is a valuable way of supporting reflection. At its simplest, learning styles can be divided into three categories: visual, auditory and kinaesthetic.

Visual

If you are a visual learner, you learn best through what is seen. Visual learners enjoy and learn from reading, taking notes, making lists, colour-coding information and seeing videos, films, graphs and diagrams. They normally enjoy a quiet place to learn. You can often spot visual learners as they will close their eyes in order to remember or recall. They may remember faces but not names and enjoy interpreting graphical data. Useful tips for a visual learner are to:

- write things down
- take detailed and clear notes
- use highlighters and underlining techniques to organise and mark up notes
- study on your own.

Auditory

If you are an auditory learner, you learn best through what is heard. Auditory learners enjoy and learn from what they hear in lectures or discussions and through the listening elements of DVDs or CD-ROMs. They enjoy talking, listening and music. Auditory learners may remember names and forget faces. They may not mind a noisy background so much as other learners. Auditory learners find it more difficult to learn through written material (e.g. graphs and books) but are helped by reading out loud and listening to audio tapes. Useful tips for an auditory learner are to:

- study with others and discuss information
- speak out loud things you want to recall and remember
- record lessons or material.

Kinaesthetic

If you a kinaesthetic learner, you learn through hands-on involvement. Kinaesthetic learners remember what was done and what they themselves do in a practical sense. They enjoy textures, space, role plays and human contact. Kinaesthetic learners learn through doing and hands-on instruction. They often use hand gestures and need to move around and take regular breaks. Useful tips for a kinaesthetic learner are to:

- use tips from other learning styles, such as writing down and discussing with others
- walk or pace around while looking at notes
- translate your reading into what can be touched, such as tapping a rhythm or kneading a soft ball
- type up notes
- eat, drink or listen to music if it helps.

Most people use different learning styles but may have a clear preference for one.

When you are aware of how you learn, this can help you in your reflection. Make sure that you build on your strengths and reflect on your learning style and whether your way of working is effective for you.

Case Study

Andreas is undertaking a piece of work on the subject of why mothers-to-be continue to smoke during pregnancy. He decides to interview mothers-to-be, their partners and health professionals to get a clearer picture and then to present his data in a series of graphs and written commentaries.

Andreas is an auditory learner and he finds great difficulty in turning his data into written form, although he has a clear grasp of his findings. He persists with the graphs as he feels they enhance his work and decides to record his commentaries on tape. After completing all the work, he transcribes the taped commentaries into text, improving on it as he listens and inputs the findings. Andreas understands his own learning style and works with it to get the best result.

As he is an auditory learner, was this the most efficient way for Andreas to develop his piece of work?

What would be the best strategies for a visual learner to use?

Reflect on the importance of identifying sources of information

As you reflect on the process of identifying information sources, consider whether:

- you could have done this work without knowing sources of information
- you could have given the subject better coverage by extending information sources
- you selected the right information sources
- the information you gained from different sources improved your work

- the information used was from the most useful, valid and reliable sources
- you have learned and enhanced your understanding of the topic through the information sources used.

Reflect on the importance of gathering information

As you reflect on the importance of gathering information, consider whether:

- you were able to utilise study skills, such as speed-reading and skimming
- you used the internet effectively
- you used libraries and other resources to help you.

Reflective practice

Write a reflective account of how you identified and gathered information. Use the above lists to help you to structure your account.

Reflect on the importance of planning

As you reflect on the importance of planning your work, consider whether:

- planning was necessary for you to undertake the work
- you planned effectively
- you used the stages of planning a project in ways that enhanced your work
- you took note of the task word in your planning (e.g. 'evaluate')
- you planned effectively to cover all the main points
- your planning in terms of the length, breadth and depth of your work was successful (e.g. did you cover the work in the right detail?)
- your planning enabled you to come to a conclusion
- your planned references and reading met your needs
- your piece of work met all your goals
- your planning led to the piece of work being fit for purpose.

Activity

Write a short critique of the way you planned to gather and present information. Reflect on your own learning style and how you were able to work to your strengths.

Reflect on the importance of presenting information

As you reflect on the importance of your presentation, consider whether:

- your work was well presented in terms of the task
- your work was relevant to the audience as indicated in the task
- your work was spell-checked, formatted and proofread
- your references were presented using an accepted format
- your bibliography was complete and accurate
- you used diagrams, graphs and other supportive presentation formats accurately so they added value to your work.

Reflect on the importance of analysing information

As you reflect on the importance of your analysis of information, consider whether:

- your analysis included reference to existing research and good practice
- your analysis was based on the information/data you had gathered

- your analysis took into account all sides of the argument
- your analysis clearly indicated evidence of your own thinking and understanding
- your analysis flowed logically and smoothly as you developed your points
- your analysis was unbiased
- your analysis was convincing and enjoyable to read.

Reflective practice

Reflect on the process of how you present and analyse information. Use the above list to help you. Use the reflective account to consider your feelings about how you are managing the processes and your confidence in developing your ideas and conclusions. Reflect on whether you would approach the process differently in future.

Useful resources

Organisations and websites

The Teaching Agency
www.education.gov.uk/aboutdfe/armslengthbodies/b0077806/the-teaching-agency

Department for Education
www.education.gov.uk

Books

Buzan, T. (1996) *The mind map book*, New York: Penguin Books.
Buzan, T. (2003) *The speed reading book,* Harlow: BBC Active.
Gibbs, G. (1988) *Learning by doing: a guide to teaching and learning methods*, Oxford: Further Educational Unit, Oxford Polytechnic.
Kolb, D.A. (1984) *Experiential learning: experience as the source of learning and development*, Upper Saddle River, NJ: Prentice Hall.
Sylva, K., Melhuish, E., Sammons, P., Siraj-Blatchford, I. and Taggart, B. (2004) *The effective provision of pre-school education (EPPE) project: final report*, London: DfES and Institute of Education, University of London.
Tolman, E.C. (1948) 'Cognitive maps in rats and men', Psychological Review, 55(4): 189–208.
'Bournemouth University Guide to Citation in the Harvard Style' (September 2010, accessed September 2011), www.bournemouth.ac.uk/library/citing_references/docs/Citing_Refs.
'Child and family: the case study', Research Mindedness in Social Work and Social Care, www.resmind.swap.ac.uk/content/08_case_studies/case_studies_01_01.htm

Chapter 6 Working with families of children and/or young people (Unit CP 6)

Working with families is a key aspect of work with children and young people and will influence how the best outcomes for the child or young person can be achieved. Although some children and young people are alone in the world, most are part of a wider family group, even when they do not live together. Families are basic units in our society and family relationships significantly affect the lives of children and young people, forming an important context for practitioners. The world of the family and community is a 'life support' system for a child or young person. Families provide for the basic needs of their young, and the young learn in the family setting about themselves and how they relate to the outside world. For most children and young people, the family is the safe base from which they interact with the rest of the world and learn their values, gender and ethnic identities, as well as what is acceptable social behaviour. Many things affect the families' ability to care for their young and this is explored further in this chapter.

There are no 'one size fits all' definitions of the family. Definitions are varied and sometimes confusing. However, the family is normally understood to be the people who are legally related

Figure 6.1 A multi-generational family

to the child or young person and those who, through relationships, have become an accepted part of their family. This will include, for example:

- biological mothers and fathers, married or unmarried
- biological brothers or sisters
- non-resident parents
- live-in partners
- step-parents and step-siblings
- grandparents or other family carers
- adoptive and foster parents
- gay and lesbian parents and their partners
- residential care workers
- carers of young offenders in secure units.

Some families do not have children or young people and others may consist of groups of individuals in various living arrangements.

Learning outcomes

1. Understand the role of the practitioner when working with families of children and young people.
2. Know the differences in family structure.
3. Understand the importance of working in partnership with parent(s)/carer(s).
4. Understand factors which influence life experiences.
5. Know how practitioners who work with children and/or young people can support families in times of crisis.

Evidence-based practice

In all work with children, young people and families, it is important to be aware of the evidence base for practice. Why do practitioners do what they do? How do practitioners know that what they are doing is right and will achieve the best possible outcomes? These questions form part of ongoing reflective practice and evaluation for the setting and service. There is information on the internet regarding evidence-based practice and research into work with families. For more information, you can refer to the Centre for Excellence and Outcomes in Children's and Young People's Services (C4EO) website (www.c4eo.org.uk), which will signpost to further reliable information.

Section 1: The role of the practitioner when working with families of children and young people

Currently, work with families emphasises the provision of support at an early stage when possible difficulties are identified to prevent more substantial difficulties developing. Early intervention can take place for any age, at any time; it is not just for the very young child. A key goal is to work in partnership with families to support their parenting role and to help build strength, health and resilience into the family.

Key term

Early intervention – intervening early and as soon as possible to tackle problems emerging for children, young people and their families or with a population most at risk of developing problems. Effective intervention may occur at any point in a child or young person's life. (Taken from C4EO expert group definition.)

There are different models or ways of working with families. For example:

- the partnership model, where parents, families and practitioners actively work together, value each other's contribution and each participates in decision making
- the expert model, where the practitioner is seen as expert with superior knowledge and parents and families have little say in what happens
- the befriending model, where practitioners are seen as friends and there are no clear boundaries or expected outcomes.

Figure 6.2 Different practitioner roles for those working with families

The partnership model is the most widely recognised and thought of as good practice, but there may be occasions when it is appropriate to use the other models. Practitioners have very clear sets of values and principles to use when working with families. The principles and values for the National Occupational Standards for practitioners who work with parents can be found at www.parentinguk.org.

Power relationships are very important when working with families. It is easy for organisations involved to fall into the trap of reproducing all the inequalities that exist in society. Organisations may discriminate against families because, for example, they are poor or have English as an additional language, without being aware of it. Settings and services need to make sure their policies and procedures work towards equality and inclusion. Individual managers and practitioners need to be aware that they may hold attitudes that value some families more than others – for example, based on social class or race. Work with families must be based on mutual respect and partnership where views are exchanged and valued.

What is the aim of your organisation's work with families? Observe how families are welcomed into the setting and suggest ways to improve their experience. Consider how your own practice could be improved in this area.

The processes of working with families in relation to the role of the practitioner

The processes of working with families will vary with the nature of individual job roles and the purpose of the setting or service. For example, someone who is working with children in a day nursery, caring for children of fee-paying parents, will work with families differently from the person providing targeted support to a family where violence is suspected or alleged. In the first case, working with families, although important, may not be the main focus of the job role. In the second case, the focus of the job role may be direct work with the family.

As can be seen from Table 6.1, there are many different job roles in working with families/ parents with different purposes. These can be divided into:

- practitioners whose main role is work with parents and families – for example, parent support advisors in schools, outreach workers in Sure Start centres, children's centres or justice settings
- practitioners whose main work is with children and young people but who interact with parents/ families on a daily basis
- practitioners whose work with families is part of a broader work role – for example, health visitors
- practitioners whose contact with the wider family may be incidental to their main roles, such as some teachers or police officers.

In practice, the distinction is not always clear-cut as services will overlap and may be co-located.

Research Activity

Find out about different job roles where the main work is with families. Compare the type of work undertaken and highlight similarities and differences.

Levels of family need

Families will vary in their level of need, as Figure 6.3 indicates. Tier 1 includes universal services with no major additional needs. Tier 2 is where families need additional support to prevent problems in the future. Families within Tiers 3 and 4 have greater needs and the role of the practitioner will be different. There may be a high level of intervention and support required.

Family needs	Examples of types of services required	Examples of job roles
Families requiring universal services (the majority)	Early years provision, health services, play and leisure services, youth services, education and schools	Teachers, nursery officers and assistants, Early Years Professionals, GPs, health visitors, playworkers, youth workers
Families needing additional information and support at different stages	As above; some families may also require speech and language therapy or learning support	As above, and speech and language therapists, specialised teachers or learning support assistants; Sure Start or Family Centre practitioners
A smaller number of families who have disabled children or young people needing targeted support	As above, some families may also require services such as Portage or use of assistive technology; some may require local authority family services or respite services	As above, and specialist disability practitioners; SENCOs in schools, educational psychologists, child psychologists
A minority of families who find difficulty in their parenting role and in providing a safe environment where children and young people will develop and flourish	As above; some families may also require support from multiple agencies, such as social services, health services such as CAMHS, drug and alcohol services, probation or youth offending teams	As above, and social workers, mental health practitioners, foster parents, residential childcare practitioners, youth offending workers

Table 6.1 Working with families

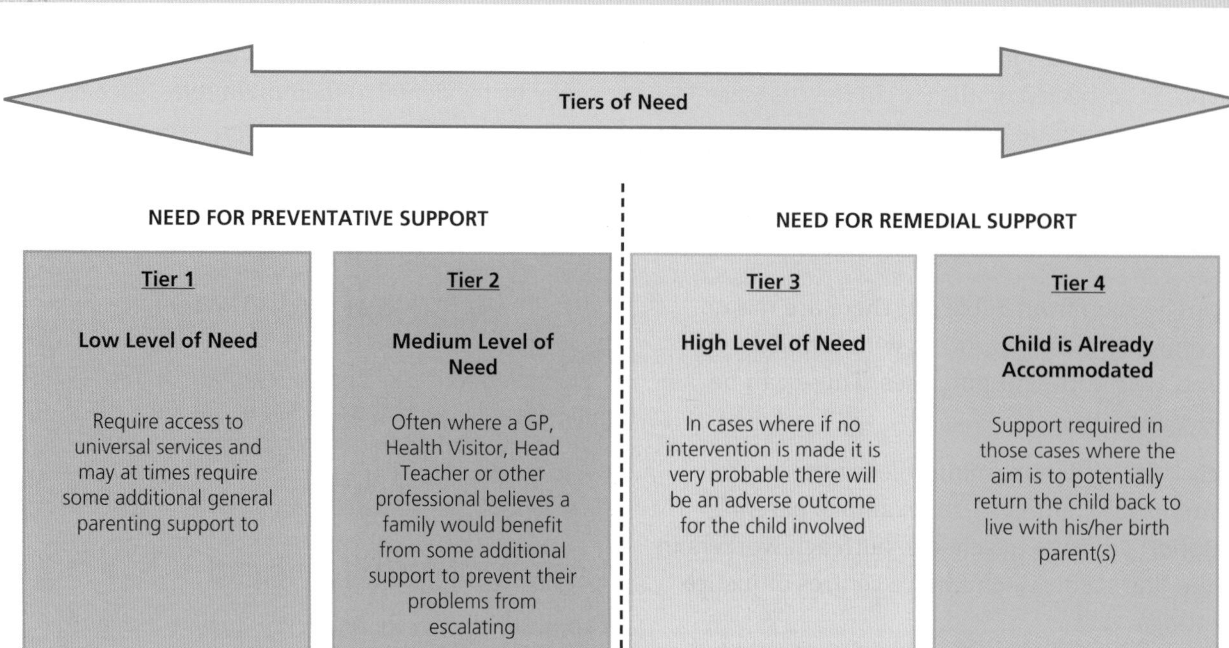

Figure 6.3 Levels of family need (taken from DfES Children's Services, The Market for Parental & Family Support Services. 2006, PriceWaterhouseCoopers)

Research Activity

Investigate the role of the lead professional. Find out different ways a lead professional may work with families.

Common processes in work with families

As well as differences, there are many similarities in the processes of work with families, regardless of role. Table 6.2 includes some of the processes that are commonly involved.

Process	Comment	Practitioner role
Developing and maintaining positive relationships with families	This includes setting up effective, positive communications based on family needs and agreeing how to share information and work in partnership together. It will include maintaining positive relationships over a period of time.	Initial and ongoing meetings or arrangements for contact, e.g. home visits, email, phone calls, formal or informal meetings. Setting up and maintaining information exchange/records for families, such as day books/diaries for young children. Establishing communication support where required. Revisiting arrangements to make sure they remain positive and effective. Dealing with disputes.
Establishing and updating goals and boundaries	Ensuring families understand • why they are working with the service • why they have may have been referred • who has referred them. Working in partnership to negotiate what the desired outcomes will be. These outcomes are sometimes set externally and are not negotiable, such as legal cases	Setting up formal contracts and agreements. Agreeing progress checks against outcomes. Checking and adapting desired goals and outcomes as circumstances change.

Process	Comment	Practitioner role
	involving access or safeguarding. Outcomes should, where possible, be measurable. Work with families will include setting boundaries, e.g. what can/cannot be confidential, what can be expected, what is included or not included, timescales and/or costs involved.	
Engaging with issues of power and control	This involves recognising that the setting or service could intimidate some families. Settings need to ensure their service is inclusive and does not create barriers for some families. It is important that families are fully involved in the service or setting and their views respected and taken into account.	Setting out to involve families as partners means ensuring barriers to their participation are removed. It is important to use clear and accessible communications and avoid jargon. Providing a warm and personalised welcome to families and making them aware of their rights and responsibilities. Enabling and supporting families to participate fully in making or influencing decisions that affect their child or young person.
Ensuring that the voice of the child or young person is heard	It is good practice for children and young people to be able to participate fully in decisions affecting their lives. Hearing the child's or young person's voice is an important principle and part of their rights. It is important to make sure that the welfare of the child or young person comes first. This often means supporting families to meet their child's needs.	Not making assumptions based on age and abilities. Very young and/or disabled children are often able to make their needs and preferences very clear.
Working effectively with other agencies if this is required	Working with families sometimes requires a multi-agency approach, e.g. with the NHS, schools, voluntary agencies or social services.	Making sure that lines of communication are clear and appropriate referrals are made.
Following policies and procedures	It is important that policies and procedures reflect current best practice and are regularly updated. Following these protects the practitioner and the family.	Making sure families are aware of policies and procedures, including complaints procedures.
Reviewing progress	Regular reviews and amendments/updates are required.	To set up reviews on a regular basis. Ensuring families, colleagues, children and young people are aware of reviews and are helped to participate and attend.
Reflecting on practice	Reflecting on practice is a key area for practitioners to check their practice is effective, meets current best practice and highlights any areas for additional training.	Including reflective practice as part of normal service delivery. This will include obtaining feedback from families, colleagues, children and young people. Keeping an up-to-date, professional development plan.
Having a planned exit strategy	For some types of work with families, an exit strategy is required. This is a planned way of bringing the service provision to an end.	The exit strategy will often be agreed with the goals and boundaries. It forms an important part of the process of work with families.

Table 6.2 Common processes in work with families

Communication boundaries that need to be adhered to when working with families

Key term

Communication boundaries – these are the ways individuals or organisations regulate and share private information with others – that is, who has access to different types of information. They involve balancing a need for disclosure with the need for privacy. Communication boundaries are necessary to protect practitioners as well as families and are closely related to confidentiality issues.

All of us have our own personal communication boundaries that allow us to control what we want people to know about us. These are necessary to help us protect ourselves and others. In our society, communication boundaries normally work to a set of agreed 'rules'. If people deliberately or unknowingly break the rules, this leads to conflict. In the context of the work setting, communication boundaries are normally set by the organisational policies and procedures, not by practitioners' own personal views. They affect all forms of communication (e.g. written, electronic, verbal). They can be set legally (e.g. what the law allows and what people are entitled to keep private). The UK Data Protection Act 1998 helps practitioners to understand communication boundaries and what can be shared. The Act distinguishes between ordinary personal data and sensitive personal data, which is subject to much stricter conditions. It is important to be able to determine different types of personal information. For example:

- personal information
- sensitive personal information
- confidential personal information.

Confidential personal information is likely to include (but is not limited to) information about a person's:

- physical or mental health or development
- social or family circumstances
- financial standing and financial details
- education, training and employment experience
- religious beliefs
- racial or ethnic origin
- criminal convictions
- sexuality.

Information relating to children and their families is particularly difficult, since it requires the rights of the child to be balanced with the rights of others, usually their parents or families. For example, a child has a right to be protected from harm and this is identified in the UN Convention on the Rights of the Child and in UK laws. It may be necessary, in order to protect a child, to disclose information about siblings or parents who themselves have rights to privacy.

Practitioners and families can, to some extent, exercise their right to communicate in certain ways and within their own boundaries. For example, a practitioner may not wish to share their religious views or a family may not wish to share the HIV status of some of its members. These issues are sensitive but only become a problem if they affect the behaviour of the person or offend or put others at risk.

When working with families in an organisational context, communication boundaries should be:

- clear and transparent
- sensitively implemented
- based on a 'need to know' principle
- agreed between practitioners and families, except where the child or young person's welfare is at risk
- within the policies and procedures of the setting.

Progress check

1. Explain the 'need to know' principle when working with children and families.
2. Give examples of circumstances:
   - when this principle may affect the work of practitioners
   - where the principle could be breached and the possible effects of this.

Communication boundaries when working with a family

Communication boundaries form part of the way in which overall goals and boundaries are agreed with families and will depend on the nature of the setting and individual family circumstances. Information about families is normally kept confidential and only released with the knowledge and permission of appropriate family members. Families have a right to understand what the communication boundaries are, who will have information about them and why this is necessary.

Families may request that communication boundaries are maintained between family members. For example, parents may request that information about a child or young person is not shared with the wider family – for example, in cases of family breakdown. Each request will be different and the professionals involved, in partnership with families, will decide the way forward. In some cases, families will not wish other agencies to have specific types of information and this should generally be respected.

Practitioners should never discuss families they are working with inappropriately or gossip inside or outside work. It is important that families can trust practitioners to respect their privacy and maintain appropriate communication boundaries.

Case Study

Ryan is seven years old and at school. He has started using inappropriate language at home and at school and his behaviour has deteriorated. Ryan's parents, along with others, believe the inappropriate language has come from Ethan, who has a number of problems at home. Several complaints are made to the school and a meeting is set up with concerned parents, the class teacher and the head. The school staff acknowledge that Ethan has been the source of some of the behavioural issues in the class but are unwilling to share details of Ethan's background and problems or to attribute blame to him. This leaves the parents frustrated and concerned and there is a frank exchange of views in the meeting. The head explains that it is not possible to discuss details of individual families with others.

How do you think this matter can be resolved? Is the head right to keep this information private?

Reflective practice

Reflect on the way you communicate with families. How do you know that your communication is effective?

Communication boundaries within the work team

It is important to identify and recognise the communication boundaries that exist within the work setting. The 'need to know' principle is important and will relate to individual job responsibilities. For example, if a child or young person has been bereaved, it would be appropriate to inform people who have direct responsibility for the child so they could recognise distress and offer support if required. It is not appropriate for practitioners to chat about families and individual children or young people in the staff room or in front of other children.

Communication boundaries with external agencies

Practitioners at different agencies should work together and recognise the communication boundaries that affect each agency. There should be a commitment to sharing information appropriately for the safety and well-being of children. The 'need to know' principle applies here, as elsewhere. It is important to understand and respect legislation and ethics that underpin confidentiality and security of information.

Communication boundaries with external agencies are normally included within policies and procedures of the setting and depend on circumstances. For example, communication boundaries with the library service may include informing the library staff of specific learning needs but not about family circumstances.

Confidentiality when working with families

Key term

Confidentiality – the duty to maintain confidence and thereby respect privacy. A person's right to privacy is enshrined in Article 12 of the United Nations (UN) Universal Declaration of Human Rights (1948).

Confidentiality is very important in work with families. It is closely related to communication boundaries, as discussed earlier. Practitioners should work with families sensitively and, where possible, encourage consent to the sharing of information where this is appropriate.

Families will need to understand what must be shared with other people and what can be confidential and they need to be aware of the principles, policies and procedures surrounding information sharing. They must be made aware of their rights and the implications of sharing or not sharing information.

The following are examples of cases where information may need to be shared and confidentiality cannot always be maintained.

- In cases of child protection, there is a requirement to share information across agencies, either in existing cases or where there are allegations of abuse. Practitioners will be required to follow the policies and procedures of the setting. If there are issues internal to the setting (e.g. where managers are involved in allegations), practitioners may be required to take action themselves and contact appropriate people or agencies.
- In cases where there are concerns about a child or young person's health, development or learning, these are normally shared first with the family but may also need to be shared with practitioners or others on a 'need to know' basis.
- Where there are legal issues, such as substance abuse, the practitioner may not able to keep the information confidential.
- Where there have been complaints from other families, children or young people, information may need to be shared.

In organisations, there are a number of practical steps that can be taken to ensure confidentiality is maintained:

- Keep desks clear from any personal or confidential information.
- Exercise care when replying to emails from people or organisations or when sending emails.
- Lock computers when leaving the area.
- Never leave visitors alone.
- Lock cabinets at night and during the day when you are not using them.
- Keep passwords private.
- Shred sensitive information.
- Be careful where you send information to print.
- Do not have private conversations in public places.

Progress check

Check how confidential information is dealt with in your setting. Familiarise yourself with the policies and procedures for sharing information.

Confidentiality when working with children and young people

Organisations often have their own policies and procedures for confidentiality when working with children and young people. These must be followed and will be set within the legal requirements for data protection. However, each situation needs to be considered on its own merits and in the context of the policies and procedures. It is not possible to assume that a 'one size fits all' approach will work or bring about the best outcomes for the child or young person.

Establishing a positive relationship with a child or young person is very important for practitioners. Practitioners need to be able to communicate effectively and sensitively with children and young people. As the relationship develops, or even early in the relationship, the child or young person may share sensitive personal information. The practitioner then has to exercise professional judgement about what to do with the information. It is also important that certain issues are shared with parents and often the practitioner can support the child or young person to do that. Practitioners can sometimes suggest sources of advice or further help.

It is important to be sensitive to the wishes of the child or young person in keeping their confidence, but there are occasions when this cannot be done. In cases of safeguarding where children or young people allege abuse, especially where a parent or family member is involved, they must be made aware immediately that what they have shared cannot be kept confidential.

In some cases, however, the issues are difficult to interpret or manage. Practitioners can discuss issues with their managers to gain advice or to enable referrals to other agencies.

Confidentiality when working with parents/carers

Many of the points made above when working with children and young people also apply to parents and carers – that is, those with legal responsibility for the child or young person. It is important to make positive relationships with parents and carers but they also need to be made aware that certain types of shared information cannot remain confidential – for example, safeguarding or legal issues.

Sometimes it is not appropriate to share information with parents and carers that has come from their child or young person. Sharing this information may have to be agreed with the child or young person first.

Confidentiality when working with the wider family

Sometimes situations arise that involve the wider family – that is, those who do not have legal responsibility for the child or young person but who may have a close relationship with them. Policies and procedures will provide general guidance on how confidentiality issues are dealt with but individual circumstances will influence the detail.

Confidentiality within the work team

The section covering communication boundaries on page 194 includes issues of confidentiality within the work team. However, it is important to recognise that, even where there are clear boundaries, there is sometimes a need to share confidential information to protect the welfare of children or young people. Their welfare should always be paramount.

Case Study

Liam is four years old and his mother cares for him. At weekends and in emergencies, Liam's paternal grandparents often care for him. Liam's mother tells the setting that Liam is being investigated for Hepatitis B but asks them not to tell his grandparents. She is concerned that they will tell his father, who will blame her as she is an ex drug addict.

What advice should the setting give to Liam's mother?

How attachment theory affects work with children and/or young people and families

Attachment is an important concept for those caring for children. Over the last decades, the idea of attachment theory has grown and developed. Secure attachments are beneficial for the child's overall development and enable the child to grow into a more stable and secure adult. Although different researchers have different views on attachment, its basic concepts have been recognised as crucial for healthy development. Taking attachment needs into account affects practice today and has transformed the way young children are cared for in institutions, such as hospitals, residential care and day care.

Key term

Attachment – attachments are emotional bonds that infants develop with their parents and other primary caregivers, such as their key person in an early childhood setting. These emotional bonds are central to a child's well-being.

The importance of attachment is emphasised in guidance to early years and care settings – for example, in the Early Years Foundation Stage (EYFS).

Key term

Separation anxiety – a normal developmental stage during which a child experiences anxiety when separated from the primary carer. Separation anxiety is normal between eight months of age and may last until 14 months old, or may occur later at 18–36 months.

John Bowlby (1965)

There are a number of theorists who have contributed to attachment theory; the most influential is John Bowlby. Bowlby was a psychologist, psychoanalyst and psychiatrist with an interest in child development who researched and published work between the 1950s and 1970s.

Bowlby felt that secure attachments are the basis of our evolutionary survival as babies are completely dependent on adults to meet their needs. Bowlby found that babies and children under three years old could be psychologically damaged by being in an institution and needed a close, consistent relationship for healthy emotional development. Bowlby called this psychological damage 'maternal deprivation', as he felt this relationship should be with the mother (or permanent mother substitute)

According to Bowlby, attachment takes place in the early years of life and has four key features:

1. Proximity maintenance (wanting to be physically close to the attachment figure)
2. Separation distress/anxiety
3. Safe haven (retreating to mother/carer when sensing danger or feeling anxious)
4. Secure base (exploration of the world knowing that the attachment figure will protect them from danger).

Mary Ainsworth (1978)

Mary Ainsworth was a colleague of Bowlby's. Ainsworth used a laboratory experiment called the 'strange situation'. In the strange situation, 12-month-old babies and their parents were brought to the laboratory and systematically separated from and reunited with one another. Babies fell into at least three categories:

1. Babies who were securely attached. These babies were upset when the parent left but on their return they went to them and were easily comforted.
2. Babies who were 'anxious resistant'. These babies were extremely distressed on separation and, when reunited, were difficult to soothe and demonstrated conflicting behaviours, which sometimes showed a desire to 'punish' the parent for leaving them (e.g. turning away, then clinging to them).
3. Babies who were 'avoidant'. These babies did not seem distressed when the parent left and actively avoided contact on their return, continuing to play with toys on the laboratory floor.

Ainsworth's research found that how babies behaved in the strange situation was linked to their experiences at home. Securely attached babies tended to have parents who were responsive to their needs.

J. Robertson and J. Robertson

The Robertsons worked closely with Bowlby and made a series of films that highlighted the plight of young children in hospital or who were separated from their main carers. It was their work that helped to change the experiences of young children in hospital, who previously were taken away from their parents for extended periods and, as a result, experienced high levels of separation anxiety/distress. In severe separation anxiety, the child goes through three stages (see Table 6.3).

Research Activity

Investigate how children were treated in hospital 50 years ago and compare that to the way they are treated today. Identify the key differences. If you can, talk to people who experienced hospital in those days and make a note of their memories.

Bowlby and the Robertsons felt that, when the child became detached, the damage to their emotional well-being could be significant and long-lasting.

A weakness of Bowlby's and his fellow researchers' work was that they looked only at mothers in a narrow section of society in a western context. The emphasis on mothers placed huge pressure on women not to return to the workplace and had an impact on social policy in terms of the provision of day care. Less day care was provided by the state as it was felt that mothers should stay at home with their children.

Stages	Signs of distress
Protest	Frustration, anger and protest, e.g. child struggles to escape, bangs on the door, kicks and cries.
Despair	Child appears to be accepting of the situation. They are calmer, withdrawn and seem sad. Many use comfort objects or thumb suck.
Detachment	Plays alone, withdrawn from others, may appear outwardly to have adjusted. The child is attempting to deal with the situation by forgetting – this may make it hard for them to trust people in the future.

Table 6.3 Stages of separation anxiety

Activity

Observe children in your setting as they settle in or cope with a big change. Explain how you know when a child is well attached:

1 to the parent, and

2 to the key person.

Multiple attachments

M. Rutter (1981) investigated the work of Bowlby and concluded it was only partially correct. Rutter concluded that children will also suffer psychological damage through family difficulties such as divorce, and not solely through separation from the mother. Rutter also concluded that infants can make multiple attachments, as in most societies a range of people are involved in care.

Neuroscience/brain development

A. Schore (1996) found that the stress hormone cortisol floods the baby's brain during intense crying and other stressful events. The release of cortisol is a normal response to stress but, when levels are high for prolonged periods, difficulties begin to arise for babies. When babies are subjected to extended periods of stress, they can begin to experience anxiety and panic. This destroys nerve connections in critical portions of an infant's developing brain. Schore concluded that, when the parts of the brain responsible for attachment and emotional control are not stimulated during infancy (e.g. when a baby is repeatedly neglected), these sections of the brain will not develop and this can lead to the baby becoming a violent, impulsive, unattached child. Schore stated that it is the sensitivity and responsiveness of a parent that helps shape parts of the brain responsible for emotional well-being.

Neuroscience also shows us that, when babies experience separation stress (e.g. from their parents/family), they have lower levels of growth hormone. This may damage the baby's growth and immune system.

Reflective practice

Engage with or observe a child who is distressed because of separation from a parent or key person and write a reflective account of the experience, drawing on attachment theory.

Summary of attachment theory

Despite criticisms of Bowlby's work, most researchers acknowledge that it was groundbreaking and has brought with it real insights into children's needs.

- Bowlby's attachment theory remains important to enable understanding of the social and emotional development of babies and young children.
- Newer research builds on Bowlby's theory and shows that babies who experience high-quality responsive care from a small number of people are able to make secure attachments.
- Babies are able to make attachments to people other than the mother, and older babies especially are capable of multiple attachments.
- Babies make attachments to those who are sensitive to their cues and who share not only in their care but also in their play and learning.
- Neuroscience and investigations into babies' brain development support attachment theory and demonstrate that neglect and severe separation stress can damage a baby's brain development, as well as their immune system and overall growth.
- Secure attachments are important to help babies and young children make the most of learning and development opportunities.

How attachment theory affects practice

Bowlby (1965) and subsequent attachment theorists have demonstrated that an understanding of the importance of attachment theory is key to positive practice with babies and children in their early years. The issue for practitioners has been how to make this work in the management and organisation of settings.

Key persons

A key person approach is designed to make sure good-quality attachments are made between the

Figure 6.4 Good attachment

child and the adult who is their key person. This means each baby or child feels special and cared for when they are away from home. Although the relationship is professional, being a key person is also an emotional and loving role, and practitioners will experience intense relationships with a child with all the feelings that may bring about. In the setting, there should be others who know the child well and can step in to a key person role in cases where the key person leaves or is away from work.

Settings find that the key person approach provides the best possible experience for the child, as well as giving job satisfaction to practitioners and customer satisfaction to parents/families.

Activity

Find out from key persons how they cope with the emotional demands of attachment to a child they work with. What help do they need to enable them to remain attached yet professional?

Settling in

It will take time for babies and young children to learn to trust new people, and practitioners need to be prepared to invest time and effort to support settling in.

Key persons usually know when new attachments have been made because the child:

- seeks them out, exploring and returning to check they are still there
- has the confidence to explore freely in their presence
- seeks their approval
- shows pleasure when they appear and distress when they go
- goes to them for comfort or is comforted by their presence.

Listening and responding to children

In order to support secure attachment and build up a special relationship, it is necessary for the practitioner to listen and respond to the child. This includes picking up and responding to the child's verbal and non-verbal cues, such as early signs of distress, boredom or need (e.g. facial expression, quivering lip, distressed crying). Parents will have provided detailed information on their child's feelings, preferences, life story and early experiences. Learning from this is vital for practitioners to be able to respond sensitively to a child.

Everyday practice

When the child is well attached to a key person, this relationship comes first. Young children need familiarity, consistent and predictable routines, and the opportunity to play freely. This, together with secure attachments, gives them the foundation for their positive learning and development.

Attachment theory and looked-after children

The quality and continuity of care for a 'looked-after' child is extremely important and is now seen as vital when making decisions for and with the child. The child's existing attachments and attachment needs are taken into account when courts are deciding about the future of the child.

Reflective practice

Reflect on how your practice and that of your setting support children to make secure attachments.

Section 2: The differences in family structure

Different family structures in society today

There are definitions of what constitutes a 'family' in the introduction to this chapter. These definitions reflect the fact that there are many different family structures in society today. As society has changed over the last century, the law has moved to recognise different family forms.

Case Study

The new Human Fertilisation and Embryology Act 2008 includes in law, for the first time, the idea of a two-mother family, where in a lesbian couple one woman carries the child and is the mother and the second woman is classed as the legal 'parent' and can be named on the birth certificate. Previously the woman who did not carry the child had no legal rights as a parent. There are extra rules that apply to people who are not in civil partnerships.

1 What does this new law say about society and its attitudes to families?
2 Give examples from your own experience of different family structures.

Family type	What it means
Nuclear family	A mother and father with their children who live together. A version of this is known as the 'cereal packet family': the woman is a housewife and full-time mother and the man is the 'breadwinner', i.e. he is the one who goes to work to earn money.
Extended family	A family group often of three generations living in close proximity, consisting of parents, children and other close relatives. This could include those who may not be related by blood or marriage.
Blended family (step-family or reconstituted family)	A social unit consisting of two previously married parents and the children of their former marriages. This will include those who have never married but who have been in committed relationships.
Lone (single) parent family	This family consists of one parent (usually female) and children.
Living apart together	Often following failed marriages or cohabitations. Initial estimates suggest that around two million people have regular partners in other households (Ipsos MORI, 2009).
Civil partnerships	Same-sex couples have created a new type of family. Civil partnerships were granted under the Civil Partnership Act 2004, giving same-sex couples rights and responsibilities identical to civil marriage.

Table 6.4 Examples of family types found in the UK today

The possible effects of different parenting styles

Key term

Parenting style – parenting refers to the rearing of a child or young person and the care, love, and guidance given by a parent. The style (way) in which parents rear their child or young person has been found to be linked to their well-being, development and behaviour.

Parenting styles

Looking at parenting styles is increasingly popular. For many years, the democratic (or authoritative) style of parenting has been seen as the most suitable for today's children and young people. As we explain below, authoritative parenting should not be confused with authoritarian parenting. The words are similar but these are two separate and very different parenting styles.

Baumrind (1967) suggested that the majority of parents display one of three different parenting styles. Further research also suggested the addition of a fourth parenting style (Maccoby and Martin, 1983). These styles are described in Table 6.5. These describe a normal range of parenting and are not describing neglectful or abusive families, except where indicated.

Although the original work by Baumrind was undertaken some years ago, it remains relevant today. In 2011, the Department for Education and Department of Health quoted from Utting (2009). The quote discusses the critical factors during the early years and states that:

> 'Effective, warm, authoritative parenting gives children confidence, a sense of well-being and self-worth. It also stimulates brain development and the capacity to learn.'

Although parenting styles are described below, it is important to see that each family is unique and may not fit neatly into a particular type. Parents within one family may have different styles – for example, a father may support a very strict approach and a mother a permissive one. Both may feel their style is the best for the child. The styles of individual parents will vary with circumstances and sometimes they will be stricter or more permissive than at other times.

Parenting style	Key features
Authoritarian	This describes strict and controlling parenting, relying on giving orders without room for explanation if challenged by the child or young person. Parents place high demands on the child or young person, tell them what to do, how to behave and when to do so, usually without flexibility. They are less responsive, e.g. there is limited use of feedback, discussion or input from the children. The parents may provide an ordered and highly structured environment. Children and young people from authoritarian families tend to perform moderately well in school and be uninvolved in problem behaviour, but they have poorer social skills, lower self-esteem and higher levels of depression.
Permissive	Permissive parents are the opposite of authoritarian parents and are sometimes thought of as indulgent. They are very responsive to their children but demand very little. There is little or no structure for their children, who are allowed to do as they please. There may be few, if any, rules in the home and those that exist may not be enforced, or are enforced inconsistently. The child or young person who has experienced this parenting style may be creative and original, with positive self-esteem. Their social skills may be poor because they do not empathise well with others. Other children or young people may find them self-centred and difficult. They may lack boundaries and have little, or no, idea of right and wrong and may not be 'happy' children or young people.

Parenting style	Key features
Authoritative	This style is sometimes called democratic. Like the authoritarian style, these parents place high demands on the child and expect them to behave appropriately according to clear boundaries. The difference is that these parents are responsive to the child. They will use more explanations and allow children to make decisions on issues that are appropriate for their age and abilities. They will also allow them to experience the outcome of those decisions. This style encourages children to be assertive, responsible and cooperative. It sets reasonable rules and guidelines that are in the best interests of the child. The rules provide structure, while still allowing room for the child to explore, test and begin the process of learning what constitutes acceptable behaviour. Authoritative parenting is also a model that allows parents to express love and affection without concerns that they are losing control. Authoritative parenting is thought to be the best for children as they learn to accept responsibility, make wiser choices and cope better with change. They have positive self-esteem, fit in and achieve well at school or nursery and, in most cases, accept the rules if they are explained and are reasonable.
Uninvolved	Some uninvolved parents still have basic boundaries, whereas others are clearly neglectful. Uninvolved/emotionally distant parents do not demand much from their child or respond to them. There is often little communication and the parent may avoid the child or young person. Parents may fulfil basic needs but are emotionally detached from the child's life. They may not supervise them and have few expectations for achievement or behaviour. Sometimes their own problems (e.g. mental health, social circumstances) are so overwhelming that they cannot deal with the child or young person. Others may find they are too busy to become involved or they themselves may have been brought up by uninvolved parents and do not know how to respond to their child or young person. The outcomes for this parenting style are likely to be the worst of all. These children tend to lack self-control, have low self-esteem and are less competent than their peers. They tend to have more delinquent behaviour as they grow older. Children may come to school or nursery in dirty or ill-fitting clothes. Their personal hygiene may not be maintained.

Table 6.5 Parenting styles

Activity

Helicopter parents are overprotective and continually hover over their child. Some children may find this very embarrassing and may want their parents to 'back off'. A contrast is sometimes called 'submarine' parenting, where parents remain hidden, only surfacing when needed. Make a note of the pros and cons of each approach for the parent and for the child or young person.

How and why parents rear their children in particular ways are complex and individual. Some influences are:

- culture
- ethnicity
- current circumstances
- the child or young person's personality, behaviour or individual needs
- the parents' own childhood experiences.

Research Activity

The Ipsos MORI report 'Families in Britain' (2009) finds that the decline of the traditional family has led to greater instability and that many children experience different family forms while they are growing up. Find out about other research into changing family structures and how this is affecting children and young people growing up in Britain.

Reflective practice

Think of children you work with who have experienced different parenting styles. Reflect on how your practice changes to meet their individual needs.

Case Study

The recent controversial book *Battle Hymn of the Tiger Mother* by Amy Chua, which supports a controlling parenting style, has challenged the view that the authoritative parenting style is best. Chua describes how she raised her children to achieve excellence and would never let them waste time on social media, TV or computer games. She ensured her children spent hours on maths and spelling drills and daily piano practice and would never accept a grade lower than 'A'. Her view is that the tiger mother's cubs are better prepared for a harsh world than those who have had an indulgent upbringing.

Discuss the advantages and disadvantages of Amy Chua's approach.

The Millennium Cohort Study (2001 and ongoing)

The Millennium Cohort Study (MCS) is a multi-disciplinary research project following the lives of around 19,000 children born in the UK in 2000–01. The findings of this study so far indicate that the authoritative parenting style best prepares children and young people to do well in life. The second most successful parenting style was the permissive, followed by the authoritarian. The children of uninvolved parents were set to do least well.

How different parenting styles may influence the practitioner's ways of working with children and/or young people

Professional work with children and young people is not the same as parenting because the basic relationship is different. However, practitioners act in 'loco parentis' and need to understand how parenting styles affect the learning, development and behaviour of the children and young people in their care. They need to take parenting styles into account when dealing with individual children, young people and families. For example, not all parents will understand or support a more democratic approach that underpins much good practice in settings and services. Always remember that most parents want the best for their child or young person, regardless of parenting style.

Where parents do not support the values of the setting, it is important for practitioners not to make negative judgements. This is a sensitive area. Social and cultural issues need to be taken into account and respect shown to the parents. Many issues are straightforward to handle. For example, where children are allowed at home to do what they like, in the setting they are encouraged to share. There are more challenging issues, such as whether it is right to encourage a child or young person to make choices or express opinions that contradict their parents' views.

In Practice

In an early years setting, the boys are playing happily in the domestic play area. A father comes to collect his son who is play 'ironing'. The father comments that letting his son play in this way will turn him into a girl and he does not want that. He pulls the child away from the domestic play area and speaks sternly to him.

What are the issues raised by the father's comment?

How should the practitioner respond?

Although one incident cannot tell you about the parenting style, what might this father's behaviour indicate?

Many settings undertake work with parents to increase understanding and, where possible, help to change behaviour that may be damaging for the child or young person. This can lead to ethical dilemmas for practitioners who need to respect a parent's beliefs and culture. Policies and procedures or a statement of the ethos of the setting may be a good starting point. It is important to remember that children or young people are all different and should not be labelled just because they have parents with particular parenting styles. In the case of uninvolved parents in particular, there may be a need for active intervention if children are neglected or suffering psychological damage.

Authoritative (democratic) parenting style

Good professional practice has many similarities with the authoritative style of parenting. Although every child and young person is different, those brought up with an authoritative parenting style may find it easier to settle in and take advantage of the learning and development opportunities in a setting. Parents who understand this type of parenting will generally understand and support the aims and goals of the setting.

Activity

Being a parent

Write a job description and person specification for a parent.

Authoritarian parenting style

Children and young people who have experienced authoritarian parenting may appear to behave well and not challenge what they are told. This sounds good but is not often in the child or young person's best interests. Practitioners can support children and young people by:

- giving clear and consistent directions until they feel able to take decisions for themselves and show independence
- providing a structured framework that will build on their strengths and gradually permit more flexibility
- understanding that they may be more dependent on adults for approval and direction and may need extra support
- giving opportunities to enable them to think for themselves
- looking beyond the 'good behaviour'
- building up self-esteem by giving praise and encouragement
- encouraging them to make choices
- modelling and encouraging assertive behaviour
- modelling appropriate language to help them to challenge effectively
- giving opportunities for them to succeed
- giving opportunities for risk taking in a safe environment.

Parents who are authoritarian in their approach may find it difficult to agree with the values of the setting or understand the purpose of the way the child or young person is treated. Practitioners need to work with parents to assist their understanding without implying criticism or being patronising.

Permissive parenting style

Children or young people who have experienced permissive parenting may have high self-esteem but can be unrealistic about themselves. They may find it difficult to settle into a consistent routine and to consider others. Practitioners can support children and young people by:

- working with them to negotiate, set and consistently maintain boundaries
- encouraging turn taking, sharing and fairness
- modelling consideration for others
- encouraging empathy
- encouraging them to have realistic expectations
- praising and rewarding appropriately
- building on their creativity and strengths
- providing a structured environment.

Parents who use this style may consider that the rules, policies and procedures of the setting are restrictive and may push the boundaries of what is acceptable for their child or young person. Practitioners will need to work carefully with the family and be prepared to explain clearly why things are expected and in some cases required.

Uninvolved parenting style

The child or young person who has experienced this parenting style has poorer outcomes than with any other parenting style. Practitioners can support children and young people by:

- providing extensive support to help them to overcome their disadvantage so far as is possible
- supporting referrals for specialist help – for example, psychologists, play therapists or social workers
- providing age appropriate nurture groups/facilities
- providing a structured environment
- providing consistent one-to-one as well as group support
- being interested and concerned for their welfare
- providing praise and encouragement
- providing consistent routines.

Progress check

Work alone or in a group to prepare a leaflet explaining the advantages of an authoritative parenting style.

Section 3: The importance of working in partnership with parent(s)/carer(s)

The outcomes for children and young people are better when settings and services work in partnership with parents/carers. Partnerships are so important they have been recognised in law. In 2006, the Scottish Parliament passed the Scottish Schools (Parental Involvement) Act. The Act was introduced to help parents, carers and schools work together as partners in children's learning. In England, there is a statutory requirement for partnership working within the EYFS (2012). Parent partnership schemes (PPS) for children and young people with special educational needs or disabilities have been in existence since 1994. Local authorities (LAs) have a duty to ensure that parents in their area have access to a PPS, which has a role in making sure that parents' views are heard and understood and that these views inform local policy and practice.

Partnership can take different forms and does not just 'happen'. It requires time, effort, skill and training. Partnership should be embedded in all aspects of the setting or service involved. Examples of partnership activities that take place are:

- undertaking 'hands on' activities with children in the setting
- involvement in the leadership and management of the setting
- parents observing their own children at home and reporting back
- regular information exchange and feedback
- encouraging participation in decision-making for their own children and for the way the setting works.

A number of different projects have been set up to research and support parent partnerships. The following are examples but there are many more:

- The Youth Justice Board has responded to the introduction of 'Parenting Orders' for parents of young people who are at risk of, or known to be, offending or who are failing to attend school by developing a parenting programme.
- The Peers Early Education Partnership (PEEP) is an early learning programme which aims to improve the life chances of children, particularly in disadvantaged areas. Its purpose is to raise educational attainment, especially in literacy, by supporting parents and carers in their role as the first educators of their children.
- Parents as partners in children's early learning and development (PEAL) project: this supports the EPPE research (2004, 2007) and shows that a good home learning environment is the most effective way of enhancing a child's learning.

Figure 6.5 Parent partnerships in action

The responsibilities of the practitioner when working with parent(s)/carer(s)

The responsibilities of practitioners when working with parents/carers will depend on the type of setting or service and their work role. However, there are some responsibilities that apply to all who work with parents/carers, although there may be different emphases. Practitioners have to work with both mothers and fathers who are the parents of the child or young person. Often work with fathers requires different strategies to engage them and support them in their parenting role. It is important to note that fathers are often more involved with their children than in previous years. The Department for Education and Department of Health (2011) state that:

'Mothers still devote more time to childcare than fathers, but more fathers are involved in childcare now and are spending more time on it than they used to – by as much as 200 per cent between 1974 and 2000.

Gray, A. (2006)

Examples of practitioner responsibilities are listed below, but these will vary with the job role:

- understanding the meaning of partnership with parents and working towards this
- reflecting the rights of the child as set out in the UN Convention on the Rights of the Child (1989) and placing the child's welfare at the heart of the process
- understanding the needs of both parents, including those of non-resident fathers and minority ethnic groups
- having effective key worker/person systems in place
- assessing need

Figure 6.6 Fathers are important

- supporting design of better services and interventions
- making sure services are conveniently located
- showing respect for the parent/carer regardless of their behaviour or attitudes
- respecting diversity and the parents' culture, language and beliefs
- recognising that the parents have unique information about their child or young person and are their primary educators
- building on parents' strengths and experience
- establishing and maintaining positive relationships
- welcoming and valuing parents
- effectively exchanging information with parents
- taking time to get to know parents and families
- encouraging active participation of parents (and the child or young person) in decision-making
- providing relevant resources and information for parents
- supporting parents through difficulties and/or when the child or young person has to be referred to other agencies
- having clear and accessible policies and procedures for work with families and parents
- being able to improve own skills and knowledge
- being aware of and using evidence-based practice.

Power relationships

It is important to remember that, when working with families, there is often an imbalance of power. Parents may feel powerless and practitioners often have to work hard to make partnerships work.

Developing effective working with families when supporting children and/or young people

Effective working means that practitioners will meet the individual and unique needs of the families they work with. They are likely to use methods and strategies that have an evidence base and they will have built in regular evaluation of their work. An effective assessment of need will be required to determine the most appropriate support. The list of examples of processes in Table 6.2 covers many of the ways of working, such as developing effective relationships and positive communication.

The key person/worker approach is a very important way in which practitioners work with families. Key persons/workers know the family well. This knowledge can prevent an over-reaction to family problems and may prevent families being labelled 'in need' or 'problem families' when in fact they have no issues that cannot be sorted out.

Families may feel it is an 'us' and 'them' situation and be worried about sharing with practitioners in case they and their children are 'labelled' or worse are taken into care. Practitioners must be open and transparent about the individual situation and its possibilities.

Benefits of partnership working with parents and carers

Sometimes it is easier to look at a question by considering what would happen if partnerships did not exist. If this were the case, and it sometimes is, even these days, this is likely to negatively affect all concerned. We know from research (see below) that outcomes for children are worse when parents and carers are uninvolved in their learning and development. Parents and carers will become frustrated and disempowered and may not support the values of the setting, leading to hostility. Practitioners may be disengaged from their clients/customers and may, for example, feel that a professional distance is appropriate when in fact they need to develop a firm attachment to a child.

Activity

Remember the last time a professional talked down to you or told you what to do without discussion. How did this make you feel? How might parents feel if a setting did this to them in regard to their child? How might a young person feel and behave?

Benefits of partnership working for children and young people

Parents and carers are a young child's first and most enduring educator. They know more about the child than anyone else and are deeply involved in their own child's life and well-being. Partnership working with parents will benefit children and young people's learning and development. Various projects focused on early years have demonstrated the benefits (e.g. PEAL and EPPE discussed above). EPPE found that children with strong home learning environments are already ahead in both social and intellectual development at the age of three. This advantage continues through to age seven, and the latest EPPE report suggests that the positive effect is maintained through to age ten. The benefits are evident across all social classes and ethnic groups, and levels of parental involvement have a greater impact on achievement for 5–11-year-olds than the variation in school quality. Partnerships with parents mean that the learning and development approach from the setting can be continued in the home and this improves the outcomes for children. This applies to learning, development and behaviour. Mutual respect as demonstrated through partnership provides a strong message to children and young people of the value of school or other services.

Partnerships with parents often lead to the empowerment of parents, who then are able to participate in the development of services that they and others require. This directly benefits the child and young person. Parents and carers find their own self-esteem and confidence grow alongside their child's.

Behaviour issues are far better dealt with when families are working in partnership with the setting. When the same approach is taken to behaviour management, this increases the child or young person's sense of self-worth.

Benefits of partnership working for the practitioner

Working in partnership with parents has many benefits for the practitioner. A positive partnership will make the work more fulfilling and the child or young person is likely to progress well. Partnerships will often allow parents and carers to be honest about the service they receive and they have a positive input to the quality improvement cycle.

If you have a genuine partnership, this will also lead to a mutual and open dialogue. This means feelings and issues can be expressed in a non-judgemental way. An atmosphere of openness and acceptance leads to less hostility and more involvement from parents.

Parents and carers often provide practical help in settings in many different ways and this is encouraged in the best settings. They can help with learning activities and bring their own special skills to the setting. For example, a parent who is a chef in an ethnic restaurant can undertake cooking activities with children, which would not only increase their learning and skills but tell them about different cultures. Partnerships with parents and carers from different ethnic groups allow settings to build on the strengths of different parts of society.

Close relationships with families and children and young people can become very demanding and sometimes difficult to handle. Practitioners should remain approachable and involved, while maintaining their professional role.

Benefits of partnership working for parents/carers

Developing close and supportive relationships with practitioners is beneficial to parents/carers:

- It gives them the confidence that their child or young person is well cared for.
- It opens doors to information and support.

For a parent lacking confidence or trust in services, forming a positive partnership with practitioners can be a way to get the help and information they need. Parents value a partnership approach where they are involved, not judged and where their views are respected. They want practitioners to get alongside them and show interest in their child or young person and the life of the family.

Parent partnerships not only assist them in their parenting role but can go beyond. For example, they can:

- increase their confidence and self-esteem
- empower them to take decisions themselves
- open doors into work or further training
- provide a way of developing new skills and knowledge.

If a child or young person has special educational needs or disabilities, partnerships are very important. Parents may have a lead professional or someone to help deal with the multiple problems that may arise. This must be firmly based in partnership to enable the parents/carer to grow in confidence and understand the issues affecting their child. The days of 'being done to' should be long gone.

Case Study

Alison has seven-year-old twins. She left school at 16 with no qualifications and has never worked. When the twins were three, she started to help at the local pre-school and, although it took time, practitioners got alongside her and encouraged her to develop herself. Within nine months, Alison was on the management committee. In order to support the twins, she took literacy classes and these improved her confidence and self-esteem. Now the twins are at school, Alison is working as a teaching assistant and has nearly completed her Level 3 qualification. She takes time to be involved in the local parent partnership scheme.

Section 4: Factors which influence life experiences

There are many different factors that influence life experiences and, although these may be common, they are individual and unique to each family. Certain life experiences are expected, such as the experience of bereavement, but they will all have an impact on a child or young person's emotional well-being. Good support will help the child or

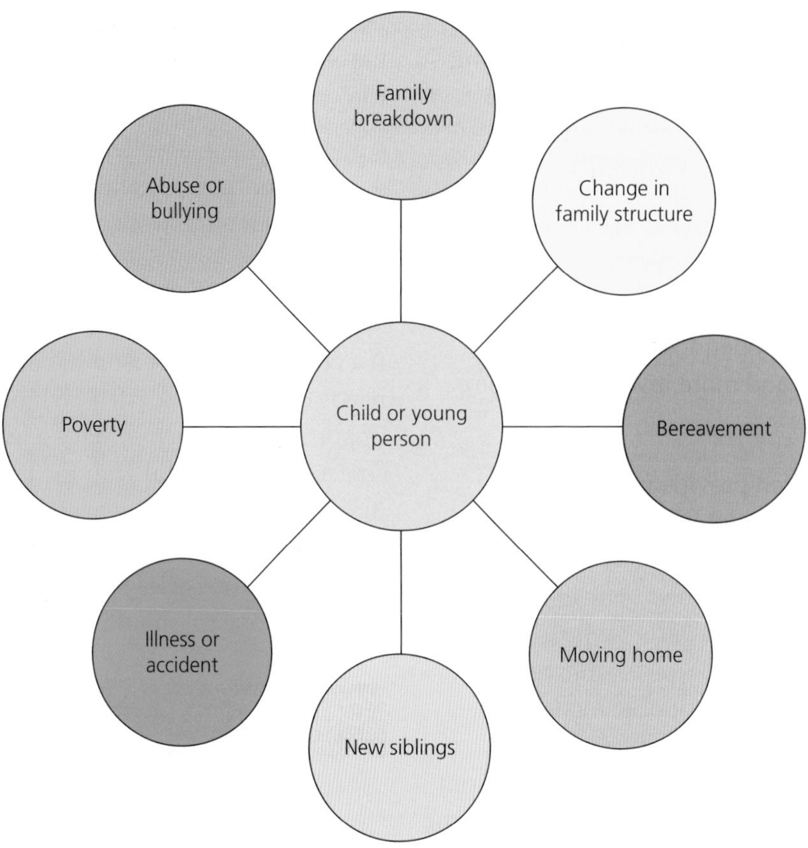

Figure 6.7 Commonly experienced major life events for children and young people

young person to adjust and make sense of the situation.

Some children and young people will experience extreme events in their lives, such as abuse, domestic violence or civil war. These children may require specialist help. Even where children and young people and families have no direct involvement, things such as natural disasters or terrorism can cause fear.

Major life events affect children, young people, parents and families in similar ways but the impact on their emotional and social well-being will vary according to:

- the severity of the experience
- the availability of high-quality support
- the resilience of the individual or family concerned.

It is important to emphasise that, with or sometimes without support, most children, young people, parents and families will cope well with major life events.

Key term

Resilience – resilience is the ability to recover from, 'bounce back', succeed and prosper after facing severe hardships, rejection and pressure. Some people think resilience is inborn and others think it is partly inborn but also influenced by life experiences.

Possible effects of major life events

It is important to recognise that practitioners will from time to time have to support children and young people who experience mental health and psychological well being issues. This is regardless of dealing with major life events but may become worse during difficult periods. Parents, carers and families may also require support.

Possible effects of major life events on the child

To mature emotionally and socially, children interact with people outside their home (e.g. close relatives, friends, neighbours, people at day care settings, schools, sports and leisure activities). By coping with common daily conflicts, stresses and strains, children gradually acquire the skills to handle more significant life events. Children also learn by watching how adults deal with stress in their lives. Children need to be made aware that to be anxious or to feel sad is normal and that these feelings will ease over time.

The child under stress during major life events may exhibit the following types of behaviour:

- withdrawn behaviour
- aggressive behaviour
- overactive or passive behaviour
- sleep problems
- irritability or a 'short fuse'
- reverting to behaviour associated with a younger child
- changes in their relationships with families and friends
- being preoccupied with what happened to them
- disruption to their learning
- exaggerated reactions to events.

Major life events, such as chronic illness and divorce, will challenge a child's abilities to cope. These events may also interfere with the child's emotional and social development. For example, a chronic illness may prevent a child from participating in activities and also impair performance in school.

Children who have experienced a major traumatic life event may take longer to recover or adapt than after a less major event. However, if a child lacks support from their family or the setting or is lacking in resilience, they may struggle to recover well whatever the severity of the life event and may exhibit many of the behaviours listed above.

Possible effects of major life events on the young person

Much of the above paragraph on the effects of life events on children also apply to young people. Young people may also experience additional major life events. For example:

- becoming a young carer of a parent or family
- experiencing relationship difficulties
- developing sexuality
- underage pregnancy
- exposure to drugs and alcohol abuse
- personal mental health issues
- leaving home or care settings.

The young person under stress during major life events may demonstrate any of the behaviours listed above for children but may also:

- abuse drugs or alcohol
- get into trouble with the law
- engage in antisocial behaviour
- make inappropriate relationships
- find themselves being groomed for sexual purposes
- play truant and be excluded from school.

Research Activity

Explain the factors that influence how children or young people cope with major life events. Find out different views on what makes a child or young person more resilient. How can practitioners support children and young people to become more resilient?

Possible effects of major life events on parent(s)/carers(s)

Parents and carers will vary in their response to life events but are often reluctant to ask for support. The types of major life events are similar to those of young people and children but from an adult perspective. How they cope will depend on their own resilience, their support networks and practical issues, such as having enough money to pay the bills.

Additional issues affecting parents/carers may include:

- domestic violence
- money worries
- chronic ill health (physical or mental)
- unemployment
- isolation

- caring responsibilities for their own parents
- poverty
- drug and alcohol abuse.

Adults may suffer stress for many reasons. One of the key pressures is concern about their children and young people. On their website, the charity Family Lives (www.familylives.org.uk) reports that, in 2010, there was an increase in parents calling into their 'Parentline'. Parents were worried about their own or their children's mental health and were suffering general stress, depression and anxiety. Depending on circumstances, practitioners can support parents by:

- recognising need
- sensitive and timely intervention
- personalising the outcomes approach to problems
- offering a listening ear
- providing information
- signposting to specialist help
- supporting a multi-agency approach if required.

Sometimes parenting programmes can be helpful to parents. The Department for Education and Department of Health (2011) states that:

> 'Supporting parents with parenting programmes has a positive impact on both parents' and children's wellbeing and mental health. The Healthy Child Programme also includes breastfeeding support and a range of proven preventive services.'

Department of Health (2011)

Possible effects of major life events on the family

Families consist of all the groups mentioned above (i.e. children, young people and adult parents) but may also include other types of relationships, as identified at the beginning of the chapter. They are subject to all the major life events described and may react to stress in any of the ways outlined.

The Ipsos MORI report (2009) states that:

> 'Families are now less stable than in previous generations. Children often grow up with different parents, in stepfamilies, or with one parent figure missing. These children are more likely to experience poverty, poor health and wellbeing and be involved in antisocial behaviour. Families will go on evolving. As more women have careers and seek more egalitarian relationships, men and women frequently need to negotiate their roles within the family. This is likely to be heightened as the economic downturn takes its toll on employment and families have to be flexible about who is in work.'

This lack of stability means families are often vulnerable to the effects of major life events. Families are reliant on the individual members to work together and support each other. Whole families will be deeply affected by events such as loss of income, poor housing or ill health of individual members. The consequences of stress vary with the nature and severity of the events, the family's emotional resilience and the availability of appropriate support.

Progress check

Families come under stress for many reasons. Describe the life events that cause stress for families today. How should services respond to these increased stresses?

The effects of socio-economic factors on families

Key term

Socio-economic factors – relating to both economic (e.g. income, expenditure, balancing the budget) and social factors (e.g. family, religion, housing, locality, health).

Socio-economic factors are closely related to the major life events discussed earlier and include:

- unemployment
- family breakdown
- low pay
- financial deprivation/poverty
- family debt
- housing instability.

Socio-economic factors that affect families are often related to poverty. Poverty in the UK is normally measured by household income. It is defined as a household earning less than 60 per cent of the median after housing costs have been paid (taken from Child Poverty Action Group, 'Poverty in the UK', London, 2011, www.cpag.org.uk/povertyfacts). It is recognised that poverty in families does change over time – for example, if a mother returns to employment after caring for young children, the family may move out of poverty. Useful information about poverty can be found on several websites, two of which are listed at the end of the chapter.

Children and young people from families that are poor are less likely to stay on at school, more likely to suffer health problems and more likely to become involved in crime. Although unemployment brings poverty, families in work who are on low wages are also frequently in poverty. Families living in very low-income households are often unable to afford basic necessities or to give children the same opportunities that others take for granted.

Families living in poverty can be affected in different ways. For example:

- living from hand to mouth
- having no money for emergencies
- being unable to replace broken furniture, equipment or toys
- being unable to afford social activities
- being unable to keep their houses heated
- having no money for holidays, sports or leisure activities
- having no money for school uniforms
- being unable to afford school trips or any extras
- being unable to afford healthier food options, which may be more expensive.

Progress check

The Child Poverty Action Group (CPAG, 2011) highlights the inequalities behind child poverty and suggests ways that government and others can take action to deal with it. Investigate child poverty in your home country and prepare a report highlighting your findings.

Section 5: How practitioners who work with children and/or young people can support families in times of crisis

It is difficult to define the term 'crisis' as this will vary for different families. For this section, we understand a crisis to mean a critical, overwhelming event for a family. This could include events such as:

- a major accident, death or serious illness
- sudden unemployment or loss of income.

Some families experience a crisis in 'normal' situations, such as new baby or a young person leaving home. This type of event means members have to change and adapt, and other families may not see this as a crisis. A crisis can also be an unexpected, 'out of the blue' event. A stressful event in itself does not constitute a crisis, but is determined by the family members' view of the event and their response to it.

A crisis is when people have tried their usual coping strategies to deal with the events without success. If families are not flexible and willing to support each other and make changes, this can lead to family disorganisation. In turn, this can lead to actions being taken which harm the family, such as alcoholism, abuse or neglect.

There are common patterns of response to most crises. An individual's reaction to a crisis can include:

- emotional reactions, such as grief, fear, anger or guilt
- behavioural reactions, such as sleep and appetite problems, withdrawal or restlessness
- mental reactions, such as difficulty concentrating, confusion or nightmares
- physical reactions, such as tiredness, panic attacks, headaches, dizziness or digestive problems.

Strategies to support families in times of crisis

Families will deal with all crises according to:

- the severity of the crisis
- their ability to change things
- the ability of the family to support one another
- the availability of high-quality support
- the flexibility and resilience of the family concerned.

If family members are severely affected by a crisis, they may:

- demonstrate behaviour that has a damaging effect, physically or emotionally, on themselves or other people
- demonstrate non-compliant or over-compliant behaviour (e.g. sabotaging attempts to help or being passive, disengaging completely)
- apparently cooperate but work to undermine the process of change
- become depressed or even suicidal
- become disorientated
- become critical or hostile.

Crisis intervention for major incidents

This section refers to incidents such as sudden death, war, violence, fire or major accidents. If appropriate support is given soon after a crisis event, this helps to reduce its effects. In some parts of the UK, when there is a major incident, there are specially trained people who can support families and individuals – for example, crisis support officers or police family liaison officers. Inter-agency working is very important in these circumstances to make sure families receive the initial and post-crisis support they need. Immediate crisis support can take place in a range of settings – for example, hospital emergency rooms, crisis/counselling centres, mental health clinics, schools, police stations and social service agencies. Local and national helplines are available to address crises related to suicide, domestic violence, sexual assault and other crises. After this type of severe crisis has settled down, some families will require long-term support. The NHS has services that can assist in situations where there is or is likely to be an impact on a child or adolescent's mental health or psychological well being. **A key** provider is the **Child and Adolescent Mental Health Service** (CAMHS). These are locally based, and you can find more information about your local area on the Internet, e.g. www.camhscares.nhs.uk for some areas in south London.

Strategies that could be used to support the child and/or young person in times of crisis

If a child or young person has been involved in a family crisis, they will need support to make sense of what has happened. If they have been severely affected, they may need specialist help from health or social care teams or other forms of support. Good leadership is required to make sure services work together effectively. Some children and young people may have witnessed violence, pain and destruction and this may have been over a long period of time. Sometimes it is easy to overlook children or young people's needs as they may not express them in the same way as adults. The NHS has recognised that children can suffer from post-traumatic stress disorder and the National Institute for Health and Clinical Excellence (NICE) has provided guidance on treatment for both children and adults. This can be found on the NICE website at www.nice.org.uk/CG26. CAMHS also has useful information as they specialise in providing help and treatment for children and young people with emotional, behavioural and mental health difficulties.

Any strategy that is used should be tailored to the needs of the individual child, young person or family. A thorough assessment of need is required to determine what support a child or young person requires. Practitioners should be trained to identify risks and warning signs when working with distressed children or young people.

Practitioners will need to be tolerant of stress reactions in the child or young person, which may include:

- not sleeping well
- anxiety
- whining and clinging
- being aggressive or withdrawn
- getting upset easily
- regressing to an earlier stage, such as bed wetting
- losing some skills
- acting out worrying scenarios, such as violence through pretend/dramatic play
- replaying one or two key areas of their experience over and over again.

Observing and assessing

Children and young people may display signs of distress all the time but they are more likely to be intermittent. Careful structured observations of behaviour and development over a period of time will give a more accurate picture than occasional anecdotal observations, although these can also be useful.

Assessment of need through the use of observations and feedback from other sources, including the child, young person or family, is important. If a child or young person does not seem to be improving or is displaying more worrying behaviour and developmental outcomes, they may need to be referred to other agencies.

Formal assessment of risk tailored to young people and children experiencing crisis may go alongside observations and assessments. This is important where children or young people show signs of becoming suicidal or engaging in other forms of self-harm or harm to others.

Routine

Children make sense of their world through significant people in their lives so maintaining a familiar, predictable routine is important. So far as possible, routines should not be rushed or disrupted. It is important that the child or young person's physical and emotional needs are met. It can help to provide a countdown system or daily diary so that the child knows what will happen next during the daily routines. It is also important to ensure that the child or young person has responsive and consistent care from a small group of people. This allows the child or young person to take comfort from familiarity. Attending nursery or school or engaging in sports activities as normal is reassuring. Encouraging children and young people to take on their normal responsibilities, as they are ready, is also helpful.

Information

Children and young people need to have the right amount of information to know what has happened. Too much information may mean they cannot take it in or make sense of it; too little can lead to their imagination taking over.

Talking/communicating

Allowing children and young people to talk through how they feel can be helpful but should never be forced. Let the child or young person lead the interaction but show that you are available and willing to listen to them and to hear what they have to say. Give time to active listening and interpreting what the child or young person is trying to communicate. In some cases, gentle and sensitive encouragement may be required. Let them know it is fine to feel angry, sad or confused. Helping the child or young person to express feelings verbally may need practitioners to provide them with the right words by reflecting back to them in conversations. Many children and young people will use other forms of expression, such as creative activities or play.

Nurturing and supporting

Practitioners may need to offer the child or young person extra support, and time should be allowed for this. For example, the child or young person may need things doing for them that they could previously cope with. A nurturing environment is important, in which the child or young person can feel warmth and concern from the people around. Physical contact, such as cuddling a young child or giving a hug to an older child, may be most appropriate but practitioners will need to follow their own setting policies and protocols concerning this. Keeping contact with familiar people and communities from before the crisis is an important part of nurturing, especially if the language and culture is different from that of practitioners.

Reassurance

Practitioners and others involved should provide sensitive reassurance about the future. It can be difficult to support children who are worrying about 'adult problems', such as finance, or where a child experiences guilt about things that are not their fault. Being honest is often the best way to deal with this, without blaming other family members. Being positive is helpful, while not denying the reality of what has happened and how the child or young person may feel.

Expressing emotion

It is helpful to allow the child or young person to express their emotion but this needs to be in a supportive environment. If, for example, they have witnessed a violent crime, they may feel helpless or guilty as they could not stop their friends or family being affected. Children and young people will need a safe environment to express emotions where they will not feel judged or condemned. It is sometimes appropriate for practitioners to let the child or young person know that they are also shocked and saddened; each case is different.

Play

Play can act as therapy and children and young people should be provided with opportunities to express themselves in age appropriate ways – for example, through talking, circle time, role playing, painting and creative activities, according to their individual needs and abilities. Play with dough or clay can help release feelings, as can vigorous outdoor play or sports.

Advocacy

Some children and young people may need people to act as advocates for them. Advocates are independent people who speak for the child or young person when, for whatever reason, they cannot speak for themselves.

Relaxation activities or techniques

This can take many forms – for example, listening to music, outdoor play to release tensions, deep breathing and laughing together. Others may use meditation techniques, prayer and spirituality.

Build on strengths

It is difficult for people who are feeling afraid or helpless to feel they have strengths to build on. Remind the child or young person of ways in which they have coped in the past. Reinforce appropriate behaviour through praise and encouragement.

Strategies that could be used to support parents/carers in times of crisis

Many of the strategies that can be used with children and young people will be suitable for parents/ carers. These will need to be tailored for adults, who may express their feelings differently and struggle with feelings of guilt and inadequacy. An initial assessment of the situation and quick action can often prevent unnecessary problems arising. It is important that adult services liaise with children's services to avoid the family falling through the net. If parents' additional support needs are not met, this will affect the rest of the family, including the child or young person. Parents/carers are more likely to ask for help if it is flexible and does not carry a stigma.

Information, resources and support

A key strategy for parents/carers is to make sure they have the necessary information, resources and support they require at the time they require it. Brokerage may be required and a practitioner may have to act as an intermediary to broker a deal for access to support services. If a family is experiencing a major crisis, they may need to access vast amounts of new information. The stress of doing this should not be underestimated. Solving problems may seem difficult at the point of crisis, but practitioners modelling problem-solving, solution-focused approaches may help.

Partnership working with parents/ carers

Working in partnership with parents has already been discussed within this chapter (see pages 210–11). When families are in crisis, partnership working remains important. However, families are more vulnerable and involving them fully in all decisions and discussions may take more time and commitment.

Goal setting

When working with parents/carers, it is sometimes appropriate to help them set goals for the future. Recognising their strengths and existing resources may assist them to plan for the future. This needs to be done with sensitivity. Barriers should be identified and, where possible, overcome.

Provision of practical support

Practical support, such as childcare, is often helpful. Being flexible and realistic about what can be offered is important. Practitioners may be able to support access to other services and demonstrate using support materials with the child or young person.

Psychological therapy

This will depend on the nature of the crisis. For example, for serious trauma, there is a form of cognitive behavioural therapy that can be used (and other therapies are also available). The National Institute for Clinical Excellence's (NICE) 2005 and 2006 guidelines may be helpful for this situation (see www.nice.org.uk/CG26 and www.nice.org.uk/nicemedia/live/11568/33191/33191.pdf).

Strategies that could be used to support the family in times of crisis

Many of the strategies that have been identified for children and young people and for parent/carers are also useful for families. Initial assessment is key to unlocking appropriate support and raising awareness in families about how things are and how they could be improved. Dealing with the stigma that can be associated with services is important to ensure families are not put off asking for help and support.

Families themselves can be seen as systems and are greater than the sum of the individual parts. What affects one person affects everybody. For example, if one member of the family is an alcoholic, they can sometimes control the whole family through their violence, mood swings and unpredictability. The whole family then works together to adapt itself to the drinking and supports the alcoholic by bailing them out if they drink and drive. Families, without realising it, will try to keep things unchanged and, when a crisis occurs, they may resist change in relationships and the balance of power. Each family member may assume different roles when under stress (e.g. a child may become a carer). There is a great deal of published research into families as systems.

It is important to encourage every family member involved to share their views and how they want things to change and develop. It can take a long time to understand complex family interactions and help the family to move on. Family therapy and other professional help may be needed.

Work with families in crisis who have multiple or complex needs

Key term

Multiple or complex needs – families with many complicated and related needs and/or serious, severe and intense needs. For example, families with children with many impairments, abusive families, families with a child or young person with a life-limiting condition.

Families with multiple or complex needs may benefit from a family-focused approach to assessing their needs and this often involves use of the Common Assessment Framework (CAF). The whole family assessment model usually means:

- a greater level of family involvement
- better understanding of the range of needs
- practitioners and families getting to know one another and building relationships
- both children and adult services becoming involved, giving better information.

This often involves providing intense support to whole families. There is usually a key worker appointed to each family, who may have to work in chaotic surroundings with uncooperative or hostile family members. Practitioners in this situation need to be well trained and need to have effective support networks. This section does not include details on specialist therapies and support that families may need but acknowledges that everyone involved with the family will have a support role to play.

When intervention can be used to support children and/or young people and their families in times of crisis

In severe emergency situations, such as war or major earthquakes, many governments offer psychological and social help to children, families and communities, as well as practical assistance with basic needs. The basic aims are to:

- restore and support normal development
- protect children and young people from accumulating more and more stress from harmful events
- support families to care for their children and young people
- empower children and young people to become actively involved in their own future (e.g.by building communities and looking for positive ways forward).

It is important that the needs of children, young people and families are considered at the planning-for-emergencies stage and not after a major crisis has taken place.

Individual families in crisis

For some families, targeted support and intervention is required. Keeping the family functioning is often the best way to support the child or young person. Intervention is most effective when it is timely and prevents a difficult situation becoming a crisis. The major life events described earlier in the chapter outline the type of situation that could become a crisis. See Section 1.1 and the whole of Section 4. Intervention often takes the form of a short period

Figure 6.8 Disasters affecting families occur frequently and need a positive response

of intensive support that focuses on the immediate needs of the family. It may be followed by long-term monitoring and additional support. Family support workers or social workers may visit and assess family needs and a period of support will be negotiated with the family. Family or Sure Start centres may offer a range of different services, such as 'drop in' group work or individual counselling.

When a crisis occurs, information or signposting to sources of help may be useful. Examples of the types of help available include the following:

- local authority: social services, housing, children's services
- NHS: physical and mental health treatment and support, CAMHS
- National Domestic Violence Helplines: these offer help and advice on how to stay safe and how to get access to emergency refuge accommodation, as well as advice for those worried about the safety of someone
- NSPCC: there is a free, confidential service for anyone concerned about children
- Samaritans: for those feeling distress and despair
- Victim Support : for victims and witnesses of crime
- Respect: for men experiencing domestic violence and perpetrators who wish to change their violent behaviour
- Support for minority and ethnic groups, such as Jewish Women's Aid
- Barnardo's: helps children and young people and families over the long term to deal with severe problems, such as abuse, homelessness and poverty
- Parentline Plus: provides help and support for anyone caring for children
- Young Minds: committed to improving the mental health of children and young people
- Gingerbread: support for single-parent families
- ChildLine: for children and young people who need to talk about problems they are experiencing
- Action for Children: works with some of the UK's most vulnerable and excluded children and young people.

Research Activity

Action for Children has developed preventative services that allow children and young people to live safely at home. Their crisis intervention service helps families with children at risk of entering the care system. Action for Children describes the importance of having such services available to families in 'crisis' and the benefits that a period of challenging and intensive support can have on both parents and children.

Investigate the work of Action for Children or similar organisations. Look at:

- their range of services
- their evidence base for practice.

Crisis intervention for parents of babies and young children

The arrival of a new baby has a major impact on a family. If the family is vulnerable, this can push them into a crisis. Some interventions, such as individual or group ante-natal education, are commonly provided. Some families require home visiting and regular support in the home. Where there have been allegations of physical child abuse and neglect, interventions such as individual and group-based parenting programmes are used. In the worse cases, the baby or child is placed in care. If there have been attachment problems and the parents have difficulty bonding with the baby, attachment-based interventions can be used. If babies or young children have serious illnesses, disabilities or sensory impairments, this can also lead to a crisis in the family. Early intervention can assist these families to help them come to terms with the situation and many will need ongoing support.

Crisis intervention for families of older children and teenagers

A number of interventions have been developed specifically for older children and young people. These can be school or community based and include:

- reducing substance abuse, violence and delinquency through various programmes of intervention, often through the justice system
- interventions for behavioural disorders (e.g. anger management)
- practitioners modelling positive behaviour and encouraging and working with families to do the same – this can be supported through group work or one-to-one counselling
- support for teenage pregnancy and/or young carers (e.g. schools based to help them complete their education)
- multi-systemic therapy – an intensive family- and community-based treatment programme that focuses on the entire world of chronic and violent juvenile offenders, including their homes and families, schools and teachers, neighbourhoods and friends
- media-based therapy – this includes cognitive therapies which are sometimes used with children and young people with behavioural issues
- programmes for coping and dealing with bullying.

These interventions are found across the country but not all are available everywhere.

How practitioners can work with families in times of crisis to access support from a range of professionals

The Department for Education Early Support website (www.education.gov.uk/childrenandyoungpeople/sen/earlysupport) states that families with a disabled child often say it is difficult to:

- find out about the services that are available to help them
- make sense of the role of different agencies and the many different people they meet
- manage multiple contacts with service providers
- get professionals to understand their child's needs in the context of the whole family
- have their own knowledge of their child recognised
- negotiate a better service when delay and bureaucracy seems to be affecting their child.

It is very important that services for children and young people of all ages are aware of the difficulties experienced by many families and take steps to make sure they offer an effective multi-agency or integrated team. When they become aware that a family is in crisis, practitioners need to be sensitive to the situation and aware of the boundaries of their own role and expertise. They need to be aware of the roles and responsibilities of other professionals and agencies and the potential for referrals.

Referrals

Settings and practitioners need to know about how referrals work, who is involved and the stages that they go through (e.g. the work of multi-agency panels, Team Around the Child (TAC) approaches, the role of lead professionals). They need to be able to support families to refer themselves where this is possible.

Depending on circumstances, referrals can be made to a range of agencies, including:

- children and families teams in local authorities
- health services
- social services
- education services
- police and probation services
- behaviour and education support teams (BESTs)
- youth offending teams
- early support services
- early intervention teams.

Case Study

Gemma is a nursery officer in a children's centre and a key person for three-year-old Sam. Sam's behaviour has changed recently; he is alternately aggressive and then withdrawn and has reverted to needing nappies during the day. Sam does not want to go home with his mother's partner. Gemma talks to the partner, who states that after being very depressed Sam's mother has been in hospital, having taken an overdose of prescription drugs, but no follow-up has taken place since she returned home. The partner asks for this information to remain confidential.

Is this family in crisis?
How should Gemma respond to the information she has received from the mother's partner?
What agencies might support this family?

Useful resources

Organisations and websites

National Statistics Focus on Families
Office for National Statistics, 2007.
www.ons.gov.uk/ons/rel/family-demography/focus-on-families/2007/index.html

Department for Education
www.education.gov.uk

CAMHS
www.camhscares.nhs.uk

Family Rights Group
A charity in England and Wales that advises parents and other family members whose children are involved with or require children's social care services because of welfare needs or concerns.
www.frg.org.uk

Contact a Family
For families with disabled children.
www.cafamily.org.uk

Family Lives
A national charity providing help and support in all aspects of family life.
www.familylives.org.uk

Family Action
A leading provider of services to disadvantaged and socially isolated families since its foundation in 1869.
www.family-action.org.uk

Family and Parenting Institute
An independent charity that exists to make the UK a better place for families and children.
www.familyandparenting.org

Useful resources (cont.)

Centre for Excellence and Outcomes (C4EO)
C4EO aims to help those working in children's services improve the life chances of all children and young people, in particular those who are most vulnerable.
www.c4eo.org.uk

Social Care Institute for Excellence (SCIE)
The purpose of the SCIE is to collect and synthesise up-to-date knowledge about what works in social care.
www.scie.org.uk

Save the Children
'Families in Crisis Briefing', 2009.
www.savethechildren.org.uk/sites/default/files/docs/Briefing_Families_in_Crisis_PDF.pdf

Concord Video and Film Council
Robertson, J. and Robertson, J. (1968) A complementary series of five films entitled 'Young Children in Brief Separation'.
www.concordmedia.co.uk

Parents as Partners in Children's Early Learning and Development: (PEAL) project
Started in 2005, PEAL is ongoing. PEAL training supports all early years settings to meet requirements of the Early Years Foundation Stage (EYFS) and Children's Centre Practice Guidance to work in partnership with parents to enhance children's learning and development.
www.peal.org.uk

The Poverty Site
The UK site for statistics on poverty and social exclusion.
www.poverty.org.uk

Child Poverty Action Group
'Poverty in the UK', 2011.
www.cpag.org.uk/povertyfacts

Books

Ainsworth, .M., Blehar, M.C., Waters, E. and Wall, S. (1978) *Patterns of attachment: a psychological study of the strange situation*, Hillsdale, NJ: Erlbaum.
Baumrind, D. (1967) 'Child-care practices anteceding three patterns of preschool behavior', *Genetic Psychology Monographs*, 75(1): 43–88.
Bowlby, J. (1965) *Child care and the growth of love,* London: Penguin.
Department for Education (2012) *Statutory framework for the Early Years Foundation Stage*. London: Department for Education.
Department for Education and Department of Health (2011) *Families in the Foundation Years – evidence pack*, London: Department for Education, Department of Health.
Department of Health (2009) *Healthy child programme: pregnancy and the first five years of life,* London: Department of Health.
Doherty, J. and Hughes, M. (2009) *Child development: right from the start,* London: Pearson.
Elfer, E., Goldschmied, E. and Selleck, D. (2003) *Key persons in the nursery: building relationships for quality provision*, London: David Fulton.

Useful resources (cont.)

Evangelou, M., Brooks, G., Smith, S. and Jennings, D. (2005) *Birth to school study: a longitudinal evaluation of the Peers Early Education Partnership* (PEEP), Oxford: DfES Publications.

Gray, A. (2006) 'The time economy of parenting', *Sociological Research Online*, 11(3), available at www.socresonline.org.uk/11/3/gray.html.

Ipsos MORI (2009) *Families in Britain*, London: Ipsos MORI.

Maccoby, E.E. and Martin, J.A. (1983) 'Socialization in the context of the family: parent–child interaction', in P.H. Mussen (ed.) and E.M. Hetherington (vol. ed.), *Handbook of child psychology: Vol. 4. Socialization, personality and social development*, 4th ed., New York: Wiley, pp. 1–101.

Ofsted (2008) *Early years: leading to excellence*, Manchester: Ofsted.

Rutter, M. (1981) *Maternal deprivation reassessed*, 2nd ed., Harmondsworth: Penguin.

Sammons, P., (2007) *Summary report. Influences on children's attainment and progress in Key Stage 2: cognitive outcomes in Year 5: Effective Pre-school and Primary Education 3–11 Project (EPPE 3–11)*, London: Institute of Education, University of London and DfES.

Schore, A.N. (1996) 'The experience-dependent maturation of a regulatory system in the orbital prefrontal cortex and the origin of developmental psychopathology', *Development and Psychopathology*, 8: 59–87.

Sylva, K., Melhuish, E., Sammons, P., Siraj-Blatchford, I. and Taggart, B. (2004) *The effective provision of pre-school education (EPPE) project: final report*, London: DfES and Institute of Education, University of London.

Utting, D. (2009) *Parenting services: assessing and meeting the need for parenting support services*, London. Family and Parenting Institute, literature review.

Youth Justice Board (2005) *Sharing personal and sensitive information on children and young people at risk of offending. A practical guide*, London: Youth Justice Board.

Chapter 7 Working as part of more than one team (Unit CP 7)

Most people have some experience of teams, through watching them or being in them. At its simplest, a team is a group of people who come together to do something. However, when working with children and families, working as an effective team may be anything but simple.

Most parents do not need a team of people to bath their child. However, if the child has complex health needs and is too big to be carried upstairs, bathing can be a problem. It can involve: occupational therapists, physiotherapists, paediatricians, nurses, doctors, health visitors, social workers, educationalists, family support workers, outreach workers, architects, structural engineers, planning departments, builders, joiners, plumbers, electricians, decorators and even the Citizens Advice Bureau.

Now imagine if everyone gave different, possibly conflicting, information, advice and guidance on how best to support that child. There could be chaos and confusion, which could well put the child at risk of harm.

Working as a team is therefore critical for children and young people. Failing to work as a team may put their health and well-being at risk.

We live in a complicated world. Professionals need specialist expertise to understand complex situations and develop high-level skills. No-one would want heart surgery to be undertaken by a plumber, no matter how good they were at their job! This development of experts focusing on specific issues means that some problems can only be solved when experts work together. Communication can be difficult, however, as we will identify.

The problems of misunderstanding or disagreement, confusion or conflict, duplication or omission of activity can all be overcome by effective team approaches. We will explore what helps or hinders team working and provide some solutions to the most common challenges.

Learning outcomes

1. Understand the value of team working.
2. Understand the rationale for working as part of more than one team when working with children and/or young people.
3. Understand the reasons for multi-agency working amongst organisations that are involved with children and/or young people.
4. Understand the benefits of cross-functional working to an organisation when working with children and/or young people.
5. Know how teams and organisations contribute to integrated working.

Section 1: The value of team working

Understanding the language of teams

The following list of words to describe teams is not exhaustive:

- inter-professional
- inter-disciplinary
- inter-agency
- cooperative
- collaborative
- coordinated

- joined up
- partnership
- multi-agency
- multidisciplinary
- integrated.

With so many labels that sometimes appear to be used randomly and interchangeably, it is not surprising that people struggle to understand what working as a team means.

To use language effectively, we must explain our terms and ask others, who may not be using our definitions, to do the same.

Key terms

Sector – a term which is often used to categorise agencies designed to address the same areas of need; for example, the education sector or health sector.

Agencies – schools and colleges would be examples of agencies within the education sector.

Services – in turn, each agency may be made up of different services, so a school may have an attendance service and a mentoring service.

Disciplines – within the services, different professionals may come from different disciplines. Each discipline would have its own training and qualifications frameworks. For example, the mentoring service may have education welfare officers or educational psychologists whose qualifications, training and professional development would be different from each other.

Team – any group of people coming together within or across sectors.

Partnership – term for a group that is more formal or permanent. A partnership has a clear remit and purpose agreed by all members and formalised in a contract or constitution.

Inter-agency and **multi-agency** – a partnership may be inter-agency, which usually means between two agencies, or it may be multi-agency, which would indicate a larger number of different agencies coming together.

The structure of teams

Teams are structured differently for different purposes. Team structures are designed to support the activity each team undertakes.

One team's structure may consist, for example, of several people who have similar roles for the purpose of delivering training activities. Another team may have several people with different roles that together perform several functions. These may include providing information, delivering workshops, assessing skills and administering tests.

Teams may be physically located in the same place or they may work in different settings but come together for regular meetings. It is important to measure how effectively the structure supports the team in fulfilling its purpose if it is to develop and improve.

The characteristics of teams

A team is something more than a collection of individuals. The whole is more than the sum of the parts. A team can be identifiable by evidence of some or all of the following:

- a shared purpose, vision, aim, objective or outcome
- an agreed set of values and principles that underpin activity
- a shared understanding of roles and responsibilities
- a contract, agreement, plan or framework to work to
- a schedule of formal or informal meetings that help direct activity
- shared processes everyone uses for:
  - identifying priority outcomes
  - monitoring activity
  - evaluating effectiveness
  - managing and supervising team members.

Consider your own experience of teams. How might a local sports team demonstrate the characteristics described above? How do the rules of the game, training sessions, the different positions they play and the 'game plan' they use all count as evidence?

The growth and development of teams

A forming–storming–norming–performing model proposed by Bruce Tuckman (1972) identifies stages that teams go through. Teams may go backwards and forwards through these stages. Their ability to move from one stage to the next both determines and is determined by their ability to realise benefits and overcome challenges.

Forming

When any group of people first comes together to form a team, each person is likely to focus on the need to be accepted by the others and avoid conflict. They will, at the same time, be building a picture about each other. They will be assessing each other's skills and attitudes and noting any weaknesses. Serious issues and feelings are likely to be avoided in the early days. People focus instead on routines, such as setting meetings and producing timetables. Team members tend to behave quite independently of one another. This can be useful for a manager to see how each member works and responds to pressure on an individual basis.

Storming

As teams agree their vision and begin to function collectively they may 'storm'. The *storming* stage is necessary for people to participate fully and feel able to express their opinions. It can be a challenging stage if it gets out of hand. It is important that members expect some storming. Leaders need to reassure people that they will be listened to and can discuss their individual needs in supervision. If they can put the collective needs of the team first, they will be able to focus on achieving results.

Members are likely to respond in different ways to these challenges. Often individuals begin to adopt particular roles related to their personality types as well as professional functions. There will be the peace makers and challengers, 'bigger picture' people and others who focus more on details.

Team members may need strong leadership in order to resolve their differences. Unfortunately some teams can spend far too long in this stage without ever really resolving individual differences. This will have a negative impact on the long-term team functioning. It can be an ongoing challenge expressed in different ways, from disruptive behaviour to long-term sickness due to stress.

Norming

At this stage, the team achieves a clear vision and plan that uses the combined skill and expertise of all members. Some necessary compromise is achieved as individuals acknowledge the need to give up some of their own ideas in order to allow the effective functioning of the team. Each member feels valued as an individual and contributes their skills and knowledge to the collective functioning of the team. Everyone takes responsibility for the team's goals. Leaders can ask team members to participate more in decision-making because they have worked through their differences. Agreed policies and procedures can provide a safe and effective framework through which issues can be resolved.

Performing

At the *performing* stage, teams are able to function as a unit. Team members have become interdependent, motivated and knowledgeable. They are now competent and able to handle the decision-making process successfully. Disagreement is expected and allowed because it is seen as appropriate to challenge respectfully in order to promote more effective working. Team members have sufficient mutual trust and tolerance to manage conflict positively and resolve issues as a team without individuals taking things personally.

As previously identified, other stages may be revisited as the team adapts to changes and challenges that may come from internal or external factors, such as staffing or funding.

Reflective practice

How were you inducted as a new member of a team? How might induction help to minimise potential storming?

The different roles of team members

The roles people adopt within teams can be experienced as a benefit or challenge by others. This may be influenced by the personalities involved, the maturity and understanding of other team members and an individual's effectiveness. Some roles are clearly nominated, such as administrative assistant; others are subtle and characterised by particular behaviours. Dr R. Meredith Belbin (2010) discovered that often the difference between success and failure for a team was not just dependent on factors such as intellect, but more on behaviour. His research identified how distinct team roles can impact on the team's performance. Table 7.1 highlights the benefits and challenges of different roles.

Belbin's research identified that people can take on different roles at different times and play more than one role at any one time. Not all teams will have all the roles 'covered' but good leaders can encourage members to fill in the missing functions. Understanding the theory of team roles can identify where the challenges to teams' effectiveness are because critical functions performed by 'roles' are missing.

Reflective practice

Explore your own role in the teams you are part of. Do you play different roles in different teams?

Team role	Benefits of the role	Challenges of the role
Plants	Highly creative people who are good at solving problems in new ways and see the bigger picture.	Can be argumentative, often overlook details, are unconventional and do not like to play by the rules.
Monitor evaluators	Effective at times of crucial decision-making, able to be impartial, not swayed by emotions. They assess situations carefully and take pride in never being wrong.	May appear overcritical, dry and boring, and not good at inspiring others.
Coordinators	Able to get on well with people, trusting, accepting, respected leaders who focus on the team's overall goals. They draw out the skills and experience of team members and delegate work appropriately. They listen to others but are strong enough to reject advice.	In coordinating the skills of others, their own individual skill set may not be apparent.
Resource investigators	The executive who is always networking, exploring opportunities and developing contacts. They are good negotiators who manage to get key information from others, provide inside knowledge on the opposition and make sure that the team's ideas are carried to the world outside.	Tend to lose interest after initial fascination with an idea and need others to complete projects and attend to details.
Implementers	Work for the team in a practical, realistic way and figure prominently in positions of responsibility. They can do the jobs that others do not want to do and do them well – for example, disciplining employees.	Weaknesses include being too conservative, inflexible and slow to respond to new possibilities.
Completer finishers	Dot the i's and cross the t's, pay close attention to detail and are steady and consistent. They are most effectively used at the end of a task, to 'polish' and scrutinise the work for errors.	According to Belbin, they tend to be overanxious and have difficulty letting go and delegating work.

Team role	Benefits of the role	Challenges of the role
Team workers	Their diplomacy and humour help in coping with awkward people. They deflect potential friction and enable difficult members within the team to use their skills positively. They frequently have a variety of skills and can fill any gaps in the work being undertaken and complete it on behalf of the team.	They tend to be indecisive in moments of crisis and are reluctant to do things that might hurt others.
Shapers	Provide the drive to ensure the team does not lose focus or momentum. They are task-focused and abound in energy with high motivation. They are committed to achieving ends and will 'shape' others into achieving the aims of the team.	Will frequently challenge, argue or disagree and two or three shapers in a group, according to Belbin, can lead to conflict, aggravation and in-fighting.
Specialists	Tend to be self-starting, dedicated and committed and can often provide specialist knowledge and technical skills.	Their single-mindedness and lack of interest in other people's subjects can be challenging.

Table 7.1 The benefits and challenges of different team roles

Progress check

Describe a person you know and the role they play. Describe the benefit to an early years team of having a particular role (e.g. a monitor evaluator).

The benefits and challenges of working as a team

When people work effectively together as a team, the benefits can be experienced by people at different levels within the organisation and by partner organisations as well. There are different challenges and benefits to different kinds of teams, but some potential benefits and challenges are common to all.

The benefits

An important benefit to any team is the combined contributions of effective team members. The collective commitment, passion, creativity and experience of the whole team can inspire and motivate individual members to achieve more.

For leaders and managers, effective teams greatly enhance the flexibility required to deliver services which are tailored to meet the needs of clients. They allow creative groupings of staff to come together to tackle issues in different ways and find various alternative solutions.

As teams develop in maturity they take responsibility, use their initiative, challenge respectfully and monitor their own effectiveness. Teams able to perform a wider range of tasks show more adaptability than an individual practitioner undertaking a specific, separate, set of tasks is able to do.

There are also motivational advantages to the collective spirit built within teams and the healthy competitive spirit between teams. Teams may be empowered with the authority to organise their own work in order to meet targets. Many are responsible for monitoring the quality of their own work.

The need for specific knowledge, skills and understanding to support practitioners in their roles can rarely be achieved by one person or role alone. Only by coming together are the necessary resources available to achieve success.

A wide variety of different skills mixed within the team can greatly enhance the opportunities for individual professional development. Team members can shadow one another and work cooperatively on shared tasks. This advantage can be experienced by team members and by leaders, who can come to a greater understanding of one another's roles.

For individual team members, the ability and opportunity to seek support from trusted colleagues with different perspectives can enhance their understanding of an issue. Equally, the opportunity to be approached by another team member to consider issues outside their current experience can be stimulating. The experience may even encourage new ideas and ways of thinking about their own work and so enhance their own practice.

In summary, when a group of people come together as a strong, cohesive team, they have at their disposal a richness of skill, talent, expertise, energy, enthusiasm, passion, creativity, imagination, commitment, knowledge and understanding that can become mutually enhancing so that the team grows from strength to strength.

The challenges

Challenges are to be expected alongside benefits. Some are external to the team, such as managing funding, coping with changes in legislation and guidance, adapting to changes in local policy and practice or responding to changes in the make-up of the local population.

A mixed team of professionals is likely to experience more challenges more frequently. Internally, team members are likely to have differences on personal, political, philosophical and practical levels. These differences do not have to become challenges. This often depends on the effectiveness of structures in place to support a team to communicate effectively, manage change and resolve their differences.

Some practitioners' attitudes may present challenges if they see themselves working *in* teams, as opposed to working *as* teams. Employees might simply work alongside others, sharing a common work experience but not truly engaging in the give-and-take of working *as* teams. It is working *as* a team that brings the full range of motivational benefits.

The structure and make-up of the team itself can be a challenge. Belbin found that teams with no 'plant' struggled to come up with the initial spark of an idea. With no 'shaper', the team was likely to cruise along without drive and direction, missing key opportunities and failing to meet deadlines. Too many 'plants' in the team could mean bad ideas concealed good ones. Too many 'shapers' could lead to in-fighting and lower morale.

Challenges themselves may impact negatively on team members. Stress can make people feel any combination of anxious, frustrated, unmotivated, undervalued, disempowered, underpaid, overworked, isolated or ignored. Individuals may even experience bullying and victimisation if they do not fit in, or they underperform or appear different in some way.

The ways in which leaders, managers and team members themselves can support teams in overcoming problems will be discussed throughout the rest of the chapter.

Section 2: The rationale for working as part of more than one team when working with children and/or young people

Case Study: Support for a mother and her newborn child

Corinne recently gave birth to Ben. She had no problems during the pregnancy but admits to being a bit of a worrier. The support from her Mum was invaluable after the birth of her first child, James, and she is worried about coping with the new baby on her own.

Corinne's main concern is breastfeeding Ben. The midwife gives her support with

Case Study Support for a mother and her newborn child (cont.)

breastfeeding and a copy of Ben's health record to share with practitioners supporting him. She visits Corinne and her family two days after her discharge from the hospital to see how they are coping. They appear to be doing well and the midwife updates the health visitor, who is based at the children's centre, with details of her visit.

Building on the midwife's information, the health visitor makes a new-birth visit. Corinne is worried that Ben is not gaining weight. She is also feeling tired as he is waking during the night and she has difficulty getting him back to sleep. All this is making James, her older son, irritable and his behaviour is becoming quite challenging.

The health visitor reassures Corinne that Ben's weight is fine and explores possible activities to engage James when Ben is feeding. She suggests the children's centre outreach worker could call with toys from the toy library and she reminds Corinne about local activities, such as the weekly postnatal drop-in, the mother and baby café and baby massage classes. They discuss Home Start, who visit families in their own home to offer practical support and friendship.

Corinne agrees that the Home Start worker can be given information about the family in order to request the service. She decides to attend the mother and baby café while James is happily settled at the nursery. It provides space for mothers to relax, feed their babies and socialise with other mothers. Staff know that Corinne may attend and make her feel welcome.

Corinne finds out more about one of the parent and toddler groups in the children's centre. The group is run by the local parenting support team. It is facilitated by a play worker and family support worker. It aims to promote positive parenting through building on the existing expertise of parents themselves and increasing their confidence and skills.

Corinne feels well supported by the local team of professionals, who work together seamlessly.

Progress check

Consider how people in the case study make an effort to work as a team.

How might the outcome differ if professionals did not speak to each other?

How would you describe the benefits of team working to a parent to gain consent to share information with relevant professionals?

Reflective practice

Give examples of the ways in which your setting ensures important information is shared with relevant staff to support effective working.

Working with different teams within an organisation

Sometimes it is difficult to distinguish between different teams within an organisation. People may say, 'We are all one big team.' Although this may support a sense of belonging and can be useful when bringing different teams together, it can also be confusing. The boundaries between one team and another within a large organisation are usually determined by their different accountabilities. We will use terms from the following 'Key terms' box to distinguish between different levels of team structures, functions and accountabilities.

Case Study — Integrated processes service (cont.)

sometimes to have the credibility of an 'insider'. Whoever led the work brought the learning back to the whole team.

Everyone was aware of their individual responsibility to communicate key messages and utilise their unique perspective effectively.

Evaluation

Evaluation demonstrated similarly complementary and overlapping functions undertaken by team members. Everyone undertook telephone interviews to collate evaluation data but more specialist staff followed up more complex cases. Sometimes staff would deliberately interview colleagues from their own service and at other times from different services and then colleagues would discuss their insights. Technical staff collated and then presented data in different charts and diagrams for interpretation by other colleagues.

The team worked successfully together to provide a service very positively evaluated by professionals and public alike.

The benefits

There were many advantages to the mix of expertise and experience team members brought to problem-solving issues for practitioners working with families. It was frequently apparent that such a diverse mix allowed both new perspectives and changes to existing perspectives.

A 'non expert' could sometimes trigger a revelation in an expert because something they said added to the understanding of a situation. Each team member from a different professional culture would perceive a different set of problems, solutions, costs and benefits to a given situation.

When people problem-solve as a collective, they embark on a shared journey. Learning together allows new ideas to be seen as belonging to the group. This is often a more effective way to bring about change. It is not then seen as one group imposing change on another, but an organic development that requires change from everyone.

Each member of the team brought not only their own personal expertise but also provided a bridge between their home agency and the team. A youth worker in the team was not only able to suggest effective resources to a teacher, they also ensured extra support was made available from the youth service.

As practice developed and improved with new ways of working, team members could more effectively disseminate learning to their own services because they were seen as credible.

When practitioners rang, for example from health, they could speak directly to a health colleague, so they had confidence they would understand their perspective. As time went on, the team had a better understanding of each other's agency's practices. They found they could use appropriate language and increase their credibility, and their advice demonstrated they understood the particular issues faced by different agencies. This helped greatly to break down barriers, not only directly with the team but more broadly among different agencies.

Finally, family members were positive about being able to discuss issues with one person who could bring a wider knowledge and understanding into one holistic view and provide comprehensive support.

Overcoming challenges and finding solutions

The following solutions to challenges are relevant to the discussions relating to the various structures of teams discussed throughout the chapter and usefully summarises learning.

- If individuals do not understand what is expected of them, it is important to ensure leaders and managers clearly communicate expectations. This can begin with communicating overall outcomes to show the links to clear performance measures for teams, which are then translated into targets for individuals.
- If individuals cannot see the bigger picture, communicate the overall role and function of the organisation to which the team belongs. Provide a team planning template that shows the whole organisation's aims and how the team's objectives fit within the overall vision.
- If there is a lack of commitment, ensure the value of the team is emphasised, successes are celebrated and individuals' contributions are recognised. Encourage opportunities for skills to grow and develop and build in excitement, promotion and challenge wherever possible.
- If there is a lack of skills and experience, ensure the team has the appropriate resources and people participating with the knowledge, skill and capability to address the issues it faces. Alternatively, provide training and development opportunities to skill staff appropriately.
- If ownership and responsibility are issues, encourage the team to participate fully in team planning, agree team performance measures, and discuss and negotiate how individuals' performance will be challenged or celebrated in order to get the most out of people.
- If teams feel they lack control, encourage the team to identify where they do have control – for example, how they resolve internal issues, how they allocate work and how they can negotiate flexible working patterns between them. Identify specific areas where they feel control is an issue and, where necessary, explain the rationale for any limitations on their control.
- If individuals do not work effectively together, support the team to understand group processes, including the Tuckman stages of group development and Belbin's team roles. Ensure everyone understands the responsibilities of individual team members and agree processes for conflict resolution and decision-making.
- If there is no creative innovation, demonstrate the value of creativity and new ideas. Reward people who take reasonable risks to make improvements and provide the training, education and professional development necessary to stimulate new thinking.
- If coordination is poor, ensure central leadership teams assist the teams to obtain what they need for success and resource appropriately.
- If teams are challenging the necessary cultural change, support staff to recognise that the team-based, collaborative, empowering, enabling culture is different to the traditional, hierarchical organisation they may be used to. Demonstrate how the process of change can reward, develop and motivate people more effectively to improve outcomes.
- If there is too much blame, plan to use failures for learning and encourage and support reasonable risk.

Research Activity

Use the websites given in the 'Useful resources' section at the end of the chapter to further explore the work of Tuckman and Belbin.

Summary of support mechanisms to enhance team functioning

A number of components within a team's or agency's structure can support effective team working. Many have been discussed throughout the chapter. Here is a summary:

- strong and effective leadership and management
- clear processes for developing the team
- alignment of contracts of employment
- shared structures for professional development
- transparent pay scales to ensure fairness and equity
- balancing generic and specific roles and functions
- balancing workload within and across the team
- effective conflict resolution
- mediation procedures for risks and issues
- effective supervision and management that takes account of specific and generic skills
- clarity around communication and information sharing
- clear criteria for service involvement with families
- agreed policies and procedures reflecting best practice
- a team handbook containing key guidance
- a respected authority figure to resolve disputes
- explicit vision and values
- clear and fair accountability and responsibility of staff for their own activity
- a robust performance management process with quality assurance mechanisms recognised by all team members.

Reflective practice

Consider the supports already in place for your team and then identity five additional ways of supporting the team's growth and development.

Summary

There is a continuum of increasing cooperation in team working and the overall advantages and disadvantages at each stage of the continuum are often very similar. There is also a similarity in the characteristics that demonstrate good practice at each stage.

One of the most important learning points is the power of the individual to contribute their own qualities within any structures and the importance of leadership and management.

Different structures facilitate different functions but all are needed. Complex structures facilitate the more complex service delivery. When each professional's activity is inextricably linked to others, a cross-functional, multi-agency structure is most effective.

Useful resources

Organisations and websites

Teamworking skills, University of Kent
www.kent.ac.uk/careers/sk/teamwork.htm

Teamworking factsheet, CIPD
www.cipd.co.uk/hr-resources/factsheets/teamworking.aspx

How to be an effective team member
www.effectivemeetings.com/teams/teamwork/effective.asp

'Multidisciplinary teamworking: Beyond the barriers? A review of the issues'
Paper by Valerie Wilson and Anne Pirrie.
https://dspace.gla.ac.uk/bitstream/1905/227/1/096.pdf

Belbin® team roles
www.belbin.com

Basic team working
www.innovativeteambuilding.co.uk/pages/articles/basics.htm

Useful resources (cont.)

Twelve tips for team building: how to build successful work teams
http://humanresources.about.com/od/involvementteams/a/twelve_tip_team.htm

Business management
www.jrank.org/business/pages/1635/teamworking.html

Books

Atkinson, M., Jones, M. and Lamont, E. (2007) *Multi-agency working and its implications for practice: a review of the literature*, Reading: CFBT Education Trust.

Belbin, R.M. (2010) *Management teams: why they succeed or fail,* 3rd edition, Oxford: Butterworth Heinemann.

Friedman, M. (2005) *Trying hard is not good enough: how to produce measurable improvement for customers and communities*, Bloomington, IN: Trafford Publishing.

Tuckman, B.W. (1972) *Conducting educational research,* New York: Harcourt Brace Jovanovich (5th edition, 1999, Wadsworth).

Chapter 8 Supportive approaches to behaviour management (Unit CP 8)

> 'We see the development of pupils' social, emotional and behavioural skills as integral to good learning and teaching. It is also integral to making classrooms orderly places for learning. This means teaching all pupils from the beginning of education to manage strong feelings, resolve conflict effectively and fairly, solve problems, work and play cooperatively, and be respectful, calm, optimistic and resilient.'
>
> Sir Alan Steer (2005)

Although the quotation above refers to schools, its meaning can be applied to early years and other settings and emphasises the importance of behaviour management. Behaviour is an action that you can see and describe. Behaviour management is a term that is used in different ways but usually means how acceptable behaviour is promoted and reinforced and unacceptable behaviour is discouraged. Different terms are used to describe behaviour – for example, acceptable, unacceptable, positive or negative, unwanted, good, constructive, poor, normal and misbehaviour. All of these and more are used in research and in everyday practice and you will find a range of terms used in this chapter.

Concerns about behaviour have led to the development of different models of behaviour management, some of which are explored later in the chapter. Settings and practitioners, as well as researchers, often feel strongly about which model to use and this can be seen in the media, where arguments about who is right are played out. Understanding of behaviour management models need to take into account the strong feelings held by people on different sides of the debate. This chapter does not take the view that one model is right and others are wrong but accepts that there are many grey areas, especially in how models are implemented, and it is important for learners to come to their own conclusions based on the evidence from their own research.

Learning outcomes

1. Understand models of behaviour management.
2. Understand the detail of a behaviour management model.
3. Understand positive support strategies within a behaviour management model.
4. Understand why a safe environment for children and/or young people supports positive behaviour.

Activity

Listen to how children's and young people's behaviour is described:

- in your setting
- among your friends and family
- in the media.

Question people and make notes on how behaviour is described. Work out whether there are similarities and differences among the groups included. What does this tell you about how children and young people are viewed in our society?

Key term

Positive behaviour – positive behaviour is that which is seen as socially, culturally and developmentally acceptable and approved by most of the people in the society.

Challenging behaviour – challenging behaviour includes unacceptable negative behaviour that is extreme, frequent and intense and can threaten the quality of life or physical safety of the child or young person and others. The competence and capacity of settings can influence when a child or young person's behaviour is defined as challenging. For example, if practitioners are under stress themselves through low staffing levels or lack of training, they are more likely to label behaviour as challenging.

Figure 8.1 There was a time when children were regularly beaten

Historically, behaviour was managed (e.g. in schools and in the home) through the use of corporal punishment, such as smacking, beating or caning. Corporal punishment is now banned in most of Europe and in parts of the USA because it is thought to be ineffective. The International Court of Human Rights (1982) ruled that corporal punishment is a violation of the basic human rights of children. Schools in England are required to have a robust behaviour policy to ensure children and young people's welfare. The Early Years Foundation Stage (EYFS) Statutory Guidance requires that children's behaviour is managed effectively and in a manner appropriate to their particular individual needs. It states that providers must not use or threaten to use physical/corporal punishment or any form of punishment which could have an adverse impact on the child's well-being. The use of physical or corporal punishment is an offence under regulations made under the Childcare Act 2006 and can lead to prosecution.

Behaviour issues are not clear-cut. For example, unwanted behaviour may be positive for the person concerned, such as the safe release of anger. What is seen as acceptable behaviour by different groups and individuals will vary to some extent but there are certain basics which most people agree with.

Acceptable (positive) behaviour includes:

- prosocial behaviour, such as sharing, helping others and cooperation
- honesty
- respect for others and for property
- consideration and empathy
- taking responsibility for own actions.

Unacceptable (negative) behaviour includes:

- verbal aggression/abuse, such as racist or sexist comments, threats and bullying
- physical aggression/abuse, such as assaulting others or damaging property
- behaviour which is destructive to the child or young person
- illegal or antisocial behaviour
- repetitive or obsessive behaviour
- disruptive behaviour
- withdrawn behaviour.

Challenging behaviour can include any of the above. Unacceptable behaviour is context specific. For example, in schools, it is unacceptable to run in corridors, chew or shout.

Causes of unacceptable behaviour

There are many biological, psychological and environmental factors that contribute to unacceptable behaviour.

- Biological factors, such as genetics, temperament, developmental delays or disorder, chronic illness and learning disability.
- Psychological factors, such as low self-esteem, mental illness and poor coping skills.
- Environmental factors, such as poor role models, dysfunctional families, poor diet, exposure to violence and aggression through media, peer pressure, gang culture, bullying and abuse.

Other causes are also blamed. For example:

- the child or young person believes it is an appropriate means of expressing emotions
- pressure from peers, parents, families and communities
- learned behaviours – that is, children and young people have learned that challenging behaviour is the way to act when difficulties, frustration or anxieties arise.

Motivation

Some practitioners feel that the major motivations behind the way children and young people behave are:

- attention seeking (e.g. a whole range of behaviours designed to gain adult attention)
- control (e.g. a child controls a whole family through refusing to eat).

Children and young people who are motivated in this way are often responding to the difficult circumstances of their lives. However, there is concern about behaviour in settings and when children and young people are at home or out and about. Antisocial behaviour is a problem for some communities and this has been highlighted again by the riots in some of England's towns and cities. In schools and other settings, some children and young people are too talkative, avoid work and disrupt the learning of others. This low-level disruption can be very difficult for practitioners to manage. Incidents of extremely challenging behaviour are less common.

Other research has highlighted the effect of unacceptable behaviour on a child or young person's life chances. The Joseph Rowntree Foundation (2010) cites behavioural problems as one factor in explaining the gap in attainment between children from rich and poorer families. Where children and young people exhibit negative or challenging behaviour, they will not be able to take best advantage of their learning experiences at school or elsewhere.

In Practice

Find out by talking to children or young people the reasons why they may behave in an unacceptable way. Think of what it was like when you were at school and the pressures you experienced. Do you think things have changed for children and young people? What are the main pressures on them to misbehave?

Behaviour management is undertaken in one form or another in all work with children and young people. At one extreme, environments can be permissive and highly tolerant, whereas others can be much more restrictive. The least restrictive principle is sometimes used as a baseline – that is, allow maximum freedom with minimum rules so that children and young people learn to take responsibility for their own behaviour. In everyday practice, most children and young people will try to work within frameworks of acceptable behaviour, some will severely test the boundaries and some will consistently exhibit challenging behaviour. The ability to communicate is a key factor as children and young people who cannot express themselves experience greater degrees of stress.

Behavioural disorders

Behavioural disorders make it more difficult for children and young people to work within frameworks of acceptable behaviour. Behavioural disorders are conditions in which a child or young person experiences changes in thinking and emotions that result in challenging behaviours. Challenging behaviours can include arguments, occasionally violence, tantrums, lying, cheating and so forth. Almost all children behave in these ways from time to time but it is the frequency and severity that can lead to a diagnosis of a behavioural disorder. Practitioners need to know something about the behavioural disorders of children and young people they work with.

Type of behavioural disorder	Description	Examples of signs and symptoms	Examples of possible treatment
Adjustment disorders	A stress-related emotional reaction to a difficult event, such as a death or divorce.	Emotional and behavioural, such as depression, anxiety, apathy, crying. Conduct disturbance, such as truancy, vandalism.	Counselling, play therapy, medication.
Attachment disorder	A result of a lack of emotional bonding with carers.	Lack of eye contact, poor impulse control, little smiling or laughter, poor interaction or self-soothing behaviour, like rocking. Lack of expectation of care or excessive familiarity, even to strangers.	In extreme cases residential care, parenting classes for carers, therapeutic settings for children to experience a more loving and nurturing environment.
Attention deficit hyperactivity disorder	Behaviour is characterised by lack of attention, hyperactivity and impulsivity.	Unable to make decisions, easily bored, cannot attend to detail, disorganised, fidgets and difficulty in turn taking.	Behaviour management programmes, counselling, medication such as Ritalin.
Autism	Autism is a lifelong developmental disability that affects how a person communicates with, and relates to, other people and the world around them.	It is a spectrum condition, which means that all people with autism share certain areas of difficulty, such as communication and social interaction. It will affect a child or young person in different ways and severity (e.g. some will not speak). Asperger syndrome is a form of autism.	Speech and language therapy, giving clear, literal instructions, praise and reward of appropriate behaviour.
Conduct disorders	Type of behavioural disorder in which a child or young person violates the personal rights of others and their property. Onset can be in childhood or adolescence.	Aggression, defiance, antisocial behaviour, destructive behaviours, such as smoking and drug and alcohol abuse, unprotected sex.	Cognitive behavioural therapy, impulse control and anger management, family therapy, medication.
Childhood schizophrenia, obsessive compulsive disorder and Tourette's, as well as others, all significantly affect behaviour but are not included here.			

Table 8.1 Behavioural disorders

The education of children and young people with behavioural, emotional and social difficulties

The Special Educational Needs (SEN) Code of Practice (paragraph 7:60) describes behavioural, emotional and social difficulties (BESD) as learning difficulties where children and young people demonstrate features such as being withdrawn or isolated, disruptive and disturbing, being hyperactive and lacking concentration, having immature social skills or presenting challenging behaviours arising from other complex special needs. Severe BESD can lead to substantial learning difficulties as the child or young person cannot, for example, concentrate on work or cope with relationships or routines.

Section 1: Models of behaviour management

A model of behaviour management is a description of the systems, processes, concepts or theories underpinning a particular approach. This section will compare and contrast models that are used with children and young people. Often the model used is decided by settings or by a local authority. This can be informed by specialist guidance that may be available or by policy in particular areas of work. It is important to note that practitioners, researchers and managers/policy makers may have very different views about what constitutes an effective and ethical system to manage behaviour. In practice, settings may use a 'what works' approach, which takes ideas from several models and blends them to use in their setting.

Key term

Behaviourism – a school of psychology that believes only observable behaviour can be studied and measured, trained and changed. Thinking skills were thought to be too subjective to study. Important concepts such as reinforcement have developed from behaviourism and influence behaviour management systems today. Behaviourists believe that reinforcement of behaviour, either negative or positive, can bring about changes in behaviour.

Compare and contrast models of behaviour management

There are many models of behaviour management, some of which are considered below.

The assertive discipline model of behaviour management

Assertive discipline (AD) is a behaviour management programme created by Marlene and Lee Canter (1992) and is widely used in the USA in schools and in some places in the UK. The basis of AD is the idea that no child or young person has a right to prevent a teacher from teaching or another child or young person from learning. AD is a behaviour-modification system developed from behaviourism. It also draws on assertiveness techniques for practitioners to use in the setting. Although it may be implemented differently in different settings, a key assumption is that in order to motivate children or young people to behave positively, the teacher should use predictable and repeated reinforcement. A whole-organisation approach is most effective as administrative and other staff should understand the model and be required to assist with its implementation. Parents need to sign up to AD as their cooperation is important, especially when, for example, notes are sent home or the child or young person is excluded.

Key term

Reinforcement of behaviour – this is often explained as a simple feedback system. If a reward or reinforcement follows a behaviour, then the behaviour becomes more probable in the future. For example, when a child behaves well and is rewarded by the carer with a smile and hug (positive reinforcement), it is likely that the child will behave well in the future. Negative reinforcement, such as being shouted at, may also lead to behaviour being repeated in order to gain attention. This system is called behaviour modification and positive reinforcement techniques are used widely with children and young people to modify their behaviour.

Assertiveness – a person who is assertive can be described as someone who expresses their needs

Key term (cont.)

and views clearly without being aggressive or passive. Assertive people express their feelings in ways that are honest and respectful to themselves and others. Assertiveness can be taught and uses specific techniques, such as the 'broken record' (i.e. repeating the rule or consequence in response to an incident).

Discipline – discipline is about training children or young people to behave appropriately in different situations and to act in accordance with rules and instructions. Punishment is not the same, although it may be used as a form of discipline.

Rules and rewards

AD is based on rules to be applied in the setting, usually no more than five. Rules are consistently applied and, although there is a small amount of negotiation with children or young people about the rules, they are set mainly by settings and practitioners.

Examples of rules are:

- following directions first time
- walking, not running in certain areas
- keeping appropriate noise level
- staying on task
- not talking at the same time as the practitioner.

The rules should be clear and easily understood by children and young people and will vary between settings.

AD uses praise and reward as a key way of managing behaviour. It provides children or young people who are keeping to the rules with positive reinforcement of their good behaviour. The same positive reinforcement is used with children and young people who have broken the rules but who then behave well. Children and young people know what to expect if they obey the rules. Visual cues should be a part of early years practice or where written communication is not possible. Whole class/group rewards can be given and these will include the child or young person who has broken the rules. To make the model work, parents should be involved and should agree in advance to cooperate in discipline techniques. The partnership of home and setting is said by supporters of AD to be effective in reducing negative behaviour.

Rewarding positive behaviour is done in different but predictable ways. For example:

- genuine and age-appropriate praise
- star charts, badges and certificates
- more free time
- positive notes home.

Consequences (sanctions)

There is a stepped programme of consequences for inappropriate/negative behaviour, each becoming more restrictive (a hierarchy of discipline). For example:

- Consequences 1 and 2 – warnings
- Consequence 3 – loss of free time, such as detention
- Consequence 4 – temporary removal from room to isolation room
- Consequence 5 – contact parents
- Consequence 6 – remove temporarily or permanently from setting.

These consequences are just examples and they will vary between settings. Extreme behaviour may be dealt with by going straight to the final step. The focus of the discipline is on the behaviour, not the child. Sometimes practitioners will talk to the child or young person rather than go through the steps, depending on whether this will defuse the situation.

The consequences of negative behaviour must be offered as a choice to the child or young person. The consequences should not be enjoyable, but at the same time they should not be humiliating, destructive or damaging to a child or young person's development and well-being.

Practitioner's role

The practitioner should frequently praise the children and young person by using scanning techniques while moving around the room. Praise should be given to every child every day. Praise should not be 'robotic'. It should be sincere and the reasons for it given – for example, 'Well done, George, for sitting quietly and waiting your turn.' The practitioner should always use positive support to encourage children and young people to continue appropriate behaviour. Consequences must be followed through each time a child or young person chooses to break the rules. The consequences must be administered in a firm, calm manner. Shortly after the consequence is given, practitioners should try to find something positive the child or young person is doing to get them back on track.

Practitioners using this system are encouraged not to show emotion but to remain calm and to apply consequences to undesirable behaviour by being assertive, not hostile or angry. They should remain calm and quiet and deal with the situation without giving the child or young person any particular attention. Maintaining eye contact and speaking in a firm tone of voice is important, both for praise and reward but also when reminding the child of the rules. Repeating positive statements is a way of repeating your rules so that all children or young people know what to do – for example, 'Very good. Rowan put his hand up to ask a question, and so did Tom and Ruby.' Using 'proximity control' is also an effective way of reinforcing the rules – that is, moving to be closer to the child or young person who is choosing to break the rules. For younger children, moving nearby and praising those children who are keeping to the rules can be effective. With adolescents, it may be better to talk to them outside the room to remind them of the rules to avoid embarrassment.

Being assertive is a key part of AD. Assertive practitioners react confidently, consistently and quickly in situations that require behaviour management. They do not see the child or young person as the enemy, nor do they use sarcasm or hostility. Assertive practitioners need to avoid non-assertive behaviour to make the system work (i.e. they should not react in a passive, inconsistent or timid manner). Assertive practitioners do not plead with children and young people to behave. Getting into a debate with angry and arguing children or young people is not an appropriate response in most situations.

Practitioners using the AD model need to learn to:

- use assertive responses
- avoid negative statements (e.g. 'how many times have I told you…?')
- set and apply rules consistently
- consistently follow through on the rules and consequences
- offer consequences as a choice
- use a broken record technique (i.e. repeating the rule or consequence in response to an incident)
- make positive assertions (e.g. 'it is good when we all work quietly').

Although AD can be seen as a rather uninvolved model, supporters claim that practitioners do build positive, trusting relationships with their children and young people and teach appropriate behaviour through direct instruction, modelling behaviour and other means. Although they demand positive behaviour and do not allow excuses for bad behaviour, they are respectful to the child or young person.

How the AD system is applied is important. In some settings, AD is applied more strictly than in others. Some practitioners allow for discussion with children and young people to help them find a way out outside the predictable consequences. This is important for children and young people who are upset. They treat the 'consequences' as a guide not a law. One-to-one meetings with a child or young person are used so that the practitioner can show empathy and try to find the root of the problem and agree a way forward.

Case Study

In a setting, raffle tickets are given to children or young people for acceptable behaviour. The child or young person writes their name on a piece of paper and puts it into a box for a daily prize. All children can participate if they have been able to show acceptable behaviour.

Do you feel this is a positive way of encouraging acceptable behaviour? Discuss with others to get their viewpoints and develop a list of strategies to encourage acceptable behaviour you could use in your setting.

Criticisms of the assertive discipline approach

It is important to remember that criticisms are sometimes expressed by people who do not agree with the basis of AD or the way it is used in schools and other settings. Some people who use AD are also concerned about aspects. Many people do not share these views and concerns.

- It may not suit practitioners who see themselves as facilitators, rather than having an authoritarian, traditional role.
- It is a compliance-based model, which some see as unethical.
- It focuses on the needs of the majority and does not deal with the individuals with problems (i.e. a vulnerable minority).
- Parents and families may not agree to support the system (e.g. they are not willing to take the child or young person home when difficult behaviour escalates to an unacceptable level).
- It relies on external reinforcement rather than internal motivation to change behaviour.
- It does not address the reason for the problem behaviour, often blaming the child or young person instead of considering what is going on in their lives.
- Practitioners have to be there in person for it to work (i.e. there is no transfer of learning of the positive behaviour).
- Children and young people have to comply in settings or lessons that are boring and unimaginative.
- It does not support developing self-esteem, how to act responsibly and how to solve problems.
- There is no room to meet individual needs and there is little adaptation for children or young people with diverse needs.
- Children or young people may underperform.
- Children or young people may become disengaged due to spending a lot of time away as a result of 'consequences'.
- AD techniques are forms of control that do not encourage critical thinking in the child or young person.

Progress check

It has been said that assertive discipline is a system of bribes and threats to make sure buses run to time in the classroom, regardless of who might get run over or left behind. Do you think this statement is accurate? Is assertive discipline ethical? Check whether you use assertive discipline in your practice. Prepare a list of advantages and disadvantages of the system.

Case Study

In an organisation caring for children and young people, practitioners and managers are divided about which behaviour management model best suits their setting. There is a heated debate and both parties criticise the other. Some practitioners wish to use the AD model, which they have seen used effectively elsewhere. They argue that there must be a consequence or punishment for poor behaviour, otherwise it will continue to be repeated. They feel the threat of consequences helps to ensure better behaviour. Others feel that this approach makes children and young people selfish as they do not worry about the impact of their behaviour on others but only on themselves.

Discuss and debate this matter with others. Outline your views, giving reasons for them.

Supportive behaviour management

Key term

Emotional intelligence (EI) – emotional intelligence describes the ability to understand and recognise your own and others' feelings and to manage feelings appropriately. Emotionally intelligent people respond appropriately to other people's emotions and can use their feelings to motivate, plan and achieve.

Supportive behaviour management (SBM) aims to help organisations change or modify their overall culture from being punitive to being supportive. SBM does not rely on behaviour modification but takes as a basis that children and young people need to become emotionally intelligent in order to make the most of their lives and learning opportunities. Mike Temple (2008) is the founder of SBM in the UK. He is a behaviour consultant and says that schools often treat badly behaved children and young people like criminals or like people whose emotions occasionally get in the way. He suggests that punishments meted out to children and young people perpetuate misbehaviour. Mike Temple suggests that compliance-based behaviour management, such as AD, fails to work for at least 5 to 10 per cent of young people and this number is growing.

The focus of SBM is on supporting children and young people to become emotionally intelligent through coaching and other activities and by organisational change, moving towards a more supportive approach. It looks at the context for that child or young person and considers what is going on in their lives. For example, there may be problems in the family or health problems and this may influence how the child or young person is feeling. Behaviour is a reflection of a person's emotional state and there is a need to consider the underlying issues behind the negative or unwanted behaviour and take these into account.

SBM is designed to be an emotionally intelligent approach to managing some of the negative or challenging behaviours that some children and young people exhibit. It recognises that all children will make mistakes and that adults should look at this not as a negative experience but as a positive opportunity to build new skills and neural (brain) connections. Adults should coach children and young people, not simply act as instructors. Coaching children and young people on how to mend relationships, resolve conflicts and find solutions is a key part of SBM. Practitioners may require specific training to operate this model.

The social and emotional aspects of learning (SEAL) are linked to SBM. There is much greater emphasis on SEAL in today's schools and this remains a cornerstone of work in the early years. SEAL recognises that to develop and learn successfully, children and young people need to feel happy and secure in their environment. Critics of SEAL (e.g. Craig 2007) say it is a pessimistic, over-controlling approach that could alienate children and young people. They claim that there is too much emphasis on children being told what they should think or feel and this could bring about problems of dependency on adults to tell them how to feel and relate to others.

Key term

Coaching – coaching is the support given to help children and young people identify the skills and capabilities that are within them and enable them to use them to the best of their ability. It encourages positive actions and the ability to learn from experience and build on success. It is not the same as counselling or therapy. Coaching is performed with individuals and groups, in person and sometimes over the phone or online.

Practitioner's role

Practitioners are required to have a supportive, listening ear in this model. This applies to teachers in classrooms or other practitioners. Supporting the development of emotional intelligence in children and young people is achieved by one-to-one or group activities where they can explore and understand their feelings and reactions. Some practitioners feel that 'circle time' can help achieve this outcome. Coaching children and young people on how to mend relationships, resolve conflicts and find solutions is a key part of SBM. Practitioners may require specific training to operate this model.

The SBM model also supports children and young people who have a positive attitude and behaviour. Practitioners will praise and reward positive behaviour – for example, using verbal acknowledgment, reward points or specific activities.

SBM follows the principle that, if a practitioner requires support with particular behaviour issues, this will be available to them – for example, short-term support or positive exit strategies if things get too difficult. If there is a stand-off between a child or young person and the practitioner, it assumes that there needs to be a means of providing distance between them. This requires 'time-out' rooms in settings staffed by, for example, teaching assistants or other suitable practitioners. Time-out spaces are helpful to put distance between the teacher and the child or young person. A child or young person might be asked by time-out staff to describe what happened. Practitioners might respond to the child or young person by saying, 'I understand how you feel and why you reacted as you did. How will you react next time?' This type of approach is based on coaching and is thought to enable the child or young person to reflect on their reactions and learn from the incident. Teachers or practitioners are also offered coaching by the time-out staff as to how to receive the child back into the classroom to avoid a repeat of the incident.

Some children or young people take several hours to become calm enough to return but gradually learn that there is a quiet place for them to go if things become difficult. After the policy has been in place a while, some children or young people ask to go to the time-out room or a teacher suggests it before things become fraught. Each incident is given individual attention and practitioners listen to and support the child or young person.

It is claimed that SBM is particularly effective with children or young people with challenging behaviour. It has been estimated that around 10 per cent of children and young people experience some sort of mental disorder, which can include challenging behaviour (source: www.mentalhealth.org.uk/information/mental-health-overview/statistics). For example:

- depression
- anxiety
- post-traumatic stress disorder
- self-harm
- eating disorder
- being a victim of abuse
- diagnosed disorder, such as ADHD
- Asperger syndrome
- autistic spectrum disorder.

High-quality, personalised support is required to help children and young people with these additional needs. Children and young people with emotional issues may try to hide their feelings through low-level disruption to divert attention away from themselves. Low-level disruption will vary by age but includes behaviour such as being late, not having their bags or equipment, disrupting others, shouting or swearing. SBM practitioners would offer a child or young person the chance to have a discussion about their feelings, rather than increasing the level of sanctions.

Key term

Circle time – a time in the day when about 6–18 children or young people sit in a circle, usually with a trained practitioner as facilitator. Circle time may have different formats and rules but its goal is to create a safe, inclusive and nurturing space where children and young people can explore and share their feelings and find solutions to problems. It provides them with the language and vocabulary to describe feelings. Circle time is designed to encourage children and young people's:

- emotional intelligence
- supportive listening
- empathy with others.

Criticisms of SBM

As with criticisms of AD, it is important to remember that these are expressed by people who do not agree with the basis of SBM or the way it is used in schools and other settings. Many people will not share these views and concerns.

- It can be expensive to set up and operate.
- It can be time consuming.
- To ensure children or young people do not fall back in their learning due to time-out needs, this approach requires high levels of cooperation – for example, teachers need to provide time-out practitioners with learning materials.
- It needs well-trained and dedicated practitioners to operate.
- It may need external expertise from behavioural specialists.
- It can be seen as rewarding bad behaviour (e.g. giving time and focused attention).
- It can be seen as unfair to children and young people who do behave well and exhibit a good attitude.
- It can be seen as individualistic.

- It can be seen as offering 'therapy', which is inappropriate for settings that are not set up for this.
- It requires a whole-school/organisation approach.
- The focus is on both academic subject teaching and teaching good behaviour (behaviour coaching), which might not be compatible.
- It could jeopardise 'standards' in its support for inclusion.

Examples of other behaviour management models

The Kounin model (1970/1977)

This model suggests that behaviour management can have a 'ripple effect', meaning that correcting one child's or young person's behaviour changes the behaviour of others. The practitioner also needs to effectively manage groups and avoid boredom by introducing variety.

The Glasser model (1965, 1998)

This model sees children and young people as 'rational beings' that are capable of making their own choices and controlling their own behaviour. They learn responsible behaviour by examining the consequences for their behaviour. Behaviour is seen as an effort to satisfy personal needs and increase self-esteem.

The Dreikurs model (1998, 2nd edition)

This model suggests that misbehaviour is a result of a child's or young person's mistaken belief that it will gain them recognition from their peer group and is directed at 'mistaken goals', such as attention-seeking, revenge and power-seeking. The model also emphasises encouragement, rather than focusing on the end result. Dreikurs emphasised logical consequences – for example, if work has not been done in school, it would have to be completed after school.

Nurture groups

The nurture group approach has some links to the supportive behaviour management model described in detail later in the chapter. Nurture groups are small, structured teaching groups for children and young people who have or may have behavioural, social or emotional needs. These needs may be linked to children and young people's challenging life circumstances. Nurture groups aim to provide a consistent and predictable environment in which children and young people can build trusting relationships with adults and gain the skills they need to learn in larger classes or groups. The Ofsted (2011) report 'Supporting children with challenging behaviour through a nurture group approach' explains the benefits and challenges of this model.

Positive behavioural support (PBS)

This is an evidence-based approach grounded in behaviourism. Its aim is to work with children and young people, often with learning disabilities, who have challenging behaviours and replace them with prosocial skills. It claims to decrease the need for punishment-based approaches, such as exclusion or physical interventions. PBS targets an individual child or young person or a whole organisation. In operation, it does not focus exclusively on an individual, but also looks at the environment, changing it to be more suitable for the child or young person.

As a starting point, PBS assumes that all behaviour has a function for the child or young person – for example, is being disruptive, the only way a child or young person can gain attention? When a child or young person finds communication difficult, they may use challenging behaviour to express themselves. They may have needs, such as boredom, hunger, tiredness or agitation, and these needs may be reflected in their behaviour as they cannot communicate them any other way. Practitioners need to understand the importance of getting to know the child or young person well and observing and drawing conclusions about feelings and behaviour. PBS assesses the function of the behaviour for the individual child or young person to find out why it occurs. It then helps practitioners, families and children and young people to develop strategies that do not reward negative or unwanted behaviour but encourage the positive.

The restorative justice model

Restorative justice brings into contact those who have caused harm and those who have been harmed. It is believed that this approach will identify the impact of an incident and contribute to a solution. It also helps to decide the immediate next steps. Usually with a practitioner's support, each side of a conflict is encouraged to give an account of what happened from their point of view and they are encouraged to:

- explain their thoughts and feelings at the time
- consider who was affected or harmed and in what way.

The outcomes of this meeting of both parties are important as they need to come to an agreement about how to restore the situation and repair any harm caused. Resolving issues through restorative justice is seen as 'fair' by most people and it can help to prevent resentment and a repeat of the situation.

Research Activity

Research how practitioners deal with behaviour issues in early years settings. Do they use punishment and rewards as tools for managing children's behaviour? When behaviour problems arise, how do they deal with these? What outcomes do they look for in the children and in the setting?

Research Activity

Research behaviour management policies from different settings. Find out if they are based upon a particular behaviour management model, or if they use elements from many different models. Explain your findings.

Progress check

Develop a table that compares two models of behaviour management of your own choosing. You could use the following headings as a guide:

1. Principles of model
2. What is the evidence base?
3. How do the models operate in settings?
4. Why are these models chosen by settings?
5. Are there any similarities and, if so, what are they?
6. What are the key differences?
7. How do these models relate to your own setting?

Progress check

In her book *21st Century Boys: Modern life is driving them off the rails and how we can get them back on track* (2009), Sue Palmer says: 'In overvaluing systems as opposed to empathy, we've been blinded to the significance of trust in human relationships.' She goes on to say that: 'We have to accept that empathy, emotional engagement and eye contact matter just as much to human progress as systems, status and success.'

Which behaviour management models would support this statement? Give reasons for your reply.

Benefits for real work environments

There are benefits for real work environments when children and young people are ready to cooperate and learn. In order for this to happen, behaviour management policies are needed and, when consistently implemented by well-trained practitioners, they will all work to some extent. However, there is a cost in time and resources to implement many of these models. Many people argue that this is time and money well spent, both for the child or young person concerned but also for the rest of the group or class. The group are freer to learn and develop without frequent disruption. The children and young people with behavioural issues thrive in an environment that meets their needs.

Assertive discipline

AD is used widely and is seen as working in schools and organisations. Its advantages in the workplace are that:

- its basis is that practitioners have a right to teach and children and young people have a right to learn, so there is clarity of purpose
- there is an increased sense of calm in the organisation
- assertive behaviour is empowering for practitioners, who feel a sense of purpose and control
- practitioners are not hostile to individuals but apply the rules consistently and impartially

Figure 8.2 Learning to manage behaviour

- noise levels are down and general behaviour, including low-level disruption, is improved
- children and young people know and understand the rules and consequences
- children and young people feel they are being treated fairly as everyone is given a choice about their behaviour
- children and young people feel their efforts are valued
- children and young people have clear structures and boundaries to observe when things may be difficult outside the school or organisation
- parents and other practitioners understand and support the system, so there is no playing one off against the other.

Supportive behaviour management

SBM puts forward a different model of behaviour management that does not rely on behaviour modification. Its advantages in the workplace are that:

- children and young people learn emotionally intelligent behaviour, which can be transferred to other situations
- children and young people learn to take responsibility for their feelings and behaviour
- children and young people have a safe environment to explore their feelings and to obtain support, such as coaching

- time out means that there is a recognised method of removing an angry or troubled child or young person in order to avoid a major confrontation
- after time out, there is support for practitioners and for children and young people to re-enter the classroom or area in a safe and controlled way
- practitioners know they have support in dealing with unacceptable behaviour as there are dedicated support staff and separate rooms or spaces to support the child or young person
- escalating support is more positive for the whole organisation than escalating consequences/ sanctions
- a blame culture is minimised as there is an acceptance that conflicts will arise from time to time
- individual needs and circumstances are recognised and individualised support is offered
- conflict is seen as an accepted part of life and mistakes are an opportunity to learn
- children, young people and involved adults learn the benefits and techniques that support solutions and conflict resolution
- it fits well with the social and emotional learning approach in schools
- it increases support, not consequences or sanctions, as the behaviour becomes more challenging.

Nurture groups

Nurture groups are closely linked to SBM and are a way of supporting vulnerable children outside the mainstream environment. Sometimes nurture groups are full-time but they can also be for part of the day or week. In a real work environment, a nurture group can give a child much-needed personal space, time and support.

Positive behavioural support

This model:

- is often used with children or young people with learning disabilities and challenging behaviour and aims to replace these behaviours with prosocial behaviour
- decreases the need for punishment
- changes the environment to support the child
- looks at the roots of disruptive behaviour and aims to find solutions
- allows practitioners to get to know the child or young person, which leads to more rewarding work.

Restorative approaches

Restorative approaches:

- are seen to be fair to both sides
- support the development of emotional intelligence and the ability to see others' points of view and therefore enjoy many of the advantages of supportive behaviour management.

How are human rights fully respected in behaviour management systems?

Children and young people have human rights, just like anyone else. The rights of children and young people have been identified in the UN Convention on the Rights of the Child 1989 (UNCRC). The UK also has its own general framework for rights within the Human Rights Act (1998). It is important to ensure that models of behaviour management do not affect the human rights of children and young people. Any proposals regarding behaviour and discipline must comply with the UK's legal obligations under human rights legislation.

Children and young people have rights to:

- be listened to
- be involved in decision-making
- be respected for themselves and for their race, culture, language and religion
- be in contact with their families if they are 'looked after'
- have concerned, consistent and caring adults involved in their lives who have their best interests at heart

- have personalised care that includes effective and appropriate behaviour management, even though they may not always like or want this.

As well as rights, children and young people also have responsibilities and they should be encouraged to respect the rights of others – for example, the right not to be ill-treated but the responsibility not to treat others badly.

Activity

In your setting, look at how the rights of children or young people are respected. For every right, there is a responsibility. How do children or young people learn their responsibilities?

Behaviourist approaches, such as assertive discipline or positive behavioural support, and human rights

Assertive discipline and positive behavioural support are based on behaviour modification systems. Behaviour modification relies on a system of rewards and sanctions and has been found to be effective in changing behaviour and in supporting positive behaviour. However, some people believe that behaviour modification is a system of 'mind control' and takes away individual freedom. They believe that:

- behaviour modification is 'done to' children or young people, not with their best interests in mind but rather to control unwanted behaviour and perhaps make life easier for those working with them
- using behaviour modification techniques requires specific objectives for behaviour to be defined and this, to some extent, takes away the rights of the child or young person to do what they wish
- behaviour modification does not teach ethical or caring behaviour
- behaviour modification does not encourage children and young people to think for themselves, which is the basis of rights.

Extreme forms of behaviour modification exist, such as behaviour modification camps that claim to sort out young people's behaviour problems but are emotionally and physically abusive. The use of extreme forms of behaviour modification is also found in some prisons in different parts of the world. This type of intervention can be seen to go against the UNCRC, especially Article 37 – the right not to be tortured or treated in an inhuman or degrading way.

Many would argue that using behaviour modification within assertive discipline in UK schools and organisations is a far less extreme version and its effectiveness makes it justified. They would argue that children and young people who exhibit unacceptable or challenging behaviour take away the human rights of others who want to learn and engage with the setting. Behaviourist practitioners argue that children deserve structure and limits to help them to get the best out of their education. Children and young people need to recognise that, as well as rights, they have responsibilities to others. Practitioners believe that they can utilise this behaviour management method fairly and with compassion. For example:

- ground rules are discussed with children, young people and families
- there is clarity in what is expected from each child and young person
- there is an emphasis on the positive
- there is acceptance that some children with additional needs may need extra support
- diversity is recognised and accommodated fairly.

Supportive behaviour management, restorative approaches and human rights

Practitioners and organisations who use these methods say that they fully respect human rights as they meet individual needs and empower children and young people to become emotionally intelligent (i.e. able to gain control over their emotions and manage their own behaviour). They do not use 'mind control' techniques and support children and young people to see why and how they behave in certain ways. Critics may argue that supporting the rights of children and young people may lead to greater tolerance of poor behaviour and this will in turn infringe the rights of others who wish to learn.

Human rights and behaviour management

Practitioners need to question the way in which they work with children and young people in order to support positive behaviour. Is there a need for intervention? Why is this child considered to have challenging behaviour? Is the way we do this in order to make it easier for the setting or for the benefit of the child or young person? A reflective attitude to these questions will assist in providing the best possible service to children and young people. This is an ethical issue and each setting and practitioner will have a view.

Activity

Develop an ideal behaviour management policy for a real or imagined setting of your choice. Discuss the policy with others.

Progress check

Analyse key factors that might influence a child or young person's behaviour.

Reflective practice

Reflect on your own practice in dealing with a child or young person who regularly demonstrates negative behaviour. Consider your emotional response – are you angry or punitive in your reactions? Do you engage with the child or young person effectively? Are you able to respond assertively? Does your response mean you need to reconsider your own practice? Would you value more training?

Section 2: The detail of a behaviour management model

The principles which underpin a chosen behaviour management model

Section 1 of this chapter explains the principles and provides details of behaviour management models. This learning outcome requires that you select, explain and analyse a model. Your learning provider will guide you on this requirement.

Analyse the chosen behaviour management model

Section 1 of this chapter provides an analysis of behaviour management models. The analysis covers the following areas:

- introduction
- goals of the model
- the model in operation
- the practitioner's role
- criticism of the model
- benefits of the model for the real work environment
- how the model respects human rights.

It is important to note that *how* any particular model is applied will affect the roles of the children, young people and practitioners involved. Any analysis must take this into account. If any model is applied with compassion and respect for individual needs, it may lessen its impact on behaviour but make it more acceptable to those concerned about human rights. Settings and practitioners need to make sure that they reflect on these ethical issues and regularly review their policies and procedures. For example, as we have seen earlier, extreme examples of behaviour modification may breach human rights and could lead to impaired emotional and social development in a child or young person. A more thoughtful application, such as assertive discipline that is applied in many settings, is considered to benefit children and young people.

Different roles in relation to behaviour management systems

The role of children and young people in models of behaviour management

Assertive discipline

In AD, children and young people can be seen as needing to be moulded into a particular shape to fit the needs of the school, organisation or society. There is less emphasis on the individual and their needs and more on the compliant majority. Children and young people who experience AD may respond well to it but they do need to comply with the rules. Their role tends to be passive as they are less involved in setting the behaviour framework, which is external to them. Some settings allow discussion with children and young people about the rules that they set but this might be minimal in other settings. AD has been called a 'compliance' model, based on a compliant majority being more important than the disruptive minority. In AD, children and young people's behaviour is moulded by an ever more tough series of sanctions (i.e. negative reinforcement). For some children and young people, especially those with behavioural disorders, this model could lead to increasing frustration. For example, impulsive or hyperactive children and young people will not respond well to negative consequences. These children and young people do not think through the impact of their behaviour prior to executing the behaviour. When they then receive negative sanctions for behaviour that is largely outside their self-control, they respond with anger, anxiety and frustration. There is a view that the basis for many challenging behaviours is neurological differences. These differences make a 'one size fits all' model difficult to work with for this group.

Supportive behaviour management

In SBM, children and young people are seen as more active, needing to be 'unfolded' rather than moulded. (Temple 2009). They are seen as being able to actively manage their own behaviour if given the right support and coaching, including taking responsibility for their own feelings and behaviour.

The role of staff in models of behaviour management

The role of the practitioner is detailed in Section 1 of this chapter.

The role of parents/carers in models of behaviour management

Parents/carers have a role in all models of behaviour management. Many parents/carers go along with what is required of them by the organisation without being presented with real alternatives. They may be distressed because their child or young person has behavioural issues and want to support the setting. Some parents may feel alienated and hostile to the setting and do not support the consequences or proposed solutions that exist for poor behaviour. This creates difficulties for any behaviour management model.

Organisations have to work hard to build partnerships with parents/carers, especially those who are hard to reach. Where partnerships work, this helps with children and young people's learning and development and can be an empowering process for parents and carers. Partnerships are especially important for behaviour issues because these can be sensitive as parents/carers may feel guilty or hostile. Where organisations can involve parents/carers, the outcomes for children and young people are better.

In AD, parents/carers are an integral part of the model. In order for the model to work, parents/carers have to support the consequences (e.g. detentions, being excluded). In SBM, there is a less obvious role in the model itself but parent support is seen as important. Some settings will provide dedicated parenting support, including classes and one-to-one counselling. In some cases, family learning opportunities will exist for those people who need literacy and numeracy support.

Regardless of any particular behaviour management model, some school settings will have parent support advisers. These practitioners work in partnership with parents/carers to improve children's lives, by involving them in identifying appropriate support for the child and family. This can be a positive way of delivering early intervention and preventative support to families. Parent support advisers can also support referrals to other services and provide a range of information for parents. In settings where there are established methods of behaviour management, the parent support adviser will take this into account but will have a range of alternative strategies they can offer.

Parent partnership services (PPS) also exist to support parents/carers of children or young people with special educational needs (SEN). These are statutory services offering information, advice and support to parents and carers of children and young people with SENs. PPS make sure that parent/carer views are heard and understood and that these views inform local policy and practice.

The ESRC (2003, updated 2006) report 'Group-based parenting programmes can reduce behaviour problems in children aged 3–12 years' provides a useful evidence base for the effectiveness of parenting programmes. This research draws together evidence from different sources and finds that children with behaviour problems are more likely to be living in lone-parent families, with parents who have no educational qualifications, in families where neither parents are employed, in low-income households or in social sector housing. The report states that there is research evidence that group-based programmes can be effective in improving the behaviour of children from these higher-risk backgrounds. For example, single parents in receipt of benefits, mothers reporting depression, alcoholism or drug abuse, and parents with previous involvement with child protection services. Although they are more likely to drop out, all these groups have participated in programmes that have been found to improve their children's behaviour. Many children from these backgrounds do well and it is important not to label families or have lower expectations.

The role of multi-agency workers in models of behaviour management

The role of the multi-agency team in behaviour management is very important. The need to refer difficult and challenging behaviour to specialist services may become urgent, especially if early intervention is required to prevent things getting worse. There are many agencies and professionals involved in behaviour management and this can be confusing for parents, families and practitioners. The lead practitioner or key person role is designed to simplify this for the child, young person and family. A lead professional takes a primary role to ensure frontline services are coordinated, coherent and achieve intended outcomes. The Children's Workforce Development Council's information factsheet 'The lead professional' states that:

> 'The lead professional is not a new role. Instead, s/he delivers three core functions as part of their work:
>
> - acts as a single point of contact for the child or family
> - coordinates the delivery of the actions agreed
> - reduces overlap and inconsistency in the services received.'

The roles of the professionals and services in Table 8.2 will vary slightly but they are likely to be involved in some form wherever there are behaviour management issues for individuals and for groups in schools and other settings.

It is often difficult for practitioners to record and share information about behaviour. Although practitioners may be aware of a child or young

Service	Purpose
Special educational needs coordinators (SENCOs)	Employed mainly in early years and schools and includes children with or without a Statement of Special Educational Needs. Includes children or young people with behavioural, emotional and social difficulties (BESD). Liaises between setting and parents/carers. Ensures that individual education plans (IEPs) are in place where needed, regardless of whether child or young person has a Statement of Educational Needs. Supports and drives setting policies for SEN. Advises other practitioners and puts in place a graduated response for each child or young person to meet their needs.
Educational psychologists (EPs)	Helps a child or young person who has problems in an educational setting (e.g. social, emotional problems or learning difficulties). Advises teachers, parents, social workers and other professionals on how best to help a child or young person. Assesses a child or young person through observation, interviews and test materials. EPs offer a wide range of appropriate interventions, such as learning programmes and collaborative work with teachers or parents.
Primary care (e.g. health visitors or GPs)	Professionals such as doctors and nurses who work in local primary care services (e.g. GP surgeries). Health visitors promote health in the whole community. Primary care teams may be the first port of call for parents and carers where children or young people have behavioural issues.
Child and Adolescent Mental Health Services (CAMHS)	NHS-provided services for children in the mental health arena in the UK. Issues of challenging behaviour and mental health issues are included in scope of services. CAMHS is for children and young people from birth to 18, and for their families, where there is concern about emotional or behavioural difficulties.
Paediatricians	Hospital or community-based doctors who specialise in work with children and young people.
Speech and language therapists (SLTs)	The role of a speech and language therapist is to assess and treat speech, language and communication problems in people of all ages to enable them to communicate to the best of their ability. They may work with children and young people at home or in schools or early years and other settings.
Parent support advisers	Parent support advisers promote good parenting and encourage parents and children to have conversations and communicate. They also encourage appropriate styles of establishing discipline and boundaries, often using coaching strategies.
Parent partnership services	Provide impartial support for children and young people with special educational needs and their families outside the decision-making system for SEN. All local authorities (LAs) have a duty to provide information, advice and support to parents of children with SENs through dedicated staff working separately from the LA's SEN team.
Youth offending teams (YOTs)	These are multi-agency teams coordinated by a local authority. They deal with young offenders and attempt to prevent reoffending and prison. Antisocial behaviour is a key part of their remit in many areas.
Behaviour education and support teams (BESTs)	A multi-agency team dedicated to preventing the development of emotional, social, behavioural and/or attendance difficulties in children and young people. BESTs provide support where there are early signs of such difficulties developing and aim to prevent this getting worse.
Clinical psychologists	Work as part of multidisciplinary teams, often in health or social care settings, to assess a child or young person's needs or behaviour. They may use psychometric tests, interviews and direct observation of behaviour. They may offer direct therapy and treatment or provide advice to other professionals as part of their role.
Family therapists	Family therapy is a special form of psychotherapy that focuses on changes within a family and recognises that family relationships have an impact on the feelings and behaviour of every family member. Instead of meeting with one individual, all or most family members are involved in the therapy process.

Service	Purpose
Specialist social workers	These are social workers who specialise in children, young people and families.
Family support workers	Family support workers provide emotional and practical help and advice to families who are experiencing long- or short-term difficulties. They aim to help children (who may otherwise be taken into care) stay with their families. They may work for a local authority or the voluntary sector in Sure Start projects, children's centres or schools, depending on their exact role. They may support children and families in severe difficulties, including behavioural issues.
Ethnic minority agencies	These are agencies set up to support children and families from ethnic minorities. They are valuable to ensure clear communication and cultural sensitivity.

Table 8.2 Examples of professionals and services that may be involved in behaviour management

person receiving behavioural support, there may be no recognised format or procedures to share information. Observation and assessment of children and young people and recording of incidents should be systematic and reliable, preferably using a proforma, either paper-based or electronic. In this way, all concerned will begin to understand the strategies being used.

Research Activity

Investigate which multi-agency services are involved in your own setting in respect to behaviour management. Identify the roles of each professional group involved and explain how they fulfil their roles.

Section 3: Understand positive support strategies within a behaviour management model

Key term

Self-esteem – self-esteem involves an individual making decisions about their experience of the world and using these to judge or compare their own value. If personal experiences are constantly negative, this can lower self-esteem.

Positive support strategies

Building the child's or young person's self-esteem

Policy makers, researchers and practitioners all emphasise the value of positive self-esteem. Self-esteem underpins the child or young person's ability to learn and their developmental progress in all areas. Children and young people with poor self-esteem do not often achieve their potential. Children or young people with positive self-esteem:

- value themselves
- have positive and enduring friendships
- believe they can solve problems and find solutions
- recognise they can improve and achieve
- believe they are likeable and worthy
- will see challenging situations as opportunities to try new things
- are more likely to take care of themselves physically and emotionally
- will persist in achieving their goals, even through difficulties
- feel they have positive skills they can offer others.

Children and young people who have poor self-esteem:

- feel undeserving, helpless and with nothing to lose
- may feel ashamed, embarrassed, guilty, sad, or angry about themselves

- may feel unsure of themselves and lack confidence
- may not be able to take physical risks and push themselves to succeed in sports and academic work
- may make inappropriate and exploitative relationships
- may not have the confidence to interact with others or to develop independence.

All models of behaviour management would claim some success in building self-esteem as practitioners recognise its importance for overall development and learning.

In terms of behaviour, a child or young person with positive self-esteem is more likely to be emotionally intelligent – that is, be able to assess, manage and control their own emotions and respond appropriately to others. Emotional intelligence is explicitly associated with SBM. The goals of the AD model of behaviour management for children and young people also include being able to manage their own behaviour and develop self-discipline and self-worth. Almost all behaviour management systems emphasise the benefits to children and young people of having a sense of control over their world and the benefits to settings through less low-level disruption and challenging behaviour.

Acknowledging positive behaviour

It is important that, when a child or young person behaves well, this is acknowledged. If practitioners only respond when a child or young person is disruptive and are constantly negative, this is disheartening to those who are trying hard. As most children and young people do want to gain approval from adults, acknowledgements of positive behaviour serve to motivate the child or young person to continue the positive behaviour. Almost all forms of behaviour management include an acknowledgement of positive behaviour and this should take up much more time each day than dealing with negative behaviour. Models of behaviour management that are based on behaviourism, such as AD, use acknowledgment of positive behaviour as an integral part of the model. Other models, such as SBM, also use acknowledgment of positive behaviour.

Only where the child or young person has behavioural disorders or other serious issues may acknowledging positive behaviour be less effective. In these cases, and where children or young people are seen to have behavioural, emotional and social difficulties (BESDs), specialist support may be needed. BESD teams exist in local areas to support children, young people, families and practitioners. Even in the worst of situations, acknowledging positive behaviour will form part of the individual behaviour plan and is still important and worthwhile. It remains important to criticise the behaviour and not the child or young person. For example, 'I do not like the way Ali has become upset', rather than 'You have been very naughty and upset Ali.'

Acknowledgments can take many forms, including:

- giving appropriate and genuine praise and encouragement
- using a personalised approach (e.g. use the child or young person's name)
- being specific about what has been positive
- highlighting what a child or young person does well
- giving rewards during the day, such as more choice
- giving rewards for good behaviour during the whole week, such as golden time in a primary school (a time for relaxation and fun as a reward for good behaviour during the week)
- using star/sticker charts.

Behaviour is reinforced by what happens after particular behaviour is demonstrated. For example:

- a one-year-old who receives smiles and hugs after she waves and claps is likely to repeat that behaviour
- a teenager who helps in the garden is taken somewhere special afterwards
- a four-year-old is shouted at for snatching toys and repeats that behaviour if it is the only way to get attention.

Children and young people may need to be taught what positive behaviour is required. They may not know what constitutes positive behaviour in the situation. For example, where children do not clean up after activities and are threatened with loss of play time, they may need to be taught how to clean up. Regular and consistent acknowledgement of positive behaviour should be part of normal everyday practice.

When practitioners provide acknowledgment of positive behaviour, they should explain why they are doing so. For example, 'Thank you, Niall, for sitting quietly and waiting for Talia to finish.' This rewards Niall but reminds everyone else of what is expected. It is important to regularly teach, remind, model, discuss and reward all your positive expectations.

In Practice

Check over a session how often you or others use positive and negative interactions with a child or young person. Are they about equal? Are you emphasising the positive sufficiently? What are the reasons for your results? What action can be taken to improve the situation?

Handling conflict calmly

When conflict begins and escalates, it is easy to panic and become alarmed. Conflict can be between children or young people, between adults and children or young people or between adults. The priority for practitioners faced with conflict is to try to stay calm and defuse the situation. Appropriate intervention may prevent deterioration into violence or destructive behaviour. How adults deal with conflict provides a model for the child or young person.

All conflict situations require practitioners to be as calm as possible. You may need to practice self-calming, using techniques such as deep breathing, before these situations arise.

The following are to be avoided when trying to deal with conflict:

- becoming anxious and agitated
- using inappropriate language
- being verbally aggressive
- not listening
- not respecting others' points of view
- raising your voice
- showing lack of respect in non-verbal ways, such as shrugging shoulders
- staring
- walking out in a rage
- being confrontational
- being inconsistent
- trying to set unreasonable boundaries
- being vague and unclear.

In the assertive discipline model, a key focus is on the practitioner remaining calm yet assertive when poor behaviour takes place. Assertiveness is a powerful tool for self-control and remaining calm in difficult circumstances. In the supportive behaviour management model, remaining calm and assertive is also important but this model recognises that, when behaviour becomes very challenging, time out may be required to allow all concerned to calm down.

Physical intervention

Sometimes physical intervention is required – for example, when an angry toddler is lying on the floor in a public place or a young person is engaged in violent confrontation. There are strict rules about physical intervention and these are normally made clear in a setting's policies and procedures. Remaining calm in these circumstances can be difficult for practitioners, who should access support from managers and others, including parents and families.

Teaching by example

Almost all theories of children and young people's learning recognise that there is some element of teaching and learning by example. Modelling positive behaviour is thought to be a powerful way of encouraging children and young people to change or adapt their behaviour. Albert Bandura's Bobo doll studies (1961, 1965) demonstrated how nursery children displayed more aggressive behaviour simply by watching adults being aggressive. They were less aggressive when they had seen the adult

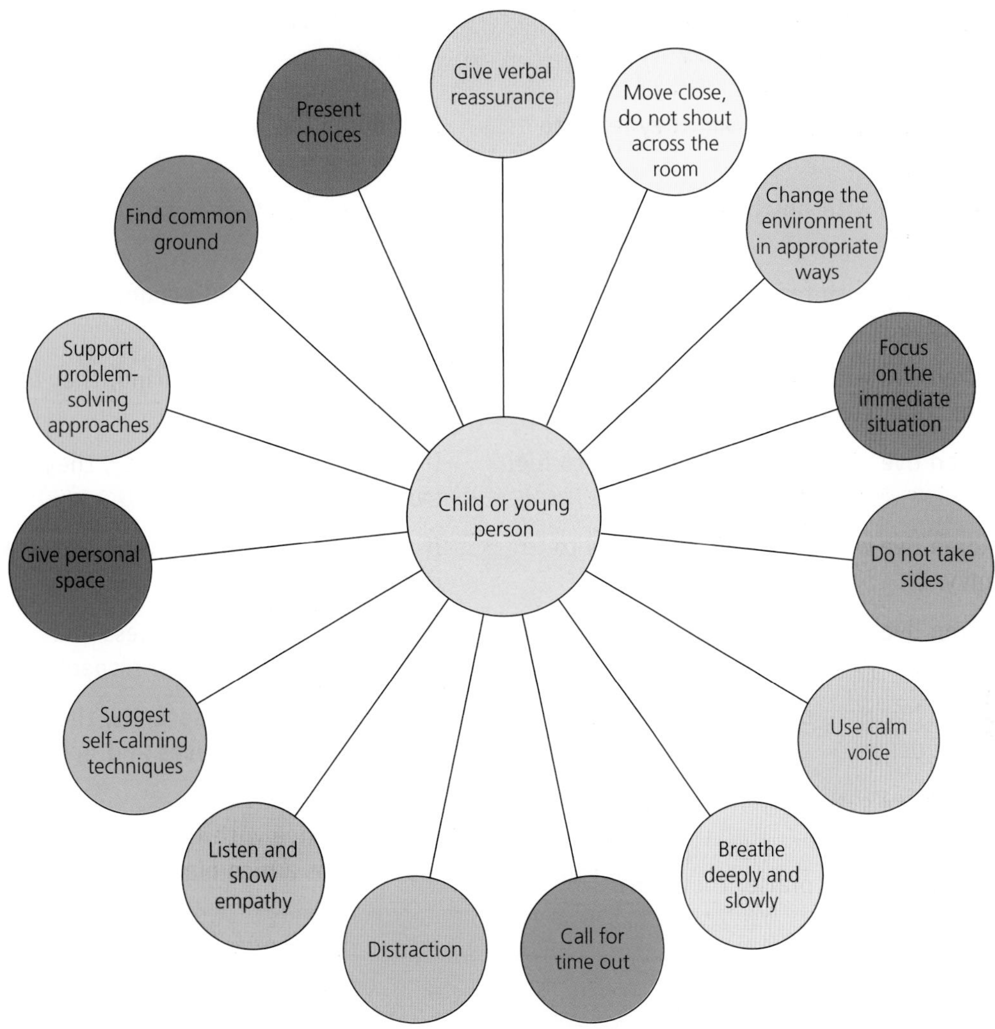

Figure 8.3 Techniques to support handling of conflict

being punished for aggressive behaviour. Although critics state that social learning theory does not take account of individual differences (e.g. genetic, brain and learning differences), the Bobo doll experiment (part of social learning theory) has been influential. Another common example of social learning is advertising, which may suggest, for example, that wearing branded trainers will make us more popular. A child or young person may accept this and feel very upset if they cannot have what they have 'learned' are items that will raise their status. This can be the basis for bullying and difficulties can arise when particular brands are common in a young person's peer group and are necessary to 'belong' to that group.

Children learn from adults' words and actions, especially adults who are important to them. They learn far more from the behaviour they see modelled than they do from 'being told'. They learn social, emotional and practical skills by observing adults and they learn values and principles from seeing adult's actions and how they manage everyday life. Adults can show children and young people that they respect others and demonstrate compassion and concern when others are suffering. They can demonstrate empathy, self-discipline and positive behaviour when dealing with the children and young people in their care. They do need to demonstrate consistency in their reactions and avoid saying one thing and doing another.

'Children learn what they live'

'If children live with criticism, they learn to condemn.

If children live with hostility, they learn to fight.

If children live with fear, they learn to be apprehensive.

If children live with pity, they learn to feel sorry for themselves.

If children live with ridicule, they learn to feel shy.

If children live with jealousy, they learn to feel envy.

If children live with shame, they learn to feel guilty.

If children live with encouragement, they learn confidence.

If children live with tolerance, they learn patience.

If children live with praise, they learn appreciation.

If children live with acceptance, they learn to love.

If children live with approval, they learn to like themselves.

If children live with recognition, they learn it is good to have a goal.

If children live with sharing, they learn generosity.

If children live with honesty, they learn truthfulness.

If children live with fairness, they learn justice.

If children live with kindness and consideration, they learn respect.

If children live with security, they learn to have faith in themselves and in those about them.

If children live with friendliness, they learn the world is a nice place in which to live.'

Dorothy Law Nolte, PhD

Ensuring genuine care

Children and young people will see immediately if the care they are offered is not genuine or just offers a 'one size fits all' approach. Genuine care is personalised and should meet the individual needs of children and young people. There have been many research projects focusing on what children and young people want from their carers and high on the list is always 'someone who knows me'.

Many children in social care settings have suffered abuse and neglect and have been raised in environments where they may have been repeatedly criticised and experienced little love and warmth. They will have repeatedly received negative messages about themselves, which will have impacted on their self-esteem and self-confidence. Such children and young people need to know that adults really care and may severely test the boundaries of the practitioner's skills and patience before they believe it.

In other settings, it is not unusual to find a child or young person who has suffered from similar, possibly milder, forms of neglect and abuse. Providing positive messages and building self-esteem, as described earlier in the chapter, is essential for children and young people to become happy and confident achievers.

An important aspect of ensuring genuine care is building positive relationships and trust between practitioners and children or young people. All interactions should include the message 'I like you,' even though those words are not used. Practitioners may not like the child or young person's behaviour but this should be communicated without saying 'I do not like you.' Building positive relationships will have already been covered in other parts of your course but the simple rules are:

- show genuine interest in all aspects of the child or young person's life
- learn their name
- greet them appropriately
- listen to them without interruption
- ask questions in a supportive way
- affirm them as individuals
- be consistent and approachable
- involve families as partners
- encourage participation by the child or young person in decisions affecting their life.

Case Study

A ten-year-old boy is in residential care after being neglected by his parents, who have not been able to care for themselves or him. He moved from his parents' home to live with his grandparents, who found his behaviour too difficult to deal with. Even though he is young, he has had three different social workers and has tried to run away.

How is the child likely to be feeling? What does this situation mean for him? Do you think he will be able to trust adults? What might help him to learn to manage his behaviour and feel better about himself?

Learning styles

Learning styles are included here because knowing a child or young person's learning style helps practitioners to know how to work with them. A real advantage for all concerned is where teaching, learning, promoting development and managing behaviour reflects the learning style of children and young people in the setting. This means practitioners who wish to offer personalised and genuine care really must know the child or young person well and respond in practical ways to their learning styles. It is impossible in most settings to meet everyone's needs all the time but considering learning styles will help with behaviour management.

Learning styles include:

- verbal: children and young people learn best through speech and the written word
- aural: children and young people learn best through sound and/or music
- kinaesthetic: children and young people learn best through 'doing' (i.e. movement and the sense of touch)
- social: children and young people learn best through group work or with a partner
- individual: children and young people learn best in private, through individual study.

Knowing the children or young people well and understanding their learning styles can help practitioners to incorporate these into the management of behaviour. As well as this, using their knowledge of learning styles in everyday work can help practitioners to ensure interest and involvement from the children or young people and encourage them to stay 'on task'.

The importance of clear expectations for children or young people consistent with their development capacity

Key term

Developmental capacity – what a child or young person is capable of understanding or doing based on their stage of development.

In dealing with behaviour, practitioners need to take into account a child or young person's age, needs and development capacities. Expectations of behaviour must be realistic for the children and young people concerned. For example, some new parents expect their 18-month-old toddler to share and are dismayed when they are not willing to do this. While it is fine to encourage sharing, it is inappropriate to expect a child of this age to share and to understand the reasons for sharing. Another example is when a child or young person has a disability or impairment and may not be able to function at the level expected of their age group.

Practitioners working with children or young people need to understand the stages and sequence of children's development in order to set realistic expectations of their behaviour. As well as this, they need to be clear about any developmental delay or additional needs. Work with children and young people is based on this information as it underpins how practitioners promote learning and development. Even within a class of children or young people in school or in an early years setting, expectations of behaviour have to take into account individual children's ages and developmental capacities. Doing this demands a wide range of expertise and skill from practitioners. Children who are consistently violent and abusive may require individual behaviour management plans. These are similar to individual education plans and are developed in consultation with other practitioners, management, parents, carers and families.

Where expectations of behaviour are too high or too low for individual children or young people, this will cause problems. Too high expectations will lead to disappointment and frustration and ultimately to low self-esteem and possibly worse behaviour. Too low expectations may have similar consequences and will give the wrong message to children and young people about what is acceptable behaviour. Getting the balance right is a matter of experience and professional expertise.

Another key issue is checking to make sure that your expectations of behaviour are clear. You can do this in many ways. For example:

- have minimum rules to remember
- make sure reminders are fit for the age group and individual needs in the group
- use written reminders, such as posters
- use pictures and stories
- give verbal reminders at every opportunity
- make conscious use of non-verbal reminders (e.g. facial expression, hand signals)
- check understanding by questioning and feedback
- gain family and colleague support.

The above represents only a small range of strategies, so continue to add your own and assess their effectiveness.

Activity

Using your knowledge of child development, prepare a table of behaviours that can be expected at the age or stage of development you are working with – for example, sharing, considering others and understanding the importance of being truthful.

Reflective practice

Reflect on your own attitude to a child or young person who constantly misbehaves. Are your expectations of their behaviour realistic and appropriate? Does the child or young person understand clearly what is expected of them? How could you improve the way you support positive behaviour? Continue your reflective practice by contrasting your attitude to a compliant child or young person.

Section 4: Why a safe environment for children and/or young people supports positive behaviour

All settings where practitioners work with children or young people have to meet strict safety requirements – for example, the Children Act 1989 and subsequent regulations and amendments. The EYFS Statutory Framework lists safety requirements for early years settings in England. Practitioners will need to understand the law and to be well trained in dealing with behaviour, including challenging behaviour where this is relevant.

A safe and well-planned environment is important for all children and young people but is especially important where children and young people have difficulties with their behaviour. A safe environment is not only about hygiene or equipment but includes:

- activities and the whole physical environment
- the emotional and social environment
- practitioners and others in the setting.

A physical environment includes activities that help both children and young people to express their emotions in a safe and controlled way using the equipment, spaces and people in the setting to facilitate this. This will include, for example:

- physical play – letting off steam, vigorous outdoor play and/or sport for those who wish to make use of it, equipment such as dough, clay or hammer and peg for younger children
- creative play, such as drawing, painting, making/building things, music, dance and movement
- pretend/dramatic play, such as dressing up, small world and home play areas
- quiet spaces where a child can feel peaceful or private.

Figure 8.4 Physical play

Figure 8.5 Being creative

The environment should encourage independence and allow the child or young person to feel a sense of ownership. They need to feel relaxed and at home in the setting with no fear of bullying or intimidation. Expectations of the child or young person should be realistic. A child or young person must be given goals that they can achieve. Sometimes this is through many small steps. If they cannot achieve the goals set, this will lead to frustration and possibly anger. As they are ready, a child or young person should be given more challenging activities and goals. They need to learn to take risks and adapt to challenges at a pace that suits them individually. The key message is for practitioners to get to know the child or young person well and deal with them as individuals. The skills of observation and assessment are crucial for this to happen and ensure personalised provision is available for each child or young person. In dealing with unacceptable or challenging behaviour, practitioners need to be clear about their role and what they can do. Following the behaviour policy and procedures of the setting is important. When there are incidents of unacceptable or challenging behaviour, strategies can be preventative or reactive.

Figure 8.6 Pretending

Preventative strategies

It is obviously best if incidents of unacceptable or challenging behaviour can be prevented. Preventative strategies will be individual for each child or young person and based on risk assessment. Risk assessments for each child or young person are developed so a clear plan can be put into action if required. Preventative strategies can include:

- changing the environment
- counselling
- cognitive behavioural therapy (solution focused)
- anger management
- learning new skills
- individual and small group work
- supporting different self-expression (e.g. play, art or music therapy)
- letting go of bad memories and looking to the future
- making good choices
- having positive thoughts.

Reactive strategies

Reactive strategies are used when behaviour has become challenging or when there is an incident. These strategies should be well planned and staff should agree to use them as required. Practitioners often see early warning signs and try to calm the child before escalation takes place (i.e. defuse the situation). Interrupting and redirecting at the first warning signs of poor behaviour can be effective – for example, changing the situation, using humour or diverting attention.

Reactive strategies will not result in any future change in a child or young person's behaviour. Their aim is to help practitioners achieve rapid, safe and effective control of challenging behaviour. Reactive strategies are not used on their own but alongside

Figure 8.7 Relaxing and quiet

plans for changing behaviour and preventative strategies.

Sometimes when violence or threat is taking place, physical intervention has to be used to protect the child/young person and others in the environment. There are strict rules and laws affecting physical intervention. The decision whether to intervene physically will rely on professional judgement based on risk assessment. Physical intervention can take the form of:

- direct physical contact, such as safe touch, holding and restraint strategies
- barriers, such as locked doors, to limit freedom of movement
- materials or equipment to restrict or prevent movement, such as the use of arm splints to reduce self-injury
- prescribed medication, which is a frequently used method of intervention in these circumstances.

In 1996 (and revised in 2008), the British Institute for Learning Disabilities developed policy guidelines to help services improve their practice in this area. Some of the key principles are that:

- restrictive physical interventions should only be used in the best interests of the person with learning disabilities
- they should only be used in conjunction with other strategies to help people learn to behave in non-challenging ways
- they should be individualised and subject to regular review
- they should employ minimal force and not cause pain.

Some settings have detailed regulations, such as never withholding food or drink, no locking in rooms, no sleep deprivation, no withholding of medical or dental care and no intimate physical searches, although searching for potentially dangerous items is allowed.

Case Study Asher and Sara

Asher is three years old and continually bites and physically attacks other children in the nursery. If he is prevented from doing this, he throws himself to the ground and screams, sometimes for long periods, until he becomes racked with sobs and very unhappy. Practitioners have tried several techniques but are at their wits' end. They decide to take action by observing the behaviour each time it occurs and assessing what the triggers are. His key person, supported by his concerned mother, observes and records incidents of the behaviour, while making sure the other children are kept safe. They notice a pattern emerging as Asher seems to have the worst outbursts first thing in the morning and just before lunch. They also notice the behaviour follows periods of outdoor play. The observations help them to try different strategies. They make sure Asher has regular healthy snacks to keep his blood sugar at a constant level and his mother starts to give him oat-based cereals instead of sugary breakfast cereals. After a few days, there has been a noticeable improvement. After Asher has been playing outdoors, practitioners make sure he is engaged in one-to-one activities or remains in close proximity to a staff member.

Sara

Sara is at an after-school club and is often heard name calling and verbally bullying another child. When challenged, she lies about the incidents, saying it was the other person's fault. Practitioners plan a strategy to deal with this each time it happens by immediately bringing together both parties to explain what happened and include others who may have observed the incident. This is sometimes called a restorative approach.

Consider both case studies and discuss the following questions.

1 Are the strategies preventative or reactive?
2 Are there other strategies that could be used for each child?
3 Do these strategies support a safe environment for the children?

Key term

Physical intervention – the term 'physical intervention' usually refers to the method of responding to challenging behaviour that involves some direct physical force limiting or restricting movement.

Research Activity

Summarise the laws and regulations that apply to physical intervention or restraint in work with children or young people within the UK.

Social and emotional safety

Children and young people's emotional and social well-being should be a key feature in all environments. A supportive and safe environment will protect them from bullying and abuse and provide help and support for them and their families. Most good provision, including schools and early years settings, plan activities to help the development of emotional and social skills and some offer support for parents and families. Practitioners normally have in-depth knowledge of development and can see when a child or young person is struggling and needs emotional support.

A sensitive and effective settling-in process is vital for a child or young person. If this is badly handled, children and young people may react with inappropriate behaviour. Meeting a child or young person's emotional and social needs must be at the centre of the process. Feeling overwhelmed, distressed and frustrated by a deluge of new experiences is not the best way to encourage positive behaviour. It is the relationships made with adults that provide the basis for a positive settling-in experience. For younger children, and in many settings for older children and young people, the 'key person' approach is used and this is vital to encourage attachment and help cope with separation anxiety.

Work with children and young people will often mean that practitioners have to draw on all their skills and knowledge to support acceptable behaviour. Routines, predictability, structure and consistency in their environment are key to settling in and remain important, ongoing features of emotional well-being.

The most important feature is the relationships that are made in the setting. In order to take risks and learn to manage themselves and their behaviour in the setting, children and young people need a safe base. This is usually an adult, who may be a key person or someone to whom they look up to, relate well and respect. Children and young people will use the 'safe base' in different ways. Some will go to the practitioner for advice or to help through difficulties. Others find that knowing they have someone is enough and they rarely go for support.

This 'safe base' supports positive learning and development experiences as secure children and young people are more able to learn and take appropriate and managed risks in learning and relationships. Sometimes siblings or other young people who are consistent and reliable fulfil this 'safe base' role. On other occasions, more unsuitable influences take over, such as street gangs, which provide this security but are often negative influences on the young people. Young people need a sense of purpose and belonging to help them navigate through this stage of their lives.

Progress check

Explain in detail the importance of relationships and a safe base and how this supports children and young people's positive behaviour.

Reflective practice

Reflect on how your own setting provides a safe environment that supports positive behaviour.

Useful resources

Organisations and websites

Parent Partnership Services
Parent Partnership Services (PPS) are statutory services offering information advice and support to parents and carers of children and young people with special educational needs.
www.parentpartnership.org.uk

Behaviour Matters
Series of papers on behaviour management for teachers but useful for all practitioners.
www.teachingexpertise.com/behaviour-management

Quality Circle Time
Developed by Jenny Mosley over the past 25 years as a whole-school approach to enhancing self-esteem and positive behaviour
www.circle-time.co.uk

High/Scope
An introduction to High/Scope and its work.
www.high-scope.org.uk

Practical Parent
Provides practical advice for parents.
www.practicalparent.org.uk

Primary Resources
Provides behaviour, rewards and motivational resources.
www.primaryresources.co.uk/behaviour/behaviour.htm

NSPCC
The NSPCC's vision is to end cruelty to children in the UK. They campaign to change the law and offer advice for adults, and much more.

Useful resources (cont.)

Search for 'behaviour management' on the following website to bring up a number of useful resources.
www.nspcc.org.uk

Department for Education
The lead professional role and schools: fact sheet (2008)
www.education.gov.uk/publications/standard/Teachersandschoolworkforce/Page5/IW46/0708

Books

Bandura, A. (1965) 'Influence of models' reinforcement contingencies on the acquisition of imitative responses', *Journal of Personality and Social Psychology*, 1: 589–595.

Bandura, A., Ross, D. and Ross, S.A. (1961) 'Transmission of aggression through imitation of aggressive models', *Journal of Abnormal and Social Psychology*, 63: 575–582.

Canter, L. and Canter, M. (1992) *Assertive discipline: positive behavior management for today's classroom*, Bloomington, IN: Canter and Associates.

Carr, E.G., Horner, R.H., Turnbull, A.P., Marquis, J.G., McLaughlin, D.M., McAtee, M.L., Smith, C.E., Ryan, K.A., Ruef, M.A., Doolabh, A. and Braddock, D. (1999) *Positive behaviour support for people with developmental disabilities: A research synthesis*, Washington: American Association on Mental Retardation.

Craig, C. (2007) *The potential dangers of a systematic, explicit approach to teaching social and emotional skills*, Glasgow: Centre for Confidence and Well-Being.

Department for Education (2010) *Guidance on school behaviour and attendance partnerships*, London: Department for Education.

Department of Health (2007) *Mansell report. Services for people with learning disabilities and challenging behaviour or mental health needs*, revised edition, London: Department of Health.

Dreikurs, R. (1998) *Maintaining sanity in the classroom: classroom management techniques*, 2nd edition, Philadelphia, PA: Taylor & Francis.

Evans, J., Harden, A., Thomas, J. and Benefield, P. (2003) *Support for pupils with emotional and behavioural difficulties (EBD) in mainstream primary school classrooms: a systematic review of the effectiveness of interventions*, EPPI-Centre (part of the Social Science Research Unit, Institute of Education, University of London) and The National Foundation for Educational Research.

Gibbs, J., Underdown, A., Stevens, M., Newbery, J. and Liabo, K. (2003, updated 2006) *Group-based parenting programmes can reduce behaviour problems of children aged 3-12 years*, What Works for Children group, Evidence Nugget, April, Economic and Social Research Council.

Glasser, W. (1965) *Reality therapy: a new approach to psychiatry*, New York: Harper & Row.

Glasser, W. (1998) *Choice theory: a new psychology of personal freedom*, New York: HarperCollins.

Goodman, A. and Gregg, P. (2010) *The importance of attitudes and behaviour for poorer children's educational attainment*, York: Joseph Rowntree Foundation.

Kounin, J. (1970/1977) *Discipline and group management in classrooms*, New York: Holt, Rinehart and Winston.

Life Skills Company (2008) 'Exit strategy for the overheated', *TES*, 7 November.

Ofsted (2005) *Healthy minds: promoting emotional health and well-being in schools*, HMI 2457, Manchester: Ofsted.

Ofsted (2011) *Supporting children with challenging behaviour through a nurture group approach*, report number 100230, Manchester: Ofsted.

Palmer, S. (2009) *21st century boys: modern life is driving them off the rails and how we can get them back on track*, London: Orion Books.

Steer, A., Sir and the Practitioners' Group on School Behaviour and Discipline (2005) *Learning behaviour: the report of the Practitioners' Group on School Behaviour and Discipline*, London: Department for Education and Skills

Steer, A., Sir (2009) *Learning behaviour: a review of behaviour standards and practices in our schools*, London: Department for Children, Schools and Families.

Temple, M. (2008) *An emotionally intelligent approach to behaviour management*, The Life Skills Company.

Temple M. (2009) *Emotionally intelligent behaviour management*, The Life Skills Company.

Chapter 9 Formal recording for use within the work environment (Unit CP 9)

Early years, care and education settings have a legal duty to keep accurate formal records to ensure compliance with relevant legislation.

Providers must maintain records and obtain and share information (with parents and carers, other professionals working with the child, and the police, social services and Ofsted as appropriate) to ensure the safe and efficient management of the setting and to help ensure the needs of all children are met (3.67 Statutory Framework for the Early Years Foundation Stage, Section 3 – The Safeguarding and Welfare Requirements 2012).

Key terms

Informed decision – when you have lots of relevant information about something which helps you to make a decision.

Conditions of registration – when a provider is given permission to operate (for example, from Ofsted), there are many rules and regulations that must be followed by the provider to ensure they work within the law and can remain registered.

Objectivity – not being influenced by thoughts or feelings, not taking into account prior conclusions.

Pro forma – a pre-designed form or document.

Authoritative organisations such as Ofsted, the Department for Education and the Health and Safety Executive set down rules and regulations which settings must adhere to as a condition of registration. It is a requirement that settings have policies and procedures in place that ensure the accurate recording of a wide range of information. The records kept by a setting include those related to children and young people using a setting, staff, visitors, the physical environment and the activity that takes place within and outside the environment.

It is of paramount importance that all records are accurate and recorded in a timely manner so that the information is recorded while it is fresh in the writer's mind. This is vitally important as the records may be used as evidence when making significant decisions about a child's education or well-being or they may even form part of the 'evidence' related to legal action being taken by individuals or authorities.

The appropriate sharing and safe storage of any records are a major consideration for any organisation. Under the Data Protection Act 1998, there is a legal requirement for the maintaining of confidentiality related to all personal information. Therefore, settings must have a written policy outlining the procedures they have in place to comply with this legal requirement.

Learning outcomes

1. Understand the rationale for recording information in a formal format.
2. Understand which format should be used relevant to target reader.
3. Be able to use formal recording in the real work environment.

Section 1: Understand the rationale for recording information in a formal format

Formal record keeping is of paramount importance for supporting the effective management of a setting and ensuring the education and well-being of the children and young people within it.

There are many benefits to recording information formally, particularly in relation to practitioners undertaking their role effectively. By following setting procedures when recording, practitioners will understand how to record certain types of information correctly.

The benefits of recording information formally include:

- upholding legal requirements related to record keeping
- supporting consistency of quality of recording
- informing reflective practice
- ensuring relevant information is available to support informed decision making
- supporting appropriate sharing of information
- maintaining setting policies and procedures.

Legal requirement

Schools are required by law, through the Education Regulations (2008), to keep records related to the education of each pupil and the curriculum.

Early years settings must abide by the Early Years Foundation Stage (EYFS) Statutory Guidance (2012). The guidance explains the records and policies which must be kept to support the effective management of an early years provision to ensure children's safety, development and well-being.

Information related to children's social care, which must be formally recorded, is regulated by the Children and Families Services. All documents and policies specified in the legislation should be properly maintained and available for inspection if an inspector requests to see them.

Recording information formally supports practitioners in a setting to comply with legislation, and these records become the evidence that demonstrates the setting is operating according to legal requirements.

Research Activity

The Statutory Framework for the Early Years Foundation Stage (2012) sets out the standards for learning, development and care for children from birth to five (available online at http://education.gov.uk).

Look at the guidance and identify three statements that direct the provider to keep formal records.

Consistency of quality

Formal recording in an agreed format, such as a pro-forma (pre-designed form), ensures that there is a consistency in the quality and content of information recorded.

When all practitioners use a similar method of recording certain events or documenting information, it ensures consistency within the setting, which supports professionalism. For example, if practitioners in a nursery made individual judgements on what information to include and how they gave feedback to parents/carers at the end of a young child's day, there would be no consistency. Some staff might write down a lengthy account of the child's day in the setting, other staff might make brief notes or decide just to give verbal feedback. The information given might differ in detail for the parents/carers each day and vital information could be missed out altogether. Therefore, having one agreed method that suits the parents/carers, such as a daily diary or fro-forma, which is completed for each child, ensures a more consistent approach.

When information is always recorded and presented to parents/carers in the same way, such as accident forms or children's progress reports, parents/carers know what to expect and it helps the setting to be perceived as a well-organised and professional provision.

Reflection

Written records within a setting are often used by practitioners when reflecting back, perhaps to reflect on how well they handled a situation or to consider if an activity they provided for the children was suitable and enjoyable. Practitioners reflect back on the children's observations and development records and use them when planning for the child's next steps. Records such as practitioner's activity plans or observations might be reviewed by supervisors when deciding what training might be beneficial for an individual practitioner or team of practitioners.

Informing decisions

Records kept in a consistently similar format, such as registers, forms or charts, allow a reader to review information quickly and make rapid, informed decisions. For example recording information about the number of children booked into a session in a register allows staff to quickly determine the number of staff required to ensure ratios are maintained.

A risk assessment record check may highlight where changes are necessary within a setting. For example, if a review of the risk assessment records highlights a piece of equipment as being responsible for a number of minor injuries, a decision may be made, based on the evidence within the records, to remove the equipment from the setting to avoid further injury.

Following policies and procedures

Formal recording might be an integral part of a procedure that has been put in place within the setting to comply with a legal requirement. A written procedure outlines what steps the setting takes to fulfil their legal responsibility, including the recording process undertaken. For example, it is the legal responsibility of all provisions to have a fire safety policy. The policy will acknowledge that the setting is required to carry out regular fire evacuation practices, along with ensuring the firefighting equipment is inspected annually. The records should document the dates and times that the practices took place and should include particular details, such as the length of time taken to evacuate the building. A record detailing the firefighting equipment inspection, confirming it was undertaken by a registered fire safety expert, will also need to be kept. The accurate records will confirm that the provision is following the written procedure and conforming to health and safety legislation. The records will need to be made available for inspection on request by the fire safety officer.

Sharing information

A multi-agency approach brings together practitioners from different sectors and professions, who work together to provide the additional support that some children, young people and families need. Formal records often form the basis of the discussions and decisions made related to safeguarding or support required by a child or family. Therefore, all relevant information should be recorded accurately and shared appropriately. Remember, the Data Protection Act 1998 should be adhered to at all times!

Many settings provide parents and carers with information about the setting, including policies and procedures, information about the daily routine, introductions to the staff and other general information about the service they provide. This information is often contained in a brochure or information pack, and/or on a website. Giving all parents and carers information in this way ensures that everyone has access to the same information and the information recorded is up-to-date and accurate.

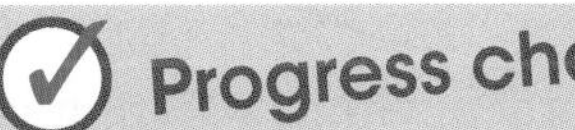

You should now understand that the value of recording information formally includes the following:

- Adhering to legal requirements. This means making sure that the conditions of registration as a care/education provider are fully met by recording all necessary information in an appropriate format.

- Ensuring consistency of quality. By recording certain types of information in a similar way or on a pre-designed form, consistency in quality is more likely to be achieved.
- Supporting reflective practice. When information is recorded in a set way, it is easier to find particular pieces of information to review details of a situation or to review performance.
- Informing decisions. When information is written in a format that is easy to read and relevant information is accessible when required, it supports practitioners to make informed decisions.
- Ensuring policies and procedures are followed. When practitioners follow a set procedure (for example, when recording information), it helps to ensure that all the relevant facts are always included whoever carries out the recording and that all practitioners are following the setting's procedures. This relates to ensuring information is stored appropriately.
- Supporting the sharing of valid information. There are many occasions when information is shared appropriately between practitioners, parents and other professionals. Formal recording helps to ensure the information is valid and written in a format that is understandable by all.

Section 2: Understand which format should be used relevant to target reader

When information is recorded within a setting, it is imperative that it is documented in a suitable way. A wide range of information needs to be formally recorded and the way it is recorded, shared and stored depends on a number of factors, including the purpose of the record and the target reader. Professionals will be required to record information in a variety of formats, including:

- reports
- pro forma
- formal letters
- observations
- records of telephone calls/memos
- minutes of meetings/meeting agenda
- numerical documents
- charts and diagrams.

The contents of all records must be:

- timely
- informative
- accurate
- presented in the appropriate format clearly understood by the target reader.

Pro forma (pre-written forms)

Pro forma are most often used when it is essential to include certain facts when recording – for example, when recording children's personal information or recording accidents in a setting. The form sets out exactly what information is required and will ensure the writer records all the relevant facts, which may be needed to comply with legislation (see an example of an accident/incident form on page 295).

Pro forma usually support the writer to record a lot of important information concisely, rather than give a long descriptive account. When reviewing information on a pro forma, the reader knows where to look to quickly gain the information they require. It is easier to compare information from a selection of records when the information is recorded in the same format – for example, when reviewing where in the setting accidents happen most frequently.

Examples of pro forma used for recording include:

- children's personal information, including safeguarding issues
- children's attendance
- children's daily routines
- staff rotas
- accidents/incidents
- medication

- risk assessments
- fridge temperature recording
- activity plans
- observation of children
- complaint investigation procedure.

Activity

Choose one of the examples listed above and design a pro forma to ensure all of the relevant information is recorded. Suggest how/why the record should be reviewed, shared and appropriately stored.

Remember to consider data protection issues!

Formal risk assessments are a way of recording the evidence that staff within a setting have identified any potential hazards and have put control measures in place to reduce the risk of harm. Risk assessment is a specific legal requirement within all early years, care and education settings and should be undertaken to ensure the safety of everyone who works in or uses them.

Risk assessments are used to inform others of risks and identify what they must do to keep themselves and others within the setting safe. For example, within early years provision, 'The Statutory Framework for the Early Years Foundation Stage' sets out legal requirements relating to risk assessment that all providers must meet. This includes identifying:

- the risk
- control measures to reduce the risk
- the person responsible for implementing and undertaking the review.

It is important to record risk assessments on a chart so that information is presented in a clear and logical way to ensure that it is correctly understood by everyone. Risk assessments should be regularly reviewed and revised if necessary; for example, a review must always take place to check that the control measures are adequate when situations change – such as when a new piece of equipment is brought into the setting or a child with an additional need or disability joins the setting. These changes should be recorded accurately and these records must be available for inspection by the relevant authorities, such as Ofsted.

It is important to record when risk assessments are undertaken and reviewed as they are evidence of good practice and meet the legal requirements of registration. For example, if a serious accident happens or a child or adult in the setting suffers a serious injury which requires investigation by the Health and Safety Executive, risk assessment records will be the main focus of the investigation.

If risk assessments are not available for inspection or have not been appropriately recorded, the setting could be held responsible in the event of injury. The registered person in the setting could even have action taken against them by the registering authority, such as Ofsted, or be prosecuted for negligence by the Health and Safety Executive

Activity

You are planning to carry out a baking activity with children aged seven years. You will be using a small electric oven to bake the cakes/biscuits. In pairs, plan the activity and, using the 'How to complete a risk assessment' instructions shown below, design and complete a risk assessment.

How to complete a risk assessment

There are six main steps to completing a risk assessment.

1. Identify the task/hazards.
2. Consider what the risk might be.
3. Decide who might be harmed.
4. Decide on control measures.
5. Consider the level of risk – how likely it is to happen.
6. Set a review date and say who will be responsible for this review.

Task/ action or hazard	What are the risks?	Who could be affected?	What control measures could be put in place?	Risk is: high; medium; low?	Person responsible + review period	Review date/ action	Review date/ action
Staff drinking hot drinks in the setting	Burns and scalds Slipping on spills	Children and adults	• Hot drinks only to be served and consumed in the staff area, away from the children. • A 'caution sign' placed to alert others to any spill and all spills to be cleaned up immediately.	Low	D. Jones (Company Health and Safety Officer) 12-month review		
Children using scissors	Cuts to: • skin • hair • clothing Stab wounds	Children and adults	• Children to be shown safe use of scissors. • Children to be supervised at all times. • Scissors to be stored out of the reach of the children.	Low	S. Barker (Nursery Manager) 6-month review		
Playing with the dressing-up box	Strangulation Trips Choking	Children	• Close supervision when children are playing with scarves, necklaces or bags with long handles. • Necklaces with beads are regularly checked for damage. • Help is given to children to ensure dressing-up clothing is not long enough to cause trips. • Dressing-up mirror is fitted with safety film.	Medium	S. Barker (Nursery Manager) 6-month review		

Table 9.1 Example of a risk assessment

Reports

A report is a document which describes or records a subject or problem and supports the writer to gather relevant information and facts and present them as accurately as possible. A report may include analysis, judgement, conclusions and recommendations. Reports can vary in length depending upon the purpose of the report – from one or two pages to hundreds of pages.

It is important to consider who will read the report, so you use language that is at the correct level for the target reader to understand. For example, a health professional may use medical words that are not familiar to some parents/carers; therefore, if parents/carers were the target readers of a report, such words would need to be explained.

A report needs to be:

- logically structured – set out clearly
- informative
- understandable – aimed at the target reader
- accurate, written objectively
- written in the past tense – the report is a summary of what has happened in the past
- signed and dated at the end.

Often a report will begin with a brief introduction outlining:

- a clear objective/why the report was carried out
- a brief history/background to the report.

The report will usually include:

- a background outline – sometimes referred to as 'terms of reference'
- a procedure
- findings
- conclusions
- recommendations.

Example of a report

A report on the standard of snacks offered within Teddy Barker's Childcare

1. Terms of reference

Teddy Barker's Childcare is a company which operates five day nurseries/wrap-around clubs for up to 250 children aged 0–8 years within the Yorkshire area (Applegate, Sunshine House, Bear House, Bridge End and Back Lane). The directors of Teddy Barker's Childcare wanted to investigate the quality of snacks offered within the settings and make changes if necessary to ensure that each setting offers a wide range of healthy snacks.

2. Procedure

The Senior Nursery Manager was asked by the directors to arrange a visit to each setting over a two-week period to gather information about the range and quality of snacks being offered to the children. The manager was also asked to report on the way the snacks were presented and how often they were offered to children.

3. Findings

(a) The range of snacks offered to the children

There was found to be a difference between the types of snacks offered within the five settings. Applegate setting had the largest range: six different fruits, three vegetable choices and four dairy options. Back Lane setting only offered three choices in total; apples, cheese and carrot sticks. Sunshine House had a good range of snacks but crisps and biscuits were sometimes offered. Sunny House and Bear House both offered five fruits and one vegetable snack.

(b) The quality of the snacks

The five settings all ensured that the produce offered was fresh. Four settings had fruit and vegetables delivered from a supermarket weekly and Bear House bought produce from the local farm shop twice each week.

(c) The presentation of the snacks

Three settings presented the children with ready-prepared snacks on a plate at the snack table. Two settings encouraged the children to select their snack and help to prepare it themselves. For example, children at Back Lane helped to peel the carrots and wash the fruit.

(d) The availability of snacks during the day

Bear House offered snacks for the longest period of time – between 9.45am and 11.15am and then again in the afternoon between 1.30pm and 2.45pm.

4. Conclusions

There are differences between the range of snacks and the length of time the snacks are offered within the five settings.

The experience the children in each setting gain varies greatly.

5. Recommendations

- A company policy is required to ensure consistency.
- All settings should source produce locally and purchase twice weekly to ensure freshness.
- Children should be included in the selection and preparation of snacks wherever practical.
- Snack time should be used as an opportunity to educate children about healthy food choices.

Signed S. Smith (Manager) 19th January 2013

Formal letters

An open letter might be used when writing to a number of people about the same topic and is mainly used when the contents are not related to individuals or do not contain information of a confidential matter. For example:

- a letter from the manager of a setting inviting all parents/carers to come and watch their child perform in a concert.

A formal letter might be written in response to a question or enquiry, to inform others or to request information. A letter written to an individual will usually be treated as confidential and any copies stored in compliance with the Data Protection Act 1995. For example:

- a manager writes a response to a letter received from a parent of a young baby, who is considering using the nursery. The parent works unusual shift patterns, so has requested that her baby attends different sessions each week. As this letter contains information that is personal to the parent, the letter should be stored and responded to in a confidential manner.

Teddy Barker's Childcare Company
Email: tbs@teddybarkers.com
Telephone: 07533269

Ref. CJB /NTR

6th December 2013

Mrs P. Nutter
20 Fishing Lane
Utley
UT1 0UT

Dear Mrs Nutter

Request for Flexible Attendance

Thank you for your recent letter of 4th December 2013 regarding Stevie's attendance at Teddy Barker's Childcare.

I am happy to inform you that we are able to accommodate your request for flexible attendance and request you make an appointment with me to discuss your exact requirements.

Thank you for choosing our nursery to care for your son. You can be assured that we will do our very best to ensure his happiness.

I look forward to meeting with you soon.

Yours sincerely,

Teddy Barker
T. Barker

Activity

Write a letter to a supplier informing them that the equipment that you purchased from them is faulty and you are requesting they collect the equipment and either repair it or replace it. Remember to set out the letter correctly and include all the relevant information.

Recording for meetings

Meetings are held for many reasons and the numbers attending can range from only two or three people to large gatherings of hundreds of people. Therefore, the format of a meeting or where a meeting might take place will depend on the purpose of the meeting. For example, a meeting with a supervisor or parent might take place in an office or quiet area of a setting, whereas a meeting to which large numbers of parents are invited might take place in a large hall or conference room. Meetings can be an excellent opportunity for a group of people to get together to discuss objectives, share information or find solutions to problems. Meetings which are well planned and effectively managed are more likely to have a positive outcome.

When a formal meeting is planned, an agenda will often be drawn up and sent to those invited to attend. This allows time for the items to be considered by individuals before the meeting.

Example of an agenda

AGENDA

Teddy Barker's Nursery
September 17th, 2013
7.00–8.45pm

Meeting called for by: Robert Fish
Minutes taken by: Susan Smith

Invited to attend: Corinne Thatcher, Victoria Tims, Rebecca Issac, Lesley Leader, Susan Herring, Fiona James, Sally Bell, Brigid Thomas, Susan Smith, Stephen Joiner

Time	Item	Owner
7.00–7.05	Welcome	Robert
7.05–7.15	Approval of last meeting's minutes	Robert
7.15–7.40	Parents' evening	Lesley
7.40–8.00	Craft material budget	Fiona
8.00–8.30	Children's learning journeys	Corinne
8.30	Any other business	Close

Minutes of a meeting

When a meeting takes place, it is important to keep a record of the information shared and the topics discussed within the meeting. These records are referred to as 'minutes'. During a meeting, minutes should be taken by one person and written up as soon as possible after the event. Minutes of a meeting might be shared with others within an organisation or group – for example, a parent committee in a school might share the minutes of a general meeting with staff and other parents/carers. However, if the meeting included information relating to a child, young person or family – for example, professionals meeting to discuss a child's behaviour or progress – then the minutes of the meeting must be treated as a confidential document and stored in compliance with the Data Protection Act 1998.

Minutes of a meeting should include:

- time and place of the meeting
- who attended
- who was invited and did not attend
- what topics were discussed (an agenda may identify the topics intended to be discussed; other topics might have been brought up in the 'any other business' section of the meeting)
- what was decided
- what actions were agreed
- who is responsible for the actions
- time and date of next meeting.

Minutes of a meeting might be read by others not present at the meeting, possibly months or even years after the event – for example, to gain information about a discussion that took place or to find out who was responsible for an action. Therefore, they need to be accurate. The person who is responsible for taking the minutes needs to ensure that they are clear about what is being said and should ask for clarification if necessary. The information recorded should be brief and written objectively – that means only including the facts and not the minute writer's opinion. Minutes of a meeting should be typed up immediately after the meeting ends so that the content is still fresh in the writer's mind. It is important that participants get a copy of the minutes promptly to enable them to carry out any actions they have taken responsibility for.

Recording children's development

The Early Years Foundation Stage (2012) identifies the importance of formative and summative assessment of children's development and makes it a legal requirement for practitioners to keep accurate records of children's progress.

The framework requires early years practitioners to review children's progress and share a summary with parents at two points:

- between the ages of 24 and 36 months
- at the end of the EYFS in the EYFS profile.

Therefore, it is of paramount importance that practitioners are able to undertake formative assessment by objectively observing and accurately recording children's development.

The EYFS also states that practitioners are required to undertake summative assessment of children. Both approaches support information sharing with staff, parents/carers, other settings and multi-agency professionals.

Summative assessment requires practitioners to make objective, accurate, short written accounts of children's development and progress, which are referred to as 'summaries'.

Observation

Observation of children can be recorded in a number of ways, including:

- written narrative observation
- Post-it notes
- tick lists
- media recording (photos, videos and sound recordings).

Recording children's development accurately and objectively is vitally important for a number of reasons. Being objective means only recording the facts as they are presented and not allowing personal opinions, beliefs or feelings to impact on the recording of those facts.

Take, as an example, a practitioner undertaking a tick-list observation of a child. He observes the child trying to climb onto a small, three-wheeled bike. The child is struggling to get on and then gives up. The practitioner is sure he saw that same child riding on the exact bike yesterday, so puts a tick next to the box which reads 'The child can climb onto and ride a three-wheeled bike'. The information is then added to the child's learning journey or development record. However, a practitioner might have lifted the child onto the bike yesterday or another child might have helped. Therefore, what has been recorded is incorrect information. The practitioner actually recorded his own opinion or belief, rather than what he saw the child doing that day.

Children's observation records are used by practitioners to gain an understanding of the child's current stage of development. The information practitioners get from reviewing the observations of a child is invaluable when providing experiences, planning activities and considering the support a child may need to strengthen and extend their learning and development. If this information is not recorded accurately, incorrect decisions may be made for the child – for example, it could result in a child being given activities that are too challenging and therefore could have the potential to damage the child's self-esteem.

Information about a child's development gained from observation is used when an individual education plan (IEP) is required to support a child's development. Therefore, observations must be recorded in a manner that ensures the reader gains an exact picture of the child's current level of development – be it a parent or a professional planning for the child's particular need.

Practitioners need to carefully consider the most appropriate form of observation. Observations recorded by practitioners may be viewed by external agencies such as doctors, psychologists or other health professionals when gaining an understanding of a child's development or behaviour. If observations are not recorded accurately or the observer has failed to record a vital piece of information, planning for a child may not be suitable and this could affect a child's progression or well-being.

Reflective practice

Look at a piece of information you have recorded – for example, a child observation or information about a child's day. Think about how you recorded the information and reflect on the following:

- Was all the information relevant?
- Did you record the information objectively?
- Could you have recorded the information in a more suitable format?

Research Activity

Research the following:

- Data Protection Act 1998
- Health and Safety Executive (HSE)
- Reporting of Injuries, Diseases and Dangerous Occurrences Regulations 1995 (RIDDOR).

Think about how each of these pieces of legislation impacts on care/education provision.

Accident and incident reporting

Practitioners within early years, care and education settings have a legal duty under the 'Reporting of Injuries, Diseases and Dangerous Occurrences Regulations 1995' (RIDDOR) to ensure accurate and consistent recording of all incidents and accidents within the setting.

Accident and incident records are important documents that are required for a number of reasons, including:

- informing other staff in the setting
- notifying parents/carers of the child/children concerned
- providing information to assist doctors or other health professionals, if medical assistance is required
- informing the risk assessment process
- providing the relevant facts when an investigation is undertaken by a regulatory authority (e.g. Ofsted or the Health and Safety Executive)
- informing insurance companies when a claim is made against the setting.

The records need to contain all the relevant information, recorded objectively, clearly and accurately. Accident or incident forms should be completed as soon as possible after the event to ensure facts are recalled and recorded accurately. Information should be concise, with only the relevant details given, so that the reader can quickly get a clear picture of the situation.

Information to be recorded on an accident/incident form:

- name of child
- date and time of accident/incident
- names of practitioners present
- what happened (where/how)
- nature of injury and which part of the child was injured
- what action was taken by the practitioners
- who was informed
- details of person reporting the accident/incident.

Accident and incident records must be reviewed regularly by the person in the setting responsible for health and safety. Reviews will assist in the identification of areas or equipment within the setting that might be contributing factors to accidents or incidents within the setting. Reviewing records might help to highlight where control measures, put

Name of child: *Include child's full name*	Date: *The date the accident/ incident happened*	Time: *The time of the accident/incident*
Name/s of practitioners present: *Include all the names of those present*		
What happened: *State what was happening before the accident/incident, how the accident/incident happened, where it happened.* *Example:* *Zac was playing with three other children in the outdoor area. The children were digging in the raised beds using small spades.* *Zac was sitting on the ground holding his spade when another child stood on Zac's hand.*		
Nature of injury: *Provide details of the injury* *Example:* *Zac has small cut/graze to right index finger where he was holding the spade and a swelling on his knuckles where the child stood on his hand.*		
Action taken: *Include details of what action the practitioner took, such as calling a first aider or seeking medical assistance if the injury was serious.* *Example:* *Jenny reassured Zac that he was going to be fine. A first aider washed the wound, checked the movement in Zac's hand, which appeared good, and then applied a cold compress.* *After ten minutes, Zac seemed OK and asked to go back out to play, so a small plaster was applied to the cut.* *Zac was observed by practitioners and seems to be using his hand in the way he normally would.*		
Details of person reporting the accident: *Rebecca Issac (nursery nurse)* Manager/Health and Safety Officer: *Stephanie Barker (manager)*		Signed: *Rebecca Issac* Signed: *S. Barker*
Is this a reportable accident/incident (yes/no)? If yes, add details of when and to whom the accident was reported.		
Advice/information given to parent/carer: *This should include information such as what to do if the child seems to be getting worse. For example, if the child has suffered a bump to the head, the parents/carers should be advised to seek immediate medical attention if the child:* • *has a headache which gets worse or does not go away within four to six hours of the accident or incident* • *becomes drowsy or difficult to wake up* • *feels sick or vomits.*		
Name of parent/carer:		Signed:

Table 9.2 Example of an accident/incident form

in place following a risk assessment, are not proving effective.

Accident and incident forms should be stored safely (complying with the Data Protection Act 1998) for a minimum of three years and be available for inspection as requested by a regulatory authority.

In some circumstances where the injury is significant – for example, when bones are broken or an injured person requires hospital treatment – the accident must be reported verbally to the relevant external authorities, such as Ofsted and/or the Health and Safety Executive (to comply with RIDDOR) within 24 hours and a copy of the report sent within seven days. Authorities may then decide to carry out an investigation, based on information recorded at the time of the incident, to ensure that the setting has taken the correct steps to try and ensure the safety of all children and adults in the setting.

Remember, the accident or incident record may be referred to when a formal investigation is undertaken or it may be used as evidence in a legal prosecution. Therefore, facts *must* be accurate!

Case Study

18th January at 2pm: Toni, aged four years, is playing in the outdoor area of a day nursery. Toni falls off a small bike and as she falls lands on her wrist. Sofia, the nursery supervisor, sees it happen and goes straight over to Toni to see if she is all right and to comfort her. Sofia is concerned because Toni's wrist looks red and swollen and she is obviously in a lot of pain.

Sofia asks another member of staff to go and get the trained first aider, who decides that Toni may have a serious injury and needs to be taken to the local hospital straight away. Toni's carer is contacted and he goes straight to the hospital to be with Toni. At the hospital, an X-ray confirms that Toni's arm is broken and an operation is required to straighten the bone before a plaster cast is applied.

In pairs, complete an accident form accurately and decide which external agencies should be notified.

Charts and diagrams

Some information recorded within a setting will be recorded in a chart or diagram. This information is very easy to read and can give the reader an instant picture or overview of a situation. For example, a pie chart might give the management a quick overview of the occupancy.

COSHH records containing information related to cleaning products or chemicals used within the setting may also be displayed on charts and should be read by all staff and available for inspection in line with Health and Safety Executive (HSE) regulations.

It is the duty of the person responsible for health and safety within the setting to ensure that accurate and up-to-date records are kept and all staff have access to these records.

Numerical records

Some information is most appropriately recorded in the form of a numerical record. Staff-to-child ratios are calculated by counting how many children at

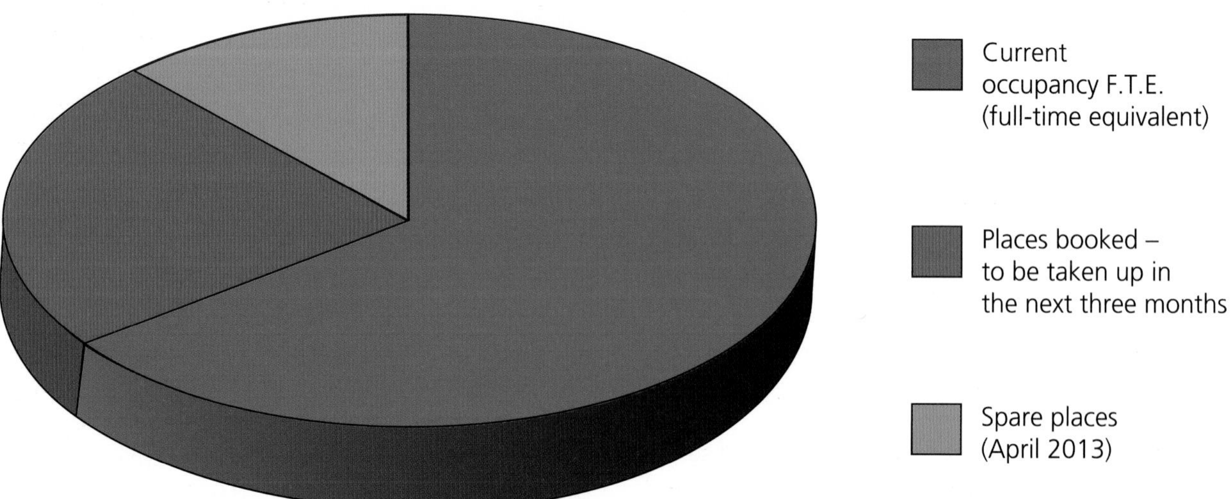

Figure 9.1 Total number of places available in the pre-school room

what age will be attending a given session and then calculating the number of staff required to maintain at least the legal minimum ratio.

It is a requirement that all settings keep a record of attendance of both children and staff. Often this information is gained in the form of a register or a signing in and out time sheet. This is a legal record so should be maintained accurately and stored appropriately. It might be that a setting is required to produce the record for inspection or to give details about a particular child's attendance. Any inaccuracies could have potentially severe consequences for either the setting or children/staff within the setting. For example, a safeguarding investigation may need to have information related to a child's attendance on a particular day. Therefore, this information must be recorded accurately and available for inspection.

Fees and accounts are often calculated using a computer spreadsheet in which the data is formatted to give the reader the exact information they require. These records might be kept solely on the computer but also need to be stored in line with data protection legislation.

Numerical data recorded to comply with legislation or operational procedure may include:

- attendance records (including numbers of staff/ children at any one time)
- year calendar, highlighting holidays, closure days and parents/carers meetings, etc.
- fridge and freezer temperature records (recorded daily)
- room temperature records
- occupancy figures (total places available/numbers of children attending)
- staff time sheets and salary calculations
- food quantity calculations/costs (based on the number of children/meals provided)
- accounts (income and expenditure)
- invoices (fees/purchases/payments)
- dates related to reviews.

When the data is recorded in a logical format such as a chart or diagram, information can be easily found and used to make comparisons, identify trends or make informed operational decisions.

Activity

You have been asked to work out the number of staff required in an afternoon session within a nursery setting.

- For children aged under two: there must be at least one member of staff for every three children.
- For children aged two: there must be at least one member of staff for every four children.
- For children over the age of three: there must be at least one member of staff for every eight children.

You check the records and, on this particular afternoon, there are 29 children booked in to attend. Five children are under two, nine children are two years old and 15 children are over the age of two years.

All of the staff hold a relevant qualification at Level 3 or above.

1 Work out the minimum number of staff required in the setting to maintain the required ratios.

2 Design a form to help you to record the information for the setting's records.

Recording for multi-agency working

Multi-agency working aims to ensure that children and young people who need extra support have exactly the right professionals supporting their needs. The range of practitioners working together to provide this support is vast and may include anyone whose job brings them into contact with children, young people and their families. Professionals from a range of agencies, such as early years, education, health, social work and police, might be involved in providing support.

Where professionals work together to provide support, effective communication between agencies is vital and may involve regular meetings between professionals, written communication and formal reports.

Confidentiality is paramount. This means that no information about children, young people or their families must be shared outside the multi-agency team of professionals involved. A breach of this confidentiality might put children, young people or their families at risk and could result in disciplinary action being taken against the person/s breaching confidentiality. Therefore, the professional must share personal records only with other professionals involved in supporting the child, young person or family and never with other people. Written communication must be stored safely so the contents of the report or document remain confidential. This will ensure the principles of the Data Protection Act 1998 are upheld.

To ensure that the support given is appropriate and will benefit the child, young person or their family, all of the facts and information used to make decisions must be accurate and up-to-date.

It is important to remember that information recorded by practitioners and shared between professionals or organisations may be used to make very significant, perhaps difficult, decisions about a child's future. For example, professionals are concerned that a child is not being cared for adequately within the family. Decisions about the type of support which needs to be put in place, both for the child and child's family, will be taken after all the records related to the child/family are thoroughly reviewed. Therefore, it is essential that the facts are recorded accurately and records are reviewed objectively.

Section 3: Using formal recording in the real work environment

There is a range of skills a practitioner is required to develop in order to record information formally, including:

- accurate recording
- following setting policies and procedures
- writing clearly, at the appropriate level
- time management
- objectivity
- recording relevant information.

Accurate recording

It is very important to ensure that information is recorded accurately – for example, the time a baby has his lunchtime feed and the amount of milk he drank. If information is not recorded accurately, decisions made based on the information could be wrong; for example, if a child's daily diary record indicated that the child had eaten most of the food she was offered at the setting, when actually the child had hardly eaten anything during that day, the fact that the child was perhaps unwell may not be picked up on as soon as it could have been.

Recording relevant information

It is important that the information is recorded in a clear-to-read way – this is writing succinctly, which means giving the relevant details rather than giving very long accounts that perhaps include information that is not necessary. For example, when recording an accident, information on how well the child was playing prior to the accident is not relevant, only what the child was doing at the actual time of the accident – any unnecessary information just stops the reader getting to the important parts.

Objectivity

When recording information, it is very important to do so objectively. This means not allowing your own thoughts, feelings or prior knowledge to affect your judgement. For example, you are observing a child's social development for his learning journey and you recall that yesterday he was arguing with another child over a toy car. Today the child is playing in the water tray and sharing the equipment well, but when you record the information you include what you saw yesterday.

Reflective practice

Think about the importance of being objective. Reflect on how well you record information objectively. How do you know you are being objective when recording information?

Time management

When recording information, the sooner after the event the information is recorded, the more likely it is to be correct. For example, it is harder the day after an event to recall exactly what happened and when. Recording information soon after the event also ensures the information is immediately available to others to support them to make informed decisions.

Writing clearly, at the appropriate level

Information is recorded for many different reasons and for a range of people. Therefore, it is crucial that the language used is appropriate for the reader. For example, using very academic words within an assignment or professional report would be appropriate. However, when designing a poster to inform all parents about an upcoming visit, the information would need to be written in a clear and concise way. This would allow parents to quickly get the information they needed. When handwriting information, it is important to write clearly so that others can easily read what has been written. If the writing is poor and you or others have to try and guess what is written at a later date, it could result in inaccurate interpretation and therefore wrong decisions being made.

Following setting policies and procedures

By using the correct recording formats, the information recorded is more likely to be relevant and useful to the reader. Having systems in place that highlight the recording procedure will help to ensure all practitioners are familiar with when and how to record information in line with setting policies. When all practitioners understand how to follow the recording procedure, it ensures that all similar situations are recorded in the same way, whichever practitioner is recording the information.

Progress check

You should understand the following:

- Recalling and recording information accurately means including the relevant facts.
- Writing succinctly is often important. Giving long, detailed accounts is not necessary when a brief overview, including relevant details, is adequate.
- Being objective is crucial. Recording only the facts and not including feelings, beliefs or prior judgements support objectivity.
- Time management skills are essential to ensure records are written up in a timely manner, so that facts are easily recalled accurately.
- Using an appropriate level of language should be considered so the records are clearly understood by the target reader.
- Writing clearly when handwriting ensures the record can be read easily and is not misunderstood by others.
- Following setting procedures is very important to ensure that information is recorded in the appropriate format.

- A sound understanding of confidentiality and data protection is necessary to protect the practitioner, the setting, children and families.
- Reflective practice is supported by effective formal recording as reviewing records supports practitioners to make informed decisions based on facts.

The above list identifies just some of the skills practitioners need to develop when recording in a real work environment. However, the most important considerations are to ensure that records are objectively written, accurate, recorded in the correct format, stored appropriately and only shared in line with the setting's confidentiality policy. Remember, records within a setting are often kept as a legal requirement and therefore every practitioner has a legal responsibility to make sure that they follow the setting policy in all aspects of record keeping.

Useful resources

Early Years Foundation Stage Statutory Framework
www.education.gov.uk/schools/teachingandlearning/curriculum/a0068102/early-years-foundation-stage-eyfs

Early Education – the British Association for Early Childhood Education
www.early-education.org.uk

HSE: investigations
www.hse.gov.uk/foi/internalops/og/ogprocedures/investigation/report.htm

Using English: formal letter writing
www.usingenglish.com/resources/letter-writing.php

Safety First Aid: reporting accidents – information for schools
www.safetyfirstaid.co.uk/first-aid-guides/Reporting-Accidents-In-Schools.aspx

ATL: accident reporting
www.atl.org.uk/health-and-safety/accidents-and-first-aid/accident-reporting.asp

Ealing Early Years Childcare and Play: summarising and tracking children's progress
www.childrenscentres.org.uk/ey_tracking_tools.asp

Childcare: improving observation skills
www.newchildcare.co.uk/observing.html

Teaching Expertise: observing, recording and planning young children's learning
www.teachingexpertise.com/articles/observing-recording-and-planning-young-childrens-learning-3352

Teaching Expertise: record keeping for efficient child protection
www.teachingexpertise.com/e-bulletins/record-keeping-efficient-child-protection-8273

The Meeting Minutes: how to write a good meeting agenda
http://themeetingminutes.com/how-to-write-a-good-meeting-agenda

How to write meeting minutes
www.dcs.warwick.ac.uk/~doron/course/cs223/minutes.html

Chapter 10 Research to support practice when working with children and/or young people (Unit CP 10)

This chapter will help you to understand what is meant by the term 'research', how research is carried out and how it can be used, particularly in relation to your work with children and young people. Research contributes to many specialist areas of work and study and is central to many disciplines, but this chapter will focus on the contribution made by research to work with children and young people.

You will begin to understand how research, and the results of research, can be used in your work with children and young people – for example, to improve practice. You will become familiar with the way in which research findings are presented in different styles and in different formats to suit particular audiences. In addition, you will be able to plan and carry out your own research project from start to finish, developing your project so that the information produced through your research investigations is fit for your intended purpose.

You will understand the particular issues that must be taken into consideration when doing research with children and young people, and how you can use more than one approach to ensure your findings are legitimate. Reflecting on the process, you will consider how you might use your conclusions to inform your work with children and young people, or that of your organisation.

Learning outcomes

1. Understand research and its value when working with children and/or young people.
2. Understand the role of a hypothesis in research.
3. Understand methodologies in research.
4. Be able to identify a research hypothesis.
5. Be able to plan and implement research in relation to working with children and/or young people
6. Be able to present data in relation to the hypothesis.
7. Be able to reflect on the research undertaken.

Section 1: The value of research when working with children and/or young people

Most research with children and young people is aimed at improving their life chances and opportunities and enabling all children to reach their full potential, rather than just adding to the sum of knowledge. It does this by helping us reach a better understanding of children and young people's development and experiences and how they see the world, so that we begin to recognise how to contribute to their development in our practice.

Children and young people's services include:

- childcare provision and nursery services
- education, school and boarding school services
- children's health services, including child and adolescent mental health services (CAMHS)

- children's social services for looked-after children, including fostering and adoption services and residential childcare services
- voluntary and charitable organisations providing specialist services for children and young people.

All organisations concerned with children and young people can use the results of research to help improve their services.

What is research?

Often when we think of research, we imagine someone in a laboratory wearing a white coat, surrounded by test tubes and machines, doing complicated experiments. In fact, some research, particularly scientific research, can be exactly like this but it is important to recognise that there are many different ways of doing research and it can actually be part of everyday life. The overall aim of research is to add to the sum of human knowledge. Research does this by asking questions to find things out, then producing data that can be measured and tested. Consequently, research can be thought of as a process for finding things out in an organised and systematic way.

Key term

Data – the facts, figures and numbers that, when analysed, provide meaningful information.

For example, we all undertake a form of research when we make decisions about things. If you were planning to buy a new car, you would think about the reasons for needing a car; for instance, it would be no use buying a two-seater sports car if you regularly need to drive your three children to school. Because there are so many cars available and you cannot research them all, you might then draw up some criteria to narrow down your requirements, such as how much you could afford and whether to consider a new car or buy second hand, your preference for manual or automatic gears, petrol or diesel engine; all these factors will affect the type of car you are prepared to consider. You would probably look at reviews of several models to see which seem to be the best fit to your needs and consider how reliable they are and how much they cost to run, tax and insure, and so on. Your decision will be affected by all these factors.

Research can be defined as:

- organised study, or the act of studying something methodically
- investigating or studying a subject closely; a course of critical or scientific inquiry; an investigation directed to the discovery of some fact by careful study of a subject.

The Shorter Oxford English Dictionary, vol. 2, third edn.

Research includes both the search for knowledge and the process through which new knowledge is gained and understanding increased; by the time you have researched your new car, you will certainly be very knowledgeable about different types of cars!

Some research, such as academic or medical research, may be carried out to investigate a particular issue or specialist area, to find out new information, for example, or seek to better understand a particular disease so that new treatments can be developed. Research might be carried out in organisations working with children and young people, including those such as charitable organisations or social services, to see how well new practices, policies or ways of doing things are working; other research is carried out to test the feasibility of new ideas or thinking.

Using the internet to find things out is not research because there is usually no way of checking the accuracy of information or the validity of the studies that such information may be based on. However, it can be useful as part of the research process.

Types of research

- **Applied research** – this uses the outcomes of research to decide what interventions (treatments, actions, ways of working) are effective. Organisations that use applied research include the National Institute for Health and Clinical Excellence (NICE), the Social Care Institute for Excellence (SCIE) and the Institute of Education.

- **Biomedical research** – this is the study of living things and research into their life processes (activities necessary to sustain life and reproduce), so it is relevant to all the life sciences. An example of biomedical research is the Human Genome Project (www.ornl.gov/hgmis/home.shtml).
- **Clinical research** – this is usually the final stage of a clinical trial for testing new drugs or treatments, in which the new product is tested on humans for the first time to measure its effectiveness and check for unwanted side effects.
- **Outcomes research** – this is the name for research which focuses on the effects of disease on individuals and society, the causes of ill health and the factors that determine health outcomes (how healthy people are). An example of this type of research is the Marmot Review (Fair Society, Healthy Lives), available at www.marmotreview.org.
- **Directed research** – this type of research is carried out on request in order to explore a specific topic or area of study. This is often used by governments to inform policy making.
- **Investigator-initiated research** – in this type of research, a topic or phenomenon is chosen by the researcher. The researcher defines the hypothesis (research question) and the structure of the research, as well as carrying it out. This is what you will be helped to do in this chapter.

The term 'research' can also be used to describe the specific activities carried out in order to find facts, to gather information, to increase understanding or to prove or disprove something. We carry out research 'to prevent ourselves from being misled by our own atomized experiences and prejudices' (Goldacre 2008). This means that we need to have an open mind when investigating new things, recognising that our personal experience, while valid, is limited. We must approach new information critically, questioning its origins. Research is therefore carried out according to a set of agreed, recognised principles to ensure that the information and knowledge coming out of the research are accurate.

The difference between primary research and secondary research

Primary research

You carry out primary research yourself, as the researcher. You will use primary research during your own research project for this unit. It involves all the stages of research, such as planning, information gathering and delivery of the research. Sometimes the researcher will have help from other people. However, they will have control over all stages of the research project, providing direction and designing the methodology. They will also have responsibility for the timescale, budget, data analysis and the conclusions drawn from the research findings. The information gathered during primary research is first hand – known as the primary source (of data/information). Therefore, primary sources are those that are directly involved (e.g. a witness or an original account of something, such as a diary).

Primary research with children and young people will involve you as the researcher interacting with the children directly, depending on the type of methodology you use for your particular research project.

Secondary research

This involves using the research other people have done in your chosen area of investigation to inform your own work in some way. For example, you may decide to carry out a review and critique of someone else's work to demonstrate that the conclusions they have drawn are not valid or are biased. Secondary sources are 'one step removed' from direct involvement and may draw their own, different, conclusions from primary sources. You will usually use information from a variety of different secondary sources, such as research papers, when engaging in secondary research. Very often the first stage of a project is what is known as a 'literature review', in which you read what others have written about the area you wish to study. It is rather like looking at all those manufacturers' brochures and reviews in car magazines when you were researching your new car.

Secondary research with children and young people will involve you seeing what others have written, what other research in and around your topic area has been carried out and what the findings show. Secondary sources of data may come from the parents or carers of the children and young people who are the subject of research, for example. Other secondary sources you could use include official statistics and publications by the Office for National Statistics (www.ons.gov.uk), such as Annual Abstracts, Social Trends and the Census.

If you design a questionnaire, carry out interviews using the questionnaire, then review and assess the responses and summarise your findings in an article, you have carried out primary research. The people you interview are your primary sources of data. If someone else then reads your article and uses it in their research project, they are using secondary sources (your work, your research findings and reports) and must acknowledge you as the author; otherwise, they would be guilty of plagiarism.

Key term

Plagiarism – passing off someone else's work as if it were your own.

Primary and secondary research are not mutually exclusive; in fact, it is a key part of the research process to use secondary sources, such as books, journal articles, reviews and newspaper articles, in the early stages of a project. Secondary sources can help you identify or refine a research question or help in the development of a research hypothesis.

It is important that you are able to assess whether research done by other people is properly carried out and their conclusions sound. There are agreed research criteria (the standards against which research is judged), which, if met, give weight and validity (strong, rational and sound argument, based on logic) to the findings.

The value of research

Research adds to the sum of human knowledge and gives us the tools to find out how and why things work, such as what interventions are effective, by providing us with evidence. When we act on the results of research, it is known as evidence-based practice, and this applies to areas of work covered by both the physical and the social sciences – from preventing disease to preventing youth offending, for example.

It can be argued, for example, that 'evidence-based medicine, the ultimate applied science, contains some of the cleverest ideas from the past two centuries, it has saved millions of lives' (Goldacre 2008).

Research in the social sciences (see 'What is research methodology?' on page 312) is concerned with the social world and human interaction – social research (for more information, see the Economic and Social Research Council website: www.esrc.ac.uk). The importance of research lies in the fact that it provides new knowledge or confirms existing knowledge. This provides value to society as a whole through increasing understanding and benefits governments, organisations and individuals when the knowledge is used to improve the systems, structures and processes that help society function, or to improve the health and well-being of individuals.

Research in the natural sciences (see 'What is research methodology?' on pages 310–12), such as medical research, helps to increase knowledge and understanding of conditions that either affect children specifically or are inherited genetic disorders. When things go wrong for children, research can help us identify how things can be improved.

Research uses specific methods of inquiry to:

- acquire new knowledge – research for discovery
- look again at existing knowledge to correct or modify it – critical enquiry
- draw together different strands of new and/ or existing research to develop a new theory – integration of knowledge.

Activity

Many academic and scientific journals regularly report the results of research. For example, *Nature* (www.nature.com) and *New Scientist* (www.newscientist.com). You can find many other journals at www.oxfordjournals.org. The British Library also has an online facility that enables you to see what is published – go to www.bl.uk/eresources/jnls/ejournals.html. There are also many social science journals, such as the *British Journal of Social Work*, available at http://bjsw.oxfordjournals.org. National newspapers such as the *Guardian* and the *Independent* also summarise recent advances and discoveries in research.

Working in pairs or small groups, find examples of research that:

- discovered something new (new knowledge)
- examined existing research and produced something new, such as a different interpretation of the original findings (critical enquiry)
- developed a new theory (integration of knowledge to extend understanding).

Try not to be put off by the technical language, which may seem complicated at first. You should be able to find relevant articles covering research in medicine, health and social care, childcare, child psychology or families that are both interesting and useful.

Academic organisations carry out research in all specialist areas as part of their role in developing and expanding knowledge. University funding from the government is linked to the amount of research published by universities. Universities are research specialists and often carry out research projects on behalf of other organisations, including government and commercial enterprises. This can be a source of additional funding.

The government frequently uses research information to make decisions when developing policies and to direct government spending according to their priorities. The Office for National Statistics (now UK National Statistics) carries out research for and on behalf of government departments. You can access the website and see which government departments have responsibility for collecting and publishing statistical information at www.statistics.gov.uk.

Commercial organisations also use research to identify sales and marketing opportunities, to see if there is a market for new products or services or to find out what people want in order to develop new products and services – for example, new smart phone applications (apps) and games.

Research can uncover facts, find out people's opinions and intentions or identify trends. Research can also help to prove or disprove something – facts, opinions, theories and ideas, for example.

Facts

Research is used to discover facts, such as how many children and young people there are in the UK and what proportion of the population they represent. Research tells us how many babies are born and how many people die per year, etc. A typical survey of this kind is the Census, which is carried out every ten years in the UK. The Census is essentially a population count of every household in England and Wales. People are required by law to answer a range of questions about themselves and their household on the same day, to ensure consistency. The Census provides a wealth of information, which can be used for many different purposes, and it shows how society has changed over time (see www.neighbourhood.statistics.gov.uk/HTMLDocs/dvc13/census1911_2001.html). You might have been involved in the last Census, which took place in 2011. Because these types of facts are concerned with numbers, they are often presented as statistics (numbers/numerical data) – for example, percentages. The study of population is called demography.

Opinions

Sometimes it is important to investigate or challenge 'common sense' assumptions or received opinion – things that are taken for granted – or to look deeper into an issue to see why some people think as they do, in order to increase understanding. Research can help to frame assumptions into a theory that can be tested to see what opinions people hold – for instance, about children and young people – and how these are formed. An example of how opinions are identified through research is the 'British Social Attitudes Survey' (http://data.gov.uk/dataset/british-social-attitudes-survey), carried out annually by the government. Opinions are also tested through market research, the results of which help companies and businesses to make decisions that respond to people's opinions, needs and preferences, increasing sales and profits. However, it is only recently that children and young people have begun to be asked their opinions and views directly.

Trends

Surveys are used to predict trends, events and people's behaviour by asking about an individual's intentions, such as how they would vote in an election, how likely they are to use private health services or whether they intend to return to work after having a baby. They may ask questions about people's lifestyles – for example, how they travel to work and whether they have a car, how many children are in the household, their household income and expenditure. It is important for governments to be able to identify trends in order to plan services and allocate resources (see http://data.gov.uk/dataset/social_trends). Again, it is only more recently, as a result of the adoption of the principles contained in the United Nations Convention on the Rights of the Child (UNCRC), that children and young people have become involved in helping to shape services that affect them. Prior to this, their views were not usually sought.

Companies also like to have information about consumer (customer) buying habits to identify new trends so that they can produce products that people, including children and young people, want to buy; this is an aspect of market research.

Research in children and young people's services

Identifying needs

For example, school readiness, literacy and numeracy, care facilities for children with life-threatening and life-limiting conditions, childhood bereavement (e.g. Winston's Wish), services for older children and young adults, bullying and child protection services. Needs might be identified for individuals or groups and/or geographically – locally, regionally or nationally across the different countries of the UK.

Highlighting gaps in provision

Research has previously identified gaps in services, such as respite care for children with additional needs (short-break foster care) and Child and Adolescent Mental Health Services (CAMHS). Services for child carers supporting disabled or sick parents might be insufficient to meet current or predicted demand or may not be offered locally if the provision is non-statutory (not legally required to be offered by local authorities). Often charities are involved in providing some services to make up for gaps in provision – for example, for unaccompanied child refugees entering the country and seeking asylum (see www.refugeecouncil.org.uk). There is often overlap between identifying needs and highlighting gaps in provision.

Planning health, education and care services

The use of research by government to evaluate current service levels or respond to significant issues, such as child deaths resulting from safeguarding failures. An example is the Laming Report, in which Lord Laming was commissioned by the government to examine how safeguarding children could be improved following the high-profile death of a child. Lord Laming's recommendations led to the 'Every Child Matters' policy, which aimed to improve integrated working between all the agencies involved with safeguarding children and young people – health, social services and education. Research also informs the provision of maternity and child health services, schools and early years services – for example, to see whether the number of school places, maternity beds or midwives is likely to be sufficient to meet the predicted changes in population.

Evaluating existing provision

For example, the Steer Review was a government-commissioned review of behaviour standards and practices in schools. The researchers examined a large amount of evidence on different ways of managing children's behaviour in schools, using a range of methodologies, and made a number of recommendations to help schools improve their practice.

Discovering new knowledge

The Human Genome Project is an example of large-scale research leading to new knowledge. Research was carried out over a number of years to identify the chemical construction of DNA (deoxyribonucleic acid – the basic building block of human existence), together with the 20,000–25,000 genes that carry specific DNA information, and create the uniqueness of each human. Indeed, so big is this research that we keep discovering more information that can potentially benefit humans. One recent example is the discovery of the gene responsible for Duchenne muscular dystrophy (DMS) – an inherited condition causing progressive muscle weakness in boys and that severely shortens their lives. This discovery has helped further research to identify a drug which may encourage the body to ignore the genetic mutation (defect) which causes DMS.

In summary:

- Research can confirm facts and things already known – for example, it can replicate experiments that confirm existing theories.
- Research clarifies and improves our understanding of the world and how it works.
- Research provides opportunities to explore ideas and follow our interests, stimulating debate and new thinking.
- Research provides evidence and answers to questions – that is, evidence-based practice, such as 'why we do this (X) and not this (Y)' (i.e. what works and what does not).

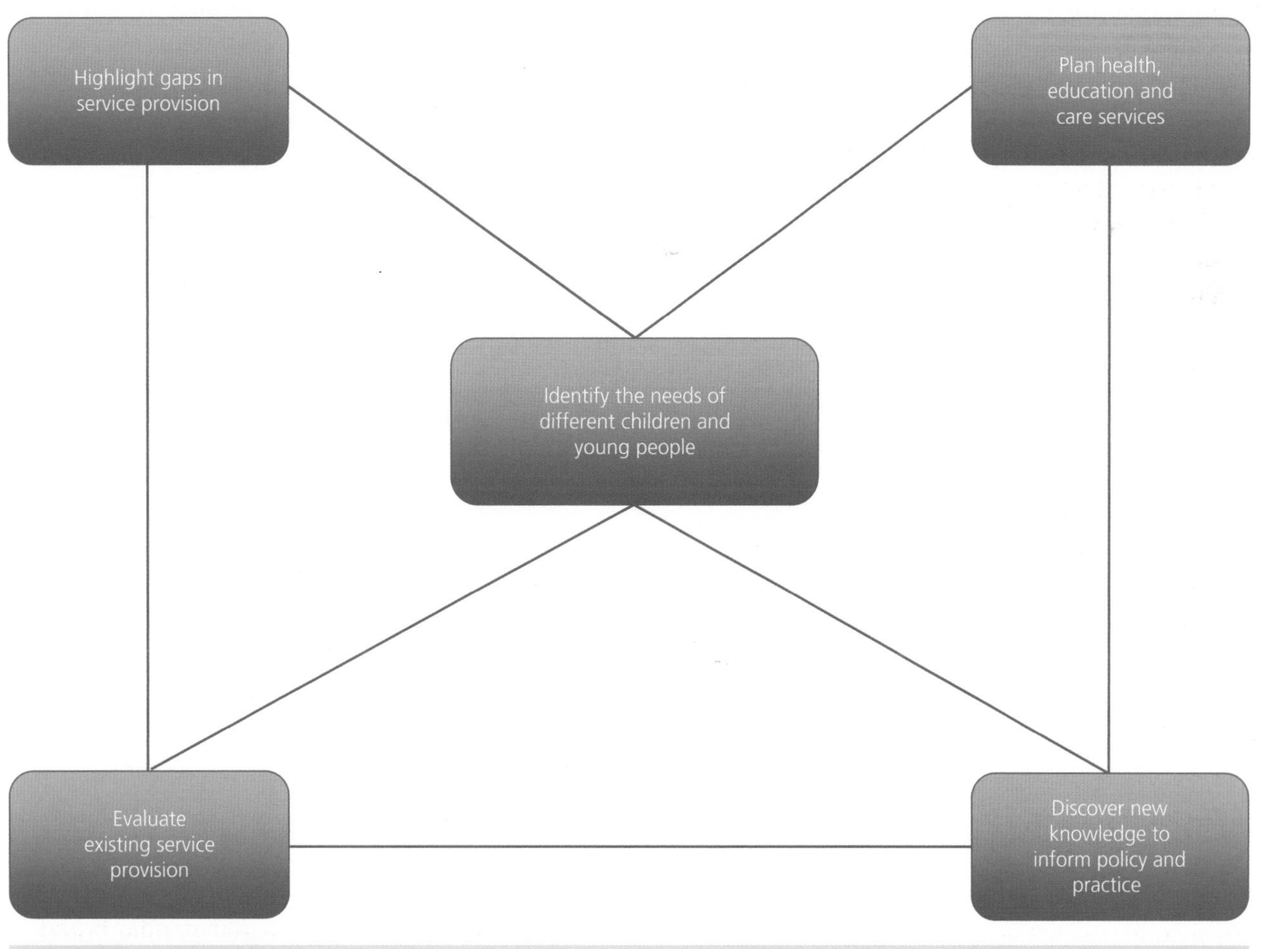

Figure 10.1 Uses of research

- New questions that need to be asked can emerge from research and additional areas that need to be better understood may be identified, triggering further research investigations. For example, data from large-scale studies may highlight small areas that do not fit the common pattern. Further research may then be carried out in these areas to understand why and in what ways they differ from the general pattern, improving understanding and adding depth to the knowledge base developed from the initial proposal.

Section 2: The role of a hypothesis in research

The area you choose to study is likely to be one in which you have a particular interest. It is important to recognise that your research will therefore be influenced, consciously or unconsciously, by what you already believe to be true about what you are investigating. This is particularly true when working with children and young people because how children are perceived historically, culturally and within different disciplines affects the whole approach to research, from the topic you choose to study, to the methodology you use and the way in which you undertake your research. This will influence the analysis of your findings and, ultimately, the outcome of your research, including any recommendations you make.

For example, if you believe that children and young people need strict discipline in order to learn right from wrong, your views on parenting will be influenced by this. If you undertake research in this area, you may be tempted (without being aware of it) to choose a methodology that is most likely to deliver the results that confirm your views. This is why it is important to try and screen out any researcher bias in the way the research is carried out. Using a hypothesis is one way in which unintentional bias can be minimised.

What is a hypothesis?

A hypothesis is an assumption or a suggested explanation which has been made on the basis of limited evidence and which becomes a starting point for further investigations. It is basically a way of asking a research question – you formulate a research question to find things out.

A hypothesis starts as a suggested explanation for something that is observed – a phenomenon. This explanation might be based on a belief, an idea, an assumption or a supposition. Much social science is about trying to find the reasons for behaviour and how society works, so while behaviour can be observed, the reasons for behaviour are not always clear. Therefore, you have to use deductive reasoning (see 'What is research methodology?' on pages 313–14) to develop a testable theory, starting with a general theory or universal statement – for example, 'all seven-year-old boys play football', which must then be examined to see if it can be proved.

If, after all the experiments and investigation have been completed, the statement holds true, then the hypothesis is valid. A hypothesis needs to be tested to see if it can be proved or disproved through investigation. The accepted way of doing this is to use the logical stages of the research process to reach a conclusion. It is important to recognise and accept that a hypothesis can only contribute to an overarching theory if the results are the same (can be replicated) when the experiment is repeated. This, of course, is rather difficult when doing social science research because people are individuals and there are so many variables that could affect the outcome. As a result, various techniques and methodologies have been developed, tried and tested with the aim of minimising any differences in the results that can be caused by variables.

Key term

Phenomenon (plural: phenomena) – an observable fact, something that can be seen or that you have noted, such as an incident, occurrence, experience or event.

Developing a hypothesis

When developing a hypothesis, you need to choose the subject you intend to test very carefully. You then have to think about exactly what you want to find out because you can usually only test one thing at a time. Types of hypothesis include the following:

- **Causal hypothesis** – this is an assumption that one thing causes another. In other words, it predicts a cause and effect: X causes Y.
- **Null hypothesis** – this a reverse way of thinking, in which you make a statement that you then try and disprove through your research.
- **Alternative hypothesis** – this is the opposite of a null hypothesis and claims that there is a difference.

For example, suppose you believe that children who attend nursery have a better vocabulary at three years old than those who do not. Your null hypothesis statement might say:

> There is no difference in the vocabulary of three-year-old children who attend nursery and those who do not.

In other words, the null hypothesis makes the claim of *no difference.*

The results of your research, depending on what you find, will either reject the statement or not. In other words, there will either be a difference or there will be no significant difference. A significant difference means *statistically significant* (see Section 6). The idea behind a null hypothesis is that it is easier to disprove than prove something, especially in a subject area that is as broad as social science. You can continue experimenting and researching the area until you have a body of knowledge.

Of course it would be impossible to test all three-year-old children who go to nursery, so you would have to take a representative sample of three-year-olds in nursery. To ensure you were comparing like with like, you would have to choose your sample carefully, allowing for variables such as sex, cultural background, family structure and so on (see Section 5), as well as the type of nursery they attend. There may be geographical differences or other variables that you would need to consider. You would also need to define what you mean by vocabulary – for example, do you mean words understood or words used? Are you examining speech patterns? All this is part of designing your methodology and planning your research and takes considerable preparation.

A common example of how a hypothesis works is to think of a court.

- Someone has been accused of a crime (the hypothesis statement).
- The prosecution presents the evidence (following research).
- The defence tries to discredit the evidence (challenging the validity of the evidence).
- The jury find the person either guilty or not guilty *according to the evidence presented.*

This does not mean that the person is innocent – they may have actually committed the crime but there is insufficient evidence to prove it beyond all reasonable doubt.

Section 3: Methodologies in research

How do we know that what we are told or see in the paper is true, when we read 'research has shown that…' or 'studies indicate that…'?

We can evaluate the work being referred to by using research criteria, the standards against which any research should be judged.

Methodology means the systematic approach to doing research, and different disciplines will use different methodologies – social science uses different methodologies from those of the natural sciences. The methodology will include the way in which research is undertaken (the process of research), including:

- the stages of the research process and a chronology or timeline
- the activities to be carried out during the research (e.g. literature review, data collection, fieldwork, statistical analysis)
- the approach to collecting data and the tools used by researchers to find out information, such as questionnaires or interviews
- the way in which the research is reported depending on the intended audience.

Key term

Methodology – a particular way of doing things or a set of techniques for gathering evidence, such as facts, figures or observations.

The methodological framework (how you approach and carry out the research) used when carrying out a research project is usually outlined in the first part of the final report (called an abstract or synopsis) by:

- describing what the activity or subject of research is
- providing a rationale for undertaking the research
- stating how the project was approached – the stages in the process
- stating how progress was measured
- outlining what represents a successful outcome.

The different tools and methods which are used to obtain raw data, such as numbers, the answers to questions or the things people say, are also included under the methodology. This data is then analysed and turned into meaningful information, which can then be used to suggest an explanation for something and which then may go on to inform further research. It is important to understand the difference between data and information. Data tells us how many and what of, what people say and believe; information tells us why things are as they are. Analysis of the data can identify patterns which suggest a possible explanation.

For example, demographics (the study of population) is concerned with both the statistics of the population (how many) and what this means. From the Census, it is possible to identify that men born during the late 1920s and still alive today are much fewer in number than would be expected compared to those a few years younger and a few years older, and compared to women of the same age. The number of people within a given age group is known as a cohort. It is also possible to see from historical data that this cohort is not small because there were fewer men born in the 1920s or because they died of illness and disease. We can also see from data on births and deaths that men born in the 1920s were no more likely to die from ill health than anyone else in their early life. However, the numbers also tell us that few of these men survived into middle and old age. All this is statistical (numerical) data.

So what is the reason for so comparatively few men in this age group? The reason is that they were all in their teens and early twenties at the start of the Second World War and many were killed in action. This additional knowledge is arrived at through the process of deductive reasoning; in this case, putting together the data from statistics with thinking about a reason why so many men failed to survive (e.g. war). This is a theory – war killed many men in their youth and young adulthood – that is suggested by examining historical information, which tells us that there was a war at about the time when these men were eligible for active service. The fact that this cohort was decimated by the war shows up clearly in population graphs and could be confirmed by further research (e.g. by interviewing those who survived).

You can explore interactive graphs of the Census for different years at: www.neighbourhood.statistics.gov.uk/HTMLDocs/dvc13/census1911_2001.html.

What is research methodology?

In order to understand why different methodologies and approaches to research are used in different disciplines, it is important to understand that there are broadly two categories of science – natural sciences, sometimes described as the physical and life sciences, and the social sciences, sometimes referred to as the social and behavioural sciences.

The natural sciences include:

- mathematics, which includes the study of areas such as logic, statistics and theoretical computer science
- physics and chemistry, branches of which are known as the physical sciences (the study of non-living systems); subject areas include disciplines (branches) such as astrophysics (the study of space) and pharmaceuticals (chemistry)

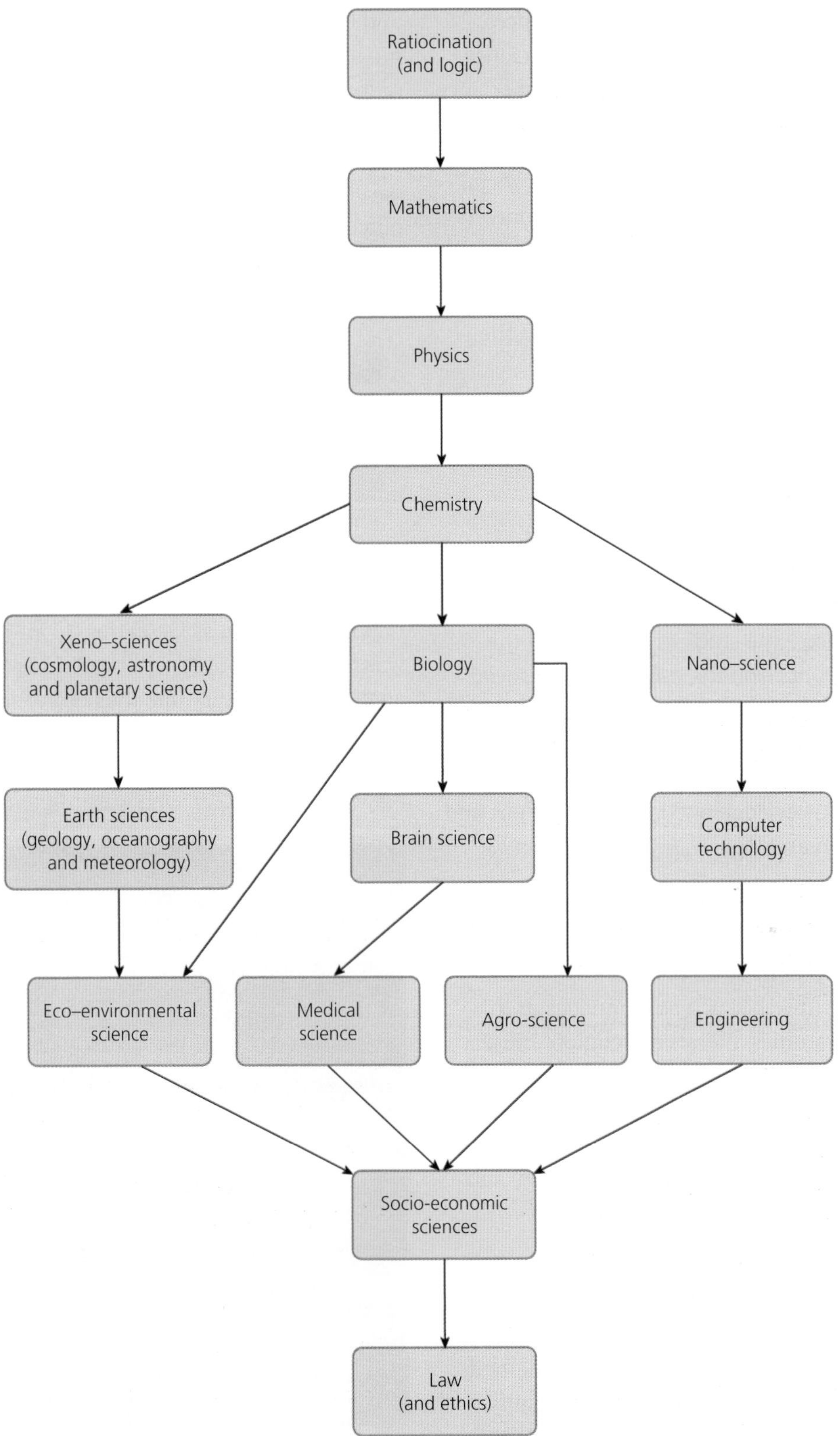

Figure 10.2 The sciences

Source: Adapted from original diagram by Alexandru T. Balaban & Douglas J. Klein in article "Is chemistry the central science?" (*Scientometrics*, 2006). Redrawn by Keenan Pepper and available on Wikipedia – published under the terms of the GNU Free Documentation License, Version 1.2 (copyright holder M. Stone)

- biology, sometimes known as the life sciences, which includes disciplines such as neuroscience (the study of the brain) and environmental science (study of the natural world).

The social sciences are sometimes known as social and behavioural sciences because they are concerned with the study of people and society. The social sciences broadly include:

- anthropology – the study of humanity and the origins of humanity
- sociology – the study of societies, including theories of how societies function
- psychology – the study of human behaviour, including social psychology and child development
- history (especially social history) – the study of the past, including politics and society in the past
- political science – the study of politics and the influence of politics on the economic and social world
- philosophy – the study of meaning; for example, the meaning of life and problems concerned with, for example, knowledge and language, values and morals, reason and logic.

Because the social sciences are concerned with human beings and the societies they create, there is inevitable overlap with other disciplines, especially the humanities subjects, such as languages and communication studies, literature, religion, music, theatre and the performing arts. In addition, some disciplines overlap with one or more of the social sciences described above – for example, social work will include elements of sociology, psychology and political science.

The scientific method

Research has traditionally been based on a set of principles which is known as the scientific method. The scientific method was developed as a result of work in the natural, or physical, sciences and remains the only approach used in these areas of specialism.

The scientific method is a way of questioning what we are seeing or being told and relies on critical thinking to distinguish those beliefs that are logical, and therefore reasonable, from other beliefs that are not supported by any evidence and do not have a rational foundation. Once you understand how to apply critical thinking to your work with children and young people, you will be able to make decisions based on evidence, justifying those decisions and the outcome of your decision making with confidence, knowing that your actions were based on evidence from sound research.

Key term

Critical thinking – the process of questioning common beliefs and explanations for things (including one's own).

The scientific method has been used since the seventeenth century, emerging from work by philosophers such as Descartes (1596–1650). It was further developed as a result of investigations and scientific inquiry into the natural sciences – mathematics, biology, chemistry and physics – in the early nineteenth century by scientists such as Isaac Newton (1642–1727), who was influenced by Descartes.

Figure 10.3 Sir Isaac Newton

Although subject to much debate over the years, the scientific method is based on the idea that the truth or facts can be discovered logically, through rational, reasoned arguments, rather than feelings or experience. By using a set of recognised and agreed principles and a logical, step-by-step approach, ideas and thoughts can be tested out to see if they are true.

The sequence of stages in the scientific method consists of the following:

- **Observation**. This may be natural observation using the naked eye or observation using scientific equipment, such as a microscope, or in the form of experiments, such as those carried out in a laboratory (e.g. mixing two substances in a test tube and applying heat). The subject of investigation has to be capable of being seen and reproduced.
- **Description**. The next stage is an accurate description of what has been observed; this is sometimes known as a phenomenon.
- **Hypothesis**. Once the phenomenon has been observed and described, a hypothesis (an educated guess, sometimes known as a premise) is developed. This is an attempt to explain the reason for what has been observed and predict what might happen.
- **Testing**. The hypothesis is then tested, using the same methods and processes – observation or experiment – as the original. If the hypothesis (statement or premise) conflicts with what actually happens, it does not hold true, the prediction was wrong and the hypothesis must be changed. In other words, 'if the map does not agree with the ground, the map is wrong' (Livingston 2006).
- **Theory**. The hypothesis continues to be tested and the results repeated by other scientists. It becomes a theory or a scientific law (e.g. Boyle's Law, which describes the relationship between the pressure and volume of a gas within a closed system).

To be considered as scientific, investigations must be objective – that is, not biased against or towards the likely or possible outcome – as this could affect the way the results are interpreted and lead to wrong conclusions being drawn. The methods used must be capable of producing evidence that can be measured.

If the findings from a research experiment are valid, they can be replicated and the results are therefore said to be reliable. All of the answers must be able to be proved and the results repeated by other scientists using exactly the same methods and procedures. The scientific method has generally been seen as the main method of academic and scientific discovery. You have probably used it yourself if you studied chemistry or physics and carried out experiments which gave the same results each time the correct process was followed.

Key term

Replicated – findings can be reproduced when the experiment is repeated.

We know that the findings are accurate because, if the research has followed the principles, the results are based on evidence and are therefore valid. It is, however, important to recognise that, in science, nothing is ever proved conclusively; it is merely accepted as fact until it is proved otherwise.

The scientific method is an example of inductive reasoning, sometimes known as a 'bottom up' approach to research because it starts with observations, seeks to find a pattern, then offers an explanation for this before finally developing a theory after the explanation has been tested and found to be reasonable. It moves from the specific to the general.

The main problem with inductive reasoning is that not everything can be observed. For example, when atoms were first discovered, their existence had to be assumed or deduced from the facts available to scientists because they could not be observed. This approach is called deductive reasoning, which is also based on reason and logical analysis but is the opposite approach from inductive reasoning because it starts from a general principle and follows this logically to a conclusion. When deductive reasoning is used, a pattern is identified, a tentative explanation or premise is put forward to explain the pattern and a hypothesis is developed to test the theory using a range of techniques or methodologies, including observation, before conclusions are made. The most famous practitioner of deductive reasoning (though a fictional character) was Sherlock Holmes. See, for example, http://en.wikipedia.org/wiki/A_Study_in_Pink.

Figure 10.4 A practitioner of deductive reasoning – Sherlock Holmes

Deductive reasoning is the approach most used in the social and behavioural sciences because human behaviour is complex and the workings of the brain and mind cannot be directly observed.

In order to use deductive reasoning, it is often the case that you might need some previous knowledge in order to make sense of different pieces of information.

Case Study Deductive reasoning

It was a Sunday evening in midsummer and Sue and Roger were travelling on the underground, returning from a shopping trip in west London. When the tube train stopped at Paddington, a young man got on with a rucksack. He was slightly sunburned, had the beginnings of a beard and was wearing shorts, hiking boots and a hat decorated with several colourful pin badges. He was also carrying a large, circular, flat object and had a plastic bracelet on his wrist.

Sue observed him for a while before turning to Roger and stating that she was glad the weather had been nice for the music festival before confirming with the young man that he had indeed been to a music festival that weekend.

Using different sources of information, can you find out what prior knowledge Sue would need in order to conclude that the young man was returning from a music festival? As this is based on real information, you might be able to identify the music festival in question!

Different research methodologies

The social sciences are concerned with human beings and the societies they create, so there is inevitable overlap with other disciplines, such as languages, literature, religion and the performing arts. Also, some disciplines overlap with one or more of the social sciences previously described – for example, social work will include elements of sociology, psychology and political science.

All of these disciplines will have something to say about children and young people in society – for example, how children were seen and treated at different times in history (e.g. being seen as small adults and sent to work); theories of how children develop and how they are socialised into society (e.g. Bowlby's theory of attachment); and how politics has influenced children's lives (e.g. through education and compulsory schooling).

Although the scientific method is difficult to apply to much social science research, social sciences do apply scientific methods, such as experiments or trials, to social investigation. It is interesting to note that the early sociological investigations into how society functions used scientific methods to ensure that their findings were taken seriously and comparable to scientific experiments in the natural sciences. This school of sociological perspective was known as positivism.

However, there are difficulties involved in applying the scientific method to social research because it is important when carrying out experiments to compare things that are the same – 'like with like – to ensure your research has validity. Things that could affect validity are called variables and might, when carrying out scientific experiments on inanimate objects, include things such as temperature or other physical conditions in which the experiment takes place.

However, people are not inanimate objects; they are all unique individuals, so when trying to make comparisons, you cannot compare like with like – there are many variables. It is therefore very important to consider the differences between people that could influence the outcome (e.g. age, gender, culture and ethnicity). These will be the variables that could affect the outcome. Social scientists often try to place people into common groups (e.g. all children between the age of five and 12 years in school). They can then use more defined categories to make comparisons (e.g. all boys aged seven years without siblings, or all primary-school children living with a single parent). This helps to minimise variability.

The social and natural sciences have developed different methodologies to ensure that the results of their investigations are scientifically rigorous. There are two main methodological approaches to carrying out research.

Quantitative methods

Based on the model used in the natural sciences, this is the standard method used by most scientific disciplines and is concerned mainly with number and measurement. The aim is to collect facts to see whether a hypothesis can be disproved; it is a key aspect of the scientific method. Quantitative research tends to focus on numerical measurement and assessment – how many, how often, etc. – and therefore it relies mainly on the analysis of statistics. Quantitative approaches have generally been regarded as the dominant approach to research. An example of a quantitative approach to research might be a large-scale survey that uses a questionnaire to identify how many children live in two-parent households, or how many primary-school children learn to swim. The Census is another example of quantitative methodology. It is usual for governments to invite specialist research or academic organisations to tender (place bids) to undertake such large-scale, population-wide research.

Qualitative methods

What quantitative approaches cannot shed light on is the reason *why* something is as it seems – for example, why there might be more or fewer children in two-parent households in some neighbourhoods than others or why some children learn to swim and others do not. This type of information is obtained using qualitative methods and is subjective in its approach. The primary aim of qualitative methods is to provide a complete and detailed description of the research topic; it is often used in social science research. The researcher is very much concerned with understanding and consequently tends to use very different methods of data collection, sometimes even becoming involved in the social area being studied (ethnography).

Mixed methods approach

Sometimes a research project will use both quantitative and qualitative types of methodology in order to obtain a much broader understanding of the issues being studied. For example, a quantitative study might count how many portions of fresh fruit children in a group (e.g. a reception class) eat per week as one measure of a healthy diet. The results will be presented in numerical form, such as a graph or pie chart. What this cannot tell you is why some children eat more fruit than others; however, if you supplemented the survey with interviews with the children and their parents – a qualitative approach – you might find the reasons for the difference (e.g. cost, personal preference or access to shops).

Mixed methods can be useful to discover the reasons for differences in the data collected through quantitative research and can provide a more rounded picture. It is important to recognise that the results might be conflicting, however, and further investigation may be needed. Mixed methods use more than one approach, combine more than one kind of research data and ask questions that aim to both explore and explain the area under study.

Ethnography

Ethnography is a qualitative methodology that has its roots in anthropology. The word comes from *ethnos*, which means folk or people in Greek, and *graph*, which is also Greek and refers to writing.

It is an interactive approach in which the researcher has a central role, living among the research subjects and within their culture for several months, in order to better understand the perspective of the group and the issues that are important to them. The aim is to understand and explain the world as seen through the eyes of the subject group. It is important that the researcher is honest about their motives and role, and that they are accepted into the group. The researcher will observe, interact with and participate in the activities of the group, sharing the experience in order to understand and explain it – this is known as participant observation.

For research purposes, data is also collected through interviews and questioning, taped conversations and video, with the researcher keeping detailed notes. It is important that the researcher tries to remain impartial, even when participating. In some cases, researchers have 'gone native' and actually joined the groups they were originally researching.

The formats of some popular television shows are based loosely on this type of research methodology – for example, *Secret Millionaire*, in which individuals wishing to donate money to worthy causes join in with charities and communities to see what work they do and how a donation could assist their work. *Undercover Boss* is similar, in that an owner or senior manager of a company spends time in disguise working with the workers in different parts of the company to get a more rounded picture of how the company is operating and what improvements could be made.

Grounded theory (Glaser and Strauss 1967)

The key feature of this methodology is that the theory is allowed to emerge from the data, the assumption being that this is more likely to be true or real than any theory suggested by an external researcher. Hence, grounded theory is essentially a method for the collection and analysis of data, with both taking place simultaneously, and ultimately providing a theory or explanation of the area being studied.

Grounded theory research starts with the researcher's area of interest. There is a difference of opinion as to whether a literature search should be used in order to identify an area of interest – Glaser advised against it, fearing it might unduly influence the way in which the data was analysed, with other people's research unconsciously influencing the researcher. Others have suggested a general reading of literature may help narrow the focus, identify the issues already covered and identify gaps in the existing body of research.

The data may be qualitative or quantitative, or a mixture of the two, and as the data is collected it is coded, which means collecting different pieces of information with similar content and allocating a level of importance to each category of information. For example, if during interviews or questioning, many people mentioned the same issue, you could reasonably assume it was important to the subject group and would code it accordingly. From the identification of similar concepts, key issues can be identified according to their importance, and grouping these together can generate a theory.

Once the data has been collected and collated (put in order) and an initial theory has been deduced, it is tested using focus groups. Depending on the outcome of the focus group, the theory may be validated (held as true), gaps in the data may be identified that require more data or further research, or the theory may be modified. It is important that the focus group is made up of the right people – they must be representative (e.g. children and young people whose lives or areas of interest are being studied or those with specialist knowledge of the area of research).

The key stages in grounded theory research are:

- Identify research area – brief, general literature search.
- Collect data using a range of methods (tools).

- Code the data according to themes, frequency, importance, etc.
- Write memos and notes detailing the relationship between codes.
- Collate data into concepts and categories.
- Develop theory from this and your notes.
- Test theory using focus groups – at least three are needed to validate the theory.
- Collect more data, add/change concepts, modify theory.
- Test again.
- Repeat last two stages until theory is confirmed.

Grounded theory is a mixed method because it can use both quantitative and qualitative data. However, it is usually considered as qualitative because, although statistics may be used as part of the data collected, it does not use statistical methods for analysis and figures are not presented as part of a theoretical explanation for the area of study.

Action research (Paulo Friere)

Action research has its roots in the work of Brazilian educator Paulo Friere, who laid the foundation for critical pedagogy, in which children are recognised as active participants in their own learning and not 'blank slates' or 'empty vessels' to be filled with facts and information decided by adults. Friere saw children as actively engaged with shaping their own world and defining their place within it.

Action research is a methodology that is used most frequently with communities to support community development. It works by involving members of the community as co-researchers, using their knowledge and engaging them in interventions that are intended to promote change and development within the community or group. The essential feature is that people are involved in the research process, rather than being separate subject matters.

Action research can be described as 'the systematic collection of information that is designed to bring about social change' (Bogdan and Biklen 1992).

The researcher or practitioner is actively involved in the cause they are researching. This type of methodology can be used effectively with young

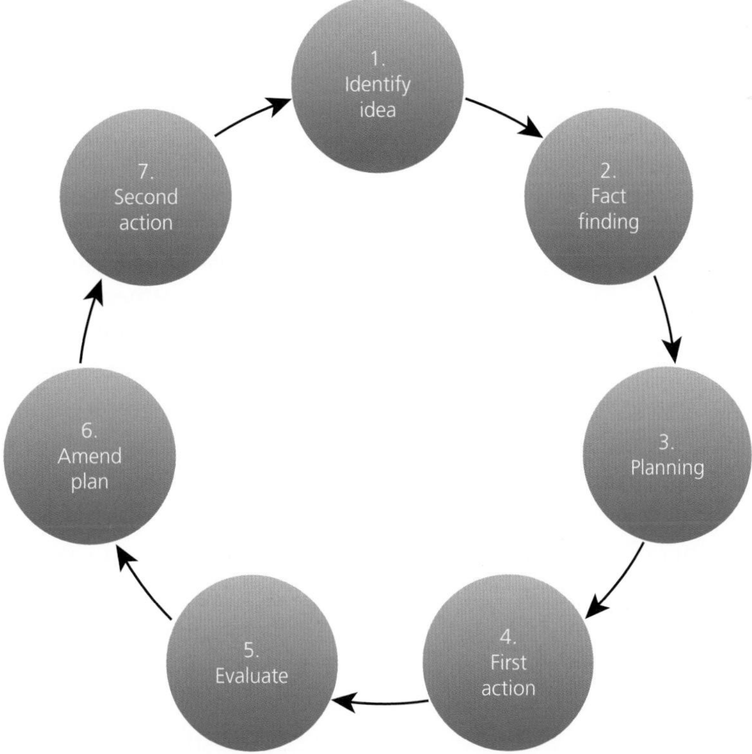

Figure 10.5 The key stages of action research. Stages 5, 6 and 7 are repeated until the goal is reached (informed by Kurt Lewin's change process)

people, for example, when they feel that their community is not meeting their needs.

Activity

In small groups, examine the publication 'An overview of child well-being in rich countries' from UNICEF (United Nations Children's Fund), available at www.unicef-irc.org/publications/pdf/rc7_eng.pdf, and the UK government's website on 'Measuring national well-being', available at http://webarchive.nationalarchives.gov.uk/20110422103457/http://www.ons.gov.uk/well-being (NB, the content of this website is archived and may be available for a limited time only).

- Identify and list which of the approaches used are quantitative and which are qualitative. Which approach is used most often in each?
- Discuss and write down the merits of each approach for understanding well-being.

Data collection tools

There is a range of methods you can use to collect data – facts, figures, statistics, numbers, etc. It is usual to use several data sources as this gives greater weight to the findings, providing validity and consistency. However, the methodology you choose will influence the types of data you need.

Controlled experiments

These are used primarily during scientific experiments in order to prevent unintended bias affecting the results. There are several aspects to controlled experiments:

- **Using a control group**. Two groups are chosen, each having the same characteristics and profile (e.g. age, sex, economic status) so that they are, as far as possible, identical. One group is the control group and the other is the experimental group, which is active in the experiment. For example, the experimental group might be given a drug being tested and the control group given a placebo (a non-active substance, such as a sugar pill).
- **Blind experiment**. This is where only the researcher knows who is participating. For example, blind tasting of foods to identify preference, famously used to advertise a margarine – 'I can't believe it's not butter.'
- **Single-blind experiment**. This is where some of the facts are withheld from the participants if they would be likely to influence the outcome. However, the researcher has all the facts.
- **Double-blind experiment** (randomised, placebo-controlled, double-blind trial) – this is commonly used in clinical trials of new drugs. Patients are randomly assigned either to the control group or to the experimental group by the study coordinator (not the researcher) and the treatment they receive is coded so that no one knows whether they received the actual drug or an identical-looking placebo (non-active substance) until the experiment is completed.

There are ethical difficulties in using controlled experiments as part of research with children and young people because it is unacceptable to withhold treatment or interventions from some children – the control group – if they are expected to be effective.

Surveys

A survey is, strictly speaking, a research strategy rather than a data collection method. It refers to the population or group from which the data will be collected. For example, you might decide to carry out a survey of young people in your area to see how many use youth clubs, what they think of them and what improvements they would like to see. You might decide to survey two year groups in three schools – this would be your sampling frame as it would be broadly representative of all the schools in your area. The size of your sample is important – the larger the sample, the more representative it is, but large-scale surveys can be expensive and time-consuming to carry out. It is important, however, to consider the number of responses you are likely to get; it is not unusual to receive only a 30 per cent response to questionnaires, so if you need 100 responses, you would need to send out at least 334 questionnaires (30 per cent of 334 = 100.2), even more if you allow for some to be incomplete or spoiled.

Case studies

Case studies are often used to illustrate a point or as the focus of research. Like surveys, they are not a data collection tool but a research strategy; they can provide a focus for the research problem. The cases to be studied must be chosen carefully, after the research objective has been defined, and may be representative of either a group or a problem, or they may be exceptions to the norm. They can be used in the development of a theory, to challenge a theory or to illustrate a theory or phenomenon.

Questionnaires

Questionnaires are used as part of a survey and need to be carefully designed to ask questions in such a way that they are not open to misunderstanding and will give valid responses. Key aspects of questionnaire design include the following:

- **Defining what you want to find out** from your respondents (people completing the questionnaire). It is a good idea to write this down, perhaps as a statement.
- **Deciding on the questions you will ask**. Sometimes these can be grouped to cover different aspects of what you are aiming to find out. All the questions should contribute to your overall research objective and allow you to test your hypothesis.
- **Deciding on the structure and layout** of the questionnaire to make it easy to understand and complete. You may have to provide instructions and a brief introduction, outlining the purpose of the questionnaire and reassuring people that their replies will remain confidential, especially if you have asked for personal information. The layout should be both interesting and straightforward and respondents should be thanked at the end. Sometimes it is a good idea to say how the information you have asked for will be used.
- **Deciding on the type of questions**. The main types of questions are closed questions and open questions. It is not unusual to have both types of questions to obtain the best response and minimise the disadvantages of using just one type of question. Sometimes you may want to know how respondents feel about an issue and you can ask them to give answers according to a scale (e.g. from 'not important' to 'extremely important' – a rating scale). These are useful in qualitative research because they can measure opinions.

Question type	Characteristics	Advantages	Disadvantages
Closed	Requires a yes/no response or a tick in a box.	Easy to answer for respondents. Easy to classify for researcher.	Reliant on the quality and scope of questions. Does not allow a different response.
Open	Requires the respondents to write the response in their own words.	Not influenced by researcher and allows respondent free expression.	Depends on ability of respondent to provide written explanation. The question may not be answered or they may forget crucial points. Harder for researcher to code/collate.
Mixed	Provides a choice of answers for respondents to tick and a box for additional comments.	Avoids problems of memory and articulation by providing prompts.	Researcher needs a good knowledge of the subject area to ask the right questions.
Ratings scale	Offers a range from low to high or important to not important.	Respondents choose the option that best represents their view. They are easy to code.	If there is a neutral option (neither agree nor disagree), respondents can 'sit on the fence'.

Table 10.1 Types of questions

Once you have put together your questionnaire, it is a good idea to pilot it with a few members of your target group, but not necessarily your sampling frame. You want to know, for example:

- Is the wording of the questions clear and explicit?
- Will they get the desired response?
- Are they in the right order?
- Are there any gaps?
- Are the instructions adequate and easy to understand?
- Is it clear how the completed questionnaires should be returned?

Interviews

Interviews are extremely useful for obtaining an in-depth understanding of issues that are important to people and obtaining their personal perspective. An interview is basically an organised conversation between two people, in which the interviewer asks questions that aim to understand the interviewee's point of view and the world as they see it.

There are several types of interviews, as outlined below.

Unstructured interviews

These are open and informal. They tend to be conversational, using open questions but based around a number of themes or topics, often in the form of a checklist. They are qualitative and are often used in ethnography and for case studies.

The main advantage of this type of interview is that the interviewee is relaxed and likely to be more open.

The disadvantages of unstructured interviews are that they require a degree of skill on the part of the interviewer, it is more difficult to maintain consistency in the responses and they are more difficult to analyse.

Semi-structured interviews

These are also fairly informal. While the same open-ended questions may be covered, the interviewer is free to ask additional questions and explore issues raised by asking for clarification (e.g. 'just to clarify, you feel that…') or for more information (e.g. 'tell me a little more about…'). They are a rich source of data and are frequently used in qualitative studies.

The advantages of semi-structured interviews are that they allow a relaxed atmosphere and the development of a relationship between researcher and interviewee, they can be used for telephone interviewing and they allow a lot of data to be collected

The disadvantages of semi-structured interviews are that they can be time-consuming, they require skill on the part of the interviewer and they can be more difficult to analyse because not all the data collected may be relevant.

Structured interviews

These have rigid rules and strict protocols in which sometimes the interviewer is required to remain neutral and disengaged, maintaining the same body posture and facial expression for each interview. They ask the same, closed questions, which must be read as written, and the interviewer should not react to interviewee responses.

The advantages of structured interviews are that the strict protocols minimise unconscious researcher bias, the responses are consistent and easy to analyse quantitatively and they are useful when looking for specific information.

The disadvantages of structured interviews are that the information is limited by the questions, interviewers will only be able to obtain information that is included in the questions set by the researcher and interviewees may be put off by the formality.

Interviews are very useful when working with children and young people but care should be taken when choosing an interview style to ensure that the child or young person can remain relaxed and untroubled.

Observation

This is one of the most effective methods of data collection used in qualitative studies. Observation can be used as an initial exploration to inform further research – for example, whom to observe, when, where and how.

Types of observation include the following.

Field observation

This is informal and direct (face to face), carried out in everyday situations and in the natural setting. It is unstructured and unsystematic so that the researcher/observer notes down everything, then looks for additional evidence and may clarify or confirm initial theories by questioning. In participant observation (a form of field study), the researcher actively engages with the subjects of the research, often becoming an accepted part of the community and working with them for long periods.

Scientific observation

This is usually carried out in a laboratory or controlled environment using a planned methodology – for example, setting out the length of time the subject is observed and looking for particular phenomena. It can involve both direct and indirect (e.g. via one-way mirror or camera) observation.

This approach is considered more scientific and is non-participatory – that is, the researcher does not engage with the subject of the research at all and the subject is unaware they are being observed. It is often used in psychology with children or animals. An example of this is a famous experiment carried out by psychologist Albert Bandura in 1961. To watch a programme about Bandura's Bobo doll experiments, go to www.bbc.co.uk/iplayer/episode/b008fxv9/Mind_Changers_The_Bobo_Doll.

Autobiographical accounts (diaries)

Some autobiographical accounts are produced by the researcher as part of the research process – for example, field notes from ethnographers or some aspects of grounded theory. In these cases, the researcher considers themselves as both subject and object of the research process, particularly when engaging in participant observation.

However, personal accounts, either of specific situations or daily accounts of life, can provide rich data for study. Clearly it is important to have a focus for the research project. However, autobiographical accounts provide an insight into the research subject's world and how they perceive it. Other data collection methods will need to be used to clarify issues and validate the theories emerging from the data. This approach is similar to interviews, except that it can be carried out over a period of time relatively cheaply.

An example of autobiographical accounts is the Mass Observation project (see www.massobs.org.uk/menu_about_mass_observation.htm).

Focus groups

Focus groups are made up of people and individuals that are representative of the sample population and they can be a good way of checking initial findings from the data. Focus groups are a crucial part of grounded theory methodology. However, they can also be used alongside other methods and are particularly effective to use with children and young people, since the assumptions adults make about the way children think and feel can often be wrong. It is helpful to have small groups of no more than 6–12 participants to ensure there can be agreement about the findings.

It is important that focus groups are well managed and made as easy as possible for the participants. It can take both skill and practice, for example, to remain neutral, to keep your views and opinions to yourself – you are not a participant – to make sure everyone gets the opportunity to speak and to be able to manage any conflict. It is important to have a clear aim (what you want from the group), which is shared with the group at the beginning. This can be returned to from time to time with the group to make sure you are still on track.

When working with children and young people, depending on the age group, it is helpful to encourage practical and creative ways of facilitating, such as using mind maps/spidergrams, drawing and collage, or coloured sticky notes and pens, so that the young people's views are both seen and heard. The process should be as interactive as possible. At the conclusion, it is important to summarise what has been achieved and thank participants for their help.

Longitudinal studies

Because longitudinal studies carry out research over an extended period of time, they are impractical for individual practitioners to undertake; teams of researchers headed by a specialist usually carry them out. As a result, it is common for governments to commission an organisation or academic institution, such as a university, to carry out longitudinal studies to identify trends. They examine a set of issues over time so that meaningful comparisons can be made. An example of a longitudinal study is the Avon Longitudinal Study of Parents and Children (ALSPAC), carried out by Bristol University (www.bristol.ac.uk/alspac/).

Choosing your methodology

A good approach to take when researching issues relating to children and young people is to use several methodological approaches and data collection tools. Children and young people are likely to have a very different perspective from adults about, for example, what is important to them, how they believe social issues affect them and the things that are important in their lives. It is, therefore, important when considering research with children and young people that you find meaningful and valid methods of representing their views, including involving them in the research process and interpretation and analysis of the data.

When thinking about your methodology, there are several things to consider:

- **Relevance** – how relevant is your research aim to your practice? How will your findings be used?
- **Feasibility** – will there be a financial cost to doing the research (e.g. will you have to travel to do interviews)? Do you have enough people to help or will you need to do all the work yourself? Can you get access to the potential subjects of your research (your sampling frame) and any documents you might need to supplement your data?
- **Coverage** – can you get enough people to participate and provide an adequate sample? Timing can be an issue; are you likely to get enough responses? Sometimes holidays like Christmas or summer holidays can cause problems with people being away or busy.
- **Validity** – how will you ensure that your data is measurable and accurate?
- **Objectivity** – how will you avoid researcher bias influencing your results (consciously or unconsciously)?
- **Ethics** – how will you ensure confidentiality? How will you avoid deceiving your subjects?

(Denscombe 2010)

Your methodology will also depend on whether you intend to involve children and young people directly, as part of the research process, or not. Generally speaking:

- if you are testing an existing theory, your approach is likely to be deductive, using quantitative methods
- if you are trying to generate a theory of your own, you will use an inductive approach and qualitative methods to collect data.

As we have seen, qualitative and quantitative methods are not mutually exclusive. You may wish to start with a quantitative analysis, examining official statistics – for example, to identify a trend – before following it up with qualitative, in-depth interviews to provide a reason for the trend.

However, your choice of research methodology will be affected by working from a hypothesis. For example, grounded theory is incompatible with developing a hypothesis because grounded theory is an inductive approach to developing a theory, using qualitative methods, whereas a hypothesis is concerned with testing a theory – the hypothesis is a theoretical statement and the process is therefore deductive.

Section 4: Identifying a research hypothesis

Developing a hypothesis, while crucial to the research process, is not usually the first stage. The starting point is for you, the researcher, to think about an area you wish to study and formulate a general question. For example, you may be thinking about feeding patterns and eating habits in young children; it is important to recognise that even if an area that interests you has already been subject to research, it is still worth investigating again because every researcher will bring their own ideas and perspectives to an area of study and, therefore, add to the body of knowledge, maybe identifying new areas for study. You may even be lucky and make a new discovery! The following quote from the Greek philosopher Heraclitus explains this: 'You could not step twice into the same river, for other waters are ever flowing on to you' (Heraclitus, 540 BC–480 BC, On the Universe, hwww.quotationspage.com).

A hypothesis is a good approach to take when carrying out a small-scale research project. In order to find an area to study, you may have to carry out some preliminary research from which to develop your hypothesis to test.

Literature search

A literature search aims to find and review published research, opinion and articles relating to a particular research topic, particularly those in professional journals. It often includes a review and analysis of official statistics and may also include searching the bibliography of books broadly related to the topic in question. The information must then be collated, assessed and narrowed down through a process of elimination until it can be distilled into a research question.

In scientific research, it is usual to do a systematic review, which involves identifying, assessing and pulling together all the research evidence relevant to the research question. The quality of the research is assessed using a scoring system, known as the Jadad or Oxford quality scoring system, to independently check the methodology. Systematic reviews often use statistical analysis, called meta-analysis, to combine the results of all the studies to form the evidence base for interventions. It is most frequently used in medicine and healthcare: for example, the Cochrane Collaboration – for more information, see www.cochrane.org/cochrane-reviews.

Developing your hypothesis

When developing your hypothesis, you will need to be able to show clearly that it is relevant to your practice. If you are currently a childcare practitioner, you might wish to identify areas in your work with children or young people that would help them with issues that they feel important.

In addition, there are many organisations that aim to help children and young people get their point across and have their views heard and for these views to be taken into account when adults are planning things that affect them. For example:

- Young Children's Voices Network: www.ncb.org.uk/ycvn
- Young Voices: http://youngvoices.co.uk/
- Funky Dragon: www.funkydragon.org/index.php?option=com_joomdragdrop&view=custom&Itemid=18.

You might wish to start by looking at relevant websites for ideas of the issues of importance to children and young people in general. You can also look at professional journals, such as *Nursery World* and *Childcare in Practice*. Also see Social Care Online at: www.scie-socialcareonline.org.uk/profile.asp?guid=608a27fd-5d79-4447-a686-32a8b9a8b590.

Aims of hypothesis in relation to work with children and young people

You should be able to demonstrate that your research is relevant to your practice. You need to develop a clear statement that states your aims. For example, if you are interested in helping children make healthy food choices, you might wish to understand how some children become 'fussy' eaters. Following an initial literature search, your research question might ask whether 'food choices when weaning affect "food fussiness" in toddlers'. You could then turn this into a null hypothesis and aim to test it.

Clearly in this example, you would be working with parents and it is a sensitive area, so you would need to ensure that your plan was ethical and feasible. The results of your research could help you develop a plan for helping such children in the childcare setting.

The aim of your research should be to improve your practice for the benefit of the children or young people you work with.

Section 5: Plan and implement research in relation to working with children and/or young people

There are a number of steps to undertaking a research project, which can be summarised as follows:

- Define your research question; formulate your research hypothesis.
- Identify sources of information (secondary research) and evaluate.
- Assess and adjust the scope of the project – make sure it is do-able.
- Refine the hypothesis based on your initial findings to fit the scope of your project.
- Select your methodologies.
- Develop a project plan – timescale.

When planning your research, it is vital that you have an understanding of the importance of ethics to research practice and that you are able to incorporate ethical practice into each stage of your research.

Ethics

'Ethics' means the moral principles that inform your actions and behaviour, acting as a guide to your conduct – a 'moral compass'. Ethics underpin conscience and allow you to distinguish between right and wrong.

In research, ethics are crucial to avoid researchers intentionally or unintentionally exploiting research subjects and participants. They aim to 'embed the principles of justice, respect and avoidance of harm into research by using agreed standards' (Morrow 2009).

By taking an ethical approach to your research, you are aiming to balance the interests of children and young people with the goals of the research project. You can only do this by building trust between the participants and the researcher/s.

Principles

Organisations may have their own ethical codes that researchers must work to. However, there are a number of principles that are generally agreed to inform an ethical approach to any research project.

Approval

You must seek approval before undertaking any research. Sometimes, especially in larger organisations, such as medical establishments, there will be an ethics committee. Researchers need to submit research proposals to the committee for approval and permission to proceed. However, it is important that you get permission from the organisation/s that you intend to approach as part of your research.

Consent

You also need to obtain consent from those participating in your research; in the case of children and young people under 18 years of age, you will also need consent from parents. It is crucial that consent is informed – this means that parents and children should be made aware of why the research is being undertaken, what benefits you hope to achieve for children and young people, any risks the research may pose to them and how you will minimise such risks. Consent must be informed, understood and freely given (i.e. without any pressure to participate).

Honesty

When undertaking research, it is crucial that you are honest in order to gain trust. This has implications for the more covert types of methodology – for example, where children or young people are being observed unknowingly.

Independence

You should be able to demonstrate that you are acting independently and have no conflict of interest – that is, that you are not going to gain in any way, whatever the outcome of the research.

Non-discrimination

You must make sure that you treat everyone involved with your research project fairly and equally. This means being aware of power relationships, especially between children and young people and the adults involved in the project. For example, adults may make assumptions about children's experience, competence and capability, knowledge and understanding, depending on their age and ability/disability. As a researcher, you should not let any assumptions you may hold influence the research – it is safer to assume ability and competence until proven otherwise and you may want to do a small pilot of your methodology to check this.

Confidentiality

As you will be collecting information for and about individuals, it is crucial that you are able to keep it confidential. You must be clear to participants about how you will use their information and who will have access to it. You must be able to ensure the confidentiality of information and also be aware of the requirements of the Data Protection Act. This will mean making arrangements to store your data securely, including any audio or video recordings. You must also ensure that children and young people cannot be identified and, if video is used, parental consent must be obtained.

Respect

You need to demonstrate that you are respecting children and young people and their privacy, ensuring that by undertaking your research you do no harm – physical or emotional. This is especially relevant if your research is to be published and in the public domain. For example, some research in sensitive areas such as drug use, teenage pregnancy, gang culture, sexual habits, youth crime, etc. can stigmatise whole groups of young people, leaving them with feelings of embarrassment, humiliation and anger. You need to be careful that you are not making assumptions about all young people based on a sample group.

Child protection

You must follow the requirements, procedures and protocols for protecting children according to the organisation in which you are working. If you are interviewing or observing children outside the boundaries of organisational rules, you must make sure you put in place arrangements for protecting and safeguarding children and make parents, children and young people and other participants aware of these protocols.

Ethics should inform the whole of your approach to research, including your choice of methodology.

Developing your research plan

Once you have decided on your area of research, you need an action plan so that you can undertake your research in an orderly and systematic way – for example, by setting out a time frame. When developing your research (action) plan, you need to state who will be involved and what each person's role is if you are not working alone. It is sometimes helpful to divide the project into stages. For example:

- Stage 1: the preliminary stage is usually the collection of secondary data, such as statistics and/or a literature search. It can be helpful to write down the aims of this first stage (e.g. to identify a research topic and inform your hypothesis).
- Stage 2: this might be to identify your sampling frame – who are you going to approach and who do you need permission from?
- Stage 3: this might identify the steps in the data collection process – for example, developing questionnaires and how you will carry out any interviews.

- Stage 4: this section should outline how you will collect, analyse and store data, including the methods of analysis you will use and how you will maintain confidentiality.
- Stage 5: this should cover how you will present your results – for example, will it be a presentation or a written report?

When drawing up your plan, you should take an ethical approach and think about the ethical implications of implementing your plan. You should be able to say how you have embedded ethics into your project when you write up the final report or present your findings.

Choosing your methodology

Once you have decided on your hypothesis, you will need to consider what methodological approach you will take and the tools you will use to collect your data. As we have seen in Section 3, the two are closely related. It is likely you will need to use a deductive approach as you will be trying to show your hypothesis can be either accepted or rejected and you will need sufficient evidence to do this. You may choose to use mixed methods, examining existing statistics and following this up with interviews or questionnaires.

Rationale for chosen methodology

The rationale for your research should show why you have chosen your particular methodology and data collection tools and why other approaches were unsuitable. You should aim to show clearly how it will improve your practice.

Implementation of methodology

By following your research plan, you can show how you implemented your methodology. You will need to seek permission and consider all the ethical issues as you do your fieldwork – that is, go out and do your interviews. You will need to take comprehensive notes of everything that happens, so that you can review and evaluate the project. It might be helpful

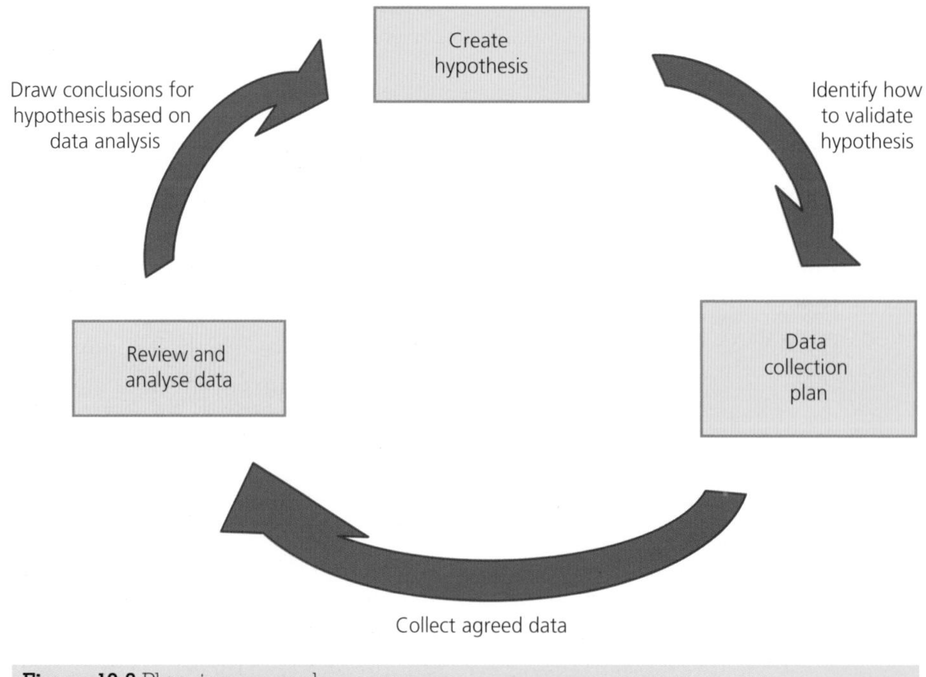

Figure 10.6 Planning research

to keep a diary (audio or written) to help you remember.

Gathering and recording research data

This aspect involves gathering in questionnaires, interview responses, and facts and figures gleaned from both primary and secondary research, and then grouping the responses together into categories or issues raised in order to analyse them. You need to make sure you have a system for keeping records.

Section 6: Present data in relation to the hypothesis

There are agreed criteria for scientific research, known as the CONSORT (Consolidated Standards of Reporting Trials) statement, which is an evidence-based set of minimum recommendations offering a standardised way of reporting randomised controlled trials (RCTs). The aim of such standards is to prevent problems arising from poor trial design, analysis and interpretation. Although the CONSORT criteria focus mainly on clinical trials (medical and pharmaceutical research), the guidelines can equally apply to all types of research.

> The CONSORT Statement is intended to improve the reporting of a randomized controlled trial (RCT), enabling readers to understand a trial's design, conduct, analysis and interpretation, and to assess the validity of its results. It emphasizes that this can only be achieved through complete transparency from authors.
>
> www.consort-statement.org

CONSORT includes broad criteria covering how aspects of research should be reported, so these are helpful to use as a basis for thinking about how to write a report of your findings. For example:

- **Title and abstract** – this is a summary of the research and findings, rather like an executive summary.
- **Introduction, background and objectives** – an explanation of the aims of and rationale for the research and choice of methodology.
- **The methodology** – how the research was carried out. You would include your literature search here, how you developed your hypothesis, etc., what interventions were carried out and the types of methods used to collect the data (e.g. questionnaires).
- **The sample size** – this should include eligibility criteria, setting and locations. For example, how participants were recruited and where the research took place.
- **Control for variables** – identifying things that could affect the objectivity of the outcome (including researcher bias) and how these were managed: for example, by having clear criteria for participants and randomly selecting them to either a control group or an active group.
- **Implementation** – how the research was carried out and by whom. For example, how children and young people were included and involved in the implementation.
- **Statistical methods** – how the data was analysed, the significance of the statistical results and what this means (this will be explored further when we look at presenting data).
- **Results** – what conclusions can be drawn from the results and how can they be used? You might include some recommendations – these might even be for further research if your results were inconclusive.
- **Bibliography and references** – it is crucial to name your sources to avoid any charge of plagiarism.

Methods of analysing data

This will depend on the methodology used. Quantitative methods require analysis of the numbers. There are software packages that can be used to analyse large amounts of numerical data (e.g. SPSS – Statistical Package for the Social Sciences) and which provide statistical analysis. However, it is also possible to collate data using an Excel spreadsheet or similar standard computer program.

It is important to have some understanding of statistics to be able to examine and assess quantitative data. Statistical methods can be applied to data in order to analyse and interpret it. Some examples that can be used to understand numerical data include the following:

- **Mean** – this is the average. You can work out the mean by dividing the total sum of the figures (number of sweets) by the number of individual representations (number of children). See Table 10.2.

	Number of sweets each child has
Chloe	6
Jack	4
Bethany	8
Joe	2
Alice	5
Total number of sweets = 25	
Total number of children = 5	
Mean value of sweets = 25 divided by 5 = **5**	

Table 10.2 Working out the mean

- **Median** – this is the middle value in a list or data set. In the example above, the numbers are 2, 4, 5, 6, 8, so the middle value is **5**.
- **Mode** – this is the number occurring most frequently. In the example shown, there is no mode as all the numbers are different.
- **Standard deviation** – this shows how close the whole data set (number of sweets) is to the average (mean) value – in this example, 5. A data set with a small standard deviation has data within a narrow range, whereas a data set with a large standard deviation has data spread out over a wide range of values.
- **Range** – this is simply the highest value and the lowest value; in the example above, this is the difference between 2 and 8 = **6**.

Microsoft Excel has built-in functions to analyse a set of data for all these values. You can use this by selecting 'Insert Function' and one of the following:

- For the Mean function, choose AVERAGE (starting cell : ending cell).
- For the Median, choose MEDIAN (starting cell : ending cell).
- For the Mode, choose MODE (starting cell : ending cell).
- For the Standard Deviation, choose STDEV (starting cell : ending cell).

Interpreting your data

Interpreting statistics can be fraught with problems, mainly because when looking at reported statistics we often do not have the full information to make a judgment. For example, see the following article:

www.guardian.co.uk/science/blog/2010/sep/29/statistics-lies-abuse.

Once you have your information, you have to be able to interpret your data and understand what might be statistically significant. This just means that any difference has not happened by chance. It is important to recognise that, with a large sample size, small differences will show up but they may not be important.

Drawing conclusions

Once you have analysed your data, you can draw conclusions by comparing various aspects of the information – using percentages, for example.

Activity

Examine the information presented on the height of boys aged between 11 and 18 years in Figures 10.7 and 10.8.

- Write down all the facts you can about how boys grow over this period.
- State three things you can deduce from the information.

		Age							
		11	**12**	**13**	**14**	**15**	**16**	**17**	**18**
	1.2	1							
	1.25	3	1						
	1.3	8	1	1	1				
	1.35	11	4	2	1				
	1.4	13	7	3	1	1	1	1	
	1.45	9	12	6	3	1	1	1	1
	1.5	6	11	10	7	2	3	2	1
Height	**1.55**	4	11	11	10	5	5	4	4
	1.6	3	7	11	13	10	8	5	5
	1.65	1	3	7	11	12	9	9	6
	1.7	1	1	4	7	11	12	12	10
	1.75		1	3	3	8	10	10	11
	1.8		1	1	1	4	6	8	11
	1.85			1	1	3	3	4	5
	1.9				1	2	1	2	4
	1.95					1	1	1	1
	2							1	1

Age	**11**	**12**	**13**	**14**	**15**	**16**	**17**	**18**
Mean	1.413	1.502	1.563	1.601	1.677	1.681	1.689	1.732
Median	1.450	1.525	1.575	1.600	1.675	1.675	1.700	1.775
Mode 1	1.400	1.450	1.550	1.600	1.650	1.700	1.700	1.750
Mode 2			1.600					1.800

Figure 10.7 Data for boys' height, by age (11–18 years)

Making recommendations

Recommendations will very much depend on the rationale for your research. If you have undertaken a project aimed at identifying an issue of importance to children and young people, you should be able to use the conclusions from your research to make some recommendations on how the issue could be addressed. For example, if you researched how many young people use youth clubs and find out from research that the youth clubs are poorly used (from your quantitative data) but that the activities on offer do not appeal to young people (from your qualitative data), you may recommend that young people are consulted and involved in upgrading the existing facilities. You may recommend that more research is carried out to find out what sort of facilities would attract more young people. A piece of action research would involve children and young people in community-led change – perhaps to raise funding

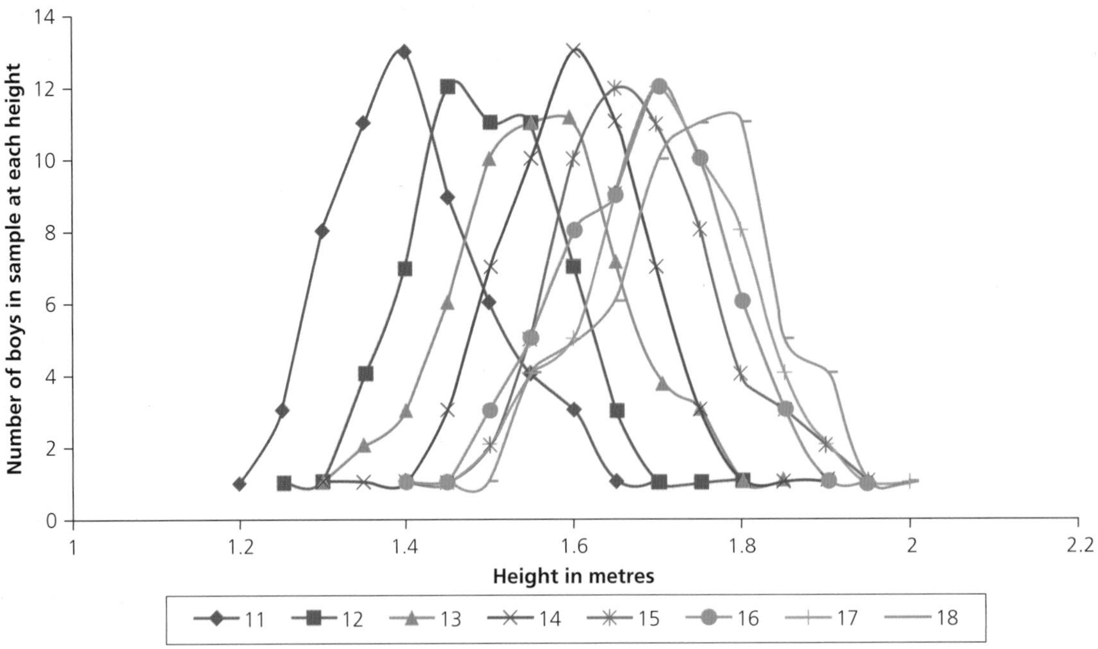

Figure 10.8 Boys' height, by age (11–18 years)

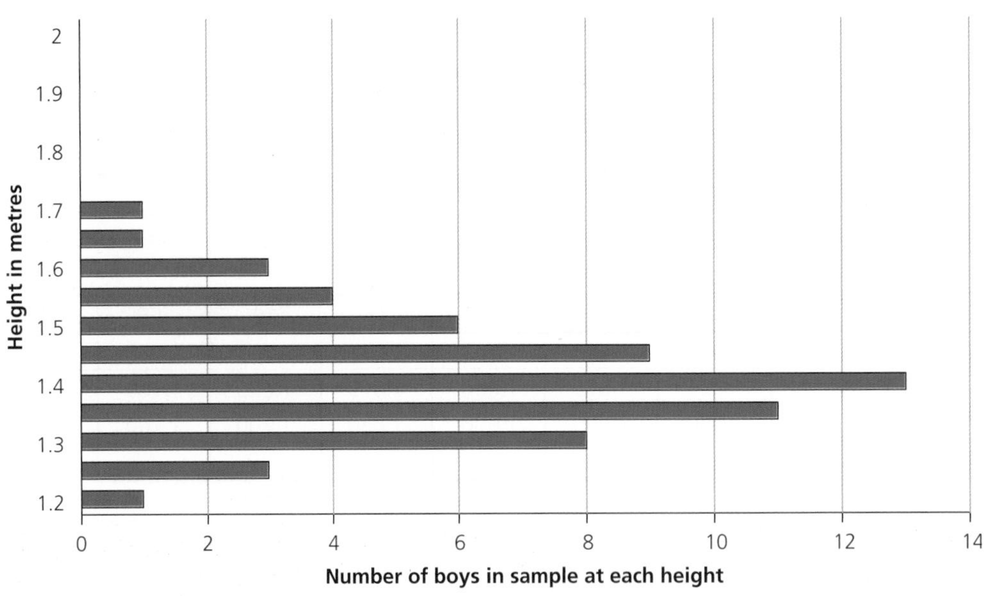

Figure 10.9 Height distribution of boys aged 11

for a new facility or to engage with the local council to upgrade existing clubs.

If your research was aimed at improving your practice, you should be able to use your conclusions to change the way you work to improve working practices for the benefit of children and young people.

Presenting your findings

You can present your data either statistically or in the form of graphs or charts. It is usual to present your findings visually and with a written explanation. You will probably wish to incorporate this into the report of your research.

See Figures 10.7, 10.8 and 10.9 for examples of how data can be presented.

Section 7: Reflect on the research undertaken

One of the main advantages of undertaking your own research is that you can learn from your experience by reflecting on the process and considering what aspects went well and what could be improved.

Methodological strengths and weaknesses

The validity of any research can be undermined by weak methodology. Common criticisms include the following:

- **Sample size** – a very small sample is unlikely to be statistically representative of the larger population. Many advertisements for cosmetics and beauty products are guilty of this. For example, if the sample is only 75 women on whom the product has been tried, 90 per cent satisfaction is fairly meaningless!
- **Assumptions** – the basic hypothesis is derived from assumptions that are false or the rationale for the hypothesis is inadequate.
- **Generalisability** – the results only apply to the specific sample and are not applicable to the wider population.
- **The results cannot be replicated** – a common criticism of qualitative studies.
- The researcher was not independent or the results show **bias**.

You need to have a sound rationale for your research and clearly state its limitations – do not make exaggerated claims for your research! If your results are not what you expected, you need to consider why and be honest about this in your report. You may suggest that further research is necessary.

Making improvements to your research

Your research can only be improved through the process of reflection. It is possible for you to improve your technical research skills by practising – for example, by examining data, especially official data, which usually has an explanation. You could also look at medical research as this is subject to much scrutiny and peer review. This will help you think about how to approach research next time. For example, there is a whole section on evidence-based health living on the following website: www.medicine.ox.ac.uk/bandolier.

Reflecting on your learning

It is unusual for research to go smoothly and without problems. However, as part of the reflective process, you need to go back over the stages of your research, examine your notes, and talk to the participants and other people involved to see where you could make improvements. It is not unreasonable to include this in your report, perhaps as an Appendix, as this will show your awareness of any issues and give you the chance to explain how you overcame any difficulties.

The impact of your research on practice

If you are only undertaking a small piece of research, it may not have a big impact overall. However, the aim of research with children and young people is primarily to improve their lives and the best way for you to do this is to improve your personal practice. If you learn from the experience of undertaking a research project, it will benefit your practice in future.

Useful resources

Organisations and websites

National Institute for Health and Clinical Excellence (NICE)
www.nice.org.uk

The Social Care Institute for Excellence (SCIE)
www.scie.org.uk

Human Genome Project
www.ornl.gov/hgmis/home.shtml

Marmot Review (Fair Society, Healthy Lives)
www.marmotreview.org

Office for National Statistics
www.ons.gov.uk

Economic and Social Research Council
www.esrc.ac.uk

Nature
www.nature.com

New Scientist
www.newscientist.com

Oxford Journals
www.oxfordjournals.org

British Library Electronic Resources and Journals
www.bl.uk/eresources/jnls/ejournals.html

British Journal of Social Work
http://bjsw.oxfordjournals.org

Snapshots from the Census years
www.neighbourhood.statistics.gov.uk/HTMLDocs/dvc13/census1911_2001.html

British Social Attitudes Survey
http://data.gov.uk/dataset/british-social-attitudes-survey

Social Trends
http://data.gov.uk/dataset/social_trends

'An overview of child well-being in rich countries'
www.unicef-irc.org/publications/pdf/rc7_eng.pdf

'Measuring national well-being'
http://webarchive.nationalarchives.gov.uk/20110422103457/http://www.ons.gov.uk/well-being

Mind Changers: The Bobo Doll
www.bbc.co.uk/iplayer/episode/b008fxv9/Mind_Changers_The_Bobo_Doll/

Mass Observation: Recoding everyday life in Britain
www.massobs.org.uk/menu_about_mass_observation.htm

Avon Longitudinal Study of Parents and Children (ALSPAC)
www.bristol.ac.uk/alspac

Useful resources (cont.)

'The simple truth about statistics'
www.guardian.co.uk/science/blog/2010/sep/29/statistics-lies-abuse

Bandolier: evidence-based thinking about health care
www.medicine.ox.ac.uk/bandolier

Books

Bogdan, R. and Biklen, S. K. (1992) *Qualitative research for education*, Boston: Allyn and Bacon.
Denscombe, M. (2010) *The good research guide for small-scale social research projects*, 4th edition, Buckingham: Open University Press.
Glaser, B.G. and Strauss, A.L. (1967) *The discovery of Grounded Theory: strategies for qualitative research*, Chicago: Aldine Publishing Company.
Goldacre, B. (2008) *Bad science*, London: Fourth Estate.
Livingston, G. (2006) *Too soon old, too late smart*, London: Hodder & Stoughton.
Morrow, V. (2009) 'The ethics of social research with children and families in young lives: practical experiences', *Working paper no. 53*, Oxford: Young Lives.

SECTION 2

Optional units

11 Support children and/or young people's development of art, drama and music (CP 11)

12 Learning about planning from a given framework of curricula (CP 13)

13 Supporting numeracy and literacy development in children and/or young people (CP 14)

Chapter 11 Support children and/or young people's development of art, drama and music (Unit CP 11)

The aim of this chapter is to enable the learner to support children and/or young people's development of art, drama and music.

Learning outcomes

1. Understand art, drama and music development when working with children and/or young people.
2. Understand learning needs of individual children and/or young people when supporting the development of art, drama and music.
3. Be able to plan and implement art, drama and music activities for children and/or young people.
4. Be able to reflect on own practice.

Section 1: Understand art, drama and music development when working with children and/or young people

The study and experience of art, drama and music are universally considered to be an indispensable part of a well-rounded education. Art, drama and music form part of the compulsory curriculum up to the end of the lower secondary stage (at about 14–16 years of age) and then are usually offered as elective subjects for upper secondary students. (Sharp and Le Métais 2000, p. 5)

However, schools (and other settings working with children and/or young people) are facing problems of curriculum overload. The changing nature of society means that schools are under immense pressure to ensure that young people have the necessary knowledge and skills for adult life (for example, languages, information technology, citizenship, drugs education and sexual health). Some countries (e.g. England) place a greater emphasis on developing the basic skills of literacy and numeracy, and this has led to pressures on the balance between compulsory and elective subjects as well as the content and organisation of the arts within the curriculum. Some of the important features of a curriculum that are beneficial to high-quality learning experiences in the arts include a strong focus on three principles of entitlement, openness and flexibility. (Sharp and Le Métais 2000, p. 10)

The curriculum for arts education is intended to be delivered within school time; pupils are entitled to the full range of arts activities at school. There is also a lot of exciting practice taking place outside school hours, where pupils attend groups and clubs out of interest and are usually well motivated (e.g. art groups, choirs, orchestras, drama clubs and theatre trips). Arts activities should encourage openness and flexibility, regardless of whether they take place during or outside school hours. The challenge is to provide children and young people with an arts experience of sufficient depth and quality, of relevance to their lives and which they find enjoyable and stimulating. This has to happen within an environment that values the arts and celebrates their contribution to society. (Sharp and Le Métais 2000, p. 11)

Curriculum frameworks to support art, drama and music

You need to be able to summarise educational curricula or frameworks which support children and/or young people's learning in art, drama and music within your home country: England, Northern Ireland, Scotland or Wales. For example, in England, the curriculum frameworks for education are the Early Years Foundation Stage (0–5 years) and the National Curriculum Key Stages 1 to 4 (5–16 years).

The Early Years Foundation Stage

The Early Years Foundation Stage (EYFS) is the statutory framework that sets the standards for the care, development and learning of children from birth to five years old. Orders and regulations under section 39 of the Childcare Act 2006 brought the EYFS into force in September 2008. This framework includes six areas covered by the early learning goals and educational programmes. None of these areas can be delivered in isolation from the others. They are equally important and depend on each other to support a rounded approach to child development. All the areas must be delivered through planned, purposeful play, with a balance of adult-led and child-initiated activities (DCSF 2008).

The six areas of learning and development are:

- personal, social and emotional development
- communication, language and literacy
- problem solving, reasoning and numeracy
- knowledge and understanding of the world
- physical development
- creative development.

Creative development in the EYFS

Art, drama and music are included within creative development within the EYFS. Children's creativity must be extended by the provision of support for their curiosity, exploration and play. They must be provided with opportunities to explore and share their thoughts, ideas and feelings – for example, through a variety of art, music, movement, dance, imaginative and role-play activities, mathematics, and design and technology.

By the end of the EYFS, children should have achieved these early learning goals in creative development:

- Respond in a variety of ways to what they see, hear, smell, touch and feel.
- Express and communicate their ideas, thoughts and feelings by using a widening range of materials, suitable tools, imaginative and role play, movement, designing and making, and a variety of songs and musical instruments.
- Explore colour, texture, shape, form and space in two or three dimensions.
- Recognise and explore how sounds can be changed, sing simple songs from memory, recognise repeated sounds and sound patterns and match movements to music.
- Use their imagination in art and design, music, dance, imaginative and role play and stories.

(DCSF 2008)

The 2012 Early Years Foundation Stage

On 6 July, a revised draft EYFS framework was issued for consultation, taking forward Dame Clare Tickell's proposals for reform: reducing paperwork and bureaucracy for professionals; focusing strongly on the three prime areas of learning most essential for children's healthy development and future learning (with four specific areas in which the prime areas are applied); simplifying assessment at age five, including to reduce the early learning goals (ELGs) from 69 to 17; and providing for earlier intervention for those children who need extra help, through the introduction of a progress check when children are aged two (DfE 2011, p. 1).

This revised EYFS was published on 27 March 2012 and will be implemented from September 2012. (The 2008 EYFS will continue to be in force until 31 August 2012.) There are seven areas of learning and development that must shape educational programmes in early years settings. Three areas are particularly important for igniting young children's curiosity and enthusiasm for learning, and for building their capacity to learn and to thrive. These three areas, known as the *prime* areas, are:

- personal, social and emotional development
- physical development
- communication and language.

Early years providers must also support young children in four *specific* areas of learning and development, through which the three prime areas are strengthened and applied. The specific areas are: literacy; mathematics; understanding the world; and expressive arts and design.

Expressive arts and design in the revised EYFS

Expressive arts and design involve enabling children to explore and play with a wide range of media and materials, as well as providing opportunities and encouragement for sharing their thoughts, ideas and feelings through a variety of activities in art, music, movement, dance, role play, and design and technology (DfE 2012, p. 5).

By the end of the EYFS, children should have achieved these early learning goals in expressive arts and design:

- **Explore and use media and materials**: sing songs, make music and dance, and experiment with ways of changing them; safely use and explore a variety of materials, tools and techniques, experimenting with colour, design, texture, form and function.
- **Be imaginative**: use what they have learnt about media and materials in original ways, thinking about uses and purposes; represent their own ideas, thoughts and feelings through design and technology, art, music, dance, role play and stories.

(DfE 2012, p. 9)

(For detailed information about the EYFS, see Chapter 13.)

Research Activity

Find out more about art, drama and music in the EYFS. For example, have a look at The Foundation Years website: www.foundationyears.org.uk.

The National Curriculum in England

The National Curriculum sets out the statutory requirements for the knowledge and skills that every child is expected to learn in schools. The National Curriculum applies to children of compulsory school age in schools in England. The National Curriculum sets out what pupils should study, what they should be taught and the standards that they should achieve. It is divided into four key stages:

- Key Stage 1: Year groups 1 and 2 (5–7-year-olds)
- Key Stage 2: Year groups 3, 4, 5 and 6 (7–11-year-olds)
- Key Stage 3: Year groups 7, 8 and 9 (11–14-year-olds)
- Key Stage 4: Year groups 10 and 11 (14–16-year-olds).

In Key Stages 1 and 2 of the National Curriculum, the compulsory subjects consist of: English; mathematics; science; information and communication technology; design and technology; history; geography; art and design; music; and physical education.

In Key Stage 3, the compulsory subjects are: English; mathematics; science; information and communication technology; design and technology; history; geography; art and design; music; physical education; citizenship; and modern foreign languages.

In Key Stage 4, the compulsory subjects are: English; mathematics; science; information and communication technology; physical education; and citizenship. Secondary schools must make entitlement curriculum areas (e.g. the arts, design and technology, the humanities and modern foreign languages) available to all students who wish to study them. In addition, there is a statutory requirement for work-related learning and a non-statutory framework setting out the minimum experience that schools should provide for work-related learning. In January 2011, the Secretary of State for Education announced a review of the National Curriculum in England. While the review is being conducted, the existing National Curriculum requirements for both primary and secondary schools will remain in force. (Detailed information is given in Chapter 13.)

Art in the primary years

In the primary years, supporting children's development in art should ensure that 'investigating and making' include 'exploring and developing ideas' and 'evaluating and developing work'. 'Knowledge and understanding' should inform this process.

In **Key Stage 1**, the curriculum should provide opportunities for pupils to:

- develop their creativity and imagination by exploring the visual, tactile and sensory qualities of materials and processes
- learn about the role of art, craft and design in their environment
- begin to understand colour, shape and space and pattern and texture, and use them to represent their ideas and feelings.

(DfE 2011)

In **Key Stage 2**, the curriculum should provide opportunities for pupils to:

- develop their creativity and imagination through more complex activities
- build on their skills and improve their control of materials, tools and techniques
- increase their critical awareness of the roles and purposes of art, craft and design in different times and cultures
- become more confident in using visual and tactile elements and materials and processes to communicate what they see, feel and think.

(DfE 2011)

Figure 11.1 Young children involved in art and design

Research Activity

Find out more about art in Key Stage 1 and Key Stage 2. For example, have a look at the section about primary 'Art and Design' on the Department for Education website:

www.education.gov.uk/schools/teachingandlearning/curriculum/primary/b00198792/art.

Art in the secondary years

In **Key Stage 3**, art and design are a statutory part of the curriculum. In art, craft and design, pupils explore visual, tactile and other sensory experiences to communicate ideas and meanings. They work with traditional and new media, developing confidence, competence, imagination and creativity. Pupils should be provided with opportunities to:

- work independently and collaboratively, taking different roles in teams
- explore areas that are new to them, including ideas, techniques and processes
- respond to the school's location and local cultural influences
- engage with contemporary art, craft and design, working with creative individuals and in creative environments where possible
- work with a variety of genres, including contemporary practice
- engage in interdisciplinary and multidisciplinary practice within the arts
- make links between art and design and other subjects and areas of the curriculum.

(DfE 2011)

In **Key Stage 4**, pupils study a mix of compulsory and optional subjects, including entitlement areas such as arts subjects (e.g. art and design, music, dance, drama and media arts). Pupils opting to study art and design can choose from a variety of qualifications depending on what is available in their school – for example, GCSE courses in art, craft and/or design that require students to complete two units: one is a portfolio of selected coursework, including a full project that meets four assessment objectives; the second is an external examination completed in ten hours at school. In addition, selected schools offer the Diploma for 14–19-year-olds, which is a qualification that combines academic and vocational learning. There are 14 Diplomas available to schools and colleges, including 'Creative and Media'.

Art choices for 16–18-year-olds in England include continuing in full-time education, either at school/college through studying for academic qualifications such as AS or A levels (e.g. fine art, media studies, photography and textiles) or vocational qualifications (e.g. BTEC Diplomas in art and design, computer games design, fashion and textiles, graphic design and photography). Selected colleges also offer the Diploma qualification for 14–19-year-olds (see above).

Research Activity

Find out more about art in Key Stage 3, Key Stage 4 and beyond. For example, have a look at the following Department for Education web pages:

- Art and Design in secondary schools: www.education.gov.uk/schools/teachingandlearning/curriculum/secondary/b00199239/art
- GCSEs: www.education.gov.uk/schools/teachingandlearning/qualifications/gcses
- The 14 to 19 Diploma: www.education.gov.uk/a0064416/what-is-the-diploma.

Drama in the primary years

In the primary years, there is no separate curriculum subject for drama – it is included as part of the English programme of study.

In **Key Stage 1**, as part of the knowledge, skills and understanding for 'speaking and listening' in English (under the subheading 'Drama'), pupils should be provided with opportunities to participate in a range of drama activities, including:

- using language and actions to explore and convey situations, characters and emotions
- creating and sustaining roles individually and when working with others

Figure 11.2 Secondary pupils involved in art and design

- commenting constructively on drama they have watched or in which they have taken part.

In **Key Stage 2**, as part of the knowledge, skills and understanding for 'speaking and listening' in English (under the subheading 'Drama'), pupils should be provided with opportunities to participate in a wide range of drama activities, including:

- creating, adapting and sustaining different roles, individually and in groups
- using character, action and narrative to convey story, themes, emotions, ideas in plays they devise and script
- using dramatic techniques to explore characters and issues (for example, hot seating, flashback)
- evaluating how they and others have contributed to the overall effectiveness of performances.

(DfE 2011)

Research Activity

Find out more about drama in Key Stage 1 and Key Stage 2. For example, have a look at the section about primary English on the Department for Education website: www.education.gov.uk/schools/teachingandlearning/curriculum/primary/b00198874/english.

Drama in the secondary years

In the secondary years, there is no separate curriculum subject for drama – it is included as part of the English programme of study.

In **Key Stage 3**, the curriculum should provide opportunities for students to: participate in individual and group improvisation and performance; devise, script and perform plays; evaluate and respond constructively to their

Figure 11.3 Young children engaged in drama activities

own and others' performances; watch live performances in the theatre wherever possible to appreciate how action, character, atmosphere, tension and themes are conveyed; participate actively in drama workshops and discuss with actors, playwrights, directors and other drama professionals the impact and meaning of different ways of performing and staging drama, wherever possible. As part of the key processes for 'speaking and listening' in English, students should be able to:

- use different dramatic approaches to explore ideas, texts and issues
- use different dramatic techniques to convey action, character, atmosphere and tension
- explore the ways that words, actions, sound and staging combine to create dramatic moments.

(DfE 2011)

In **Key Stage 4**, the curriculum should provide opportunities for students to: evaluate and respond constructively to their own and others' performances; watch live performances in the theatre wherever possible and consider how action, character, atmosphere, tension and themes are conveyed that are integral to their learning and enhance their engagement with the concepts, processes and content of the subject. As part of the key processes for 'speaking and listening' in English, students should be able to:

- use a range of dramatic approaches to explore complex ideas, texts and issues in scripted and improvised work
- select different dramatic techniques to convey action, character, atmosphere and tension, and justify choices
- evaluate drama performances that they have watched or taken part in.

(DfE 2011)

In addition to drama being included as part of the English curriculum, which is compulsory until age 16, students may opt to study drama as an elective subject depending on what is available in their school – for example, GCSE Drama.

Drama choices for 16–18-year-olds in England include continuing in full-time education, either at school/college through studying for academic qualifications such as AS or A levels (e.g. drama and theatre studies, film studies) or vocational qualifications (e.g. BTEC Diplomas in drama, performing arts, production arts). Selected colleges also offer the Diploma qualification for 14–19-year-olds (e.g. Creative and Media).

Figure 11.4 Young people engaged in drama activities

Research Activity

Find out more about drama in Key Stage 3, Key Stage 4 and beyond. For example, have a look at the following Department for Education web pages:

- English in secondary schools: www.education.gov.uk/schools/teachingandlearning/curriculum/secondary/b00199101/english
- GCSEs: www.education.gov.uk/schools/teachingandlearning/qualifications/gcses
- The 14 to 19 Diploma: www.education.gov.uk/a0064416/what-is-the-diploma.

Music in the primary years

In the primary years, teaching music should ensure that 'listening, and applying knowledge and understanding' are developed through the interrelated skills of 'performing', 'composing' and 'appraising'.

In **Key Stage 1**, the curriculum should provide opportunities for pupils to:

- listen carefully and respond physically to a wide range of music
- play musical instruments and sing a variety of songs from memory, adding accompaniments and creating short compositions, with increasing confidence, imagination and control
- explore and enjoy how sounds and silence can create different moods and effects.

(DfE 2011)

In **Key Stage 2**, the curriculum should provide opportunities for pupils to:

- sing songs and play instruments with increasing confidence, skill, expression and awareness of their own contribution to a group or class performance
- improvise, and develop their own musical compositions, in response to a variety of different

stimuli with increasing personal involvement, independence and creativity
- explore their thoughts and feelings through responding physically, intellectually and emotionally to a variety of music from different times and cultures.

(DfE 2011)

Figure 11.5 A young child participating in a musical activity

Research Activity

Find out more about art in Key Stage 1 and Key Stage 2. For example, have a look at the section about primary Music on the Department for Education website: www.education.gov.uk/schools/teachingandlearning/curriculum/primary/b00199150/music.

Music in the secondary years

Music education encourages active involvement in different forms of music making. Music learning develops students' critical skills: their ability to listen, to appreciate a wide variety of music, and to make judgements about musical quality. It also increases self-discipline, creativity, aesthetic sensitivity and fulfilment.

In **Key Stage 3**, students should be provided with opportunities to:

- develop individual performance skills, both vocal and instrumental, including the use of music technology
- develop listening and aural perception skills in practical activities, including composing and performing
- develop creative and compositional skills, including songwriting, arranging and improvising
- work with a range of musicians and watch and listen to live musical performances where possible, to extend their musical learning
- work individually, in musical groups of different sizes and as a class
- build on their own interests and skills, taking on different roles and responsibilities and developing music leadership skills
- make links between music and other subjects and areas of the curriculum.

(DfE 2011)

In **Key Stage 4**, pupils study a mix of compulsory and optional subjects, including entitlement areas such as art and design, music and drama. Pupils may opt to study music depending on what is available in their school – for example, GCSE Music, in which students are required to complete three units: performing music; composing music; and appraising music. In addition, selected schools offer the Diploma for 14–19-year-olds, which is a qualification that combines academic and vocational learning. There are 14 Diplomas available to schools and colleges, including 'Creative and Media'.

Figure 11.6 Secondary pupils participating in musical activities

Music choices for 16–18-year-olds in England include continuing in full-time education, either at school/ college through studying for academic qualifications such as AS or A levels in music or vocational qualifications such as BTEC Diplomas in music practice and music technology). Selected colleges also offer the Diploma qualification for 14–19-year-olds (see above).

Research Activity

Find out more about music in Key Stage 3, Key Stage 4 and beyond. For example, have a look at the following Department for Education web pages:

- Music in secondary schools: www.education.gov.uk/schools/teachingandlearning/curriculum/secondary/b00199601/music
- GCSEs: www.education.gov.uk/schools/teachingandlearning/qualifications/gcses
- The 14 to 19 Diploma: www.education.gov.uk/a0064416/what-is-the-diploma.

Curriculum frameworks in Northern Ireland, Scotland and Wales

You should know the relevant national curriculum guidelines for teaching and learning relevant to the pupils you work with. The above information relates to England.

Northern Ireland

The revised Northern Ireland Curriculum was introduced in September 2007. The Northern Ireland Curriculum sets out the minimum requirements that should be taught at each key stage while giving practitioners the flexibility to provide a broad and balanced curriculum that meets children's individual needs with opportunities for every child to experience success in learning in order to achieve as high a standard as possible. The primary phase consists of:

- The Foundation Stage: Years 1 and 2 (4–6-year-olds)
- Key Stage 1: Years 3 and 4 (6–8-year-olds)
- Key Stage 2: Years 5, 6 and 7 (8–11-year-olds).

The secondary phase consists of:

- Key Stage 3: Years 8, 9 and 10 (11–14-year-olds)
- Key Stage 4: Years 11 and 12 (14–16-year-olds).

The relevant section of the curriculum is the Area of Learning entitled 'The Arts', which includes art and design, music and drama. (More detailed information about curriculum frameworks in Northern Ireland is given in Chapter 13.)

Scotland

In Scotland, the national guidance 'Pre-Birth to Three: Positive Outcomes for Scotland's Children and Families' replaces 'Birth to Three: Supporting our Youngest Children'. It includes important information on pre-birth and brain development and it reflects the principles and philosophy which underpin the Early Years Framework and Curriculum for Excellence. For more information, visit: www.ltscotland.org.uk/earlyyears/prebirthtothree/index.asp.

The curriculum in Scotland has been under review and, from August 2010, all schools are expected to adopt the new 'Curriculum for Excellence'. The Curriculum for Excellence is Scotland's curriculum for children and young people aged 3 to 18, which replaces 'A Curriculum Framework for Children 3 to 5' and the '5–14 Curriculum'. The Curriculum for Excellence includes:

- Early Level: Nursery and P1 (3–6 years)
- First Level: P2, P3 and P4 (5–9 years)
- Second Level: P5, P6 and P7 (8–12 years)
- Third and Fourth Level: S1, S2 and S3 (11–15 years)
- Senior Phase: S4, S5 and S6 (14–18 years).

(More detailed information about curriculum frameworks in Scotland is given in Chapter 13.)

Wales

At the moment, there is no statutory framework for 0–3-year-olds in Wales, although in January 2011 the Deputy Minister for Children agreed to work to take forward a 'Progress and Development Framework' for 0–3-year-olds, focusing on the needs of the child before they enter into the Foundation Phase. However, there is an early learning programme, Flying Start, which is targeted at 0–3-year-olds in the most disadvantaged communities in Wales. It aims to create positive outcomes in the medium and long term. It is a prescriptive programme, based on international evidence of what works. For more information, see: http://wales.gov.uk/topics/childrenyoungpeople/parenting/help/flyingstart/?lang=en.

In Wales, the revised school curriculum for 3 to 19-year-olds has been implemented since September 2008. This includes:

- The Foundation Phase: Nursery, Reception and Years 1 and 2 (3–7-year-olds)
- Key Stage 2: Years 3, 4, 5 and 6 (7–11-year-olds)
- Key Stage 3: Years 7, 8 and 9 (11–14-year-olds)
- Key Stage 4: Years 10 and 11 (14–16-year-olds).

(More detailed information about curriculum frameworks in Wales is given in Chapter 13.)

Research Activity

Find out more about the curriculum frameworks for art, drama and music in Northern Ireland, Scotland or Wales. For example, have a look at the following:

- Northern Ireland Curriculum website: www.nicurriculum.org.uk/
- Curriculum for Excellence website: www.ltscotland.org.uk/curriculumforexcellence/curriculumoverview/index.asp
- Welsh Government website: http:/wales.gov.uk/topics/educationandskills/schoolshome/curriculuminwales/arevisedcurriculumforwales/?lang=en.

Supporting the development of art, drama and music skills when working with children and/or young people

It is vital that *all* children and young people have access to a stimulating environment which enables learning to take place in exciting and challenging ways. To develop into healthy, considerate and intelligent adults, all children and young people require intellectual stimulation as well as physical care and emotional security. Intellectual stimulation through play and other learning opportunities allows children and young people to develop their cognitive abilities and fulfil their potential as individuals.

The children and/or young people you work with will be constantly thinking and learning (e.g. gathering new information and formulating new ideas about themselves, other people and the world around them). When supporting the development of art, drama and music skills, you should provide children and/or young people with opportunities to:

- explore their environment and/or investigate new information/ideas
- discover things for themselves through a wide variety of experiences
- feel free to make mistakes in a safe and secure environment using 'trial and error'
- develop autonomy through increased responsibility and working independently
- encourage and extend their knowledge and skills with appropriate support from adults (and other children/young people)
- learn to make sense of new information within an appropriate curriculum framework.

Developing imagination and creativity

Imagination involves the individual's ability to invent ideas or to form images. Children express their imagination through imitative play to begin with and then gradually through imaginative play (e.g. pretend play or role play). As children explore their environment and find out what objects and materials can do, they use their imagination to increase their understanding of the world and their role within it. For example, through imaginative play, children can become other people by dressing up and behaving like them. Imaginative play assists the development of children's imagination through activities such as dressing up, small-scale toys, doll play, shop play and hospital play.

Creativity is the *use* of the imagination in a wide variety of activities, including play, art, design technology, music, dance, drama, stories and poetry. Children can express their creativity through creative activities such as painting, drawing, collage, play dough, clay, cooking, design and model making. Creativity involves a process rather than an end product. It cannot be measured by the end result of an activity, but is based upon *how* the child works and *why*. Creativity involves: exploring and experimenting with a wide range of materials; learning about the properties of materials (e.g. colour, shape, size and texture); developing fine motor skills to manipulate materials; developing problem-solving techniques; and developing an understanding of the world and our personal contribution to it.

Key terms

Creativity – the *use* of the imagination in a wide variety of activities, including play, art, design technology, music, dance, drama, stories and poetry.

Imagination – the individual's ability to invent ideas or to form images.

Examples of opportunities to encourage children's imagination and creativity

1. **Painting** with brushes, sponges, string; finger painting, bubble painting, 'butterfly' or 'blob' painting, marble painting, wax resist painting; printing (e.g. with leaves, potatoes, cotton reels) and pattern making (e.g. with rollers, stamps).
2. **Drawing** using pencils, crayons, felt tips or chalks on a variety of materials, including

different kinds of paper, card, fabric and wood. Include colouring activities linked to the children's interests by drawing your own colouring sheets, buying ready-made colouring books or using free printable colouring pages from the internet.

3. **Model making** using commercial construction kits (e.g. *Lego Explore, Mega Bloks* or *Stickle Bricks*), wooden blocks or clean and safe 'junk' materials to enable children to create their own designs.
4. **Collage** using glue and interesting materials to create pictures involving different textures, colours and shapes, and provide an enjoyable sensory experience too.
5. **Clay, play dough and plasticine** can be used creatively; they are tactile too.
6. **Cooking** provides a similar experience to working with play dough or clay, except that the end product is (usually) edible. Remember to include 'no cook' activities, such as icing biscuits, making sandwiches or peppermint creams.
7. **Making music** can provide opportunities for children to explore different sounds and to experiment freely with the musical instruments. Provide a portable box/trolley with a range of percussion instruments, including: drum, tambourine, castanets, wood blocks, shakers, bell stick, Indian bells, triangle, xylophone and chime bars.
8. **Water play** with plain, bubbly, coloured, warm or cold water helps children learn about the properties of water (e.g. it pours, splashes, runs, soaks). Provide small containers to fill and empty, as well as a sieve and funnel.
9. **Sand play** provides opportunities for exploring the properties of sand (e.g. wet sand sticks together and can be moulded, while dry sand does not stick and can be poured). Use 'washed' or 'silver' sand (not builder's sand, which might contain cement). Provide small containers, buckets, sieves and funnels.

(There is more detailed information on creativity in Unit CYPOP7 of *CACHE Level 3 Diploma Children and Young People's Workforce: Early Learning and Child Care, available at www.hoddereducation/cache.*)

Activity

1. Give an example of an activity (one each for art, drama and music) which encourages a group of children to express themselves freely in an imaginative and creative way.
2. Suggest ways to support the development of children's imagination and creativity.

Supporting the development of art skills

Supporting the development of art skills in children and young people includes providing opportunities for spontaneous painting and drawing, undirected by adults. Children should be offered frequent opportunities to paint and draw when they feel like it. For very young children especially, spontaneous painting and drawing are a valuable means of expression. The benefit of children being able to express themselves in this way is reduced if adults insist on questioning children about their paintings or drawings, suggesting additions to the work and wanting titles for every painting or drawing (Hobart and Frankel 2009, p. 71).

Children and young people also need opportunities to engage in art activities, which are generally adult directed. Children and young people should be allowed to use their own ideas, even when following adult-directed activities. Art activities will help to stimulate children's imagination and an aesthetic awareness. Art activities encourage children's creativity as well as their social development by sharing materials

Figure 11.7 Children exploring and experimenting with materials

Figure 11.8 Young child participating in an adult-directed art activity

and turn-taking, learning about the properties of various materials and developing language skills as the children have to understand instructions and ask questions. Children usually work in small groups with an adult supervising, and sometimes the whole class is involved as part of a theme that is being explored, providing links to other areas of the curriculum (Hobart and Frankel 2009, p. 77).

Understanding children's paintings and drawings

Adult interpretations of children's paintings and drawings may often be incorrect. Most children love to do all dark, one-colour paintings at some stage in their development. This does not necessarily mean that something terrible has happened to them that they wish to forget! However, understanding what stage of development children might have reached by interpreting their paintings and drawings is interesting (Hobart and Frankel 2009, p. 71).

Children's paintings and drawings are often used as indicators of children's intellectual abilities. For example, intelligence tests such as Florence Goodenough's 'draw-a-man' test (1926), and the updated test of drawing a man, woman and self by Dale Harris (1963) had been used to measure children's intelligence according to the presence of set criteria (e.g. head, mouth, fingers, etc.): the more detailed the drawings, the more intelligent the child (Kamen 2000, p. 122).

The difficulty with this is that children's drawing and painting abilities depend on a number of factors, such as:

- physical ability, e.g. fine motor skills in holding and using a pencil, crayon or brush
- opportunities for mark making
- interest in drawing and painting activities
- concentration levels
- visual input from books, television, displays, posters
- the teaching of drawing and painting skills
- adult reactions to children's artistic attempts.

(Kamen 2000, pp. 122 and 123)

None of these factors is related to IQ (intelligence quotient). Children can demonstrate obvious intelligence in other ways (e.g. reading ability and comprehension skills), but fail to complete the drawing of a recognisable person with the detail expected from a child of their particular age. The validity of such tests has been challenged and their use has declined. Research also shows that some children with cognitive and language difficulties (e.g. children on the autistic spectrum) have exceptional drawing abilities, perhaps because this is their only means of self-expression (Kamen 2000, p. 123).

Children's drawings (and paintings) are also used as a way to assess young children's emotional development. For example, preoccupation with the use of black may be seen as a warning sign of emotional trauma but could equally be a reflection of the child's interest in exploring dark colours, and nothing more sinister. Similarly, anatomically correct drawings of people do not necessarily indicate that a child is being sexually abused; they may have seen people in quite natural situations (e.g. bath time or getting dressed). We need instead to look at *what children mean to express* through their drawings and paintings, rather than use adult interpretations of their creative activities. This is easier once children have language to express their ideas verbally as well as pictorially, but it is more difficult with babies, toddlers and children with communication difficulties (Kamen 2000, p. 123).

Another factor to consider is that Western society does not place much importance on the *teaching* of drawing or painting. Especially for young children, the emphasis is on allowing children to develop their drawing and painting skills in their own way. Children do not see many adults drawing and painting, unless they receive a Rudolf Steiner education, where specific artistic techniques are taught from five years old upwards (Kamen 2000, p. 123).

Activity

Find out more about teaching children to draw and/or paint. For example, have a look at Rudolf Steiner education, where drawing is an integral part of children and young people's learning, including their academic studies: www.steinerwaldorf.org. This website includes the 2010 ITN short film *The Gift of Learning*, which shows how art, music, play and active learning are central to the curriculum: www.steinerwaldorf.org/thegiftoflearningdvd.html.

Figure 11.9 A child's version of a famous painting

The National Curriculum has promoted the idea of introducing young children to the work of famous artists, such as Van Gogh and Monet, and encouraging children to try out different artistic techniques. The results have been surprising; children have produced paintings with detail far exceeding the children's usual artistic output (Kamen 2000, p. 123).

You may have noticed that if an adult draws or paints alongside the children in your setting and talks about what they are all doing, the detail in the children's drawings or paintings increases quite markedly. The *process* of drawing or painting, and the *context* in which the art activity takes place, is as important as the drawing/painting itself – that is, the end *product* (Kamen 2000, p. 124).

Drawing is often seen as children's first attempts at writing. While the same skills (e.g. hand–eye coordination and pencil control) are required for both, drawing and writing are actually two distinct activities. Writing is speech written down, while drawing is an individual's pictorial representation of their world. Both activities *do* involve the use of symbols. The simplistic and stylised nature of young children's drawings shows more about their *use of drawing* rather than their cognitive abilities or drawing skills. Young children use their drawings to convey meaning in the same way as they will later use words – for example, a young child's drawing is a pictorial symbol for 'bird' in the same way as the written word *bird* (Kamen 2000, p. 124).

From the age of seven years, visual realism becomes more important as children's understanding of the function of drawings changes. Through drawing and painting, children express themselves, their understanding of the world around them and their relationship to it. Limitations for this expression are imposed by the medium used (e.g. crayons or paints) and the ability to translate 3D objects into the images. For example, even adults have problems with perspective in drawings/paintings and plans or maps rely on symbolic representation rather than realism.

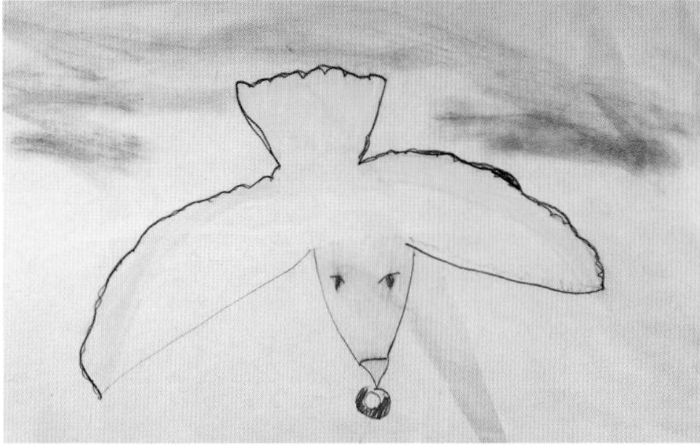

Figure 11.10 A child's drawing of a bird

How young children's drawings and paintings develop

Drawing and painting are important to children's development because they help:

- the expression of feelings, fears and fantasies
- hand–eye coordination and pencil control
- represent the people and the world around them
- the recall of memorable events, e.g. birthdays, holidays, falling off the swings!

Age	Characteristic abilities	Example of child's drawing/painting
12 to 18 months	• Cannot lift crayon off paper, moves it up and down in random marks. • Has no control of stroke direction. • Experiments with sensation of feeling paint, rather than creating pictures.	A
18 months to 2 years	• Cannot lift crayon off paper, draws round and round in circular movements. • Very limited control of stroke direction. • Explores sensation of paint textures, rather than creating pictures. • Imitates adults' and other children's artistic efforts.	B

Age	Characteristic abilities	Example of child's drawing/painting
2 to 3 years	• Can lift a crayon off paper and continue in different place, makes lines, circles and dots. • Begins to control stroke direction. • Begins to draw shapes representing objects and people. • Does not know what they are drawing beforehand, but will say what they have drawn afterwards once they can see a resemblance between the marks they have made and an object or person. • Experiments with textures and colours.	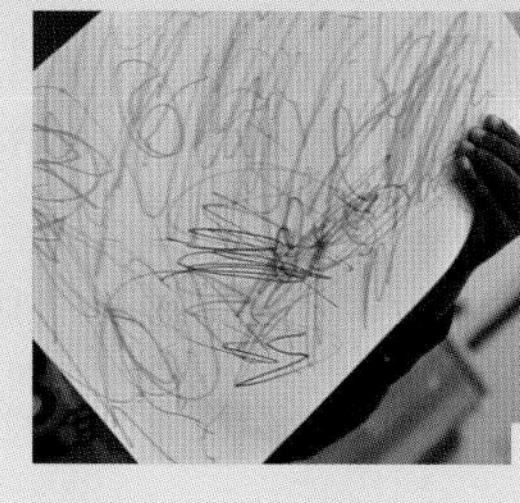 C
3 to 4 years	• Can start and finish lines, draws dashes and dots. • Does plan drawings, but objects may not always be recognisable. • Draws recognisable people, e.g. 'tadpole' person with circular body/head, arms and legs (which may or may not be joined to the body), basic facial features, possibly hair, fingers may be present (but maybe too few/too many), possibly has feet.	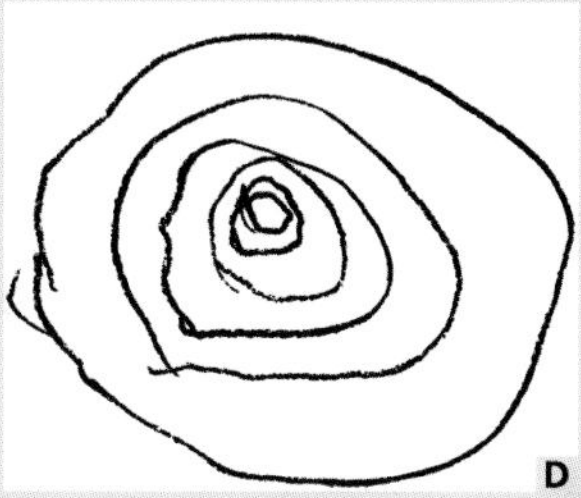 D
4 to 5 years	• Drawings are right way up. • More like adult representations, but still childlike, e.g. sun always shining with rays coming out. • Drawings of people are more detailed, e.g. 'tadpole' person and includes more obvious body shape, solid arms and legs, hair on head, more detailed facial features, including eyebrows, five fingers on each arm, etc.	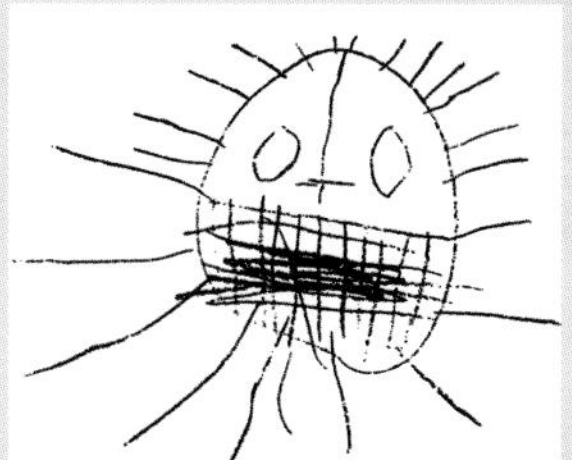 E
5 to 6 years	• People have more detailed bodies, e.g. neck, two-part bodies, ears, fingers, eyelashes, etc. • People with details of clothes, e.g. skirt styles, etc. • Scenes have ground and sky. • More adult representations, but still child stylised, e.g. 'classic' house with roof, chimney, four windows and a central door.	 F
6 to 7 years	• More adult representations, e.g. clearly recognisable people and scenes. • Gradually more and more detailed pictures. • Very detailed people, e.g. facial features, including chins, freckles, etc., details on clothes. • Background detail is increasingly important, e.g. flowers, vehicles, fences, trees, birds, etc. • Houses become more elaborate, reflecting reality, e.g. child who lives in a flat will draw block of flats, where before they drew a classic house, as described above. • Some children may be reluctant to draw or become frustrated at an inability to accurately represent what they see; they become self-critical and want to get details just right.	 G

Figure 11.11 The development of young children's drawings and paintings (images A, D, E and F reproduced from *Understanding Children's Drawings: Tracing the Path of Incarnation* by Michaela Strauss, published by Rudolf Steiner Press, 2007)

Activity

1 Observe a child drawing or painting a picture of a person.

2 In your assessment, comment on the child's: imaginative/creative skills; concentration level; use of colour; and fine motor skills (e.g. pencil or brush control). You might also consider the emotional value of the activity.

3 Compare to the usual pattern of development for drawing/painting for a child of this age. See Figure 11.11 and the timeline of drawing development in children aged 2 years to 16 years available online: www.learningdesign.com/Portfolio/DrawDev/kiddrawing.html#anchor2480790.

Opportunities to support the development of art skills

1. Provide lots of paper, crayons and pencils. Chunky crayons and thick-stemmed pencils are best for young children.
2. Encourage children to hold the pencil/crayon as best they can. They will control these better with a grip about two centimetres from the point.
3. Keep drawing sessions short. Be guided by the child's interest and concentration. A child's first attempt is usually their best, so do not ask them to do a picture over and over to get a better copy.
4. Let the children in your setting see *you* drawing and painting.
5. Draw outlines for children to fill in details (e.g. adding facial features to a circle). However, do not do this all the time; children also need freedom to draw what they like, how they like, when they like!
6. Encourage observation skills by getting children to copy patterns and shapes. As children get older, encourage them to represent 3D objects in 2D and pay attention to detail (e.g. self-portraits, drawing pictures of their own models and still life such as flowers, fruit and toys).
7. Provide variety in drawing and painting activities by offering different materials, tools and techniques (e.g. chalks, pastels, charcoal, felt tips; sponges, different-sized brushes, rollers; different-sized paper, shaped paper, different textures).
8. Provide plenty of interesting experiences, including outings to provide stimuli for drawing and painting activities.
9. Provide opportunities for children to see and appreciate the work of famous artists (such as Pollock, Picasso, Monet, Van Gogh, Toulouse-Lautrec, Dali and Warhol) through books with examples of their work, displaying copies of famous artwork and visiting art galleries.
10. Provide opportunities for children to experiment with using different art styles (e.g. abstract, cubism, impressionism, post-impressionism, realism, surrealism, pop art), including those from other cultures, and creating their own art galleries and/or art portfolios.

Activity

1 Suggest ways to support the development of children's art skills. Use your own experiences of working with children if possible. You could use your observation of a young child drawing or painting as the starting point for this activity.

2 Visit an art gallery in your local area. Which art styles/artists are displayed at the gallery? Does the gallery have an educational department, provide art workshops for children or have an artist-in-residence programme?

3 Think about how you could use a visit to an art gallery with the children from your setting to develop their art skills.

Figure 11.12 Children visiting an art gallery

Supporting the development of drama skills

For young children, the development of drama skills starts with imaginary play. Imaginary play grows out of imitative play. Babies from a very early age imitate adults in games of peek-a-boo, waving goodbye and copying actions. Later, children do not need a direct role model in front of them, but will use their memory – for example, pouring out imaginary cups of tea for everyone and pretending to eat non-existent food. At around two years, children start to take on different roles – for example, one child will be the 'mummy' and another the 'daddy'; this will gradually extend to include the 'baby', the 'big sister', the 'little brother' or a visiting 'grandparent'. As children become older, role play will be extended to other people who are familiar in their lives or from books and television. The provision of dressing-up clothes (that can be used in many different ways) helps to stimulate the children's imagination (Hobart and Frankel 2009, p. 63).

The provision of play and drama activities

- **Role play**, such as: domestic play (e.g. playing/imitating 'Mum' or 'Dad'); pretending to be a baby while other children act as parents; later imitating other role models, such as carers, play workers, teachers, characters from television, books; shop play (e.g. post office, hairdresser's, café, where they can explore other roles); other role-play environments (e.g. pretending to visit the dentist, clinic, optician or hospital, setting up a home corner, a health centre or hospital). This also includes drama activities (see below).
- **Dressing-up activities**, such as: pretending to be parents, carers, play workers, teachers, film/television superheroes, characters from games

consoles, kings and queens, which allows children to experiment with being in power and in control; pretending to be someone else can also help children to understand what it is like to be that person and encourages empathy and consideration for others.

- **Dolls and puppets** to help children to deal with their feelings – for example, jealousy over a new baby can be expressed by shouting at a teddy or doll; puppets are also a useful way of providing children with a 'voice' and may encourage shy or withdrawn children to express themselves more easily.
- **Miniature worlds**, such as: play with small-scale toys (e.g. dolls' houses, toy farms and toy zoos), as well as vehicle play, where children can act out previous experiences or situations while sharing ideas and equipment with other children; this can also help them establish friendships.
- **Drama activities**, such as: working in role; presenting drama and stories to others (for example, telling a story through tableaux or using a narrator); improvisation during role-play scenarios; responding to performances.

Activity

1. Observe a child involved in a drama activity.
2. In your assessment, comment on the child's: language and communication skills; social interaction; imaginative/creative skills; concentration level; and memory skills. You might also consider the emotional value of the activity. Also comment on the level of adult support provided during the activity.
3. Suggest ways to encourage and extend the development of the child's drama skills.

Figure 11.13 Children participating in play activities

Opportunities to support the development of drama skills

1. Provide opportunities for imaginative/role play which encourages children to explore different roles in positive ways, as well as encouraging language and communication (e.g. role/pretend play such as dressing-up, home corner, shop play).
2. Provide a variety of resources for children to engage in imaginary play (e.g. clean, unwanted clothing for dressing-up activities, not just commercially produced outfits); commercially produced resources which are well made, durable and safe for children's use, such as child-sized domestic play equipment; dressing-up clothes, cooking utensils, dolls and puppets that reflect different cultures; space for children's imaginary games that require few or no props.
3. Provide activities which encourage children to express themselves and to develop self-confidence – for example, circle games such as *The name game*, where each child takes it in turn to say 'My name is ... and I like to ... because ...' or *Circle jump*, where each child takes a turn at jumping into the circle, making an action that they feel expresses them and saying 'Hello, I'm ...'; then the rest of the children copy the action and reply 'Hello...[repeating the child's name]'.
4. Let the children in your setting see *you* engaging in imaginative play, including role play.
5. Provide plenty of interesting experiences, including books, stories and outings to provide stimuli for imaginative play and drama activities. For example, invite parents/grandparents to read or tell stories in community languages.
6. Provide opportunities for children to act out their favourite stories or to create their own variations of popular tales. For example, read *The True Story of the Three Little Pigs* (by Jon Scieszka). This tells the 'Three Little Pigs' story from the wolf's point of view. Then ask the children to write and then act out their own version of a traditional story from a different point of view (e.g. *Little Red Riding Hood* from the wolf's point of view or *Jack and the Beanstalk* from the giant's point of view).
7. Provide scenarios for children to act out – for example, exploring common themes such as risk taking through stories (e.g. *Jack and the Beanstalk*) or television programmes. Children can think about and discuss the risks taken by their favourite characters. Puppets and role play can be used to help them deal with potentially risky situations (e.g. dealing with bullying).
8. Provide opportunities for children to see and appreciate the work of famous playwrights (such as Ayckbourn, Bennett, Brecht, Chekhov, Coward, Jonson, Miller, Shakespeare, Shaw, Stoppard and Wodehouse) through reading books and play scripts, watching plays on DVDs, visiting theatres, inviting theatre-in-education companies or local theatre groups to perform within the setting.
9. Provide opportunities for children to experiment with different acting styles (e.g. drama, comedy, tragedy, fantasy, science fiction, farce, black comedy, comedy of manners and improvisation). This includes those from other countries/cultures, such as: traditional African theatre including storytelling, drama, music and dance; Chinese shadow play (shadow puppetry) and Chinese opera; ancient Greek theatre; Italian *commedia dell'arte*; traditional Japanese theatre, e.g. Bunraku, Kabuki, Kyogen, Noh; producing and performing plays; filming and reviewing their own drama activities.
10. Provide children with opportunities to create their own scripts. You can use class or group topics as well as the children's own interests to stimulate their ideas for stories and plays (e.g. weather, transport, festivals, our nursery or school, holidays, animals, spaceships, dragons, wizards, monsters, haunted house).

Activity

1. Suggest ways to support the development of children's drama skills. Use your own experiences of working with children if possible. You could use your observation of a child involved in a drama activity as the starting point for this activity.
2. Visit a local theatre. What type of productions does the theatre stage? Does the theatre have an educational department, provide drama workshops for children or give performances in local settings, such as nurseries, schools and colleges?
3. Think about how you could use a visit to the theatre with the children from your setting to develop their drama skills.

Supporting the development of music skills

Music is a familiar part of everyday life. From a very young age, babies will respond without discrimination but with enjoyment to a wide range of musical and rhythmic sounds. Lullabies are often used to soothe babies to sleep. As children grow older, their musical taste is formed by outside influences, particularly those of the family, the culture they are born into and the media, as well as their primary carers and peers. Experimenting with musical instruments and singing helps children discriminate sounds and aids their language development. In some classrooms and homes, singing or rhyming is quite natural and carries on between the children and adults as a way of normal communication (Hobart and Frankel 2009, p. 105).

Music activities can provide an outlet for children's feelings and ideas. Most children have an interest in sounds from birth (unless born with a profound hearing loss) and show pleasure at hearing music. Children develop their own musical abilities by listening to and participating in a range of musical activities from an early age (Kamen 2000, p. 56).

The provision of music activities

- Listening to adults singing songs and rhymes.
- Listening to songs and rhymes on CDs.
- Singing songs and rhymes with adults and other children.
- Making music on home-made instruments, such as upturned pots and pans, wooden spoons and shakers (remember safety!), or with commercial percussion instruments, such as a xylophone, triangle, tambourine or drum.
- Experiencing a range of live and recorded music from different times and cultures (for example, from the British Isles, from classical, folk and

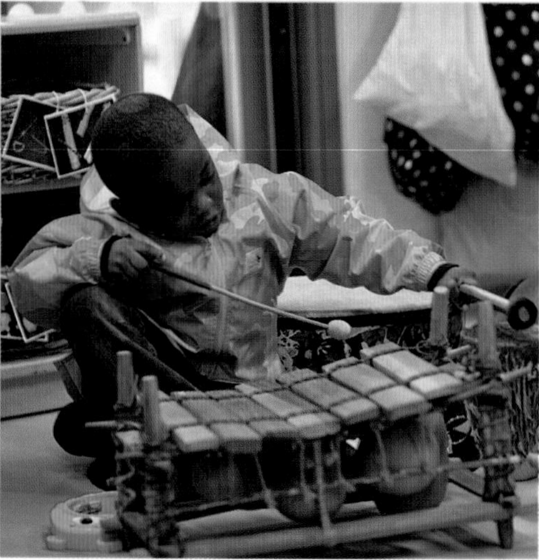

Figure 11.14 Children participating in music activities

popular genres, by well-known composers and performers).

- Using ICT to capture, change and combine sounds.
- Learning to play a musical instrument (e.g. recorder, piano, guitar, violin, cello, etc.).
- Integrating performing, composing and appraising.

Activity

1 Observe a child involved in a music activity.

2 In your assessment, comment on the child's: language and communication skills; auditory discrimination; imaginative/creative skills; concentration level; and memory skills. You might also consider the emotional value of the activity. Also comment on the level of adult support provided during the activity.

3 Suggest ways to encourage and extend the development of the child's music skills.

Opportunities to support the development of music skills

1. Provide activities to encourage children's listening skills and auditory discrimination. For example: listening in silence – 'What can you hear?' (such as clock ticking, wind blowing, rain falling); 'What's that sound?' – identifying everyday sounds on CD or from behind a screen; playing sound lotto.
2. Introduce children to rhyme by clapping out the beat of a rhyme, a song, a simple sentence or the syllables in each child's name. These skills will also help with the children's language and communication skills, especially their early reading skills.
3. Let children dance to music to develop a sense of rhythm.
4. Music provides an interesting and exciting way for children to be creative – for example, making their own combinations of different sounds plus simple rhythmic patterns and tunes.
5. Use percussion instruments, especially with young children, as it is easy for them to make rhythmic and melodic sounds without the experience and expertise required for more complex instruments such as recorders, guitars and pianos (see below).
6. Provide a portable box or trolley with a range of percussion instruments, including drums, tambourines, castanets, woodblocks, shakers, bell sticks, Indian bells, triangles, xylophones and chime bars.
7. To begin with, provide young children with opportunities to play along with their favourite songs and rhymes. Encourage the children to decide which instruments might be suitable for particular songs (e.g. triangles and bells for *Twinkle, Twinkle Little Star*). Also provide opportunities for children to experiment freely with the musical instruments.
8. Children enjoy the experience of making music using a wide range of musical instruments. As well as percussion instruments (see above), introduce children to string instruments (e.g. guitars, pianos, violins, zithers); wind instruments (e.g. flutes, harmonicas, recorders, whistles); and brass instruments (e.g. trumpets, French horns, trombones, tubas).
9. Provide opportunities for children to listen to and appreciate the work of famous composers (e.g. Bach, Beethoven, Brahms, Chopin, Haydn, Mozart, Schubert, Stravinsky, Tchaikovsky and Wagner) and influential musicians (such as The Beatles, Bob Dylan, Elvis Presley, The Rolling Stones, Chuck Berry, Jimi Hendrix, James Brown, Little

Richard, Aretha Franklin and Ray Charles) through listening to CDs, watching concerts etc. on DVDs, visiting concert halls and other suitable music venues, and inviting music groups to perform within the setting.

10. Provide opportunities for children to identify and explore a variety of music genres from past and present (e.g. Bach and the Baroque Suite, Haydn and the Classical Symphony, Brahms and the Romantic Concerto, Lennon and McCartney and '60s pop songs). This includes those from different countries/cultures, such as traditional: African music (Apala, Benga and Fuji); Balinese music (Gamelan); Brazilian music (capoeira music, choro, bossa nova, samba, lambada); Chinese music (Beijing Opera); Irish and Scottish folk music (Gaelic music and dancing); Spanish music (flamenco, jota, trikiti); and Welsh music contests (Eisteddfodau). In addition, provide opportunities for children to produce and perform music, as well as film and review their own musical activities.

11. Gradually encourage children to create their own music by getting them to copy clapping patterns, making clapping patterns using their own names etc. Use pictures, stories and rhymes as a stimulus for the children to make their own musical creations, on their own, with a partner or as a group. Encourage them to represent their music using symbols and/or words before introducing them to formal music scores. For example:

clap *wave* *clapclap wavewave clapclapclap wavewavewave*

() W ()() WW ()()() WWW

shakeshake woosh woosh shake shake woosh woosh

SS # # S S # #

bangbangbang BOOM bangbangbang BOOM

ooo O ooo O

Activity

1. Suggest ways to support the development of children's music skills. Use your own experiences of working with children if possible. You could use your observation of a child involved in a music activity as the starting point for this activity.
2. Visit your local concert hall. What type of musical events does the concert hall present? Does the concert hall have an educational department, provide music workshops for children or give performances in local settings, such as nurseries, schools and colleges?
3. Think about how you could use a visit to the concert hall with the children from your setting to develop their music skills.

The benefits of developing art, drama and music skills for children and/or young people

For all children, at all abilities, the arts (art, drama and music) play a central role in cognitive, motor, language and social-emotional development. The arts motivate and engage children in learning, stimulate memory, facilitate understanding, enhance symbolic communication, promote relationships and provide an avenue for building competence. The arts are natural for young children. Child development specialists note

Figure 11.15 Children enjoying a musical performance

that play is the business of young children; play is the way children promote and enhance their development. The arts are a most natural vehicle for play (Goldhawk 1998, p. 7).

The arts are also a source of joy and wonder, which bid students to touch, taste, hear and see the world. Children are powerfully affected by storytelling, music, dance and the visual arts. They often construct their understanding of the world around musical games, imaginative drama and drawing (Hamblen 1993).

Children and young people learn to appreciate and value images and artefacts across times and cultures and to understand the contexts in which they were made. In art, craft and design, pupils reflect critically on their own and other people's work, judging quality, value and meaning. They learn to think and act as artists, crafts people and designers, working creatively and intelligently (DfE 2011, p. 1).

To succeed in today's economy of ideas, students need to have the ability to use words, images, sounds and motion to communicate. Active participation and learning in the arts also improve overall academic achievement, socialisation and preparation for college and the workforce. A child's education is not complete unless it includes the arts. A comprehensive strategy for a complete education includes high-quality, continuing arts instruction in the classroom, as well as participation and learning in community-based arts programmes (Americans for the Arts 2001).

The benefits of art for children and young people

Childhood represents a very productive period of picture making; children create a massive collection of pictures, particularly paintings and drawings. What are the benefits of children and young people engaging in art, both in terms of their own creations and appreciation of pictures made by others? There are many general benefits of art for children and young people, such as: encouraging a sense of achievement and pride in learning a skill; improving concentration, patience, motor skill and hand–eye coordination; developing social skills in group art projects; and providing relaxation and fun! (Jolley 2010)

The benefits of developing art skills for children and/or young people

1. **Stimulating imagination and creativity**: children can take their experiences of the world and transform these by making new connections and relationships through their inventive minds. Their knowledge, memories and fantasies all feed their imagination, and art allows children to explore, build on and record their own creative and imaginative ideas.
2. **Providing a means of expression**: making pictures allows children to express their feelings and ideas, both as a means of self-expression and to communicate to others. These may include reliving a happy event they recently experienced (e.g. a birthday party or a day out) or drawing out some sad feelings as a therapeutic exercise. In addition, older children may use pictures for conceptual purposes – that is, for expressing their concerns and ideas.
3. **Encouraging visual thinking**: pictures encourage us to think about and understand the world visually, instead of only thinking about things in terms of what name they are called and their function.
4. **Developing observational skills**: making pictures helps children observe more closely the subject matter from the real-world scene they are drawing from, and therefore makes them more observant of the details in the world around them. Together with visual thinking, developing observational skills through picture making facilitates the child's visual sensitivity of the world.
5. **Learning problem-solving and analytical skills**: pictures enable children to explore and test out ideas, while making decisions on how they choose to represent them. For instance, children will learn problem-solving skills as they grapple with trying to create a three-dimensional scene from the world on a two-dimensional page. With practice, children learn that through concentration and persistence they can produce more successful pictures of what they are trying to achieve.
6. **Increasing autonomy**: a child's picture is his or her own. It has worth in its own right, without having to be measured or judged by others as right or wrong. The child has the authority to say what the picture is of, or what it communicates, therefore building up the child's confidence and self-esteem.

(Jolley 2010)

The benefits of drama for children and young people

Drama is not only about the product (the performance); it also helps in the process of language learning. Using drama and drama activities has clear advantages for language learning. It encourages children to speak and gives them the chance to communicate, even with limited language, using non-verbal communication, such as body movements and facial expressions. There are also a number of other factors which make drama a very powerful tool in the language classroom. This is because drama involves children at many levels, through their bodies, minds, emotions, language and social interaction (Phillips 1999, p. 6).

The benefits of developing drama skills for children and/or young people

1. **Motivation**: drama activities are very motivating and can be fun. The same activity can be done at different levels at the same time, which means that all children can do it successfully. The end product (the performance) is clear and so children feel safe and have a goal to work towards (even though this might not coincide with their teacher's aims). Children are motivated if they know that one or two groups will be asked to show what they have done, or if they are being videoed or putting on a public performance.
2. **Familiar activities**: dramatising is part of children's lives from an early age. Children act out scenes and stories from the age of about three or four years. They play at being adults in situations which are part of their everyday lives (like shopping and visiting the doctor). Many of these day-to-day situations are predictable. Children try out different roles in make-believe play. They rehearse the language and the 'script' of the situation and experience the emotions involved, knowing that they can switch back to reality whenever they want to. Such pretend play prepares children for the real-life situations they will meet later on: play is a rehearsal of the real thing. Make-believe encourages children's creativity and develops their imagination, and at the same time gives them the opportunity to use language that is outside their daily needs. For example, by acting out situations such as being Little Red Riding Hood, Aladdin's Magic Carpet or a bank robber and then using all the language that grows out of that personality or role.
3. **Confidence**: by taking on a role, children can escape from their everyday identity and lose their inhibitions. This is useful with children who are shy about speaking, who do not like joining in group activities or who speak English as an additional language. If you give them a special role, it encourages them to be that character and abandon their shyness, reluctance or embarrassment. This is especially true when you use puppets and masks. The teacher can use roles to encourage children who would otherwise hold back, and control children who dominate the weaker ones.
4. **Group dynamics**: children often work in pairs or groups when engaged in drama activities. This group work may be very structured, where children reproduce a model, or it may mean children taking responsibility for their own work. Children have to make decisions as a group, listen to each other and value each other's suggestions. They have to cooperate to achieve their aims, find ways of settling their differences and use the strengths of each member of the group.
5. **Language personalisation**: drama can help bring texts to life, making them more meaningful – for example, dramatising allows children to add an emotion or personality to a text that they have read or listened to. Take any word, sentence or short dialogue (two to four lines) and ask the children to practise saying it 'in character'. It is surprising how the meaning of something as simple as 'What's your name?' can be changed according to how and where you say it. For example, think about how a policeman asks a robber and how Father Christmas asks a hopeful child the same question. By interpreting the words, the children make them their own. This also makes language memorable.
6. **Cross-curricular content**: when using drama, your aims can be more than linguistic. You can use topics from other subjects: the children can act out scenes from history or the life cycle of a frog. You can work on ideas and issues that run through the curriculum, such as sexism, respect for the environment or road safety. Important messages can be conveyed and explored through sketches and role play. Drama can also be used to introduce the culture of new languages through stories and customs, and with the context working on different kinds of behaviour.

(Phillips 1999)

The benefits of music for children and young people

Recent advances in the study of the brain have enhanced the understanding of the way that active engagement with music may influence other activities. The cerebral cortex self-organises as children and young people engage with different musical activities. Skills in these areas may then transfer to other activities if the processes involved are similar. Increasing the amount of music within the curriculum can enhance relationships within the group/class, improve self-reliance and enable better social adjustment and more positive attitudes, particularly in low ability, disaffected pupils. The positive effects of engagement with music on personal and social development will only occur if, overall, it is an enjoyable and rewarding experience (Hallam 2010).

Research Activity

Analyse the benefits of developing art, drama and music skills for young children. You could start by looking at the following:

- Goldhawk's report *Young Children and the Arts: Making Creative Connections – A Report of the Task Force on Children's Learning and the Arts: Birth to Age Eight, available at:* www.eric.ed.gov/PDFS/ED453968.pdf
- Hallam's article 'The power of music: its impact on the intellectual, personal and social development of children and young people', available at: www.devon.gov.uk/dms-powerofmusic.pdf
- Ofsted's report *Making a Mark: Art, Craft and Design Education*, available at: www.education.gov.uk/publications/eOrderingDownload/110135.pdf.

The benefits of developing music skills for children and/or young people

1. **Developing perceptual, language and literacy skills**: speech and music have a number of shared processing systems. Musical experiences which enhance processing can therefore impact on the perception of language, which in turn impacts on learning to read. Active engagement with music sharpens the brain's early encoding of linguistic sound. Musical training develops skills which enhance perception of auditory patterns. Learning to play an instrument enhances the ability to remember words through enlargement of the left cranial temporal regions. Children experiencing difficulties with reading comprehension have benefited from training in rhythmical performance.
2. **Stimulating intellectual development and numeracy**: research exploring the relationships between mathematics and active musical engagement has had mixed results, in part, because not all mathematics tasks share underlying processes with those involved in music. Transfer is dependent on the extent of the match; for instance, children receiving instruction on rhythm instruments scored higher on part–whole maths problems than those receiving piano and singing instruction. Learning an instrument has an impact on intellectual development, particularly spatial reasoning.
3. **Enhancing general attainment and creativity**: there is a consistent relationship between active engagement in music and general attainment. Two nationally representative data sources in the USA with data from over 45,000 children found that associations between music and achievement persisted even when prior attainment was taken into account. Music participation enhances measured creativity, particularly when the musical activity itself is creative – for instance, improvisation.
4. **Influencing personal and emotional development**: general attainment may be influenced by the impact that music has on personal and social development. Playing an instrument can lead to a sense of achievement; an increase in self-esteem; increased

confidence; persistence in overcoming frustrations when learning is difficult; self-discipline; and provide a means of self-expression. These may increase motivation for learning in general, thus supporting enhanced attainment. Music has been linked to the capacity to increase emotional sensitivity. The recognition of emotions in music is related to emotional intelligence.

5. **Encouraging social development**: participating in musical groups promotes friendships with like-minded people; self-confidence; social skills; social networking; a sense of belonging; teamwork; self-discipline; a sense of accomplishment; cooperation; responsibility; commitment; mutual support; bonding to meet group goals; increased concentration; and provides an outlet for relaxation. Working in small musical groups requires the development of trust and respect and skills of negotiation and compromise. In adolescence, music makes a major contribution to the development of self-identity and is seen as a source of support when young people are feeling troubled or lonely.
6. **Improving physical development, health and well-being**: rhythmic accompaniment to physical education enhances the development of physical skills. Learning to play an instrument enhances fine motor coordination. There may be particular health benefits for singing in relation to the immune system, breathing, adopting good posture, improved mood and stress reduction. The research has been carried out with adults but these benefits could equally apply to children.

(Hallam 2010)

Section 2: Understand learning needs of individual children and/or young people when supporting the development of art, drama and music

Effective planning for children's early learning is based on each child's individual needs, abilities and interests; this is why accurate observations and assessments are so important. These needs have to be integrated into the curriculum requirements for your particular setting and the age group(s) of the children you work with – for example, in England, the Early Years Foundation Stage or the National Curriculum (see page 337). The curriculum sets out the standards to be used to measure the progress and performance of children/young people in each subject to help practitioners plan and implement learning activities that meet the individual learning needs of the children and/or young people they work with. (Detailed information about curriculum planning is given in Chapter 13.)

As a practitioner, you will need to plan, implement and evaluate plans for supporting the development of art, drama and music according to the requirements of your setting. When planning, implementing and evaluating these plans, your overall aims should be to:

- support *all* the children you work with
- ensure each child has full access to the relevant curriculum
- encourage participation by all children
- meet children's individual learning and development needs
- build on children's existing knowledge and skills
- help all children achieve their full potential.

The individual learning needs of visual, auditory and kinaesthetic learners

Children and young people have different ways of processing information. They use the skills of looking, listening or touching in varying amounts depending on their individual learning style. For example, some children require visual stimulation, some respond well to verbal instructions, while others need more 'hands-on' experiences. In addition, different times of the day affect individual levels of concentration. Some children work better in the morning, others in the afternoon. You need to be aware of the individual learning styles of the children you work with in order to plan and provide appropriate learning activities. Recognising learning styles will help you to understand the ways children learn and to assist them in achieving educational success.

Different learning styles

We receive and process information in different ways. The main ways, though, are through sight (visual), hearing (auditory) and physical bodies (kinaesthetic). One of these channels tends to be more dominant in each of us. If we receive new information through this channel, it is easier for us to understand and use; if it is presented through a weaker channel, we tend to find the ideas more difficult. For example, when engaged in drama activities, children use all the channels, and each child will draw on the one that suits them best. This means they will all be actively involved in the activity and the language will 'enter' through the channel most appropriate them (Phillips 1999, p. 7).

Visual learners gather information through observation and reading. According to research, about 65 per cent of people have this learning style.

Auditory learners gather information by listening carefully and then repeating instructions either out loud or mentally in order to remember what they have learned. Research suggests that about 30 per cent of people use this style of learning.

Kinaesthetic learners gather information through touch and movement. All young children rely on this learning style to a large extent, hence the importance of active learning, especially in the early years. About 5 per cent of people continue to use this style as adults.

You can find further information about visual, auditory and kinaesthetic learning styles in Chapter 5 (pages 184–5).

People are not restricted to learning in only one way. For example, children can learn to use different learning styles for different activities within the curriculum. However, research shows that working outside their preferred learning style for extensive periods can be stressful. Providing opportunities for children to use their preferred learning style, wherever practical, increases their chances of educational success (Tobias 1996).

As well as relying on one particular style of learning, people also tend to use one of two styles of processing information: either analytic or global. Analytic learners process information by dividing it into pieces and organising it in a logical manner (e.g. making lists, putting things in order, following clear instructions or rules, completing/handing in work on time). Analytic learners prefer order and a planned, predictable sequence of events or ideas.

Global learners process information by grouping large pieces of information together and focusing on the main ideas rather than details (e.g. drawing spidergrams, using pictures or key words, ignoring or bending rules, including missing deadlines). Global learners prefer spontaneity and activities which allow them creative freedom.

Key terms

Visual learners – gather information through observation and reading, responding well to visual aids, such as pictures, diagrams and charts.

Auditory learners – gather information by listening carefully and then repeating instructions either out loud or mentally in order to remember what they have learned.

Kinaesthetic learners – gather information through touch and movement, benefiting from physical interaction with their environment with plenty of emphasis on *learning by doing*.

Activity

1 Think about a group of children that you work with. Are they visual, auditory or kinaesthetic learners? Think about how the children you work with gather information. Do they prefer to:
- work as an individual or in a group?
- follow step-by-step instructions or have open-ended projects?
- read and talk about work?
- engage in practical activities and experiment for themselves?

2 Think about how the children you work with process information. For example, are they analytic or global learners?

The benefits of acknowledging individual learning needs to identify support

It is vital that all children have access to a stimulating learning environment that enables them to learn in exciting and challenging ways. Intellectual stimulation through appropriate learning activities allows children to develop their intellectual abilities and to fulfil their potential as individuals.

Research into how children think and learn has made adults more aware of the need to observe and assess children's development very carefully, to listen to children and the way they express ideas and to take account of children's interests and experiences when planning learning opportunities.

The adult supports children's learning and development by:

- providing learning experiences within a meaningful context
- adapting tasks and learning experiences
- selecting appropriate materials for each child's needs and abilities
- encouraging children to make choices about what they want to do and when.

An understanding of intellectual development is essential for practitioners because it helps them to work with others in supporting learning activities through: a well-organised and structured learning environment; careful planning and preparation of learning activities; the provision of appropriate learning resources; effective communication with children during learning activities; high adult expectations for learner development; and accurate evaluation of learning activities and assessment of children's abilities.

Section 3: Plan and implement art, drama and music activities for children and/or young people

Encouraging creativity requires careful planning so that children and/or young people are helped to respond creatively to challenges that have been set for them. Practitioners need to place the activity in a context that will be relevant to their lives, select an interesting challenge and ensure that the children and/or young people have the necessary artistic skills to meet the challenge. Providing choice, ensuring the children and/or young people can work independently, encouraging teamwork, allowing experimentation and encouraging children and/or young people to persevere are key components of fostering creativity in art, drama and music (Sharp and Le Métais 2000, p. 9).

Planning and implementing activities to enhance children's development should be based on your observations of each child, your relationship with each child and your understanding of holistic development and learning. Effective planning for young children involves:

- viewing children as powerful and competent learners
- using your knowledge of children as active learners to inform your planning
- observing children closely and respecting them as individuals in order to plan rich, meaningful experiences
- recognising that an experience must be holistic to be meaningful and potentially rich in learning
- planning a rich learning experience around the whole child, not around a specific area of learning
- taking a holistic approach to the planning process by recognising and building on the child's needs, skills, interests and earlier experiences
- making your planning flexible and flow with the child.

(Abbott and Langston 2005)

(More detailed information about holistic development can be found in Chapter 5 'Understand child and young person development' in *CACHE Level 3 Diploma Children and Young People's Workforce: Early Learning and Child Care*, pp. 49–66.)

Key term

Holistic – looking at the 'whole' child or young person (e.g. *all* aspects of the child or young person's development).

Implementing curriculum plans involves working with other people (e.g. parents, colleagues and other professionals) to deliver the appropriate curriculum for the children in your setting. You should implement planned curriculum activities and experiences that meet the needs of the children in your setting by:

- providing a stimulating, enjoyable and carefully planned learning environment, including using indoor and outdoor spaces
- using everyday routines to enhance learning
- ensuring a balance between structured and freely chosen play
- supporting and extending play to encourage learning by using your knowledge of individual children and their preferred learning styles
- using appropriate materials and support strategies for each child's needs and abilities
- encouraging children's participation and providing assistance at an appropriate level for each child, including supporting children with special needs
- having high expectations of children and commitment to raising their achievement based on a realistic appraisal of their capabilities and what they might achieve
- encouraging children to make choices about their own learning
- changing and adapting plans as required to meet the needs of all the children.

Planning art, drama and music activities for children and/or young people

You will need to plan the provision of art, drama and music activities for the children you work with based on your assessment of their developmental progress. You should recognise that children's developmental progress depends on each child's level of maturation and their prior experiences. You should take these into account and have realistic expectations when planning activities and routines to promote children's development. (See Chapter 6 'Promote child and young person development' in *CACHE Level 3 Diploma Children and Young People's Workforce: Early Learning and Child Care*.)

This includes regularly reviewing and updating plans for individual children and ensuring that plans balance the needs of individual children and the group as appropriate to your setting. You should know and understand that children develop at widely different rates but in broadly the same sequence. When planning provision to promote children's development, you need to recognise that children's development is holistic, even though it is divided into different areas (e.g. **S**ocial, **P**hysical, **I**ntellectual, **C**ommunication and language, and **E**motional). You should remember to look at the 'whole' child. You need to look at *all* areas of children's development in relation to the particular aspect of development or learning you are focusing on when planning provision to promote children's development. (More detailed information is in Chapter 5 'Understand child and young person development' in *CACHE Level 3 Diploma Children and Young People's Workforce: Early Learning and Child Care.*)

Identifying the aims of art, drama and music activities

Following your observation and assessment of a child's development, learning and/or behaviour, your recommendations can provide the basis for planning appropriate activities to encourage and extend the child's skills in specific areas, such as art, drama and music. Effective planning is based on children's individual needs, abilities and interests, hence the importance of accurate and reliable child observations and assessments. Depending on the type of setting, you will also need to plan provision based on the requirements for the relevant curriculum frameworks for art, drama and music (see page 337).

You can also look at Figure 1.22 (the Planning cycle for observations and assessments of activities) on page 42.

When planning art, drama and music activities, your overall aims should include:

- supporting the care and development of *all* the children you work with
- ensuring every child has full access to the appropriate curriculum
- meeting children's individual developmental and learning needs
- building on each child's existing knowledge, understanding and skills.

In Practice

Describe how *you* plan the provision of art, drama and music activities to promote children's development in your setting. Include examples of any planning sheets you use.

Recognising individual needs when planning art, drama and music activities

When planning art, drama and music activities, it is essential to recognise the individual needs of children and/or young people. For example, the overarching principles of the EYFS emphasise the importance of taking individual needs into consideration when planning for children's early learning: 'Every child is a unique child…' and 'Children develop and learn in different ways and at different rates…' (DfE 2011, p. 4).

The unique child

This principle celebrates the uniqueness of every child and encourages practitioners to take the time to observe, listen and tune in to individual children, in order to understand what it is that makes each child tick. As young children's strengths, interests, preferences and different developmental pathways begin to unfold, practitioners can respond by planning to capture experiences that are meaningful and tailored to individual needs (Jaeckle 2008).

Children develop and learn in different ways and at different rates

Children learn from everything they do. The EYFS affirms that young children learn best through carefully planned, play-based experiences that start with their strengths, interests and capabilities. It acknowledges that young children are active learners and that they need opportunities to explore and make sense of the world, supported by knowledgeable, interested and sensitive adults. The EYFS places the child firmly at the heart of the learning experience and demands an informed approach to supporting children's learning and development, gained through observational assessment and genuine partnerships with parents (Jaeckle 2008).

Activity

Think about how planning in your setting is underpinned by the EYFS principles of 'Every child is a unique child…' and 'Children develop and learn in different ways and at different rates…'. For example:

- How does the setting celebrate the uniqueness of every child?
- Do practitioners take the time to observe, listen and tune in to individual children?
- How do practitioners identify the children's strengths, interests and preferences?
- How do practitioners identify the children's different developmental pathways?
- How do practitioners plan for meaningful experiences which are tailored to the children's individual needs?

Relating art, drama and music activities to other areas of learning

When planning art, drama and music activities, it is essential to relate each activity to at least one other area of learning. For example, one of the central principles of the EYFS emphasises the connections between all areas of learning and development: 'All areas of learning and development are important and are interconnected' (DfE 2011, p.4).

All areas of learning and development are important and are interconnected

This principle recognises that all areas of learning are interconnected and that, while children will need to be taught new skills, these should always be balanced by opportunities for them to independently apply, practise and combine their new learning through a well-resourced environment, inside and out (Jaeckle 2008).

How are art, drama and music activities connected to other areas of learning?

Learning in the expressive arts offers rich and exciting opportunities for combining art and design, dance, drama and music with other areas of the curriculum. Examples include dance activities that contribute to children and young people's physical activity; therefore the experiences and outcomes in dance can be linked with those for physical education. Films and DVDs provide opportunities to experience dance, drama, music, art and design within the context of a story. Children and young people will develop, enhance and apply skills gained in the expressive arts in a very broad range of activities, including role play and participation in whole-school events, community events and outdoor learning. Such activities promote the development of skills in areas such as talking and working with others and contribute to children and young people's mental, emotional, social and physical well-being (Education Scotland 2012, p. 4).

Activity

Think about how planning in your setting relates art, drama and music activities to other areas of learning. For example:

- How does the setting plan play-based experiences?
- How do practitioners plan art, drama and music activities?
- How are these activities connected to other areas of the relevant curriculum framework?

Implementing art, drama and music activities for children and/or young people

Good preparation and organisation are essential when implementing art, drama and music activities for children and/or young people. These may include: having any instructions and/or questions for the child or

Links to the EYFS	Art	Drama	Music
Personal, social and emotional development	Children learn to share and take turns to work cooperatively on a group project and to understand the rules of working in a group. It provides enjoyment, a sense of achievement, independence, autonomy and self-esteem. The sense of purpose is developed in older children when producing a piece of finished work. Painting, especially, allows children to express emotions that they may find difficult to put into words.	Children experience the roles of others. Children may play together in large and small groups and some activities require social interaction. Children take turns and share equipment. Children can display caring and social skills (e.g. nursing, parenting and showing hospitality) and explore different cultural backgrounds (e.g. the use of multicultural domestic equipment and clothes). Children start to form their own identity through role play. Children can express and release positive and negative emotions. It gives them confidence and allows self-esteem to develop. Playing roles empowers children and lets them glimpse and come to terms with the adult world.	Music is an opportunity to share experiences and to provide a musical introduction to diverse cultures. It is a non-competitive activity and helps build relationships. Children learn to share and take turns and to have consideration for others. Music encourages freedom of expression and the release of emotions such as pleasure, fear and frustration. It can be relaxing and therapeutic and can raise self-esteem and confidence, especially in older children when performing. Music and songs from all cultures will help children to develop positive feelings of acceptance and a sense of belonging and this also encourages respect.
Communication, language and literacy	New vocabulary is learnt, particularly positional language such as 'under' and 'over'. Understanding the instructions and asking questions develops comprehension and expressive speech. They can discuss what they are doing with an adult or another child. Printing encourages symbol recognition through mark-making. Symbolic blobs lead to the foundation of reading and writing.	Imaginative play stimulates language and the use of new vocabulary, particularly with the involvement of a sympathetic and sensitive adult. It promotes discussion of life experiences. Imaginative play presents opportunities for children to direct and organise activities, promotes creativity, and may lead to writing imaginative stories and plays. Symbolising everyday objects leads to an understanding of print.	Singing develops expressive language, articulation, vocabulary, diction and expressive use of the voice. Music develops listening skills and heightens a feeling for language, exploring a new means of expression.

Links to the EYFS	Art	Drama	Music
Problem solving, reasoning and numeracy	The exploration of materials, textures and techniques expands knowledge of colour and shapes. It helps children to understand spatial relationships and composition. Children use their imagination and creativity in planning and producing their artwork. Children's concentration span is often extended in a well-thought-out, enjoyable activity.	Domestic play offers mathematical experiences in matching and sorting and one-to-one correspondence, by laying tables and putting crockery and cutlery away in the correct place. Graded dolls and doll's clothes help children to understand the concepts of small, medium and large, and can give children a range of mathematical experiences. Imaginative play aids problem solving by encouraging a child to invent new ways of doing things.	Music aids memory, concentration, sequencing, classification and discrimination. There should be opportunities to match and copy sounds and movements.
Knowledge and understanding of the world	Children experiment with a variety of materials and observe the changes in the materials (e.g. mixing powder paints). The exploration and experimentation of different materials lead to an understanding of design and technology, as well as encouraging the effective and skilful use of tools. Creative art activities link in well with festivals and celebrations.	Imaginative play and drama activities present opportunities to participate in other cultures and encourage an appreciation of other children's life experiences.	Children will be interested in volume and vibration, and in exploring how and why sounds change, and in exploring the properties of various instruments.
Physical development	Painting at the easel develops large muscles in the arms of the younger child. As the child gains more control, fine motor skills are developed, aiding hand–eye coordination. Many of the materials and textures used in creative art activities will encourage tactile development, and colours will stimulate vision.	Imaginary play and drama activities can be very energetic, particularly when acting as superheroes. Large muscles are used when dressing up. Fine motor skills and hand–eye coordination are used in fastening clothes, dressing dolls, handling domestic equipment, and in playing with small-world toys.	Using instruments develops body and spatial awareness, balance, coordination and agility. Playing instruments and executing finger rhymes help to develop fine motor skills and hand–eye coordination. Hearing is sharpened by the practice of discriminating sounds. Touch is stimulated by handling well-made instruments.

Links to the EYFS	Art	Drama	Music
Creative development	Creative art activities stimulate aesthetic awareness of composition, colour, shape, patterns, spatial relationships and attractive materials. They encourage imagination and creativity, as well as the beginning of art appreciation.	Rich materials give tactile experiences (e.g. in handling clothing and fabrics). Using objects in imaginative ways, not necessarily for the function for which they were designed, helps children to have fun and indulge in fantasy, with no expected end result.	Music can be an anaesthetic and spiritual experience and is often uplifting.

Table 11.1 Art, drama and music – links to the EYFS (adapted from Hobart & Frankel, 2009)

group of children ready (e.g. prompt cards, worksheet, work card or written on the board); ensuring sufficient materials, including any specialist equipment; setting out the materials and equipment on the table ready or letting the children get the resources out for themselves, depending on their ages and abilities.

Implementing an activity may involve:

1 Giving out any instructions to the children.
2 Showing children what to do (e.g. demonstrate a new technique).
3 Keeping an individual child and/or group on task.
4 Clarifying meaning and/or ideas (e.g. explaining any difficult words or concepts to the children).
5 Assisting children with any special equipment (e.g. hearing aid or a Dictaphone).
6 Providing any other appropriate assistance.
7 Encouraging the children to tidy up afterwards as appropriate to the ages and abilities.
8 Remembering to maintain the children's safety at all times.

Evaluating the activities implemented in relation to children's learning

After you have planned and implemented the art, drama or music activity, you will need to evaluate it. Some evaluation also occurs during the routine or activity, providing continuous assessment of a child's performance. It is important to evaluate each activity so that you can:

- assess whether the activity has been successful (e.g. have the aims and objectives or outcomes been met?)
- identify possible ways in which the activity might be modified/adapted to meet the individual needs of the child or children
- provide accurate information for the senior practitioner, setting manager or other professionals about the success of a particular routine or activity.

The senior practitioner, setting manager or your college tutor/assessor should give you guidelines on how to present your activity plans. If not, you could use the suggested format on page 43 in Chapter 1.

In Practice

1. Plan an **art activity** for children and/or young people that will include: the aim of the activity; recognition of individual needs; how the activity relates to one other area of learning. (As the starting point for this activity, you could use your observation of a child drawing or painting, plus your suggestions to support children's art skills from page 354.)
2. Implement the art activity planned for children and/or young people.
3. Analyse the outcome of the activity implemented in relation to the children and/or young people's learning.
4. Evaluate the outcome of the activity implemented in relation to the aim and the one other area of learning identified.

In Practice

1. Plan a **drama activity** for children and/or young people that will include: the aim of the activity; recognition of individual needs; how the activity relates to one other area of learning. (As the starting point for this activity, you could use your observation of a child involved in a drama activity from page 356, plus your suggestions to support children's drama skills from page 358.)
2. Implement the drama activity planned for children and/or young people.
3. Analyse the outcome of the activity implemented in relation to the children and/or young people's learning.
4. Evaluate the outcome of the activity implemented in relation to the aim and the one other area of learning identified.

In Practice

1. Plan a **music activity** for children and/or young people that will include: the aim of the activity; recognition of individual needs; how the activity relates to one other area of learning. (As the starting point for this activity, you could use your observation of a child involved in a music activity from page 359, plus your suggestions to support children's music skills from page 360.)
2. Implement the music activity planned for children and/or young people.
3. Analyse the outcome of the activity implemented in relation to the children and/or young people's learning.
4. Evaluate the outcome of the activity implemented in relation to the aim and the one other area of learning identified.

Section 4: Reflect on own practice

Effective practice requires committed, enthusiastic and reflective practitioners with a breadth and depth of knowledge, skills and understanding. To be an effective, reflective practitioner, you should use your own learning to improve your work with children and their families in ways which are sensitive, positive and non-judgemental. Through initial and ongoing training and development, you can develop, demonstrate and continuously improve your:

- relationships with both children and adults
- understanding of the individual and diverse ways that children develop and learn
- knowledge and understanding in order to actively support and extend children's learning in and across all areas and aspects of learning
- practice in meeting all children's needs, learning styles and interests
- work with parents, carers and the wider community
- work with other professionals.

(DfES 2005)

Reflecting on the planning process for each art, drama and music activity

As a practitioner, you need to know and understand the techniques of reflective analysis: questioning what, why and how; seeking alternatives; keeping an open mind; viewing from different perspectives; thinking about consequences; testing ideas through comparing and contrasting; asking 'what if?'; synthesising ideas; and seeking, identifying and resolving problems (NDNA 2004).

Self-evaluation is needed to improve your own professional practice and to develop your ability to reflect upon activities and modify plans to meet the individual needs of the children and/or young people you work with. When evaluating your own practice you should consider the following:

- Was your own particular contribution appropriate?
- Did you choose the right time, place and resources?
- Did you intervene enough or too much?
- Did you achieve your goals (e.g. objectives/ outcomes for the child or children and yourself)?

If not, why not? Were the goals too ambitious or unrealistic?
- What other strategies/methods could have been used? Suggest possible modifications.
- Who should you ask for further advice (e.g. senior practitioner, setting manager, other professional)?

Reflecting on own practice in supporting the delivery and outcome of the activities

You need to know and understand clearly the exact role and responsibilities in supporting the delivery and outcome of art, drama and music activities. Review your professional practice by making regular and realistic assessments of how well your working practices match your role and responsibilities. Share your self-assessments with those responsible for managing and reviewing your work performance – for example, during your regular discussions/meetings with your colleagues or with your line manager. You should also ask other people for feedback about how well you fulfil the requirements and expectations of your role. You can also reflect on your own professional practice by making comparisons with appropriate models of good practice (e.g. the work of more experienced practitioners within the setting).

Drawing conclusions which show how to extend and refine future practice

You should work together with your colleagues and other professionals to create a learning community that includes art specialists, artists (e.g. painters, sculptors, illustrators, designers, actors, composers, musicians), parents, families, carers, teachers and educational consultants. You should assist parents and carers in understanding the importance of the arts and the role of the arts in supporting children's creativity in all aspects of their development. You should work with parents and carers in designing and implementing activities that will foster creativity in all aspects of their children's development.

You can extend and refine future practice by:

- planning arts activities that reinforce the learning activities within the appropriate curriculum, both in the setting and in the home (including cultural events and customs)
- knowing and understanding the arts curriculum within the setting
- being familiar with children's stages of development
- participating in art activities with children where they feel comfortable and where they feel their talents exist
- recognising that play is a critically important vehicle to children's social, emotional and cognitive development, as well as a reflection of their development
- guiding children and avoiding rigid performance or presentation rules and structures
- facilitating developmentally appropriate, child-initiated and child-centred activities in the arts
- providing guidance to young people on using materials (e.g. media, musical instruments and technology)
- providing activities and materials to create, perform and respond to their own and others' works of art
- providing ongoing opportunities and materials for creative reading and storytelling activities (e.g. puppet shows, books, stories read by adults, role playing)
- using a child's language in as many experiences as possible (e.g. labelling objects and works of art)
- recognising the child's efforts and works (e.g. displaying artwork and giving positive feedback) and having a place for all children's efforts, not just the 'best'
- recording and communicating each child's progress and achievements in the arts

- being a good listener and observer and encouraging others to be the same
- communicating regularly with parents, colleagues and other practitioners about arts activities
- being a strong advocate for quality arts education experiences
- participating in programmes which connect young children, older children, young people and older members of the community (such as grandparents).

(Goldhawk 1998, p. 5)

Activity

1 Give examples of how you reflect on the planning process, delivery and outcome of art, drama and music activities, including:

- self-evaluation
- reflections on your interactions with others
- sharing your reflections with others
- using feedback from others to improve your own evaluation.

2 Describe how you have used reflection to extend and refine future practice.

Useful resources

Organisations and websites

Arts on the move

This website provides a one-stop-shop for drama ideas for those working with children and young people of all ages.

www.artsonthemove.co.uk/index.php

Earlyarts

The national network for people working creatively with children and families in the arts, cultural and early years sectors.

www.earlyarts.co.uk

Education Scotland

This website provides detailed information about the expressive arts, including principles and practices, experiences and outcomes, as well as support materials.

www.educationscotland.gov.uk/learningteachingandassessment/curriculumareas/expressivearts/index.asp

Foundation Years

This website (developed by 4Children) is the 'one-stop-shop' for resources, information and the latest news on the foundation years. The website provides advice and guidance for practitioners on working effectively with parents as partners in their children's learning.

www.foundationyears.org.uk

National Grid for Learning Cymru

The teaching resources area of the NGfL Cymru website provides access to a range of teaching materials which can be selected according to age range and then subject (for example, click on 'Early Years', then 'Creative Development').

www.ngfl-cymru.org.uk/vtc-home.htm

Useful resources (cont.)

Progress in the Arts
This website provides support and guidance for delivering The Arts Area of Learning within the Northern Ireland Curriculum. It contains suggestions for activities in art and design, music and drama, from Foundation Stage through to Key Stage 3. www.nicurriculum.org.uk/microsite/the_arts.

Siren Films
Siren Films produces high-quality DVDs covering a wide range of topics, such as the first year of life, two-year-olds, three- and four-year-olds, learning through play, exploratory play, pretend play, outdoor play, and learning and development.
www.sirenfilms.co.uk.

Teaching Ideas
This website provides free ideas, resources, information and advice for teaching and learning, including art, drama (as part of speaking and listening) and music. www.teachingideas.co.uk.

Books

Abbott, L. and Langston, A. (2005) *Birth to three matters: supporting the framework of effective practice*, Maidenhead: Open University Press.

Americans for the Arts (2001) *Making the case to Congress for federal support of arts education, Arts Advocacy Day 2001, available at:* www.americansforthearts.org/get_involved/advocacy/aad/issue_briefs/2001/advocacy_issuebrief_004.asp (accessed May 2012).

Bance, L. (2012) *Music for early learning: songs and musical activities to support children's development*, London: Routledge.

Booth, D. and Hachiya, M. (eds) (2000) *The arts go to school: classroom-based activities that focus on music, painting, drama, movement, media, and more*, illustrated edition, Ontario: Pembroke Publishers Limited.

Bruce, T. (2011) *Cultivating creativity: for babies, toddlers and young children*, 2nd edition, London: Hodder Education.

Bruce, T. (2011) *Learning through play: for babies, toddlers and young children*, 2nd edition, London: Hodder Education.

DCSF (2008) *Statutory framework for the Early Years Foundation Stage: setting the standards for learning, development and care for children from birth to five*, London: Department for Children, Schools and Families.

DfE (2011) *Secondary curriculum subjects: art and design*, London: Department for Education, available at: www.education.gov.uk/schools/teachingandlearning/curriculum/secondary/b00199239/art (accessed April 2012).

DfE (2012) *Statutory framework for the Early Years Foundation Stage: setting the standards for learning, development and care for children from birth to five*, London: Department for Education, available at: http://media.education.gov.uk/assets/files/pdf/e/eyfs%20statutory%20framework%20march%202012.pdf (accessed April 2012).

DfES (2005) *Primary national strategy: KEEP – Key Elements of Effective Practice*, London: Department for Education and Skills, available at: http://dera.ioe.ac.uk/7593/1/pns_fs120105keep.pdf (accessed May 2012).

Drake, J. (2009) *Planning for children's play and learning*, London: David Fulton Publishers.

Education Scotland (2012) *Curriculum for excellence – expressive arts: principles and practice*, Edinburgh: Scottish Government, available at: www.educationscotland.gov.uk/Images/expressive_arts_principles_practice_tcm4-540037.pdf (accessed May 2012).

Useful resources (cont.)

Goldhawk, S. (1998) *Young children and the arts: making creative connections – a report of the task force on children's learning and the arts: birth to age eight, Washington:* Arts Education Partnership, available at: www.eric.ed.gov/PDFS/ED453968.pdf (accessed May 2012).
Griffiths, F. (2009) *Supporting children's creativity through music, dance, drama and art*, London: Routledge.
Hallam, S. (2010) 'The power of music: its impact on the intellectual, personal and social development of children and young people', *International Journal of Music Education,* 38(3): 269–289, available at: www.devon.gov.uk/dms-powerofmusic.pdf (accessed May 2012).
Hamblen, K.A. (1993) 'Theories and research that support art instruction for instrumental outcomes', *Theory into Practice,* 32(4): 191–198.
Hobart, C. and Frankel, J. (2009) *A Practical Guide to Activities for Young Children*, 4th edition, London: Nelson Thornes.
Hutchin, V. (2012) *The EYFS: A Practical Guide for Students and Professionals*, London: Hodder Education.
Jaeckle, S. (2008) 'The EYFS principles: a breakdown', *Early Years Update*, September, available at: www.teachingexpertise.com/articles/eyfs-principles-breakdown-4117 (accessed February 2012).
Jolley, R.P. (2010) *Children and pictures: drawing and understanding*, Oxford: Wiley-Blackwell.
Kamen, T. (2000) *Psychology for childhood studies*, London: Hodder & Stoughton.
Meggitt, C., Kamen, T., Bruce, T. and Grenier, J. (2011) *CACHE Level 3 Diploma: Children and young people's workforce: early learning and child care*, London: Hodder Education.
Melling, B. (2006) *Creative activities for the early years: thematic art and music activities*, Dunstable: Brilliant Publications.
National Advisory Committee on Creative and Cultural Education (NACCCE) (1999) *All our futures: creativity, culture and education*, London: Department for Culture, Media and Sport/Department for Education and Employment (this is a lengthy report – 243 pages – but a helpful summary is available at: www.creativetallis.com/uploads/2/2/8/7/2287089/all_our_futures_summary.pdf or you can access the full report at: http://sirkenrobinson.com/skr/pdf/allourfutures.pdf).
NDNA (2004) *National occupational standards in children's care, learning and development*, Brighouse: NDNA.
Ofsted (2012) *Making a mark: art, craft and design education*, Manchester: Office for Standards in Education, Children's Services and Skills, available at: www.education.gov.uk/publications/eOrderingDownload/110135.pdf (accessed May 2012).
Phillips, S. (1999) *Drama with children*, Oxford: Oxford University Press.
Sharp, C. and Le Métais, J. (2000) *The arts, creativity and cultural education: an international perspective*, London: Qualifications and Curriculum Authority, available at: www.inca.org.uk/pdf/finalreport.pdf (accessed May 2012).
Swale, J. (2009) *Drama games for classrooms and workshops*, London: Nick Hern Books.
Tobias, C. (1996) *The way they learn*, Colorado Springs: Focus on the Family Publishing.
Williams, D. (2007) *Creative art activities for the early years foundation stage*, Preston: Topical Resources.

Chapter 12 Learning about planning from a given framework of curricula (Unit CP 13)

The aim of this unit is to enable the learner to gain an understanding of planning for children or young people's learning within a given framework or curriculum.

Learning outcomes

1. Understand the rationale for working within given frameworks or curricula.
2. Understand a range of models used when planning for children and/or young people's learning.
3. Be able to plan to a framework or curriculum.

Section 1: Understanding the rationale for working within given frameworks or curricula

As a practitioner, you need to be able to understand the rationale for working within given frameworks or curricula. As appropriate to your particular role, you will need to plan, implement, monitor and evaluate curriculum plans according to the relevant curriculum framework(s) as appropriate to the ages, needs and abilities of the children you work with and the requirements of your setting. This includes preparing, implementing and monitoring curriculum plans according to the curriculum frameworks to support learning for your home country: England, Northern Ireland, Scotland or Wales.

When planning, implementing and evaluating curriculum plans, your overall aims should be to:

- support *all* the children you work with
- ensure each child has full access to the relevant curriculum
- encourage participation by all children
- meet children's individual learning and development needs
- build on children's existing knowledge and skills
- help all children achieve their full potential.

Key terms

Curricula – programmes of study provided by a school, college or other education setting.

Frameworks – structures for supporting the concepts, values and practices relating to the development, care and learning of children and/or young people.

Rationale – the logical basis for a course of action (e.g. the fundamental reasons for working within given frameworks or curricula).

Effective planning for children's learning is based on each child's individual needs, abilities and interests; this is why accurate observations and assessments are so important. (See Chapter 6: 'Promote child and young person development' in Meggitt *et al.*, 2011). These needs have to be integrated into the curriculum requirements for your particular setting and the age group(s) of the children you work with.

As appropriate to your particular role, you will need to prepare curriculum plans according to the curriculum frameworks for children and/or young people for your home country: England, Northern Ireland, Scotland or Wales. For example, in England, the curriculum framework for children is the Early Years Foundation Stage (0–5 years) or the National Curriculum (5–16 years).

Frameworks or curricula to support children's learning in England

The Department for Education is responsible for education and children's services in England.

The Early Years Foundation Stage

The Early Years Foundation Stage (EYFS) is the statutory framework that sets the standards for the care, development and learning of children from birth to five years old. All maintained and independent schools or registered early years providers in the private, voluntary and independent sectors caring for children from birth to five must use the EYFS. The current framework includes six areas covered by the early learning goals and educational programmes. None of these areas can be delivered in isolation from the others. They are equally important and depend on each other to support a rounded approach to child development. All the areas must be delivered through planned, purposeful play, with a balance of adult-led and child-initiated activities. The six areas of learning and development are:

- personal, social and emotional development
- communication, language and literacy
- problem solving, reasoning and numeracy
- knowledge and understanding of the world
- physical development
- creative development.

The revised 2012 Early Years Foundation Stage

A revised EYFS was implemented from September 2012. The revised EYFS 2012:

- simplifies the statutory assessment of children's development at age five
- simplifies the learning and development requirements by reducing the number of early learning goals from 69 to 17
- has a stronger emphasis on the three prime areas which are most essential for children's healthy development: communication and language; physical; and personal, social and emotional development
- has a new progress check at age two on their child's development for parents; this links with the Healthy Child review carried out by health visitors, so that children get any additional support they need before they start school
- strengthens partnerships between professionals and parents, ensuring that the new framework uses clear language.

(DfE 2012)

As a result of the Tickell Review, the revised EYFS includes a strong endorsement of the principles and themes of the original EYFS with support for play as the route through which the areas of learning should be delivered. There is also an increased focus on the characteristics of effective teaching and how children learn through developing the characteristics of learning: play and exploration; creating and critically thinking; and active learning. At the same time, it is made clear that play alone does not lead to successful learning and the supportive role of practitioners and parents is emphasised as fundamental in children's learning (Langston 2011).

In planning and guiding children's activities, practitioners should be guided by the different ways that children learn. Three characteristics of effective teaching and learning are as follows:

- **Playing and exploring** – children investigate and experience things, and 'have a go'.
- **Active learning** – children concentrate and keep on trying if they encounter difficulties, and enjoy achievements.
- **Creating and thinking critically** – children have and develop their own ideas, make links between ideas and develop strategies for doing things.

(DfE 2012, pp. 6 and 7)

Key term

Active learning – learning by doing; participation in activities in meaningful situations.

The EYFS principles are designed to celebrate the importance of play and learning, by putting the young child back at the heart of early years practice (Jaeckle 2008).

Four guiding principles should shape practice in early years settings:

- Every child is a unique child, who is constantly learning and can be resilient, capable, confident and self-assured.
- Children learn to be strong and independent through positive relationships.
- Children learn and develop well in an enabling environment, in which their experiences respond to their individual needs and there is a strong partnership between practitioners and parents and/or carers.
- Children develop and learn in different ways and at different rates. The framework covers the education and care of all children in early years provision, including children with special educational needs and disabilities.

(DfE 2012, p. 3)

*Every child is a **unique child**, who is constantly learning and can be resilient, capable, confident and self-assured.*

This principle celebrates the uniqueness of every child and advocates that practitioners take the time to observe, listen and tune in to individual children, in order to understand what it is that makes each child tick. As young children's strengths, interests, preferences and different developmental pathways begin to unfold, practitioners can plan responsively to capture experiences that are meaningful and tailored to individual needs. The EYFS encourages practitioners to constantly build on their previous best practice, through an ongoing process of reflection and self-evaluation to improve the quality of their provision. This means that practitioners also need to be aware of their own unique strengths, capabilities and learning preferences (Jaeckle 2008).

Figure 12.1 Every child is a unique child

In Practice

Think about how curriculum planning in your setting is underpinned by the principle of 'a unique child'. For example:

- ❑ How does the setting celebrate the uniqueness of every child?
- ❑ Do practitioners take the time to observe, listen and tune in to individual children?
- ❑ How do practitioners identify the children's strengths, interests and preferences?
- ❑ How do practitioners plan for meaningful experiences which are tailored to the children's individual needs?
- ❑ What are *your* unique strengths, capabilities and learning preferences?

Children learn to be strong and independent through ***positive relationships****.*

Creating a secure emotional environment is paramount if everyone in the setting is to flourish. No one learns effectively when they are worried or afraid; both adults and children should be able to try new experiences, explore new resources and share their thoughts and feelings in an atmosphere of mutual trust and respect. When we are encouraged to think creatively and know that our ideas and contributions will be valued, we develop positive attitudes to learning and confidence in ourselves as learners. Mistakes are then seen in a positive light, as a natural part of the learning

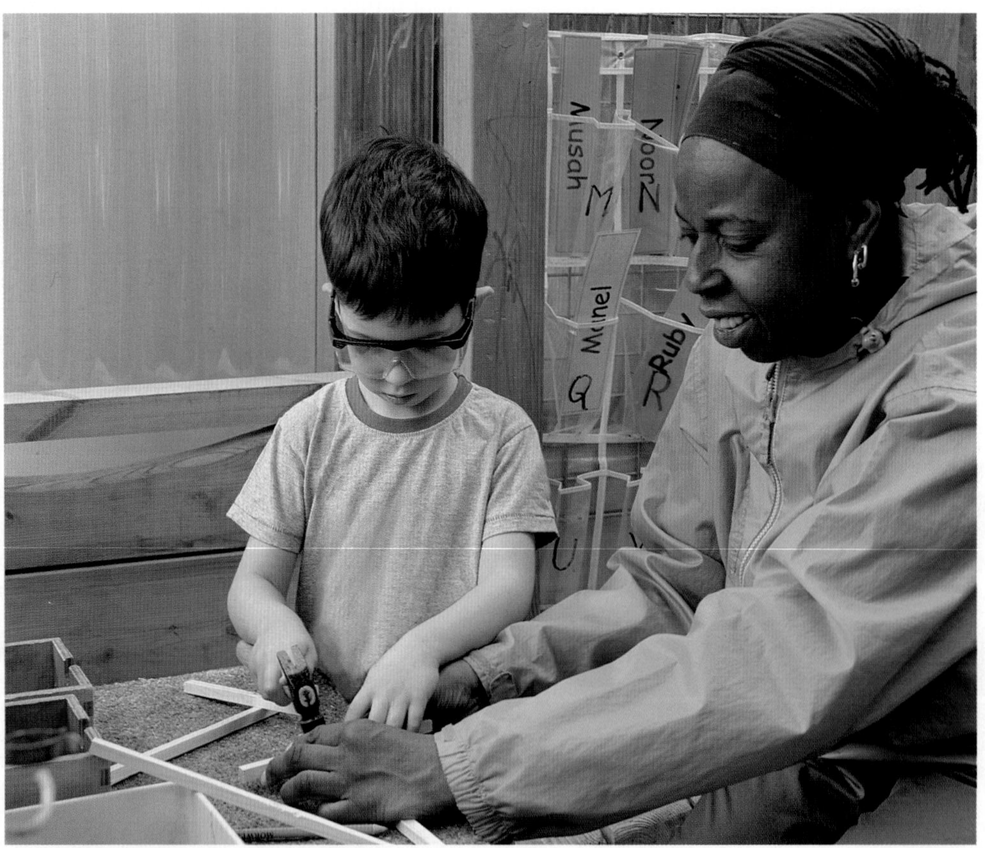

Figure 12.2 Children learn to be strong and independent through positive relationships

journey and an opportunity to grow and learn. A happy 'can do' attitude is infectious and everyone benefits – children, practitioners and parents (Jaeckle 2008).

In Practice

Think about how curriculum planning in your setting is underpinned by the principle of 'positive relationships'. For example:

- ❑ How does the setting create a secure emotional environment?
- ❑ Does the setting provide opportunities for both adults and children to try new experiences, explore new resources and share their thoughts and feelings?

Children learn and develop well in ***enabling environments****, in which their experiences respond to their individual needs and there is a strong partnership between practitioners and parents and/or carers.*

In the Reggio Emilia approach, the environment is sometimes referred to as the third teacher, and thoughtful planning, inside and out, is the key to really effective early years provision. The EYFS acknowledges the critical importance of both the emotional and the physical environment. Practitioners who view themselves as co-researchers working alongside the children will be able to see the environment from the child's point of view and

Figure 12.3 Children learn and develop well in enabling environments

reflect on the possibilities that it has to offer. When the environment is right, there is a contagious sparkle in the air, the children are deeply engaged in their learning and practitioners' confidence soars as they are free to support each child constructively on their learning journey (Jaeckle 2008).

In Practice

Think about how curriculum planning in your setting is underpinned by the principle of 'an enabling environment'. For example:

- ❏ Are there sufficient opportunities for children to get deeply involved, discover new lines of enquiry, experiment, explore and solve problems?
- ❏ Is the environment full of inspiration, with provocations for learning that will capture the child's imagination?
- ❏ Does the environment enable children to be independent and make their own choices of materials and resources?
- ❏ Are there quiet spaces where children can ponder and play, as well as larger, open spaces for them to test their new physical skills?

Children develop and learn in different ways and at different rates. *The framework covers the education and care of all children in early years provision, including children with special educational needs and disabilities.*

Figure 12.4 Children develop and learn in different ways and at different rates

Children learn from everything they do. The EYFS affirms that young children learn best through carefully planned, play-based experiences that start with their strengths, interests and capabilities. It acknowledges that young children are active learners and that they need opportunities to explore and make sense of the world, supported by knowledgeable, interested and sensitive adults. This principle recognises that all areas of learning are interconnected and that, while children will need to be taught new skills, these should always be balanced by opportunities for them to independently apply, practise and consolidate their new learning through a richly resourced environment, inside and out. The EYFS places the child firmly at the heart of the learning experience and demands an informed approach to supporting children's learning and development, gained through observational assessment and genuine partnerships with parents. (Jaeckle 2008)

In Practice

Think about how curriculum planning in your setting is underpinned by the principle of 'children develop and learn in different ways and at different rates'. For example:

- ❏ How do practitioners identify the children's different developmental pathways?
- ❏ How does the setting plan play-based experiences?
- ❏ How does the setting involve parents in the planning process?

There are seven areas of learning and development that must shape educational programmes in early years settings. There are three prime areas:

- personal, social and emotional development
- physical development
- communication and language.

Providers must also support children in four specific areas of learning and development, through which the three prime areas are strengthened and applied. The specific areas are:

- literacy
- mathematics
- understanding the world
- expressive arts and design.

Each area of learning and development must be implemented through planned, purposeful play and through a mix of adult-led and child-initiated activity. Play is essential for children's development, building their confidence as they learn to explore, to think about problems and to relate to others. Children learn by leading their own play and by taking part in play which is guided by adults. There is an ongoing judgment to be made by practitioners about the balance between activities led by children and activities led or guided by adults. Practitioners must respond to each child's emerging needs and interests, guiding their development through warm, positive interaction. As children grow older, and as their development allows, it is expected that the balance will gradually shift towards more activities led by adults, to help children prepare for more formal learning, ready for Year 1 (DfE 2012, p. 6).

Alongside the updated EYFS framework, there are additional support materials, including:

- guidance and exemplification for completing the Early Years Foundation Stage Profile
- best-practice models for presenting information from the progress check at age two
- a chart covering child development from birth to age five (covering both the prime and specific areas)
- a summary of the EYFS for parents.

The National Curriculum

The education system in England is undergoing major changes due to the coalition government. For example, the Education Bill was introduced into the House of Commons on 26 January 2011. The Education Bill takes forward the legislative proposals in the Schools White Paper (2010) *The Importance of Teaching*, which set out a reform programme for the schools system. For more information, see: www.education.gov.uk/aboutdfe/departmentalinformation/educationbill/a0073748/education-bill.

As part of the government's reform programme for schools, the Secretary of State for Education announced on 20 January 2011 that the government has launched a review of the National Curriculum in England with the aim of developing a coherent curriculum which supports transition from Key Stage 1 through to Key Stage 4. For more detailed information, visit: www.education.gov.uk.

The National Curriculum applies to children of compulsory school age in schools in England. The National Curriculum sets out the statutory requirements for the knowledge and skills that every child is expected to learn in schools. The National Curriculum framework enables practitioners to provide all school-aged children with challenging learning experiences, taught in ways that are both balanced and manageable. The National Curriculum sets out the standards to be used to measure the progress and performance of pupils in each subject to help practitioners plan and implement learning activities that meet the individual learning needs of pupils.

The National Curriculum sets out what pupils should study, what they should be taught and the standards that they should achieve. It is divided into four key stages:

- Key Stage 1: 5–7-year-olds (Year groups: 1 and 2)
- Key Stage 2: 7–11-year-olds (Year groups: 3, 4, 5 and 6)
- Key Stage 3: 11–14-year-olds (Year groups: 7, 8 and 9)
- Key Stage 4: 14–16-year-olds (Year groups: 10 and 11).

The primary curriculum

In Key Stage 1 and Key Stage 2, the National Curriculum consists of these compulsory subjects: English, mathematics, science, information and communication technology, design and technology, history, geography, art and design, music and physical education. In addition, there is a non-statutory framework for personal, social and health education (PSHE) and citizenship. Primary schools must also provide religious education, although parents may withdraw their children from this if they wish to do so. Primary schools must also provide sex education but again parents can withdraw their children from these lessons. For more information, see: http://education.gov.uk/publications/standard/KS1ES/Page1/QCA/99/457.

The secondary curriculum

In Key Stage 3 of the National Curriculum, the compulsory subjects are: English, mathematics, science, information and communication technology, design and technology, history, geography, art and design, music, physical education, citizenship and modern foreign languages.

In Key Stage 4, the compulsory subjects are: English, mathematics, science, information and communication technology and physical education. Secondary schools must make entitlement curriculum areas (e.g. the arts, design and technology, the humanities and modern foreign languages) available to all students who wish to study them. In addition, there is a new statutory requirement for work-related learning and a non-statutory framework setting out the minimum experience that schools should provide for work-related learning.

In Key Stages 3 and 4, there is a non-statutory framework for personal, social and health and economic education, as well as religious education, which is a statutory subject with a non-statutory programme of study. As in primary schools, parents may withdraw their children from religious education and sex education lessons if they wish to do so, except for the aspects of sex education (e.g. human reproduction) included as part of the science programme of study. For more information, see: http://education.gov.uk/publications/standard/publicationDetail/Page1/QCA/04/1374.

Why frameworks or curricula are required

Frameworks and curricula set out the statutory requirements for children's development and learning in early years settings and schools. For example, the Childcare Act 2006 requires the Secretary of State to specify learning and development requirements and welfare requirements for early years provision. The learning and development requirements are given legal force by an order made under Section 39

(1) (a) of the Childcare Act 2006. The safeguarding and welfare requirements are given legal force by regulations made under Section 39 (1) (b) of the Childcare Act 2006. Together, the order, the regulations and the statutory framework document make up the legal basis of the EYFS (DfE 2011a).

Frameworks and curricula provide structured approaches to supporting the learning of children and young people. They form the basis for each setting's curriculum planning, including how they meet the statutory requirements for all children and/or young people and any variations to meet the needs of individuals.

Activity

Explain why frameworks or curricula are required.

Why it is important to adhere to and work within given frameworks or curricula

As a practitioner, it is important that you understand and follow the frameworks or curricula which support the learning of the children that you work with. This includes knowing and following policies and procedures relating to teaching and learning. Every setting should have policies and procedures which put into practice the legal requirements under which they work. You should have access to copies of the policies and procedures relevant to your work in the setting. For example, in an early years setting, you should know what your role and responsibilities are to implement the EYFS.

Detailed information about a setting's curriculum planning can be found in: policy statements for the whole curriculum and for each area of the curriculum; schemes of work and teaching plans for each key stage; class or group timetables; weekly and daily planning grids; activity plans; and individual education plans.

Curriculum planning is the detailed process of working out how, and using what methods, a setting is going to put the relevant framework or curricula into practice in the day-to-day running. Curriculum planning should influence and determine decisions and actions relating to supporting learning and development.

The first stage in this is to create a curriculum policy. A curriculum policy provides a set of guidelines and these guidelines give a general overview of the kind of action which will be taking place in the setting and will be consistently followed by all staff members.

Curriculum policies provide the basis upon which more detailed procedures and plans can then be built. Curriculum policies also give practitioners an indication of what their particular roles and responsibilities are in implementing the policies. Curriculum policies are not only a legal requirement but they also distinguish the setting as a unique organisation tailored to the particular needs and abilities of its staff, children, their families and the local community.

As a practitioner, you need to ensure that children and/or young people are provided with activities at the appropriate level for their development and learning. For example, there should be a balance between encouraging younger children to develop their own problem-solving skills through play with minimal adult intervention and complying with the early learning goals in the EYFS.

Adhering to and working within the given frameworks or curricula which support the learning of the children and/or young people are important because they improve:

- the quality of the education provision
- the structure of the learning environment
- the provision of materials and equipment
- the communication between adults and children during learning experiences
- the adult expectations of children's development.

Adhering to and working within the given frameworks or curricula also increase the practitioner's awareness and understanding of the importance of: very carefully observing and assessing children's development; listening to children and the way they express ideas; and taking account of children's interests and experiences when planning learning opportunities.

Activity

Explain why it is important to adhere to and work within given frameworks or curricula.

Section 2: Understanding a range of models used when planning for children and/or young people's learning

You must prepare plans for supporting children and young people's learning according to requirements by basing your planning on information from the relevant curriculum documents (see above) and consulting with relevant colleagues. You should include children, parents and other professionals in the planning process as appropriate to your setting. You must ensure that your plans reflect anti-discriminatory practice and inclusive practice. (See the section 'Understand how to support diversity, inclusion and participation in early years settings' on pages 317–321 of Meggitt *et al.* 2011).

Key terms

Anti-discriminatory practice – taking positive action to counter discrimination and prejudice.

Inclusive practice – identifying barriers to participation and taking positive action to eliminate those barriers and encourage participation in the full range of activities provided by the setting.

Different curriculum planning models

Developing curriculum plans involves planning activities that provide all children and/or young people with appropriate opportunities to learn which reflect the range of needs, interests and the past achievements of individuals in each year group at each key stage. Curriculum plans include:

- **policy statements** showing the balance between different parts of the curriculum at each key stage or level of development
- **practical guidelines** for staff assisting the delivery of each curriculum subject (e.g. general information about resources and important teaching points)
- **long-term plans** showing the content and skills in the programmes of study for every area/subject at each key stage and how these are covered, including links between subjects as well as progression, consolidation and diversification for children across units
- **medium-term plans** defining the intended learning outcomes for units of work, including information on learning activities, recording and assessment methods
- **short-term plans** setting out detailed information on learning activities for children and/or young people in each group/class on a weekly and daily basis, including lesson plans and/or activity plans with details of specific targets, organisation, resources and strategies to support learning.

(QCA 2001)

You must draw up long-term, medium-term and short-term plans according to the requirements of the curriculum framework in your home country. Depending on your role and the setting, you will be involved in the planning and preparation of schemes of work and teaching plans by having regular planning meetings with colleagues (e.g. weekly, monthly, every half-term or once a term). You will need to prepare plans which take into account the pattern of children's attendance (e.g. part-time or full-time) and their need for a balanced programme of activities.

Effective planning involves the appropriate sequencing of the curriculum content and learning activities that build on children and young people's previous learning and achievements. Long-term and medium-term curriculum plans should show progression from year group to year group within each key stage. These plans enable practitioners to devise and implement learning activities in their short-term planning that promote progress and achievement for all children and/or young people.

Long-term plans

Long-term plans are usually drawn up in preparation for the year ahead. A long-term plan should provide an overview of the range of learning opportunities for children/young people and should include the content and skills in each curriculum area or subject – for example, the areas of learning in the Foundation Stage or the programmes of study for every subject at each key stage of the National Curriculum.

Long-term and medium-term curriculum plans set out the intentions for learning for each term, for each year group in a key stage. Practitioners may need to adjust the balance in the curriculum to focus on particular areas of learning so that their planning takes account of group or individual education plans. The setting will have long-term and medium-term plans for each curriculum area or subject. There will also be plans for other aspects of the curriculum, including:

- the development of literacy and numeracy skills (e.g. during specific literacy and numeracy activities/lessons, as well as opportunities to develop these skills in other subject areas)
- the development of personal and social skills (during lessons on PSHE, sex and relationship education, and citizenship)
- children's spiritual, moral, social and cultural development (e.g. during RE lessons and acts of collective worship, as well as through the school ethos and day-to-day activities).

Long-term plans may include an overall curriculum plan (usually linked to a topic or theme), demonstrating how the setting intends to encourage and extend children's learning within a curriculum framework (e.g. the Early Years Foundation Stage). Long-term plans should include links between subjects/areas of learning as well as progression, consolidation and diversification for children. Long-term plans should show progression for children's learning and development (e.g. from year group to year group within each key stage).

Many settings (including early education settings and schools) use a central topic or theme to link teaching and learning across the curriculum. A topic web can be a useful starting point for schemes of work and activity/lesson plans. Using a topic web can help ensure that you cover each area of the curriculum and emphasises an integrated approach to curriculum planning with play at the heart of children's learning and development.

An effective long-term plan for the Early Years Foundation Stage will usually include:

- an indication of when you plan to teach areas/aspects of learning
- an indication of how regularly you plan to teach areas/aspects of learning
- an indication of how you will link areas/aspects of learning in a relevant and interesting way for children (e.g. through themes or topics)
- special events and activities that provide a meaningful context and enhance learning (e.g. a visit to a city farm, a cultural or religious festival).

In Practice

Give examples of the long-term plans (e.g. overall curriculum plan, topic web) used within the curriculum framework applicable to the children and/or young people in your setting.

Medium-term plans

Some settings may only have long-term and short-plans with the content of medium-term plans included as part of their long-term plans. Other settings may use medium-term plans to bridge the gap between the outline of the long-term plan and detailed short-term plans. Medium-term plans define the intended learning outcomes for areas of learning or units of work, including information on learning activities, recording and assessment methods – for example, the intentions for learning for each school term, for each year group in a key stage.

Medium-term plans involve the detailed planning and preparation of schemes of work that are central to the effective delivery of the curriculum (especially in schools) and to the provision of appropriate support for children's learning. These plans enable staff to devise and implement learning activities in

Prime areas

Topic: All Around the World	**Personal, social and emotional development**	**Physical development**	**Communication and language**
	Role-play areas – Bedouin tent, Inuit igloo. Invite visitors to talk about other cultures and religions. Look at different national or religious costumes/head coverings. Circle times. Puzzles and games depicting pictures from around the world. Learn to say 'hello' in different languages. Make contact with an early years setting in another country and write/draw pictures to them. Collect water in containers in the garden and talk about the importance of water in different countries and how we need to use water carefully. Stories and songs.	Simple origami. Use chopsticks. Dressing up in different costumes from other countries. Have a go at tai chi or yoga. Play children's games from other countries. Action songs from around the world. Carry things in baskets on your head/water in a bucket/bundles of washing on your back. Dance to music from around the world.	Role-play areas – Bedouin tent, Inuit igloo, market stall from another country, sari shop. Collect artefacts from around the world – Russian dolls, African drums or masks, bells, Indian sari material, etc. Memory games – 'I went to market and I bought…'. Holiday photos from abroad. Small-world toys – e.g. airport. Boats to travel in water tray/desert in sand tray. Stories and songs from other countries. Storytelling using props. Talk about festivals and celebrations from other countries.
Literacy	**Mathematics**	**Understanding the world**	**Expressive arts and design**
Tell stories of journeys using these props. Book making. Storytelling with props and puppets. Get relatives who are abroad to send postcards – display them on a world map. Arabic and Chinese writing. Make up a global alphabet using words associated with other countries. Books, rhymes and songs from other countries. Non-fiction books.	Russian dolls and other things that fit inside each other. Foreign coins. Role-play areas – shops from other countries, e.g. African market stall and Indian sari shop. Patterns and shapes – Mehndi and rangoli patterns from India/Tangrams from China. Look at the patterns on different national flags. Sorting artefacts to their appropriate country. Counting songs and books from other countries. Learn to count to five or 10 in another language.	World maps, globes and atlases. Role-play areas – Bedouin tent, Inuit igloo, sari shop. Taste food from other countries – Indian sweets, German Stollen cake, French croissants, Chinese rice, etc. Label a world map with children's names of places they have been/their relatives live. Link up with a setting from another country and write/send pictures to them. Posters and pictures showing scenes from other countries. Collection of hats from other countries – sombrero, Australian bush hat, Russian fur hat, British sun hat, etc. Hold a Japanese tea ceremony. Sand and water play. Discuss the importance of water to everyone.	Role-play areas. Play with Indian sari material. Music from around the world. Songs from around the world. Instruments from other countries. Make Japanese folded paper fans. Face painting – look at how people in other countries decorate their bodies. Weaving. Chinese writing. African print making. Make clay pots.

Specific areas

Figure 12.5 Topic web based on the 2012 Early Years Foundation Stage (adapted from an article by J. Mickelburgh from: http://www.eyfs.info/resources/topics/topic.php?Around-the-world-4)

their short-term planning that promote progress and achievement for all children. Staff may need to adjust the balance in the curriculum to focus on particular areas of learning so that their planning takes account of group or individual education plans.

Medium-term plans also include:

- **a group/class timetable** outlining when and where the play and learning activities will take place, periods when children can rest and restore energy (e.g. story time), and routines that must be done at specific times (e.g. registration, break/ playtime, lunchtime, tidying-up time, home time)
- **practical guidelines** for staff assisting the delivery of each curriculum subject or area of learning (e.g. general information about resources and important teaching points)
- **structured learning programmes for individual children**, including particular activities to encourage the development of children with special educational needs (e.g. individual education plans).

Individual education plans

All childcare and education settings should differentiate their approaches to activities to meet the needs of individual children/young people. The strategies used to enable individual children with special educational needs (SEN) to make progress during learning activities should be set out in an individual education plan (IEP) whether they receive additional support in the school as part of Early Years Action, Early Years Action Plus or a statement of special educational need.

Key term

Special educational needs – all children/young people have *individual* needs, but some children may have *additional* needs due to physical disability, sensory impairment, learning difficulty or emotional/behavioural difficulty.

A child or young person's IEP should identify three or four individual targets in specific key areas – for example, communication, literacy, numeracy or behaviour and social skills. When helping to develop individual educational plans, remember to have high expectations of children and a commitment to raising their achievement based on a realistic appraisal of children's abilities and what they can achieve. You may be involved in regular reviews of individual educational plans in consultation with the child or young person's class teacher/form tutor, the SENCO, the child/young person and their parents (e.g. at least three times a year).

A child or young person's IEP should include the following information:

- the child or young person's strengths
- priority concerns
- any external agencies involved
- background information, including assessment details and/or medical needs
- parental involvement/child participation
- the short-term targets for the child/young person
- the provision to be put in place (e.g. resources, strategies, staff, allocated support time)
- when the plan is to be reviewed
- the outcome of any action taken.

Documentation and information about the Special Educational Needs Code of Practice, including Early Years or School Action, Early Years or School Action Plus and Statutory Assessment, should be available from the school office or the SENCO.

In Practice

Give examples of the medium-term plans (e.g. schemes of work, timetables, IEPs) used within the curriculum framework applicable to the children and/or young people in your setting.

Short-term plans

Short-term plans should be based on the long-term plan *and* ongoing observations and assessments of children, as well as discussions with colleagues and parents. You should use this information to plan appropriate activities and experiences for children. Short-term plans set out detailed information about play and learning activities for each class, group or individual child on a weekly and daily basis, including lesson or activity plans with details of specific learning objectives or intentions for the children based on the

<table>
<tr><th colspan="4">Individual Education Plan</th></tr>
<tr><td>Name</td><td>Fred Jones</td><td>Stage</td><td>Statutory Assessment</td></tr>
<tr><td>Area/s of Concern</td><td>Literacy, Maths, Behaviour</td><td>Year Group/IEP No.</td><td>Year 2, Class 7/IEP No 2</td></tr>
<tr><td>Class Teacher</td><td>Mrs J Smith</td><td>Start Date</td><td>April 2010</td></tr>
<tr><td>Supported by</td><td>Mr H Brown (TA)</td><td>Review Date</td><td>June 2010</td></tr>
<tr><td>Proposed Support</td><td>Twice a week</td><td>Support Began</td><td>October 2009</td></tr>
<tr><td colspan="3">Targets to be Achieved:
1. To read/spell c-v-c words with vowel sounds 'a' and 'o'.
2. To understand and use number bonds to 10.
3. To sit still on the mat during class/group sessions.
4. To give verbal answers of more than one word.</td><td>Achieved:
1.
2.
3.
4.</td></tr>
<tr><td colspan="4">Achievement Criteria:
1. Accurate when tested at random on three separate occasions.
2. Use number bonds to answer sums accurately on three separate occasions.
3. Achieved on 6 out of 10 occasions over a period of a week.
4. Achieved on 4 occasions.</td></tr>
<tr><td colspan="4">Possible Resources and Techniques:
1. Wooden/plastic letters. Phonic workbooks. Card games. Computer programs. Tracking. Dictation.
2. Additions games e.g. bingo, snap, dice game. Lists of number bonds for reference. Textbooks/worksheets.
3. Clear expectations of behaviour at story time/discussion time. Reward chart.
4. Open-ended questions.</td></tr>
<tr><td colspan="4">Possible Strategies to use in Class:
1. Encourage Fred to write the sounds he hears in a spoken word and to read c-v-c words accurately.
2. Set verbal and written questions for practising using number bonds. Provide apparatus for support if needed.
3. Minimise the time spent sitting still at first, gradually build up. Seat Fred away from distractions.
4. Question and answer sessions. Encourage full sentence answers.</td></tr>
<tr><td colspan="4">Ideas for Support Teacher or Teaching Assistant:
1. Use multi-sensory methods for teaching c-v-c words. Set rhyming activities.
2. Provide practical activities to practise number bonds e.g. find different ways of splitting 10 objects.
3. Look at the reward chart with Fred. Praise achievement.
4. Use individual discussion.</td></tr>
<tr><td colspan="4">Parents/Carers need to:
Make sure the words sent home are practised.
Use money to add to 10p.
Encourage Fred to speak in whole sentences.</td></tr>
<tr><td colspan="4">Pupil needs to:
Try to apply spellings he has learnt to his own written work.
Try to sit still.
Try to speak in whole sentences.</td></tr>
</table>

Figure 12.6 Example of individual education plan (from *Teaching Assistant's Handbook Level 3*, page 257, Hodder Education, 2011)

early learning goals as appropriate to each child's level of development. Short-term plans should also include details of the proposed implementation of each activity, including organisation and staff required, resources needed, including any specialist equipment, and strategies to be used to support children's learning and development.

Short-term planning provides the details of activities to support learning on a weekly, daily and lesson-by-lesson basis. To plan appropriate activities, you need to:

- identify the intended learning outcomes that promote inclusion, participation and achievement for all children
- use information about children's interests, skills and prior achievements to structure the content and progress of activities/lessons
- take into account children's individual learning needs, including their different learning styles
- include targets from individual education plans for children with special educational needs
- define the roles and responsibilities of those involved
- ensure that adequate and appropriate resources are available
- use ICT to support children's learning and development.

Short-term plans should include an appropriate balance between familiar activities and new learning challenges. Children and young people need to be motivated and stimulated by a wide range of activities to support learning in a variety of contexts. Some children/young people may need frequent repetitions of the same activity in the same context so that they begin to notice events and start to learn. Others may need to repeat similar experiences over an extended period. A particular activity may remain relevant to a group for many months or even years, but its context should be modified according to the subject, motivation, current interest and age of the children and/or young people. This is especially relevant to supporting children/young people with learning difficulties. (Information about supporting children with disabilities can be found on pages 188–194 in Chapter 11 of Meggitt *et al.* 2011.)

Children and young people have different learning styles and will learn at different rates. They will have different preferences for the presentation of learning activities and materials. For example, they may prefer to learn through visual, auditory or kinaesthetic stimuli. Planning for learning activities needs to take account of these learning needs. (See Chapter 11, page 366.)

Working with others is an important aspect of learning. Short-term planning can help practitioners to group children together during different activities to support learning in a variety of ways: whole class, cross-class groups (e.g. within the same year group), ability sets, mixed-ability or 'friendship' groups, pairs or one-to-one (adult and child/young person).

The new EYFS framework makes clear that practitioners should observe and respond to each child in their care on an ongoing basis. It gives a broad steer that there should be a focus on prime areas for younger children, with gradual building-in of support in the specific areas for older age ranges, as children develop, and as appropriate to their individual level of development and progress. This reflects the importance of the prime areas of learning for other areas, but practitioners should of course be flexible in their approach, responding to each child as an individual. There is nothing in the framework that holds back a practitioner from introducing specific areas to a particular child's learning experience earlier than they might for other children, if they judge that to be appropriate. Experiences which support younger children's learning in the prime areas, moreover, will also support their learning in the specific areas. Sharing rhymes and picture books, for example, lays the foundations for reading and writing, as well as for communication and language (DfE 2011b, Section 4).

An effective short-term plan for young children will usually include:

- clear learning intentions for individual or groups of children informed by observations and based on the early learning goals
- a brief description of the range of activities and experiences, including adult-directed and child-initiated activities, indoors and outdoors
- how activities and experiences can be adapted for individual or groups of children

Example of planning based upon children's interests

EYFS: Planning for continuous provision and children's experiences

Key points from observations week ending: ____________
Zara: Using the train set and mimicking/verbalising alongside adult, moving in response to music, using emerging language to communicate.
Tilly: Investigating balls/cylindrical objects, using/exploring dolls and pushchair.
Jimmy: Stacking with blocks and constructing/deconstructing towers, moving rhythmically to music, using emerging vocal sounds to communicate.

Additions to Continuous Provision/The Physical Environment | **Focused Activities and Experiences**

Resources	Adults Role/Effective Practice	Activities and Experiences	Adult's Role/Effective Practice
A range of different-sized/textured balls.	Resources relating to circles, balls and sphere-shaped objects, introduce a 'Lazy Susan' to the floor space. Introduce circular floor mats – indoors/outdoors. Introduce bells sealed inside a hamster ball – indoors/outdoors.	**Support play – rolling balls to and fro, introducing a range of different sizes, textures and noises throughout the week.** **Building towers with small blocks.**	Note what it is that Tilly enjoys. Is it the rolling motion or circular objects in general? What is her response to the addition of bells? Involve Jimmy in this much-loved activity, encourage others to participate, note children's ability to stack one item upon another.
Train set	**Support Zara's play/exploration and encourage parallel play with other children to support her development of positive relationships during the first weeks at a new setting.**	Use music of varying pace and rhythm throughout the week for children to move in response to music. In all situations, support and encourage children's emerging communication skills, both gesture and verbal (babbling/forming first words).	Observe carefully – what styles of music do the children respond to most expressively? Calm, quiet, loud, fast etc.
Dolls and pushchairs	Engage in imaginative play initiated by the children and model the dolls enjoying healthy snack- and mealtimes to support/encourage Tilly to engage in a wider variety of foods.		Note which stage of language development your key children may be at.

Links to EYFS

PSED: Learn that their voices and actions have effects on others/feel safe and secure within healthy relationships with key people.
CLL: Enjoy babbling and increasingly experiment using sounds and words to represent objects around them.
PSRN: Through their manipulations of objects.
PD: Use increasing mobility to connect with toys, objects and people.
CD: Move their whole bodies to sounds they enjoy, such as music or a regular beat.

PSED: Show a strong sense of self as a member of different communities, such as their family or setting.
CLL: Use single-word and two-word utterances to convey simple and more complex messages.
PSRN: Use blocks to create their own simple structures and arrangements.
KUW: Are curious about the environment.
PD: Express themselves through action and sound.
CD: Begin to move to music, listen to or join in with songs and rhymes.

Figure 12.7 Example of planning based upon children's interests
Source: http://www.ndna.org.uk/

Activity plan: Around the World Story Bag **Date:**

EYFS link(s):
Main focus on the prime area – communication and language.

Learning objectives:
Extend children's vocabulary, exploring the meanings and sounds of new words.
Use language to imagine and recreate roles and experiences.

Resources:
A colourful and exotic-looking bag.
Five artefacts from other countries put into the bag – e.g. a French croissant, an African drum, an Indian sari, a Japanese fan, a Mexican hat.
A story rug and cushions to sit on.

How the activity will be carried out:
Invite the children to sit on the story rug. Explain to them that they are going to help tell a story that takes them all around the world. Show them the bag and tell them that it contains some things to help us tell the story. To begin with, which country are we in? (England). What do we know about England? What is the weather like? What is the food like? What do we like to do? Where are we going next? Ask a child to choose something from the bag. What have they chosen? A croissant. Where is it from? How did we get to France? What time of day do they eat croissants? What do we like about France? Then choose another object… What shall we do in Mexico? Continue to support the children as they use the objects to talk about each country. When the last object has been chosen and discussed, ask them how they would like to travel back home. Is it good to be back?

Questions to ask:
Different places – what do you see?
How did we get here?

Language to use:
Travel, journey, smells, sounds, things to do, things to eat.

Differentiation (birth to three):	**Extension:**
Give the children the opportunity to explore the objects in the bag. Make breakfast with the croissants, wear a hat, play the drum, etc.	Put together a different story bag and leave the rug and cushions out in a quiet space as a place where the children can go to tell their own 'around the world' stories. Add books about other countries.

Evaluation:

Figure 12.8 Example of an activity plan (adapted from focus plan by J. Mickelburgh from: http://eyfs.info/cmsAdmin/uploads/CLL-Around-the-World-Story-Bag.pdf)

- how the children will be organised
- the resources and equipment required
- the role of the adult(s), including parents
- questions and/or vocabulary that the adult(s) will use during the activity
- opportunities for observation and informal assessments of individual or groups of children.

In Practice

Give examples of the short-term plans (e.g. activity plans, lesson plans) used within the curriculum framework applicable to the children and/or young people in your setting.

Involving children in planning activities

Being flexible and allowing for children's choice in planning activities help their learning and development by promoting: discussion and effective communication skills; cooperative group work; opportunities for first-hand experiences and exploration; and information skills (including referencing skills, finding and using different resources).

High/Scope

Some early years settings take children's involvement in planning as the central basis for structuring their learning activities. The High/Scope philosophy encourages children to make decisions about their own choice of activities by involving them in the planning, doing and reviewing of activities. The children still participate in some adult-directed activities, such as story time, PE and other larger group activities, as well as work to develop specific skills, such as literacy and numeracy in small groups or as individuals. (See section from page 403 on adult-directed activities.)

The High/Scope 'plan–do–review' cycle of planning looks something like this:

1. **Plan**: in a small group with an adult, children discuss which activities they intend to do that session. For example, a child might say: 'I'm going to build a sandcastle first, next I will paint a picture for my mum and then I will play in the shop.'
2. **Do**: the children participate in the activities of their choice and are encouraged to talk during this time, with adults helping to extend the children's language and learning.
3. **Review**: at the end of the session, the group come together again to look back on the session's activities, including talking about what they liked best and giving reasons why they made any changes to their original choices. For example, a child might say: 'I enjoyed making a really big sandcastle with my friend Tom. Then I painted a red dinosaur for my mum. I didn't play in the shop today as Tom wanted to play with the cars instead. We made a great big traffic jam with all the cars and trucks!'

The Montessori method

Maria Montessori (1869–1952) was an Italian educator and physician who became one of the best known and most influential early childhood educators. She began by working with children with special needs. She designed carefully graded self-teaching materials which stimulate children's learning through the use of their senses. Montessori believed that children learn best by doing things independently without adult interference and children also concentrate better when engaged in a self-chosen activity. Adults working with young children need to be specially trained to give the appropriate support to children's independent learning. The learning environment was considered to be especially important. Montessori believed the equipment should be specifically designed for children (e.g. small, child-sized furniture, kitchen utensils, tools) and that children should have freedom to move and explore their environment. Central to the Montessori methodology are the specialised Montessori learning materials – carefully designed and beautifully made equipment to encourage young children's development, knowledge, understanding and practical skills.

Steiner education

Rudolf Steiner (1861–1925) was a philosopher and scientist who inspired a worldwide movement of schools that promote meaningful teaching and learning opportunities. The ideas and principles which inform a Steiner education provide an

Figure 12.9 The Montessori method

unhurried and creative learning environment where equal attention is given to the physical, emotional, intellectual, cultural and spiritual needs of each child and that is designed to work in harmony with the different phases of the child's development. The core subjects of the curriculum are taught in thematic blocks and all lessons include a balance of artistic, practical and intellectual content. Whole-class, mixed-ability teaching is the norm. A Steiner education takes account of the needs of the whole child and sees artistic activity and the development of the imagination as integral to learning. A Steiner education provides children and young people with opportunities to develop a strong sense of self with varied skills that enable them to become independent and socially responsible adults (SWSF 2008).

In Practice

Give examples of children and/or young people's involvement in planning activities within the curriculum framework applicable to your setting.

The benefits of each curriculum planning model described in relation to supporting the delivery of children and/or young people's learning

Advanced planning and the detailed preparation of work are central to the effective delivery of the curriculum and to providing appropriate support for both teaching and learning. Practitioners should involve others (e.g. colleagues, students and parent helpers) in the planning and preparation of their work by having regular planning meetings about once a term or every half term. In addition, each day the practitioner and other members of their team should discuss:

- the activities planned for that day/session

Figure 12.10 Steiner education

- the objectives of the activities
- each team member's contribution to the activities
- the type and level of support for the children and/ or young people
- the specific strategies for supporting activities.

When planning and implementing learning activities for children, you should ensure that you make accurate and detailed records of what has been planned and/or implemented in order to: clarify the aims and learning objectives of activity plans; avoid contradictory strategies and unnecessary duplication of work; use the time available more effectively; evaluate the success of plans/activities; and provide continuity and progression for future planning.

Regular planning meetings and discussions will help to avoid confusion as the practitioner and others in the team will be clear about the exact tasks to be performed and the level of support to be provided. Short discussions after activities are also helpful to provide feedback about the progress of children during group- or individual-learning activities. This feedback can make a valuable contribution to the assessment of children and help with the future planning of activities to support learning.

There should be very close teamwork in the setting and all staff should know all the children. There should be continual liaison between members of staff. You should liaise with others who will use your assessment information to inform planning for the children concerned. Some reporting to colleagues may be verbal and all records should be passed on to the relevant member of staff (e.g. the child's next teacher). Working with senior colleagues, you will need to ensure that full and complete records are provided for the new setting when children transfer to another nursery or primary school. You must follow your setting's policies and procedures for sharing information, including any confidentiality and data protection requirements. (See the section 'The principles and practices relating to confidentiality' on pages 13–16 in Chapter 1 of Meggitt *et al.* 2011.)

Figure 12.11 Planning meeting with colleagues

You should report children's progress to their parents on a regular basis depending on the requirements of your setting. You should provide information about their children's achievements and targets for future development and learning, as well as any difficulties they may have. This may include, in consultation with children and parents, seeking additional support from appropriate sources if children are not progressing as expected and, where necessary, referring to external agencies.

In Practice

1. Outline your setting's policy and procedures for reporting children's progress to colleagues and other professionals.
2. What are your responsibilities for reporting children's progress to colleagues and other professionals?
3. What are your responsibilities for reporting children's progress to their parents?

When planning and implementing activities to support learning, your overall aims should be to:

- support all the children you work with according to the relevant framework (e.g. EYFS)
- ensure each child has full access to the curriculum
- encourage participation by all children
- meet children's individual learning needs
- build on children's existing knowledge and skills
- enable all children to achieve their full learning potential.

Evaluating each model identified in relation to clarity of information and ease of use within the workplace

Evaluating planning models to support children's development and learning will help you to identify implications for practice – for example: ensuring assessment opportunities are built into the planning provision to promote children's development and learning; providing support for individual staff members as necessary; and reviewing assessment outcomes and data in order to evaluate overall standards throughout the setting.

Monitoring and reflecting on the implementation of curriculum frameworks involve developing monitoring strategies and documentation as required by the relevant curriculum framework in your home country. You should regularly communicate with parents and colleagues to support monitoring of curriculum frameworks. You should check that each area of the curriculum is implemented to a consistent quality according to the requirements of your setting and the relevant inspection regime. You should monitor the participation and learning of all the children in the setting. You should reflect on your practice in the light of your work in planning and implementing curriculum frameworks.

In Practice

Outline the monitoring strategies and documentation required by the curriculum framework relevant to your setting. Include information on how you:

- ❏ communicate with parents/colleagues
- ❏ monitor children's participation and learning
- ❏ reflect on practice.

Keeping planning flexible

Despite careful planning, you may find that a learning activity is not appropriate for all the children you are working with. You need to monitor children's responses to learning activities and take appropriate action to modify or adapt activities to achieve the intended learning goals/objectives or provide additional activities to extend their learning. You may need to provide an alternative version of the activity or you might be able to present the materials in different ways or offer a greater/lesser level of assistance. You may need to modify or adapt learning activities for the following reasons:

- The child lacks concentration.
- The child is bored or uninterested.
- The child finds the activity too difficult or too easy.
- The child is upset or unwell (if so, you may need to abandon/postpone the activity).

Children's responses should also be considered when providing support for learning activities. You should be sensitive to children's needs and preferences. You should take notice of non-verbal responses and preferences demonstrated by the children; these are just as important as what they say. Remember to give the children positive encouragement and feedback to reinforce and sustain their interest and efforts in the learning process. You can use children's positive or negative responses to modify or extend activities to meet each child's needs more effectively. For example, if the learning intentions prove too easy or too difficult, you may have to set new goals. By breaking down learning activities into smaller tasks, you may help individual children to achieve success more quickly. In modifying plans, you are continuing a cycle of planning and implementing activities.

Even in settings where children are working within the National Curriculum framework or towards the 'early learning goals', your planning needs to be flexible enough to allow for children's individual interests and unplanned, spontaneous opportunities for promoting children's development and learning. For example, an unexpected snowfall can provide a wonderful opportunity to talk about snow and for children to share their delight and fascination for this type of weather. Or a child might bring in their collection of postcards, prompting an unplanned discussion about the collections of other children; this might be developed into a 'mini-topic' on collections if the children are really interested. It is important that children have this freedom of choice to help represent their experiences, feelings and ideas. Adults may still be involved in these activities, but in more subtle ways, such as encouraging children to make their own decisions and talking with children while they are engaged in these types of activities.

Figure 12.12 Flexible planning

In Practice

How have you made use of an unplanned learning opportunity?

Section 3: Planning to a framework or curriculum

The children you work with will be constantly thinking and learning – for example, gathering new information and formulating new ideas about themselves, other people and the world around them. When implementing curriculum plans, you should provide children with opportunities to: explore their environment and/or investigate new information/ideas; discover things for themselves through a wide variety of experiences; feel free to make mistakes in a safe and secure environment using 'trial and error'; develop autonomy through increased responsibility and working independently; encourage and extend their knowledge and skills with appropriate support from adults (and other children); and learn to make sense of new information within an appropriate curriculum framework.

It is vital that *all* children have access to a stimulating environment which enables learning to take place in exciting and challenging ways. To develop into healthy, considerate and intelligent adults, all children require intellectual stimulation, as well as physical care and emotional security. Intellectual stimulation through play and other learning opportunities allows children to develop their cognitive abilities and fulfil their potential as individuals. Planning and implementing activities to enhance young children's development should be based on your observations of each child, your relationship with each child and your understanding of holistic learning. Effective planning for young children involves:

- viewing children as powerful and competent learners
- using your knowledge of children as active learners to inform your planning
- observing children closely and respecting them as individuals in order to plan rich, meaningful experiences
- recognising that an experience must be holistic to be meaningful and potentially rich in learning
- planning a rich learning experience around the whole child, not around a specific area of learning
- taking a holistic approach to the planning process by recognising and building on the child's needs, skills, interests and earlier experiences
- making your planning flexible and flow with the child.

(Abbott and Langston 2005)

Planning for child-initiated activities

Play provides opportunities for children to choose activities in which they can interact with other children or adults, or sometimes play alone. During these activities, children learn by first-hand experience – by actively 'doing'. Children experience play physically and emotionally. Young children especially need sufficient space, time and choice with a range of play activities, both indoors and outdoors. Using their observations of individual children's current interests, developmental needs and play needs, practitioners should plan and prepare opportunities for child-initiated play, as well as adult-directed activities (from page 403).

Practitioners need to use their knowledge of the children in their care to ensure a balance of child-initiated and adult-directed play activities. When a child engages in a self-chosen pursuit, this is child-initiated activity. For example, a child might elect to play with a fire engine – fitting the driver behind the steering wheel, extracting the driver, replacing the driver, throwing the driver back into a box and introducing a different driver. Another instance of a child-initiated choice may be where a child takes ownership of an activity and 'subverts' it to a different purpose than intended. For example, a child might prefer to pour water into a hole to make a puddle rather than watering the plants as the adult intended. Other child-initiated activities may be instigated when the child brings something to the setting – such as an experience of having been on a bus or visiting hospital. This might lead to the provision of resources, stories and pictures to support this interest. Whatever children bring is an indication of their current interest and should be supported (DCSF 2008, p. 7).

Key term

Child-initiated play – self-chosen activities in which children and young people follow their own ideas, in their own way and for their own reasons.

The benefits of child-initiated play

Child-initiated play has important benefits for children's development – for example, it helps to promote their self-confidence and independence. It provides opportunities for children to: try things out; solve problems; be creative; take risks; and use trial and error to find things out. In their play, young children use the experiences they have and extend them to build up ideas, concepts and skills. While playing, children can express their fears and relive anxious experiences in a safe and secure environment. For example, role play allows children to take on and rehearse new and familiar roles.

In Practice

- ❑ Observe a child or small group of children involved in child-initiated play.
- ❑ Make notes on what the child/children are doing and what the developmental benefits are.

Provision for child-initiated play

Children need a combination of real and imaginary experiences to encourage language and learning. This is why play is such an important aspect of young children's thinking and learning. Young children need to handle objects and materials to understand basic concepts. For example, water play can help young children to learn about volume and capacity in fun ways. Through active learning, children use play opportunities to encourage and extend the problem-solving abilities which are essential to developing their intellectual processes. Suggested play opportunities include:

- **creative play activities**, such as painting, drawing and model making, etc.
- **imaginative play activities**, such as role play, dressing-up, dolls, puppets, etc.
- **physical play activities**, like outdoor play, ball games, climbing and using apparatus
- **manipulative play activities**, involving matching, grading and fitting; jigsaws and table-top games.

Figure 12.13 Example of opportunity for child-initiated play

Activity

What opportunities for child-initiated play are provided in your setting?

The role of the adult in supporting child-initiated play

You should aim to provide minimum intervention in child-initiated play while keeping children safe from harm. For example, you will need to intervene when boisterous play becomes unsafe. You should support rather than direct child-initiated play. You should help to create a play environment that will stimulate child-initiated play and provide maximum opportunities for children to experience a wide variety of play types.

Activity

Create an information pack about child-initiated play. Include information on the following:

- what child-initiated play is
- what the benefits of child-initiated play are
- examples of opportunities for child-initiated play
- a list of resources that might support child-initiated play
- the role of adults in planning for child-initiated play
- examples of how an adult could support child-initiated play.

Planning adult-directed activities

Early years settings should ensure a balance of child-initiated play (see above) and adult-directed activities. Practitioners use their judgment and knowledge of the children in their care to decide what this balance should be. Examples of adult-directed activities include small group times in which an adult selects the time to encourage

Figure 12.14 Adult supporting child-initiated play

a particular aspect of learning or to discuss a particular topic. The adult may introduce a particular material, skill or idea. Often when an adult initiates an activity – for example, demonstrates the skill of weaving – the child's need for adult involvement will decrease over time as they master the skill (DCSF 2008, p. 7).

Key term

Adult-directed activities – activities in which adults provide specific opportunities to encourage a particular aspect of learning, discuss a particular topic or introduce a particular material, skill or idea.

Activity

What is the difference between child-initiated and adult-directed activities?

The benefits of adult-directed activities

Through play, in a secure but challenging environment with effective adult support, children can: explore, develop and represent learning experiences that help them to make sense of the world; practise and build up ideas, concepts and skills; learn how to understand the need for rules; take risks and make mistakes; think creatively and imaginatively; and communicate with others as they investigate or solve problems (DCSF 2008, pp. 7–8).

Adult-directed activities provide opportunities for children to experience sustained learning and shared thinking, as well as develop specific skills, such as literacy and numeracy. The benefits of adult-directed activities include opportunities for children to:

- work together during activities that involve turn-taking and sharing

- listen to others, such as singing a short song, sharing an experience or describing something they have seen or done
- develop phonological awareness (awareness of sounds), particularly through rhyme and alliteration (e.g. the *h*appy *h*ippo *h*opped) and their knowledge of the alphabetic code
- talk for a wide range of purposes – for example, to present ideas to others as descriptions, explanations, instructions or justifications
- focus on mathematical learning – for example, exploring shape, size and pattern during block play
- experiment with a number of objects, the written numeral and the written number
- develop number skills through matching activities with a range of numbers, numerals and a selection of objects
- learn scientific skills during practical activities – for example, learning about the characteristics of liquids and solids by melting chocolate or cooking eggs
- use a range of ICT to include cameras, photocopiers, CD players, tape recorders and programmable toys, in addition to computers
- participate in physical challenges during opportunities for physical activity
- enjoy energetic play, both indoors and outdoors
- enjoy creative activities, such as painting, drawing and model making using a wide variety of equipment and resources in a variety of ways.

(DCSF 2008)

Activity

- Observe a child or small group of children involved in adult-directed activity.
- Make notes on what the child/children are doing and what the developmental benefits are.

Provision of adult-directed activities

When planning adult-directed activities, practitioners should consider the following: the age of the children; the children's levels of development and their developmental needs; the children's interests; diversity (e.g. ensuring activities reflect the cultural diversity of the setting); inclusion (e.g. ensuring activities are accessible to children with disabilities/special needs); and links to the relevant early years curriculum (e.g. EYFS).

You can write down your plans for play opportunities on a planning sheet or in an activity file. Your plans may be brief or detailed depending on the requirements of your setting. Some activities may require more detailed preparation and organisation than others (e.g. arts and crafts, cooking, outings, etc.).

A plan for a play activity could include the following:

1 **Title:** A brief description of the activity.
2 **When?** Date and time of the activity.
3 **Where?** Where the activity will take place – for example, indoor play area, outdoor play area, local park or playground.
4 **Why?** Outline why you have selected this particular activity – for example, identifying children's play needs and preferences through research, observation or consultation.
5 **What?** What you need to prepare in advance – for example, selecting or making appropriate resources and buying ingredients, materials or equipment.
6 **How?** How you will organise the activity. Consider any safety requirements. Think about tidying up after the activity (e.g. encouraging the children to help tidy up).

Evaluate the activity afterwards – for example, the children's response to the activity, the skills and/or learning demonstrated by the children and the effectiveness of your preparation, organisation and implementation. Make a note of your evaluation on the planning sheet or in the activity file. These notes will prove helpful when planning future play opportunities and for providing information to colleagues at regular meetings. (More detailed information is in the section 'Planning activities to support learning' from page 406.)

Activity

What opportunities for adult-directed play are provided in your setting?

Figure 12.15 Example of opportunity for adult-directed play activity

The role of the adult in supporting adult-directed activities

The role of the practitioner is crucial in observing and reflecting on children's spontaneous play and building on this by planning and providing resources to support and extend specific areas of children's learning. Take a look at Figure 1.16 'Adult supporting child's learning' diagram on page 27.

Activity

- Plan an adult-directed activity for a young child.
- Discuss the benefits of the planned adult-directed activity in supporting the child's learning.
- Include a list of resources for the activity.
- Give examples of how the adult will support the child's learning

Planning activities to support learning

Effective planning is based on children/young people's individual needs, abilities and interests, hence the importance of accurate observations and assessments (see the section 'Assessing the development needs of children or young people and preparing a development plan' on pages 89–99 in Chapter 6 of Meggitt *et al.* 2011). These needs should be integrated into the activities to support the learning of the children and/or young people you work with. These activities must be related to the relevant curriculum requirements applicable in your own country and workplace (see section on curriculum frameworks from page 379).

Planning activities to support learning involves a continuous cycle of: identifying learning needs; preparing, organising and implementing learning activities; observing and recording child responses; evaluating learning activities; and identifying future learning needs.

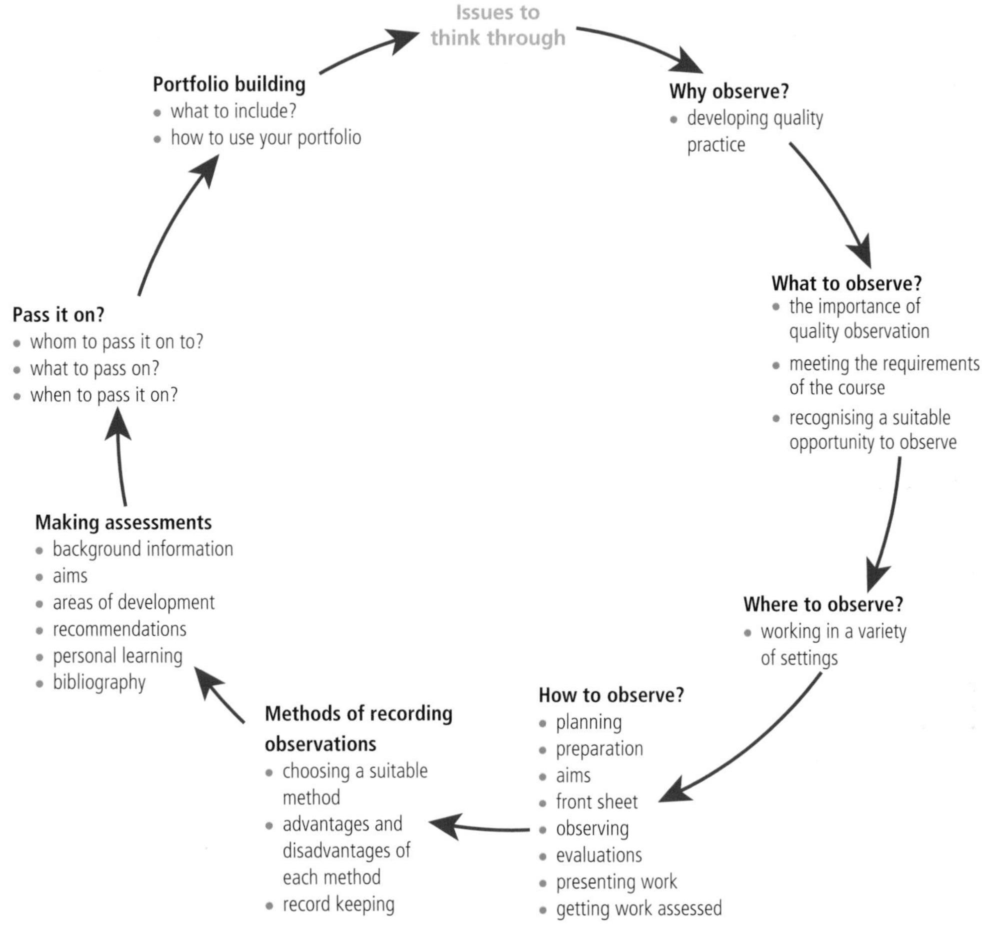

Figure 12.16 Thinking about observing, by Jackie Harding and Liz Meldon-Smith (from *Teaching Assistant's Handbook Level 3*, page 2, Hodder Education, 2011)

The planning process

1. Specify intended learning outcomes for the child or children:

- What is the main purpose of the activity?
- How will it encourage the child or children's learning and development?
- What will the child or children gain from participating in the activity?
- How does the activity link with the early learning goals or National Curriculum subjects?

2. Prepare for the activity:

- What do you need to prepare in advance?
- Will you need to make work cards or photocopy worksheets?
- What instructions and/or questions will you require for the child or children?
- Do you need prompt cards for instructions or questions?

3. Select resources for the activity:

- What materials and equipment will you need?
- Do you need any specific audio, visual or tactile aids?
- Where will you obtain the necessary resources?
- Are there any special resources required for children with special educational needs?

4. Organise the activity:

- How will the activity be organised?
- Where will the activity be implemented?
- How long will the activity take?
- How will you give out any instructions to the child or children?
- Will you work with the children one at a time or as a group?
- How will you set out the resources?
- Are there any particular safety requirements?
- How will you organise any tidying up after the activity?
- Will the children be encouraged to help tidy up?

5. Identify your role:

- Are there any specific instructions from a senior practitioner (e.g. class teacher)?
- What strategies will you use to support learning?
- How will you promote independent learning?

6. Implement the activity:

- How does/do the child or children respond to the learning activity?
- Do you need to adapt the original plan (e.g. change the resources or the timing of the learning activity)?

7. Observe responses:

- Observe the child's or children's responses during the activity.
- Did the child or children find the activity too hard or too easy?
- If possible, make brief notes during the activity.

8. Record achievements/difficulties:

- Make a note of the child's or children's achievements and/or any difficulties.
- Record these using methods as appropriate to your role.
- Report achievements, difficulties or concerns to the senior practitioner/setting manager.

9. Evaluate the activity:

- Did the child or children achieve the intended learning outcomes?
- How effective were the preparation, organisation and implementation of the activity?

10. Identify future learning needs:

- Have you identified any future learning needs for the child or children as a result of their responses during this activity?
- Are there any possible modifications you could make for future activities?
- Discuss your ideas with other people who work with the child or children.

Planning provision based on observations and assessments

You will need to plan provision for the children you work with based on your assessment of their developmental progress. You should recognise that developmental progress depends on each child's level of maturation and their prior experiences. You should take these into account and have realistic expectations when planning activities and routines to promote children's development. This includes regularly reviewing and updating plans for individual children and ensuring that plans balance the needs of individual children and the group, as appropriate to your setting. You should know and understand that children develop at widely different rates but in broadly the same sequence. When planning provision to promote children's development, you need to recognise that children's development is holistic, even though it is divided into different areas (e.g. **S**ocial, **P**hysical, **I**ntellectual, **C**ommunication and language, and **E**motional). You should remember to look at the 'whole' child. You need to look at *all* areas of children's development in relation to the particular aspect of development or learning you are focusing on when planning provision to promote children's development. (More detailed information is in Chapter 5 'Understand child and young person development' in Meggitt *et al.* 2011.)

Activity

Observe a child involved in an activity to support learning. In your assessment, you should:

- specify the learning objectives for the activity
- identify the development and skills demonstrated by the child during the activity (e.g. social, physical, intellectual, communication and language, and emotional)
- comment on the level of adult support provided during the activity
- suggest ways to encourage and extend the child's learning and development.

Following your observation and assessment of a child's development, learning and/or behaviour, your recommendations can provide the basis for planning appropriate routines and/or activities to encourage and extend the child's skills in specific areas. Effective planning is based on children's individual needs, abilities and interests, hence the importance of accurate and reliable child observations and assessments. (See Figure 1.22 'Planning children's activities' in Chapter 1, page 42.) Depending on the type of setting, you may also need to plan provision based on the requirements for curriculum frameworks for early education.

When planning activities to support the learning of children and/or young people, your overall aims should be to:

- support the care and development of *all* the children you work with
- ensure every child has full access to the appropriate curriculum
- meet children's individual developmental and learning needs
- build on each child's existing knowledge, understanding and skills.

You need to plan, in consultation with your colleagues, the strategies and resources to be used to promote children's independent learning. This includes: encouraging and supporting children in making decisions about their own learning; providing appropriate levels of assistance for individual children; using ICT to enable children to work more independently; providing challenges to promote independent learning; and encouraging children to review their own learning strategies, achievements and future learning needs.

In Practice

Describe how *you* plan provision to support children's learning in your setting. Include examples of any planning sheets you use.

Preparation and organisation

Good preparation and organisation are essential when implementing plans to promote children's development, including: having ready any instructions and/or questions for the child or group of children (e.g. prompt cards, worksheets, work cards or written on the board); ensuring sufficient materials and equipment, including any specialist equipment; and deciding on whether to set out the materials and equipment on the table ready or to let the children get the resources out for themselves, depending on their ages and abilities.

Short-term plans (e.g. individual lesson plans and/or activity plans) should include information about your role in preparing and organising activities. These plans should include the learning objectives and what the intended learning outcomes for the children/young people might be. Use your personal timetable, the group/class timetable and the available systems of communication within the setting to help you know and understand: what you have to do before you implement the activity; where, when and with whom the activity will take place; and why the activity is being implemented.

You need the relevant activity/lesson plans at least the day before so that you have time to prepare what you need for the activities. This preparation may involve: finding resources; doing some photocopying; checking equipment and its availability; reading up on a subject; finding artefacts or reference books for the children/young people; and asking a senior colleague for further information.

The learning resources in the setting should support learning activities across the full range of the curriculum. A wide variety of learning resources will help to maintain interest in the curriculum area and help to support individual learning needs. The setting should decide on spending priorities when allocating resources as some areas of the curriculum may require more substantial or expensive learning materials than others. Careful criteria should be set for selecting and using learning resources. For example, health and safety, ages/ability levels of the children or young people, quality and durability, versatility and value for money, special educational needs (e.g. specialist or modified learning materials) and equal opportunities (e.g. resources reflecting positive images of cultural diversity, gender roles and people with disabilities).

The organisation of learning resources is also an important consideration. For example, to encourage independent learning, resources should be organised in ways that allow children and/or young people to locate the learning resources they need and to put them away afterwards. Learning resources should be clearly labelled and stored where they are accessible to the children/young people. Learning resources must be regularly maintained, cleaned and checked for damage. Items that are incomplete, unhygienic or past repair should be appropriately discarded.

Implementing plans

Implementing curriculum plans involves working with other people (e.g. parents, colleagues and other professionals) to deliver the appropriate curriculum for the children and/or young people in your setting. To provide effective support for children and/or young people's learning, you must know and understand the objectives of the activities and the strategies to support their learning.

As a practitioner, you should be aware of your experience and expertise in relation to supporting activities and how these relate to the planned activities. You should ensure that you are adequately prepared for your contribution to the activities, such as understanding the relevant subject knowledge and support strategies, as well as obtaining appropriate resources. This may mean discussing development opportunities to improve your skills in areas where you currently lack experience or expertise (see the section on 'Learning opportunities and personal development' on pages 23–25 in Chapter 2 of Meggitt *et al.* 2011).

Your role will depend on the setting you work in, as well as your own experience and/or qualifications. As a practitioner, you may have a general role working with different classes in a year group/key stage or specific responsibilities for a child/young person, subject area or age group. When working with a specific child or children, you should have information regarding their special educational needs and any special provision, including details of statements of special educational needs, individual education plans and/or behaviour support plans. You may be involved in implementing a structured programme designed by a specialist, such as a speech and language therapist (see the section 'Develop a plan with an individual child or young person to support learning, play or leisure needs' on pages 456–458 in Chapter 21 of Meggitt *et al.* 2011).

When implementing activities, you should ensure that you make accurate and detailed records of what has been planned and delivered in order to: clarify the aims and learning objectives of activity plans; avoid contradictory strategies/unnecessary duplication of work; use the time available more effectively; evaluate the success of plans/activities; and provide continuity and progression for future planning.

Implementing an activity may involve: giving out any instructions to the children; showing children what to do (e.g. demonstrating a new technique); keeping an individual child and/or group on task; clarifying meaning and/or ideas; explaining any difficult words to the children; assisting children with any special equipment (e.g. hearing aid or Dictaphone); providing any other appropriate assistance; encouraging the children to tidy up afterwards as appropriate to the ages and abilities; and remembering to maintain the children's safety at all times.

Figure 12.17 Implementing a plan to support the learning of a child with disabilities

Implementing activities

You should implement planned activities that meet the needs of the children in your setting by:

- providing a stimulating, enjoyable and carefully planned learning environment, including using indoor and outdoor spaces
- using everyday routines to enhance learning
- ensuring a balance between structured and freely chosen play
- supporting and extending play to encourage learning by using your knowledge of individual children and their preferred learning styles
- using appropriate materials and support strategies for each child's needs and abilities
- encouraging children's participation and providing assistance at an appropriate level for each child, including supporting children with special needs
- having high expectations of children and a commitment to raising their achievement based on a realistic appraisal of their capabilities and what they might achieve
- encouraging children to make choices about their own learning
- changing and adapting plans to meet the needs of all the children as required.

Describe your role in implementing activities to support the learning of children and/or young people.

Evaluating plans

After you have planned and implemented an activity, you will need to evaluate it. You should use all the available relevant information to evaluate the effectiveness of your planning and implementation of the activity – for example, responses and/or information from parents, colleagues and other professionals.

Some evaluation also occurs during the activity, providing continuous assessment of a child's performance. It is important to evaluate the activity so that you can: assess whether the activity has been successful (e.g. whether the aims or outcomes have been met); identify possible ways in which the activity might be adapted to meet the individual needs of the child or children; and provide accurate information for the senior practitioner, setting manager or other professionals about the success of a particular activity.

Evaluating activities to support learning

When evaluating activities to support the learning of an individual or group of children/young people, remember these important points:

- How did the child or children respond to the activity?
- Did you need to adapt the original plan (e.g. change the resources or the timing of the learning activity)?
- Did the child or children achieve the intended learning objectives?
- How effective was the preparation and delivery of the activity?
- Make a note of any achievements and/or difficulties.
- Record these using methods as appropriate to your role.
- Report achievements, difficulties or concerns to the senior practitioner.
- Have you identified any future learning needs for the child or children as a result of their responses during this activity?
- Are there any possible modifications you could make for future activities to support learning?
- Discuss your ideas with colleagues and/or the child's parents.

You will need to keep accurate records of children's progress and responses to activities in order to feed back information to the teacher and other relevant people. You can record significant aspects of child participation and progress during the activity (if possible) or shortly afterwards so that you remember important points. You can provide information on children's progress and responses by considering these questions:

1. Did the child or children achieve the objectives/outcomes set? If not, why not?
2. If the child or children did achieve the objectives, what effect has it had (e.g. on behaviour, learning or any special need)?
3. Were the objectives too easy or too hard for the child or children?
4. How did any staff involvement affect the child or children's achievement?
5. Was the activity plan successful? If not, why not?

The senior practitioner, setting manager or your college tutor/assessor should give you guidelines on how to present your plans for activities to support the learning of children and/or young people. If not, use the examples of plans in this chapter as a guide; you could also use the suggested format for an activity plan on page 43 in Chapter 1. Your work must be presented using a recognised method of academic referencing with supporting bibliography to validate your work. If you are not sure how to do this, the straightforward guide 'How to Cite References – Study Skills' is available at: www.bized.co.uk/reference/studyskills/references.htm.

In Practice

1. Develop a **long-term** plan: for example, a topic web for half-term. Ensure that you provide links to the relevant framework or curriculum, such as the EYFS.
2. Produce a **medium-term** plan: for example, a weekly plan of activities. You could use the observation from page 409 as the basis for your plan. Include information on: the intended learning outcomes/objectives for each activity; organisation, resources and staff required; any special requirements (e.g. specialist equipment); and the support to be provided by adults.
3. Devise, implement and evaluate a **short-term** plan: for example, activity plans. Describe **two** activities you have planned, implemented and evaluated (one with the focus on child-initiated play and one adult-directed activity). Include: a brief description of each learning activity; the objectives of each learning activity; a list of materials and/or equipment used; your contribution to the learning activities; the type and level of support for the child or children; the specific strategies for supporting learning activities; and an evaluation of each learning activity. Include copies of planning and evaluation sheets.

Useful resources

Organisations and websites

Foundation Years

Developed by 4Children, this is the 'one stop shop' for resources, information and the latest news on the foundation years. The website provides advice and guidance for practitioners on working effectively with parents as partners in their children's learning.
www.foundationyears.org.uk

Books

Abbott, L. and Langston, A. (2005) *Birth to three matters: supporting the framework of effective practice*, Maidenhead: Open University Press.

DCSF (2008) *Practice guidance for the Early Years Foundation Stage*, London: Department for Children, Families and Schools.

DCSF (2009) *Learning, playing and interacting: good practice in the Early Years Foundation Stage*, London: Department for Children, Families and Schools.

DfE (2011a) *Statutory framework for the Early Years Foundation Stage: setting the standards for learning, development and care for children from birth to five*, draft for consultation, 6 July 2011, London: Department for Education, available at: http://kathybigio.com/pdf/revised_early_years_foundation_stage.pdf (accessed February 2012).

DfE (2011b) *Reforming the Early Years Foundation Stage (the EYFS): government response to consultation 20 December 2011*, London: Department for Education, available at: www.education.gov.uk/consultations/downloadableDocs/Government%20response%20doc%20191211%201630%20finaltext%20KM%20CB%201808(v2).pdf (accessed February 2012).

DfE (2012) *Statutory framework for the Early Years Foundation Stage: setting the standards for learning, development and care for children from birth to five*, London: Department for Education, available at: www.education.gov.uk/publications/standard/AllPublications/Page1/DFE-00023-2012 (accessed March 2012).

Gillespie Edwards, A. (2002) *Relationships and learning: caring for children from birth to three*, London: National Children's Bureau.

Useful resources (cont.)

Harding, J. and Meldon-Smith, L. (2001) *How to make observations and assessments*, 2nd edition, London: Hodder & Stoughton.

Hobart, C. and Frankel, J. (2005) *A practical guide to activities for young children*, 3rd edition, Cheltenham: Nelson Thornes.

Hutchin, V. (2012) *The EYFS: A Practical Guide for Students and Professionals*, London: Hodder Education.

Jaeckle, S. (2008) 'The EYFS principles: a breakdown', *Early Years Update*, September, available at: www.teachingexpertise.com/articles/eyfs-principles-breakdown-4117 (accessed February 2012).

Langston, A. (2011) 'EYFS Review special – what it means for you and your practice', *Nursery World*, 30 March, available at: www.nurseryworld.co.uk/news/1062969/EYFS-REVIEW-special—means-practice (accessed March 2012).

Lindon, J. (2012) *Understanding child development: linking theory and practice*, 3rd edition, London: Hodder Education.

Meggitt, C., Kamen, T., Bruce, T. and Grenier, J. (2011) *CACHE Level 3 Diploma: Children and young people's workforce: early learning and child care*, London: Hodder Education.

QCA (2001) *Planning, teaching and assessing the curriculum for pupils with learning difficulties*, Coventry: Qualifications and Curriculum Authority.

Sheridan, M.D. (1997) *From birth to five years: children's developmental progress*, London: Routledge.

SWSF (2008) *What is Steiner education?*, Stourbridge: Steiner Waldorf Schools Fellowship, available at: www.steinerwaldorf.org/whatissteinereducation.html (accessed May 2012).

Chapter 13 Supporting numeracy and literacy development in children and/or young people (Unit CP 14)

The aim of this unit is to enable the learner to support the development of numeracy and literacy skills in children and/or young people.

Learning outcomes

1. Understand numeracy and literacy learning when working with children and/or young people.
2. Understand learning needs of individual children and/or young people when supporting the development of numeracy and literacy skills.
3. Be able to plan and deliver numeracy and literacy activities for children and/or young people.
4. Be able to reflect on own practice.

Section 1: Understanding numeracy and literacy learning when working with children and/or young people

At the centre of all learning are two key skills: literacy and numeracy. As a practitioner, you will be involved in helping children and/or young people to develop their numeracy and literacy skills. Working within the relevant curriculum framework, you should provide support for numeracy and literacy learning during whole-class, group- and individual-learning activities, including: discussing with colleagues how these learning activities will be organised and what your particular role will be; providing the agreed support as appropriate to the different learning needs of children/young people; and giving feedback to colleagues, parents and other professionals about the progress of children in developing numeracy and literacy skills.

What is literacy?

Literacy means the ability to read and write. The word 'literacy' has only fairly recently been applied as the definitive term for reading and writing (especially when the National Literacy Strategy was introduced in schools). It makes sense to use the term 'literacy' as the skills of reading and writing do complement one another and are developed together. Reading and writing are forms of communication based on spoken language. Children need effective speaking and listening skills in order to develop literacy skills. Literacy unites the important skills of reading, writing, speaking and listening.

What is numeracy?

The term 'numeracy' was introduced in about 1982 to describe what was previously called arithmetic. Individuals who are competent at arithmetic have always been described as 'numerate'; now this competency is called 'numeracy'. Numeracy is more than an ability to do basic arithmetic. Numeracy is a proficiency that involves confidence and competence with numbers and measures. It requires an understanding of the number system, a repertoire of computational skills and an inclination and ability to solve number problems in various contexts. Numeracy also demands practical understanding of the ways in which data is gathered, by counting and measuring, and is presented in graphs, diagrams and tables.

Key terms

Numeracy – competency in arithmetic.

Literacy – the ability to read and write.

Curriculum frameworks which support numeracy skills and literacy skills

You should know the relevant national regulatory frameworks and curriculum guidelines for supporting numeracy skills and literacy skills which are relevant to the children and/or young people you work with. In England, the relevant statutory frameworks are the revised Early Years Foundation Stage and the National Curriculum in England.

In the schools white paper *The Importance of Teaching*, published on 22 November 2010, the coalition government set out its plans to reduce the amount of guidance and materials offered to schools. The government believes that schools should be free to use their own professional judgment about how they teach, without unnecessary prescription. Non-statutory materials and guidance (such as the Literacy Framework and Every Child a Writer) have been removed from the National Curriculum website and the site restructured accordingly. All material previously available is preserved on the UK government web archive: http://webarchive.nationalarchives.gov.uk/20110809091832/http://www.teachingandlearningresources.org.uk.

Practitioners can make their own judgment about the resources they use to prepare and teach the curriculum or other related topics. Where guidance is required, online copies of QCDA materials are still available for schools and other settings to access if they wish: http://archive.teachfind.com/qcda/www.qcda.gov.uk/default.html.

The revised 2012 Early Years Foundation Stage

On 6 July 2011, a revised draft EYFS framework was issued for consultation, taking forward proposals for reform: reducing paperwork and bureaucracy for professionals; focusing strongly on the three prime areas of learning most essential for children's healthy development and future learning (with four specific areas in which the prime areas are applied); simplifying assessment at age five, including to reduce the early learning goals (ELGs) from 69 to 17; and providing for earlier intervention for those children who need extra help, through the introduction of a progress check when children are age two (DfE 2011a, pp. 1 and 2).

This revised EYFS was published on 27 March 2012 and will be implemented from September 2012. (The 2008 EYFS will continue to be in force until 31 August 2012.) There are seven areas of learning and development that must shape educational programmes in early years settings. Three areas are particularly important for igniting young children's curiosity and enthusiasm for learning and for building their capacity to learn and to thrive. These three areas, known as the *prime* areas, are: personal, social and emotional development; physical development; and communication and language. Early years providers must also support young children in four *specific* areas of learning and development, through which the three prime areas are strengthened and applied. The specific areas are: literacy, mathematics, understanding the world, and expressive arts and design.

Prime area: communication and language

Communication and language development involves giving children opportunities to experience a rich language environment; to develop their confidence and skills in expressing themselves; and to speak and listen in a range of situations. By the end of the EYFS, children should have achieved these early learning goals in communication and language:

- **Listening and attention:** children listen attentively in a range of situations. They listen to stories, accurately anticipating key events and respond to what they hear with relevant comments, questions or actions. They give their attention to what others say and respond appropriately, while engaged in another activity.

- **Understanding:** children follow instructions involving several ideas or actions. They answer 'how' and 'why' questions about their experiences and in response to stories or events.
- **Speaking:** children express themselves effectively, showing awareness of listeners' needs. They use past, present and future forms accurately when talking about events that have happened or are to happen in the future. They develop their own narratives and explanations by connecting ideas or events.

(DfE 2012, pp. 7 and 8)

Specific area: literacy

Literacy development involves encouraging children to link sounds and letters and to begin to read and write. Children must be given access to a wide range of reading materials (books, poems and other written materials) to ignite their interest. By the end of the EYFS, children should have achieved these early learning goals in literacy:

- **Reading:** children read and understand simple sentences. They use phonic knowledge to decode regular words and read them aloud accurately. They also read some common irregular words. They demonstrate understanding when talking with others about what they have read.
- **Writing:** children use their phonic knowledge to write words in ways which match their spoken sounds. They also write some irregular common words. They write simple sentences which can be read by themselves and others. Some words are spelt correctly and others are phonetically plausible.

(DfE 2012, pp. 8 and 9)

Figure 13.1 Young children engaged in a communication and language activity

Figure 13.2 Young children engaged in a literacy activity

Specific area: mathematics

Mathematics involves providing children with opportunities to develop and improve their skills in counting, understanding and using numbers, calculating simple addition and subtraction problems and describing shapes, spaces and measures. By the end of the EYFS, children should have achieved these early learning goals in mathematics:

- **Numbers:** children count reliably with numbers from 1 to 20, place them in order and say which number is one more or one less than a given number. Using quantities and objects, they add and subtract two single-digit numbers and count on or back to find the answer. They solve problems, including doubling, halving and sharing.
- **Shape, space and measures:** children use everyday language to talk about size, weight, capacity, position, distance, time and money to compare quantities and objects and to solve problems. They recognise, create and describe patterns. They explore characteristics of everyday objects and shapes and use mathematical language to describe them.

(DfE 2012, p. 9)

(For detailed information about the EYFS, see Unit CP 13 in Chapter 12.)

Development Matters in the EYFS

Development Matters in the Early Years Foundation Stage (EYFS) provides non-statutory guidance to support early years practitioners in implementing the statutory requirements of the EYFS. Other guidance is also available at www.foundationyears.org.uk.

Children are born ready, able and eager to learn. They actively reach out to interact with other people

Figure 13.3 Young children engaged in a mathematics activity

and in the world around them. Development is not an automatic process, however. It depends on each unique child having opportunities to interact in positive relationships and enabling environments (Early Education 2012, p. 2).

The four themes of the EYFS (A Unique Child, Positive Relationships, Enabling Environments, and Learning and Development) underpin all early years practice. *Development Matters* shows how these themes, and the principles that inform them, work together for children in the EYFS.

Research Activity

Find out more about supporting numeracy and literacy in the EYFS. For example, have a look at the Foundation Years website: www.foundationyears.org.uk.

The National Curriculum in England

The National Curriculum sets out the statutory requirements for the knowledge and skills that every child is expected to learn in schools. The National Curriculum applies to children of compulsory school age in schools in England. The National Curriculum sets out what pupils should study, what they should be taught and the standards that they should achieve. Supporting the learning of numeracy and literacy skills is part of the compulsory subjects of mathematics and English in all key stages. In January 2011, the Secretary of State for Education announced a review of the National Curriculum in England. While the review is being conducted, the existing National Curriculum requirements for both primary and secondary schools will remain in force. (Detailed information is given in Chapter 12.)

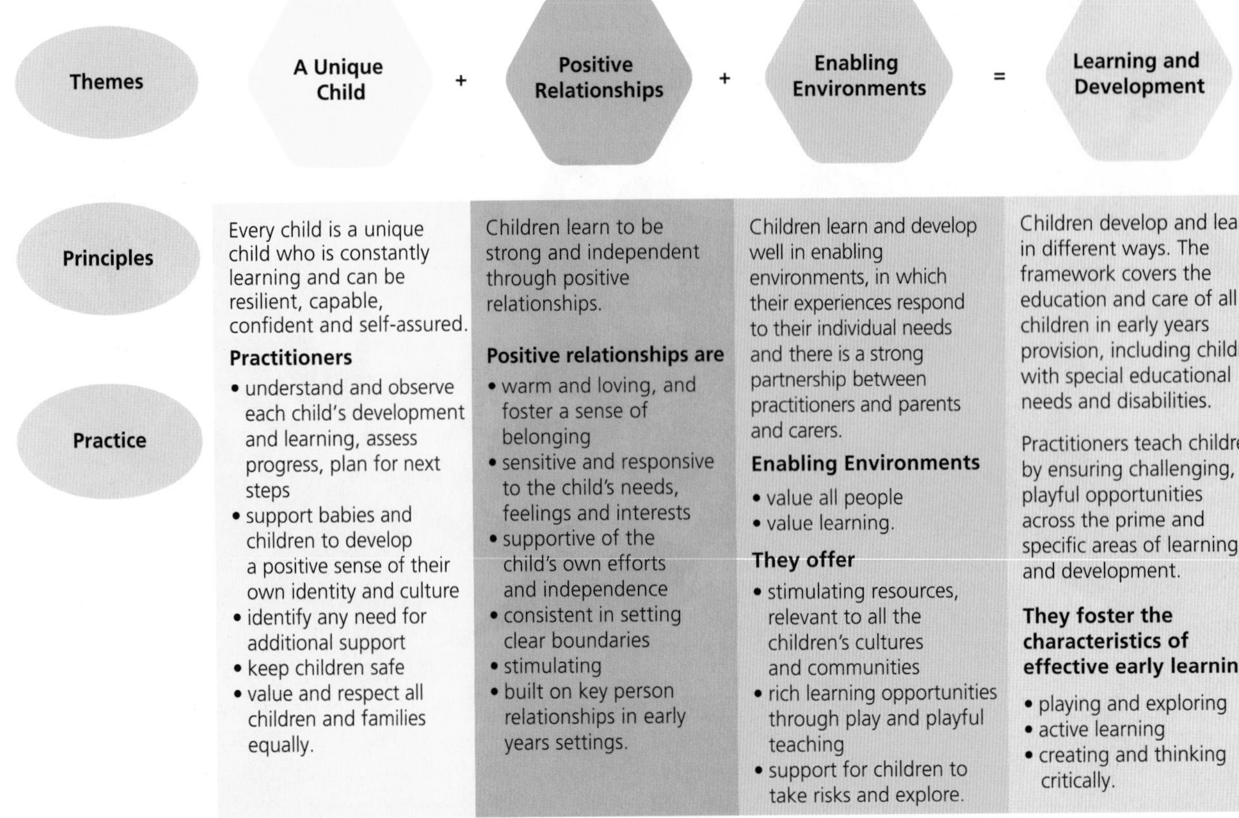

Figure 13.4 How the four themes of the EYFS underpin all early years practice (adapted from'Development Matters in the Early Years Foundation Stage', p. 2, available at: http:// www.media.education.gov.uk/assets/files/pdf/d/development%20matters%20 in%20the%20eyfs.pdf)

English in the primary years

Teaching should ensure that work in 'speaking and listening', 'reading' and 'writing' is integrated. The programme of study for English and the National Literacy Strategy Framework for teaching are closely related. The framework provides a detailed basis for implementing the statutory requirements of the programmes of study for reading and writing.

In English, during **Key Stage 1**, pupils learn to speak confidently and listen to what others have to say. They begin to read and write independently and with enthusiasm. They use language to explore their own experiences and imaginary worlds. For example:

- **Speaking and listening:** pupils learn to speak clearly, thinking about the needs of their listeners. They work in small groups and as a class, joining in discussions and making relevant points. They also learn how to listen carefully to what other people are saying, so that they can remember the main points. They learn to use language in imaginative ways and express their ideas and feelings when working in role and in drama activities.
- **Reading:** pupils' interest and pleasure in reading is developed as they learn to read confidently and independently. They focus on words and sentences and how they fit into whole texts. They work out the meaning of straightforward texts and say why they like them or do not like them.
- **Writing:** pupils start to enjoy writing and see the value of it. They learn to communicate meaning in narrative and non-fiction texts and spell and punctuate correctly.

(DfE 2011b, pp. 1–5)

In English, during **Key Stage 2**, pupils learn to change the way they speak and write to suit different situations, purposes and audiences. They read a range of texts and respond to different layers of meaning in them. They explore the use of language in literary and non-literary texts and learn how language works. For example:

- **Speaking and listening:** pupils learn how to speak in a range of contexts, adapting what they say and how they say it to the purpose and the audience. Taking varied roles in groups gives them opportunities to contribute to situations with different demands. They also learn to respond appropriately to others, thinking about what has been said and the language used.
- **Reading:** pupils read enthusiastically a range of materials and use their knowledge of words, sentences and texts to understand and respond to the meaning. They increase their ability to read challenging and lengthy texts independently. They reflect on the meaning of texts, analysing and discussing them with others.
- **Writing:** pupils develop understanding that writing is essential to both thinking and learning, and enjoyable in its own right. They learn the main rules and conventions of written English and start to explore how the English language can be used to express meaning in different ways. They use the planning, drafting and editing process to improve their work and to sustain their fiction and non-fiction writing.

(DfE 2011b, pp. 6–9)

The Department for Education has published draft primary National Curriculum programmes of study for English, mathematics and science; the final programmes will be introduced into primary schools in September 2014. In English, children will be taught to read using systematic phonics and there will be a stronger emphasis on reading for pleasure. In grammar, children will be expected to understand how to use apostrophes correctly and how to use

Figure 13.5 Primary pupils involved in an English activity

the subjunctive. Learning to recite poems and taking part in debates and presentations will also be expected (Gaunt 2012).

Research Activity

Find out more about English in Key Stage 1 and Key Stage 2. For example, have a look at the section about primary 'English' on the Department for Education website: www.education.gov.uk/schools/teachingandlearning/curriculum/primary/b00198874/english.

English in the secondary years

During **Key Stage 3**, pupils should continue to extend the effective use of the four key English skills by speaking clearly, listening closely, reading carefully and writing fluently. These skills will help pupils to express themselves creatively and increase their confidence about speaking in public and writing for others. Pupils should read classic and contemporary prose and poetry from around the world, examining how writers use language and considering the social/moral issues raised.

During **Key Stage 4**, pupils learn to use language confidently, both in their academic studies and in the world beyond school. Pupils use and analyse complex features of language; they are keen readers who can read many kinds of text and make articulate and perceptive comments about them.

Research Activity

Find out more about English in Key Stage 3, Key Stage 4 and beyond. For example, have a look at the following sections on the Department for Education website:

- English in secondary schools: www.education.gov.uk/schools/teachingandlearning/curriculum/secondary/b00199101/english
- GCSEs: www.education.gov.uk/schools/teachingandlearning/qualifications/gcses
- The 14 to 19 Diploma: www.education.gov.uk/a0064416/what-is-the-diploma.

Mathematics in the primary years

During **Key Stage 1**, pupils learn to count and do basic number calculations, such as addition and subtraction. Pupils learn how to talk about mathematical problems and work out how to solve them through practical activities. Pupils demonstrate their thinking and problem-solving skills by using objects, pictures, diagrams, simple lists, tables, charts, words, numbers and symbols. They do mental calculations (e.g. work out sums in their heads) without relying on calculators. They handle and describe the various features of basic shapes. They learn to estimate and measure a range of everyday objects.

During **Key Stage 2**, pupils learn more about numbers and the number system, including doing more difficult number calculations, such as multiplication and division. Pupils talk about mathematical problems and decide on strategies to tackle them. Pupils demonstrate their thinking and problem-solving skills by using mathematical language, diagrams, words, numbers and symbols. Pupils learn how to use calculators to solve certain mathematical problems but they are expected to solve most problems using mental calculations (e.g. working out sums in their heads) or writing them down on paper. They handle and describe the various features of more complex shapes. They learn to answer questions by selecting, organising and presenting appropriate data using tables, charts, and graphs.

Research Activity

Find out more about mathematics in Key Stage 1 and Key Stage 2. For example, have a look at the section about primary 'mathematics' on the Department for Education website:www.education.gov.uk/schools/teachingandlearning/curriculum/primary/b00199044/mathematics.

Mathematics in the secondary years

During **Key Stage 3**, pupils learn more about numbers and the number system, more complex calculations, different ways of solving mathematical problems and algebra. Pupils talk about mathematical problems and decide on strategies to tackle them. Pupils demonstrate their thinking and problem-solving skills by using more complex mathematical language, diagrams, words, numbers and symbols. Pupils learn to use scientific calculators to solve complex mathematical problems but they are still expected to solve most problems using mental calculations (e.g. working out sums in their heads) or writing them down on paper. They learn more about shapes and coordinates, constructing shapes (geometry) and measurement. They continue to answer questions by selecting, organising and presenting appropriate data using tables, charts and graphs. Pupils learn to solve increasingly demanding mathematical problems, including problems that require a step-by-step approach to reach a solution.

In **Key Stage 4**, there are two programmes of study for mathematics: foundation and higher. Pupils may be taught either the foundation or higher programme of study. The foundation programme of study is intended for those pupils who have not attained a secure Level 5 at the end of Key Stage 3. Pupils studying at the foundation level should: consolidate their understanding of basic mathematics, which will help them to tackle unfamiliar problems in the workplace and everyday life and develop the knowledge and skills they need in the future; become increasingly proficient in mathematical calculations; and collect data, learn statistical techniques to analyse data and use ICT to present and interpret the results.

The higher programme of study is intended for students who have attained a secure Level 5 at the end of Key Stage 3. Pupils studying at the higher level should: use short chains of deductive reasoning, develop their own proofs and begin to understand the importance of proof in mathematics; see the importance of mathematics as an analytical tool for solving problems; refine their calculating skills to include powers, roots and numbers expressed in standard form; learn to handle data through practical activities, using a broader range of skills and techniques, including sampling; and develop the confidence and flexibility to solve unfamiliar problems and to use ICT appropriately.

Research Activity

Find out more about mathematics in Key Stage 3, Key Stage 4 and beyond. For example, have a look at the following sections on the Department for Education website:

- Mathematics in secondary schools: www.education.gov.uk/schools/teachingandlearning/curriculum/secondary/b00199003/mathematics
- GCSEs: www.education.gov.uk/schools/teachingandlearning/qualifications/gcses
- The 14 to 19 Diploma: www.education.gov.uk/a0064416/what-is-the-diploma.

Curriculum frameworks in Northern Ireland, Scotland and Wales

You should know the relevant National Curriculum guidelines for supporting the learning of numeracy and literacy skills relevant to the children/young people you work with. The above information curriculum relates to England.

Northern Ireland

The revised Northern Ireland Curriculum was introduced in September 2007 and sets out the minimum requirements that should be taught at each key stage. The relevant sections of the curriculum are the areas of learning entitled: language and literacy, and mathematics and numeracy.

Scotland

The Curriculum for Excellence is Scotland's curriculum for children and young people aged 3–18. The relevant curriculum areas are languages and mathematics. Curriculum areas are not structures for timetabling; settings have the freedom to think imaginatively about how the experiences and outcomes might be organised and planned for in creative ways which encourage deep, sustained learning and which meet the needs of their children and young people.

Wales

In Wales, the revised school curriculum for 3–19-year-olds has been implemented since September 2008. The relevant areas of learning in the Foundation

Phase are: language, literacy and communication skills, and mathematical development. The requirements for English at Key Stages 2, 3 and 4 are set out in 'English in the National Curriculum for Wales'. The requirements for Welsh at Key Stages 2, 3 and 4 are set out in 'Welsh in the National Curriculum for Wales'. The requirements for mathematics at Key Stages 2, 3 and 4 are set out in 'Mathematics in the National Curriculum for Wales'.

Research Activity

Find out more about the curriculum frameworks for numeracy and literacy in Northern Ireland, Scotland or Wales. For example, have a look at the following websites:

- Northern Ireland Curriculum website: www.nicurriculum.org.uk
- Curriculum for Excellence website: www.ltscotland.org.uk/curriculumforexcellence/curriculumoverview/index.asp
- Welsh Government website: http://wales.gov.uk/topics/educationandskills/schoolshome/curriculuminwales/arevisedcurriculumforwales/?lang=en.

Supporting children and/or young people's numeracy learning

Being able to do number calculations confidently is an essential life skill; it helps people function effectively in everyday life. It is also very important as a first step in learning mathematics. We use numeracy in everyday life, including shopping (e.g. checking change, buying the right quantities, getting value for money), cooking (e.g. weighing ingredients), decorating (e.g. calculating the amount of wallpaper, paint, carpet or other materials needed for the required areas), sewing (e.g. measuring materials, using graph paper to plot designs),and journeys and holidays (e.g. understanding transport timetables, planning the best route, calculating mileage or the time a journey will take, working out how much petrol is needed for a car journey).

Supporting the development of numeracy skills

Learning numeracy skills is the central part of mathematics, but children are also taught about geometry (e.g. space and shapes) and the beginnings of algebra (e.g. number patterns). Children need to develop numeracy skills that involve confidence and competence with numbers and measures, including:

- using and applying mathematics
- counting and understanding number
- knowing and using number facts
- calculating
- understanding shape
- measuring
- handling data.

Using and applying mathematics

Children learn to select an appropriate mathematical skill to tackle or solve a problem. They learn to use words, symbols and basic diagrams to record and give details about how they solved a problem. Children develop problem-solving skills in order to work out the best approach to finding a mathematical solution. They learn which *questions* to ask, as well as developing the appropriate skills to answer mathematical problems, such as: What is the problem? Which mathematical skill needs to be used? Will a graph, chart or diagram help find the solution?

Counting and understanding number

Many children learn number names and how to count before they begin school. At home and/or in early years settings (e.g. day nursery or playgroup), they do counting activities and sing number songs and rhymes. During the primary school years, children develop and extend their counting skills. Younger children begin with numbers 0 to 20, which are the most difficult to learn as each number name is different. Numbers from 20 onwards have recognisable patterns, which makes learning numbers up to 100 and above much easier.

Children begin by counting forwards and then backwards from 20. Once they are confident with this, they learn to count forwards and backwards in sets of 2, 5 and 10, which helps with doing sums and the early stages of learning multiplication.

Figure 13.6 Young children using and applying mathematics

Knowing and using number facts

Primary pupils should learn to recognise and use:

- number symbols and words for whole numbers 1 (one) to 20 (twenty) by 4–5 years
- all the whole numbers to 100 (hundred), plus halves and quarters, by 6–7 years
- numbers to 10,000, including more fractions and decimal places, by 8–9 years
- all whole numbers, fractions, decimals and percentages by 10–11 years.

During the primary school years, children also develop knowledge and understanding of the mathematical language relevant to numbers: smaller, bigger; more/less than; even and odd numbers; factors and prime numbers, etc.

From about four or five years old, children begin to learn how to make mathematical calculations using real objects to add and subtract small whole numbers. Gradually, they recognise number patterns, which make doing calculations easier. For example, being able to add 4 + 8 means they can also add 400 + 800. Memorising number facts also helps with calculations – for example, learning multiplication tables by heart.

Figure 13.7 Young children knowing and using number facts

Calculating

By age 10–11 years, children should have learned addition, subtraction, multiplication and division using whole numbers, fractions, decimals and negative numbers. As well as learning mental calculations, children also learn the standard written methods for calculation operations.

Remember, the aim for older children is to calculate mentally and to become less reliant on fingers and apparatus. Older children should be encouraged to consider mental methods first through strategies such as: 'Think first, and try to work it out in your head. Now check on your number line' (DfES 1999). Children with special needs may need particular equipment, books and materials for mathematics activities. (See section on page 443 on supporting children with special numeracy needs.)

Understanding shape

In addition to developing competency with numbers, children learn to recognise and name geometrical shapes. They also learn about the properties of shapes – for example, a triangle has three sides; a square has four right angles. Children learn about directions, angles and plotting points on a graph.

Measuring

Children learn to measure mass, distance, area and volume using appropriate units (e.g. kilograms, metres, centimetres or litres). Measuring also includes learning to tell the time in hours and minutes.

Handling data

Handling data is an essential skill in this technological age and using computers is an important aspect of mathematics today. Children learn to gather, arrange and convert data into useful information: for example, working out the likelihood of rain so we know when to wear a raincoat or take an umbrella.

The Department for Education has published draft primary National Curriculum programmes of study for English, mathematics and science; the final programmes will be introduced into primary schools in September 2014. In mathematics, children will be expected to add, subtract, multiply and divide fractions, in line with the way children are taught in high-performing countries such as Singapore and Hong Kong. By the age of nine, children will be expected to know their times tables up to 12 x 12, as is the case in Massachusetts. Currently children only need to know their ten times table by the end of primary school. By the age of seven, children should know number bonds up to 20, such as 9 + 9 = 18. (Gaunt 2012)

Figure 13.8 Young children understanding shape

Activity

- How did you develop your numeracy skills? How did your own children (if you have any) develop their numeracy skills? (For example: singing number songs and rhymes; practical mathematics activities, such as sorting shapes, measuring or shopping; playing number games; learning by rote, such as reciting times tables; learning formal number operations, such as addition, subtraction, multiplication and division.)
- What are the methods used to support the development of numeracy skills in your setting?
- Consider the similarities and differences between these methods.

Activity

Observe a young child during a numeracy activity. Then answer these questions:

- Did the child achieve the learning objectives set? If not, why not?
- If the child has achieved the learning objectives, what effect has it had (e.g. on the child's behaviour, learning, any special need)?
- Were the learning objectives too easy or too hard for the child?
- How did any staff involvement affect the child's achievement?
- Was the activity plan successful? If not, why not?

Opportunities to support the development of numeracy skills

You can help children to develop their numeracy skills by:

1. **Using numbers in everyday activities with babies and toddlers**, such as counting stairs, and finger and toe games.
2. **Encouraging children to use and apply mathematics to tackle and solve everyday, practical mathematical problems** – for example, giving change in shop play and real shopping trips (addition and subtraction);exploring volume and capacity during sand and water play, filling various containers to encourage understanding of full, empty, half-full, half-empty, nearly full, nearly empty, more/less than, the same amount, then introduce idea of standard measures (e.g. litre of juice, pint of milk); using weighing and measuring activities, such as shop play (using balance scales to compare toys and other items), real shopping (helping to weigh fruit and vegetables), sand play (heavy and light) and cooking activities (weighing ingredients to show importance of standard measures).
3. **Providing opportunities for children to use and apply mathematics in the setting and wider environment**, such as through orientation exercises, nature walks and geography and environmental studies, can develop numeracy skills; educational visits can also contribute to mathematics across the curriculum (e.g. visits to science museums).
4. **Encouraging young children to explore numbers** through playing games like dominoes, snakes and ladders and other simple board games; looking for shapes/ sizes and making comparisons, price tags and quantities in shop play and real shopping trips; number songs and rhymes like *'One, two, three, four, five, Once I caught a fish alive...'*.
5. **Supporting children engaged in counting, calculating and solving mathematical problems** – for example, addition and subtraction, then multiplication and division. Supporting older children in employing standard methods to perform mental and written calculations, including addition, subtraction, multiplication and

division using whole numbers, fractions, decimals and percentages.

6. **Prompting children to communicate their reasoning about problems and explaining their solutions** using objects, pictures, diagrams, numbers, symbols and relevant mathematical language: for example, using letter symbols in algebra and setting up and using simple equations to solve problems.
7. **Supporting children's use of calculator functions to complete complex calculations** and understand the answers calculators give in relation to the initial mathematical problem.
8. **Encouraging children to compare, estimate and measure a range of everyday objects** – for example, developing an understanding of length by comparing everyday objects/toys and using mathematical language, such as tall/taller/tallest, short/shorter/shortest, long/longer/longest, same height, same length; and measuring objects using appropriate units, such as centimetres, metres, kilograms or litres.
9. **Helping children to tell the time** – o'clock, half past and quarter past the hour; with older pupils telling the time in hours and minutes and solving problems relating to time using a 12-hour or 24-hour clock.
10. **Encouraging children to explore shape and space** through activities such as games involving shape recognition; handling and describing the various features of basic shapes (e.g. using correct names for basic 2D and 3D shapes and knowing how many sides, corners or right angles a shape has); and physical activities involving whole turns, half turns and quarter turns or right angles, as well as spatial awareness (e.g. PE, movement, dance). Helping older children to learn more about shapes and coordinates, constructing shapes (geometry) and measurement, including using a ruler, protractor and compass to create lines, angles and 2D or 3D shapes.
11. **Using information and communication technology (ICT) to encourage or extend children's knowledge, understanding and skills in mathematics** – for example, playing shape recognition games; writing instructions to create and change shapes on a computer; and providing opportunities for children to select, collect, organise and present appropriate data using lists, charts, graphs, diagrams, tables, surveys, questionnaires and CD-ROMs.

Activity

1. Suggest ways to support the development of children's numeracy skills. Use your own experiences of working with children if possible. You could use your observation of a young child engaged in a numeracy activity as the starting point for this activity.
2. Visit a post office in your local area. What activities are available to support children's numeracy learning? Does the post office have an educational department or provide workshops for children?
3. Think about how you could use a visit to a post office with the children from your setting to develop their numeracy skills.

Supporting children and/or young people's literacy learning

Developing literacy skills is an essential aspect of development and learning. Without literacy skills, individuals are very restricted in their ability to: function effectively in school, college or at work; access information and new ideas; communicate their own ideas to others; and participate fully and safely in society. Education depends on individuals being able to read and write. Nearly all jobs and careers require at least basic literacy (and numeracy) skills. Our society also requires

Figure 13.9 Young children visiting a post office

people to use literacy skills in everyday life: reading signs (e.g. street names, shop names, traffic signs and warning signs); reading newspapers, magazines, instructions, recipes, food labels; dealing with correspondence (e.g. reading and replying to letters, household bills, bank statements, wage slips and benefits); using computers, the internet and e-mail; and writing shopping lists, memos and notes.

Supporting the development of literacy skills

Speaking and listening are part of the National Curriculum programme of study for English, which also includes reading and writing. These three areas all focus on language and how it is used in the different modes. The different modes of language are:

- non-verbal communication
- thinking
- listening
- speaking
- reading
- writing.

Each mode has its own distinct features but speaking and listening, reading and writing are interdependent. (See section on developing communication skills and addressing speech, language and communication needs on pages 329–320 in Chapter 16 of Meggitt *et al.* 2011.)

Developing speaking and listening skills

All areas of the curriculum provide opportunities for the development of children's speaking and listening skills. The skills used will vary according to the curriculum area. For example, children may be involved in learning activities that encourage them to: describe, interpret, predict and hypothesise in mathematics and science; express opinions and discuss design ideas in art, design and technology;

discuss cause and effect in history and geography; and discuss social or moral issues in PSHE and RE.

Speaking and listening skills involve:

- **speaking**: being able to speak clearly and to develop and sustain ideas in talk
- **listening**: developing active listening strategies and critical skills of analysis
- **group discussion and interaction**: taking different roles in groups, making a range of contributions and working collaboratively
- **drama**: improvising and working in role, scripting and performing, and responding to performances.

(DfES 2003a)

Developing reading skills

Reading is the process of turning groups of written symbols into speech sounds. In English, this means being able to read from left to right, from the top of the page to the bottom and being able to recognise letter symbols and their combinations as words. Reading is not just one skill; it involves a variety of different abilities: visual and auditory discrimination; language and communication skills; word identification skills; conceptual understanding; comprehension skills; and memory and concentration.

Being able to read does not happen suddenly. Reading is a complex process involving different skills, some of which (e.g. visual discrimination and communication skills) the individual has been developing since birth. Being able to use and understand spoken language forms the basis for developing reading skills. A child who has a wide variety of language experiences will have developed many of the skills needed for learning to read. Children who are pushed too hard by being forced to read and write before they are ready may actually be harmed in terms of their literacy development as they can be put off reading, writing and other related activities. The prime area 'communication and language' and the specific area 'literacy' included in the revised Early Years Foundation Stage provide guidelines to help early years staff (and parents) understand the importance of informal approaches to language and literacy.

There is no set age at which children are magically ready to read, although most children learn to read between the ages of four and a half and six years old. The age at which a child learns to read depends on a number of factors: physical maturity and coordination skills; social and emotional development; language experiences, especially access to books; interest in stories and rhymes; concentration and memory skills; and opportunities for play.

Reading skills checklist

1. Can the child see and hear properly?
2. Are the child's coordination skills developing within the expected norm?
3. Can the child understand and follow simple verbal instructions?
4. Can the child cooperate with an adult and concentrate on an activity for short periods?
5. Does the child show interest in the details of pictures?
6. Does the child enjoy looking at books and joining in with rhymes and stories?
7. Can the child retell parts of a story in the right order?
8. Can the child tell a story using pictures?
9. Can the child remember letter sounds and recognise them at the beginning of words?
10. Does the child show pleasure or excitement when able to read words in school?

If the answer is 'yes' to most or all of these questions, the child is probably ready to read; if the answer is 'no' to any of the questions, the child may need additional support or experiences in those areas before they are ready to read.

Reading approaches

Most adults helping children to develop reading skills use a combination of the 'look and say' approach to introduce early sight vocabulary and then move on to the more intensive phonics approach to establish the children's reading vocabulary. It is important for you to be flexible to meet the individual literacy needs of children. You should also work with parents to develop their children's reading skills.

Whole-word or 'look and say' approach

Children are taught to recognise a small set of key words (usually related to a reading scheme) by means of individual words printed on flashcards. Children recognise the different words by shape and other visual differences. Once children have developed a satisfactory sight vocabulary, they go on to the actual reading scheme. The whole-word approach is useful for learning difficult words which do not follow the usual rules of the English language. The drawback is that this approach does not help children to work out new words for themselves.

Phonics approach

With this approach, children learn the sounds that letters usually make. This approach helps children establish a much larger reading vocabulary fairly quickly as they can 'sound out' new words for themselves. The disadvantage is that there are many irregular words in the English language; one letter may make many different sounds – for example, bough, rough, through. However, children do better with the phonics approach than any other approach.

Apprenticeship approach

This approach, also known as the 'story' or 'real books' approach, does not formally teach children to read. Instead the child sits with an adult and listens to the adult read; the child starts reading along with the adult until the child can read some or the entire book alone. This approach does not help children with the process of decoding symbols. There has been much criticism of this approach, but it has proved effective in this country and New Zealand as part of the 'Reading Recovery' programme for older, less able readers.

Activity

1. How did you learn to read? How did your own children (if you have any) learn to read?
2. What are the approaches to developing reading skills in your setting?
3. Consider the similarities and differences between these approaches.

Developing writing skills

Writing is the system we use to present 'speech in a more permanent form' (Moyle 1976). There are two elements to writing: the **mechanical skill of letter formation** – that is, writing legibly using recognised word and sentence structures, including appropriate spaces between words and punctuation marks – and the **creative skill of 'original composition'**–that is, deciding what to write and working out how to write it using appropriate vocabulary to express thoughts and ideas, which may be fact or fiction (Taylor 1973).

Children will experience written language through books and stories and learn that writing is made up of symbols or patterns organised on paper in a particular way. In English, this means 26 letters in the alphabet, written from left to right horizontally. Children also learn by watching adults and other children, whether at home, in the childcare setting and/or in school, that writing can be used for:

- recording past events and experiences (e.g. news, outings, visitors, special events)
- exchanging information (e.g. notes, memos, letters, postcards)

- functional writing (e.g. shopping lists, recipes, menus, recording experiments or data)
- sharing stories and ideas (e.g. story writing, poetry).

Children do not learn to write just through exposure to a writing environment. Writing is a skill that has to be taught. Learning to write involves learning specific conventions with regard to letter shapes, the sequence of letters in words, word order in sentences, the direction of writing, etc. It is usual to teach writing skills alongside reading. This helps children to make the connection between written letters and the sounds they make when reading. Most of the activities used to develop children's reading skills will also help their writing skills. In addition, children need plenty of opportunities to develop the coordination skills necessary for writing – for example, hand–eye coordination, fine manipulative skills for pencil control and being able to sit still with the correct posture for writing.

Developing writing skills is much more difficult then reading because of the considerable physical and cognitive demands of writing – for example, coordinating movements to write; writing legibly (e.g. letters of consistent size and shape); leaving gaps between words; using the correct punctuation and sentence structure; following the correct spelling requirements; and writing material of the required length, which also makes sense. Remember that some children may have special needs which require them to use alternative means or specialist equipment (e.g. Braille, voice-activated computer or word processor).

Activity

1. How did you learn to write? How did your own children (if you have any) learn to write?
2. What are the opportunities provided to develop children's writing skills in your setting?
3. Consider the similarities and differences between these experiences.

Figure 13.10 A young child developing his writing skills

Activity

Observe a young child during a literacy activity. Then answer these questions:

- Did the child achieve the learning objectives set? If not, why not?
- If the child has achieved the learning objectives, what effect has it had (e.g. on the child's behaviour, learning, any special need)?
- Were the learning objectives too easy or too hard for the child?
- How did any staff involvement affect the child's achievement?
- Was the activity plan successful? If not, why not?

Figure 13.11 Children sharing books in the book corner

Opportunities to support the development of literacy skills

You can help children to develop their literacy skills by:

1. **Providing plenty of opportunities for children to talk** – children who are effective communicators often transfer these skills to reading and writing. Provide plenty of opportunities for discussion, such as: circle time; story time; problem solving during activities; follow-up to activities (e.g. after television programmes or stories); cooperative group work; games and puzzles; and talking about key features when on outings.

2. **Sharing books, stories, poems and rhymes to introduce children to different literary styles or genres**, including picture books, storybooks, 'big' books, novels, poetry books, information books, dictionaries, encyclopaedias and atlases. This also includes looking at other types of printed materials (e.g. newspapers, magazines, comics, signs). These will encourage children's listening skills and auditory discrimination and provide stimulus for discussion and literacy activities, as well introducing or extending their vocabulary.
3. **Encouraging children to participate in appropriate opportunities for play**, especially activities that encourage language and communication – for example, role/pretend play, such as dressing-up, home corner, shop play, creative activities.
4. **Using displays as a stimulus for discussions and to consolidate learning**– for example, wall and interactive tabletop displays with interesting objects to talk about, look at and/or play with, as well as recorded sounds to listen to, including voices, music, songs, rhymes and musical instruments.
5. **Providing opportunities for children to follow and give instructions**, such as: introducing or extending knowledge on a specific skill; specifying tasks (verbal and/or written on a board); listening to step-by-step instructions; explaining worksheets, work cards or textbooks; verbal instructions during an activity to keep children on task or providing extra support for individual children; and delivering verbal/written messages or errands.
6. **Encouraging children to participate in games to develop auditory and visual discrimination**, like sound lotto and 'guess the sound' using sounds of everyday objects or musical instruments. Encourage children to participate in matching games and memory games to develop visual discrimination and memory skills (e.g. snap, matching pairs, jigsaws and games like 'I went shopping...'). Provide fun activities to develop letter recognition, such as 'I spy...' using letter sounds; going on a 'letter hunt' (looking around the classroom for things beginning with a particular letter); hanging up an 'alphabet washing line'; and singing alphabet songs and rhymes.
7. **Providing opportunities for the children to write for different purposes and for different audiences**, such as: writing about their own experiences as appropriate to their age and level of development (e.g. news and recording events); creating their own stories and poems as a means of expressing their feelings and ideas; using class or group topics as well as the children's own interests to stimulate their ideas for stories and poems; and using storybooks as a starting point for the children's own creative writing. Provide children with opportunities to write in different styles, such as: writing letters; writing reports; writing step-by-step instructions; and designing posters, signs and notices. Encourage children to use independent spelling techniques (e.g. word banks, personal word books and dictionaries).
8. **Using alternative writing methods** to release younger children or those with coordination difficulties (such as dyspraxia) from their physical limitations of writing – for example, allowing them to dictate their ideas while an adult acts as scribe or use a tape recorder or word processor.
9. **Considering the individual interests and abilities of children**, including valuing children's home experiences/cultural backgrounds and being aware of possible developmental or psychological difficulties that may affect their speaking and listening skills by carefully observing children's development and learning. (See section on supporting children with special numeracy and/or literacy needs on page 441.)

10. **Using ICT to encourage or extend children's literacy skills**, including television, CD-ROMs and the internet as additional stimuli for discussions and ideas. ICT can also be used to introduce or reinforce information on topics and themes within the setting. Remember that ICT is not a substitute for other forms of communication, such as conversation and children's play.

Figure 13.12 Children visiting the local library

Activity

1. Suggest ways to support the development of children's literacy skills. Use your own experiences of working with children if possible. You could use your observation of a young child engaged in a literacy activity as the starting point for this activity.
2. Visit a library in your local area. What activities are available to support children's literacy learning? Does the library have an educational department or provide workshops for children?
3. Think about how you could use a visit to a library with the children from your setting to develop their literacy skills.

Section 2: Understanding the learning needs of individual children and/or young people when supporting the development of numeracy and literacy skills

Effective planning to support the development of children's numeracy and literacy skills is based on each child's individual needs, abilities and interests. This is why accurate observations and assessments are so important. These needs have to be integrated into the curriculum requirements for your particular setting and the age group(s) of the children you work with – for example, in England, the Early Years Foundation Stage or the National Curriculum (see page 416). The curriculum sets out the standards to be used to measure the progress and performance of children/young people in each subject to help practitioners plan and implement learning activities that meet the individual learning needs of the children and/or young people they work with. (Detailed information about curriculum planning can be found in Chapter 12.)

Potential individual learning needs in relation to numeracy and literacy

Children and young people have different ways of processing information. They use the skills of looking, listening or touching in varying amounts depending on their individual learning style. For example, some children require visual stimulation (visual learners), some respond well to verbal instructions (auditory learners), while others need more 'hands-on' experiences (kinaesthetic learners). In addition, different times of the day affect individual levels of concentration; some children work better in the morning, others in the afternoon. You need to be aware of the individual learning styles of the children you work with in order to plan and provide appropriate learning activities. Recognising learning styles will help you to understand the ways children learn and to assist them in achieving educational success. (See 'Different learning styles' on page 366 in Chapter 11.)

Visual learners

Visual learners learn best by seeing the learning material – for example, looking at charts, tables, illustrated textbooks, overhead transparencies, videos, flip charts, handouts and maps. Visual learners need clear sight lines without irrelevant obstructions, such as other people's heads. Visual learners should look at the practitioner when they are speaking, participate in group/class discussions and take detailed notes during lectures. Visual learners enjoy watching the practitioner's body language and facial expression as this helps them to understand the content of the topic under discussion.

Visual learners often have trouble working while having a conversation, even if the discussion directly relates to the subject matter. When studying, visual learners tend to work alone in a quiet place and try to transcribe their material on paper, including making designs, drawings, graphs or tables of complex, abstract ideas. Completing tasks using diagrams, time lines, charts or graphs helps visual learners to remember important concepts. Visual learners need to either take written notes or underline important facts and dates in colours. When they are learning auditory concepts such as phonics, visual learners need to see the letters to learn. (Morris 2011)

Auditory learners

Auditory learners tend to learn mainly by hearing information. They learn best through their ears, especially via verbal discussions, talking things through and listening to the words of others. They interpret the underlying meanings of speech through listening to tone of voice, pitch, speed and other nuances. When they have pages to read, they need to quietly say the words aloud in order to hear the words as they read. Often written information has little meaning until it is heard. When they are learning concepts such as phonics, they need to hear the similarities – for example, they may not realise that 'ph' sounds just like 'f' unless they say the sounds out loud.

Reading aloud, going over class notes and talking to oneself about the relevant points are important to auditory learners. Before reading, auditory learners need a purpose with clear verbal instructions as to what is required. After they have finished a task, they should summarise out loud what was just read. These learners often benefit from reading text aloud and using a tape recorder. Taping notes and playing them back to learn the information can be quite an effective way for auditory learners to understand and remember the information. Auditory learners should have opportunities to talk to their peers about the learning material. Auditory learners sometimes encounter problems keeping columns aligned, so encouraging them to set out mathematical calculations on graph paper may help. (Morris 2011)

Kinaesthetic learners

Kinaesthetic learners learn best through a hands-on approach – for example, they like to be physically involved as they find it extremely difficult to sit still. They often pace around the classroom and want to have music or television playing in the background. ICT can be very helpful as kinaesthetic learners work well on computers where they can touch the keys as they type. They learn well when they can physically do things, such as handling materials and exploring their properties (e.g. sand and/or water play and construction activities). They need to actually use their hands and bodies while learning.

Kinaesthetic learners may need to walk around, pace or hop while reading. When studying, they need to make flash cards to remember important dates and facts. Kinaesthetic learners often experience difficulties in more formal learning situations such as school because they have to sit still and listen to a teacher. They need to learn to take notes in class in order to have something for their hands to do. (Morris 2011)

Supporting children during numeracy and literacy activities according to their learning styles

You can help to support the development of children's numeracy and literacy skills by using these practical suggestions relating to the different learning styles.

With visual learners:

- use visual materials, such as photographs, pictures, charts, maps, graphs, etc.
- ensure they have a clear view of you when you are speaking so they can see your body language and facial expression
- use colour to highlight important points in the text
- provide handouts or, if applicable, encourage the learner to take notes
- illustrate ideas as a picture or brainstorming bubble before writing them down
- use books and stories with clear illustrations
- use ICT (e.g. computers and videos)
- provide a quiet place for study away from verbal disturbances
- encourage them to read illustrated books
- encourage them to visualise information as a picture to aid their memory.

With auditory learners:

- encourage them to participate in group/class discussions
- provide opportunities for them to talk and make presentations
- use a tape recorder during important lessons instead of taking notes/using handouts
- read text out aloud
- create musical jingles to aid memory

- create mnemonics to aid memory (e.g. the mnemonic **SPICE** to help learners remember the different aspects of children's development: **S**ocial, **P**hysical, **I**ntellectual, **C**ommunication, **E**motional)
- provide opportunities for them to discuss their ideas verbally
- get them to dictate while you write down their thoughts
- use verbal analogies and storytelling to demonstrate your point.

With kinaesthetic learners:

- provide plenty of opportunities for active learning, such as play activities
- provide opportunities for learners to take frequent breaks from more formal learning
- encourage them to handle learning materials (e.g. 3D models, props during story time)
- allow them to move around to learn new things (e.g. read while on an exercise bike, mould a piece of clay to learn a new concept)
- allow them to work at a standing position
- use bright colours to highlight reading material
- play music in the background to aid concentration during activities
- provide space for freedom of movement
- use the local environment to provide a stimulus for learning (e.g. outings to the park).

In Practice

Suggest ways to support the following children's numeracy and literacy skills according to their learning styles.

Visual learners:

- ❑ Lucy is a fairly quiet child who needs lots of encouragement to participate in group/class discussions but who works well in individual and small-group situations. She particularly likes learning activities that involve ICT graphics. She needs extra support for numeracy activities.
- ❑ Tom is a very able, articulate child with a lively imagination and sense of humour. He has excellent language and communication skills. He loves books and stories, especially those with an historical or religious background.

Auditory learners:

- ❑ Rebecca is a studious and articulate child who participates fully in group/class discussions. She is very competent in both literacy and numeracy activities. She can be distracted during some learning activities by chatting too much with her best friend, Miriam.
- ❑ Johnson is a studious but very talkative child. He has very good language and communication skills and is always a keen participant in group/class discussions. He particularly enjoys history and geography activities.

Kinaesthetic learners:

- ❑ Chrissie is a capable child who enjoys learning activities involving practical construction skills, such as design technology. She needs extra support for literacy activities.
- ❑ Peter finds it difficult to concentrate during some learning activities and can be easily distracted by his best friend, Jonas. He likes practical activities and enjoys PE, particularly games involving climbing or ball skills. He requires some additional support for both literacy and numeracy skills.

The benefits of acknowledging individuals' learning needs to identify support

Research has concluded that we do not all learn in the same way. Some teachers still teach a large number of pupils one way by using traditional teaching styles that might appear to be successful for the teacher but are often unsuccessful for a large majority of the learners seated in front of them. If individuals are expected to learn in ways that interfere with their preferred learning style, this creates artificial stress, reduces motivation and limits performance. Some research even suggests that many children with special educational needs are being assessed and taught incorrectly in terms of their dominant learning style. For example, some children who have been formally identified as having learning disabilities may simply be learning differently! (Morris 2011)

An effective practitioner will tend to offer learning experiences in many different ways in order to reach all learners. Most learners can learn the same content, but how they best receive and then perceive that content are determined largely by their individual learning styles. A learning style defines the main way in which a learner processes, concentrates, internalises and retains new and/or complex information. Understanding how each individual best learns information must be taken into account in order to provide appropriate opportunities for learning. (Morris 2011)

Activity

In your own words, summarise the benefits of acknowledging learning needs of individuals to identify support.

Section 3: Planning and delivering numeracy and literacy activities for children and/or young people

As a practitioner, you should consider the individual needs, interests and stage of development of each child in your care. You should use this information to plan a challenging and enjoyable experience for each child in all of the areas of learning and development. When working with the youngest children, you should focus strongly on the three prime areas (personal, social and emotional development; physical development; and communication and language), which are the basis for successful learning in the other four specific areas (literacy; mathematics; understanding the world; and expressive arts and design). The three prime areas reflect the key skills and capacities all children need to develop and learn effectively. As children grow in confidence and ability within the three prime areas, the balance will shift towards a more equal focus on all areas of learning. Throughout the early years, if a child's progress in any prime area gives you cause for concern, you should discuss this with a senior member of staff, according to your setting's policies and procedures. If it is determined that a child may have a special educational need or disability, specialist support will then be required and the setting should link with, and help families to access, relevant services from other agencies, as appropriate. (DfE 2012, p. 6)

Planning and implementing numeracy and literacy activities for children

Planning and implementing numeracy and literacy activities for children should be based on your observations and assessments of each child's development and learning, your relationship with each child and your understanding of holistic development and learning. (More information about holistic development can be found on pages 49–66 of Chapter 5 'Understand child and young person development' in Meggitt *et al.* 2011.)

Following your observation and assessment of a child's development, learning and/or behaviour, your recommendations can provide the basis for planning appropriate activities to encourage and extend the child's skills in specific areas, such as numeracy and literacy. Effective planning is based on children's individual needs, abilities and interests, hence the importance of accurate and reliable child observations and assessments. (See Figure 1.22 'Planning children's activities' on page 42.)

Depending on the type of setting, you will also need to plan provision based on the requirements for the relevant curriculum frameworks for numeracy and literacy. Providing numeracy and literacy activities for young children involves the following:

- **Planning**: defining aims and objectives, including planned and possible outcomes in play. Building on previous outcomes from play.
- **Organisation**: indoor and outdoor environments: space, resources, time, daily routines, activities, what adults do, what children do.
- **Implementation**: the ways in which adult-initiated activities and tasks are presented in order to support intended and possible learning outcomes and build on previous learning experiences and interests. The ways in which

Planning and implementing numeracy and literacy activities for children

Planning

At the planning stage, practitioners decide on the aims and intentions of the activity, which may be long-, medium- or short-term. Practitioners' intentions can include responding to children's intentions and meanings, as well as allowing for unplanned developments.

Organisation

At the organisation stage, practitioners decide how the learning environment (both indoors and outdoors) will be set out, what resources will be available, where they will be located, how much choice children have and whether materials and activities can be combined. How the day, or session, is structured also influences the amount of time available for play.

Implementation

At the implementation stage, practitioners decide where and how they will spend their time, which should allow opportunities to follow children's own learning journeys. Awareness of children's intentions can only come about through a curriculum model that encourages them to express their intentions and follow their own learning journeys.

Assessment, documentation and evaluation

Practitioners should be sensitive to the meanings that children communicate in their play and use these to inform the next cycle of planning. Practitioners therefore need to understand the meaning of play activities in the 'here and now' and decide what the next significant steps are. In practice, this may shift the emphasis more towards short-term planning so that the curriculum is responsive to learners. Children's interests and ideas may also form the impetus for planning a short topic or informing adult-initiated activities. Such an approach can be enabling and empowering for children and practitioners, particularly where there is a continuum between work and play, and between adult- and child-initiated activities.

(Wood and Attfield 2005, pp. 139 and 140)

adults allow time for and follow play and child-initiated activities.

- **Assessment, documentation and evaluation**: understanding patterns of learning, interests, temperaments. Identifying learning outcomes from adult- and child-initiated activities. Documenting learning in order to provide a feedback loop into planning. Using evidence from all adults in the setting to evaluate the quality and effectiveness of the curriculum.

(Wood and Attfield 2005, p. 139)

When planning numeracy and literacy activities, your overall aims should include:

- supporting the care and development of *all* the children you work with
- ensuring every child has full access to the appropriate curriculum
- meeting children's individual developmental and learning needs
- building on each child's existing knowledge, understanding and skills.

In Practice

Describe how you plan the provision of numeracy and literacy activities to promote children's development in your setting. Include examples of any planning sheets you use.

Recognising individual needs when planning numeracy and literacy activities

When planning numeracy and literacy activities, it is essential to recognise the individual needs of the children. The practitioner has a key role in providing support for children during numeracy and literacy activities. You need to understand how numeracy and literacy activities are organised in your setting and your specific role in supporting various learning activities, including class discussions, group work and tasks for individuals.

When planning numeracy and literacy activities, you need to be able to:

- understand the intended learning outcomes for the children
- agree on the support strategies to be used for each child
- obtain the resources required for the activity
- implement the agreed strategies to develop children's numeracy or literacy skills
- provide feedback and encouragement during the numeracy or literacy activity
- monitor the progress of the children during the numeracy or literacy activity
- report achievements and any problems relating to the children's numeracy and/or literacy development to the relevant people (e.g. colleagues, parents, specialists).

Supporting children with special numeracy and/or literacy needs

Some children may have special numeracy and/or literacy needs because the language used in numeracy and literacy activities may be too complex for them to understand. Lack of concentration and/or poor memory skills can prevent some children from learning important techniques, such as times tables or letter sounds. Frequent experiences of failure during numeracy or literacy activities can make some children anxious, discouraged and lacking in confidence so that they fall behind in their numeracy or literacy development.

Mathematical skills involve a wide range of specific capabilities, any of which can prove difficult for particular children and affect their numeracy development. It is important to find out what the child knows and where the problem lies. It is important to make sure that the child's problem with numeracy is not in fact a problem with literacy. For example, some children may: not be able to understand the written question; have handwriting or directional problems, resulting in inaccurate recording and errors; or have poor motor skills, causing miscalculations when using a calculator.

Support strategies to help children to develop their numeracy skills

The following support strategies can be used to help children to develop their numeracy skills (appropriate for their age, ability and individual needs):

- Using questions and prompts to encourage mathematical skills.
- Repeating instructions as necessary.
- Taking notes for a child while a colleague is talking.
- Explaining and reinforcing correct mathematical vocabulary.
- Reading and clarifying textbook/worksheet activity for a child.
- Introducing follow-on tasks to reinforce and extend learning (e.g. problem-solving tasks, puzzles).
- Playing a mathematical game with an individual child or small group.
- Helping children to use computer software and learning programmes.
- Helping children to select and use appropriate mathematical resources (e.g. number lines, measuring instruments).
- Assisting children with special equipment (e.g. a hearing aid or a Dictaphone).
- Encouraging shy or reticent children to participate in conversations and discussions.
- Providing any other appropriate assistance during an activity.
- Monitoring children's progress during an activity.
- Reporting problems and successes to colleagues, parents and other professionals.

Support strategies to help children to develop their literacy skills

The following support strategies can be used to help children to develop their literacy skills (appropriate for their age, ability and individual needs):

- Using targeted prompts and feedback to encourage independent reading and writing.
- Encouraging children to participate in shared reading and writing activities.
- Developing phonic knowledge and skills to help children read and spell accurately.
- Using specific reading or writing support strategies (e.g. paired reading, writing frames).
- Using specific reading or writing support programmes (e.g. graded reading books).
- Repeating instructions as necessary.
- Taking notes for a child while another practitioner is talking.
- Explaining difficult words and phrases to a child.
- Promoting the use of dictionaries.
- Reading and clarifying textbook/worksheet activity for a child.
- Reading a story to an individual child or small group.
- Playing a word game with an individual child or small group.
- Directing computer-assisted learning programmes.
- Assisting children with special equipment (e.g. a hearing aid or a Dictaphone).
- Encouraging shy or reticent children to participate in conversations and discussions.
- Providing any other appropriate assistance during an activity.
- Monitoring children's progress during an activity.
- Reporting problems and successes to parents, colleagues and other professionals.

Some children may have special numeracy and/or literacy needs due to special educational needs (SEN), such as cognitive and learning difficulties, sensory impairment, physical disabilities or behavioural difficulties. The range of children with SEN varies from setting to setting. Many children with SEN may not have special numeracy or literacy needs and will not require extra or different numeracy or literacy support. However, many groups/classes will have one or more children with identified SEN who require a modified approach to developing numeracy and literacy skills.

The two broad groups of children with special numeracy and literacy needs

1. The first, larger group comprises children who experience minor difficulties in learning, which is reflected in their attainment of levels of numeracy and/or literacy, which are below those expected for children of their age. These children can usually overcome these difficulties through normal teaching strategies and will soon develop the essential numeracy and literacy skills that will enable them to catch up and work at a comparable level to the rest of their year group.
2. The second, smaller group includes children with severe and complex learning difficulties that require the use of different teaching strategies. These children may require different levels of work from the rest of their year group. They may need to be taught at a different pace for all or most of their school years. Some children with SEN will always need access to systems such as symbols, signing, Braille or electronic communicators.

(DfES 1999)

Many children with special educational needs (e.g. those with physical disabilities or sensory impairment) will not require a separate learning programme for developing numeracy and/or literacy skills. For most of them, access, materials, equipment and furniture may require adapting to meet their particular needs so that they can work alongside the rest of their group or class. They should work on the same objectives for their year group with emphasis on access and support. Adaptations that may be necessary include sign language, Braille and symbols, tactile materials, technological aids and adapted measuring equipment. Some children will need to work on the development of particular numeracy or literacy skills for longer than others – for example, children with speech and language difficulties may need to work on programmes devised by a speech therapist or specialist language teacher.

Assisting children with special numeracy and literacy needs

You may provide assistance for children with special numeracy and literacy needs by:

- signing to support a child with hearing impairment during shared numeracy/literacy activities
- supporting a child during group work to develop specific numeracy or literacy skills
- asking questions aimed at the appropriate level
- giving the child some extra help in a group
- sitting next to the child to keep them on task.

Figure 13.13 Adult supporting a child with special literacy needs

Supporting children with learning difficulties

Children with learning difficulties usually require constant repetition and revision of previous learning in numeracy and literacy. This is especially important in terms of language and mental calculations. For example, the understanding of the language of mathematics and the ability to calculate mentally are essential to the development of numeracy skills. Children with learning difficulties may not have adequate language and mental strategies, which may affect their ability to do calculations in the same way as other children. Real objects and experiences are important for all children, but especially for children with learning difficulties, as these can help them develop an understanding of the abstract concepts used in mathematics. For example, a 'post office' role-play situation, using play money, can help support the teaching of addition and subtraction.

Children with specific learning difficulties show problems in learning in one particular area of development; some children with specific learning difficulties (such as dyslexia or dyscalculia) may have difficulties in developing key skills in numeracy and literacy. Possible difficulties are outlined below. Remember that many young children make similar mistakes; specific learning difficulties are only indicated where the difficulties are severe and persistent or grouped together.

Children with dyslexia may have difficulty with:

- their speech development, which may be delayed
- coordination and/or concentration
- selecting and using correct words and phrases
- letter and numeral recognition/formation (e.g. 'b' for 'd', or 51 for 15)
- telling left from right
- learning the alphabet and multiplication tables

- remembering sequences (e.g. days of the week/ months of the year)
- following verbal and/or written instructions.

Strategies to support children with dyslexia

The following strategies may help to support children with dyslexia:

- Ensure the child is near you or at the front of the class/group.
- Check unobtrusively that copy-writing, note-taking, etc. are done efficiently.
- Use a 'buddy' system (i.e. another child copies for the child with dyslexia).
- Give positive feedback and encouragement, without drawing undue attention to the child.
- Use computers to help the child (e.g. word processing with spell-check facility).
- Help the child to develop alternative strategies and study skills.
- Get specialist advice and support (e.g. British Dyslexia Association, educational psychologist, health visitor, special needs advisor, specialist teacher, occupational therapist).

(BDA 1997)

Children with dyscalculia will have difficulty:

- understanding key mathematical concepts and the relationships of numbers, as well as using application procedures
- distinguishing between digits that are similar in shape (e.g. 6 and 9, 7 and 1, 2 and 5)
- sequencing (e.g. saying times tables, predicting next number in a series, use of number line, following a sequence of instructions)
- with mathematics word problems, including reading and language processing difficulties or losing track of number operation mid-process
- organising and setting out calculations in writing
- memorising and recalling maths facts (e.g. recalling tables, mental arithmetic).

Strategies to support children with dyscalculia

The following strategies may help to support children with dyscalculia:

- Provide real objects to support learning, such as building blocks, cones, toys and number apparatus.
- Use flash cards and illustrated wall displays to demonstrate the specific mathematical vocabulary for a particular task.
- Keep written instructions and explanations on worksheets to a minimum.
- Mathematics has a strong visual element so make frequent use of a number line, 100 square, number apparatus, pictures, diagrams, graphs and computer programs.
- Use games and puzzles in which pupils can quickly pick up the rules after watching a demonstration.

(DfES 2003b)

Key terms

Dyslexia – a specific learning difficulty involving particular difficulties in learning to read, write and spell.

Dyscalculia – a specific learning difficulty involving the ability to do or learn mathematics.

Activity

1. Describe how to provide support for children with special numeracy and literacy needs.
2. Use examples from your own experience if applicable.

Figure 13.14 Adult supporting children with special numeracy needs

Supporting children with English as an additional language

Bilingual means 'speaking two languages', which applies to some children (and staff) in settings throughout the United Kingdom. 'Multilingual' is used to describe someone who uses more than two languages. The term 'bilingual' is widely used for all children who speak two or more languages. The EYFS uses the term 'children whose home language is not English', while the National Curriculum's preferred term for bilingual children is 'children with English as an additional language (EAL)'.

For young children whose home language is not English, practitioners must take reasonable steps to provide opportunities for children to develop and use their home language in play and learning, supporting their language development at home. Practitioners must also ensure that young children have plenty of opportunities to learn and reach a good standard in English during the EYFS. When assessing communication, language and literacy skills, practitioners must assess children's skills in English. If a child does not have a strong grasp of English language, practitioners must explore the child's skills in the home language with parents and/or carers, to establish whether there is cause for concern about language delay (DfE 2012, p. 6).

There is a broad range of school-aged children with EAL, including children who are:

- literate and numerate in English and do not require extra provision
- able to converse in English but need help to use language in their written work
- literate and/or numerate in languages other than English but need a little extra support with literacy and numeracy activities

- learning to speak English as well as learning to read and write it
- below the levels of literacy or numeracy expected for their age and require adapted materials to meet their literacy or numeracy needs.

It is important to distinguish between children who have additional language learning needs and those who also have special educational needs (SEN). It is also important not to underestimate what children can do mathematically simply because they are learning English as an additional language. They should be expected to make progress in their mathematical learning at the same rate as other children of the same age. Some children with EAL may also be assessed as having SEN (see above).

Activity

Describe how you have (or could have) provided support for the development of numeracy and literacy skills for children with English as an additional language.

Relating numeracy and literacy activities to other areas of learning

When planning numeracy and literacy activities, it is essential to relate each activity to at least one other area of learning. For example, one of the overarching principles of the EYFS emphasises the importance of the interconnectivity between all areas of learning and development: 'All areas of learning and development are important and are interconnected' (DfE 2011a, p. 4).

How are numeracy and literacy activities connected to other areas of learning?

Children's numeracy and literacy skills should be developed across all curriculum areas. Practitioners working with children should actively seek out

Strategies to support children with English as an additional language

You can support children with English as an additional language by:

- encouraging the children to use their home or community languages some of the time – this promotes security and social acceptance, which will make learning English easier
- inviting parents/grandparents to read or tell stories in community languages or to be involved with small groups for cooking, sewing or craft activities
- using songs and rhymes to help introduce new vocabulary or concepts
- using other areas of the curriculum to develop language skills in a meaningful context (e.g. focus on words used when working on the computer or during science experiments)
- using play activities and/or games to encourage and extend language
- using group work to provide opportunities for intensive, focused teaching input
- repeating instructions for children with English as an additional language (EAL)
- speaking more clearly, emphasising key words, particularly when you are describing tasks that they are to do independently
- encouraging them to join in things that all children do in chorus: counting, reading aloud whole number sentences, chanting, finger games, songs about numbers, and so on (the structure of rhymes and the natural rhythm in songs or poems play an important part in developing number sense in any culture)
- using stories and rhymes from a range of cultural backgrounds.

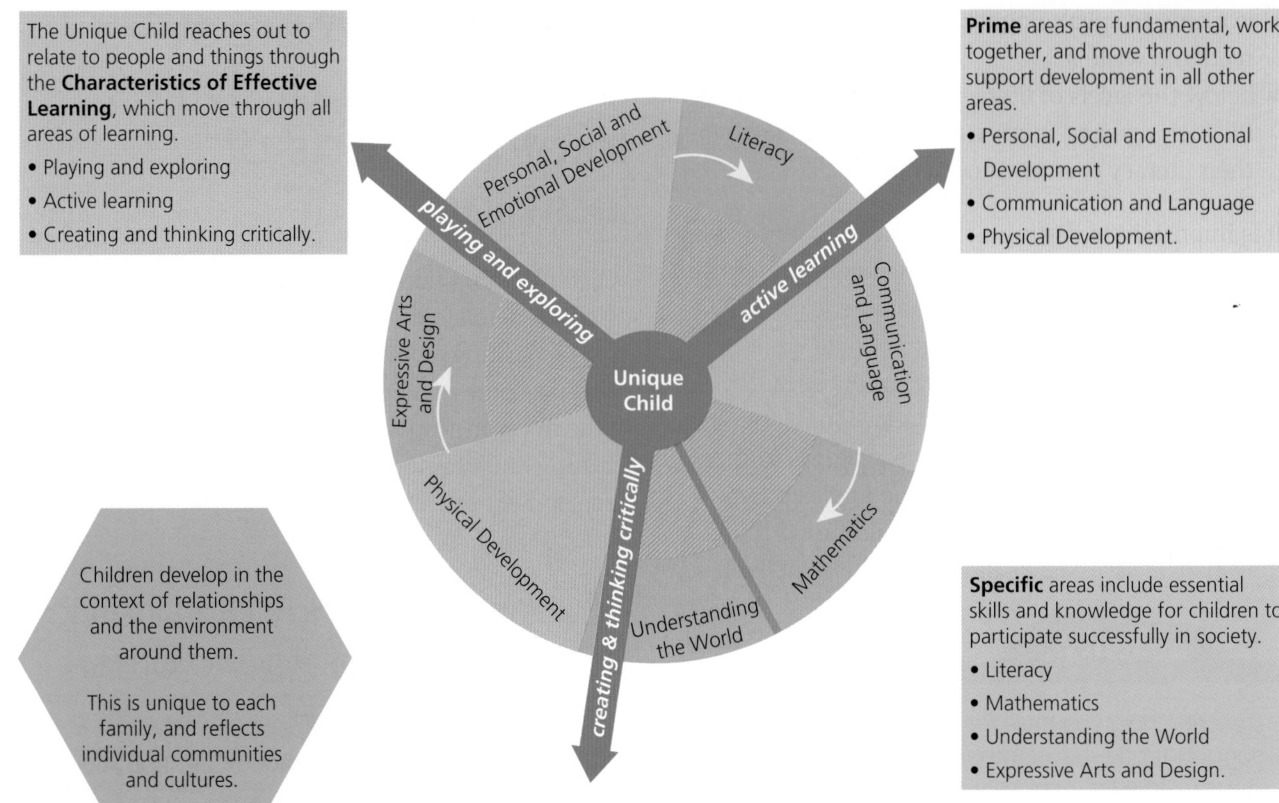

Figure 13.15 The prime and specific areas of learning and development are all interconnected (adapted from 'Development Matters in the Early Years Foundation Stage', p. 4, available at link provided in Figure 13.4 caption, page 420)

opportunities which will allow children to reflect on, use and develop their literacy and numeracy skills – in the early years setting, this is delivered through play (see below). Children should be involved in discussions about what they are good at and what they need to do to improve and extend their learning. Practitioners should plan how best to enhance children's literacy skills, given that the opportunities to do so are embedded across the curriculum – especially through speaking and listening. Effective planning should ensure that numeracy is highlighted in relevant and meaningful ways across learning – and not simply forced to fit into every learning activity. (LTS 2010, p. 7)

Helping children to develop their literacy and numeracy skills through play

Although play is a process rather than a subject, many play activities provide opportunities for learning through curriculum subject areas. These subject areas provide children with powerful tools for making sense of the world and incorporate distinctive, as well as interconnected, ways of learning. (Wood and Attfield 2005, p. 122) Practitioners need a good understanding of the structures of the subject areas of the curriculum – the concepts, skills, tools for enquiry and investigation, and ways of thinking and reasoning. They also need to understand the way that different curriculum subjects are connected – how these connections can be made and what connections children make through their own activities. (Wood and Attfield 2005, p. 137)

Playing with numeracy

Children become real-world mathematicians by participating in everyday practices in different contexts – home, community and school. Children invent their own strategies that enable them to solve a variety of addition and subtraction word problems. These strategies are often evident in play contexts as children encounter problems and develop their own solutions. Practitioners can build on children's invented strategies and create contexts in which they move through different stages of learning to explore the relationships between ideas and to link their own informal strategies to the more formal symbol system of mathematics. Like all the subject areas, mathematics has its own language, ways of thinking, reasoning, problem solving, methods, rules and procedures. Children's success in solving mathematical problems depends on their ability to relate mathematics to familiar, everyday practices. Play activities can provide a range of contexts for integrating mathematics into everyday practices that children encounter in and out of the setting.

Playing with literacy

Play integrates speaking, listening, reading and writing and provides contexts for meaningful literacy practices. Children use a wide variety of literacy-related skills, concepts and behaviours in their play and show interest in, and knowledge of, the many functions and purposes of print. When engaging in playful literacy, children are not just pretending to read and write; they are acting as readers and writers. This is a fundamental distinction which enables children to see the meaning and relevance of such activities. Play, pretending and language are symbolic activities that support and share many characteristics with the development of reading and writing. Socio-dramatic play can be a particularly rich context for literacy development because of the connections between story making and telling, and symbolic activity. For example, role play can involve complex, novel and detailed play narratives in which children interweave reality and fantasy, drawing on their social and cultural worlds. Play narratives can be inspired by stories (both fact and fiction) that adults tell to children, as well as stories that children invent. (Wood and Attfield 2005, pp. 143–145)

Linking play and literacy involves imaginative planning, varied resources and engaging with children to provide an appreciative audience and support their developing skills and confidence. Provision that has breadth and relevance to children's lives helps them to engage in reading and writing for a variety of purposes in real situations. Playing their way into literacy provides powerful stimuli for learning. Practitioners can extend children's understanding of the literacy events which take place in real-world contexts. For example:

- writing a menu
- reading a recipe
- filling out cheques, signing receipts
- reading brochures and filling out booking forms in a travel agency
- drawing maps and plans of journeys
- drawing plans for buildings, parks, playgrounds
- designing cards, posters, badges, clothes, book covers
- developing comic strips and storyboards (drawing and writing)
- using websites and other ICT.

(Wood and Attfield 2005, pp. 147–149)

Activity

Think about how planning in your setting relates numeracy and literacy activities to other areas of learning. For example:

- How does the setting plan play-based experiences?
- How do practitioners plan numeracy and literacy activities?
- How are these activities connected to other areas of the relevant curriculum framework?

Activity

Describe how you plan to provide a broad range of experiences to develop children's numeracy and literacy skills, both in and outside the setting. For example, using a variety of play opportunities and outings to develop children's numeracy and literacy skills.

Numeracy across all areas of learning

You can help children to develop numeracy skills in different areas of the curriculum by providing opportunities for them to know, understand and use aspects of the following:

1. **Number and number processes to**:
   - calculate accurately, where appropriate, using efficient mental strategies
   - estimate and round appropriately
   - use calculators and other ICT resources appropriately and efficiently.
2. **Applying numeracyto**:
   - identify and use an efficient strategy for the calculations they need to do
   - confidently measure and estimate measurements
   - work confidently with money and time
   - choose suitable units
   - find, select, sort, collate and link information from a variety of sources.
3. **Information handling to**:
   - organise information appropriately
   - present graphs, charts and diagrams to suit purpose and audience
   - read numbers accurately from a range of diagrams, tables, graphs and real-life objects
   - make inferences, informed decisions and draw valid conclusions
   - use information for different purposes.
4. **Understanding, analysing and evaluating to**:
   - work in groups or individually to solve problems
   - confidently judge the reasonableness of solutions, checking them out when necessary
   - explain their thinking and share their approaches and solutions
   - form and respond to questions
   - interpret and use information effectively.
5. **Creating text to**:
   - present information/data clearly and effectively.

(Adapted from LTS 2010, p. 10)

Literacy across all areas of learning

You can help children to develop literacy skills in different areas of the curriculum by providing them with the following literacy experiences:

1. **Knowledge and use of technical aspects of**:
   - interacting/collaborating: communicating with others in group and class discussions, during question and answer sessions and when making presentations
   - reading increasingly complex or unfamiliar ideas, structures and vocabulary: using knowledge of context clues, punctuation, grammar and layout to help access new/unfamiliar texts
   - effective writing: spelling and punctuating with sufficient accuracy and varying sentences and paragraphs appropriately/effectively; reviewing and editing written work; presenting work effectively to suit purpose and audience.
2. **Finding and using information**:
   - speaking and listening: preparing for and participating in class and group discussions; comparing/contrasting sources; using information for different purposes
   - reading: finding, selecting, sorting, summarising and linking information from a variety of sources.
3. **Organising and using information**:
   - writing: effective note making, developing ideas, acknowledging sources appropriately in written work, developing and using appropriate and effective vocabulary.

Literacy across all areas of learning (continued)

4. Understanding, analysing and evaluating:
- speaking and listening: forming and responding to questions; engaging in increasingly complex discussions (literal, inferential, evaluative); exploring factors which influence/persuade to help consider the reliability of information
- reading: considering the purpose and main concerns in texts, making inferences, discussing similarities and differences between types of text, forming questions.

5. Creating texts:
- speaking and listening: listening/discussing attentively to help share information and points of view, explain processes, summarise and clarify
- writing: producing increasingly complex texts (ideas, structures and vocabulary); using language effectively to persuade, argue, explore ideas and express points of view.

(Adapted from LTS 2010, p. 17)

Evaluating the numeracy and literacy activities implemented in relation to children's learning

After you have planned and implemented the numeracy or literacy activity, you will need to evaluate it. Despite careful planning and organisation, you may have problems in providing support for children during learning activities. You should know and understand the sorts of problems that might occur. For example, difficulties with the quantity, quality, suitability or availability of learning resources; issues relating to space, comfort, noise levels or disruptions within the learning environment; and factors that may affect a child's ability to learn – for example, social and cultural background or special educational needs, such as learning difficulties or behaviour problems (see section from page 424 on 'Supporting children with special numeracy and literacy needs').

You will need to be able to deal with any problems you may have in providing support for children as planned. For example, modifying or adapting an activity; providing additional activities to extend their learning; providing an alternative version of the activity; presenting the materials in different ways; offering a greater or lesser level of assistance; coping with insufficient materials or equipment breakdown; and dealing with uncooperative or disruptive children. The senior practitioner, setting manager or your college tutor/assessor should give you guidelines on how to present your activity plans. If not, you could use the suggested format on page 43 in Chapter 1.

In Practice

Plan a numeracy activity for young children that will include:

- the aim of the activity
- recognition of individual needs
- how the activity relates to one other area of learning.

(As a starting point, you could use your observation of a young child engaged in a numeracy activity from page 427, plus your suggestions to support the development of children's numeracy skills from page 428.)

Implement the numeracy activity planned for the children.

Analyse the outcome of the activity implemented in relation to the children's learning.

Evaluate the outcome of the activity implemented in relation to the aim and the one other area of learning identified.

In Practice

Plan a literacy activity for young children that will include:

- the aim of the activity
- recognition of individual needs
- how the activity relates to one other area of learning.

(As a starting point, you could use your observation of a young child involved in a literacy activity from page 433, plus your suggestions to support the development of children's literacy skills from page 435.)

Implement the literacy activity planned for children.

Analyse the outcome of the activity implemented in relation to the children's learning.

Evaluate the outcome of the activity implemented in relation to the aim and the one other area of learning identified.

Section 4: Reflecting on own practice

Professional knowledge is not static: skilled practitioners reflect critically on their planning, provision and children's learning journeys, and are willing to improve their practice. They use evidence from their own evaluations, from their peers and from research studies to support development.

Effective practice requires committed, enthusiastic and reflective practitioners with a breadth and depth of knowledge, skills and understanding in order to provide numeracy and literacy activities appropriate to children's learning needs. To be an effective, reflective practitioner, you should use your own learning to improve your ability to support the development of children's numeracy and literacy skills.

Through initial and ongoing training and development, you can develop, demonstrate and continuously improve your:

- own numeracy and literacy skills as necessary
- relationships with children and their families to encourage the development of numeracy and literacy skills outside the setting (e.g. reading at home, shopping trips, cooking activities)
- understanding of the individual and diverse ways that children develop and learn
- knowledge and understanding in order to actively support and extend children's numeracy and literacy skills in and across all areas of learning
- practice in meeting all children's needs, learning styles and interests
- work with parents, carers and the wider community to develop children's numeracy and literacy skills in meaningful contexts (e.g. visits to local library, local shops, the post office)
- work with other professionals to support children with special numeracy and literacy needs.

Reflecting on the planning process for each numeracy and literacy activity

As a practitioner, you need to know and understand the techniques of reflective analysis: questioning what, why and how; seeking alternatives; keeping an open mind; viewing from different perspectives; thinking about consequences; testing ideas through comparing and contrasting; asking 'what if?'; synthesising ideas; and seeking, identifying and resolving problems (NDNA 2004).

Self-evaluation is needed to improve your own professional practice and to develop your ability to reflect upon and modify plans for numeracy and literacy activities to meet the individual needs of the children you work with. When evaluating your own practice, you should consider the following:

- Was your own particular contribution appropriate to the activity?
- Did you choose the right time, place and resources?
- Did you intervene enough or too much?
- Did you achieve your goals (e.g. objectives/outcomes for the child or children and yourself)?

If not, why not? Were the goals too ambitious or unrealistic?

- What other strategies/methods could have been used? Suggest possible modifications.
- Who should you ask for further advice (e.g. senior practitioner, setting manager, other professional)?

Reflecting on own practice in supporting the delivery and outcome of the activities

You need to know and understand clearly your exact role and responsibilities in supporting the delivery and outcome of numeracy and literacy activities. Review your professional practice by making regular and realistic assessments of how well your working practices match your role and responsibilities. Share your self-assessments with those responsible for managing and reviewing your work performance (e.g. during your regular discussions/meetings with your colleagues or with your line manager). You should also ask other people for feedback how well you fulfil the requirements and expectations of your role. You can also reflect on your own professional practice by making comparisons with appropriate models of good practice (e.g. the work of more experienced practitioners supporting the development of children's numeracy and literacy skills within the setting).

Drawing conclusions which show how to extend and refine future practice

You should work together with your colleagues and other professionals to create a learning

Extending and refining future practice

You can extend and refine future practice by:

- knowing and understanding the relevant curriculum within the setting
- planning numeracy and literacy activities that reinforce learning within the appropriate curriculum, both in the setting and in the home (including cultural events and customs)
- being familiar with children's levels of development
- recognising that play is a critically important vehicle in supporting the development of children's numeracy and literacy skills
- facilitating developmentally appropriate child-initiated and child-centred activities to develop young children's early numeracy and literacy skills
- providing ongoing opportunities and materials for reading and storytelling activities (e.g. puppet shows, books, stories read by adults, role playing)
- using a child's language in as many experiences as possible (e.g. labelling objects)
- recognising the child's efforts and works (e.g. displaying work and giving positive feedback), and having a place for all children's efforts, not just the 'best'
- recording and communicating each child's progress and achievements in numeracy and literacy
- being a good listener and observer and encouraging others to be the same
- communicating regularly with parents, colleagues and other practitioners about numeracy and literacy activities
- participating in inter-generational programmes which connect young children, older children, young people and older members of the community (such as grandparents).

(Adapted from Goldhawk 1998, p. 5)

environment that demonstrates examples of best practice in developing numeracy and literacy skills. You should assist parents and carers in understanding the importance of being numerate and literate. You should work with parents and carers in designing and implementing activities that will foster children's numeracy and literacy skills in all aspects of their development and learning.

Activity

1 Give examples of how you reflect on the planning process, delivery and outcome of numeracy and literacy activities, including: self-evaluation; reflections on your interactions with others; sharing your reflections with others; and using feedback from others to improve your own evaluation.

2 Describe how you have used reflection to extend and refine future practice.

Useful resources

Organisations and websites

Foundation Years

This website (developed by 4Children) is the 'one-stop-shop' for resources, information and the latest news on the foundation years. The website provides advice and guidance for practitioners on working effectively with parents as partners in their children's learning.www.foundationyears.org.uk

Siren Films

Siren Films produces high-quality DVDs covering a wide range of topics, such as the first year of life, two-year-olds, three- and four-year-olds, learning through play, exploratory play, pretend play, outdoor play, and learning and development.
www.sirenfilms.co.uk

Teaching Ideas

This website provides free ideas, resources, information and advice for teaching and learning, including numeracy and literacy activities.
www.teachingideas.co.uk

Books

Abbott, L. and Langston, A. (2005) *Birth to three matters: supporting the framework of effective practice*, Maidenhead: Open University Press.
Alcott, M. (2002) *An introduction to children with special needs*, London: Hodder & Stoughton.
BDA (1997) *Dyslexia: an introduction for parents, teachers and others with an interest in dyslexia*, Bracknell: British Dyslexia Association.
Bruce, T. (2011) *Learning through play: for babies, toddlers and young children*, 2nd edition, London: Hodder Education.
DCSF (2008) *Statutory framework for the Early Years Foundation Stage: setting the standards for learning, development and care for children from birth to five*, London: Department for Children, Schools and Families, available at: www.education.gov.uk/publications/eOrderingDownload/00267-2008BKT-EN.pdf.
DfE (2011a) *Reforming the Early Years Foundation Stage (the EYFS): government response to consultation 20 December 2011*, London: Department for Education, available at: www.education.gov.uk/consultations/downloadableDocs/Government%20response%20doc%20191211%201630%20finaltext%20KM%20CB%201808(v2).pdf (accessed February 2012).
DfE (2011b) *Primary curriculum subjects – English*, London: Department for Education, available at: www.education.gov.uk/schools/teachingandlearning/curriculum/primary/b00198874/english(accessed May 2012).

Useful resources (cont.)

DfE (2011c) *Primary curriculum subjects – Mathematics*, London: Department for Education, available at: www.education.gov.uk/schools/teachingandlearning/curriculum/primary/b00199044/mathematics(accessed May 2012)

DfE (2012) *Statutory framework for the Early Years Foundation Stage: setting the standards for learning, development and care for children from birth to five*, London: Department for Education, available at: www.education.gov.uk/publications/standard/AllPublications/Page1/DFE-00023-2012 (accessed March 2012).

DfES (1999) *The national numeracy strategy – framework for teaching mathematics from reception to Y6*, London: Department for Education and Skills.

DfES (2003a) *Primary national strategy – speaking, listening, learning: working with children in Key Stages 1 and 2 handbook*, London: Department for Education and Skills.

DfES (2003b) *Electronic adult numeracy core curriculum with access for all*, London: Department for Education and Skills.

DfES (2005) *Primary national strategy: KEEP – Key Elements of Effective Practice*, London: Department for Education and Skills, available at:http://dera.ioe.ac.uk/7593/1/pns_fs120105keep.pdf (accessed May 2012).

Drake, J. (2009) *Planning for children's play and learning*, London: David Fulton Publishers.

Early Education (2012) *Development matters in the Early Years Foundation Stage (EYFS)*, London: The British Association for Early Childhood Education, available at: http://media.education.gov.uk/assets/files/pdf/d/development%20matters%20in%20the%20eyfs.pdf (accessed June 2012).

Gaunt, C. (2012) 'Primary curriculum overhaul for maths, science and English', *Nursery World*, 11 June, available at: www.nurseryworld.co.uk/news/bulletin/nurseryworldupdate/article/1135745/?DCMP=EMC-CONNurseryWorldUpdate (accessed June 2012).

Godwin, D. and Perkins, M. (2002) *Teaching language and literacy in the early years*, London: David Fulton Publishers.

Goldhawk, S. (1998) *Young children and the arts: making creative connections – a report of the task force on children's learning and the arts: birth to age eight*, Washington: Arts Education Partnership, available at:www.eric.ed.gov/PDFS/ED453968.pdf (accessed May 2012).

Hobart, C. and Frankel, J. (2005) The EYFS: *A Practical Guide for Students and Professional children*, 3rd edition, Cheltenham: Nelson Thornes.

Hutchin, V. (2012) *The EYFS: A Practical Guide for Students and Professionals*, London: Hodder Education.

LTS (2010) *Developing literacy and numeracy across learning – professional development pack*, Glasgow: Learning and Teaching Scotland, available at: www.educationscotland.gov.uk/Images/Developingliteracyandnumeracyacrosslearning_tcm4-645064.pdf(accessed June 2012).

Meggitt, C., Kamen, T., Bruce, T. and Grenier, J. (2011) *CACHE Level 3 Diploma: Children and young people's workforce: early learning and child care*, London: Hodder Education.

Morris, C. (2011) *Best way to learn*, 'Success is working smarter and harder' website, available at:www.igs.net/~cmorris/best_way_to_learn.html (accessed June 2012).

Moyle, D. (1976) *The teaching of reading*, East Grinstead: Ward Lock Educational.

NDNA (2004) *National occupational standards in children's care, learning and development*, Huddersfield: National Day Nurseries Association.

Palmer, S. and Bayley, R. (2004) *Foundations of literacy: a balanced approach to language, listening and literacy skills in the early years*, Stafford: Network Educational Press Ltd.

Siraj-Blatchford, J. and Clarke, P. (2000) *Supporting identity, diversity and language in the early years*, Maidenhead: Open University Press.

Useful resources (cont.)

Taylor, J. (1973) *Reading and writing in the first school*, London: George Allen and Unwin.
Tobias, C. (1996) *The way they learn*, Colorado Springs: Focus on the Family Publishing.
Topping, K. and Bamford, J. (1998) *The paired maths handbook: parental involvement and peer tutoring in mathematics*, London: David Fulton Publishers.
Whitehead, M.R. (2004) *Language and literacy in the early year*, London: Sage Publications Ltd.
Williams, S. and Goodman, S. (2000) *Helping young children with maths*, London: Hodder & Stoughton.
Wood, E. and Attfield, J. (2005) *Play, learning and the early childhood curriculum*, 2nd edition, London: Sage Publications Ltd.
Wright, R.J., Martland, J., Stafford, A.K. and Stanger, G. (2002) *Teaching number: advancing children's skills and strategies*, London: Paul Chapman Publishing.

Index